THE RECORDS OF THE FEDERAL CONVENTION OF 1787

VOLUME III

THE RECORDS

OF THE

FEDERAL CONVENTION

OF 1787

EDITED BY

MAX FARRAND

REVISED EDITION IN FOUR VOLUMES

VOLUME III

NEW HAVEN AND LONDON · YALE UNIVERSITY PRESS

Published with assistance from
the John Ben Snow Memorial Trust.

Printed in the United States of America by
The Murray Printing Co., Westford, Mass.

International standard book numbers: 0–300–00449–4 (cloth)
0–300–00082–0 (pbk.)
Library of Congress catalog card number: 86–50311

12   11   10   9   8   7   6   5   4   3

APPENDIX A

SUPPLEMENTARY RECORDS OF PROCEEDINGS IN CONVENTION

CONTENTS

SUPPLEMENT

I. RESOLUTION OF CONGRESS.[1]

1787, February 21.

Whereas there is provision in the Articles of Confederation & perpetual Union for making alterations therein by the Assent of a Congress of the United States and of the legislatures of the several States; And whereas experience hath evinced that there are defects in the present Confederation, as a mean to remedy which several

---

[1] *Documentary History of the Constitution*, IV, 78.

of the States and particularly the State of New York by express instructions to their delegates in Congress have suggested a convention for the purposes expressed in the following resolution and such Convention appearing to be the most probable mean of establishing in these states a firm national government

Resolved that in the opinion of Congress it is expedient that on the second Monday in May next a Convention of delegates who shall have been appointed by the several states be held at Philadelphia for the sole and express purpose of revising the Articles of Confederation and reporting to Congress and the several legislatures such alterations and provisions therein as shall when agreed to in Congress and confirmed by the states render the federal constitution adequate to the exigencies of Government & the preservation of the Union

---

II. THE GOVERNOR OF NORTH CAROLINA [Richard Caswell] TO THE NAVAL OFFICERS OF THE PORTS OF THAT STATE.[1]

[Circular].

Kinston, 1st March, 1787.

Sir:

I find it absolutely necessary for the advantage of the State to require that you do without delay furnish me with an attested Accot. in your official capacity as Naval Officer of Port Brunswick of each & very article exported from your port in the years 1785 & 1786. I mean the amot. of each article, each year, of the growth and manufacture of this State, and if possible the no. and class of vessels that is ships, sloops, schooners, &c., with the nation to which each certain no. belongs.

Indeed three Copies will be necessary, one to be laid before Congress, one before the Convention of Deputies proposed to be held at Philadelphia the first of May next, and one to lodge with the Executive for the information of the General Assembly. Pray do not fail in furnishing me as speedily as possible otherwise it will be too late to transmit the Copy to the Convention. Any expence attending this measure must be charged to the public.

(Governor Caswell to John Walker, James Coor, Wm. Brown, M. Payne and Jno. Humphries.)

---

[1] *North Carolina State Records*, XX, 631.

III. Mr. Otto, chargé d'affaires de France, au Secrétaire d'Etat des Affaires Etrangères, comte de Montmorin.[1]

No. 85.

A New York, le 10 avril, 1787.

Monseigneur,

Délégués de la pluspart des Etats nommés pour convenir d'un nouveau système de gouvernement. Le Congrès n'est qu'un phantome de souveraineté. Résolution ci-jointe du Congrès pour suggérer l'idée d'une nouvelle Convention générale. Le Rhode-Island est le seul Etat qui ait refusé d'envoyer à Philadelphie des délégués pour cet objet. Cet Etat est méprisé en Amérique. Membres les plus distingués qui doivent composer cette assemblée á Philadelphie pour régler la nouvelle Convention générale, qui est devenue d'une

L'insuffisance de la confédération actuelle et la nécessité absolue de la refondre entièrement sont si bien senties, que la plupart des Etats ont nommé sans délai des délégués chargés de s'assembler à Philadelphie pour convenir d'un nouveau système de gouvernement moins défectueux et moins précaire que celui qui existe dans ce moment ci, ou plutôt qu *devroit* exister. Le Congrès n'est réellement qu'un phantome de souveraineté destitué de pouvoirs, d'énergie et de considération, et l'édifice qu'il doit supporter tombe en ruine. Cette assemblée, craignant de perdre le peu d'éclat qui lui reste, a du moins voulu avoir l'air de suggérer l'idée d'un nouvelle *Convention générale;* c'est dans ce but qu'elle a publié la résolution ci jointe.[2] Le Rhodeisland est jusqu'ici le seul Etat qui ait positivement refusé d'envoyer des délégués a Philadelphie; cette conduite, jointe à plusieurs autres mesures également malhonêtes et imprudentes l'ont rendu complètement méprisable en Amérique. Les papiers publics sont remplis de sarcasmes contre cette petite République, et malhereusement elle paraît mériter tout le mal qu'on en dit.

Si tous les délégués nommés pour cette Convention de Philadelphie y assistent, on n'aura jamais vu, même en Europe, une assemblée plus respectable par les talens, les connoissances, le désintéressement et le patriotisme de ceux qui la composeront. Le gal. Washington, le Dr. Franklin et un grand nombre d'autres personnages distingués, quoique moins connus en Europe, y sont appellés. On ne sauroit douter que les intérêts

---

[1] French Archives: *Ministère des Affaires Etrangères Archives. Etats-Unis Correspondance.* Vol. 32, pp. 237 ff.

[2] Résolution du Congrès du 21 février 1787. Même volume, fo 239ro. Traduction française.

nécessité indis-
pensable.

de la confédération n'y soient plus solidement
discutés qu'ils ne l'ont jamais été. Une triste
expérience de plusieurs années ne prouve que
trop qu'il est impossible que les choses restent
sur le pied actuel. Pendant la guerre, le Congrès
empruntait, pour ainsi dire, sa force des armées
angloises, qui infestoient les Etats de toutes
parts; le papier monnoye qu'il pouvoit créer à
l'infini, les subsides de la France, l'énthousiasme
et le patriotisme des individus, les confiscations,
des troupes nombreuses lui donnoient une importance qui s'est évanouie au moment de la paix.
Il s'agit donc d'adopter un nouveau plan de confédération, de donner au Congrès des pouvoirs
coercitifs, des impôts considérables, une armée,
le droit de régler exclusivement le commerce de
tous les Etats. Mais cette nouvelle assemblée
n'a elle-même que le pouvoir de *proposer*. Les
Etats voudront-ils se laisser dépouiller d'une
partie de leur souveraineté? Voudront-ils consentir à n'être plus que des provinces d'un grand
Empire? La majorité des Etats pourra-t-elle
faire la loi à ceux qui ne voudront pas sacrifier
leur indépendance actuelle? C'est ce dont on a
lieu de douter; mais je dois m'attacher, Monseigneur, à vous présenter des faits et non des
conjectures.

Je ne puis cependant m'empêcher de vous
observer que, quoique cette nouvelle *Convention*
soit l'unique moyen de réunir les membres épars
de la Confédération, les Américains les plus
instruits sont bien loin de le regarder comme
suffisant. Il règne dans la formation de ces
Etats un vice radical qui s'opposera toujours à
une union parfaite, c'est que les Etats n'ont réellement aucun intérêt pressant d'être sous un
seul chef. Leur politique, qui se borne à leurs
speculations com[m]erciales, leur inspire même
réciproquement de l'aversion et de la jalousie,
passions qui se trouvoient absorbées pendant la
guerre par l'enthousaiasme de la liberté et de
l'indépendance, mais qui com[m]encent à repren-
dre toute leur force. Ces républicains n'ont

plus de Philippe à leurs portes, et, comme ils ont secoué le joug de l'Angleterre pour ne pas payer des taxes, ils portent avec impatience celui d'un Congrès, qui ne peut que les charger d'impôts sans leur offrir aucune protection contre des ennemis qui n'existent plus. La confédération n'est réellement soutenue que par le parti aristocratique et ce parti s'affoiblit tous les jours. Les Cincinnati et tous les créanciers publics se trouvent dans cette classe, mais à mesure qu'ils sont ruinés par les intrigues du parti opposé ou par l'épuisement du trésor continental, ils deviennent plébéiens pour obtenir des places de confiance ou du moins pour avoir de quoi vivre, d'autres vont porter dans les districts occidentaux leur industrie et les foibles débris de leur fortune; un petit nombre d'entre eux passe en Angleterre.

Je suis avec un profond respect, Monseigneur, votre très humble et très obéissant serviteur,

Otto.

IV. RICHARD CASWELL TO ALEXANDER MARTIN.[1]

April 11, 1787.

Mr. Speight thinks the allowance not sufficient as 'tis probable the Convention may sit longer than we at first apprehended & as we are to acc't he thinks with me, that 'tis best to draw one months further allowance,[2] least we should be stinted as he was at Congress & obliged to run in debt. I have therefore enclosed you a Warrant for one months further allowance & as I presume you will not set out as soon as you mentioned you may have time to collect it.

V. RESOLUTION OF CONGRESS.[3]

Monday April 23. 1787

On motion of Mr Carrington seconded by Mr Johnson Resolved That the priviledge of sending & receiving letters and packets free of postage be extended to the members of the Convention to be held in Philadelphia on the second Monday in May next in the same manner as is allowed to the members of Congress. --

---

[1] *North Carolina State Records*, Vol. XX, pp. 666-7.
[2] Allowance for three months had been previously granted.
[3] *Documentary History of the Constitution* IV, 121.

VI. WILLIAM JACKSON TO GEORGE WASHINGTON.[1]

W. Jackson to His Excellency General Washington Mount-Vernon
    Flattered by the opinions of some of my friends, who have expressed a wish that I would offer myself a Candidate for the Office of Secretary to the fœderal Covention — I presume to communicate to you my intention — and to request (so far as you shall deem it consonant with the more important interests of the Public) your influence in procuring me the honor of that appointment.

To say more on this subject would be to offend against that generous friendship, which I am persuaded, if held compatible with the service of our Country, will prompt an active goodness in my favor.

[Endorsed:] From W. Jackson Esqr recd. 24th. Aprl 1787

VIa. JARED INGERSOLL TO WILLIAM SAMUEL JOHNSON.[2]

Philadelphia, April 28th. 1787
    Major Jackson this moment called on me and expressed his willingness to serve the proposed Convention in the Character of Secretary and requested I would do him the favor to write you a line upon the Subject as it is the expectation as well as wish of people here that you may be among the Delegates from Connecticut.

I comply with the Desire of Major Jackson as I find a strange Idea is prevalent that a prior application of some sort forms a preferable Title and least some other person [sho]uld be able to anticipate him. . . .

P. S.   In my haste I forgot to mention that some of your brethren in Congress, Col. Lee in particular can give you full information as to the Character of Major Jackson.

VII. SEVERAL GENTLEMEN OF RHODE ISLAND TO THE CHAIRMAN OF THE GENERAL CONVENTION.[3]

Providence May 11. 1787.
Gentlemen
    Since the Legislature of this State have finally declined sending Delegates to Meet you in Convention for the purposes mentioned in the Resolve of Congress of the 21st February 1787. the Mer-

---

[1] *Documentary History of the Constitution* IV, 121-122.
[2] Papers of W. S. Johnson, Connecticut Historical Society. Furnished to the editor through the courtesy of Mr. Edmund C. Burnett of the Department of Historical Research of the Carnegie Institution of Washington.
[3] *Documentary History of the Constitution*, I, 275-276. See also XLV and CII below.

chants Tradesmen and others of this place, deeply affected with the evils of the present unhappy times, have thought proper to Communicate in writing their approbation of your Meeting, And their regret that it will fall short of a Compleat Representation of the Federal Union. ——

The failure of this State was Owing to the Nonconcurrence of the Upper House of Assembly with a Vote passed in the Lower House, for appointing Delegates to attend the said Convention, at thier Session holden at Newport on the first Wednesday of the present Month. ——

It is the general Opinion here and we believe of the well informed throughout this State, that full power for the Regulation of the Commerce of the United States, both Foreign & Domestick ought to be vested in the National Council.

And that Effectual Arrangements should also be made for giving Operation to the present powers of Congress in thier Requisitions upon the States for National purposes. ——

As the Object of this Letter is chiefly to prevent any impressions unfavorable to the Commercial Interest of this State, from taking place in our Sister States from the Circumstance of our being unrepresented in the present National Convention, we shall not presume to enter into any detail of the objects we hope your deliberations will embrace and provide for being convinced they will be such as have a tendency to strengthen the Union, promote Commerce, increase the power & Establish the Credit of the United States.

The result of your deliberations tending to these desireable purposes we still hope may finally be Approved and Adopted by this State, for which we pledge our Influence and best exertions. ——

In behalf of the Merchants, Tradesmen &c

We have the Honour to be with perfect Consideration & Respect

Your most Obedient &
Most Humble Servant's

John Brown	Jabez Bowen	
Thos Lloyd Halsey	Nichos Brown	
Jos. Nightingale	John Jenckes,	
Levi Hall	Welcome Arnold	comtee
Philip Allen	William Russell	
Paul Allen	Jeremiah Olney,	
	William Barton	

The Honble the Chairman of the General Convention

Philadelphia

[Endorsed:] No 5.   Letter from several Gentlemen of Rhode

Island addressed to the honorable the Chairman of the General
Convention signed in behalf of the Merchants, Tradesmen &ca
dated Providence May 11. 1787.
read on Monday May 28. 1787. — Ordered to lye on the table for
farther consideration _____

VIII. GEORGE WASHINGTON: DIARY.[1]

Monday, [May] 14. — This being the day appointed for the
meeting of the Convention such members of it as were in town
assembled at the State House, where it was found that two States
only were represented, viz., Virginia and Pennsylvania. Agreed
to meet again to-morrow at 11 o'clock. . . .

Tuesday, 15. — Repaired to the State Ho. at the hour appointed
No more States represented, tho there were members (but not
sufficient to form a quorum) from two or three others, viz., No.
Carolina and Delaware, as also Jersey. Govr Randolph. of Virginia, came in to-day. _____

IX. JAMES MADISON TO THOMAS JEFFERSON.[2]

Philada. May 15th. 1787

Monday last was the day for the meeting of the Convention.
The number as yet assembled is but small.   Among the few is Genl
Washington who arrived on sunday evening amidst the acclamations
of the people, as well as more sober marks of the affection and veneration which continues to be felt for his character.   The Governor
Messrs. Wythe & Blair, and Docr. McClurg are also here. Col.
Mason is to be here in a day or two.   There is a prospect of a pretty
full meeting on the whole, though there is less punctuality in the
outset than was to be wished.   Of this the late bad weather has been
the principal cause.   I mention these circumstances because it is
possible, this may reach you before you hear from me through any
other channel, and I add no others because it is merely possible.

_____

X. GEORGE WASHINGTON: DIARY.[1]

Wednesday, [May] 16. — Only two States represented. Agreed
to meet at — o'clock.   Doctr McClurg, of Virginia, came in.   Dined
at Doctr Franklin's. . . .

Thursday, 17. — Mr. [Charles] Pinkney, of So. Carolina, coming
in from New York, and Mr. Rutledge being here before, formed a
representation from that State.   Colonel Mason getting in this

_____

[1] *Pennsylvania Magazine of History and Biography*, XI, 297.
[2] *Documentary History of the Constitution*, IV, 165.

evening from Virginia, completed the whole number of this State
in the delegation. ———————

XI. BENJAMIN FRANKLIN TO RICHARD PRICE.[1]

Philada, May 18, 1787.
We have now meeting here a Convention of the principal people
in the several States, for the purpose of revising the federal Constitution, and proposing such amendments as shall be thoroughly
necessary. It is a most important business, and I hope will be
attended with success. ———————

XII. BENJAMIN FRANKLIN TO THOMAS JORDAN.[2]

Philadelphia, May 18, 1787.
I received your very kind letter of February 27th, together
with the cask of porter you have been so good as to send me. We
have here at present what the French call *une assemblée des notables*
a convention composed of some of the principal people from the
several States of our confederation. They did me the honor of
dining with me last Wednesday,[3] when the cask was broached, and
its contents met with the most cordial reception and universal approbation. In short, the company agreed unanimously, that it was the
best porter they had ever tasted. ———————

XIII. GEORGE WASHINGTON: DIARY.[4]

Friday, [May] 18. — The State of New York was represented.
. . .
Saturday, 19. — No more States represented. Agreed to meet
at 1 o'clock on Monday. ———————

XIIIa. PENNSYLVANIA JOURNAL AND WEEKLY ADVERTISER.[5]

Saturday, May 19, 1787.
A return of the Delegates appointed to the Foederal Convention: —
The names of those who have already arrived in this City, are printed
in Italic.

---

[1] Smyth, *Writings of Benjamin Franklin*, IX, 585–586.

[2] Smyth, *Writings of Benjamin Franklin*, IX, 582.

[3] Jameson (*Studies*, 93) cites another letter of Franklin's to his sister, to the effect
that his new dining-room would enable him to have a dinner-party of only twenty-
four, which would be about the number of delegates in attendance on the 16th.

[4] *Pennsylvania Magazine of History and Biography*, XI, 297.

[5] The same item (with slight differences in spelling and omitting John Neilson
of New Jersey) is given in the *Pennsylvania Herald and General Advertiser* of
May 19.

New Hampshire. John Langdon, John Sparhawk, Pierce Long.

Massachusetts. Francis Dana, Elbridge Gerry, Nathan Gorham, Rufus King, Caleb Strong.

Connecticut. Their legislature were to meet in the beginning of this month, at which time it is supposed their delegates would be appointed.

Rhode Island. Has not made any appointment as yet.

New York. *Robert Yates, Alexander Hamilton, John Lansing.*

New Jersey. *David Brearly,* William Churchill Houston, William Patterson, John Neilson.

Pennsylvania. *Benjamin Franklin, Thomas Mifflin, Robert Morris, Thomas Fitzimmons, George Clymer, Jared Ingersol, James Wilson, Gouverneur Morris.*

Delaware. John Dickinson, *George Reed,* Gunning Bedford, Richard Basset, *Jacob Broome.*

Maryland. Robert Hanson Harrison, Charles Carroll, of Carrolton, James McHenry.

Virginia. *George Washington, Peyton Randolph,* John Blair, *James Maddison,* George Mason, *George Wythe,* Richard Henry Lee.

North Carolina. Alexander Martin, Willis Jones, *Richard Dobbs Spaight,* William Richardson Davie, William Blunt.

South Carolina. *John Rutledge,* Charles Caterworth Pinckney, Henry Laurens, *Charles Pinckney,* Pierce Butler.

Georgia. *William Few,* Abraham Baldwin, George Walton, William Pierce, William Houston, Nathaniel Pendelton.

XIV. George Washington to Arthur Lee.[1]

Philadelphia, May 20th, 1787.

My rheumatic complaint having very much abated . . . I have yielded to what appeared to be the wishes of many of my friends, and am now here as a delegate to the convention. Not more than four states were represented yesterday. If any have come in since, it is unknown to me. These delays greatly impede public measures, and serve to sour the temper of the punctual members, who do not like to idle away their time. ⸺

XV. George Mason to George Mason, Jr.[2]

Philadelphia, May 20th, 1787.

Upon our arrival here on Thursday evening, seventeenth May, I found only the States of Virginia and Pennsylvania fully repre-

---

[1] R. H. Lee, *Life of Arthur Lee,* II, 173.

[2] K. M. Rowland, *Life of George Mason,* II, 100–102.

sented; and there are at this time only five — New York, the two Carolinas, and the two before mentioned. All the States, Rhode Island excepted, have made their appointments; but the members drop in slowly; some of the deputies from the Eastern States are here, but none of them have yet a sufficient representation, and it will probably be several days before the Convention will be authorized to proceed to business. The expectations and hopes of all the Union centre in this Convention. God grant that we may be able to concert effectual means of preserving our country from the evils which threaten us.

The Virginia deputies (who are all here) meet and confer together two or three hours every day, in order to form a proper correspondence of sentiments; and for form's sake, to see what new deputies are arrived, and to grow into some acquaintance with each other, we regularly meet every day at three o'clock. These and some occasional conversations with the deputies of different States, and with some of the general officers of the late army (who are here upon a general meeting of the Cincinnati), are the only opportunities I have hitherto had of forming any opinion upon the great subject of our mission, and, consequently, a very imperfect and indecisive one. Yet, upon the great principles of it, I have reason to hope there will be greater unanimity and less opposition, except from the little States, than was at first apprehended. The most prevalent idea in the principal States seems to be a total alteration of the present federal system, and substituting a great national council or parliament, consisting of two branches of the legislature, founded upon the principles of equal proportionate representation, with full legislative powers upon all the subjects of the Union; and an executive: and to make the several State legislatures subordinate to the national, by giving the latter the power of a negative upon all such laws as they shall judge contrary to the interest of the federal Union. It is easy to foresee that there will be much difficulty in organizing a government upon this great scale, and at the same time reserving to the State legislatures a sufficient portion of power for promoting and securing the prosperity and happiness of their respective citizens; yet with a proper degree of coolness, liberality and candor (very rare commodities by the bye), I doubt not but it may be effected. There are among a variety some very eccentric opinions upon this great subject; and what is a very extraordinary phenomenon, we are likely to find the republicans, on this occasion, issue from the Southern and Middle States, and the anti-republicans from the Eastern; however extraordinary this may at first seem, it may, I think be accounted for from a very common and natural impulse of the human mind.   Men disappointed in expectations too hastily and sanguinely formed, tired and disgusted with the unexpected evils they have experienced, and anxious to remove them as far as possible, are very apt to run into the opposite extreme; and the people of the Eastern States, setting out with more republican principles, have consequently been more disappointed than we have been.

We found travelling very expensive — from eight to nine dollars per day.   In this city the living is cheap.   We are at the old *Indian Queen* in Fourth Street, where we are very well accommodated, have a good room to ourselves, and are charged only twenty-five Pennsylvania currency per day, including our servants and horses, exclusive of club in liquors and extra charges; so that I hope I shall be able to defray my expenses with my public allowance, and more than that I do not wish.   _____

XVI. George Mason to Arthur Lee.[1]

Philadelphia, May 21, 1787.

I arrived in this city on Thursday evening last, but found so few of the deputies here from the several States that I am unable to form any certain opinion on the subject of our mission.   The most prevalent idea I think at present is a total change of the federal system, and instituting a great national council or parliament upon the principles of equal, proportionate representation, consisting of two branches of the legislature invested with full legislative powers upon the objects of the Union; and to make the State legislatures subordinate to the national by giving to the latter a negative upon all such laws as they judge contrary to the principles and interest of the Union; to establish also a national executive, and a judiciary system with cognizance of all such matters as depend upon the law of nations, and such other objects as the local courts of justice may be inadequate to. . . .

I have received your favor by Major Jackson; nothing that I have heard has yet been mentioned upon this subject among the deputies now here; though I understand there are several candidates, which I am surprised at, as the office will be of so short duration, and merely honorary, or *possibly* introductory to something more substantial.   _____

XVII. George Read to John Dickinson.[2]

Philadelphia, May 21st, 1787.

It was rather unlucky that you had not given me a hint of your

[1] Rowland, *Life of George Mason*, II, 102–103.
[2] W. T. Read, *Life and Correspondence of George Read*, pp. 443–444.

wish to be in a lodging-house at an earlier day. Mrs. House's,[1] where I am, is very crowded, and the room I am presently in so small as not to admit of a second bed. That which I had heretofore, on my return from New York, was asked for Governor Randolph, it being then expected he would have brought his lady with him, which he did not, but she is expected to follow some time hence.

I have not seen Mr. Bassett, being from my lodgings when he called last evening. He stopt at the Indian Queen, where Mr. Mason, of Virginia, stays, the last of their seven deputies who came in. We have now a quorum from six States, to wit: South and North Carolina, Virginia, Delaware, Pennsylvania, and New York, and single deputies from three others, — Georgia, New Jersey, and Massachusetts, — whose additional ones are hourly expected, and also the Connecticut deputies, who have been appointed, within the last ten days, by the Legislature there. We have no particular accounts from New Hampshire, other than that the delegates to Congress were appointed deputies to this convention. Maryland you may probably have heard more certain accounts of than we who are here. Rhode Island hath made no appointment as yet.

The gentlemen who came here early, particularly Virginia, that had a quorum on the first day, express much uneasiness at the backwardness of individuals in giving attendance. It is meant to organize the body as soon as seven States' quorums attend. I wish you were here.

I am in possession of a copied draft of a Federal system intended to be proposed, if something nearly similar shall not precede it. Some of its principal features are taken from the New York system of government. A house of delegates and senate for a general legislature, as to the great business of the Union. The first of them to be chosen by the Legislature of each State, in proportion to its number of white inhabitants, and three-fifths of all others, fixing a number for sending each representative. The second, to wit, the senate, to be elected by the delegates so returned, either from themselves or the people at large, in four great districts, into which the United States are to be divided for the purpose of forming this senate from, which, when so formed, is to be divided into four classes for the purpose of an annual rotation of a fourth of the members. A president having only executive powers for seven years. By this plan our State may have a representation in the House of Delegates of one member in eighty. I suspect it to be of importance to the small States that their deputies should keep a strict watch

---

[1] On Market Street.

upon the movements and propositions from the larger States, who will probably combine to swallow up the smaller ones by addition, division, or impoverishment; and, if you have any wish to assist in guarding against such attempts, you will be speedy in your attendance. ————————

XVIII. GEORGE WASHINGTON: DIARY.[1]

Monday, [May] 21. — Delaware State was represented. . . .
Tuesday, 22. — North Carolina represented. . . .
Wednesday, 23. — No more States represented. . . .
Thursday, 24. — No more States represented.

————————

XIX. WILLIAM GRAYSON TO JAMES MADISON.[2]

24th. May 1787.

Entre nous. I believe the Eastern people have taken ground they will not depart from respecting the Convention. — *One legislature* composed of a lower-house tri ennially elected and an *Executive* & *Senate* for a good number of years. — I shall see Gerry & Johnson, as they pass & may perhaps give you a hint.

————————

XIXa. RUFUS KING TO JEREMIAH WADSWORTH.[3]

Philadelphia 24 May 87

New York, Delaware, Pennsylvania Virginia North and South Carolina, are represented by a Quorum or the whole of their Delegates — New Jersey will probably be represented Tomorrow. Should this be the Case the Convention will be able to appoint their President and Secretary. General Washington will be placed in the Chair, and Temple Franklin or Majr. Jackson will be Secretary — Georgia and Maryland will be represented in three or four Days — I am mortified that I alone am from New England — the Backwardness may prove unfortunate — Pray hurry on your Delegates — some personal Sacrifices perhaps may stand in the way of their immediate attendance — But they ought not to yield to such Considerations — Believe me it may prove most unfortunate if they do not attend within a few days —

————————

[1] *Pennsylvania Magazine of History and Biography,* XI, 298.
[2] *Documentary History of the Constitution,* IV, 167.
[3] Jeremiah Wadsworth Papers, Connecticut Historical Society. Furnished to the editor through the courtesy of Mr. Edmund C. Burnett of the Department of Historical Research of the Carnegie Institution of Washington.

XX. George Washington: Diary.[1]

Friday, [May] 25. — Another delegate comes in from the State of New Jersey. Made a quorum. And seven States being now represented the body was organized and I was called to the Chair by a unanimous vote. Major Jackson was appointed Secretary and a Com'ee. consisting of Mr. Wythe, Mr. Hamilton and Mr. Ch. Pinkney chosen to prepare rules and regulations by which the convention should be governed. To give time for this it adjourned till Monday, 10 o'clock. ————

XXI. James Madison to Edmund Pendleton.[2]

Philada. May 27. 1787.

I have put off from day to day writing to my friends from this place in hopes of being able to say something of the Convention. Contrary to every previous calculation the bare quorum of seven States was not made up till the day before yesterday. The States composing it are N. York, N. Jersey, Pena. Delaware, Virga. N. Carolina & S. Carolina. Individual members are here from Massts. Maryland & Georgia; and our intelligence promises a compleat addition of the first and last, as also of Connecticut by tomorrow General Washington was called to the chair by a unanimous voice, and has accepted it. The Secretary is a Major Jackson. This is all that has yet been done except the appointment of a Committe for preparing the rules by which the Convention is to be governed in their proceedings. A few days will now furnish some data for calculating the probable result of the meeting. In general the members seem to accord in viewing our situation as peculiarly critical and in being averse to temporising expedients. I wish they may as readily agree when particulars are brought forward. Congress are reduced to five or six States, and are not likely to do any thing during the term of the Convention. ————

XXII. James Madison to his Father.[3]

Philada. May 27th. 1787.

We have been here for some time suffering a daily disappointment from the failure of the deputies to assemble for the Convention. Seven States were not made up till the day before yesterday. Our intelligence from N. York promises an addition of three more by tomorrow. General Washington was unanimously called to

---

[1] *Pennsylvania Magazine of History and Biography*, XI, 298.
[2] *Documentary History of the Constitution*, IV, 169.
[3] *Documentary History of the Constitution*, IV, 168.

the Chair & has accepted it.   It is impossible as yet to form a judgment of the result of this experiment.   Every reflecting man becomes
daily more alarmed at our situation.

XXIII. George Mason to George Mason, Jr.[1]

Philadelphia, May 27, 1787.

It is impossible to judge how long we shall be detained here,
but from present appearances I fear until July, if not later.   I begin
to grow heartily tired of the etiquette and nonsense so fashionable
in this city.   It would take me some months to make myself master
of them, and that it should require months to learn what is not worth
remembering as many minutes, is to me so discouraging a circumstance as determines me to give myself no manner of trouble about
them.   . . .

We had yesterday, for the first time, a representation of seven
States — New York, New Jersey, Pennsylvania, Delaware, Virginia, and the two Carolinas, and it is expected that the deputies
from Massachusetts, Connecticut, and Georgia will be here by Monday or Tuesday.   The State of Rhode Island has refused to appoint
deputies, and although New Hampshire has appointed it is thought
we shall be deprived of their representation by no provision having
been made for defraying their expenses.   The State of Delaware
has tied up the hands of her deputies by an express direction to
retain the principle in the present Confederation of each State having the same vote; no other State, so far as we have yet seen, hath
restrained its deputies on any subject.

Nothing was done yesterday but unanimously appointing
General Washington President; Major Jackson (by a majority of
five States to two) Secretary; reading the credentials from the
different States on the floor, and appointing a committee to draw up
and report the rules of proceeding.   It is expected our doors will be
shut, and communications upon the business of the Convention be
forbidden during its sitting.   This I think myself a proper precaution to prevent mistakes and misrepresentation until the business
shall have been completed, when the whole may have a very
different complexion from that in which the several crude and
indigested parts might in their first shape appear if submitted to
the public eye.

---

[1] Rowland, *Life of George Mason*, II, 103–4.

XXIV. Edmund Randolph to Beverley Randolph.[1]

Philadelphia, May 27, 1787.

Seven States met on friday, appointed a committee to prepare rules, and adjourned 'till Monday. In four or five days we shall probably have every State represented, except Rhode Island, which has peremptorily refused to appoint deputies, and new Hampshire, of which we can hear nothing certain but her friendly temper towards the Union. I aught, however, to add, that a respectable minority in R. Island are solicitous that their State should participate in the Convention. ─────────

XXV. George Washington: Diary.[2]

Monday, [May] 28. — Met in Convention at 10 o'clock. Two States more, viz.: Massachusetts and Connecticut being represented, made nine more on the floor; proceeded to the establishment of rules for the government of the Convention and adjourned about 2 o'clock.

Tuesday, 29. — The same number of States met in the Convention as yesterday. ─────────

XXVI. William Blount to Governor Caswell.[3]

New York, May 28th, 1787.

Soon after the arrival of Mr. Spaight at Philadelphia he informed me by letter that he had brought with him a Commission for me to attend the Convention at the place and Stead of your Excellency. I had been for some time before, and at this time, too indisposed to undertake a journey so far as Philadelphia; at present I am much on the Recovery and shall leave this in a few days to attend the duties of that appointment. On the 24th Inst., only Six States had appeared, among which North Carolina included and had four Members present; on the 25th there were Seven and at that period the Delegates from Massachusetts had passed through this City. North Carolina being so strongly represented and no Convention being formed until this day (if to-day) my absence as yet have been certainly of no moment, indeed I have not the Vanity to suppose my presence and assistance will be of much avail in so arduous a Business as the Amending the Confederation. For some days past not more than five States have appeared on the Floor of Congress Chamber, it is Generally believed that there will not appear a Sufficient Number to form a Congress until the Convention rises.

───────────────

[1] *Virginia Calendar of State Papers*, IV, 291.
[2] *Pennsylvania Magazine of History and Biography*, XI, 299.
[3] *North Carolina State Records*, XX, 706–7.

XXVII. William Grayson to James Monroe.[1]

N York May 29th. 1787.

The draught made from Congress of members for the Convention has made them very thin & no business of course is going on here: I do not believe that this will be the case untill that body shall be dissolved, which I hardly think will be the case these three months. What will be the result of their meeting I cannot with any certainty determine, but I hardly think much good can come of it: the people of America don't appear to me to be ripe for any great innovations & it seems they are ultimately to ratify or reject: the weight of Genl. Washington as you justly observe is very great in America, but I hardly think it is sufficient to induce the people to pay money or part with power.

The delegates from the Eastwd. are for a very strong government, & wish to prostrate all ye. state legislature, & form a general system out of ye. whole; but I don't learn that the people are with them, on ye. contrary in Massachuzets they think that government too strong & are about rebelling again, for the purpose of making it more democratical: In Connecticut they have rejected the requisition for ye. present year decidedly, & no Man there would be elected to the office of a constable if he was to declare that he meant to pay a copper towards the domestic debt: — R. Island has refused to send members — the cry there is for a good government after they have paid their debts in depreciated paper: — first demolish the Philistines /i, e, their Creditors/ & then for *propriety.*

N Hamshire has not paid a shilling, since peace, & does not ever mean to pay one to all eternity: — if it was attempted to tax the people for ye domestic debt 500 Shays would arise in a fortnight. — In N. York they pay well because they can do it by plundering N Jersey & Connecticut. — Jersey will go great lengths from motives of revenge and Interest: Pensylvany will join provided you let the sessions of the Executive of America be fixed in Philada. & give her other advantages in trade to compensate for the loss of State power. I shall make no observations on the southern States, but I think they will be/ perhaps from different motives/ as little disposed to part with efficient power as any in the Union.

XXVIII. Henry Knox to General Washington.[2]

New-York 29 May 1787

As you will have states sufficient to proceed to business, we hope

---

[1] *Documentary History of the Constitution,* IV, 170-171.
[2] *Documentary History of the Constitution,* IV, 171.

to hear by the post of this day that you are completely organized. Mr Peirce, & Mr Houston from Georgia set off from this place for Philadelphia yesterday. Mr Sherman & Doctor Johnson will be in Philadelphia in the course of the week. I have not heard any thing from New Hampshire, but I am persuaded, from circumstances, that the delegates from that state will be with you by the 10th of June. I am indeed happy that the convention will be so full, as to feel a confidence that they represent the great majority of the people of the United States.

XXIX. W. R. Davie to James Iredell.[1]

Philadelphia, May 30th, 1787.

After a very fatiguing and rapid journey I arrived here on the 22d. The gentlemen of the Convention had been waiting from day to day for the presence of seven States; on the 25th the members from Jersey attended, and Gen. Washington was chosen President. Yesterday nine States were represented, and the great business of the meeting was brought forward by Virginia, with whom the proposition for a Convention had originated.

As no progress can yet be expected in a business so weighty, and, at the same time, so complicated, you will not look for any news now from this quarter.

XXX. George Washington to Thomas Jefferson.[2]

Philadelphia 30th May 1787.

But, having since been appointed by my native State to attend the national convention, and having been pressed to a compliance in a manner, which it hardly becomes me to describe, I have, in a measure, been obliged to sacrifice my own sentiments, and to be present in Philadelphia. . . .

The business of this convention is as yet too much in embryo to form any opinion of the conclusion. Much is expected from it by some; not much by others; and nothing by a few. That something is necessary, none will deny; for the situation of the general government, if it can be called a government, is shaken to its foundation, and liable to be overturned by every blast. In a word, it is at an end; and, unless a remedy is soon applied, anarchy and confusion will inevitably ensue.

---

[1] McRee, *Life and Correspondence of James Iredell*, II, 161.
[2] W. C. Ford, *Writings of George Washington*, XI, 158–159.

XXXI. George Washington: Diary.[1]

Wednesday, [May] 30. — Convention as yesterday. . . .

Thursday, 31. — Convention representation increased by coming in of the State of Georgia, occasioned by the arrival of Maj. Pierce and Mr. Houston. . . .

Friday, June 1. — Convention as yesterday.

XXXII.[2] George Mason to George Mason, jr.[3]

Philadelphia, June 1st, 1787.

The idea I formerly mentioned to you, before the Convention met, of a great national council, consisting of two branches of the legislature, a judiciary and an executive, upon the principle of fair representation in the legislature, with powers adapted to the great objects of the Union, and consequently a control in these instances, on the State legislatures, is still the prevalent one. Virginia has had the honor of presenting the outlines of the plan, upon which the convention is proceeding; but so slowly that it is impossible to judge when the business will be finished, most probably not before August — *festina lente* may very well be called our motto. When I first came here, judging from casual conversations with gentlemen from the different States, I was very apprehensive that soured and disgusted with the unexpected evils we had experienced from the democratic principles of our governments, we should be apt to run into the opposite extreme and in endeavoring to steer too far from Scylla, we might be drawn into the vortex of Charybdis, of which I still think there is some danger, though I have the pleasure to find in the convention, many men of fine republican principles. America has certainly, upon this occasion, drawn forth her first characters; there are upon this Convention many gentlemen of the most respectable abilities, and so far as I can discover, of the purest intentions. The eyes of the United States are turned upon this assembly, and their expectations raised to a very anxious degree.

May God grant, we may be able to gratify them, by establishing a wise and just government. For my own part, I never before felt myself in such a situation; and declare I would not, upon pecuniary motives, serve in this convention for a thousand pounds per day. The revolt from Great Britain and the formations of our new governments at that time, were nothing compared to the great

---

[1] *Pennsylvania Magazine of History and Biography,* XI, 299–300.

[2] For Diary of William Samuel Johnson, June 1– September 18, see Supplement to Appendix A, CCCCII.

[3] Rowland, *Life of George Mason,* II, 129–130.

business now before us; there was then a certain degree of enthusiasm, which inspired and supported the mind; but to view, through the calm, sedate medium of reason the influence which the establishment now proposed may have upon the happiness or misery of millions yet unborn, is an object of such magnitude, as absorbs, and in a manner suspends the operations of the human understanding. . . .

All communications of the proceedings are forbidden during the sitting of the Convention; this I think was a necessary precaution to prevent misrepresentations or mistakes; there being a material difference between the appearance of a subject in its first crude and undigested shape, and after it shall have been properly matured and arranged. ——————————

XXXIII. George Washington: Diary.[1]

Saturday, [June] 2. — Major Jenifer, coming in with powers from the State of Maryland authorizing one member to represent it, added another State, now eleven, to the convention.

——————————

XXXIV. Benjamin Rush to Richard Price.[2]

Philadelphia, June 2nd, 1787.

Dr Franklin exhibits daily a spectacle of transcendent benevolence by attending the Convention punctually, and even taking part in its business and deliberations. He says "it is the most august and respectable Assembly he ever was in in his life, and adds, that he thinks they will soon finish their business, as there are no prejudices to oppose, nor errors to refute in any of the body." Mr. Dickinson (who is one of them) informs me that they are all *united* in their objects, and he expects they will be equally united in the means of attaining them. Mr. Adams's book has diffused such excellent principles among us, that there is little doubt of our adopting a vigorous and compounded federal legislature. Our illustrious minister in this gift to his country has done us more service than if he had obtained alliances for us with all the nations of Europe.

——————————

XXXV. Jeremiah Wadsworth to Rufus King.[3]

Hartford, June 3, 1787.

Yours of the 24th ulto. came to hand after our delegates had set out. I am satisfied with the appointment — except Sherman,

[1] *Pennsylvania Magazine of History and Biography*, XI, 300.

[2] Massachusetts Historical Society, *Proceedings*, Second Series, XVII, 367.

[3] C. R. King, *Life and Correspondence of Rufus King*, I, 221.

who, I am told, is disposed to patch up the old scheme of Government. This was not my opinion of him, when we chose him: he is as cunning as the Devil, and if you attack him, you ought to know him well; he is not easily managed, but if he suspects you are trying to take him in, you may as well catch an Eel by the tail.

XXXV*c*. GEORGE WASHINGTON: DIARY.[1]

Monday, [June] 4. — Convention as on Saturday.

XXXVI. GEORGE WASHINGTON TO LA FAYETTE.[2]

Philadelphia, June 6th 1787.

It was, when I came here, and still is, my intention, to write you a long letter from this place before I leave it, but the hour is not yet come when I can do it to my own Satisfaction or for your information.   I therefore shall wait till the result of the present meeting is more matured, and till the members who constitute it are at liberty to communicate the proceedings more freely before I attempt it.

You will I dare say, be surprized my dear Marquis to receive a letter from me at this place, — you will probably, be more so, when you hear that I am again brought, contrary to my public declaration, and intention, on a public theatre — such is the viscissitude of human affairs, and such the frailty of human nature that no man I conceive can well answer for the resolutions he enters into.

The pressure of the public voice was so loud, I could not resist the call to a convention of the States which is to determine whether we are to have a Government of respectability under which life — liberty, and property will be secured to us, or are to submit to one which may be the result of chance or the moment, springing perhaps from anarchy and Confusion, and dictated perhaps by some aspiring demagogue who will not consult the interest of his Country so much as his own ambitious views.   What my be the result of the present deliberations is more than I am able, at present, if I was at liberty, to inform you, & therefore I will make this letter short, with the assurance of being more particular when I can be more satisfactory —

XXXVII. JAMES MADISON TO THOMAS JEFFERSON.[3]

Philada. June 6th. 1787.

The day fixed for the meeting of the Convention was the 14th.

---

[1] *Pennsylvania Magazine of History and Biography*, XI, 300.
[2] *Documentary History of the Constitution*, IV, 184.
[3] *Documentary History of the Constitution*, IV, 181–183.

ult: on the 25th. and not before seven States were assembled. General Washington was placed unâ voce in the chair. The Secretaryship was given to Major Jackson. The members present are from Massachusetts Mr. Gerry, Mr. Gorum, Mr. King, Mr. Strong. From Connecticut Mr. Sherman Doct. S. Johnson, Mr. Elseworth. From N. York Judge Yates, Mr. Lansing, Col. Hamilton. N. Jersey, Governour Livingston, Judge Brearly, Mr. Patterson, Attorney Genl. (Mr. Houston & Mr. Clarke are absent members.) From Pennsylvania Doctr. Franklyn, Mr. Morris, Mr. Wilson, Mr. Fitzimmons, Mr. G. Clymer. Genl. Mifflin, Mr. Governeur Morris, Mr. Ingersoll. From Delaware Mr. Jno. Dickenson, Mr. Reed, Mr. Bedford, Mr Broom, Mr. Bassett. From Maryland Majr. Jenifer only. Mr. McHenry, Mr. Danl. Carrol, Mr. Jno. Mercer, Mr. Luther Martin are absent members. The three last have supplied the resignations of Mr. Stone, Mr. Carrol of Carolton, and Mr. T. Johnson as I have understood the case. From Virginia Genl. Washington, Governor Randolph, Mr. Blair, Col. Mason, Docr. McClurg, J Madison. — Mr. Wythe left us yesterday, being called home by the serious declension of his lady's health. From N. Carolina, Col. Martin late Governor, Docr. Williamson, Mr. Spaight, Col. Davy. — Col. Blount is another member but is detained by indisposition at N. York. From S. Carolina Mr. John Rutlidge, General Pinkney, Mr. Charles Pinkney, Majr. Pierce Butler. Mr. Laurens is in the Commission from that State, but will be kept away by the want of health. From Georgia Col. Few, Majr. Pierce, formerly of Williamsbg. & aid to Genl. Greene, Mr. Houston. — Mr. Baldwin will be added to them in a few days. Walton and Pendleton are also in the deputation. — N. Hamshire has appointed Deputies but they are not expected; the State treasury being empty it is said, and a substitution of private resorces being inconvenient or impracticable. I mention this circumstance to take off the appearance of backwardness, which that State is not in the least chargeable with, if we are rightly informed of her disposition. Rhode Island has not yet acceded to the measure As their Legislature meet very frequently, and can at any time be got together in a week, it is possible that caprice if no other motive may yet produce a unanimity of the States in this experiment.

In furnishing you with this list of names, I have exhausted all the means which I can make use of for gratifying your curiosity, It was thought expedient in order to secure unbiassed discussion within doors, and to prevent misconceptions & misconstructions without, to establish some rules of caution which will for no short time restrain even a confidential communication of our proceedings. The names of the members will satisfy you that the States have been serious in this business. The attendance of Genl, Washington is a proof of the light in which he regards it. The whole Community is big with expectation. And there can be no doubt but that the result will in some way or other have a powerful effect on our destiny.

XXXVIII. Edmund Randolph to Beverley Randolph.[1]

Philadelphia, June 6, 1787.

The prospect of a very long sojournment here has determined me to bring up my family. They will want about thirty pounds for the expense of travelling. The Executive will therefore oblige me by directing a warrant in my favor, to be delivered to Mrs. R. for that amount. My account stands thus:

1787.	Dr.	With the Comm'lth.
May 2d — To cash received . . . . £100.00.[2]		
	57.12.	
	£ 42. 8. now in my hands.	

1787.		Cr.
June 6 — By attending from the 6th of May to this day (both inclusive), 32 days, at 6 dols. per day, which amount to 192 d's, and are equal to . . . .£57.12s.		

Twenty-three or four days more will overrun this sum, and will have elapsed before my family can arrive, so that I trust there will be no difficulty in the advance,

Mr. Wythe has left 50£ of his money to be distributed among such of his colleagues as should require it. . . . We have every reason to expect harmony in the convention, altho' the currents of opinion are various. But no man can yet divine in what form our efforts against the American crises will appear to the public eye. It will not be settled in its principles for perhaps some weeks hence.

XXXVIIIa. James Madison to William Short.[3]

Philada. June 6th. 1787

The Convention has been formed about 12 days. It contains in several instances the most respectable characters in the U. S.

---

[1] *Calendar of Virginia State Papers*, IV, 293–294.

[2] "A hundred pounds was voted for each of the Virginia delegates, and a vessel ordered to convey those residing at Williamsburg, — Blair and Wythe." (M. D. Conway, *Omitted Chapters of History*, 64.)

[3] William Short MSS., Library of Congress.

and in general may be said to be the best contribution of talents the States could make for the occasion. What the result of the experiment may be is among the arcana of futurity. Our affairs are considered on all hands as at a most serious crisis. No hope is entertained from the existing Confederacy. And the eyes and hopes of all are turned towards this new assembly. The result therefore whatever it may be must have a material influence on our destiny, and, on that of the cause of republican liberty. The personal characters of the members promise much. The spirit which they bring with them seems in general equally promising. But the labor is great indeed; whether we consider the real or imaginary difficulties within doors or without doors.

XXXIX. DAVID BREARLEY TO JONATHAN DAYTON.[1]

Philadelphia, 9th June 1787.

We have been in a Committee of the Whole for some time, and have under consideration a number of very *important* propositions, none of which, however, have as yet been reported. My colleagues, as well as myself, are very desirous that you should join us immediately. The importance of the business really demands it.

XL. EDWARD CARRINGTON TO THOMAS JEFFERSON.[2]

New York June 9. 1787

The proposed scheme of a convention has taken more general effect, and promises more solid advantages than was at first hoped for. all the States have elected representatives except Rhode Island, whose apostasy from every moral, as well as political, obligation, has placed her perfectly without the views of her confederates; nor will her absence, or nonconcurrence, occasion the least impediment in any stage of the intended business. on friday the 25th. Ult. seven States having assembled, at Philadelphia, the Convention was formed by the election of General Washington President, and Major W. Jackson Secretary — the numbers have since encreased to 11 States — N. Hampshire has not yet arrived, but is daily expected.

The Commissions of these Gentlemen go to a thorough reform of our confederation — some of the States, at first, restricted their deputies to commercial objects, but have since liberated them. the

---

[1] J. F. Jameson, *Studies in the History of the Federal Convention* in the *Annual Report of the American Historical Association* for 1902, p. 98.

[2] *Documentary History of the Constitution*, IV, 189-195.

latitude thus given, together with the generality of the Commission from the States, have doubtless operated to bring Genl. Washington forward, contrary to his more early determination — his conduct in both instances indicate a deep impression upon his mind, of the necessity of some material change — . . .

Men are brought into action who had consigned themselves to an eve of rest, and the Convention, as a Beacon, is rousing the attention of the Empire.

The prevailing impression as well in, as out of, Convention, is, that a fœderal Government adapted to the permanent circumstances of the Country, without respect to the habits of the day, be formed, whose efficiency shall pervade the whole Empire: it may, and probably will, at first, be viewed with hesitation, but, derived and patronsed as it will be, its influence must extend into a general adoption as the present fabric gives way. that the people are disposed to be governed is evinced in their turning out to support the shadows under which they now live, and if a work of wisdom is prepared for them, they will not reject it to commit themselves to the dubious issue of Anarchy.

The debates and proceedings of the Convention are kept in profound secrecy — opinions of the probable result of their deliberations can only be formed from the prevailing impressions of men of reflection and understanding — these are reducible to two schemes — the first, a consolidation of the whole Empire into one republic, leaving in the states nothing more than subordinate courts for facilitating the administration of the Laws — the second an investiture of of a fœderal sovereignty with full and independant authority as to the Trade, Revenues, and forces of the Union, and the rights of peace and War, together with a Negative upon all the Acts of the State legislatures. the first idea, I apprehend, would be impracticable, and therefore do not suppose it can be adopted — general Laws through a Country embracing so many climates, productions, and manners, as the United States, would operate many oppressions, & a general legislature would be found incompetent to the formation of local ones, as a majority would, in every instance, be ignorant of, and unaffected by the objects of legislation — the essential rights, as well as advantages, of representation would be lost, and obedience to the public decrees could only be ensured by the exercise of powers different from those derivable from a free constitution — such an experiment must therefore terminate in a despotism, or the same inconveniencies we are now deliberating to remove. Something like the second will probably be formed — indeed I am certain that nothing less than what will give the fœderal sovereignty a compleat controul over the State Governments, will be thought worthy of discussion — such a scheme constructed upon well adjusted principles would certainly give us stability and importance as a nation, and if the Executive powers can be sufficiently checked, must be eligible — unless the whole has a decided influence over the parts, the constant effort will be to resume the delegated powers, and there cannot be an inducement in the fœderal sovereignty to refuse its assent to an innocent Act of a State. the negative which the King of England had upon our Laws was never found to be materially inconvenient _____

XLI. MR. OTTO, CHARGÉ D'AFFAIRES DE FRANCE, AU SECRÉTAIRE D'ETAT DES AFFAIRES ETRANGÈRES, COMTE DE MONTMORIN.[1]

No. 91.

Monseigneur, A New York, le 10 juin 1787.

Explication sur les plans de réforme projettés dans la Convention fédérale de Philadelphie. Différens partis qui s'y opposeront. Opinion que le mieux seroit de maintenir la confédération actuelle.

Dans ma dépêche No. 85, je me suis borné à soumettre à la Cour une idée générale des changemens qui doivent être faits dans la Constitution fédérale par la *Convention* de Philadelphie. Les plans de réforme qui m'ont été communiqués depuis me mettent en état de vous informer plus amplement des innovations que les députés se proposent d'introduire. Comme il s'agit de refondre entièrement la constitution américaine, j'espère, Monseigneur, que vous excuserés les longueurs qu'il me sera impossible d'éviter. On est rarement spectateur d'une opération politique plus importante que celle-ci, et il est difficile de renfermer dans peu de pages des objets qui doivent déterminer le bonheur, la puissance et l'énergie future d'un Empire naissant.

Le premier vice de la Constitution actuelle, Monseigneur, est l'inégalite de la représentation. Tous les Etats ont une voix dans le Conseil fédéral, mais leur population, leur étendue, leurs richesses diffèrent à l'infini. La Géorgie, le Rhodeisland, le Delaware ont en Congrès la même importance que la Virginie, la Pensylvanie, le Massachussets, quoique ces derniers Etats soient au moins cinquante fois plus peuplés et plus opulens que les autres. Il

---

[1] French Archives: *Ministère des Affaires Etrangèrs. Archives. Etats-Unis. Correspondance.*Vol. 32, pp. 275 ff.

s'agit donc de diviser les Etats en districts, com-
posés d'un certain nombre d'habitans et de donner
à chaque district le droit d'envoyer un député en
Congrès. Parce moyen, la Virginie, auroit cinquante voix pour une de la Géorgie, et une résolution du Congrès exprimeroit le vœu de la *majorite
des habitans* et non de la *majorité d'une division
fortuite d'Etats*. Les députés de tous les districts
formeroient donc un corps politique semblable à
la Chambre des Communes en Angleterre. Les suffrages y seroient comptés par têtes et non collective-
ment par Etats, et les bills concernant les finances
ne pourroient être proposés que dans cette Chambre.

Mais les intrigues d'un homme entreprenant,
l'or d'une puissance étrangère, l'éloquence funeste
d'un membre accrédité ou peut être l'avidité d'un
marchand pourroient y former un parti contraire
au bien général. Pour éviter cet inconvénient, on
propose une autre branche législative qu'on pourroit
appeller le *Senat* et qui ressembleroit quant à ses
fonctions à la Chambre haute du Parlement d'Angleterre. Les sénateurs seroient élus par la Chambre
des députés en proportion des suffrages de chaque
Etat. Aucune résolution ne pourroit avoir force de
loi qu'après avoir été approuvée par la majorité des
deux Chambres.

Il seroit cependant encore possible que le grand
nombre d'affaires fît précipiter des résolutions im-
portantes. Un Président élu pour six années et
son Conseil composé des différens Ministres d'Etats
auroient donc le droit d'examiner ces résolutions
avant qu'elles fussent publiées et de les remettre
de nouveau sous les yeux des deux Chambres. Dans
ce cas, il faudroit une majorité de deux tiers des
représentans pour faire passer une loi.

Mais malgré toutes ces précautions, on ne
pourroit encore être sûr que d'une bonne *législation*,
dont le Congrès, même dans sa forme actuelle, s'est
assés bien acquitté. Il n'en est pas de même de la
branche *exécutive*, puisque cette assemblée n'a eu
jusqu'ici que le droit de *recommander*, aux différens
Etats les mesures qui lui paroissoient être les plus
avantageuses. D'après les nouveaux plans, le Prési-

dent et son Conseil auroient le droit d'exécuter par
la force les résolutions du Conseil féderal, à peu près
de la même manière dont l'Empereur fait exécuter
les décrets de la diète de Ratisbonne, en faisant
marcher des troupes ou en ordonnant à plusieurs
Etats voisins d'envahir le Gouvernment qui refuseroit
de se soumettre à la volonté collective des Etats.

Cette dernière partie du projet, Monseigneur,
éprouvera les plus grandes difficultés, et, quoique
plusieurs députés, comptent la faire passer il m'est
impossible de l'espérer. Les intérêts des petits
Etats seroient bientôt sacrifiés aux vues ambitieuses
de leurs voisins, qui, ayant l'avantage d'avoir en
Congrès une représentation beaucoup plus nom-
breuse, seroient toujours sûrs de la majorité.

Les réformateurs observent ensuite combien il
est difficile d'obtenir pour une innovation quelconque
le consentement de treize Etats, ainsi qu'il est
statué par l'ancienne Constitution. L'opposition
d'un seul Etat a empêché depuis quatre ans l'éstab-
lissement d'un droit de 5 pour o|o sur les importa-
tions, droit qui auroit suffi à tous les besoins de la
confédération. Cette faculté, presqu' aussi ruin-
euse pour les Etats-Unis que l'a été le *liberum veto*
pour la république de Pologne, est entièrement
incompatible avec un gouvernment bien ordonné.
On propose en conséquence que désormais le suffrage de dix Etats soit suffisant pour toute altéra-
tion que les circonstances pourront rendre nécessaire
dans le système général, et que tout Etat qui
refusera de s'y conformer soit exclu pour toujours
de la confédération.

Pour mettre fin aux contradictions qui se trouvent
quelquefois entre les loix des Etats particuliers et
celles du gouvernement général, on propose de nom-
mer un Committé des deux Chambres, chagré d'examiner toutes les loix des Etats individuels et de
rejeter toutes celles qui seront contraires aux maximes
et aux vues du Congrès. Les Etats seront surtout
privés de la faculté de faire aucun règlement de
commerce ou de statuer sur aucun objet relatif au
droit des gens et le Congrès se réservera exclusivement cette branche de législation.

Les deux Chambres du Congrès, de concert avec le Conseil de révision, auroient le droit exclusif de déterminer le nombre de troupes et de vaisseaux nécessaire pour soutenir la majesté de peuple américain, et, sans demander le consentement particulier des Etats, ils pourroient répartir les taxes et les impôts de la manière qui leur paroitroit la plus équitable, et, en cas de refus d'un Etat particulier, le Congrès pourroit y lever par ses propres officiers le double de son contingent pour le punir de son opposition.

Les députés, Monseigneur, qui m'ont communiqué ces différens projets, sont déterminés à les soutenir avec vigueur dans l'assemblée de Philadelphie. Je ne répéterai pas ici les doutes que j'ai exprimés ailleurs sur leur succés; mais il est de mon devoir de vous soumettre l'opinion d'une autre classe d'hommes, dont le parti sera également fort et peut être plus obstiné dans l'assemblée dont il s'agit.

Ces hommes observent que, dans la situation actuelle des choses, il est impossible de réunir sous un seul Chef tous les membres se la confédération. Leurs intérêts politiques, leurs vues commerciales, leurs habitudes et leurs loix sont si hétérogènes, qu'il n'y a pas une résolution du Congrès qui puisse être également utile et populaire au Sud et au Nord du Continent; leur jalousie même paroît être un obstacle insurmontable. Pendant la guerre, les Etats avoient un intérêt général de repousser des ennemis puissants et cruels; cet intérêt n'existe plus, pourquoi réparer un édifice qui n'a plus même de fondemens? Le commerce devient désormais la principale base du système politique de ces Etats. Les habitans du Nord sont pêcheurs et navigateurs, ceux du Centre fermiers, ceux du Sud planteurs. Leur législation doit encourager, améliorer, perfectionner les différentes branches de leur industrie. Dire que le Congrès pourra faire des règlemens particuliers et utiles pour chacune de ces branches, c'est dire que le Congrès n'aura point de passions, que l'intrigue n'aura jamais aucune part à ses mesures, que les intérêts du Nord ne seront jamais sacrifiés à ceux du Sud: chose théoriquement impossible et

reconnue fausse par l'expérience. "Dans cette
"crise, continuent les partisans de ce système, il
"ne reste qu'un moyen pour donner à chaque Etat
"toute l'énergie dont il est susceptible, c'est de
"diviser le continent en plusieurs confédérations
"dont chacune auroit un gouvernement général et
"indépendant des autres. Cette division n'est pas
"difficile; la nature paroit l'avoir indiquée. La
"confédération *du Nord* pourroit être composée du
"New-Hampshire, du Massachussets, du Rhode-
"Island, du Conecticut, du Vermont et de l'ètat
"de New York jusqu'a la rivière d'Hudson. La
"confédération *du Centre* contiendroit tout le pays
"situé entre cette rivière et le Potowmac, et celle
"*du Sud* seroit composée de la Virginie, des deux
"Carolines et de la Géorgie. Les productions, les
"intérêts, les loix, même les moeurs des habitans se
"trouveroient ainsi classés suivant leurs différentes
"nuances, et les trois Gouvernmens se fortiffieroient
"en raison de leur arrondissement et de l'identité
"de leurs vues politiques. Qu'on ne dise point
"qu'une de ces divisions tomberoit facilement sous
"le joug d'une nation étrangère; n'a-t-on pas vu
"souvent en Europe plusieurs puissances réunies
"contre une autre puissance qui menaçoit de les
"envahir? Des traites d'alliance entre les différens
"Etats serviroient d'un lien commun et produiroient
"le même effet q'une confédération générale."
Les Cincinnati, c'est à dire les officiers de l'ancienne armée américaine, sont intéressés à l'ébtab-
lissement d'un Gouvernement solide, puisqu'ils
sont tous créanciers du public, mais, considérant
la foiblesse du Conseil national et l'impossibilité
d'être payés par la présente administration, ils proposent de jeter tous les Etats dans une seule masse
et de mettre à leur tête le gal. Washington avec
toutes les prérogatives et les pouvoirs d'une tête
couronnée. Ils menacent même de faire eux mêmes
cette révolution les armes à la main, aussitôt qu'ils
seront convainous de l'inutilité de la *Convention*
actuelle. Ce Projet est trop extravaguant pour
mériter la moindre discussion. La Société des
Cincinnati, qui s'est formée sans aucune sanction

publique, s'avise aujourd'hui de régler la constitution politique, sans y avoir été authorisée par les
peuples; mais elle est trop foible et trop impopulaire
pour faire aucune impression.

Un quatrième parti, et peut être celui qui trom-
phera de tous les autres, propose de laisser les choses
sur le pied actuel. L'Etat de Rhode-Island, le
gouverneur et les principaux chefs de l'administration de New York, M. John Adams et un grand
nombre d'individus dans les différens Etats sont
de ce parti. "Nous ne trouvons pas, disent-ils,
"que la situation des Etats-Unis soit si malheureuse
"qu'on veut nous le faire accroire. Nos villes et
"notre population s'augmentent journellement, nos
"vastes territoires se défrichent, notre commerce
"et notre industrie s'étendent prodigieusement; si
"quelques districts manquent d'or et d'argent, nous
"leurs donnons du papier qui leur en tient lieu; si
"nous ne sommes pas respecté en Europe, nous ne
"le serons pas davantage apres avoir sacrifié à un
"corps souverain une partie de notre liberté. Nos
"créanciers étrangers seront payés quand nous en
"aurons les moyens et jusques là ils ne peuvent nous
"faire aucun mal. Pourquoi changer un système
"politique qui a fait prospérer les Etats, et qui n'a
"d'autre inconvénient que celui de différer le paye-
"ment de nos dettes? Un Gouvernement plus
"absolu nous exposeroit au despotisme d'une as-
"semblée aristocratique ou au caprice d'un seul
"homme, car comment s'imaginer que des membres
"du Congrès, pouvant disposer librement d'une
"armée, d'une flotte, d'un trésor grossi par les con-
"tributions de tous les Etats, veuillent rentrer au
"bout d'un an dans la classe ordinaire des citoyens,
" échanger et l'administration publique contre celle
" d'une ferme. Il importe à notre liberté que le
"Congrès ne soit qu'un simple corps diplomatique,
"et non une assemblée souveraine et absolue."

Parmi cette grande variété de projets, il sera
bien difficile pour l'assemblée de Philadelphie
d'adopter un plan qui puisse convenir à tous les
partis et à tous les Etats. S'il m'etoit permis,
Monseigneur, d'avoir une opinion, je me rangerois

du côté de ceux qui proposent de ne rien changer à
la confédération actuelle, non que je pense qu'elle
rendra plutôt justice aux créanciers étrangers ou
domestiques, ni qu'elle donnera plus d'éclat aux
Etats-Unis, ni même qu'elle conservera plus longtemps l'union et la bonne intelligence entre ses
membres, mais parce qu'elle convient mieux que
tout autre système politique à l'esprit des peuples.
Les hommes riches, les négocians, les officiers publics, les Cincinnati sont tous portés pour un gouvernement plus absolu, mais leur nombre est bien petit
quand on le compare à toute la masse des citoyens.

Quoi qu'il en soit, la Convention générale vient
de commencer ses séances après avoir élu unanimement le gal. Washington pour Président. Cette
nomination donnera certainement plus d'éclat à
tout ce qui émanera de cette assemblée importante
et respectable. On espère que ses résolutions por-
teront le sceau de la sagesse, de la modération, de
la prévoyance, qui forment les principaux traits
dans le caractère du général.

Je laisse, Monseigneur, à des personnes plus
habiles que moi le soin de démêler quelle espèce de
gouvernement conviendroit le plus à nos intérêts
en Amérique, et je me borne à leur fournir des
matériaux.

Je suis avec un profond respect, Monseigneur,
votre très humble et très obéissant serviteur,

Otto.

XLII. Elbridge Gerry to James Monroe.[1]

Philadelphia 11th June 1787

The Convention is proceeding in their arduous undertaking with
eleven States: under an Injunction of Secrecy on their Members —
New Hamshire have elected Members who are soon expected. the
object of this Meeting is very important in my Mind — unless a
System of Government is adopted by *Compact*, *Force* I·expect will
plant the Standard: for such an anarchy as now exists cannot last
long. Gentlemen seem to be impressed with the Necessity of establishing some efficient System, & I hope it will secure Us against
domestic as well as foreign Invasions —

----

[1] *Documentary History of the Constitution*, IV, 199-200.

XLIII. R. D. Spaight to Governor Caswell.[1]

Philadelphia, 12th June, 1787.

I should have done myself the pleasure of writing to your Excellency oftener than I have done, but not being at Liberty to Communicate anything that passes in the Convention, I have nothing to write about.

The time it will require for the Convention to finish the business they have before them being entirely uncertain the deputies are of opinion that a further advance of two months' Salary will be necessary, and have wrote to your Excellency on that Subject by this Post, should your Excellency think proper to grant us warrants for two months' Salary in addition to those we have already drawn.[2]

XLIV. North Carolina Delegates to Governor Caswell.[3]

Philadelphia, June 14th, 1787.

Sir:

By the date of this you will observe we are near the middle of June and though we sit from day to day, Saturdays included, it is not possible for us to determine when the business before us can be finished, a very large Field presents to our view without a single Straight or eligible Road that has been trodden by the feet of Nations. An Union of Sovereign States, preserving their Civil Liberties and connected together by such Tyes as to Preserve permanent & effective Governments is a system not described, it is a Circumstance that has not Occurred in the History of men; if we shall be so fortunate as to find this in descript our Time will have been well spent. Several Members of the Convention have their Wives here and other Gentlemen have sent for theirs. This Seems to promise a Summer's Campaign. Such of us as can remain here from the inevitable avocation of private business, are resolved to Continue whilst there is any Prospect of being able to serve the State & Union. Your Excellency is sufficiently informed that the Money of our State is subject to Considerable Decrements when reduced to Current Coin, however it may serve as an Auxiliary by which some of the inconveniencies may be relieved which must necessarily attend our continuance abroad for a much longer Time than was expected; for this Reason we submit to your Consideration the Propriety of furnishing us with an additional Draught for two months' Service, in case of our return at an earlier period than at Present we have rea-

---

[1] *North Carolina State Records*, XX, 723.

[2] See XLIV and LII below.

[3] *North Carolina State Records*, XX, 723-724. See LII below.

son to apprehend, we are to Account, and perhaps it would be more desirable that we should have Occasion to repay a small Sum into the Treasury than that we should be under the Necessity of Coming Home, the Public Service unfinished from the want of supplies.

We have the Honour to be, with the utmost Consideration, Sir, Your Excellency's most Obedt. and Very Humble Servants,

ALEX. MARTIN,
RICHARD D. SPAIGHT,
W. R. DAVIE.
HUGH WILLIAMSON.

XLV. JAMES M. VARNUM TO GENERAL WASHINGTON.[1]

Sir —   Newport June 18th 1787

The inclosed address,[2] of which I presume your Excellency has received a duplicde, was returned to me from New York after my arrival in this State.   I flatterd myself that our Legislature, which convened on monday last, would have receded from the resolution therein refer'd to, and have complied with the recommendation of Congress in sending deligates to the federal convention.   The upper house, or Governor, & Council, embraced the measure, but it was negatived in the house of Assembly by a large majority, notwithstanding the greatest exertions were made to support it.

Being disappointed in their expectations, the minority in the administration and all worthy citizens of this State, whose minds are well informd regreting the peculiarities of their Situation place their fullest confidence in the wisdom & moderation of the national council, and indulge the warmest hopes of being favorably consider'd in their deliberations.   From these deliberations they anticipate a political System which must finally be adopted & from which will result the Safety, the honour, & the happiness of the United States.

Permit me, Sir, to observe, that the measures of our present Legislature do not exhibit the real character of the State.   They are equally reprobated, & abhor'd by Gentlemen of the learned professions, by the whole mercantile body, & by most of the respectable farmers and mechanicks.   The majority of the administration is composed of a licentious number of men, destitute of education, and many of them, Void of principle.   From anarchy

---

[1] *Documentary History of the Constitution*, I, 277–279. Although the letter is unsigned it is known to have come from James M. Varnum.

[2] The address referred to was that of several gentlemen of Rhode Island pledging their support to the result of the deliberations of the Convention. For the copy of this address, see above, VII.

and confusion they derive their temporary consequence, and this they endeavor to prolong by debauching the minds of the common people, whose attention is wholly directed to the Abolition of debts both public & private. With these are associated the disaffected of every description, particularly those who were unfriendly during the war. Their paper money System, founded in oppression & fraud, they are determined to Support at every hazard. And rather than relinquish their favorite pursuit the trample upon the most sacred obligations. As a proof of this they refused to comply with a requisition of Congress for repealing all laws repugnant to the treaty of peace with Great Britain, and urged as their principal reason, that it would be calling in question the propriety of their former measures

These evils may be attributed, partly to the extreme freedom of our own constitution, and partly to the want of energy in the federal Union: And it is greatly to be apprehended that they cannot Speedily be removed but by uncommon and very serious exertions. It is fortunate however that the wealth and resources of this State are chiefly in possion of the well Affected, & that they are intirely devoted to the public good.

I have the honor of being Sir,
    with the greatest Veneration & esteem,
        Your excellencys very obedient &
            most humble servant —
His excellency
    Genl Washington   [Endorsed:]

No 6.
Letter to General Washington dated Newport June 18. 1787.

_____

XLVI. NATHAN DANE TO RUFUS KING.[1]

[New York], June 19th.
I fully agree to the propriety of the Convention order restraining its members from communicating its doings, tho' I feel a strong desire and curiosity to know how it proceeds. I think the public never ought to see anything but the final report of the Convention — the digested result only, of their deliberations and enquiries.

Whether the plans of the Southern, Eastern or Middle States succeed, never, in my opinion, ought to be known. A few reflections on the subject lead me to doubt whether one of your members, Mr. P.,[2] who two or three days since came to this city, fully under-

_____
[1] C. R. King, *Life and Correspondence of Rufus King*, I, 225.
[2] Probably William Pierce of Georgia, see Appendix B.

stood the true meaning, full and just extent of the order not to communicate &c. _____

XLVII. EDMUND RANDOLPH TO BEVERLEY RANDOLPH.[1]

Phila., June 21, 1787.

Mr. Wythe, before he left us, requested that the Executive might, if they thought proper, appoint a successor to him. I informed him that I doubted whether, at this advanced stage of the business, they would be so inclined — especially, too, as there was a hope of his return; but that I would mention the affair to you.

_____

XLVIII. ROBERT MORRIS TO HIS SONS IN LEIPZIG.[2]

June 25, 1787.

General Washington is now our guest, having taken up his abode at my house during the time he is to remain in this city. He is President of a convention of Delegates from the Thirteen States of America, who have met here for the purpose of revising, amending, and altering the Federal Government. There are gentlemen of great abilities employed in this Convention, many of whom were in the first Congress, and several that were concerned in forming the Articles of Confederation now about to be altered and amended. You, my children, ought to pray for a successful issue to their labours, as the result is to be a form of Government under which you are to live, and in the administration of which you may hereafter probably have a share, provided you qualify yourselves by application to your studies. _____

XLIX. WILLIAM SAMUEL JOHNSON TO HIS SON.[3]

Philadelphia, 27 June, 1787.

I am here attending with Mr. Shearman and Mr. Elsworth as delegates, on the part of Connecticut, a grand convention of the United States, for the purpose of strengthening and consolidating the union and proposing a more efficient mode of government than that contained in the articles of confederation. We have delegates from eleven states actually assembled, consisting of many of the most able men in America, with General Washington at our head, whom we have appointed president of the convention. It is agreed that for the present our deliberations shall be kept secret, so that I can only tell you that much information and eloquence has been displayed

_____

[1] *Virginia Calendar of State Papers*, IV, 298.
[2] *Pennsylvania Magazine of History and Biography*, II, 170.
[3] Bancroft, *History of the Constitution of the United States*, II, 430.

in the introductory speeches, and that we have hitherto preserved great temperance, candor, and moderation in debate, and evinced much solicitude for the public weal. Yet, as was to be expected, there is great diversity of sentiment, which renders it impossible to determine what will be the result of our deliberations.

L. George Mason to Beverley Randolph.[1]

Philadelphia, June 30, 1787.

The Convention having resolved that none of their proceedings should be communicated during their sitting, puts it out of my power to give you any particular information upon the subject. *Festina lente* seems hitherto to have been our maxim. Things, however, are now drawing to that point on which some of the fundamental principles must be decided, and two or three days will probably enable us to judge — which is at present very doubtful — whether any sound and effectual system can be established or not. If it cannot, I presume we shall not continue here much longer; if it can, we shall probably be detained 'til September.

I feel myself disagreeably circumstanced in being the only member of the Assembly in the Virginia delegation, and, consequently, if any system shall be recommended by the Convention that the whole weight of explanation must fall upon me; and if I should be prevented by sickness or accident from attending the Assembly, that it will be difficult for the Assembly to obtain such information as may be necessary upon the subject, as I presume that in the progress through the legislature many questions may be asked and inquiries made, in which satisfactory information, from time to time, can hardly be given but by a member of the House in his place.

We have just received information here that Mr. Wythe has made a resignation, and does not intend to return. Under these circumstances I would beg leave to submit it to the consideration of the Executive, whether it might not be proper to fill the vacancy in the delegation, occasioned by Mr. Wythe's resignation, with some member of the Assembly. Mr. Corbin being here, his appointment, if it shall be judged proper, would occasion little additional charge to the State, if the Convention should, unfortunately, break up without adopting any substantial system — that event will happen, I think — before the appointment can reach this place; if the Convention continues to proceed on the business, with a prospect of success, Mr. Corbin is on the spot; and I doubt it may be difficult to prevail

---

[1] Rowland, *Life and Correspondence of George Mason*, II, 131–132.

on any member of the Assembly, now in Virginia, to come hither
at this late stage of the business.

LI. GEORGE WASHINGTON TO DAVID STUART.[1]

Philadelphia July 1st. 1787.

Rhode Island, from our last Accts sill persevere in that impolitic
— unjust — and one might add without much impropriety scandal-
ous conduct, which seems to have marked all her public Councils
of late; — Consequently, no Representation is yet here from thence.
New Hampshire, tho' Delegates have been appointed, is also unrepresented — various causes have been assigned — whether well, or ill
founded I shall not take upon me to decide — The fact however is
that they are not here.   Political contests, and want of Money, are
amidst the reasons assigned for the non attendance of the members.

As the rules of the Convention prevent me from relating any
of the proceedings of it, and the gazettes contain more fully than I
could detail other occurrances of public nature, I have little to communicate to you on the article of News.   Happy indeed would it
be if the Convention shall be able to recommend such a firm and
permanent Government for this Union, as all who live under it may
be secure in their lives, liberty and property, and thrice happy would
it be, if such a recommendation should obtain.   Every body wishes
— every body expects some thing from the Convention — but
what will be the final result of its deliberation, the book of fate must
disclose — Persuaded I am that the primary cause of all our disorders lies in the different State Governments, and in the tenacity
of that power which pervades the whole of their systems.   Whilst
independent sovereignty is so ardently contended for, whilst the
local views of each State and seperate interests by which they are
too much govern'd will not yield to a more enlarged scale of poli-
ticks; incompatibility in the laws of different States, and disrespect
to those of the general government must render the situation of
this great Country weak, inefficient and disgraceful.   It has already
done so, — almost to the final dessolution of it — weak at home and
disregarded abroad is our present condition, and contemptible
enough it is.

Entirely unnecessary was it, to offer any apology for the sentiments you were so obliging as to offer me — I have had no wish
more ardent (thro' the whole progress of this business) than that of
knowing what kind of Government is best calculated for us to live
under.   No doubt there will be a diversity of sentiment on this

---

[1] *Documentary History of the Constitution*, IV, 223–225.

important subject; and to inform the Judgment, it is necessary to hear all arguments that can be advanced. To please all is impossible, and to attempt it would be vain; the only way therefore is, under all the views in which it can be placed — and with a due consideration to circumstances — habits — &cc. &cc. to form such a government as will bear the scrutinizing eye of criticism and trust it to the good sense and patriotism of the people to carry it into effect.— Demagogue, — men who are unwilling to lose any of their state consequence — and interested characters in each, will oppose any general government: but let these be regarded rightly, and Justice it is to be hoped will at length prevail.

LII. Governor Caswell to the North Carolina Delegates.[1]

No. Carolina, 1st July, 1787.

Agreeable to your request I have this day drawn on the Collectors for two months' allowance to each of the deputies in service of the State in Convention, in addition to the four months' allowance formerly drawn for. Your Task is arduous, your undertaking is of such magnitude as to require Time for Deliberation and Consideration, and altho' I know each Gentleman must sensibly feel for his own private concerns in being so long absent from them, Yet the future happiness of the States so much depends on the determination of the Convention I am convinced your wishes to promote that happiness to your Country are such as to induce you to attend to the completing this business if possible. Any thing I can do which may tend towards making your stay agreeable shall be most chearfully attended to & I shall be most happy at all times in rendering you service or receiving any communications or advice from you. Mr. Spaight's and Mr. Williamson's are forwarded to the Gentlemen by them directed; Mr Martin's and Mr. Davies' remain with me subject to their order.

LIII. Phineas Bond to Lord Carmarthen.[2]

Philadelphia July 2nd. 1787

The deliberations of the Convention, my Lord, are conducted with vast secrecy; and nothing is known with accuracy but that their drift is to endeavor to form such a federal constitution, as will give energy and consequence to the union. Whether this is to be done by improving the old governments or by substituting new ones — whether by continuing a power in each State to regulate

---

[1] *North Carolina State Records*, XX, 729. See XLIII and XLIV above.
[2] *Annual Report of the American Historical Association* for 1896, I, 539.

its internal policy, or to abolish all separate establishments, and to form one grand federal authority, is a matter of consideration which creates much doubt and animadversion.

. . . Even in this crisis my Lord when the sober part of the continent looks up to the Convention to prescribe some mode competent to remove existing evils, there is not a complete delegation of the States in Convention — two of the thirteen are not represented, New Hampshire did appoint delegates, but as no fund was provided for their expenses and support they declined attending — The Assembly of Rhode I positively refused to appoint, and when the motion was again lately agitated, it was negatived by a majority of 17 members. ——————

LIIIa. GEORGE WASHINGTON: DIARY.[1]

Monday, [July] 2. — Dined with some of the members of Convention at Indian Queen. ——————

LIV. ALEXANDER HAMILTON TO GEORGE WASHINGTON.[2]

July 3d. 87

In my passage through the Jerseys and since my arrival here I have taken particular pains to discover the public sentiment and I am more and more convinced that this is the critical opportunity for establishing the prosperity of this country on a solid foundation — I have conversed with men of information not only of this City but from different parts of the state; and they agree that there has been an astonishing revolution for the better in the minds of the people. The prevailing apprehension among thinking men is, that the Convention, from a fear of shocking the popular opinion, will not go far enough — They seem to be convinced that a strong well mounted government will better suit the popular palate than one of a different complexion. Men in office are indeed taking all possible pains to give an unfavourable impression of the Convention; but the current seems to be running strongly the other way.

A plain but sensible man, in a conversation I had with him yesterday, expressed himself nearly in this manner — The people begin to be convinced that their "excellent form of government" as they have been used to call it, will not answer their purpose; and that they must substitute something not very remote from that which they have lately quitted.

These appearances though they will not warrant a conclusion that the people are yet ripe for such a plan as I advocate, yet serve

---

[1] *Pennsylvania Magazine of History and Biography,* XI, 302.
[2] *Documentary History of the Constitution,* IV, 226–227.

to prove that there is no reason to despair of their adopting one equally energetic, if the Convention should think proper to propose it. They serve to prove that we ought not to allow too much weight to objections drawn from the supposed repugnancy of the people to an efficient constitution — I confess I am more and more inclined to believe that former habits of thinking are regaining their influence with more rapidity than is generally imagined.

Not having compared ideas with you, Sir, I cannot judge how far our sentiments agree; but as I persuade myself the genuineness of my representations will receive credit with you, my anxiety for the event of the deliberations of the Convention induces me to make this communication of what appears to be the tendency of the public mind. . . . I own to you Sir that I am seriously and deeply distressed at the aspect of the Councils which prevailed when I left Philadelphia — I fear that we shall let slip the golden opportunity of rescuing the American empire from disunion anarchy and misery — No motley or feeble measure can answer the end or will finally receive the public support. Decision is true wisdom and will be not less reputable to the Convention than salutary to the community.

I shall of necessity remain here ten or twelve days; if I have reason to believe that my attendance at Philadelphia will not be mere waste of time, I shall after that period rejoin the Convention.

LV. R. D. SPAIGHT TO JAMES IREDELL.[1]

Philadelphia, 3d July, 1787.

The Convention has made, as yet, but little progress in the business they have met on; and it is a matter of uncertainty when they will finish. Secrecy being enjoined I can make no communications on that head.

LVI. NATHAN DANE TO RUFUS KING.[2]

July 5th, 1787.

I am very sorry to hear you say that it is uncertain what will be the result of the Convention, because I infer there must be a great diversity of sentiments among the members. The Convention must do something — its meeting has all those effects which we and those who did not fully discern the propriety of the measure apprehended. You know the general opinion is, that our Federal Constitution must be mended; and if the Convention do not agree at least in some

---

[1] McRee, *Life and Correspondence of James Iredell*, II, 162
[2] C. R. King, *Life and Correspondence of Rufus King*, I, 227-228.

amendments, a universal despair of our keeping together, will take place. It seems to be agreed here that the Virginia plan was admitted to come upon the floor of investigation by way of experiment and with a few yieldings on this point & that it keeps its ground at present. The contents of this plan was known to some, I believe, before the Convention met. Perhaps the public mind will be prepared in a few years to receive this new system. However I leave the whole to the wisdom of the Convention.

LVII. Hugh Williamson to James Iredell.[1]

Philadelphia, July 8th, 1787.

I think it more than likely that we shall not leave this place before the middle of August. The diverse and almost opposite interests that are to be reconciled, occasion us to progress very slowly. I fear that Davie will be obliged to leave us before our business is finished, which will be a heavy stroke to the delegation. We have occasion for his judgment, for I am inclined to think that the great exertions of political wisdom in our late Governor [Martin], while he sat at the helm of our State, have so exhausted his fund, that time must be required to enable him again to exert his abilities to the advantage of the nation.

LVIII. Edmund Randolph's Suggestion for Conciliating the Small States.[2]

communicated by Mr. Randolph, July 10. as an accomodating proposition to small States

(This & the following paper to be in an appendix)

1. Resolvd. that in the second branch each State have one vote in the following cases,

 1. in granting exclusive rights to Ports.
 2. in subjecting vessels or seamen of the U. States to tonnage, duties or other impositions
 3. in regulating the navigation of Rivers
 4. in regulating the rights to be enjoyed by citizens of one State in the other States.
 5. in questions arising on the guarantee of territory
 6. in declaring war or taking measures for subduing a Rebellion
 7. in regulating Coin

---

[1] McRee, *Life and Correspondence of James Iredell*, II, 163.
[2] From the Madison Papers, XII, 60. Printed in *Documentary History of the Constitution*, V, 437–438.

    8. in establishing & regulating the post office
    9. in the admission of new States into the Union
  10. in establishing rules for the government of the Militia
  11. in raising a regular army
  12. in the appointment of the Executive
  13. in fixing the seat of Government

That in all other cases the right of suffrage be proportioned according to an equitable rule of representation.

    2. that for the determination of certain important questions in the 2d branch, a greater number of votes than a mere majority be requisite

    3. that the people of each State ought to retain the perfect right of adopting from time to time such forms of republican Government as to them may seem best, and of making all laws not contrary to the articles of Union; subject to the supremacy of the General Government in those instances only in which that supremacy shall be expressly declared by the articles of the Union.

    4. That altho' every negative given to the law of a particular State shall prevent its operation, any State may appeal to the national Judiciary against a negative; and that such negative if adjudged to be contrary to the power granted by the articles of the Union, shall be void

    5. that any individual conceiving himself injured or oppressed by the partiality or injustice of a law of any particular State may resort to the National Judiciary, who may adjudge such law to be void, if found contrary to the principles of equity and justice.

LIX. George Washington to Alexander Hamilton.[1]

Philadelphia 10th. July 87.

I thank you for your communication of the 3d. — When I refer you to the state of the Councils which prevailed at the period you left this City — and add, that they are now, if possible, in a worse train than ever; you will find but little ground on which the hope of a good establishment can be formed. — In a word, I *almost* despair of seeing a favourable issue to the proceedings of the Convention, and do therefore repent having had any agency in the business.

The Men who oppose a strong & energetic government are, in my opinion, narrow minded politicians, or are under the influence of local views. — The apprehension expressed by them that the *people* will not accede to the form proposed is the *ostensible*, not the *real* cause of the opposition — but admitting that the *present* senti-

---

[1] *Documentary History of the Constitution*, IV, 235–236.

ment is as they prognosticate, the question ought nevertheless to be, is it, or is it not, the best form? — If the former, recommend it, and it will assuredly obtain mauger opposition

I am sorry you went away — I wish you were back. — The crisis is equally important and alarming, and no opposition under such circumstances should discourage exertions till the signature is fixed. — I will not, at this time trouble you with more than my best wishes and sincere regards.

LX. William Blount to Governor Caswell.[1]

New York, July 10th, 1787

On the 18th of June Mr. Hawkins & myself left this for Philadelphia, on my arrival I took my seat in Convention and he agreed for his passage to Petersburg. After having been there a few days, we received a Letter from Charles Thomson informing us that our presence would Complete Seven States in Congress and that a Congress was absolutely Necessary for the great purpose of the Union. Whereupon we returned here on the 4th Instant & formed a Congress and we Considered ourselves bound to Continue until some other State comes up, of which we are in hourly Expectation, and then I shall proceed to the Convention and he will return home.

I conceived it more for the benefit and honor of the State, in which Opinion my Colleagues in the Convention agreed, to return with Mr. Hawkins and represent the State in Congress than to Continue in the Convention especially as my Colleagues in that Body were Generally unanimous and Competent to the Purposes of their Mission. In this instance I hope my Conduct will meet the approbation of Your Excellency and my fellow Citizens.

LXI. Edmund Randolph to Beverley Randolph, L't-Governor.[2]

Phila. July 12, 1787

The Deputation here have desired me to obtain a further sum of money. I have accordingly drawn for one hundred pounds, which the Executive will oblige us by paying. . . .

By attendance on the Convention, together with travelling Expences from 6th of May inclusive, to 19th July inclusive, being 74 days, at 6 dollars per day, which are equal to 444 dollars; which are equal to . . . . £133. 4.

[1] *North Carolina State Records*, XX, 734.
[2] *Virginia Calendar of State Papers*, IV, 315.

LXII. MANASSEH CUTLER: JOURNAL. [1]

[1787], *Friday, July* 13. This tavern (Indian Queen) is situated in Third Street, between Market Street and Chestnut Street, and is not far from the center of the city. It is kept in an elegant style, and consists of a large pile of buildings, with many spacious halls, and numerous small apartments, appropriated for lodging rooms. . . .

Being told, while I was at tea, that a number of the Members of the Continental Convention, now convened in this city for the purpose of forming a Federal Constitution, lodged in this house, and that two of them were from Massachusetts, immediately after tea, I sent into their Hall (for they live by themselves) to Mr. Strong, and requested to speak with him. We had never been personally acquainted, nor had I any letter to him, but we had both of us an hearsay knowledge of each other, and Mr. Gerry had lately mentioned to Mr. Strong that he daily expected me, in consequence of a letter he had received from Governor Bowdoin. Mr. Strong very politely introduced me to Mr. Gorham, of Charlestown, Mass; Mr. Madison and Mr. Mason and his son, of Virginia; Governor Martin, Hon. Hugh Williamson, of North Carolina; the Hon. John Rutledge and Mr. Pinckney, of South Carolina; Mr. Hamilton, of New York, who were lodgers in the house, and to several other gentlemen who were spending the evening with them. I spent the evening with these gentlemen very agreeably.

. . . Mr. Strong was up as early as myself, and we took a walk to Mr. Gerry's in Spruce street, where we breakfasted. . . . Mr. Gerry has hired a house, and lives in a family state. . . .

From Mr. Peale's we went to the State House. This is a noble building; the architecture is in a richer and grander style than any public building I have before seen. The first story is not an open walk, as is usual in buildings of this kind. In the middle, however, is a very broad cross-aisle, and the floor above supported by two rows of pillars. From this aisle is a broad opening to a large hall, toward the west end, which opening is supported by arches and pillars. In this Hall the Courts are held, and, as you pass the aisle, you have a full view of the Court. The Supreme Court was now sitting. This bench consists of only three judges. Their robes are scarlet; the lawyers', black. The Chief Judge, Mr. McKean, was sitting with his hat on, which is the custom, but struck me as being very odd, and seemed to derogate from the dignity of a judge. The hall east of the aisle is employed for public business. The chamber over it is now occupied by the Continental Conven-

---

[1] Cutler, *Life, Journals and Correspondence of Manasseh Cutler*, I, 253–271.

tion,[1] which is now sitting, but sentries are planted without and within — to prevent any person from approaching near — who appear to be very alert in the performance of their duty. . . .

Dr. Franklin lives in Market Street, between Second and Third Streets, but his house stands up a court-yard at some distance from the street. We found him in his Garden, sitting upon a grass plat under a very large Mulberry, with several other gentlemen and two or three ladies. . . . I delivered him my letters. After he had read them, he took me again by the hand, and, with the usual compliments, introduced me to the other gentlemen of the company, who were most of them members of the Convention. Here we entered into a free conversation, and spent our time most agreeably until it was dark. . . . The Doctor showed me a curiosity he had just received, and with which he was much pleased. It was a snake with two heads, preserved in a large vial. . . . The Doctor mentioned the situation of this snake, if it was traveling among bushes, and one head should choose to go on one side of the stem of a bush and the other head should prefer the other side, and that neither of the heads would consent to come back or give way to the other. He was then going to mention a humorous matter that had that day taken place in Convention, in consequence of his comparing the snake to America, for he seemed to forget that everything in Convention was to be kept a profound secret; but the secrecy of Convention matters was suggested to him, which stopped him, and deprived me of the story he was going to tell. . . . We took our leave at ten, and I retired to my lodgings.

The gentlemen who lodged in the house were just sitting down to supper; a sumptuous table was spread, and the attendance in the style of noblemen. After supper, Mr. Strong came in and invited me into their Hall, where we sat till twelve. . . .

LXIII. George Wythe to ————.[2]

16 july, 1787.

The reason which moved me, and the only one which could have moved me, to retire from the convention at Philadelphia, not only continues, but i fear is more urgent than it was. The executive, therefore, are desired to consider my letter to governour Ran-

---

[1] "The Convention which met to form the Constitution of the United States, met *up stairs*, and at the same time the street pavement along Chestnut Street was coverd with earth to silence the rattling of wheels." Watson, *Annals of Philadelphia and Pennsylvania*, (1855), I, 402.

[2] William Brotherhead, *Centennial Book of the Signers*, p. 257.

dolph, or this, sir, to you, as a resignation of the office which i was deputed to sustain in the convention —

_____

LXIV. W. R. Davie to James Iredell.[1]

Philadelphia, July 17, 1787.

The two great characters you inquire after move with inconceivable circumspection. This hint will satisfy you. Their situations, though dissimilar, are both peculiar and delicate.

I shall not stay until the business is finished. I am sorry it will be out of my power. As soon as the general principles are established I shall set out.

_____

LXV. James Madison to Thomas Jefferson.[2]

Philada. July 18. 1787.

The Convention continue to sit, and have been closely employed since the Commencemt. of the Session. I am still under the mortification of being restrained from disclosing any part of their proceedings. As soon as I am at liberty I will endeavor to make amends for my silence, and if I ever have the pleasure of seeing you shall be able to give you pretty full gratification. I have taken lengthy notes of every thing that has yet passed, and mean to go on with the drudgery, if no indisposition obliges me to discontinue it. It is not possible to form any judgment of the future duration of the Session. I am led by sundry circumstances to guess that the residue of the work will not be very quickly despatched. The public mind is very impatient for ye event, and various reports are circulating which tend to inflame Curiosity. I do not learn however that any discontent is expressed at the concealment; and have little doubt that the people will be as ready to receive as we shall be able to propose, a Government that will secure their liberties & happiness.

_____

LXVa. Pennsylvania Packet and Daily Advertiser.

July 19, 1787.

So great is the unanimity, we hear, that prevails in the Convention, upon all great federal subjects, that it has been proposed to call the room in which they assemble — Unanimity Hall.[3]

_____

[1] McRee, _Life and Correspondence of James Iredell_, II, 165.

[2] _Documentary History of the Constitution_, IV, 236.

[3] This same item appeared in several other newspapers a day or two later.

LXVI. Hugh Williamson to James Iredell.[1]

Philadelphia, July 22d, 1787.

After much labor the Convention have nearly agreed on the principles and outlines of a system, which we hope may fairly be called an *amendment* of the Federal Government. This system we expect will, in three or four days, be referred to a small committee, to be properly dressed; and if we like it when clothed and equipped, we shall submit it to Congress; and advise them to recommend it to the hospitable reception of the States. I expect that some time in September we may put the last hand to this work. And as Congress can have nothing to do with it but put the question — pass or not pass, — I am in hopes that the subject may be matured in such time as to be laid before our Assembly at its next session. . . . Two delegates from New Hampshire arrived yesterday, so that we have every State except Rhode Island.

LXVII. Benjamin Franklin to John Paul Jones.[2]

Philada. July 22, 1787.

Be pleased to present my Respects to him, and acquaint him that the Convention goes on well, and that there is hope of great Good to result from their Counsels. — I intended to have wrote to him: but three Days Illness from which I have hardly recovered have prevented me. ⸻

LXVIII. John Jay to George Washington.[3]

New York 25 July 1787

Permit me to hint, whether it would not be wise & seasonable to provide a a strong check to the admission of Foreigners into the administration of our national Government; and to declare expresly that the Command in chief of the american army shall not be given to, nor devolve on, any but a natural *born* Citizen.

LXIX. mr. otto, chargé d'affaires de france, au secrétaire d'etat des affaires etrangères, comte de montmorin.[4]

No 96.

A New York, le 25 juillet, 1787.

Monseigneur,

Particular-   Quoique la *Convention générale* de Philadelphie

---

[1] McRee, *Life and Correspondence of James Iredell*, II, 167.
[2] Smyth, *Writings of Franklin*, IX, 604–605.
[3] *Documentary History of the Constitution*, IV, 237.
[4] French Archives: *Ministère des Affaires Etrangères. Archives. Etats-Unis. Correspondance.* Vol. 32, pp. 325 ff.

ités sur la ait enjoint à ses membres le secret le plus profond
Convention sur toutes ses délibérations, on a su que, parmi les
générale étab- différens plans de gouvernement proposés, celui de
lie à Philadel- la Virginie a été considéré comme le moins imparfait
phie pour des et qu'un Committé est actuellement chargé de
changemens l'examiner en détail et d'en donner son opinion.   Ce
projettés dans plan se ressent de la modération du gal. Washing-
la Constitution. ton qui est à la tête de la délégation, mais il est
peut être encore trop rigoureux pour des peuples
incapables de supporter le moindre joug.   Après ce
que j'ai eu l'honneur de vous mander, Monseigneur,
dans ma dépêche No. 91, il seroit superflu d'ajouter
ici aucune réflexion; j'attendrai la publication des
débats de la Convention pour vous en rendre compte.

A mesure que les spéculateurs politiques avan-
cent dans leurs projets, ils suggèrent de nouvelles
idées, dont on ne s'étoit point douté.   Les petits
Etats, craignant de voir établir une représentation
proportionnée à l'éntendue et à la population de
chaque Etat, réforme qui leur seroit très préju-
diciable, proposent aujourd'hui d'y consentir, pourvu
que tous les Etats soient divisés en portions égales.
On sent combien cette clause est peu proper à satis-
faire les Etats puissans.

Les Américains ne se dissimulent plus, Mon-
Obstacles seigneur, que les difficultés que le gouvernement
qu'on craint fédéral a éprouvées depuis la paix ne soient prin-
que n'éprou- cipalement dues à l'ambition de quelques individus
vent les plans qui craignent de perdre leur influence en donnant
de la Convent- trop de pouvoirs au corps qui représente la confédé-
ion de Phila- ration.   Le gouvernement et les principaux mem-
delphie de la bers de chaque Etat se trouveroient bornés au
part de ceux maintien de la police intérieure, tandis que les
qui ont peur finances et les grands intérêts nationaux seroient
de perdre leur exclusivement confiés au Congrès.   On doit donc
influence. craindre qu'en addressant aux Etats les nouveaux
plans de la Convention de Philadelphie, les mêmes
hommes qui se sont opposés jusqu'ici à un impôt
général et à d'autres règlemens onéreux ne fas-
sent rejeter la réforme qu'il s'agit d'introduire.

Exposition Pour remédier à cet inconvénient, les membres de
que la Con- la Convention prétendent que les administrations
vention de particulièrs des Etats n'ont pas le droit de décider

Philadelphie veut faire aux peuples assemblés du désordre qui résulte du système fédéral actuel.

une question relative à la Constitution fondamentale, et que c'est aux peuples assemblés à donner leurs voix. Ils espèrent qu'en convoquant extraordinairement les habitans de chaque district, en mettant sous leurs yeux l'incohérence actuelle du système fédéral, le peu de ressources du Congrès, les suites malheureuses de l'anarchie, l'épuisement du trésor, le mépris que les nations étrangères ont pour un peuple sans chef et sans vigueur, la difficulté de faire fleurir le commerce parmi les règlemens discordans de treize républiques séparées, enfin la nécessité d'écarter par une union solide et permanente les horreurs d'une guerre civile qui naîtroit indubitablement de l'etat actuel des choses, à moins qu'on ne trouvât sans délai le moyen d'y remédier, les peuples ne manqueroient pas de blâmer les vues ambitieuses de leurs magistrats et de consentir unanimement à un système de gouvernement plus uniforme et plus énergique. Les taxes et les impôts qu'il s'agit de faire verser dans les coffres du Congrès ayant été perçus jusqu'ici par les Etats individuels, on croit que les peuples ne feront aucune difficulté de les accorder au gouvernement général. Les hommes publics qui m'entretiennent journellement de ces projets connoissent certainement mieux que moi les dispositions des peuples, mais je doute encore beaucoup de leur succès.

Le Gouverneur de New York est l'ennemi le plus dangereux de la puissance du Congrès.

Les partisans de la réforme, Monseigneur, ont soin en attendant, d'attaquer publiquement les plus redoutables de leurs autagonistes. Leurs traits sont principalement dirigés contre le Gouverneur de New York, l'ennemi le plus actif et le plus dangereux de la puissance du Congrès. Son intérêt personel le porte à ne sacrifier aucune de ses prérogatives et à conserver à son Etat tous les droits de la souveraineté.

LXX. Governor Caswell to R. D. Spaight.[1]

No. Carolina, Kinston, July 26th, 1787.

From the hint you threw out in your first letter I am induced to think that the plan of a National Parliament and Supreme Executive with adequate powers to the Government of the Union will

---

[1] *North Carolina State Records*, XX, 752.

be more suitable to our situation & circumstances than any other, but I should wish also an independent Judicial department to decide any contest that may happen between the United States and individual States & between one State and another; this however is only a hint, you may not see the necessity of it as forcible as I do and I presume 'tis now too late to offer any reasons for the establishment, as that matter I flatter myself is before this got over; all I can say respecting the Convention is to recommend a perseverence to the end, to the deputies from this State.

LXXI. ALEXANDER HAMILTON TO AULDJO.[1]

New York, July 26, 1787.

I have delivered the paper you committed to me, as it stood altered, to Major Peirce, from whose conduct I am to conclude the affair between you is at an end.   He informs me that he is shortly to set out on a jaunt up the North River.

As you intimate a wish to have my sentiments in writing on the transaction, I shall with pleasure declare that the steps you have taken in consequence of Mr. Peirce's challenge have been altogether in conformity to my opinion of what would be prudent, proper and honorable on your part.   They seem to have satisfied Mr. Peirce's scruples arising from what he apprehended in some particulars to have been your conduct to him, and I presume we are to hear nothing further of the matter.   _____

LXXII. ALEXANDER MARTIN TO GOVERNOR CASWELL.[2]

Philadelphia, July 27th, 1787.

You may think I have been remiss in making you Communications from the Federal Convention, which you had a right to expect from my engagements to you in my last Letter from Carolina.   But when you are informed that the Members of that Body are under an Injunction of Secrecy till their Deliberations are moulded firm for the public Eye, You will readily I flatter myself, excuse me.   This Caution was thought prudent, least unfavourable Representations might be made by imprudent printers of the many crude matters & things daily uttered & produced in this Body, which are unavoidable, & which in their unfinished state might make an undue impression on the too credulous and unthinking Mobility.   How long before the business of Convention will be finished is very uncertain, perhaps not before September, if then.   Believe me Sir, it is no small

---

[1] Lodge, *Works of Alexander Hamilton*, (Federal Edition) IX, 421.
[2] *North Carolina State Records*, XX, 753.

task to bring to a conclusion the great objects of a United Government viewed in different points by thirteen Independent Sovereignties; United America must have one general Interest to be a Nation, at the same time preserving the particular Interest of the Individual States. However Sir, as soon as I am at Liberty to make Communications Your Excellency shall have the earliest information.

LXXIII. GEORGE WASHINGTON: DIARY.[1]

[July] Friday — 27th.

In Convention, which adjourned this day, to meet again on Monday the 6th. of August that a Comee. which had been appointed (consisting of 5 Members) might have time to arrange, and draw into method & form the several matters which had been agreed to by the Convention, as a Constitution for the United States. —

LXXIV. JAMES MONROE TO THOMAS JEFFERSON.[2]

Fred'ricksburg — July 27, 1787.

I shall I think be strongly impressed in favor of & inclin'd to vote for whatever they will recommend. I have heard from *Becly* 'tho' not from himself (who accompanied *the Governour* up in *expectation of being appointed clerk*) they had agreed *giving the United States a negative upon the laws of the several States* * this I shod. think proper — it will if the body is well organiz'd, be the best way of introducing uniformity in their proceedings that can be devis'd, *of a negative kind* or by a power to operate *indirectly* but a few months will give us the result be it what it may.

* If it can be done consistently with the constitutions of the several States — indeed it might be well to revise them all — & incorporate the fœdl. constitution in each.

LXXV. JAMES MADISON TO HIS FATHER.[3]

Philada. July 28. 1787.

I am sorry that I cannot gratify your wish to be informed of the proceedings of the Convention. An order of secresy leaves me at liberty merely to tell you that nothing definitive is yet done, that the Session will probably continue for some time yet, that an Adjourn-

---

[1] *Documentary History of the Constitution*, IV, 239.

[2] *Documentary History of the Constitution*, IV, 237–238. The portions of the original MS. in cipher are here represented by *italics*.

[3] *Documentary History of the Constitution*, IV, 239.

ment took place on thursday last until Monday week, and that a Committee is to be at work in the mean time.

LXXVI. Nicholas Gilman to Joseph Gilman.[1]

Philadelphia, July 31st 1787 —

I have the pleasure to inform you of my having arrived at this place on the 21st instant, Mr Langdon arrived a few hours before and, notwithstanding we are so late in the day, it is a circumstance, in this critical state of affairs, that seems highly pleasing to the Convention in general. — Much has been done (though nothing conclusively) and much remains to do — A great diversity of sentiment must be expected on this great Occassion: feeble minds are for feeble measures & some for patching the old garment with here & there a shred of new Stuff; while vigorous minds and warm Constitutions advocate a high toned Monarchy — This is perhaps a necessary contrast as "all natures difference keeps all natures peace" it is probable the conclusion will be on a medium between the two extremes. —

As secrecy is not otherwise enjoined than as prudence may dictate to each individual — in a letter to my brother John,[2] of the 28th instant, I gave him (for the satisfaction of two or three who will not make it public) a hint respecting the general principles of the plan of national Government, that will probably be handed out — which will not be submitted to the Legislatures but after the approbation of Congress to an assembly or assemblies of Representatives recommended by the several Legislatures, to be expressly chosen by the people to consider & decide thereon. —

Great wisdom & prudence as well as liberallity of Sentiment & a readiness to surrender natural rights & privileges for the good of the nation appears in the southern delegates in general and I most devoutly wish that the same spirit may pervade the whole Country that the people by absurdly endeavoring to retain all their natural rights may not be involved in Calamitous factions which would end but with the loss of all

. . . I think the business of the Convention will not be completed untill the first of September —

---

[1] *New Hampshire State Papers*, XXI, 835–836.

[2] "The letter to John Taylor Gilman seems not to be extant." Jameson, *Studies of Federal Convention*, p. 91.

LXXVI*a*. PIERCE BUTLER TO WEEDON BUTLER.[1]

New York, August 1st, 1787.

My last letter from Carolina would inform you of my intended visit to Philadelphia. As I declined the honorary fellow Citizens offered me of the Chief Magistracy, I could not refuse the last Appointment of Acting as One of their Commissioners to the Convention to be held at Philadelphia. No doubt you have heard of the purport of the meeting, — to form a stronger Constitution on strict Foederal Principles, for the Governmt. of the whole — I hope we may succeed. Our Country expect much of us. We have satt every day since the 25th of May till last Saturday, when we adjourned for one week. Having placed my Family here, Philadelphia not being so healthy, I embraced the opportunity of visiting them. I go back to Philada on Sunday and shall return home the first week in November. _____

LXXVII. JAMES McCLURG TO JAMES MADISON.[2]

Richmond Augt. 5. 87.

I am much obliged to you for your communication of the proceedings of ye Convention, since I left them; for I feel that anxiety about ye result, which it's. Importance must give to every honest citizen. If I thought that my return could contribute in the smallest degree to it's Improvement, nothing should keep me away. But as I know that the talents, knowledge, and well-establish'd character, of our present delegates, have justly inspired this country with ye most entire confidence in their determinations; & that my vote could only *operate* to produce a division, & so destroy ye vote of ye State, I think that my attendance now would certainly be useless, perhaps injurious.

LXXVIII. GEORGE WASHINGTON'S DIARY.[3]

[August] Monday — 6th.

Met, according to adjournment in convention, & received the Rept. of the Committee — _____

LXXIX. W. R. DAVIE TO JAMES IREDELL.[4]

Philadelphia, August 6th, 1787

I shall leave this place on Monday next; and, probably, be in

---

[1] British Museum, Additional MSS., 16603. Copy furnished through the courtesy of the Department of Historical Research of the Carnegie Institution of Washington.

[2] *Documentary History of the Constitution*, IV, 244-245.

[3] *Documentary History of the Constitution*, IV, 245.

[4] McRee, *Life and Correspondence of James Iredell*, II, 168.

Halifax by the time you receive this, as the great outlines are now marked, and have been detailed by a committee: the residue of the work will rather be tedious than difficult.

LXXX. NORTH CAROLINA DELEGATES TO GOVERNOR CASWELL.[1]

Philadelphia, July [August] 7th, 1787.

The Convention having on the 26th of last Month finished the outline of the Amendments proposed to the Federal System, the business was of course Committed for detail and we have the pleasure to inform your Excellency that the report was received on yesterday. From the progress, which has already taken up near three months; we are induced to believe the result of our deliberations will shortly be presented to the United States in Congress and as they are only to consider whether the System shall or shall not be recommended to the States, the Business cannot Remain long before them. It is certainly to be desired that they may be ready to pass upon this subject before the end of the Federal year, otherwise the Report of the Convention, and Consequently of Congress, cannot meet our Assembly in Time next regular adjournment, and we have experienced the difficulty of calling them together at another time. We think it will therefore be of importance that the States in General, and that our State in particular be represented in Congress during the Months of September & October and submit to the Consideration of your Excellency whether it would not be proper to expedite the attendance of those Gentlemen whose duty it may be to serve in Congress at this time.

LXXXI. R. D. SPAIGHT TO JAMES IREDELL.[2]

Philadelphia, August 12th, 1787.

The Convention having agreed upon the outlines of a plan of government for the United States, referred it to a small committee to detail: that committee have reported, and the plan is now under consideration. I am in hopes we shall be able to get through it by the 1st or 15th of September.

It is not probable that the United States will in future be so ideal as to risk their happiness upon the unanimity of the whole; and thereby put it in the power of one or two States to defeat the most salutary propositions, and prevent the Union from rising out of that contemptible situation to which it is at present reduced.

---

[1] *North Carolina State Records*, XX, 733.
[2] McRee: *Life and Correspondence of James Iredell*, II, 168.

LXXXII. James Madison to his Father.[1]

Philada. Augst. 12. 1787.

The Convention reassembled at the time my last mentioned that they had adjourned to. It is not possible yet to determine the period to which the Session will be spun out. It must be some weeks from this date at least, and possibly may be computed by months. Eleven States are on the ground, and have generally been so since the second or third week of the Session. Rhode Island is one of the absent States. She has never yet appointed deputies. N. H. till of late was the other. That State is now represented. But just before the arrival of her deputies, those of N. York left us.

LXXXIII. Elbridge Gerry to General Warren.[2]

Philadelphia, Aug. 13, 1787.

It is out of my power in return for the information you have given me to inform you of our proceedings in convention, but I think they will be complete in a month or six weeks, perhaps sooner. Whenever they shall be matured I sincerely hope they will be such as you and I can approve, and then they will not be engrafted with principles of mutability, corruption or despotism, principles which some, you and I know, would not dislike to find in our national constitution. ─────────

LXXXIIIa. Pennsylvania Herald and General Advertiser.

Wednesday, August 15, 1787.

The debates of the fœderal convention continued until five o'clock on Monday evening; when, it is said, a decision took place upon the most important question that has been agitated since the meeting of this assembly. ─────────

LXXXIV. George Washington to La Fayette.[3]

Philadelphia August 15th. 1787

Altho' the business of the Fœderal Convention is not yet clos'd, nor I, thereby, enabled to give you an account of its proceedings; yet, the opportunity afforded by Commodore Paul Jones' Return to France is too favourable for me to omit informing you, that the present expectation of the members is, that it will end about the first of next month; when, or as soon after as it shall be in my power, I will communicate the result of our long deliberation to you.

─────────

[1] *Documentary History of the Constitution*, IV, 247–248.
[2] Austin, *Life of Elbridge Gerry*, II, 36.
[3] *Documentary History of the Constitution*, IV, 253.

LXXXV. George Washington to Henry Knox.[1]

Philadelphia. August 19 1787

By *slow*, I wish I could add, and *sure* movements, the business of the Convention progresses but to say when it will end, or what will be the result, is more than I dare venture to do and therefore shall hazard no opinion thereon. If some thing good does not proceed from the Cession the defects cannot with propriety be charged to the hurry with which the business has been conducted, notwithstanding which many things may be forgot — some of them not well digested — and others from the contrariety of sentiments with which such a body is pervaded become a mere nihility yet I wish a disposition may be found in Congress, the several State Legislatures — and the community at large to adopt the Government which may be agreed on in Convention because I am fully persuaded it is the best that can be obtained at the present moment under such diversity of ideas as prevail.

LXXXVI. Alexander Hamilton to Rufus King.[2]

New York, Aug. 20., 1787.

Since my arrival here, I have written to my colleagues, informing them, that if either of them would come down, I would accompany him to Philadelphia. So much for the sake of propriety and public opinion.

In the mean time if any material alteration should happen to be made in the plan now before the Convention, I will be obliged to you for a communication of it. I will also be obliged to you to let me know when your *conclusion* is at hand; for I would choose to be present at that time. _____

LXXXVII. Hugh Williamson to Governor Caswell.[3]

Philadelphia, 20th August, 1787

On Monday last Col. Davie set out from this place. I regret his departure very much as his conduct here has induced me to think highly of his abilities and political principles. On Monday next Col. Martin also proposes to leave us when we shall be reduced to a mere representation; of the five Gentlemen who were appointed by the Assembly only one will remain. I wish you in the meanwhile to believe that Col. Blount & myself are determined to persevere while there are Six other States on the Floor or until the business

---

[1] *Documentary History of the Constitution,* IV, 254–255.
[2] C. R. King, *Life and Correspondence of Rufus King,* I, 258.
[3] *North Carolina State Records,* XX, 765–766.

is finished, tho' it should last for months, we have two reasons for this resolution, either of which will be conclusive. We owe this duty to the State whose interest seems to be deeply concerned, and we owe it to the feelings of your Excellency, for we would not have it alleged that Gentlemen whom you had been pleased to honor with the Public trust had failed in a single Iota of their duty to the Public. We shall on some future occasion be at liberty to explain to your Excellency how difficult a part has fallen to the share of our State in the course of this business and I flatter myself greatly if we have not sustained it with a Principle & firmness that will entitle us to what we will never ask for, the thanks of the public. It will be sufficient for us if we have the satisfaction of believing that we have contributed to the happiness of Millions.

LXXXVIII. WILLIAM BLOUNT TO GOVERNOR CASWELL.[1]

Philadelphia, Monday, August 20th, 1787.

In a letter from New York I informed your Excellency of my reasons for leaving the Convention and returning to that place with Mr. Hawkins to represent this State in Congress. On Monday the 6th Inst. the Committee of detail made their Report to the Convention and on the Morning of Tuesday the 7th Hawkins and myself returned here and I again took my seat in Convention; so that tho' I was not present all the time the Convention were debating and fixing the principles of the Government I have been and mean to continue to be present while the detail is under Consideration, that is until the Business of the Convention is Completed. From 10 to 4 O'Clock are the invariable hours of Session and as much Unanimity as can be expected prevails, yet I believe the business will not be completed in less than a month from this Time; Mr. Davie left us on this day week, his business at the approaching Superior Court called him so pressingly that he could not stay any longer. If he could have complied with his own inclination, or those of the Delegation of the State he would have remained during the Session.

Mr. Martin informs us that on Monday next we must also submit to his leaving us. I wish it could be other ways . . .

Your Excellency is not now to be informed that I am not at liberty to explain the particulars of the mode of Government that the Convention have in Contemplation, but I will venture to assure you that it will be such a form of Government as I believe will be readily adopted by the several States because I believe it will be such as will be their respective interest to adopt.

---

[1] *North Carolina State Records*, XX, 764–5.

LXXXIX. Alexander Martin to Governor Caswell.[1]

Philadelphia, August 20th, 1787.

I have been honored with your Excellency's Letter of the 26th Ulto. in which you are pleased to suggest you have been disappointed in receiving particular information respecting the Convention; In my last I wrote your Excellency the Reasons which I flatter myself you have received and approved of, why Communications could not be made until the Business before this Body be Completed and prepared for the public Eye, much time has been employed in drawing the outlines of the Subjects of their Deliberations in which as much unanimity has prevailed as could be well expected from so many Sentiments Arising in twelve Independent Sovereign Bodies; Rhode Island not having deigned to keep company with her Sister States on this Occasion. The Convention after having agreed on some great principles in the Government of the Union Adjourned for a few days, having appointed a Committee composed of the following Gentlemen, to wit: Mr. Rutledge of South Carolina, Mr. Randolph of Virginia, Mr. Elsworth of Connecticut, Mr. Wilson of Pennsylvania, and Mr. Gorham of Massachusetts, to detail or render more explicit the chief subjects of their Discussion; on the Report of these Gentlemen the Convention again met, and are now employed taking up the same Paragraph by paragraph, and so slow is the progress that I am doubtful the Business will not be fully reduced to System and finished before the middle of September next, if then.

It is the wish of the Members of Convention that the States be fully represented in Congress at the time they will be presented with the Conventional Transactions, of which should Congress give their approbation the same may be transmitted to the Legislatures of the several States at their next meeting, that the sense of the Union be obtained as soon as possible thereupon. Colo. Ashe is alone at Congress, Colo. Burton was expected before this, but is not yet arrived; Col. Blount has been with us from Congress for some days past, as Col. Davie was under the Necessity to return Home; Mr. Hawkins is also returned. I am also obliged to be at Salisbury Superior Court in Sept. next, and propose to sett off the first of that month on my return. The State will still be represented fully in Convention by my Honourable friends Messrs. Spaight, Blount & Williamson. My absence may I think be the more easily dispenced with when I have the pleasure to inform your Excellency the Deputation from the State of North Carolina have generally been unanimous on all great questions, and I flatter myself will continue so until the Objects of their mission be finished. Tho' I have not told your Excellency affirmatively what the Convention have done, I can tell you negatively what they have not done. They are not about to create a King as hath been represented unfavourably in some of the eastern States, so that you are not to expect the Bishop Oznaburg or any prince or great man of the World to rule in this Country.[1] The Public Curiosity will no doubt be gratified at the next Assembly, perhaps before.

_____

XC. DAVID BREARLEY TO WILLIAM PATERSON.[2]

Philadelphia 21 Aug. 1787.

I was in hopes after the Committee had reported, that we should have been able to have published by the first of September, at present I have no prospect of our getting through before the latter end of that month. Every article is again argued over, with as much earnestness and obstinacy as before it was committed. We have lately made a rule to meet at ten and sit 'til four, which is punctually complied with. Cannot you come down and assist us, — we have many reasons for desiring this; our duty, in the manner we now sit, is quite too hard for three, but a much stronger reason is, that we actually stand in need of your abilities.

_____

XCI. JAMES McCLURG TO JAMES MADISON.[3]

Richmond Augt. 22. 87.

I have so much pleasure from your communications, that I shall be careful to acknowledge the receipt of them, with a view to secure their continuance.

I have still some hope that I shall hear from you of ye reinstatement of ye *Negative* — as it is certainly ye only mean by which the several Legislatures can be restrain'd from disturbing ye order & harmony of ye whole, & ye Governmt. render'd properly *national*, & *one*. I should suppose yt some of its former opponents must by this time have seen ye necessity of advocating it, if they wish to support their own principles.

_____

XCII. EXTRACT FROM THE PENNSYLVANIA JOURNAL.[2]

[August 22, 1787.]

We are informed, that many letters have been written to the

_____

[1] See XCII below.
[2] Jameson, *Studies in the History of the Federal Convention*, in the *Annual Report of the American Historical Association* for 1902, p. 99.
[3] *Documentary History of the Constitution*, IV, 264.

members of the foederal convention from different quarters, respecting the reports idly circulating, that it is intended to establish a
monarchical government, to send for the bishop of Osnaburgh, &c.,
&c. — to which it has been uniformly answered, tho' we cannot,
affirmatively, tell you what we are doing, we can, negatively, tell
you what we are not doing — we never once thought of a king.[1]

XCIII. EDMUND RANDOLPH TO THE LIEUTENANT GOVERNOR OF
VIRGINIA.[2]

Philadelphia August 22 1787.

I requested Dr. Mclurg to inform your honorable board, that
at the completion of our business we should be called upon for several expences, incurred during our session; the principal of which
would be an allowance to the secretary, and two door-keepers, and
the charge of printing and stationary. Perhaps this circumstance
may have escaped that gentleman's memory; and as it is a matter
of some consequence to us, I beg leave to mention it now, and to
ask the sense of the executive, whether it can be placed among the
contingent charges of government, or must be paid by ourselves.
When I informed you, that the balance in my hands would probably
be absorbed before my return, or something to this effect, I had in
contemplation not my own wages only, but this debt also. You
will therefore be pleased, sir, to give me the earliest answer, which
may be in your power. Should it not be expedient to allow these
expences, I shall have a small balance still in my hands, which I
will pay into the treasury immediately on my return — . . .

N. B. I failed in my attempt to take up my draught for the
100 L, as it had been sent to Virginia, contrary to the information
I first received. So that what I have said above goes upon the supposition of that sum having been debited to me.

XCIV. W. R. DAVIE TO GOVERNOR CASWELL.[3]

Halifax, August 23rd. 1787.

I left Philadelphia on the 13th Ulto., before which date we had
informed you of the progress of the business; it was not supposed
the Convention would rise before the first of September, and all
the other Gentlemen were attending and agreed to stay, and as the

---

[1] Compare phraseology with that at the close of LXXXIX above, and see
CVII below.

[2] Virginia State Library, Executive Papers. Copy furnished by the Department
of Historical Research of the Carnegie Institution.

[3] *North Carolina State Records*, XX, 766.

general principles were already fixed and Considering the State and Nature of my business, I felt myself fully at liberty to return, especially as No. Carolina was so fully and respectably represented.

XCIV*a*. PENNSYLVANIA PACKET AND DAILY ADVERTISER.

Thursday, August 23, 1787.

The punctuality with which the members of the Convention assemble every day at a certain hour, and the long time they spend in the deliberations of each day (sometimes 7 hours) are proofs, among other things how much they are entitled to the universal confidence of the people of America. Such a body of enlightened and honest men perhaps never before met for political purposes in any country upon the face of the earth.

XCV. EZRA STILES: DIARY.[1]

[August] 27. Judge Elsworth a Member of the foederal Convention just returned fr. Philada visited me, & tells me the Convent. will not rise under three Weeks.

XCVI. ALEXANDER HAMILTON TO RUFUS KING.[2]

New York, Aug. 28, 1787.

I wrote to you some days since to request you to inform me when there was a prospect of your finishing, as I intended to be with you, for certain reasons, before the conclusion.

It is whispered here that some late changes in your scheme have taken place which give it a higher tone. Is this the case?

I leave town today to attend a circuit in a neighboring County, from which I shall return the last of the week; and shall be glad to find a line from you explanatory of the period of the probable termination of your business.

XCVII. NATHANIEL GORHAM TO CALEB STRONG.[3]

Philadelphia Augt 29

I recd your favour from N York and was pleased to find that you had got on so well. . . . We have now under consideration the 18th Article which is that the United States shall guarantee, &c. &c.[4]

---

[1] *Literary Diary of Ezra Stiles*, III, 279.

[2] C. R. King, *Life and Correspondence of Rufus King*, I, 258.

[3] Jameson, *Studies in the History of the Federal Convention* in the *Annual Report of the American Historical Association* for 1902, p. 100.

[4] Taken up and passed on August 30. On August 29, Article XVII was under consideration and was continued on August 30.

I am in hopes we shall be done in about 20 days.   There are several things referred which will take some time.

XCVIII. THOMAS JEFFERSON TO JOHN ADAMS.[1]

Paris Aug. 30. 1787.

I have news from America as late as July 19. nothing had then transpired from the Federal convention. I am sorry they began their deliberations by so abominable a precedent as that of tying up the tongues of their members. nothing can justify this example but the innocence of their intentions, & ignorance of the value of public discussions. I have no doubt that all their other measures will be good & wise. it is really an assembly of demigods. Genl. Washington was of opinion they should not separate till October.

XCIX. GEORGE WASHINGTON TO JOHN JAY.[2]

Philadelphia Sept. 2d 1787

I regret not having had it in my power to visit New York during the adjournment of the Convention, last Month. — not foreseeing with any precission the period at which it was likely to take place or the length of it, I had put my carriage in the hands of a workman to be repaired and had not the means of mooving during the recess but with, or the curtisy of, others.

I thank you for the hints contained in your letter

C. EDMUND RANDOLPH TO BEVERLEY RANDOLPH.[3]

Phila., Sept. 2, 1787.

I expect to leave this place on Saturday, Seven night.

CI. JAMES MADISON TO HIS FATHER.[4]

Philada. Sepr. 4. 1787.

The Convention has not yet broken up but its Session will probably continue but a short time longer. Its proceedings are still under the injunction of secresy. . . . As soon as the tie of secresy shall be dissolved I will forward the proceedings of the Convention.

CII. JOHN COLLINS TO ARTHUR ST. CLAIR, PRESIDENT OF CONGRESS.[4]

Newport Septem ye 4th: 1787

I have not as yet lost all hopes of getting a Representation to

---

[1] *Documentary History of the Constitution*, IV, 266.
[2] *Documentary History of the Constitution*, IV, 269.
[3] *Virginia Calendar of State Papers*, IV, 338.
[4] *Documentary History of the Constitution*, IV, 270.

the General Convention timely, that their Report may be made in the name of the thirteen United States, the idea of a Report from twelve States onely appears extreem disagreeable, I shall spare no pains to prevent it —— ————

CIII. JAMES MADISON TO THOMAS JEFFERSON.[1]

Philada. Sepr. 6. 1787.

As the Convention will shortly rise I should feel little scruple in disclosing what will be public here, before it could reach you, were it practicable for me to guard by Cypher against an intermediate discovery. But I am deprived of this resource by the shortness of the interval between the receipt of your letter of June 20, and the date of this. This is the first day which has been free from Committee service, both before & after the hours of the House, and the last that is allowed me by the time advertised for the sailing of the packet.

The Convention consists now as it has generally done of Eleven States. There has been no intermission of its Sessions since a house was formed; except an interval of about ten days allowed a Committee appointed to detail the general propositions agreed on in the House. The term of its dissolution cannot be more than one or two weeks distant. A Governmt. will probably be submitted to the *people of* the *States*, consisting of a *president, cloathed* with *Executive power*; a *Senate chosen* by the *Legislatures*, and another *House chosen* by the *people of* the States, jointly *possessing* the *legislative* power; and a regular *judiciary* establishment. The mode of constituting the *Executive* is among the few points not yet finally settled. The *Senate* will consist of two *members* from each *State*, and *appointed sexennially*. The other, of *members appointed biennially* by the *people of the States*, in proportion to their number. The Legislative power will *extend to taxation, trade*, and sundry other general matters. The powers of Congress will be *distributed*, according to their *nature, among the several departments*. The States will be *restricted from paper money* and in a *few other instances*. These are *the outlines*. The extent of them may perhaps surprize you. I hazard an opinion nevertheless that the *plan, should* it *be adopted*, will neither effectually *answer* its *national object*, not prevent the local *mischiefs* which everywhere *excite disgusts* agst. the *State Governments*. The grounds of this opinion will be the subject of a future letter. . . .

Nothing can exceed the universal anxiety for the event of the

---

[1] *Documentary History of the Constitution*, IV, 273–276; Hunt, *Writings of Madison*, IV, 389–391. Italicised words were in cipher in the original.

meeting here. Reports and conjectures abound concerning the nature of the plan which is to be proposed. The public however is certainly in the dark with regard to it. The Convention is equally in the dark as to the reception wch. may be given to it on its publication. All the prepossessions are on the right side, but it may well be expected that certain characters will wage war against any reform whatever. My own idea is that the public mind will now or in a very little time receive anything that promises stability to the public Councils & security to private rights, and that no regard ought to be had to local prejudices or temporary considerations. If the present moment be lost, it is hard to say what may be our fate. ...

Mr. Wythe has never returned to us. His lady whose illness carried him away, died some time after he got home.

CIV. Jonas Phillips to the President and Members of the Convention.[1]

Sires

With leave and submission I address myself To those in whome there is wisdom understanding and knowledge. they are the honourable personages appointed and Made overseers of a part of the terrestrial globe of the Earth, Namely the 13 united states of america in Convention Assembled, the Lord preserve them amen —

I the subscriber being one of the people called Jews of the City of Philadelphia, a people scattered and despersed among all nations do behold with Concern that among the laws in the Constitution of Pennsylvania their is a Clause Sect. 10 to viz — I do believe in one God the Creature and governour of the universe the Rewarder of the good and the punisher of the wicked — and I do acknowledge the scriptures of the old and New testament to be given by a devine inspiration — to swear and believe that the new testament was given by devine inspiration is absolutly against the Religious principle of a Jew. and is against his Conscience to take any such oath — By the above law a Jew is deprived of holding any publick office or place of Goverment which is a Contridectory to the bill of Right Sect 2. viz

That all men have a natural and unalienable Right To worship almighty God according to the dectates of their own Conscience and understanding, and that no man aught or of Right can be Compelled to attend any Relegious Worship or Erect or support any place of worship or Maintain any minister contrary to or against his own free will and Consent nor Can any man who acknowledges

[1] *Documentary History of the Constitution*, I, 281–283.

the being of a God be Justly deprived or abridged of any Civil Right as a Citizen on account of his Religious sentiments or peculiar mode of Religious Worship, and that no authority Can or aught to be vested in or assumed by any power what ever that shall in any Case interfere or in any manner Controul the Right of Conscience in the free Exercise of Religious Worship —

It is well known among all the Citizens of the 13 united States that the Jews have been true and faithful whigs, and during the late Contest with England they have been foremost in aiding and assisting the States with their lives and fortunes, they have supported the Cause, have bravely faught and bleed for liberty which they Can not Enjoy —

Therefore if the honourable Convention shall in ther Wisdom think fit and alter the said oath and leave out the words to viz — and I do acknoweledge the scripture of the new testement to be given by devine inspiration then the Israeletes will think them self happy to live under a goverment where all Relegious societys are on an Eaquel footing — I solecet this favour for my self my Childreen and posterity and for the benefit of all the Isrealetes through the 13 united States of america

My prayers is unto the Lord. May the people of this States Rise up as a great and young lion, May they prevail against their Enemies, May the degrees of honour of his Excellencey the president of the Convention George Washington, be Extollet and Raise up. May Every one speak of his glorious Exploits. May God prolong his days among us in this land of Liberty — May he lead the armies against his Enemys as he has done hereuntofore — May God Extend peace unto the united States — May they get up to the highest Prosperetys — May God Extend peace to them and their seed after them so long as the Sun and moon Endureth — and may the almighty God of our father Abraham Isaac and Jacob endue this Noble Assembly with wisdom Judgement and unamity in their Councells, and may they have the Satisfaction to see that their present toil and labour for the wellfair of the united States may be approved of, Through all the world and perticular by the united States of america is the ardent prayer of Sires

Your Most devoted obed Servant

JONAS PHILLIPS

Philadelphia 24th Ellul 5547 or Sepr 7th 1787

[Addressed:] To His Excellency the president and the Honourable Members of the Convention assembled

Present

[Endorsed:]   No 8.
          Letter from Jonas Phillips a Jew, dated Sept. 7. 1787.
     to the President & Members of the Convention

<hr>

CV. Jonathan Dayton to Elias Dayton.[1]

Philadelphia, Sept. 9, 1787.

We have happily so far finished our business, as to be employed
in giving it its last polish and preparing it for the public inspection.
This, I conclude, may be done in three or four days, at which time
the public curiosity and our desire of returning to our respective
homes, will equally be gratified.

<hr>

CVI. Joseph Jones to James Madison.[2]

13 September, 1787.

The continuance of your session and some stories I have heard
since my return and on my visit to Alexandria, make me apprehensive there is not that unanimity in your councils I hoped for
and had been taught to believe. From whence it originated I know
not, but it is *whispered* here, there is great disagreement among the
gentlemen of our delegation, that the general and yourself on a very
important question were together, Mr. M — n alone and singular
in his opinion and the other two gentlemen holding different sentiments. I asked what was the question in dispute, and was answered
that it respected either the defect in constituting the Convention
as not proceeding immediately from the people, or the referring the
proceedings of the body to the people for ultimate decision and confirmation. My informant also assured me the fact might be relied
on as it came, as he expressed it, from the fountain head. I took
the liberty to express my disbelief of the fact and that from the
circumstances related it was very improbable and unworthy attention. I mention this matter for want of something else to write to
you, and more especially as it respects our delegation in particular.

<hr>

CVII. Sydney to Lord Dorchester.[3]

Whitehall, 14 Sept., 1787.

The report of an intention on the part of America to apply for
a sovereign of the house of Hanover[4] has been circulated here; and

<hr>

[1] Jameson, *Studies in the History of the Federal Convention* in *Annual Report of the
American Historical Association*, for 1902, p. 100.

[2] Massachusetts Historical Society, *Proceedings*, 2d Series, XVII, 474–475.

[3] Bancroft, *History of the Constitution of the United States*, II, 441.

[4] See XCII above.

should an application of that nature be made, it will require a very nice consideration in what manner so important a subject should be treated. But whatever ideas may have been formed upon it, it will upon all accounts be advisable that any influence which your lordship may possess should be exerted to discourage the strengthening their alliance with the house of Bourbon, which must naturally follow were a sovereign to be chosen from any branch of that family.

CVIII. JOHN DICKINSON TO GEORGE READ.[1]

Mr. Dickinson presents his compliments to Mr. Read, and requests that if the constitution, formed by the convention, is to be signed by the members of that body, Mr. Read will be. so good as to subscribe Mr. Dickinson's name — his indisposition and some particular circumstances requiring him to return home.[2]
September 15th, 1787.

CIX. GEORGE WASHINGTON: DIARY.[3]

[September], Saturday 15th.
concluded the business of Convention, all to signing the proceedings; to effect which the House sat till 6 o'clock; and adjourned 'till Monday that the Constitution which it was proposed to offer to the People might be engrossed — and a number of printed copies struck off. —

CX. GEORGE WASHINGTON: DIARY.[4]

[September] Monday — 17th.
Met in Convention when the Constitution received the unanimous assent of 11 States and Colo. Hamilton's from New York (the only delegate from thence in Convention) and was subscribed to by every Member present except Govr. Randolph and Colo. Mason from Virginia — & Mr. Gerry from Massachusetts. The business being thus closed, the Members adjourned to the City Tavern, dined together and took a cordial leave of each other. — after which I returned to my lodgings — did some business with, and received the papers from the secretary of the Convention, and retired to meditate on the momentous wk. which had been executed, after not less than five, for a large part of the time six, and sometimes 7 hours sitting every day, sundays & the ten days adjournment to give a Commee. opportunity & time to arrange the business for more than four months. —

---

[1] W. T. Read, *Life and Correspondence of George Read*, 456–457.
[2] Dickinson's signature to the Constitution is in Read's handwriting.
[3] *Documentary History of the Constitution*, IV, 277.
[4] *Documentary History of the Constitution*, IV, 281.

CXI. WILLIAM JACKSON TO GENERAL WASHINGTON.[1]

Monday evening

Major Jackson presents his most respectful compliments to General Washington. . . .

Major Jackson, after burning all the loose scraps of paper which belong to the Convention, will this evening wait upon the General with the Journals and other papers which their vote directs to be delivered to His Excellency

[Endorsed:] From Majr Wm. Jackson 17th Sep. 1787.

———————

CXIa. PENNSYLVANIA HERALD AND GENERAL ADVERTISER.

September 18, 1787.

Yesterday afternoon, about four o'clock the foederal convention . . . broke up.   ———————

CXII. NICHOLAS GILMAN TO PRESIDENT SULLIVAN.[2]

Philadelphia September 18th 1787

I have the pleasure to inform your Excellency that the important business of the Convention is closed. — their Secretary set off this morning to present the Honorable the Congress with a report of their proceedings and the Convention adjourned without day.

———————

CXIII. NICHOLAS GILMAN TO JOSEPH GILMAN.[3]

Philadelphia, September 18, 1787.

The important business of the Convention being closed, the Secretary set off this morning to present Congress with a report of their proceedings, which I hope will soon come before the State in the manner directed, but as some time must necessarily elapse before that can take place, I do myself the pleasure to transmit the enclosed papers for your private satisfaction forbearing all comments on the plan but that it is the best that could meet the unanimous concurrence of the States in Convention; it was done by bargain and Compromise, yet notwithstanding its imperfections, on the adoption of it depends (in my feeble judgment) whether we shall become a respectable nation, or a people torn to pieces by intestine commotions, and rendered contemptible for ages.

---

[1] *Documentary History of the Constitution,* IV, 281.

[2] *New Hampshire State Papers,* XXI, 836.

[3] Hunt, *Fragments of Revolutionary History* (Brooklyn, 1892), p. 156. Corrected from a photostat in the Harvard College Library.

CXIV. Edmund Randolph to Beverley Randolph.[1]

Phila., Sept. 18, 1787.

I do myself the honor of forwarding to the executive a copy of the national constitution. Altho' the names of Colo. Mason and myself are not subscribed, it is not, therefore, to be concluded that we are opposed to its adoption. Our reasons for not subscribing will be better explained at large, and on a personal interview, than by letter. ⸺⸺

CXV. North Carolina Delegates to Governor Caswell.[2]

Philadelphia, September 18th, 1787.

In the course of four Months severe and painful application and anxiety, the Convention have prepared a plan of Government for the United States of America which we hope will obviate the defects of the present Federal Union and procure the enlarged purposes which it was intended to effect. Enclosed we have the honor to send you a Copy, and when you are pleased to lay this plan before the General Assembly we entreat that you will do us the justice to assure that honorable Body that no exertions have been wanting on our part to guard and promote the particular interest of North Carolina. You will observe that the representation in the second Branch of the National Legislature is to be according to numbers, that is to say, According to the whole number of white Inhabitants added to three-fifths of the blacks; you will also observe that during the first three years North Carolina is to have five Members in the House of Representatives, which is just one-thirteenth part of the whole number in that house and our Annual Quota of the National debt has not hitherto been fixed quite so high. Doubtless we have reasons to believe that the Citizens of North Carolina are more than a thirteenth part of the whole number in the Union, but the State has never enabled its Delegates in Congress to prove this Opinion and hitherto they had not been Zealous to magnify the number of their Constituents because their Quota of the National Debt must have been Augmented accordingly. We had many things to hope from a National Government and the chief thing we had to fear from such a Government was the Risque of unequal or heavy Taxation, but we hope you will believe as we do that the Southern States in general and North Carolina in particular are well secured on that head by the proposed system. It is provided in the 9th Section of Article the first that no Capitation or other

---

[1] *Virginia Calendar of State Papers*, IV, 343.
[2] *North Carolina State Records*, XX, 777–779.

direct Tax shall be laid except in proportion to the number of Inhabitants, in which number five blacks are only Counted as three. If a land tax is laid we are to pay the same rate, for Example: fifty Citizens of North Carolina can be taxed no more for all their Lands than fifty Citizens in one of the Eastern States. This must be greatly in our favour for as most of their Farms are small & many of them live in Towns we certainly have, one with another, land of twice the value that they Possess. When it is also considered that five Negroes are only to be charged the Same Poll Tax as three whites the advantage must be considerably increased under the proposed Form of Government. The Southern States have also a much better Security for the Return of Slaves who might endeavour to Escape than they had under the original Confederation. It is expected a considerable Share of the National Taxes will be collected by Impost, Duties and Excises, but you will find it provided in the 8th Section of Article the first that all duties, Impost and excises shall *be uniform* throughout the United States. While we were taking so much care to guard ourselves against being over reached and to form rules of Taxation that might operate in our favour, it is not to be supposed that our Northern Brethren were Inattentive to their particular Interest. A navigation Act or the power to regulate Commerce in the Hands of the National Government by which American Ships and Seamen may be fully employed is the desirable weight that is thrown into the Northern Scale. This is what the Southern States have given in Exchange for the advantages we Mentioned above; but we beg leave to observe in the course of this Interchange North Carolina does not appear to us to have given up *anything* for we are doubtless the most independent of the Southern States; we are able to carry our own produce and if the Spirit of Navigation and Ship building is cherished in our State we shall soon be able to carry for our Neighbors. We have taken the liberty to mention the General pecuniary Considerations which are involved in this plan of Government, there are other Considerations of great Magnitude involved in the system, but we cannot exercise your patience with a further detail, but submit it with the utmost deference, and have the Honor to be,

Your Excellency's Most Obedient Humble Servts,

WM. BLOUNT,

RICH'D D. SPAIGHT,

HUGH WILLIAMSON.

CXVI. James McHenry: Anecdotes.[1]

18 —

A lady asked Dr. Franklin Well Doctor what have we got a republic or a monarchy — A republic replied the Doctor if you can keep it.*

* The lady here aluded to was Mrs. Powel of Philada.

Mr. Martin said one day in company with Mr Jenifer speaking of the system before Convention —

I'll be hanged if ever the people of Maryland agree to it. I advise you said Mr Jenifer to stay in Philadelphia lest you should be hanged.

CXVII. Anecdote.[2]

When the Convention to form a Constitution was sitting in Philadelphia in 1787, of which General Washington was president, he had stated evenings to receive the calls of his friends. At an interview between Hamilton, the Morrises, and others, the former remarked that Washington was reserved and aristocratic even to his intimate friends, and allowed no one to be familiar with him. Gouverneur Morris said that was a mere fancy, and he could be as familiar with Washington as with any of his other friends. Hamilton replied, "If you will, at the next reception evenings, gently slap him on the shoulder and say, 'My dear General, how happy I am to see you look so well!' a supper and wine shall be provided for you and a dozen of your friends." The challenge was accepted. On the evening appointed, a large number attended; and at an early hour Gouverneur Morris entered, bowed, shook hands, laid his left hand on Washington's shoulder, and said, "My dear General, I am very happy to see you look so well!" Washington withdrew his hand, stepped suddenly back, fixed his eye on Morris for several minutes with an angry frown, until the latter retreated abashed, and sought refuge in the crowd. The company looked on in silence. At the supper, which was provided by Hamilton, Morris said, "I have won the bet, but paid dearly for it, and nothing could induce me to repeat it.[3]

---

[1] *American Historical Review*, XI, 618. The date of this is uncertain.

[2] This anecdote is taken from James Parton, *Life of Thomas Jefferson*, (1874), p. 369.

[3] This is doubtless the same story told in another form by W. T. Read in his *Life and Correspondence of George Read* (1870, p. 441 note):

"But it appears from the following anecdote, communicated to me by Mrs. Susan

CXVIII. WILLIAM PIERCE: ANECDOTE.[1]

When the Convention first opened at Philadelphia, there were a number of propositions brought forward as great leading principles for the new Government to be established for the United States. A copy of these propositions was given to each Member with the injunction to keep everything a profound secret. One morning, by accident, one of the Members dropt his copy of the propositions, which being luckily picked up by General Mifflin was presented to General Washington, our President, who put it in his pocket, After the debates of the Day were over, and the question for adjournment was called for, the General arose from his seat, and previous to his putting the question addressed the Convention in the following manner, —
Gentlemen

"I am sorry to find that some one Member of this Body, has been so neglectful of the secrets of the Convention as to drop in the State House a copy of their proceedings, which by accident was picked up and delivered to me this Morning. I must entreat Gentlemen to be more careful, least our transactions get into the News Papers, and disturb the public repose by premature speculations. I know not whose Paper it is, but there it is (throwing it down on the table), let him who owns it take it." At the same time he bowed, picked up his Hat, and quitted the room with a dignity so severe

---

Eckard, of Philadelphia, daughter of Colonel James Read, that Mr. Morris was once frightened, embarrassed, and sensible of inferiority in the presence of a fellow-mortal:

"Gouverneur Morris, a very handsome, bold, and — I have heard the ladies say — very impudent man. His talents and services are part of American history. He wore a wooden leg. He was not related to the great financier, who was said to be a natural child. The office of Mr. [Robert] Morris was only divided from papa's by a small entry, and was constantly visited by Mr. Gouverneur Morris, and papa's also. One day the latter entered, and papa was so struck by his crest-fallen appearance that he asked, 'Are you not well?' He replied, 'I am not, — the devil got possession of me last night.' 'I have often cautioned you against him,' said papa, playfully, 'but what has happened to disturb you?' 'I was at the President's last night; several members of the Cabinet were there. The then absorbing question, ('I forget,' Mrs. E. writes, 'what it was') 'was brought up. The President was standing with his arms behind him, — his usual position, — his back to the fire, listening. Hamilton made a speech I did not like. I started up and spoke, stamping, as I walked up and down, with my wooden leg; and, as I was certain I had the best of the argument, as I finished I stalked up to the President, slapped him on the back, and said, 'Ain't I right, general?' The President did not speak, but the majesty of the American people was before me. Oh, his look! How I wished the floor would open and I could descend to the cellar! You know me,' continued Mr. Morris, 'and you know my eye would never quail before any other mortal.'"

[1] *American Historical Review*, III, 324–325, It is impossible to assign any date to the relation of this anecdote.

that every Person seemed alarmed; for my part I was extremely so, for putting my hand in my pocket I missed my copy of the same Paper, but advancing up to the Table my fears soon dissipated; I found it to be the hand writing of another Person. When I went to my lodgings at the Indian Queen, I found my copy in a coat pocket which I had pulled off that Morning. It is something remarkable that no Person ever owned the Paper.

CXIX. WILLIAM PIERCE: CHARACTER SKETCHES OF DELEGATES
TO THE FEDERAL CONVENTION.[1]

From New Hampshire.

Jno. Langdon Esqr. and Nichs. Gilman Esquire.

Mr. Langdon is a Man of considerable fortune, possesses a liberal mind, and a good plain understanding. — about 40 years old.

Mr. Gilman is modest, genteel, and sensible. There is nothing brilliant or striking in his character, but there is something respectable and worthy in the Man. — about 30 years of age.

From Massachusetts.

Rufus King, Natl. Gorham, Gerry and Jno. [Caleb] Strong Esquires.

Mr. King is a Man much distinguished for his eloquence and great parliamentary talents. He was educated in Massachusetts, and is said to have good classical as well as legal knowledge. He has served for three years in the Congress of the United States with great and deserved applause, and is at this time high in the confidence and approbation of his Country-men. This Gentleman is about thirty three years of age, about five feet ten Inches high, well formed, an handsome face, with a strong expressive Eye, and a sweet high toned voice. In his public speaking there is something peculiarly strong and rich in his expression, clear, and convincing in his arguments, rapid and irresistible at times in his eloquence but he is not always equal. His action is natural, swimming, and graceful, but there is a rudeness of manner sometimes accompanying it. But take him *tout en semble*, he may with propriety be ranked among the Luminaries of the present Age.

Mr. Gorham is a Merchant in Boston, high in reputation, and much in the esteem of his Country-men. He is a Man of very good sense, but not much improved in his education. He is eloquent and easy in public debate, but has nothing fashionable or elegant

---

[1] *American Historical Review*, III, 325-334. It is impossible to assign any exact date to the writing of these sketches. A comparison of this with the characterizations reported to the French government (see CLIX below) is interesting.

in his style; — all he aims at is to convince, and where he fails it never is from his auditory not understanding him, for no Man is more perspicuous and full. He has been President of Congress, and three years a Member of that Body. Mr. Gorham is about 46 years of age, rather lusty, and has an agreable and pleasing manner.

Mr. Gerry's character is marked for integrity and perseverance. He is a hesitating and laborious speaker; — possesses a great degree of confidence and goes extensively into all subjects that he speaks on, without respect to elegance or flower of diction. He is connected and sometimes clear in his arguments, conceives well, and cherishes as his first virtue, a love for his Country. Mr. Gerry is very much of a Gentleman in his principles and manners; — he has been engaged in the mercantile line and is a Man of property. He is about 37 years of age.

Mr. Strong is a Lawyer of some eminence, — he has received a liberal education, and has good connections to recommend him. As a Speaker he is feeble, and without confidence. This Gentn. is about thirty five years of age, and greatly in the esteem of his Colleagues.

From Connecticut.

Saml. Johnson, Roger Sherman, and W. [Oliver] Elsworth Esquires.

Dr. Johnson is a character much celebrated for his legal knowledge; he is said to be one of the first classics in America, and certainly possesses a very strong and enlightened understanding.

As an Orator in my opinion, there is nothing in him that warrants the high reputation which he has for public speaking. There is something in the tone of his voice not pleasing to the Ear, — but he is eloquent and clear, — always abounding with information and instruction. He was once employed as an Agent for the State of Connecticut to state her claims to certain landed territory before the British House of Commons; this Office he discharged with so much dignity, and made such an ingenious display of his powers, that he laid the foundation of a reputation which will probably last much longer than his own life. Dr. Johnson is about sixty years of age, possesses the manners of a Gentleman, and engages the Hearts of Men by the sweetness of his temper, and that affectionate style of address with which he accosts his acquaintance.

Mr. Sherman exhibits the oddest shaped character I ever remember to have met with. He is awkward, un-meaning, and unaccountably strange in his manner. But in his train of thinking there is something regular, deep and comprehensive; yet the oddity of his address, the vulgarisms that accompany his public speaking, and that strange New England cant which runs through his public as well as his private speaking make everything that is connected with him grotesque and laughable; — and yet he deserves infinite praise, — no Man has a better Heart or a clearer Head. If he cannot embellish he can furnish thoughts that are wise and useful. He is an able politician, and extremely artful in accomplishing any particular object; — it is remarked that he seldom fails. I am told he sits on the Bench in Connecticut, and is very correct in the discharge of his Judicial functions. In the early part of his life he was a Shoe-maker; — but despising the lowness of his condition, he turned Almanack maker, and so progressed upwards to a Judge. He has been several years a Member of Congress, and discharged the duties of his Office with honor and credit to himself, and advantage to the State he represented. He is about 60.

Mr. Elsworth is a Judge of the Supreme Court in Connecticut; — he is a Gentleman of a clear, deep, and copious understanding; eloquent, and connected in public debate; and always attentive to his duty. He is very happy in a reply, and choice in selecting such parts of his adversary's arguments as he finds make the strongest impressions, — in order to take off the force of them, so as to admit the power of his own. Mr. Elsworth is about 37 years of age, a Man much respected for his integrity, and venerated for his abilities.

From New York.

Alexander Hamilton, [Robert] Yates, and W. [John] Lansing Esquires.

Colo. Hamilton is deservedly celebrated for his talents. He is a practitioner of the Law, and reputed to be a finished Scholar. To a clear and strong judgment he unites the ornaments of fancy, and whilst he is able, convincing, and engaging in his eloquence the Heart and Head sympathize in approving him. Yet there is something too feeble in his voice to be equal to the strains of oratory; — it is my opinion that he is rather a convincing Speaker, that [than] a blazing Orator. Colo. Hamilton requires time to think, — he enquires into every part of his subject with the searchings of phylosophy, and when he comes forward he comes highly charged with interesting matter, there is no skimming over the surface of a subject with him, he must sink to the bottom to see what foundation it rests on. — His language is not always equal, sometimes didactic like Bolingbroke's at others light and tripping like Stern's. His eloquence is not so defusive as to trifle with the senses, but he rambles just enough to strike and keep up the attention. He is about 33 years old, of small stature, and lean. His manners are tinctured with stiffness, and sometimes with a degree of vanity that is highly disagreeable.

Mr. Yates is said to be an able Judge. He is a Man of great legal abilities, but not distinguished as an Orator. Some of his Enemies say he is an anti-federal Man, but I discovered no such disposition in him. He is about 45 years old, and enjoys a great share of health.

Mr. Lansing is a practicing Attorney at Albany, and Mayor of that Corporation. He has a hisitation in his speech, that will prevent his being an Orator of any eminence; — his legal knowledge I am told is not extensive, nor his education a good one. He is however a Man of good sense, plain in his manners, and sincere in his friendships. He is about 32 years of age.

From New Jersey.

Wm. Livingston, David Brearly, Wm. Patterson, and Jonn. Dayton, Esquires.

Governor Livingston is confessedly a Man of the first rate talents, but he appears to me rather to indulge a sportiveness of wit, than a strength of thinking. He is however equal to anything, from the extensiveness of his education and genius. His writings teem with satyr and a neatness of style. But he is no Orator, and seems little acquainted with the guiles of policy. He is about 60 years old, and remarkably healthy.

Mr. Brearly is a man of good, rather than of brilliant parts. He is a Judge of the Supreme Court of New Jersey, and is very much in the esteem of the people. As an Orator he has little to boast of, but as a Man he has every virtue to recommend him. Mr. Brearly is about 40 years of age.

M. Patterson is one of those kind of Men whose powers break in upon you, and create wonder and astonishment. He is a Man of great modesty, with looks that bespeak talents of no great extent, — but he is a Classic, a Lawyer, and an Orator; — and of a disposition so favorable to his advancement that every one seemed ready to exalt him with their praises. He is very happy in the choice of time and manner of engaging in a debate, and never speaks but when he understands his subject well. This Gentleman is about 34 ys. of age, of a very low stature.

Capt. Dayton is a young Gentleman of talents, with ambition to exert them. He possesses a good education and some reading; he speaks well, and seems desirous of improving himself in Oratory. There is an impetuosity in his temper that is injurious to him; but there is an honest rectitude about him that makes him a valuable Member of Society, and secures to him the esteem of all good Men. He is about 30 years old, served with me as a Brother Aid to General Sullivan in the Western expedition of '79.

From Pennsylvania.

Benja. Franklin, Thos. Mifflin, Robt. Morris, Geo. Clymer, Thomas Fitzsimons, Jared Ingersol, James Wilson, Governeur Morris.

Dr. Franklin is well known to be the greatest phylosopher of the present age; — all the operations of nature he seems to understand,– the very heavens obey him, and the Clouds yield up their Lightning to be imprisoned in his rod. But what claim he has to the politician, posterity must determine. It is certain that he does not shine much in public Council, — he is no Speaker, nor does he seem to let politics engage his attention. He is, however, a most extraordinary Man, and tells a story in a style more engaging than anything I ever heard. Let his Biographer finish his character. He is 82 years old, and possesses an activity of mind equal to a youth of 25 years of age.

General Mifflin is well known for the activity of his mind, and the brilliancy of his parts. He is well informed and a graceful Speaker. The General is about 40 years of age, and a very handsome man.

Robert Morris is a merchant of great eminence and wealth; an able Financier, and a worthy Patriot. He has an understanding equal to any public object, and possesses an energy of mind that few Men can boast of. Although he is not learned, yet he is as great as those who are. I am told that when he speaks in the Assembly of Pennsylvania, that he bears down all before him. What could have been his reason for not Speaking in the Convention I know not, — but he never once spoke on any point. This Gentleman is about 50 years old.

Mr. Clymer is a Lawyer of some abilities; — he is a respectable Man, and much esteemed. Mr. Clymer is about 40 years old.

Mr. Fitzsimons is a Merchant of considerable talents, and speaks very well I am told, in the Legislature of Pennsylvania. He is about 40 years old.

Mr. Ingersol is a very able Attorney, and possesses a clear legal understanding. He is well educated in the Classic's, and is a Man of very extensive reading. Mr. Ingersol speaks well, and comprehends his subject fully. There is a modesty in his character that keeps him back. He is about 36 years old.

Mr. Wilson ranks among the foremost in legal and political knowledge. He has joined to a fine genius all that can set him off and show him to advantage. He is well acquainted with Man, and understands all the passions that influence him. Government seems to have been his peculiar Study, all the political institutions of the World he knows in detail, and can trace the causes and effects of every revolution from the earliest stages of the Greecian commonwealth down to the present time. No man is more clear, copious, and comprehensive than Mr. Wilson, yet he is no great Orator. He draws the attention not by the charm of his eloquence, but by the force of his reasoning. He is about 45 years old.

Mr. Governeur Morris is one of those Genius's in whom every species of talents combine to render him conspicuous and flourishing in public debate: — He winds through all the mazes of rhetoric, and throws around him such a glare that he charms, captivates, and leads away the senses of all who hear him. With an infinite streach of fancy he brings to view things when he is engaged in deep argumentation, that render all the labor of reasoning easy and pleasing. But with all these powers he is fickle and inconstant, — never pursuing one train of thinking, — nor ever regular. He has gone through a very extensive course of reading, and is acquainted with all the sciences. No Man has more wit, — nor can any one engage the attention more than Mr. Morris. He was bred to the Law, but I am told he disliked the profession, and turned merchant. He is engaged in some great mercantile matters with his namesake Mr. Robt. Morris. This Gentleman is about 38 years old, he has been unfortunate in losing one of his Legs, and getting all the flesh taken off his right arm by a scald, when a youth.

From Delaware.

John Dickinson, Gunning Bedford, Geo: Richd. Bassett, and Jacob Broom Esquires.

Mr. Dickinson has been famed through all America, for his Farmers Letters; he is a Scholar, and said to be a Man of very extensive information. When I saw him in the Convention I was induced to pay the greatest attention to him whenever he spoke. I had often heard that he was a great Orator, but I found him an indifferent Speaker. With an affected air of wisdom he labors to produce a trifle, — his language is irregular and incorrect, — his flourishes (for he sometimes attempts them), are like expiring flames, they just shew themselves and go out; — no traces of them are left on the mind to chear or animate it. He is, however, a good writer and will ever be considered one of the most important characters in the United States. He is about 55 years old, and was bred a Quaker.

Mr. Bedford was educated for the Bar, and in his profession I am told, has merit. He is a bold and nervous Speaker, and has a very commanding and striking manner; — but he is warm and impetuous in his temper, and precipitate in his judgment. Mr. Bedford is about 32 years old, and very corpulent.

Mr. Read is a Lawyer and a Judge; — his legal abilities are said to be very great, but his powers of Oratory are fatiguing and tiresome to the last degree; — his voice is feeble, and his articulation so bad that few can have patience to attend to him. He is a very good Man, and bears an amiable character with those who know him. Mr. Read is about 50, of a low stature, and a weak constitution.

Mr. Bassett is a religious enthusiast, lately turned Methodist, and serves his Country because it is the will of the people that he should do so. He is a Man of plain sense, and has modesty enough to hold his Tongue. He is a Gentlemanly Man, and is in high estimation among the Methodists. Mr. Bassett is about 36 years old.

Mr. Broom is a plain good Man, with some abilities, but nothing to render him conspicuous. He is silent in public, but chearful and conversable in private. He is about 35 years old.

From Maryland.

Luther Martin, Jas. McHenry, Daniel of St. Thomas Jenifer, and Daniel Carrol Esquires.

Mr. Martin was educated for the Bar, and is Attorney general for the State of Maryland. This Gentleman possesses a good deal of information, but he has a very bad delivery, and so extremely prolix, that he never speaks without tiring the patience of all who hear him. He is about 34 years of age.

Mr. Mc.Henry was bred a physician, but he afterwards turned Soldier and acted as Aid to Genl. Washington and the Marquis de la Fayette. He is a Man of specious talents, with nothing of genious to improve them. As a politician there is nothing remarkable in him, nor has he any of the graces of the Orator. He is however, a very respectable young Gentleman, and deserves the honor which his Country has bestowed on him. Mr. Mc. Henry is about 32 years of age.

Mr. Jenifer is a Gentleman of fortune in Maryland; — he is always in good humour, and never fails to make his company pleased with him. He sits silent in the Senate, and seems to be conscious that he is no politician. From his long continuance in single life, no doubt but he has made the vow of celibacy. He speaks warmly of the Ladies notwithstanding. Mr. Jenifer is about 55 years of Age, and once served as an Aid de Camp to Major Genl. Lee.

Mr. Carrol is a Man of large fortune, and influence in his State. He possesses plain good sense, and is in the full confidence of. his Countrymen. This Gentleman is about   years of age.

From Virginia.

Genl. Geo: Washington, Geo: Wythe, Geo: Mason, Jas. Maddison junr. Jno. Blair, Edmd. Randolph, and James Mc.Lurg.

Genl. Washington is well known as the Commander in chief of the late American Army. Having conducted these states to independence and peace, he now appears to assist in framing a Government to make the People happy. Like Gustavus Vasa, he may be said to be the deliverer of his Country;—like Peter the great he appears as the politician and the States-man; and like Cincinnatus he returned to his farm perfectly contented with being only a plain Citizen, after enjoying the highest honor of the Confederacy, — and now only seeks for the approbation of his Country-men by being virtuous and useful. The General was conducted to the Chair as President of the Convention by the unanimous voice of its Members. He is in the 52d. year of his age.

Mr. Wythe is the famous Professor of Law at the University of William and Mary. He is confessedly one of the most learned legal Characters of the present age. From his close attention to the study of general learning he has acquired a compleat knowledge of the dead languages and all the sciences. He is remarked for his examplary life, and universally esteemed for his good principles. No Man it is said understands the history of Government better than Mr. Wythe, — nor any one who understands the fluctuating condition to which all societies are liable better than he does, yet from his too favorable opinion of Men, he is no great politician. He is a neat and pleasing Speaker, and a most correct and able Writer. Mr. Wythe is about 55 years of age.

Mr. Mason is a Gentleman of remarkable strong powers, and possesses a clear and copious understanding. He is able and convincing in debate, steady and firm in his principles, and undoubtedly one of the best politicians in America. Mr. Mason is about 60 years old, with a fine strong constitution.

Mr. Maddison is a character who has long been in public life; and what is very remarkable every Person seems to acknowledge his greatness. He blends together the profound politician, with the Scholar. In the management of every great question he evidently took the lead in the Convention, and tho' he cannot be called an Orator, he is a most agreable, eloquent, and convincing Speaker. From a spirit of industry and application which he possesses in a most eminent degree, he always comes forward the best informed Man of any point in debate. The affairs of the United States, he perhaps, has the most correct knowledge of, of any Man in the Union. He has been twice a Member of Congress, and was always thought one of the ablest Members that ever sat in that Council. Mr. Maddison is about 37 years of age, a Gentleman of great modesty, — with a remarkable sweet temper. He is easy and unreserved among his acquaintance, and has a most agreable style of conversation.

Mr. Blair is one of the most respectable Men in Virginia, both on account of his Family as well as fortune. He is one of the Judges of the Supreme Court in Virginia, and acknowledged to have a very extensive knowledge of the Laws. Mr. Blair is however, no Orator, but his good sense, and most excellent principles, compensate for other deficiencies. He is about 50 years of age.

Mr. Randolph is Governor of Virginia, — a young Gentleman in whom unite all the accomplishments of the Scholar, and the States-man. He came forward with the postulata, or first principles, on which the Convention acted, and he supported them with a force of eloquence and reasoning that did him great honor. He has a most harmonious voice, a fine person and striking manners. Mr. Randolph is about 32 years of age.

Mr. Mc.Lurg is a learned physician, but having never appeared before in public life his character as a politician is not sufficiently known. He attempted once or twice to speak, but with no great success. It is certain that he has a foundation of learning, on which, if he pleases, he may erect a character of high renown. The Doctor is about 38 years of age, a Gentleman of great respectability, and of a fair and unblemished character.

North Carolina.

Wm. Blount, Richd. Dobbs Spaight, Hugh Williamson, Wm. Davey, and Jno. [Alexander] Martin Esquires.

Mr. Blount is a character strongly marked for integrity and honor. He has been twice a Member of Congress, and in that office discharged his duty with ability and faithfulness. He is no Speaker, nor does he possess any of those talents that make Men shine; — he is plain, honest, and sincere. Mr. Blount is about 36 years of age.

Mr. Spaight is a worthy Man, of some abilities, and fortune. Without possessing a Genius to render him brilliant, he is able to discharge any public trust that his Country may repose in him. He is about 31 years of age.

Mr. Williamson is a Gentleman of education and talents. He enters freely into public debate from his close attention to most subjects, but he is no Orator. There is a great degree of good humour and pleasantry in his character; and in his manners there is a strong trait of the Gentleman. He is about 48 years of age.

Mr. Davey is a Lawyer of some eminence in his State. He is

said to have a good classical education, and is a Gentleman of considerable literary talents. He was silent in the Convention, but his opinion was always respected. Mr. Davey is about 30 years of age.

Mr. Martin was lately Governor of North Carolina, which office he filled with credit. He is a Man of sense, and undoubtedly is a good politician, but he is not formed to shine in public debate, being no Speaker. Mr. Martin was once a Colonel in the American Army, but proved unfit for the field. He is about 40 years of age.

South Carolina.

Jno. Rutledge, Chs. Cotesworth Pinckney, Charles Pinckney, and Pierce Butler Esquires.

Mr. Rutledge is one of those characters who was highly mounted at the commencement of the late revolution; — his reputation in the first Congress gave him a distinguished rank among the American Worthies. He was bred to the Law, and now acts as one of the Chancellors of South Carolina. This Gentleman is much famed in his own State as an Orator, but in my opinion he is too rapid in his public speaking to be denominated an agreeable Orator. He is undoubtedly a man of abilities, and a Gentleman of distinction and fortune. Mr. Rutledge was once Governor of South Carolina. He is about 48 years of age.

Mr. Chs. Cotesworth Pinckney is a Gentleman of Family and fortune in his own State. He has received the advantage of a liberal education, and possesses a very extensive degree of legal knowledge. When warm in a debate he sometimes speaks well, — but he is generally considered an indifferent Orator. Mr. Pinckney was an Officer of high rank in the American army, and served with great reputation through the War. He is now about 40 years of age.

Mr. Charles Pinckney is a young Gentleman of the most promising talents. He is, altho' only 24 ys. of age, in possession of a very great variety of knowledge. Government, Law, History and Phylosophy are his favorite studies, but he is intimately acquainted with every species of polite learning, and has a spirit of application and industry beyond most Men. He speaks with great neatness and perspicuity, and treats every subject as fully, without running into prolixity, as it requires. He has been a Member of Congress, and served in that Body with ability and eclat.[1]

Mr. Butler is a character much respected for the many excellent

---

[1] "In reference to this part of his life, Mr. Pinckney frequently spoke of the deep diffidence and solemnity which he felt, being the youngest member of the body, whenever he addressed the Federal Convention." (J. B. O'Neall, *Biographical Sketches of the Bench and Bar of South Carolina*, Charleston, 1859, II, 140.)

virtues which he possesses. But as a politician or an Orator, he has no pretentions to either. He is a Gentleman of fortune, and takes rank among the first in South Carolina. He has been appointed to Congress, and is now a Member of the Legislature of South Carolina. Mr. Butler is about 40 years of age; an Irishman by birth.

For Georgia.

Wm. Few, Abraham Baldwin, Wm. Pierce, and Wm. Houstoun Esqrs.

Mr. Few possesses a strong natural Genius, and from application has acquired some knowledge of legal matters; — he practices at the bar of Georgia, and speaks tolerably well in the Legislature. He has been twice a Member of Congress, and served in that capacity with fidelity to his State, and honor to himself. Mr. Few is about 35 years of age.

Mr. Baldwin is a Gentleman of superior abilities, and joins in a public debate with great art and eloquence. Having laid the foundation of a compleat classical education at Harvard College, he pursues every other study with ease. He is well acquainted with Books and Characters, and has an accomodating turn of mind, which enables him to gain the confidence of Men, and to understand them. He is a practising Attorney in Georgia, and has been twice a Member of Congress. Mr. Baldwin is about 38 years of age.

Mr. Houstoun is an Attorney at Law, and has been Member of Congress for the State of Georgia. He is a Gentleman of Family, and was educated in England. As to his legal or political knowledge he has very little to boast of. Nature seems to have done more for his corporeal than mental powers. His Person is striking, but his mind very little improved with useful or elegant knowledge. He has none of the talents requisite for the Orator, but in public debate is confused and irregular. Mr. Houstoun is about 30 years of age of an amiable and sweet temper, and of good and honorable principles.

My own character I shall not attempt to draw, but leave those who may choose to speculate on it, to consider it in any light that their fancy or imagination may depict. I am conscious of having discharged my duty as a Soldier through the course of the late revolution with honor and propriety; and my services in Congress and the Convention were bestowed with the best intention towards the interest of Georgia, and towards the general welfare of the Confederacy. I possess ambition, and it was that, and the flattering opinion which some of my Friends had of me, that gave me a seat in the wisest Council in the World, and furnished me with an opportunity of giving these short Sketches of the Characters who composed it.

CXX. BENJAMIN FRANKLIN TO MRS. JANE MECOM.[1]

Philada. Sept. 20. 1787

The Convention finish'd the 17th Instant. I attended the Business of it 5 Hours in every Day from the Beginning; which is something more than four Months. You may judge from thence that my Health continues; some tell me I look better, and they suppose the daily Exercise of going & returning from the State-house has done me good. — You will see the Constitution we have propos'd in the Papers. The Forming of it so as to accommodate all the different Interests and Views was a difficult Task: and perhaps after all it may not be receiv'd with the same Unanimity in the different States that the Convention have given the Example of in delivering it out for their Consideration. We have however done our best and it must take its chance.

CXXI. JAMES MADISON TO EDMUND PENDLETON.[2]

Philada., Sepr. 20 1787

The privilege of franking having ceased with the Convention, I have waited for this opportunity of inclosing you a copy of the proposed Constitution for the U. States. I forbear to make any observations on it; either on the side of its merits or its faults. The best Judges of both will be those who can combine with a knowledge of the collective & permanent interest of America, a freedom from the bias resulting from a participation in the work. If the plan proposed be worthy of adoption, the degree of unanimity attained in the Convention is a circumstance as fortunate, as the very respectable dissent on the part of Virginia is a subject of regret. The double object of blending a proper stability & energy in the Government with the essential characters of the republican Form, and of tracing a proper line of demarkation between the national and State authorities, was necessarily found to be as difficult as it was desireable, and to admit of an infinite diversity concerning the means among those who were unanimously agreed concerning the end.

CXXII. EDWARD CARRINGTON TO JAMES MADISON.[3]

New York Sept. 23. 1787

The Gentlemen who have arrived from the Convention inform us that you are on the way to join us — least, however, you may, under

---

[1] *Documentary History of the Constitution*, IV, 291.

[2] *Documentary History of the Constitution*, IV, 291–292.

[3] *Documentary History of the Constitution*, IV, 293.

a supposition that the state of the delegation is such as to admit of your absence, indulge yourself in leisurely movements, after the fatiguing time you have had, I take this precaution to apprise you that the same schism which unfortunately happened in our State in Philadelphia, threatens us here also — one of our Colleagues Mr. R. H. Lee is forming propositions for essential alterations in the Constitution, which will, in effect, be to oppose it.—Another, Mr. Grayson, dislikes it, and is, at best for giving it only a silent passage to the States. Mr. H. Lee joins me in opinion that it ought to be warmly recommended to ensure its adoption. — a lukewarmness in Congress will be made a ground of opposition by the unfriendly in the States — those who have hitherto wished to bring the conduct of Congress into contempt, will in this case be ready to declare it truly respectable.   _____

CXXIII. SHERMAN AND ELLSWORTH TO THE GOVERNOR OF CONNECTICUT.[1]

Sir,

New London, Sept. 26.

We have the honour to transmit to your excellency a printed copy of the constitution formed by the federal convention, to be laid before the legislature of the state.

The general principles, which governed the convention in their deliberations on the subject, are stated in their address to congress.

We think it may be of use to make some further observations on particular parts of the constitution.

The congress is differently organized: yet the whole number of members, and this state's proportion of suffrage, remain the same as before.

The equal representation of the states in the senate, and the voice of that branch in the appointment to offices, will secure the rights of the lesser, as well as of the greater states.

Some additional powers are vested in congress, which was a principal object that the states had in view in appointing the convention. Those powers extend only to matters respecting the common interests of the union, and are specially defined, so that the particular states retain their sovereignty in all other matters.

The objects, for which congress may apply monies, are the same mentioned in the eighth article of the confederation, viz. for the common defence and general welfare, and for payment of the debts incurred for those purposes. It is probable that the principal branch of revenue will be duties on imports; what may be

---

[1] Carey's *American Museum*, II, 434-435.

necessary to be raised by direct taxation is to be apportioned on the several states, according to the numbers of their inhabitants, and although congress may raise the money by their own authority, if necessary, yet that authority need not be exercised, if each state will furnish its quota.

The restraint on the legislatures of the several states respecting emitting bills of credit, making any thing but money a tender in payment of debts, or impairing the obligation of contracts by *ex post facto* laws, was thought necessary as a security to commerce, in which the interest of foreigners, as well as of the citizens of different states, may be affected.

The convention endeavoured to provide for the energy of government on the one hand, and suitable checks on the other hand, to secure the rights of the particular states, and the liberties and properties of the citizens. We wish it may meet the approbation of the several states, and be a mean of securing their rights, and lengthening out their tranquility.

With great respect, we are,

Sir, your excellency's

Obedient humble servants,

Roger Sherman
Oliver Elsworth,

His excellency gov. Huntington.

CXXIV. WILLIAM PIERCE TO ST. GEORGE TUCKER.[1]

New York, Sept. 28, 1787.

You ask me for such information as I can, with propriety, give you, respecting the proceedings of the Convention: In my letter from Philadelphia, in July last, I informed you that everything was covered with the veil of secrecy. It is now taken off, and the great work is presented to the public for their consideration. I enclose you a copy of it, with the letter which accompanies the Constitution.

You will probably be surprised at not finding my name affixed to it, and will, no doubt, be desirous of having a reason for it. Know then, Sir, that I was absent in New York on a piece of business so necessary that it became unavoidable. I approve of its principles, and would have signed it with all my heart, had I been present. To say, however, that I consider it as perfect, would be to make an acknowledgement immediately opposed to my judgment. Perhaps it is the only one that will suit our present situation. The wisdom

---

[1] *American Historical Review*, III. 313–314.

of the Convention was equal to something greater; but a variety of local circumstances, the inequality of states, and the dissonant interests of the different parts of the Union, made it impossible to give it any other shape or form.

CXXV. James Wilson: Address to a Meeting of the Citizens of Philadelphia on October 6, 1787.[1]

Another objection that has been fabricated against the new constitution, is expressed in this disingenuous form — "the trial by jury is abolished in civil cases." I must be excused, my fellow citizens, if, upon this point, I take advantage of my professional experience, to detect the futility of the assertion. Let it be remembered, then, that the business of the foederal constitution was not local, but general — not limited to the views and establishments of a single state, but co-extensive with the continent, and comprehending the views and establishments of thirteen independent sovereignties. When, therefore, this subject was in discussion, we were involved in difficulties, which pressed on all sides, and no precedent could be discovered to direct our course. The cases open to a jury, differed in the different states; it was therefore impracticable, on that ground, to have made a general rule. The want of uniformity would have rendered any reference to the practice of the states idle and useless: and it could not, with any propriety, be said, that "the trial by jury shall be as heretofore:" since there has never existed any foederal system of jurisprudence, to which the declaration could relate. Besides, it is not in all cases that the trial by jury is adopted in civil questions: for causes depending in courts of admiralty, such as relate to maritime captures, and such as are agitated in the courts of equity, do not require the intervention of that tribunal. How, then, was the line of discrimination to be drawn? The convention found the task too difficult for them; and they left the business as it stands — in the fullest confidence, that no danger could possibly ensue, since the proceedings of the supreme court are to be regulated by the congress, which is a faithful representation of the people: and the oppression of government is effectually barred, by declaring that in all criminal cases, the trial by jury shall be preserved.

. . . Perhaps there never was a charge made with less reason, than that which predicts the institution of a baneful aristocracy in the foederal senate. This body branches into two characters, the one legislative, and the other executive. In its legislative character, it can effect no purpose without the co-operation of the house of

[1] P. L. Ford, *Pamphlets on the Constitution*, 157–159.

representatives: and in its executive character, it can accomplish no object, without the concurrence of the president. Thus fettered, I do not know any act which the senate can of itself perform: and such dependence necessarily precludes every idea of influence and superiority. But I will confess, that in the organization of this body, a compromise between contending interests is discernible: and when we reflect how various are the laws, commerce, habits, population, and extent of the confederated states, this evidence of mutual concession and accommodation ought rather to command a generous applause, than to excite jealousy and reproach. For my part, my admiration can only be equalled by my astonishment, in beholding so perfect a system formed from such heterogenous materials.

_____

CXXVI. George Mason to George Washington.[1]

Gunston-Hall Octor. 7th. 1787.

I take the Liberty to enclose you my Objections to the new Constitution of Government; which a little Moderation & Temper, in the latter End of the Convention, might have removed. I am however most decidedly of Opinion, that it ought to be submitted to a Convention chosen by the People, for that special Purpose; and shou'd any Attempt be made to prevent the calling such a Convention here, such a Measure shall have every Opposition in my Power to give it. You will readily observe, that my Objections are not numerous (the greater Part of the inclosed paper containing Reasonings upon the probable Effects of the exceptionable Parts) tho' in my mind, some of them are capital ones.[2]

_____

CXXVIa. Pierce Butler to Weedon Butler.[3]

New York, October 8th, 1787.

After four months close Confinement, We closed on the 17th of last month the business Committed to Ús. If it meets with the approbation of the States, I shall feel myself fully recompensed for my share of the trouble, and a Summer's Confinement which injured my health much. . . . We, in many instances took the Constitution of Britain, when in its purity, for a model, and surely We cou'd not have a better. We tried to avoid what appeared to Us

_____

[1] _Documentary History of the Constitution_, IV, 315.

[2] The enclosure consisted of Mason's well known objections to the Constitution. The paper is practically identical with that printed in the _Records_ of September 15.

[3] British Museum, Additional MSS., 16603. Copy furnished through the courtesy of the Department of Historical Research of the Carnegie Institution of Washington.

the weak parts of Antient as well as Modern Republicks. How well We have succeeded is left for You and other Letterd Men to determine. It is somewhat singular yet so the fact is, that I have never met with any Dutch man who understood the Constitution of his own Country. It is certainly a very complex unwieldy piece of business. I have read different Histories of it with attention, and to this hour I have but a very inadequate idea of it. Pray give me your opinion freely of the One I had some small hand in frameing, after you have read it. In passing judgment on it you must call to mind that we had Clashing Interests to reconcile — some strong prejudices to encounter, for the same spirit that brought settlers to a certain Quarter of this Country is still alive in it. View the system then as resulting from a spirit of Accomodation to different Interests, and not the most perfect one that the Deputies cou'd devise for a Country better adapted for the reception of it than America is at this day, or perhaps ever will be. It is a great Extent of Territory to be under One free Government; the manners and modes of thinking of the Inhabitants, differing nearly as much as in different Nations of Europe. If we can secure tranquillity at Home, and respect from abroad, they will be great points gain'd. We have, as you will see, taken a portion of power from the Individual States, to form a General Government for the whole to preserve the Union. The General Government to Consist of two Branches of Legislature and an Executive to be vested in One person for four years, but elligible again — the first Branch of the Legislature to be elected by the People of the different States, agreeable to a ratio of numbers and wealth, to serve for two years. The Second to Consist of two members from each State, to be appointed by the Legislature of the States to serve for six years. One third to go out every two years, but to be Elligible again if their State thinks proper to appoint them. A Judiciary to be Supreme in all matters relating to the General Government, and Appellate in State Controversies. The powers of the General Government are so defined as not to destroy the Sovereignty of the Individual States. These are the outlines, if I was to be more minute I shou'd tire your patience.

_____

CXXVII. GEORGE WASHINGTON TO DAVID HUMPHREYS.[1]

Mount Vernon October 10th. 1787.

The Constitution that is submitted, is not free from imperfections. — but there are as few radical defects in it as could well be

_____

[1] _Documentary History of the Constitution_, IV, 320.

expected, considering the heterogenious mass of which the Convention was composed and the diversity of interests that are to be attended to,   As a Constitutional door is opened for future amendments and alterations, I think it would be wise in the People to accept what is offered to them and I wish it may be by as great a majority of them as it was by that of the Convention; but this is hardly to be expected because the importance and sinister views of too many characters, will be affected by the change.   Much will depend however upon literary abilities, and the recommendation of it by good pens should be *openly*, I mean publickly afforded in the Gazetees.   Go matters however as they may, I shall have the consolation to reflect that no objects but the public good — and that peace and harmony which I wished to see prevail in the Convention, obtruded even for a moment in my bosom during the whole Session long as it was —

CXXVIII. Letter to Jefferson [?].[1]

Philadelphia 11. Oct. 1787.

I have given two or three papers which contain the substance of what has passed here respecting the federal convention.   the connecting thread is all I shall send, except a few minutes of the proceedings of the convention.

After four months session the house broke up.   the represented states, eleven & a half, having unanimously agreed to the act handed to you, there were only three dissenting voices; one from New England, a man of sense, but a Grumbletonian.   he was of service by objecting to every thing he did not propose.   it was of course more canvassed, & some errors corrected.   the other two are from Virginia: but Randolph wishes it well, & it is thought would have signed it, but he wanted to be on a footing with a popular rival — both these men sink in the general opinion.   no wonder they were opposed to a Washington & Madison.   Dr. Franklin has gained much credit within doors for his conduct, & was the person who proposed the general signature.   he had prepared his address in writing.   the exertion of speaking being too great, they allowed another to read it.   the day previous he sent for the Pennsylvania delegates; & it was reported that he did it to acquaint them of his disapprobation of certain points, & the impossibility of agreeing to them.   his views were different.   he wanted to allay every possible scruple, & make their votes unanimous.   some of the sentiments of the address were as follows.

---

[1] A copy of this document in Jefferson's handwriting is among the Jefferson Papers in the Library of Congress.   It is printed here from *Documentary History of the Constitution*, IV, 324–327.

'We have been long together. every possible objection has been combated. with so many different & contending interests it is impossible that any one can obtain every object of their wishes. we have met to make mutual sacrifices for the general good, and we have at last come fully to understand each other, & settle the terms. delay is as unnecessary as the adoption is important. I confess it does not fully accord with my sentiments. but I have lived long enough to have often experienced that we ought not to rely too much on our own judgments. I have often found I was mistaken in my most favorite ideas. I have upon the present occasion given up, upon mature reflection, many points which, at the beginning, I thought myself immoveably & decidedly in favor of. this renders me less tenacious of the remainder. there is a possibility of my being mistaken. the general principle which has presided over our deliberations now guides my sentiments. I repeat, I do materially object to certain points, & have already stated my objections — but I do declare that these objections shall never escape me without doors; as, upon the whole, I esteem the constitution to be the best possible, that could have been formed under present circumstances; & that it ought to go abroad with one united signature, & receive every support & countenance from us. I trust none will refuse to sign it. if they do, they will put me in mind of the French girl who was always quarelling & finding fault with every one around her, & told her sister that she thought it very extraordinary, but that really she had never found a person who was always in the right but herself.' . . .

The attempt is novel in history; and I can inform you of a more novel one; that I am assured by the gentlemen who served, that scarcely a personality, or offensive expression escaped during the whole session. the whole was conducted with a liberality & candor which does them the highest honor. I may pronounce that it will be adopted. General Washington lives; & as he will be appointed President, jealousy on this head vanishes. the plan once adopted, difficulties will lessen. 9. states can alter easier than 13 agree. with respect to Rhode island, my opinion is that she will join speedily. she has paid almost all her debts by a sponge, & has more to gain by the adoption than any other state. it will enable us to gain friends, & to oppose with force the machinations of our enemies.

CXXIX.

OBSERVATIONS
ON THE
PLAN OF GOVERNMENT
SUBMITTED TO THE
FEDERAL CONVENTION,
In PHILADELPHIA, on the 28th of May, 1787.
By Mr. CHARLES PINCKNEY,
Delegate from the State of South-Carolina.
Delivered at different Times in the course of their Discussions.
NEW-YORK: — Printed by FRANCIS CHILDS.[1]

Mr. President,

It is, perhaps, unnecessary to state to the House the reasons which have given rise to this Convention. The critical and embarrassed situation of our public affairs is, no doubt, strongly impressed upon every mind. I well know, it is an undertaking of much delicacy, to examine into the cause of public disorders, but having been for a considerable time concerned in the administration of the Federal System, and an evidence of its weakness, I trust the indulgence of the House will excuse me, while I endeavor to state with conciseness, as well the motives which induced the measure, as what ought, in my opinion, to be the conduct of the convention.

There is no one, I believe, who doubts there is something particularly alarming in the present conjuncture. There is hardly a man, in, or out of office, who holds any other language. Our government is despised — our laws are robbed of their respected terrors — their inaction is a subject of ridicule — and their exertion, of abhorrence and opposition — rank and office have lost their rever-

---

[1] A reprint of the title-page. The text of the entire pamphlet is corrected from the copy of the original edition in the Library of the New York Historical Society.

From a letter of Madison (see CXXX below) it is evident that the pamphlet must have been printed before October 14. (It was also reprinted in the *State Gazette* of South Carolina, October 29—November 29, 1787, — see Jameson, *Studies*, p. 116, note.) The greater part of the document probably represents a speech prepared in advance by Pinckney to be delivered at the time of presenting his plan of government (See Professor McLaughlin's explanation of the identity of this speech in the *American Historical Review*, IX, 735 — 741). The lateness of the hour on May 29 doubtless prevented this, but portions of the speech may have been used later in the debates of the Convention. This would account for the unusual wording of the title-page.

As modifications may have been made in the original draft, it has seemed advisable to print it here, rather than with the Records of May 29.

See further, Appendix D.

ence and effect — our foreign politics are as much deranged, as our domestic economy — our friends are slackened in their affection, — and our citizens loosened from their obedience. We know neither how to yield or how to enforce — hardly anything abroad or at home is sound and entire — disconnection and confusion in offices, in States and in parties, prevail throughout every part of the Union. These are facts, universally admitted and lamented.

This state of things is the more extraordinary, because it immediately follows the close of a war, when we conceived our political happiness was to commence; and because the parties which divided and were opposed to our systems, are known, to be in a great measure, dissolved. No external calamity has visited us — we labor under no taxation that is new or oppressive, nor are we engaged in a war with foreigners, or in disputes with ourselves. To what then, are we to attribute our embarrassments as a nation? The answer is an obvious one. — To the weakness and impropriety of a government, founded in mistaken principles — incapable of combining the various interests it is intended to unite and support — and destitute of that force and energy, without which, no government can exist.

At the time I pronounce in the most decided terms, this opinion of our Confederation, permit me to remark, that considering the circumstances under which it was formed — in the midst of a dangerous and doubtful war, and by men, totally inexperienced in the operations of a system so new and extensive, its defects are easily to be excused. We have only to lament the necessity which obliged us to form it at that time, and wish that its completion had been postponed to a period better suited to deliberation. I confess myself in sentiment with those, who were of opinion, that we should have avoided it if possible, during the war. That it ought to have been formed by a Convention of the States, expressly delegated for that purpose, and ratified by the authority of the people. This indispensible power it wants; and is, therefore, without the validity a federal Constitution ought certainly to have had. In most of the States it has nothing more, strictly speaking, than a legislative authority, and might therefore to be said, in some measure, to be under the control of the State legislatures.

Independent of this primary defect, of not having been formed in a manner that would have given it an authority paramount to the Constitutions and laws of the several States, and rendered it impossible for them to have interfered with its objects or operations, the first principles are destructive, and contrary to those maxims of government which have been received, and approved for ages.

In a government, where the liberties of the people are to be preserved, and the laws well administered, the executive, legislative and judicial, should ever be separate and distinct, and consist of parts, mutually forming a check upon each other. The Confederation seems to have lost sight of this wise distribution of the powers of government, and to have concentred the whole in a single unoperative body, where none of them can be used with advantage or effect. The inequality of the principle of Representation, where the largest and most inconsiderable States have an equal vote in the affairs of the Union; the want of commercial powers; of a compelling clause to oblige a due and punctual obedience to the Confederation; a provision for the admission of new States; for an alteration of the system, by a less than unanimous vote; of a general guarantee, and in short of numerous other reforms and establishments, convince me, that upon the present occasion, it would be politic in the Convention to determine that they will consider the subject de novo. That they will pay no farther attention to the Confederation, than to consider it as good materials, and view themselves as at liberty to form and recommend such a plan, as from their knowledge of the temper of the people, and the resources of the States, will be most likely to render our government firm and united. This appears to me, far more proper than to attempt the repair of a system, not only radically defective in principle, but which, if it was possible to give it operation, would prove absurd and oppressive. You must not hesitate to adopt proper measures, under an apprehension the States may reject them. From your deliberations much is expected; the eyes, as well as hopes of your constituents are turned upon the Convention; let their expectations be gratified. Be assured, that, however unfashionable for the moment, your sentiments may be, yet, if your system is accomodated to the situation of the Union, and founded in wise and liberal principles, it will, in time, be consented to. An energetic government is our policy, and it will at last be discovered, and prevail.

Presuming that the question will be taken up de novo, I do not conceive it necessary to go into a minute detail of the defects of the present Confederation, but request permission, to submit, with deference to the House, the Draft of a Government which I have formed for the Union. The defects of the present will appear in the course of the examination I shall give each article that either materially varies or is new. I well know the Science of Government is at once a delicate and difficult one, and none more so than that of Republics. I confess my situation or experience have not been such, as to enable me, to form the clearest and justest opinions.

The sentiments I shall offer, are the result of not so much reflection as I could have wished. The Plan will admit of important amendments. I do not mean at once to offer it for the consideration of the House, but have taken the liberty of mentioning it, because it was my duty to do so.

The first important alteration is, that of the principle of Representation, and the distribution of the different Powers of Government. In the federal Councils, each State ought to have a weight in proportion to its importance; and no State is justly entitled to a greater. A Representation is the sign of the reality. Upon this principle, however abused, the parliament of Great Britain is formed, and it has been universally adopted by the States in the formation of their Legislatures. It would be impolitic in us, to deem that unjust, which is a certain and beneficial truth. The abuse of this equality, has been censured as one of the most dangerous corruptions of the English Constitution; and I hope we shall not incautiously contract a disease that has been consuming them. Nothing, but necessity, could have induced Congress to ratify a Confederation upon other principles. It certainly was the opinion of the first Congress, in 1774, to acquire materials for forming an estimate of the comparative importance of each State; for, in the commencement of that session, they gave as a reason, for allowing each colony a vote, that it was not in their power, at that time, to procure evidence for determining their importance. This idea, of a just Representation, seems to have been conformable to the opinions of the best writers on the subject, that, in a confederated system, the members ought to contribute according to their abilities, and have a vote in proportion to their importance. But if each must have a vote, it can be defended upon no other ground, than that of each contributing an equal share of the public burdens: either would be a perfect system. The present must ever continue irreconcileable to justice. Montesquieu, who had very maturely considered the nature of a confederated Government, gives the preference to the Lycian, which was formed upon this model. The assigning to each State its due importance in the federal Councils, at once removes three of the most glaring defects and inconveniences of the present Confederation. The first is, the inequality of Representation: the second is, the alteration of the mode of doing business in Congress; that is, voting individually, and not by States: the third is, that it would be the means of inducing the States to keep up their delegations by punctual and respectable appointments. The dilatory and unpleasant mode of voting by States, must have been experienced by all who were members of Congress. Seven are necessary for any question, except adjourning, and nine for those of importance. It seldom happens that more than nine or ten States are represented. Hence it is generally in the power of a State, or of an individual, to impede the operations of that body. It has frequently happened, and indeed, lately, there have rarely been together, upon the floor, a sufficient number of States to transact any but the most trifling business. When the different branches of Government are properly distributed, so as to make each operate upon the other as a check, the apportioning the Representation according to the weight of the members, will enable us to remove these difficulties, by making a majority of the Houses, when constituted, capable of deciding in all, except a few cases, where a larger number may be thought necessary. The division of the legislative will be found essential, because, in a government where so many important powers are intended to be placed, much deliberation is requisite. No possibility of precipitately adopting improper measures ought to be admitted, and such checks should be imposed, as we find, from experience, have been useful in other governments. In the Parliament of Great Britain, as well as in most, and the best instituted legislatures in the States, we find, not only two Branches, but in some, a Council of Revision, consisting of their executive, and principal officers of government. This, I consider as an improvement in legislation, and have therefore incorporated it as a part of the system. It adds to that due deliberation, without which, no act should be adopted; and, if in the affairs of a State government, these restraints have proved beneficial, how much more necessary may we suppose them, in the management of concerns, so extensive and important?

The Senate, I propose to have elected by the House of Delegates, upon proportionable principles, in the manner I have stated, which, though rotative, will give that body a sufficient degree of stability and independence. The districts, into which the Union are to be divided, will be so apportioned, as to give to each its due weight, and the Senate, calculated in this, as it ought to be in every Government, to represent the wealth of the Nation. No mode can be devised, more likely to secure their independence, of, either the people, or the House of Delegates, or to prevent their being obliged to accomodate their conduct to the influence or caprice of either. The people, in the first instance, will not have any interference in their appointment, and each class being elected for four years; the House of Delegates, which nominate, must, from the nature of their institution, be changed, before the times of the Senators have expired.

The executive should be appointed septennially, but his eligibility ought not to be limited: He is not a branch of the legislature, farther, than as a part of the Council of Revision, and the suffering him to continue eligible, will, not only be the means of ensuring his good behavior, but serve to render the office more respectable. I shall have no objection to elect him for a longer term, if septennial appointments are supposed too frequent or unnecessary. It is true, that in our Government, he cannot be cloathed with those executive authorities, the Chief Magistrate of a Government often possesses; because they are vested in the Legislature, and cannot be used or delegated by them in any, but the specified mode. Under the New System, it will be found essentially necessary to have the Executive distinct. His duties, will be, to attend to the execution of the acts of Congress, by the several States; to correspond with them upon the subject; to prepare and digest, in concert with the great departments, such business as will come before the Legislative, at their stated sessions: to acquire, from time to time, as perfect a knowledge of the situation of the Union, as he possibly can, and to be charged with all the business of the Home Department. He will be empowered, whenever he conceives it necessary, to inspect the Departments of Foreign Affairs, of War, of Treasury, and when instituted, of the Admiralty. This inspection into the conduct of the Departments will operate as a check upon those Officers, keep them attentive to their duty, and may be the means in time not only of preventing and correcting errors, but of detecting and punishing mal-practices. He will have a right to consider the principals of these Departments as his Council, and to acquire their advice and assistance, whenever the duties of his Office shall render it necessary. By this means our Government will possess what it has always wanted, but never yet had, a Cabinet Council. An institution essential in all Governments, whose situation or connections oblige them to have an intercourse with other powers. He will be the Commander-in-Chief of the Land and Naval Forces of the United States; have a right to convene and prorogue the Legislature upon special occasions, when they cannot agree, as to the time of their adjournment; and appoint all Officers, except Judges and Foreign Ministers. Independent of the policy of having a distinct Executive, it will be found that one, on these principles will not create a new expense: The establishment of the President of Congres's Household will nearly be sufficient; and the necessity which exists at present, and which must every day increase, of appointing a Secretary for the Home Department, will then cease. He will remain always removable by impeachment, and it will rest with the Legislature, to fix his salary upon permanent principles,

The mode of doing business in the Federal Legislature, when thus newly organized, will be the Parliamentary one, adopted by the State Legislatures. In a Council so important, as I trust the Federal Legislature will be, too much attention cannot be paid to their proceedings. It is astonishing, that, in a body, constituted as the present Congress, so few inaccuracies are to be seen in their proceedings; for certainly, no Assembly can be so much exposed to them, as that, wherein a resolution may be introduced, and passed at once. It is a precipitancy which few situations can justify, in deliberative bodies, and which the proposed alteration will effectually prevent.

The 4th article, respecting the extending the rights of the Citizens of each State, throughout the United States; the delivery of fugitives from justice, upon demand, and the giving full faith and credit to the records and proceedings of each, is formed exactly upon the principles of the 4th article of the present Confederation, except with this difference, that the demand of the Executive of a State, for any fugitive, criminal offender, shall be complied with. It is now confined to treason, felony, or other high misdemeanor; but, as there is no good reason for confining it to those crimes, no distinction ought to exist, and a State should always be at liberty to demand a fugitive from its justice, let his crime be what it may.

The 5th article, declaring, that individual States, shall not exercise certain powers, is also founded on the same principles as the 6th of the Confederation.

The next, is an important alteration of the Federal System, and is intended to give the United States in Congress, not only a revision of the Legislative acts of each State, but a negative upon all such as shall appear to them improper.

I apprehend the true intention of the States in uniting, is to have a firm national Government, capable of effectually executing its acts, and dispensing its benefits and protection. In it alone can be vested those powers and prerogatives which more particularly distinguish a sovereign State. The members which compose the superintending Government are to be considered merely as parts of a great whole, and only suffered to retain the powers necessary to the administration of their State Systems. The idea which has been so long and falsely entertained of each being a sovereign State, must be given up; for it is absurd to suppose there can be more than one sovereignty within a Government. The States should retain nothing more than that mere local legislation, which, as districts of a general Government, they can exercise more to the benefit of their particular inhabitants, than if it was vested in the Supreme Council;

but in every foreign concern, as well as those internal regulations, which respecting the whole ought to be uniform and national, the States must not be suffered to interfere. No act of the Federal Government in pursuance of its constitutional powers ought by any means to be within the control of the State Legislatures; if it is, experience warrants me in asserting, they will assuredly interfere and defeat its operation. That these acts ought not therefore to be within their power must be readily admitted; and if so, what other remedy can be devised than the one I have mentioned? As to specifying that only their acts upon particular points should be subject to revision, you will find it difficult to draw the line with so much precision and exactness as to prevent their discovering some mode of counteracting a measure that is disagreeable to them. It may be said, that the power of revision here asked, is so serious a diminution of the State's importance, that they will reluctantly grant it. — This, however true, does not lessen its necessity, and the more the subject is examined, the more clearly will it appear. It is agreed that a reform of our Government is indispensable, and that a stronger Federal System must be adopted; but it will ever be found, that let your System upon paper be as complete, and guarded as you can make it, yet still if the State Assemblies are suffered to legislate without restriction or revision, your Government will remain weak, disjointed, and inefficient. Review the ordinances and resolutions of Congress for the last five or six years, such I mean as they had a constitutional right to adopt, and you will scarcely find one of any consequence that has not, in some measure, been violated or neglected. Examine more particularly your treaties with foreign powers; those solemn national compacts, whose stipulations each member of the Union was bound to comply with. Is there a treaty which some of the States have not infringed? Can any other conduct be expected from so many different Legislatures being suffered to deliberate upon national measures? Certainly not. Their regulations must ever interfere with each other, and perpetually disgrace and distract the Federal Councils. I must confess, I view the power of revision and of a negative as the corner stone of any reform we can attempt, and that its exercise by Congress will be as safe as it is useful. In a Government constituted as this is, there can be no abuse of it. — The proceedings of the States which merely respect their local concerns, will always be passed as matters of form, and objections only arise where they shall endeavor to contravene the Federal Authority. Under the British Government, notwithstanding we early and warmly resisted their other attacks, no objection was ever made to the negative of the King. As a part of his Government it was considered proper. Are we now less a part of the Federal Government than we were then of the British? Shall we place less confidence in men appointed by ourselves, and subject to our recall, than we did in their executive? I hope not. Whatever views we may have of the importance or retained sovereignty of the States, be assured they are visionary and unfounded, and that their true interests consist in concentring as much as possible, the force and resources of the Union in one superintending Government, where alone they can be exercised with effect. In granting to the Federal Government certain exclusive national powers, you invest all their incidental rights. The term exclusive involves every right or authority necessary to their execution. This revision and negative of the laws is nothing more than giving a farther security to these rights. It is only authorizing Congress to protect the powers you delegate, and prevent any interference or opposition on the part of the States. It is not intended to deprive them of the power of making such laws as shall be confined to the proper objects of State legislation, but it is to prevent their annexing to laws of this kind, provisions which may in their nature interfere with the regulations of the Federal Authority. It will sometimes happen that a general regulation which is beneficial to the Confederacy, may be considered oppressive or injurious by a particular State. In a mixed Government, composed of so many various interests, it will be impossible to frame general systems, operating equally upon all its members. The common benefit must be the criterion, and each State must, in its turn, be obliged to yield some of its advantages. If it was possible, compleatly to draw the distinguishing line, so as to reserve to the States, the Legislative rights they ought to retain, and prevent their exceeding them, I should not object, but it will be found exceedingly difficult; for as I have already observed, leave them only a right to pass an act, without revision or controul, and they will certainly abuse it. The only mode that I can think of, for qualifying it, is to vest a power somewhere, in each State, capable of giving their acts a limited operation, until the sense of Congress can be known. To those who have not sufficiently examined the nature of our Federal System, and the causes of its present weakness and disorders, this curb upon the State Legislatures may perhaps appear an improper attempt to acquire a dangerous and unnecessary power. I am afraid the greater part of our Citizens are of this class, and that there are too few among them, either acquainted with the nature of their own Republic, or with those of the same tendency, which have preceded it. Though our present disorders must be attributed in the first instance, to the weakness and inefficacy of our Government, it must still be confessed, they have been precipitated by the refractory and inattentive conduct of the States; most of which, have neglected altogether, the performance of their Federal Duties, and whenever their State-policy, or interests prompted, used their retained Sovereignty, to the injury and disgrace of the Federal Head. Nor can any other conduct be expected, while they are suffered to consider themselves as distinct Sovereignties, or in any other light, than as parts of a common Government. The United States, can have no danger so much to dread, as that of disunion; nor has the Federal Government, when properly formed, anything to fear, but from the licentiousness of its members. We have no hereditary monarchy or nobles, with all their train of influence or corruption, to contend with; nor is it possible to form a Federal Aristocracy. Parties may, for a time prevail in the States, but the establishment of an aristocratic influence in the Councils of the Union, is remote and doubtful. It is the anarchy, if we may use the term, or rather worse than anarchy of a pure democracy, which I fear. Where the laws lose their respect, and the Magistrates their authority; where no permanent security is given to the property and privileges of the Citizens; and no measures pursued, but such as suit the temporary interest and convenience of the prevailing parties, I cannot figure to myself a Government more truly degrading; and yet such has been the fate of all the antient, and probably will be, of all the modern Republics. The progress has been regular, from order to licentiousness; from licentiousness to anarchy, and from thence to despotism. If we review the ancient Confederacies of Greece, we shall find that each of them in their turn, became a prey to the turbulence of their members; who, refusing to obey the Federal Head, and upon all occasions insulting, and opposing its authority, afforded an opportunity to foreign powers, to interfere and subvert them. There is not an example in history, of a Confederacy's being enslaved or ruined by the invasions of the supreme authority, nor is it scarcely possible, for depending for support and maintenance upon the members, it will always be in their power to check and prevent injuring them. The Helvetic and Belgic Confederacies, which, if we except the Gryson league, are the only Governments that can be called Republics in Europe, have the same vices with the ancients. The too great and dangerous influence of the parts — an influence, that will sooner or later subject them to the same fate. In short, from their example, and from our own experience, there can be no truth more evident than this, that, unless our Government is consolidated, as far as is practicable, by retrenching the State authorities, and concentering as much force and vigor in the Union, as are adequate to its exigencies, we shall soon be a divided, and consequently an unhappy people. I shall ever consider the revision and negative of the State laws, as one great and leading step to this reform, and have therefore conceived it proper, to bring it into view.

The next article, proposes to invest a number of exclusive rights, delegated by the present Confederation; with this alteration, that it is intended to give the unqualified power of raising troops, either in time of peace or war, in any manner the Union may direct. It does not confine them to raise troops by quotas, on particular States, or to give them the right of appointing Regimental Officers, but enables Congress to raise troops as they shall think proper, and to appoint all the officers. It also contains a provision for empowering Congress to levy taxes upon the States, agreeable to the rule now in use, an enumeration of the white inhabitants, and three-fifths of other descriptions.

The 7th article invests the United States, with the complete power of regulating the trade of the Union, and levying such imposts and duties upon the same, for the use of the United States, as shall, in the opinion of Congress, be necessary and expedient. So much has been said upon the subjects of regulating trade, and levying an impost, and the States have so generally adopted them, that I think it unnecessary to remark upon this article. The intention, is to invest the United States with the power of rendering our maritime regulations uniform and efficient, and to enable them to raise a revenue, for Federal purposes, uncontrolable by the States. I thought it improper to fix the per centage of the impost, because it is to be presumed their prudence will never suffer them to impose such duties, as a fair trade will not bear, or such as may promote smuggling. But as far as our commerce, will bear, or is capable of yielding a revenue, without depressing it, I am of opinion, they should have a right to direct. The surrendering to the Federal Government, the complete management of our commerce, and of the revenues arising from it, will serve to remove that annual dependence on the States, which has already so much deceived, and will, should no more effectual means be devised, in the end, fatally disappoint us. This article, will, I think, be generally agreed to by the States. The measure of regulating trade, is nearly assented to by all, and the only objections to the impost, being from New York, and entirely of a constitutional nature, must be removed by the powers being incorporated with, and becoming a part of the Federal System.

The 8th article only varies so far from the present, as in the article of the Post Office, to give the Federal Government a power, not only to exact as much postage, as will bear the expense of the Office, but also, for the purpose of raising a revenue. Congress had this in contemplation, some time since, and there can be no objection, as it is presumed, in the course of a few years, the Post Office, will be capable of yielding a considerable sum to the Public Treasury.

The 9th article respecting the appointment of Federal Courts, for deciding territorial controversies between different States, is the same with that in the Confederation; but this may with propriety be left to the Supreme Judicial.

The 10th article gives Congress a right to institute all such offices as are necessary for managing the concerns of the Union; of erecting a Federal Judicial Court, for the purposes therein specified; and of appointing Courts of Admiralty for the trial of maritime causes in the States respectively. The institution of a Federal Judicial upon the principles mentioned in this article, has been long wanting. At present there is no Tribunal in the Union capable of taking cognizance of their officers who shall misbehave in any of their departments, or in their ministerial capacities out of the limits of the United States; for this, as well as the trial of questions arising on the law of nations, the construction of treaties, or any of the regulations of Congress in pursuance of their powers, or wherein they may be a party, there ought certainly to be a Judicial, acting under the authority of the Confederacy; for securing whose independence and integrity some adequate provision must be made, not subject to the controul of the Legislature. As the power of deciding finally in cases of Appeal and all Maritime Regulations are to be vested in the United States, the Courts of Admiralty in the several States, which are to be governed altogether by their Regulations, and the Civil Law, ought also to be appointed by them; it will serve as well to secure the uprightness of the Judges, as to preserve an uniformity of proceeding in Maritime Cases, throughout the Union.

The exclusive right of coining Money — regulating its alloy, and determining in what species of money the common Treasury shall be supplied, is essential to assuring the Federal Funds. If you allow the States to coin Money, or emit Bills of Credit, they will force you to take them in payment for Federal Taxes and Duties, for the certain consequence of either introducing base Coin, or depreciated Paper, is the banishing Specie out of circulation; and though Congress may determine, that nothing but Specie shall be received in payment of Federal Taxes or Duties, yet, while the States retain the rights they at present possess, they will always have it in their power, if not totally to defeat, yet very much to retard and confuse the collection of Federal Revenues. The payments of the respective States into the Treasury, either in Taxes or Imposts, ought to be regular and uniform in proportion to their abilities; — no State should be allowed to contribute in a different manner from the others, but all alike in actual Money. There can be no other mode of ascertaining this, than to give to the United States the exclusive right of coining, and determining in what manner the Federal Taxes shall be paid.

In all those important questions where the present Confederation has made the assent of Nine States necessary, I have made the assent of Two-Thirds of both Houses, when assembled in Congress, and added to the number, the Regulation of Trade, and Acts for levying an Impost and raising a Revenue: — These restraints have ever appeared to me proper; and in determining questions whereon the political happiness and perhaps existence of the Union may depend, I think it unwise ever to leave the decision to a mere majority; no Acts of this kind should pass, unless Two-Thirds of both Houses are of opinion they are beneficial, it may then be presumed the measure is right; but when merely a majority determines, it will be doubtful, and in questions of this magnitude where their propriety is doubtful, it will in general be safest not to adopt them.

The exclusive right of establishing regulations for the Government of the Militia of the United States, ought certainly to be ves[t]ed in the Federal Councils. As standing Armies are contrary to the Constitutions of most of the States, and the nature of our Government, the only immediate aid and support that we can look up to, in case of necessity, is the Militia. As the several States form one Government, united for their common benefit and security, they are to be considered as a Nation — their Militia therefore, should be as far as possible national — an uniformity in Discipline and Regulations should pervade the whole, otherwise, when the Militia of several States are required to act together, it will be difficult to combine their operations from the confusion a difference of Discipline and Military Habits will produce. Independent of our being obliged to rely on the Militia as a security against Foreign Invasions or Domestic Convulsions, they are in fact the only adequate force the Union possess, if any should be requisite to coerce a refractory or negligent Member, and to carry the Ordinances and Decrees of Congress into execution. This, as well as the cases I have alluded to, will sometimes make it proper to order the Militia of one State into another. At present the United States possess no power of directing the Militia, and must depend upon the States

to carry their Recommendations upon this subject into execution
— while this dependence exists, like all their other reliances upon
the States for measures they are not obliged to adopt, the Federal
views and designs must ever be delayed and disappointed. To
place therefore a necessary and Constitutional power of defence and
coercion in the hands of the Federal authority, and to render our
Militia uniform and national, I am decidedly in opinion they should
have the exclusive right of establishing regulations for their Government and Discipline, which the States should be bound to comply
with, as well as with their Requisitions for any number of Militia,
whose march into another State, the Public safety or benefit should
require.

In every Confederacy of States, formed for their general benefit
and security, there ought to be a power to oblige the parties to furnish their respective quotas without the possibility of neglect or
evasion; — there is no such clause in the present Confederation,
and it is therefore *without this indispensable security.* Experience
justifies me in asserting that we may detail as minutely as we can,
the duties of the States, but unless they are assured that these duties
will be required and enforced, the details will be regarded as nugatory.   No Government has more severely felt the want of a coercive
Power than the United States; for want of it the principles of the
Confederation have been neglected with impunity in the hour of
the most pressing necessity, and at the imminent hazard of its existence: Nor are we to expect they will be more attentive in future.
Unless there is a compelling principle in the Confederacy, there must
be an injustice in its tendency; It will expose an unequal proportion
of the strength and resources of some of the States, to the hazard
of war in defence of the rest — the first principles of Justice direct
that this danger should be provided against — many of the States
have certainly shewn a disposition to evade a performance of their
Federal Duties, and throw the burden of Government upon their
neighbors.   It is against this shameful evasion in the delinquent,
this forced assumption in the more attentive, I wish to provide, and
they ought to be guarded against by every means in our power.
Unless this power of coercion is infused, and exercised when necessary, the States will most assuredly neglect their duties.   The consequence is either a dissolution of the Union, or an unreasonable
sacrifice by those who are disposed to support and maintain it.

The article impowering the United States to admit new States
into the Confederacy is become indispensable, from the separation
of certain districts from the original States, and the increasing population and consequence of the Western Territory.   I have also added

an article authorizing the United States, upon petition from the majority of the citizens of any State, or Convention authorized for that purpose, and of the Legislature of the State to which they wish to be annexed, or of the States among which they are willing to be divided, to consent to such junction or division, on the terms mentioned in the article. — The inequality of the Federal Members, and the number of small States, is one of the greatest defects of our Union. It is to be hoped this inconvenience will, in time, correct itself; and, that the smaller States, being fatigued with the expence of their State Systems, and mortified at their want of importance, will be inclined to participate in the benefits of the larger, by being annexed to and becoming a part of their Governments. I am informed sentiments of this kind already prevail; and, in order to encourage propositions so generally beneficial, a power should be vested in the Union, to accede to them whenever they are made.

The Federal Government should also possess the exclusive right of declaring on what terms the privileges of citizenship and naturalization should be extended to foreigners. At present the citizens of one State, are entitled to the privileges of citizens in every State. Hence it follows, that a foreigner, as soon as he is admitted to the rights of citizenship in one, becomes entitled to them in all. The States differed widely in their regulations on this subject. I have known it already productive of inconveniences, and think they must increase. The younger States will hold out every temptation to foreigners, by making the admission to office less difficult in their Governments, than the older. — I believe in some States, the residence which will enable a foreigner to hold any office, will not in others intitle him to a vote. To render this power generally useful it must be placed in the Union, where alone it can be equally exercised.

The 16th article proposes to declare, that if it should hereafter appear necessary to the United States to recommend the Grant of any additional Powers, that the assent of a given number of the States shall be sufficient to invest them and bind the Union as fully as if they had been confirmed by the Legislatures of all the States. The principles of this, and the article which provides for the future alteration of the Constitution by its being first agreed to in Congress, and ratified by a certain proportion of the Legislatures, are precisely the same; they both go to destroy that unanimity which upon these occasions the present System has unfortunately made necessary — the propriety of this alteration has been so frequently suggested, that I shall only observe that it is to this unanimous consent, the depressed situation of the Union is undoubtedly owing. Had the measures recommended by Congress and assented to, some of them by eleven and others by twelve of the States, been carried into execution, how different would have been the complexion of Public Affairs? To this weak, this absurd part of the Government, may all our distresses be fairly attributed.

If the States were equal in size and importance, a majority of the Legislatures might be sufficient for the grant of any new Powers; but disproportioned as they are and must continue for a time; a larger number may now in prudence be required — but I trust no Government will ever again be adopted in this Country, whose Alteration cannot be effected but by the assent of all its Members. The hazardous situation the United Netherlands are frequently placed in on this account, as well as our own mortifying experience, are sufficient to warn us from a danger which has already nearly proved fatal. It is difficult to form a Government so perfect as to render alterations unnecessary; we must expect and provide for them: — But difficult as the forming a perfect Government would be, it is scarcely more so, than to induce Thirteen separate Legislatures, to think and act alike upon one subject — the alterations that nine think necessary, ought not to be impeded by four — a minority so inconsiderable should be obliged to yield. Upon this principle the present articles are formed, and are in my judgment so obviously proper, that I think it unnecessary to remark farther upon them.

There is also in the Articles, a provision respecting the attendance of the Members of both Houses; it is proposed that they shall be the judges of their own Rules and Proceedings, nominate their own Officers, and be obliged, after accepting their appointments, to attend the stated Meetings of the Legislature; the penalties under which their attendance is required, are such as to insure it, as we are to suppose no man would willingly expose himself to the ignominy of a disqualification: Some effectual mode must be adopted to compel an attendance, as the proceedings of the Government must depend upon its formation — the inconveniencies arising from the want of a sufficient representation have been frequently and severely felt in Congress. The most important questions have on this account been delayed, and I believe I may venture to assert, that for six months in the year they have not lately had such a representation as will enable them to proceed on business of consequence. Punctuality is essential in a Government so extensive; and where a part of the Members come from considerable distances, and of course have no immediate calls to divert their attention from the Public business, those who are in the vicinity should not be suffered to disappoint them; if the power of compelling their attendance is necessary, it must be incorporated as a part of the Constitution which the United States will be bound to execute; at present it is contended that no such authority exists; that the Members of Congress are only responsible to the State they represent, and to this may be attributed that shameful remissness in forming the Federal Council, which has been so derogating and injurious to the Union. The Article I have inserted is intended to produce a reform, and I do not at present discover a mode in which the attendance of the Members can be more effectually enforced.

The next Article [1] provides for the privilege of the Writ of Habeas Corpus — the Trial by Jury in all cases, Criminal as well as Civil — the Freedom of the Press, and the prevention of Religious Tests, as qualifications to Offices of Trust or Emolument: The three first essential in Free Governments; the last, a provision the world will expect from you, in the establishment of a System founded on Republican Principles, and in an age so liberal and enlightened as the present.

There is also an authority to the National Legislature, permanently to fix the seat of the general Government, to secure to Authors the exclusive right to their Performances and Discoveries, and to establish a Federal University.

There are other Articles, but of subordinate consideration. In opening the subject, the limits of my present observations would only permit me to touch the outlines; in these I have endeavored to unite and apply as far as the nature of our Union would permit, the excellencies of such of the State Constitutions as have been most approved. The first object with the Convention must be to determine on principles — the most leading of these are, the just proportion of representation, and the arrangement and distribution of the Powers of Government. In order to bring a system founded on these principles, to the view of the Convention, I have sketched the one which has just been read — I now submit it with deference to their Consideration, and wish, if it does not appear altogether objectionable, that it may be referred to the examination of a Committee.

There have been frequent but unsuccessful attempts by Congress to obtain from the States the grant of additional powers, and such is the dangerous situation in which their negligence and inattention have placed the Federal concerns, that nothing less than a Convention of the States could probably prevent a dissolution of the Union.

---

[1] This paragraph hardly seems in keeping with the rest of the document, and it may well be a later insertion. These ideas were suggested by Pinckney in the Convention on August 20, see *Records* of that date.

Whether we shall be so fortunate as to concur in measures calculated to remove these difficulties, and render our Government firm
and energetic, remains to be proved. A change in our political
System is inevitable; the States have wisely foreseen this, and provided a remedy. Congress have sanctioned it. The consequences
may be serious, should the Convention dissolve without coming
to some determination. — I dread even to think of the event of a
convulsion, and how much the ineffectual assemblage of this body
may tend to produce it. Our citizens would then suppose that no
reasonable hope remained of quietly removing the public embarrassment, or of providing by a well-formed Government, for the
protection and happiness of the People. They might possibly
turn their attention to effecting that by force, which had been in
vain constitutionally attempted.

I ought again to apologize for presuming to intrude my sentiments upon a subject of such difficulty and importance. It is one
that I have for a considerable time attended to. I am doubtful
whether the Convention will at first be inclined to proceed as far
as I have intended; but this I think may be safely asserted, that
upon a clear and comprehensive view of the relative situation of
the Union, and its Members, we shall be convinced of the policy
of concentering in the Federal Head, a compleate supremacy in the
affairs of Government; leaving only to the States, such powers as
may be necessary for the management of their internal concerns.

CXXX. James Madison to George Washington.[1]

New York, Octr. 14. 1787.

I add . . . a pamphlet which Mr. Pinkney has submitted to
the public,[2] or rather as he professes, to the perusal of his friends;[3]

CXXXI. Edmund Randolph to the Speaker of the Virginia
House of Delegates.[4]

Richmond, Oct. 10. 1787.

The constitution which I enclosed to the general assembly in
a late official letter, appears without my signature. This circumstance, although trivial in its own nature, has been rendered rather
important to myself at least by being misunderstood by some, and
misrepresented by others. — As I disdain to conceal the reasons

---

[1] *Documentary History of the Constitution*, IV, 329.
[2] See CXXIX above.
[3] For Washington's comment in reply, see CXXXV below.
[4] P. L. Ford, *Pamphlets on the Constitution*, 261–276.

for withholding my subscription, I have always been, still am, and ever shall be, ready to proclaim them to the world. To the legislature, therefore, by whom I was deputed to the federal convention, I beg leave now to address them; affecting no indifference to public opinion, but resolved not to court it by an unmanly sacrifice of my own judgment.

As this explanation will involve a summary, but general review of our federal situation, you will pardon me, I trust, although I should transgress the usual bounds of a letter.

Before my departure for the convention, I believed, that the confederation was not so eminently defective, as it had been supposed. But after I had entered into a free communication with those who were best informed of the condition and interest of each State; after I had compared the intelligence derived from them with the properties which ought to characterize the government of our union, I became persuaded, that the confederation was destitute of every energy, which a constitution of the United States ought to possess.   . . .

I come, therefore, to the last, and perhaps only refuge in our difficulties, a consolidation of the union, as far as circumstances will permit. To fulfil this desirable object, the constitution was framed by the federal convention. A quorum of eleven States, and the only member from a twelfth have subscribed it; Mr. Mason, of Virginia, Mr. Gerry, of Massachusetts, and myself having refused to subscribe.

Why I refused, will, I hope, be solved to the satisfaction of those who know me, by saying, that a sense of duty commanded me thus to act. It commanded me, sir, for believe me, that no event of my life ever occupied more of my reflection. To subscribe, seemed to offer no inconsiderable gratification, since it would have presented me to the world as a fellow laborer with the learned and zealous statesmen of America.

But it was far more interesting to my feelings, that I was about to differ from three of my colleagues, one of whom is, to the honor of the country which he has saved, embosomed in their affections, and can receive no praise from the highest lustre of language; the other two of whom have been long enrolled among the wisest and best lovers of the commonwealth; and the unshaken and intimate friendship of all of whom I have ever prized, and still do prize, as among the happiest of all acquisitions.—I was no stranger to the reigning partiality for the members who composed the convention, and had not the smallest doubt, that from this cause, and from the ardor of a reform of government, the first applauses at least would be loud and profuse. I suspected, too, that there was something in the human breast which for a time would be apt to construe a temperateness in politics, into an enmity to the union. Nay, I plainly foresaw, that in the dissensions of parties, a middle line would probably be interpreted into a want of enterprise and decision. — But these considerations, how seducing soever, were feeble opponents to the suggestions of my conscience. I was sent to exercise my judgment, and to exercise it was my fixed determination; being instructed by even an imperfect acquaintance with mankind, that self-approbation is the only true reward which a political career can bestow, and that popularity would have been but another name for perfidy, if to secure it, I had given up the freedom of thinking for myself.

It would have been a peculiar pleasure to me to have ascertained before I left Virginia, the temper and genius of my fellow citizens, considered relatively to a government, so substantially differing from the confederation as that which is now submitted. But this was, for many obvious reasons, impossible; and I was thereby deprived of what I thought the necessary guides.

I saw, however, that the confederation was tottering from its own weakness, and that the sitting of a convention was a signal of its total insufficiency. I was therefore ready to assent to a scheme of government, which was proposed, and which went beyond the limits of the confederation, believing, that without being too extensive it would have preserved our tranquility, until that temper and that genius should be collected.

But when the plan which is now before the general assembly, was on its passage through the convention, I moved, that the State conventions should be at liberty to amend, and that a second general convention should be holden, to discuss the amendments, which should be suggested by them. This motion was in some measure justified by the manner in which the confederation was forwarded originally, by congress to the State legislatures, in many of which amendments were proposed, and those amendments were afterwards examined in congress. Such a motion was doubly expedient here, as the delegation of so much power was sought for. But it was negatived. I then expressed my unwillingness to sign. My reasons were the following:

1. It is said in the resolutions which accompany the constitution, that it is to be submitted to a convention of delegates chosen in each State by the people thereof, for their assent and ratification. The meaning of these terms is allowed universally to be, that the convention must either adopt the constitution in the whole, or reject

it in the whole, and is positively forbidden to amend. If therefore, I had signed, I should have felt myself bound to be silent as to amendments, and to endeavor to support the constitution without the correction of a letter. With this consequence before my eyes, and with a determination to attempt an amendment, I was taught by a regard for consistency not to sign.

2. My opinion always was, and still is, that every citizen of America, let the crisis be what it may, ought to have a full opportunity to propose, through his representatives, any amendment which in his apprehension, tends to the public welfare. By signing, I should have contradicted this sentiment.

3. A constitution ought to have the hearts of the people on its side. But if at a future day it should be burdensome after having been adopted in the whole, and they should insinuate that it was in some measure forced upon them, by being confined to the single alternative of taking or rejecting it altogether, under my impressions, and with my opinions, I should not be able to justify myself had I signed.

4. I was always satisfied, as I have now experienced, that this great subject would be placed in new lights and attitudes by the criticism of the world, and that no man can assure himself how a constitution will work for a course of years, until at least he shall have heard the observations of the people at large. I also fear more from inaccuracies in a constitution, than from gross errors in any other composition; because our dearest interests are to be regulated by it; and power, if loosely given. especially where it will be interpreted with great latitude, may bring sorrow in its execution. Had I signed with these ideas, I should have virtually shut my ears against the information which I ardently desired.

5. I was afraid that if the constitution was to be submitted to the people, to be wholly adopted or wholly rejected by them, they would not only reject it, but bid a lasting farewell to the union. This formidable event I wished to avert, by keeping myself free to propose amendments, and thus, if possible, to remove the obstacles to an effectual government. But it will be asked, whether all these arguments, were not be well weighed in convention. They were, sir, with great candor. Nay, when I called to mind the respectability of those, with whom I was associated, I almost lost confidence in these principles. On other occasions, I should cheerfully have yielded to a majority; on this the fate of thousands yet unborn, enjoined me not to yield until I was convinced.

Again, may I be asked, why the mode pointed out in the constitution for its amendment, may not be a sufficient security against its imperfections, without now arresting it in its progress? My answers are — 1. That it is better to amend, while we have the constitution in our power, while the passions of designing men are not yet enlisted, and while a bare majority of the States may amend than to wait for the uncertain assent of three fourths of the States. 2. That a bad feature in government, becomes more and more fixed every day. 3. That frequent changes of a constitution, even if practicable, ought not to be wished, but avoided as much as possible. And 4. That in the present case, it may be questionable, whether, after the particular advantages of its operation shall be discerned, three fourths of the States can be induced to amend. . . .

I should now conclude this letter, which is already too long, were it not incumbent on me, from having contended for amendments, to set forth the particulars, which I conceive to require correction. I undertake this with reluctance: because it is remote from my intentions to catch the prejudices or prepossessions of any man But as I mean only to manifest that I have not been actuated by caprice, and now to explain every objection at full length would be an immense labour, I shall content myself with enumerating certain heads, in which the constitution is most repugnant to my wishes.

The two first points are the equality of suffrage in the senate, and the submission of commerce to a mere majority in the legislature, with no other check than the revision of the president. I conjecture that neither of these things can be corrected; and particularly the former, without which we must have risen perhaps in disorder.

But I am sanguine in hoping that in every other justly obnoxious cause, Virginia will be seconded by a majority of the States. I hope that she will be seconded. 1. In causing all ambiguities of expression to be precisely explained. 2. In rendering the president ineligible after a given number of years. 3. In taking from him the power of nominating to the judiciary offices, or of filling up vacancies which may there happen during the recess of the senate, by granting commissions which shall expire at the end of their next sessions. 4. In taking from him the power of pardoning for treason at least before conviction. 5. In drawing a line between the powers of congress and individual States ; and in defining the former, so as to leave no clashing of jurisdictions nor dangerous disputes; and to prevent the one from being swallowed up by the other, under cover of general words, and implication. 6. In abridging the power of the senate to make treaties supreme laws of the land. 7. In incapacitating the congress to determine their own salaries. And 8. In limiting and defining the judicial power.

CXXXII. George Washington to Doctor Stuart.[1]

Mount Vernon October 17th. 1787

As the enclosed advertiser contains a speech of Mr. Wilson's[2] (as able, candid and honest a member as in Convention) which will place the most of — M. — objections in their true point of light, I send it to you — the republication will (if you can get it done) be Serviceable at this Juncture. His ipso facto objection does not, I believe require any answer, every mind must recoil at the idea — and with respect to the navigation act. I am mistaken if any men, bodies of men or Countries, will enter into any compact or treaty, if one of the three is to have a negative controul over the other two, but granting that it is an evil it will infallibly work *its* own cure. — there must be reciprocity or no Union. which of the two is preferable, will not become a question in the mind of any true patriot.

CXXXIII. Elbridge Gerry to President of Senate and Speaker of House of Representatives of Massachusetts.[3]

New York, Oct. 18, 1787.

Gentlemen,

I have the honour to inclose, pursuant to my commission, the constitution proposed by the federal convention.

To this system I gave my dissent, and shall submit my objections to the honourable legislature.

It was painful for me, on a subject of such national importance, to differ from the respectable members who signed the constitution: But conceiving as I did, that the liberties of America were not secured by the system, it was my duty to oppose it.

My principal objections to the plan, are, that there is no adequate provision for a representation of the people — that they have no security for the right of election — that some of the powers of the legislature are ambiguous, and others indefinite and dangerous — that the executive is blended with, and will have an undue influence over, the legislature — that the judicial department will be oppressive — that treaties of the highest importance may be formed by the president with the advice of two-thirds of a quorum of the senate — and that the system is without the security of a bill of rights. These are objections which are not local, but apply equally to all the states.

As the convention was called for "the sole and express purpose

----

[1] *Documentary History of the Constitution*, IV, 333.
[2] For extracts from this speech, see CXXV above.
[3] Carey's *American Museum*, II, 435–436.

of revising the articles of confederation, and reporting to congress, and the several legislatures, such alterations and provisions as shall render the federal constitution adequate to the exigencies of government, and the preservation of the union," I did not conceive that these powers extend to the formation of the plan proposed: but the convention being of a different opinion, I acquiesced in it, being fully convinced that to preserve the union, an efficient government was indispensably necessary; and that it would be difficult to make proper amendments to the articles of confederation.

The constitution proposed has few if any federal features; but is rather a system of national government. Nevertheless, in many respects, I think it has great merit, and, by proper amendments, may be adapted to the "exigencies of government, and preservation of liberty." [1]

CXXXIV. James Madison to George Washington.[2]

N. York Octr. 18. 1787.

I have been this day honoured with your favor of the 10th. instant, under the same cover with which is a copy of Col. Mason's objections to the Work of the Convention. As he persists in the temper which produced his dissent it is no small satisfaction to find him reduced to such distress for a proper gloss on it; for no other consideration surely could have led him to dwell on an objection which he acknowledged to have been in some degree removed by the Convention themselves — on the paltry right of the Senate to propose alterations in money bills — on the appointment of the vice President — president of the Senate instead of making the President of the Senate the vice president, which seemed to be the alternative — and on the *possibility*, that the Congress may misconstrue their powers & betray their trust so far as to grant monopolies in trade &c. If I do not forget too some of his other reasons were either not at all or very faintly urged at the time when alone they ought to have been urged; such as the power of the Senate in the case of treaties, & of impeachments; and their duration in office. With respect to the latter point I recollect well that he more than once disclaimed opposition to it. My memory fails me also if he did not acquiesce in if not vote for, the term allowed for the further importation of slaves; and the prohibition of duties on exports by the States. What he means by the dangerous tendency of the Judiciary I am at some loss to comprehend. It never was

---

[1] A reply to Gerry's "Objections" will be found in C. R. King, *Life and Correspondence of Rufus King*, I, 303–306. An extract is printed in CLXXXIII below.

[2] *Documentary History of the Constitution*, IV, 334–336.

intended, nor can it be supposed that in ordinary cases the inferior tribunals will not have final jurisdiction in order to prevent the evils of which he complains. The great mass of suits in every State lie between Citizen & Citizen, and relate to matters not of federal cognizance. Notwithstanding the stress laid on the necessity of a Council to the President I strongly suspect, tho I was a friend to the thing, that if such an one as Col. Mason proposed, had been established, and the power of the Senate in appointments to offices transferred to it, that as great a clamour would have been heard from some quarters which in general eccho his Objections. What can he mean by saying that the Common law is not secured by the new Constitution, though it has been adopted by the State Constitutions. The Common law is nothing more than the unwritten law, and is left by all the Constitutions equally liable to legislative alterations. I am not sure that any notice is particularly taken of it in the Constitutions of the States. If there is, nothing more is provided than a general declaration that it shall continue along with other branches of law to be in force till legally changed. The Constitution of Virga. drawn up by Col Mason himself, is absolutely silent on the subject. An *ordinance* passed during the same Session, declared the Common law as heretofore & all Statutes of prior date to the 4 of James I. to be still the law of the land, merely to obviate pretexts that the separation from G. Britain threw us into a State of nature, and abolished all civil rights and obligations. Since the Revolution every State has made great inroads & with great propriety in many instances on this *monarchical* code. The "revisal of the laws" by a Committe of wch. Col. Mason was a member, though not an acting one, abounds with such innovations. The abolition of the *right of primogeniture*, which I am sure Col. Mason does not disapprove, falls under this head. What could the Convention have done? If they had in general terms declared the Common law to be in force, they would have broken in upon the legal Code of every State in the most material points: they wd. have done more, they would have brought over from G. B. a thousand heterogeneous & antirepublican doctrines, and even the *ecclesiastical Hierarchy itself*, for that is a part of the Common law. If they had undertaken a discrimination, they must have formed a digest of laws, instead of a Constitution. This objection surely was not brought forward in the Convention, or it wd. have been placed in such a light that a repetition of it out of doors would scarcely have been hazarded. Were it allowed the weight which Col. M. may suppose it deserves, it would remain to be decided whether it be candid to arraign the Convention for omissions which were never suggested to them — or prudent to vindicate the dissent by reasons which either were not previously thought of, or must have been wilfully concealed — But I am running into a comment as prolix, as it is out of place.

CXXXV. George Washington to James Madison.[1]

Mount Vernon, 22 October, 1787.
Mr. C. Pinckney is unwilling, (I perceive by the enclosures contained in your favor of the 13th,) to lose any fame that can be acquired by the publication of his sentiments.

CXXXVI. Benjamin Franklin to Mr Grand.[2]

Philada. Oct. 22 — 87.
I send you enclos'd the propos'd new Federal Constitution for these States. I was engag'd 4 Months of the last Summer in the Convention that form'd it. It is now sent by Congress to the several States for their Confirmation. If it succeeds, I do not see why you might not in Europe carry the Project of good Henry the 4th into Execution, by forming a Federal Union and One Grand Republick of all its different States & Kingdoms; by means of a like Convention; for we had many Interests to reconcile.

CXXXVII. James Madison to Thomas Jefferson.[3]

New York, Octr 24, 1787.
You will herewith receive the result of the Convention, which continued its session till the 17th of September. I take the liberty of making some observations on the subject, which will help to make up a letter, if they should answer no other purpose.

It appeared to be the sincere and unanimous wish of the Convention to cherish and preserve the Union of the States. No proposition was made, no suggestion was thrown out, in favor of a partition of the Empire into two or more Confederacies.

It was generally agreed that the objects of the Union could not be secured by any system founded on the principle of a confederation of Sovereign States. A *voluntary* observance of the federal law by all the members could never be hoped for. A *compulsive* one could evidently never be reduced to practice, and if it could, involved equal calamities to the innocent & the guilty, the necessity of a military force both obnoxious & dangerous, and in general a scene

---

[1] W. C. Ford, *Writings of George Washington*, XI, 174–175.
[2] *Documentary History of the Constitution*, IV, 341–342.
[3] Hunt, *Writings of James Madison*, V, 17–35.

resembling much more a civil war than the administration of a regular Government.

Hence was embraced the alternative of a Government which instead of operating, on the States, should operate without their intervention on the individuals composing them; and hence the change in the principle and proportion of representation.

This ground-work being laid, the great objects which presented themselves were 1. to unite a proper energy in the Executive, and a proper stability in the Legislative departments, with the essential characters of Republican Government. 2. to draw a line of demarkation which would give to the General Government every power requisite for general purposes, and leave to the States every power which might be most beneficially administered by them. 3. to provide for the different interests of different parts of the Union. 4. to adjust the clashing pretensions of the large and small States. Each of these objects was pregnant with difficulties. The whole of them together formed a task more difficult than can be well conceived by those who were not concerned in the execution of it. Adding to these considerations the natural diversity of human opinions on all new and complicated subjects, it is impossible to consider the degree of concord which ultimately prevailed as less than a miracle.

The first of these objects, as respects the Executive, was peculiarly embarrassing. On the question whether it should consist of a single person, or a plurality of co-ordinate members, on the mode of appointment, on the duration in office, on the degree of power, on the re-eligibility, tedious and reiterated discussions took place. The plurality of co-ordinate members had finally but few advocates. Governour Randolph was at the head of them. The modes of appointment proposed were various, as by the people at large — by electors chosen by the people — by the Executives of the States — by the Congress, some preferring a joint ballot of the two Houses — some a separate concurrent ballot, allowing to each a negative on the other house — some, a nomination of several candidates by one House, out of whom a choice should be made by the other. Several other modifications were started. The expedient at length adopted seemed to give pretty general satisfaction to the members. As to the duration in office, a few would have preferred a tenure during good behaviour — a considerable number would have done so in case an easy & effectual removal by impeachment could be settled. It was much agitated whether a long term, seven years for example, with a subsequent & perpetual ineligibility, or a short term with a capacity to be re-elected, should be fixed. In favor of the first opinion were urged the danger of a gradual degeneracy of re-elections from time to time, into first a life and then a hereditary tenure, and the favorable effect of an incapacity to be reappointed on the independent exercise of the Executive authority.   On the other side it was contended that the prospect of necessary degradation would discourage the most dignified characters from aspiring to the office, would take away the principal motive to ye faithful discharge of its duties — the hope of being rewarded with a reappointment would stimulate ambition to violent efforts for holding over the Constitutional term — and instead of producing an independent administration, and a firmer defence of the constitutional rights of the department, would render the officer more indifferent to the importance of a place which he would soon be obliged to quit forever, and more ready to yield to the encroachmts. of the Legislature of which he might again be a member.   The questions concerning the degree of power turned chiefly on the appointment to offices, and the controul on the Legislature.   An *absolute* appointment to all offices — to some offices — to no offices, formed the scale of opinions on the first point.   On the second, some contended for an absolute negative, as the only possible mean of reducing to practice the theory of a free Government which forbids a mixture of the Legislative & Executive powers.   Others would be content with a revisionary power, to be overruled by three fourths of both Houses. It was warmly urged that the judiciary department should be associated in the revision.   The idea of some was that a separate revision should be given to the two departments — that if either objected two thirds, if both, three fourths, should be necessary to overrule.

In forming the Senate, the great anchor of the Government the questions, as they came within the first object, turned mostly on the mode of appointment, and the duration of it.   The different modes proposed were 1. by the House of Representatives. 2. by the Executive. 3. by electors chosen by the people for the purpose. 4. by the State Legislatures. — On the point of duration, the propositions descended from good behavior to four years, through the intermediate terms of nine, seven, six, & five years.   The election of the other branch was first determined to be triennial, and afterwards reduced to biennial.

The second object, the due partition of power between the General & local Governments, was perhaps of all, the most nice and difficult.   A few contended for an entire abolition of the States; Some for indefinite power of Legislation in the Congress, with a negative on the laws of the States; some for such a power without a negative; some for a limited power of legislation, with such a negative; the majority finally for a limited power without the negative. The question with regard to the negative underwent repeated discussions, and was finally rejected by a bare majority. As I formerly intimated to you my opinion in favor of this ingredient, I will take this occasion of explaining myself on the subject. Such a check on the States appears to me necessary. 1. to prevent encroachments on the General authority. 2. to prevent instability and injustice in the legislation of the States.

. . . In the American Constitution the general authority will be derived entirely from the subordinate authorities. The Senate will represent the States in their political capacity; the other House will represent the people of the States in their individual capacy. The former will be accountable to their constituents at moderate, the latter at short periods. The President also derives his appointment from the States, and is periodically accountable to them. This dependence of the General on the local authorities, seems effectually to guard the latter against any dangerous encroachments of the former; whilst the latter, within their respective limits, will be continually sensible of the abridgement of their power, and be stimulated by ambition to resume the surrendered portion of it. We find the representatives of Counties and Corporations in the Legislatures of the States, much more disposed to sacrifice the aggregate interest, and even authority, to the local views of their constituents, than the latter to the former. I mean not by these remarks to insinuate that an esprit de corps will not exist in the National Government or that opportunities may not occur of extending its jurisdiction in some points. I mean only that the danger of encroachments is much greater from the other side, and that the impossibility of dividing powers of legislation, in such a manner, as to be free from different constructions by different interests, or even from ambiguity in the judgment of the impartial, requires some such expedient as I contend for. . . . It may be said that the Judicial authority, under our new system will keep the States within their proper limits, and supply the place of a negative on their laws. The answer is, that it is more convenient to prevent the passage of a law than to declare it void after it is passed; that this will be particularly the case, where the law aggrieves individuals, who may be unable to support an appeal agst. a State to the supreme Judiciary; that a State which would violate the Legislative rights of the Union, would not be very ready to obey a Judicial decree in support of them, and that a recurrence to force, which, in the event of disobedience would be necessary, is an evil which the new Constitution meant to exclude as far as possible.

2. A constitutional negative on the laws of the States seems equally necessary to secure individuals agst. encroachments on their rights. . . .

Begging pardon for this immoderate digression I return to the third object above mentioned, the adjustments of the different interests of different parts of the Continent. Some contended for an unlimited power over trade including exports as well as imports, and over slaves as well as other imports; some for such a power, provided the concurrence of two thirds of both Houses were required; Some for such a qualification of the power, with an exemption of exports and slaves, others for an exemption of exports only. The result is seen in the Constitution. S. Carolina & Georgia were inflexible on the point of the slaves.

The remaining object created more embarrassment, and a greater alarm for the issue of the Convention than all the rest put together. The little States insisted on retaining their equality in both branches, unless a compleat abolition of the State Governments should take place; and made an equality in the Senate a sine qua non. The large States on the other hand urged that as the new Government was to be drawn principally from the people immediately and was to operate directly on them, not on the States; and consequently as the States wd. lose that importance which is now proportioned to the importance of their voluntary compliances with the requisitions of Congress, it was necessary that the representation in both Houses should be in proportion to their size. It ended in the compromise which you will see, but very much to the dissatisfaction of several members from the large States.

It will not escape you that three names only from Virginia are subscribed to the Act. Mr. Wythe did not return after the death of his lady. Docr. M'Clurg left the Convention some time before the adjournment. The Governour and Col. Mason refused to be parties to it. Mr. Gerry was the only other member who refused. The objections of the Govr. turn principally on the latitude of the general powers, and on the connection established between the President and the Senate. He wished that the plan should be proposed to the States with liberty to them to suggest alterations which should all be referred to another general Convention, to be incorporated into the plan as far as might be judged expedient. He was not inveterate in his opposition, and grounded his refusal to subscribe pretty much on his unwillingness to commit himself, so as not to be at liberty to be governed by further lights on the subject. Col. Mason left Philada. in an exceeding ill humour indeed. A number of little circumstances arising in part from the impatience which prevailed towards the close of the business, conspired to whet his acrimony. He returned to Virginia with a fixed disposition to prevent the adoption of the plan if possible. He considers the want of a Bill of Rights as a fatal objection. His other objections are to the substitution of the Senate in place of an Executive Council & to the powers vested in that body — to the powers of the Judiciary — to the vice President being made President of the Senate — to the smallest of the number of Representatives — to the restriction on the States with regard to ex post facto laws — and most of all probably to the power of regulating trade, by a majority only of each House. He has some other lesser objections. Being now under the necessity of justifying his refusal to sign, he will of course muster every possible one. His conduct has given great umbrage to the County of Fairfax, and particularly to the Town of Alexandria. He is already instructed to promote in the Assembly the calling of a Convention, and will probably be either not deputed to the Convention, or be tied up by express instructions. He did not object in general to the powers vested in the National Government, so much as to the modification. In some respects he admitted that some further powers would have improved the system. He acknowledged in particular that a negative on the State laws, and the appointment of the State Executive ought to be ingredients; but supposed that the public mind would not now bear them, and that experience would hereafter produce these amendments.

CXXXVIIa. James Madison to William Short.[1]

New York Octr. 24. 1787

The paper which I enclose for Mr. Jefferson will shew you the result of the Convention. The nature of the subject, the diversity of human opinion, and the collision of local interests, and of the pretensions of the large & small States, will not only account for the length of time consumed in the work, but for the irregularities which will be discovered in its structure and form.

CXXXVIII. James Madison to Edmund Pendleton.[2]

New York Octr. 28. 1787.

I have recd. and acknowledge with great pleasure your favor of the 8th. inst: The remarks which you make on the Act of the Convention appear to me to be in general extremely well founded. Your criticism on the clause exempting vessels bound to or from a

---

[1] William Short MSS., Library of Congress.
[2] *Documentary History of the Constitution*, IV, 352–353.

State from being obliged to enter &c. in another is particularly so. This provision was dictated by the jealousy of some particular States, and was inserted pretty late in the Session. The object of it was what you conjecture. The expression is certainly not accurate.

CXXXIX. A Landholder [Oliver Ellsworth], I.[1]

It proves the honesty and patriotism of the gentlemen who composed the general Convention, that they chose to submit their system to the people rather than the legislatures, whose decisions are often influenced by men in the higher departments of government, who have provided well for themselves and dread any change least they should be injured by its operation. I would not wish to exclude from a State Convention those gentlemen who compose the higher branches of the assemblies in the several states, but choose to see them stand on an even floor with their brethren, where the artifice of a small number cannot negative a vast majority of the people.

This danger was foreseen by the Federal Convention, and they have wisely avoided it by appealing directly to the people.

CXL. George Washington to Mrs. Macauly Graham.[2]

Mount Vernon Novber. 16th 1787

You will undoubtedly, before you receive this, have an opportunity of seeing the Plan of Government proposed by the Convention for the United States. You will very readily conceive, Madam, the difficulties which the Convention had to struggle against. The various and opposit interests which were to be conciliated — the local prejudices which were to be subdued, the diversity of opinions and sentiments which were to be reconciled; and in fine, the sacrifices which were necessary to be made on all sides for the General welfare, combined to make it a work of so intricate and difficult a nature that I think it is much to be wondered at that any thing could have been produced with such unanimity as the Constitution proposed.

CXLI. James Wilson in the Pennsylvania Convention.[3]

November 23, 1787.

Mr. Wilson then moved that the time of meeting and adjourning should be fixed, observing that with respect to the time of ad-

---

[1] P. L. Ford, *Essays on the Constitution*, 139–140. First printed in the *Connecticut Courant* of November 5, 1787.

[2] *Documentary History of the Constitution*, IV, 379.

[3] McMaster and Stone, *Pennsylvania and the Federal Constitution*, 216.

journment, it had been found necessary in the Federal Convention to make a rule that at 4 o'clock they should break up, even if a member was in the middle of his speech.

CXLII. James Wilson in the Pennsylvania Convention.[1]

November 24, 1787.

To frame a government for a single city or State, is a business both in its importance and facility, widely different from the task entrusted to the Federal Convention, whose prospects were extended not only to thirteen independent and sovereign States, some of which in territorial jurisdiction, population, and resource, equal the most respectable nations of Europe, but likewise to innumerable States yet unformed, and to myriads of citizens who in future ages shall inhabit the vast uncultivated regions of the continent. The duties of that body therefore, were not limited to local or partial considerations, but to the formation of a plan commensurate with a great and valuable portion of the globe.

I confess, Sir, that the magnitude of the object before us, filled our minds with awe and apprehension. . . . But the magnitude of the object was equalled by the difficulty of accomplishing it, when we considered the uncommon dexterity and address that were necessary to combat and reconcile the jarring interests that seemed naturally to prevail, in a country which, presenting a coast of 1500 miles to the Atlantic, is composed of 13 distinct and independent States, varying essentially in their situation and dimensions, and in the number and habits of their citizens — their interests too, in some respects really different, and in many apparently so; but whether really or apparently, such is the constitution of the human mind, they make the same impression, and are prosecuted with equal vigor and perseverance. Can it then be a subject for surprise that with the sensations indispensably excited by so comprehensive and so arduous an undertaking, we should for a moment yield to despondency, and at length, influenced by the spirit of conciliation, resort to mutual concession, as the only means to obtain the great end for which we were convened? Is it a matter of surprise that where the springs of dissension were so numerous, and so powerful, some force was requisite to impel them to take, in a collected state, a direction different from that which separately they would have pursued?

There was another reason, that in this respect, increased the difficulties of the Federal Convention — the different tempers and

---

[1] McMaster and Stone, *Pennsylvania and the Federal Constitution*, 218–231.

dispositions of the people for whom they acted. But, however widely they may differ upon other topics, they cordially agree in that keen and elevated sense of freedom and independence, which has been manifested in their united and successful opposition to one of the most powerful kingdoms of the world. Still it was apprehended by some, that their abhorrence of constraint, would be the source of objection and opposition; but I confess that my opinion, formed upon a knowledge of the good sense, as well as the high spirit of my constituents, made me confident that they would esteem that government to be the best, which was best calculated eventually to establish and secure the dignity and happiness of their country. Upon this ground, I have occasionally supposed that my constituents have asked the reason of my assent to the several propositions contained in the plan before us. My answer, though concise, is a candid and I think a satisfactory one — because I thought them right; and thinking them right, it would be a poor compliment indeed to presume they could be disagreeable to my constituents. . . . The extent of country for which the New Constitution was required, produced another difficulty in the business of the Federal Convention. It is the opinion of some celebrated writers, that to a small territory the democratical, to a middling territory (as Montesquieu has termed it) the monarchical, and to an extensive territory the despotic form of government, is best adapted. Regarding then, the wide and almost unbounded jurisdiction of the United States, at first view the hand of despotism seemed necessary to control, connect and protect it; and hence the chief embarrassment arose. For we knew that, although our constituents would cheerfully submit to the legislative restraints of a free government, they would spurn at every attempt to shackle them with despotic power.

In this dilemma, a Federal Republic naturally presented itself to our observation, as a species of government which secured all the internal advantages of a republic, at the same time that it maintained the external dignity and force of a monarchy. . . .

But while a federal republic removed one difficulty, it introduced another, since there existed not any precedent to assist our deliberations; for, though there are many single governments, both ancient and modern, the history and principles of which are faithfully preserved and well understood, a perfect confederation of independent states is a system hitherto unknown.

. . . Another, and perhaps the most important obstacle to the proceedings of the Federal Convention, arose in drawing the line between the national and the individual governments of the states.

On this point a general principle readily occurred, that whatever object was confined in its nature and operation to a particular State ought to be subject to the separate government of the States; but whatever in its nature and operation extended beyond a particular State, ought to be comprehended within the federal jurisdiction. The great difficulty, therefore, was the application of this general principle, for it was found impracticable to enumerate and distinguish the various objects to which it extended; and as the mathematics only are capable of demonstration, it ought not to be thought extraordinary that the convention could not develop a subject involved in such endless perplexity. . . .

These difficulties, Mr. President, which embarrassed the Federal Convention, are not represented to enhance the merit of surmounting them, but with a more important view, to show how unreasonable it is to expect that the plan of government should correspond with the wishes of all the States, of all the Citizens of any one State, or of all the citizens of the united continent. I remember well, Sir, the effect of those surrounding difficulties in the late Convention. At one time the great and interesting work seemed to be at a stand, at another it proceeded with energy and rapidity, and when at last it was accomplished, many respectable members beheld it with wonder and admiration. But having pointed out the obstacles which they had to encounter, I shall now beg leave to direct your attention to the end which the Convention proposed. . . .

At this period, America has it in her power to adopt either of the following modes of government: She may dissolve the individual sovereignty of the States, and become one consolidated empire; she may be divided into thirteen separate, independent and unconnected commonwealths; she may be erected into two or more confederacies; or, lastly, she may become one comprehensive Federal Republic. . . .

Of these three species of government, however, I must observe, that they obtained no advocates in the Federal Convention, nor can I presume that they will find advocates here, or in any of our sister States. The general sentiment in that body, and, I believe, the general sentiment of the citizens of America, is expressed in the motto which some of them have chosen, UNITE OR DIE; and while we consider the extent of the country, so intersected and almost surrounded with navigable rivers, so separated and detached from the rest of the world, it is natural to presume that Providence has designed us for an united people, under one great political compact. If this is a just and reasonable conclusion, supported by the wishes of the people, the Convention did right in proposing a single confederated Republic. But in proposing it they were necessary led, not only to consider the situation, circumstances, and interests of one, two, or three States, but of the collective body; and as it is essential to society, that the welfare of the whole should be preferred to the accomodation of a part, they followed the same rule in promoting the national advantages of the Union, in preference to the separate advantages of the States. A principle of candor, as well as duty, led to this conduct; for, as I have said before, no government, either single or confederated, can exist, unless private and individual rights are subservient to the public and general happiness of the nation. It was not alone the State of Pennsylvania, however important she may be as a constituent part of the union, that could influence the deliberations of a convention formed by a delegation from all the United States to devise a government adequate to their common exigencies and impartial in its influence and operation. In the spirit of union, inculcated by the nature of their commission, they framed the constitution before us, and in the same spirit they submit it to the candid consideration of their constituents. . . .

These observations have been made, Mr. President, in order to preface a representation of the state of the Union, as it appeared to the late convention. We all know, and we have all felt, that the present system of confederation is inadequate to the government and the exigencies of the United States. . . .
Has America lost her magnanimity or perseverance? No! Has she been subdued by any high-handed invasion of her liberties? Still I answer no; for dangers of that kind were no sooner seen than they were repelled. But the evil has stolen in from a quarter little suspected, and the rock of freedom, which stood firm against the attacks of a foreign foe, has been sapped and undermined by the licentiousness of our own citizens. Private calamity and public anarchy have prevailed; and even the blessing of independency has been scarcely felt or understood by a people who have dearly achieved it. . . .

The commencement of peace was likewise the commencement of our distress and disgrace. Devoid of power, we could neither prevent the excessive importations which lately deluged the country, nor even raise from that excess a contribution to the public revenue; devoid of importance, we were unable to command a sale for our commodities in a foreign market; devoid of credit, our public securities were melting in the hands of their deluded owners, like snow before the sun; devoid of dignity, we were inadequate to perform treaties on our own part, or to compel a performance on the part of a contracting nation. In short, Sir, the tedious tale disgusts me, and I fondly hope it is unnecessary to proceed. The years of languor are over. We have seen dishonor and destruction, it is true, but we have at length penetrated the cause, and are now anxious to obtain the cure. The cause need not be specified by a recapitulation of facts; every act of Congress, and the proceedings of every State, are replete with proofs in that respect, and all point to the weakness and imbecility of the existing confederation; while the loud and concurrent voice of the people proclaims an efficient national government to be the only cure. Under these impressions, and with these views, the late convention were appointed and met; the end which they proposed to accomplish being to frame one national and efficient government, in which the exercise of beneficence, correcting the jarring interests of every part, should pervade the whole, and by which the peace, freedom, and happiness of the United States should be permanently ensured. The principles and means that were adopted by the convention to obtain that end are now before us, and will become the great object of our discussion.

. . . That the supreme power, therefore, should be vested in the people, is in my judgment the great panacea of human politics. It is a power paramount to every constitution, inalienable in its nature, and indefinite in its extent. For I insist, if there are errors in government, the people have the right not only to correct and amend them, but likewise totally to change and reject its form; and under the operation of that right, the citizens of the United States can never be wretched beyond retrieve, unless they are wanting to themselves.

Then let us examine, Mr. President, the three species of simple government, which as I have already mentioned, are the monarchical, aristocratical and democratical. . . .

To obtain all the advantages, and to avoid all the inconveniences of these governments, was the leading object of the late convention. Having therefore considered the formation and principles of other systems, it is natural to enquire, of what description is the constitution before us? In its principles, Sir, it is purely democratical; varying indeed, in its form, in order to admit all the advantages, and to exclude all the disadvantages which are incidental to the known and established constitutions of government. But when we take an extensive and accurate view of the streams of power that appear through this great and comprehensive plan, when we contemplate the variety of their directions, the force and dignity of their currents, when we behold them intersecting, embracing, and surrounding the vast possessions and interests of the continent, and when we see them distributing on all hands beauty, energy and riches, still, however numerous and wide their courses. however diversified and remote the blessings they diffuse, we shall be able to trace them all to one great and noble source, THE PEOPLE.

CXLIII. JAMES WILSON IN THE PENNSYLVANIA CONVENTION.[1]

November 26, 1787.

It was observed in the convention, that the Federal convention had exceeded the powers given to them by the several legislatures; but Mr. Wilson observed, that however foreign the question was to the present business, he would place it in its proper light. The Federal convention did not act at all upon the powers given to them by the States, but they proceeded upon original principles, and having framed a constitution which they thought would promote the happiness of their country, they have submitted it to their consideration, who may either adopt or reject it, as they please.

CXLIV. THE LANDHOLDER [OLIVER ELLSWORTH], IV.[2]

By the proposed constitution the new Congress will consist of nearly one hundred men; when our population is equal to Great Britain of three hundred men, and when equal to France of nine hundred. Plenty of Lawgivers! why any gentlemen should wish for more is not conceivable.

. . . Convention foreseeing this danger, have so worded the article, that if the people should at any future time judge necessary, they may diminish the representation.

CXLV. JAMES WILSON IN THE PENNSYLVANIA CONVENTION.[3]

November 28, 1787.

Mr. President, we are repeatedly called upon to give some reason why a bill of rights has not been annexed to the proposed plan . . . But the truth is, Sir, that this circumstance, which has since occasioned so much clamor and debate, never struck the mind of any member in the late convention till, I believe, within three days of the dissolution of that body, and even then of so little account was the idea that it passed off in a short conversation, without introducing a formal debate or assuming the shape of a motion. . . .

. . . Thus, Sir, it appears from the example of other states, as well as from principle, that a bill of rights is neither an essential nor a necessary instrument in framing a system of government,

---

[1] McMaster and Stone, *Pennsylvania and the Federal Constitution*, p. 235.

[2] P. L. Ford, *Essays on Constitution*, p. 152, from the *Connecticut Courant*, of November 26, 1787.

[3] McMaster and Stone, *Pennsylvania and the Federal Constitution*, pp. 252–254.

since liberty may exist and be as well secured without it. But it was not only unnecessary, but on this occasion it was found impracticable — for who will be bold enough to undertake to enumerate all the rights of the people? — and when the attempt to enumerate them is made, it must be remembered that if the enumeration is not complete, everything not expressly mentioned will be presumed to be purposely omitted. _____

CXLVI. James Wilson in the Pennsylvania Convention.[1]

November 28, 1787.

The truth is, Sir, that the framers of this system were particularly anxious, and their work demonstrates their anxiety, to preserve the state governments unimpaired — it was their favorite object; and, perhaps, however proper it might be in itself, it is more difficult to defend the plan on account of the excessive caution used in that respect than from any other objection that has been offered here or elsewhere. . . . I trust it is unnecessary to dwell longer upon this subject; for, when gentlemen assert that it was the intention of the federal convention to destroy the sovereignty of the states, they must conceive themselves better qualified to judge of the intention of that body than its own members, of whom not one, I believe, entertained so improper an idea.

CXLVIa. James McHenry before the Maryland House of Delegates.[2]

Maryland Novr. 29th 1787 —

The Delegates to the late Convention being call'd before the House of Representatives to explain the Principles, upon which the proposed Constitution for the United States of America were formed

Mr. McHenry addressed the House in the followg. terms

Mr. Speaker,

Convention having deposited their proceedings with their Worthy President, and by a Resolve prohibited any copy to be taken, under the Idea that nothing but the Constitution thus framed and sub-

---

[1] McMaster and Stone, *Pennsylvania and the Federal Constitution*, p. 265.

[2] This document and the one following (CXLVI*b*), in the possession of the Library of Congress, were among the manuscripts of John Leeds Bozman. Mr. Bernard C. Steiner of the Enoch Pratt Free Library, Baltimore, identifies them as a part of the legislative records of Maryland and as in the handwriting of one of the clerks of the legislature. (*Maryland Historical Magazine*, December, 1909.)

The documents having become accessible since the manuscript of the present work was completed, the editor has been unable to give as complete a series of cross-references to them as their importance would warrant.

mitted to the Public could come under their consideration, I regret that at this distant period, I am unable from Memory to give this Honorable House so full and accurate information as might possibly be expected on so important and interesting a Subject. I Collated however from my Notes as soon as the Pleasure of this House was made known to me such of the proceedings as pass'd under my observation from an anxious desire I have to give this Honorable Body the information they require —

It must be within the Knowledge of this House Mr Speaker that the plan of a Convention originated in Virginia — accordingly when it met at Philadelphia the objects of the meeting were first brought forward in an address from an Honorable Member of that State. He premised that our present Constitution had not and on further experiance would be found that it could not fulfill the objects of the Confederation.

1st. It has no sufficient provision for internal defence nor against foreign invasion, if a State offends it cannot punish; nor if the rights of Embassadors or foreign Nations be invaded have the Judges of the respective States competent Jurisdiction to redress them. In short the Journals of Congress are nothing more than a History of expedients, without any regular or fixed system, and without power to give them efficacy or carry them into Execution —

2nd. It does not secure the separate States from Sedition among themselves nor from encroachments against each other —

3rd. It is incapable of producing certain blessings the Objects of all good governments, Justice, Domestic Tranquillity, Common Defence Security to Liberty and general Welfare — Congress have no powers by imposts to discharge their internal engagements or to sustain their Credit with Foreigners — they have no powers to restrain the Emission of Bills of Credit issued to the destruction of foreign Commerce — the perversion of National Justice and violation of private Contracts — they have no power to promote inland Navigation, encourage Agriculture or Manufactures

4th. They have no means to defend themselves against the most direct encroachments — in every Congress there is a party opposed to Federal Measures — In every state even there is a party opposed to efficient Government, the wisest regulations may therefore thwarted and evaded: the Legislature be treated with insult and derision and there is no power, no force to carry their Laws into execution, or to punish the Offenders who oppose them.

5th. The Confederation is inferior to the State Constitutions and cannot therefore have that controul over them which it necessarily requires — the State Governments were first formed and the

federal Government derived out of them wherefore the Laws of
the respective States are paramount and cannot be controuled by
the Acts of Congress —

He then descanted with Energy on our respective situations
from New Hampshire to Georgia, on the Situation of our joint
National Affairs at Home and abroad and drew the Conclusion that
all were on the brink of ruin and disolution — That once dissolve
the tie by which we are united and alone preserved and the prediction
of our Enemies would be compleat in the bloodshed in contending
and opposite interests — That perhaps this was the last, the only
opportunity we should ever have to avoid or remedy those impending evils — The Eyes of all actuated by hopes or fears were fixed
upon the proceedings of this Convention and if the present meeting
founded in a Spirit of Benevolence and General Good, did not correct, or reform our present Situation, it would end most assuredly
in the Shame and ruin of ourselves and the Tryumph of others —
He therefore moved that it be "Resolved the Articles of the Confederation ought to be corrected and enlarged, and for that purpose
submitted certain resolves to the further Consideration of the Convention — Convention being thus in possession of these propositions on the thirtieth of May   Resolved to go into a consideration
of them when the Honorable Gentleman who first brought them
forward moved to withdraw the two first Resolutions, and to substitute the following in lieu of them — 1st. That the Union of the
States ought to be founded on the basis of Common Defence, security to Liberty, and General Welfare. 2d. That to this end the right
of Suffrage ought to be in proportion to the value of the Property
contributing to the expence of General Government or to the free
Inhabitants that compose such Government. 3rd. That a National
Government ought to be formed with Legislative and Judicial
powers. — At this period, Mr. Speaker I was suddenly call'd from
Philadelphia by an account that one of my nearest and Dearest
Relations was at the point of Death, and did not return till the 4th
of August — Convention had formed a Committee of Detail in my
absence which on the sixth of August brought in their report, that
had for its Basis the propositions handed from Virginia, and with
some amendments is the Constitution now submitted to the People—[1]

S: 2 To this Section it was objected that if the qualifications of the
Electors were the same as in the State Governments, it would involve
in the Federal System all the Disorders of a Democracy; and it

---

[1] The third page of the MS. ends at this point, and the next page begins abruptly
with a discussion of article I, Section 2, of the completed Constitution.

was therefore contended, that none but Freeholders, permanently interested in the Government ought to have a right of Suffrage — the Venerable Franklin opposed to this the natural rights of Man — their rights to an immediate voice in the general Assemblage of the whole Nation, or to a right of Suffrage & Representation and he instanced from general History and particular events the indifference of those, to the prosperity and Welfare of the State who were deprived of it. Residence was likewise thought essential to interest the Human heart sufficiently by those ties and affections it necessarily creates to the general prosperity — at first the Report of the Committee had extended it to three Years only, but on better consideration it was altered to Seven; And the Period of Twenty five Years deemed a necessary Age to mature the Judgement and form the mind by habits of reflection and experience. — Little was said on this subject it passed without any considerable opposition and therefore I was not at the pains to note any other particulars respecting it

That the Representatives should be appointed according to Numbers occasioned a very long, interesting and serious Debate. The Larger States warmly contended for this Regulation and were seriously opposed by the lesser — by the latter it was contended it threw too much power into the hands of the former, and it was answered by the former that Representation ought to be according to property, or numbers, and in either case they had a right to such influence as their Situation gave them, on the contrary if each State had an equal voice, it would unreasonably throw the whole power in the lesser States — In the end a compromise took place by giving an equal Voice to each State in the Senate which 'till then the larger States had contended ought to be formed like the other branch by a Representation according to numbers [1]—

S: 3d. The Classing the Senate so as to produce the proposed change was established by Convention on the principle that a Rotation of power is essential to Liberty. No qualification of property was adopted, that merit alone might advance unclogged by such restriction. It did not pass however unattempted; but the proposed rate of property by the South, was thought much too high by the East, as that by the East on the Contrary was deemed too low by the South.—

The Committee of Detail by their report had at first given to the Senate the choice of their own President but to avoid Cabal

---

[1] McHenry was absent from the Convention at the time of this debate and compromise, so that this statement is not based upon his own observation.

and undue influence, it was thought better to alter it. And the power of trying impeachments was lodged with this Body as more likely to be governed by cool and candid investigation, than by those heats that too often inflame and influence more populous Assemblys.

S 4. It was thought expedient to vest the Congress with the powers contained in this Section, which particular exigencies might require them to exercise, and which the immediate representatives of the People can never be supposed capable of wantonly abusing to the prejudice of their Constituents — Convention had in Contemplation the possible events of Insurrection, Invasion, and even to provide against any disposition that might occur hereafter in any particular State to thwart the measures of the General Government on the other hand by an Assembly once a Year Security is Annually given to the People against encroachments of the Governments on their Liberty.

S 5. Respects only the particular privileges and Regulations of each branch of the Legislature.

S 6. That the attendance of Members in the General Legislature at a great distance from their respective abodes might not be obstructed and in some instances prevented either by design or otherwise in withholding any Compensation for their Services, Convention thought it most adviseable to pay them out of the General Treasury, otherwise a representation might some times fail when the Public Exigence might require that attendance — Whether any Members of the Legislature should be Capable of holding any Office during the time for which he was Elected created much division in Sentiment in Convention; but to avoid as much as possible every motive for Corruption, was at length Settled in the form it now bears by a very large Majority.

S: 7. Much was also said on the Priviledge that the immediate Representatives of the People had in originating all Bills to create a Revenue: It was opposed by others on the Principle that, in a Government of this Nature flowing from the People without any Hereditary rights existing in either Branch of the Legislature, the public Good might require, and the Senate ought to possess powers coexistive in this particular with the House of Representatives. The Larger States hoped for an advantage by confirming this priviledge to that Branch where their numbers predominated, and it ended in a compromise by which the Lesser States obtained a power of amendment in the Senate — The Negative given to the President underwent an amendment, and was finally restored to its present form, in the hope that a Revision of the Subject and the objections offered against it might contribute in some instances to perfect

those regulations that inattention or other motives had at first rendered imperfect —

S 8. The power given to Congress to lay taxes contains nothing
more than is comprehended in the Spirit of the eigth article of the
Confederation. To prevent any Combination of States, Duties, Imposts and Excises shall be equal in all, and if such a Duty is laid on
foreign Tonage as to give an advantage in the first instance to the
Eastern States, it will operate as a bounty to our own Shipbuilders.
If an oppressive Act should be obtained to the prejudice of the
Southern States, it will always be subject to be regulated by a Majority, and would be repealed as soon as felt. That at most it could
prevail no longer than 'till that Jealousy should be awakened which
must have Slept when it passed, and which could never prevail but
under a supposed Combination of the President and the two Houses
of the Legislature.

S. 9. Convention were anxious to procure a perpetual decree
against the Importation of Slaves; but the Southern States could
not be brought to consent to it — All that could possibly be obtained was a temporary regulation which the Congress may vary
hereafter.

Public Safety may require a supension of the Ha: Corpus in
cases of necessity: when those cases do not exist, the virtuous Citizen will ever be protected in his opposition to power, 'till corruption
shall have obliterated every sense of Honor & Virtue from a Brave
and free People. Convention have also provided against any direct
or Capitation Tax but according to an equal proportion among the
respective States: This was thought a necessary precaution though
it was the idea of every one that government would seldom have
recourse to direct Taxation, and that the objects of Commerce
would be more than Sufficient to answer the common exigencies of
State and should further supplies be necessary, the power of Congress
would not be exercised while the respective States would raise those
supplies in any other manner more suitable to their own inclinations
— That no Duties shall be laid on Exports or Tonage, on Vessells
bound from one State to another is the effect of that attention to
general Equality that governed the deliberations of Convention.
Hence unproductive States cannot draw a revenue from productive
States into the Public Treasury, nor unproductive States be ham-
pered in their Manufactures to the emolument of others. When
the Public Money is lodged in its Treasury there can be no regulation more consistant with the Spirit of Economy and free Government that it shall only be drawn forth under appropriation by Law
and this part of the proposed Constitution could meet with no oppo-

sition as the People who give their Money ought to know in what manner it is expended.

That no Titles of Nobility shall be granted by the United States will preserve it is hoped, the present Union from the Evils of Aristocracy.

S: 10. It was contended by many that the State sought to be permitted to Emit Bills of Credit where their local Circumstances might require it without prejudice to the obligations arising from private Contracts; but this was overruled by a vast Majority as the best Security that could be given for the Public faith at home and the extension of Commerce with Foreigners.

Article the 2nd.

S: 1st. The Election of the President according to the Report of the Committee of Detail was intended to have been by ballot of both Houses; to hold his appointment for Seven Years, and not be Capable to be reelected; but this mode gave an undue influance to the large States, and paved the way to faction and Corruption — all are guarded against by the present method, as the most exalted Characters can only be Known throughout the whole Union — His power when elected is check'd by the Consent of the Senate to the appointment of Officers, and without endangering Liberty by the junction of the Executive and Legislative in this instance.

Article the 3rd.

S: 1st. The judicial power of the United States underwent a full investigation — it is impossible for me to Detail the observations that were delivered on that Subject — The right of tryal by Jury was left open and undefined from the difficulty attending any limitation to so valuable a priviledge, and from the persuasion that Congress might hereafter make provision more suitable to each respective State — To suppose that mode of Tryal intended to be abolished would be to Suppose the Representatives in Convention to act Contrary to the Will of their Constituents, and Contrary to their own Interest.

Thus Mr. Speaker I have endeavour'd to give this Honorable House the best information in my power on this important Subject — Many parts of this proposed Constitution were warmly opposed, other parts it was found impossible to reconcile to the Clashing Interest of different States — I myself could not approve of it throughout, but I saw no prospect of getting a better — the whole however is the result of that spirit of Amity which directed the wishes of all for the general good, and where those Sentiments govern it will meet I trust, with a Kind and Cordial reception.

CXLVI*b*. Luther Martin before the Maryland House of
Representatives.[1]

Mr. Speaker.   Maryland Novr. 29th. 1787. —

When I join'd the Convention I found that Mr. Randolph had
laid before that Body certain propositions for their consideration,
and that Convention had entered into many Resolutions, respecting
their manner of conducting the Business one of which was that
seven States might proceed to Business, and therefore four States
composing a Majority of seven, might eventually give the Law to
the whole Union. Different instructions were given to Members
of different States — The Delegates from Delaware were instructed
not to infringe their Local Constitution — others were prohibited
their assent to any duty in Commerce: Convention enjoined all
to secrecy; so that we had no opportunity of gaining information
by a Correspondence with others; and what was still more inconvenient extracts from their Journals were prohibited even for our
own information — It must be remembered that in forming the
Confederacy the State of Virginia proposed, and obstinately contended (tho unsupported by any other) for representation according
to Numbers: and the second resolve now brought forward by an
Honourable Member from that State was formed in the same spirit
that characteriz'd its representatives in their endeavours to increase
its powers and influence in the Federal Government. These Views
in the larger States, did not escape the observation of the lesser and
meetings in private were formed to counteract them: the subject
however was discuss'd with coolness in Convention, and hopes were
formed that interest might in some points be brought to Yield to
reason, or if not, that at all events the lesser States were not precluded from introducing a different System; and particular Gentlemen were industriously employed in forming such a System at
those periods in which Convention were not sitting.

At length the Committee of Detail brought forward their Resolutions which gave to the larger States the same inequality in the Senate
that they now are proposed to have in the House of Representatives
— Virginia, Pennsylvania and Massachusetts would have one half —
all the Officers and even the President were to be chosen by the Legislative: so that these three States might have usurped the whole
power. The President would always have been from one of the
larger States and so chosen to have an absolute negative, not only
on the Laws of Congress but also on the Laws of each respective

---

[1] See CXLVI*a*, note 1. This document represents an earlier stage of Martin's
Genuine Information (CLVIII).

State in the Union. Should the representation from the other States be compleat, and by a Miracle ten States be so united as upon any occasion to procure a Majority; yet the President by his Negative might defeat the best intentions for the public good. Such Government would be a Government by a Junto and bind hand and foot all the other States in the Union On this occasion the House will please to remember that Mr. Bo   was in the Chair, and General Washington and the Venerable Franklin on the floor, and led by State influence, neither of them objected to this System, but on the Contrary it seemed to meet their warm and cordial approbation. — I revere those worthy Personages as much as any man can do, but I could not compliment them by a Sacrafice of the trust reposed in me by this State by acquiescing in their opinion. Then it was Mr. Speaker that those persons who were labouring for the general good, brought forward a different System — The absence of Mr. McHenry unhappily left Maryland with only two representatives, and they differed: New Hampshire Delegates were also absent. Mr. Patterson from Jersey introduced this new System, by which it was proposed, that the Laws of the Confederacy should be the Laws of each State, and therefore the State Judiciaries to have Cognizance in the first instance and the Federal Courts to have an Apelant Jurisdiction only —

The first measure that took place on the Jersey System was to pass a vote not to receive it — Three parties now appeared in Convention; one were for abolishing all the State Governments; another for such a Government as would give an influence to particular States — and a third party were truly Federal, and acting for general Equallity — They were for considering, reforming and amending the Federal Government, from time to time as experience might point out its imperfections, 'till it could be made competent to every exigence of State, and afford at the same time ample security to Liberty and general Welfare. But this scheme was so opposite to the views of the other two, that the Monarchical party finding little chance of succeeding in their wishes joined the others and by that measure plainly shewed they were endeavouring to form such a Government as from its inequality must bring in time their System forward, or at least much nearer in practice than it could otherwise be obtained —

When the principles of opposition were thus formed and brought forward by the 2d. S: respecting the manner of representation, it was urged by a Member of Pennsylvania, that nothing but necessity had induced the larger States to give up in forming the Confederacy, the Equality of Representation according to numbers —

That all governments flowed from the People and that their happiness being the end of governments they ought to have an equal Representation. On the contrary it was urged by the unhappy Advocates of the Jersey System that all people were equally Free, and had an equal Voice if they could meet in a general Assembly of the whole. But because one Man was stronger it afforded no reason why he might injure another, nor because ten leagued together, they should have the power to injure five; this would destroy all equallity. That each State when formed, was in a State of Nature as to others, and had the same rights as Individuals in a State of Nature — If the State Government had equal Authority, it was the same as if Individuals were present, because the State Governments originated and flowed from the Individuals that compose the State, and the Liberty of each State was what each Citizen enjoyed in his own State and no inconvenience had yet been experienced from the inequality of representation in the present Federal Government. Taxation and representation go hand and hand, on the principle alone that, none should be taxed who are not represented; But as to the Quantum, those who possess the property pay only in proportion to the protection they receive — The History of all Nations and sense of Mankind shew, that in all former Confederacies every State had an equal voice. Moral History points out the necessity that each State should vote equally — In the Cantons of Switzerland those of Bene & Lucerne have more Territory than all the others, yet each State has an equal voice in the General Assembly. The Congress in forming the Confederacy adopted this rule on the principle of Natural right — Virginia then objected. This Federal Government was submitted to the consideration of the Legislatures of the respective States and all of them proposed some amendments; but not one that this part should be altered. Hence we are in possession of the General Voice of America on this subject. When baffled by reason the larger States possitively refused to yield — the lesser refused to confederate, and called on their opponents to declare that security they could give to abide by any plan or form of Government that could now be devised. The same reasons that now exist to abolish the old, might be urged hereafter to overthrow the New Government, and as the methods of reform prescribed by the former were now utterly disregarded, as little ceremony might be used in discarding the latter — It was further objected that the large States would be continually increasing in numbers, and consequently their influence in the National Assembly would increase also: That their extensive Territories were guaranteed and we might be drawn out to defend the enormous extent of those States, and

encrease and establish that power intended in time to enslave ourselves — Threats were thrown out to compel the lesser States to
confederate — They were told this would be the last opportunity
that might offer to prevent a Dissolution of the Union, that once
dissolve that Band which held us together and the lesser States
had no security for their existence, even for a moment — The lesser
States threatened in their turn they they would not lay under the
imputation of refusing to confederate on equitable conditions; they
threatened to publish their own offers and the demands of others,
and to appeal to the World in Vindication of their Conduct.

At this period there were eleven States represented in Convention on the question respecting the manner of appointing Delegates
to the House of Representatives — Massachusetts, Pensylvania,
Virginia, North Carolina, South Carolina and Georgia adopted it
as now handed to the consideration of the People. — Georgia now
insignificant, with an immense Territory, looked forward to future
power and Aggrandizement, Connecticut, New York, Jersey, and
Delaware were against the Measure and Maryland was unfortunately
divided — On the same question respecting the Senate, perceiving
the lesser States would break up Convention altogether, if the influence of that branch was likewise carried against them, the Delegates of Georgia differed in sentiment not on principle but on expediency, and fearing to lose every thing if they persisted, they did not
therefore vote being divided. Massachusetts, Pensylvania, Virginia, North Carolina, and South Carolina were in the affirmative,
and New York, Connecticut, Jersey, Delaware & Maryland were
in the Negative. Every thing was now at a stand and little hopes
of agreement, the Delegates of New York had left us determined not
to return, and to hazard every possible evil, rather than to Yield
in that particular; when it was proposed that a conciliating Committee should be formed of one member from each State — Some Members possitively refused to lend their names to this measure others
compromised, and agreed that if the point was relinquished by the
larger States as to the Senate — they would sign the proposed Constitution and did so, not because they approved it but because they
thought something ought to be done for the Public — Neither General Washington nor Franklin shewed any disposition to relinquish
the superiority of influence in the Senate. I now proposed Convention should adjourn for consideration of the subject, and requested leave to take a Copy of their proceedings, but it was denied,
and the Avenue thus shut to information and reflection —

Article 1st.

S: 1st. A Government consisting of two Branches advocated by some was opposed by others — That a perfect Government necessarily requiring a Check *over them* did not require it over *States* and History could furnish no instance of such a second branch in Federal Governmts — The seperate States are competent to the Government of Individuals and a Government of *States* ought to be *Federal,* and which the object of calling Convention, and not to establish a *National Government.* It begins We the People — And the powers are made to flow from them in the first instance. That in Federal Governments an equal voice in each State is essential, as being all in a *State of Nature* with respect to each other. Whereas the only figure in this Constitution that has any resemblance to a federal one, is the equality of Senate — but the 4th Section gives the power to Congress to strike out, at least to render Nugatory this, the most valuable part of it. It cannot be supposed that any State would refuse to send Representatives, when they would be bound whether they sent Deputies or not, and if it was intended to relate to the cases of Insurrection or Invasion, why not by express words confine the power to these objects?

S: 6. By this Article the Senators when elected are made independant of the State they represent. They are to serve Six Years, to pay themselves out of the General Treasury, and are not paid by the State, nor cán be recalled for any misconduct or sacrafice of the Interest of their State that they make before the expiration of that period. They are not only Legislative, but make a part of the Executive, which all wise Governments have thought it essential to keep seperated. They are the National Council; and none can leave their private concerns and their Homes for such a period and consent to such a service, but those who place their future views on the emoluments flowing from the General Government — Tho' a Senator cannot be appointed to an office created by himself, He may to any that has been antecedently established; and by removing Old Officers, to new Offices, their places may be occupied by themselves and thus the Door opened to evade and infringe the Constitution. When America was under the British Dominion every matter was conducted within a narrow Circle in the Provincial Government, greatly to the ease and convenience of the People. The Habits thus acquired are opposed to extensive Governments, and the extent of this, as a National one, cannot possibly be ever carried into effect —

S: 2. Slaves ought never to be considered in Representation, because they are Property. They afford a rule as such in Taxation; but

are Citizens intrusted in the General Government, no more than
Cattle, Horses, Mules or Asses; and a Gentleman in Debate very
pertinently observed that he would as soon enter into Compacts,
with the Asses Mules, or Horses of the Ancient Dominion as with
their Slaves — When there is power to raise a revenue by direct
Taxation, each State ought to pay an equal Ratio; Whereas by taxing
Commerce some States would pay greatly more than others.

S: 7. It was contended that the Senate derived their powers from
the People and therefore ought to have equal priviledges to the
Representation That it would remove all ground for contest about
originating Money Bills, what Bills were so or not, and how far
amendments might be made, but nothing more could be obtained from
the power of the larger States on that subject than what appears in the
proposed Constitution.   In Great Britain the King having Hereditary rights, and being one of the three Estates that compose the
Legislature has obtained a Voice in the passage of all Acts that bear
the title of laws.   But the Executive here have no distinct rights,
nor is their President likely to have more understanding than the
two Branches of the Legislature.   Additional weight is thus unnecessarily given to the large States who voting by numbers will
cohere to each other, or at least among themselves, and thus easily
carry, or defeat any measure that requires a Majority of two thirds.

S: 8: By the word Duties in this Section is meant Stamp Duties.
This power may be exercised to any extent, but it has likewise this
dangerous tendency it may give the Congress power by establishing
duties on all Contracts to decide on cases of that nature, and ultimately draw the dicision of the Federal Courts, which will have
sufficient occupation by the other powers given in this Section.
They are extensive enough to open a sluice to draw the very blood
from your Veins.   They may lay direct Taxes by assessment, Poll
Tax, Stamps, Duties on Commerce, and excise everything else —
all this to be collected under the direction of their own Officers,
and not even provided that they shall be Inhabitants of the respective States whey they are to act, and for which many reasons will
not be the case: and should any Individual dare to dispute the conduct of an Excise Man, ransacking his Cellars he may be hoisted
into the Federal Court from Georgia to vindicate his just rights,
or to be punished for his impertinence.   In vain was it urged that
the State Courts ought to be competent to the decision of such
cases: The advocates of this System thought State Judges would
be under State influence and therefore not sufficiently independant.
But this is not all, they would either trust your Juries for altho
matters of Fact are triable by Juries in the Inferior Courts the Judges

of the Supreme Court on *appeal* are to decide on *Law* and *fact* both. In this Manner Mr. Speaker our rights are to be tried in all disputes between the Citizens of one State and another, between the Citizens and Foreigners, and between the Citizens and these Revenue Officers of the General Government. As to other cases the Constitution is silent, and it is very doubtful if we are to have the priviledge of Tryal by Jury at all, where the cause originates in the Supreme Court. Should the power of these Judiciaries be incompetent to carry this extensive plan into execution, other, and more certain Engines of power are supplied by the standing Army — unlimited as to number or its duration, in addition to this Government has the entire Command of the Militia, and may call the whole Militia of any State into Action, a power, which it was vainly urged ought never to exceed a certain proportion. By organizing the Militia Congress have taken the whole power from the State Governments; and by neglecting to do it and encreasing the Standing Army, their power will increase by those very means that will be adopted and urged as an ease to the People.

Nothing could add to the mischevious tendency of this system more than the power that is given to suspend the Act of Ha: Corpus — Those who could not approve of it urged that the power over the Ha: Corpus ought not to be under the influence of the General Government. It would give them a power over Citizens of particular States who should oppose their encroachments, and the inferior Jurisdictions of the respective States were fully competent to Judge on this important priviledge; but the Allmighty power of deciding by a call for the questjon, silenced all opposition to the measure as it too frequently did to many others.

S: 9. By this Article Congress will obtain unlimitted power over all the Ports in the Union and consequently acquire an influence that may be prejudicial to general Liberty. It was sufficient for all the purposes of General Government that Congress might lay what Duties they thought proper, and those who did not approve the extended power here given, contended that the Establishment of the Particular ports ought to remain with the Government of the respective States; for if Maryland for instance should have occasion to oppose the Encroachments of the General Government — Congress might direct that all Vessels coming into this Bay, to enter and clear at Norfolk, and thereby become as formidable to this State by an exercise of this power, as they could be by the Military arrangements or Civil Judiciaries. That the same reason would not apply in prohibiting the respective States from laying a Duty on Exports, as applied to that regulation being exercised by Congress:

in the latter case a revenue would be drawn from the productive States to the General Treasury, to t[?] ease of the unproductive, but particular States might be desirous by this method to contribute to the support of their Local Government or for the Encouragement of their Manufactures.

Article 2nd.

S: 1st. A Variety of opinion prevailed on this Article. Mr. Hamilton of New York wanted the President to be appointed by the Senate, others by both Branches, others by the People at large — others that the States as States ought to have an equal voice — The larger States wanted the appointment according to numbers — those who were for a one Genl. Government, and no State Governments, were for a choice by the People at large, and the very persons who would not trust the Legislature to vote by States in the Choice, from a fear of Corruption, yet contended nevertheless for a Standing Army, and before this point was finally adjusted I had left the Convention.

As to the Vice President, the larger States have a manifest influence and will always have him of their choice. The power given to these persons over the Army, and Navy, is in truth formidable, but the power of Pardon is still more dangerous, as in all acts of Treason, the very offence on which the prosecution would possibly arise, would most likely be in favour of the Presidents own power. —

Some would gladly have given the appointment of Ambassadors and Judges to the Senate, some were for vesting this power in the Legislature by joint ballot, as being most likely to know the Merit of Individuals over this extended empire. But as the President is to nominate, the person chosen must be ultimately his choice and he will thus have an army of civil officers as well as Military — If he is guilty of misconduct and impeached for it by the first branch of the Legislature he must be tried in the second, and if he keeps an interest in the large States, he will always escape punishment — The impeachment can rarely come from the Second branch, who are his Council and will be under his influence.

S: 3rd. It was highly reasonable that Treason against the United States should be defined; resistence in some cases is necessary and a Man might be a Traitor to the General Government in obeying the Laws of his own State, a Clause was therefore proposed that wherever any State entered into Contest with the General Governmt. that during such Civil War, the general Law of Nations, as between Independant States should be the governing rule between them; and that no Citizen in such case of the said State should be deemed guilty of Treason, for acting against the General Government, in

Conformity to the Laws of the State of which he was a member: but this was rejected.

Article 6th.

The ratification of this Constitution is so repugnant to the Terms on which we are all bound to amend and alter the former, that it became a matter of surprise to many that the proposition could meet with any countanance or support. Our present Constitution expressly directs that all the States must agree before it can be dissolved; but on the other hand it was contended that a Majority ought to govern — That a dissolution of the Federal Government did not dissolve the State Constitutions which were paramount the Confederacy. That the Federal Government being formed out of the State Governments the People at large have no power to interfere in the *Federal Constitution* Nor has the *State* or *Federal* Government any power to confirm a new Institution. That this Government if ratified and Established will be *immediately* from the *People*, paramount the *Federal Constitution* and operate as a dissolution of it.

Thus Mr. Speaker, I have given to this Honorable House such information, as my situation enabled me to do, on the Subject of this proposed Constitution. If I have spoke with freedom, I have done no more than I did in Convention. I have been under no influence from the expectation of ever enjoying any Office under it, and would gladly yield what little I have saved by Industry, and the Emoluments of my profession to have been able to present it to the Public [1] in [a] different form. I freely [own, that it did not] meet my approbation, and [   ] this House will do [   ] believe that [I have conducted myself   ] freeman and a faithful servant of the [   ] to the best of my Judgement for the Gen [   ]

CXLVII. James Wilson in the Pennsylvania Convention.[2]

November 30, 1787.

Mr. Wilson. It is objected that the number of members in the House of Representatives is too small. This is a subject somewhat embarrassing, and the convention who framed the article felt the enbarrassment. . . .

The convention endeavored to steer a middle course, and when we consider the scale on which they formed their calculation, there are strong reasons why the representation should not have been larger. On the ratio that they have fixed, of one for every thirty

[1] A part of the MS. is torn off. Words in brackets are partly legible.
[2] McMaster and Stone, *Pennsylvania and the Federal Constitution*, 287–289.

thousand, and according to the generally received opinion of the increase of population throughout the United States, the present number of their inhabitants will be doubled in twenty-five years, and according to that progressive proportion, and the ratio of one member for thirty thousand inhabitants, the House of Representatives will, within a single century, consist of more than six hundred members.   Permit me to add a further observation on the numbers — that a large number is not so necessary in this case as in the cases of state legislatures.   In them there ought to be a representation sufficient to declare the situation of every county, town and district, and if of every individual, so much the better, because their legislative powers extend to the particular interest and convenience of each; but in the general government its objects are enumerated, and are not confined in their causes or operations to a county, or even to a single state.   No one power is of such a nature as to require the minute knowledge of situations and circumstances necessary in state governments possessed of general legislative authority. These were the reasons, Sir, that I believe had influence on the convention to agree to the number of thirty thousand; and when the inconveniences and conveniences on both sides are compared, it would be difficult to say what would be a number more unexceptionable.

CXLVIII. James Wilson in the Pennsylvania Convention.[1]

December 3, 1787.

Much fault has been found with the mode of expression used in the first clause of the ninth section of the first article.   I believe I can assign a reason why that mode of expression was used, and why the term slave was not directly admitted in this constitution:—
. . . These were the very expressions used in 1783, and the fate of this recommendation was similar to all their [Congress] other resolutions.   It was not carried into effect, but it was adopted by no fewer than eleven out of thirteen States; . . . It was natural, Sir, for the late convention to adopt the mode after it had been agreed to by eleven states, and to use the expression which they found had been received as unexceptionable before.   With respect to the clause restricting Congress from prohibiting the migration or importation of such persons as any of the States now existing shall think proper to admit, prior to the year 1808, the honorable gentleman says that this clause is not only dark, but intended to grant to Congress, for that time, the power to admit the importation of slaves.

---

[1] McMaster and Stone, *Pennsylvania and the Federal Constitution*, 311–313.

No such thing was intended; but I will tell you what was done, and it gives me high pleasure that so much was done. Under the present confederation, the States may admit the importation of slaves as long as they please; but by this article, after the year 1808, the Congress will have power to prohibit such importation, notwithstanding the disposition of any State to the contrary. I consider this as laying the foundation for banishing slavery out of this country; and though the period is more distant than I could wish, yet it will produce the same kind, gradual change which was pursued in Pennsylvania.[1] It is with much satisfaction I view this power in the general government, whereby they may lay an interdiction on this reproachful trade. But an immediate advantage is also obtained, for a tax or duty may be imposed on such importation not exceeding ten dollars for each person; and this, Sir, operates as a partial prohibition. It was all that could be obtained. I am sorry it was no more; but from this I think there is reason to hope that yet a few years, and it will be prohibited altogether. And in the meantime, the new States which are to be formed will be under the control of Congress in this particular, and slaves will never be introduced amongst them. The gentleman says that it is unfortunate in another point of view: it means to prohibit the introduction of white people from Europe, as this tax may deter them from coming amongst us. A little impartiality and attention will discover the care that the convention took in selecting their language. The words are, the *migration or* IMPORTATION of such persons, etc., shall not be prohibited by Congress prior to the year 1808, but a tax or duty may be imposed on such IMPORTATION. It is observable here that the term migration is dropped when a tax or duty is mentioned, so that Congress have power to impose the tax only on those imported.   _____

CXLIX. JAMES WILSON IN THE PENNSYLVANIA CONVENTION.[2]

December 4, 1787.

A good deal has already been said, concerning a bill of rights; I have stated, according to the best of my recollection, all that passed in convention relating to that business. Since that time, I have spoken with a gentleman, who has not only his memory, but full notes, that he had taken in that body; and he assures me, that upon this subject no direct motion was ever made at all; and certainly, before we heard this so violently supported out of doors, some pains ought to have been taken to have tried its fate within;

---

[1] See CCCXXVII note below.
[2] McMaster and Stone, *Pennsylvania and the Federal Constitution*, 313–338.

but the truth is, a bill of rights would, as I have mentioned already, have been not only unnecessary, but improper. . . .

. . . Enumerate all the rights of men! I am sure, Sir, that no gentleman in the late convention would have attempted such a thing. . . .

I say, Sir, that it was the design of this system, to take some power from the State government, and to place it in the general government. It was also the design, that the people should be admitted to the exercise of some powers which they did not exercise under the present confederation. It was thought proper that the citizens, as well as the States, should be represented; . . .

. . . I am not a blind admirer of this system. Some of the powers of the senators are not with me the favorite parts of it, but as they stand connected with other parts, there is still security against the efforts of that body: it was with great difficulty that security was obtained, and I may risk the conjecture, that if it is not now accepted, it never will be obtained again from the same States. Though the senate was not a favorite of mine, as to some of its powers, yet it was a favorite with a majority in the Union, and we must submit to that majority, or we must break up the Union. It is but fair to repeat those reasons, that weighed with the convention; perhaps I shall not be able to do them justice, but yet I will attempt to show, why additional powers were given to the senate, rather than to the house of representatives. These additional powers, I believe, are, that of trying impeachments, that of concurring with the President in making treaties, and that of concurring in the appointment of officers. These are the powers that are stated as improper. It is fortunate, that in the exercise of every one of them, the Senate stands controlled; if it is that monster which it said to be, it can only show its teeth, it is unable to bite or devour. With regard to impeachments, the senate can try none but such as will be brought before them by the house of representatives.

The senate can make no treaties; they can approve of none unless the President of the United States lay it before them. With regard to the appointment of officers, the President must nominate before they can vote. So that if the powers of either branch are perverted, it must be with the approbation of some one of the other branches of government: thus checked on one side, they can do no one act of themselves.

. . . Sir, I confess I wish the powers of the senate were not as they are. I think it would have been better if those powers had been distributed in other parts of the system. . . .

CL. James Wilson in the Pennsylvania Convention.[1]

December 7, 1787

. . . I shall beg leave to premise one remark, that the convention, when they formed this system, did not expect they were to deliver themselves, their relations and their posterity, into the hands of such men as are described by the honorable gentlemen in opposition. They did not suppose that the legislature, under this constitution, would be an *association of demons.* They thought that a proper attention would be given by the citizens of the United States, at the general election, for members to the House of Representatives; they also believed that the particular states would nominate as good men as they have heretofore done, to represent them in the Senate. . . .

The Convention thought further (for on this very subject, there will appear caution, instead of imprudence, in their transactions) they considered, that if suspicions are to be entertained, they are to be entertained with regard to the objects in which government have separate interests and separate views from the interests and views of the people. To say that officers of government will oppress, when nothing can be got by oppression, is making an inference, bad as human nature is, that cannot be allowed. . . .

Whenever the general government can be a party against a citizen, the trial is guarded and secured in the constitution itself, and therefore it is not in its power to oppress the citizen. In the case of treason, for example, though the prosecution is on the part of the United States, yet the Congress can neither define nor try the crime. If we have recourse to the history of the different governments that have hitherto subsisted, we shall find that a very great part of their tyranny over the people has arisen from the extension of the definition of treason. . . .

. . . Sensible of this, the Convention has guarded the people against it, by a particular and accurate definition of treason.

It is very true that trial by jury is not mentioned in civil cases; but I take it, that it is very improper to infer from hence, that it was not meant to exist under this government. Where the people are represented — where the interest of government cannot be separate from that of the people, (and this is the case in trial between citizen and citizen) the power of making regulations with respect to the mode of trial, may certainly be placed in the legislature; for I apprehend that the legislature will not do wrong in an instance from which they can derive no advantage. These were not all the

---

[1] McMaster and Stone, *Pennsylvania and the Federal Constitution*, 351-353.

reasons that influenced the convention to leave it to the future Congress to make regulations on this head.

By the constitution of the different States, it will be found that no particular mode of trial by jury could be discovered that would suit them all. The manner of summoning jurors, their qualifications, of whom they should consist, and the course of their proceedings, are all different, in the different States; and I presume it will be allowed a good general principle, that in carrying into effect the laws of the general government by the judicial department, it will be proper to make the regulations as agreeable to the habits and wishes of the particular States as possible; and it is easily discovered that it would have been impracticable, by any general regulation, to have given satisfaction to all. We must have thwarted the custom of eleven or twelve to have accommodated any one. Why do this, when there was no danger to be apprehended from the omission? We could not go into a particular detail of the manner that would have suited each State.

Time, reflection, and experience, will be necessary to suggest and mature the proper regulations on this subject; time and experience were not possessed by the convention; they left it therefore to be particularly organized by the legislature — the representatives of the United States — from time to time, as should be most eligible and proper. _____

CLI. THE LANDHOLDER [OLIVER ELLSWORTH], VI.[1]

Just at the close of the Convention, whose proceedings in general were zealously supported by Mr. Mason, he moved for a clause that no navigation act should ever be passed but with the consent of two-thirds of both branches; urging that a navigation act might otherwise be passed excluding foreign bottoms from carrying American produce to market, and throw a monopoly of the carrying business into the hands of the eastern states who attend to navigation, and that such an exclusion of foreigners would raise the freight of the produce of the southern states, and for these reasons Mr. Mason would have it in the power of the southern states to prevent any navigation act. This clause, as unequal and partial in the extreme to the southern states, was rejected; because it ought to be left on the same footing with other national concerns, and because no state would have a right to complain of a navigation act which should leave the carrying business equally open to them all. Those who preferred cultivating their lands would do so; those who chose to

_____

[1] P. L. Ford, *Essays on the Constitution*, 161–166. First printed in the *Connecticut Courant*, December 10, 1787.

navigate and become carriers would do that. The loss of this question determined Mr. Mason against the signing the doings of the convention, and is undoubtedly among his reasons as drawn for the southern states; but for the eastern states this reason would not do.[1] . . .

There is to be no ex post facto laws. This was moved by Mr. Gerry and supported by Mr. Mason, and is exceptional only as being unnecessary; for it ought not to be presumed that government will be so tyrannical, and opposed to the sense of all modern civilians, as to pass such laws: if they should, they would be void.

The general Legislature is restrained from prohibiting the further importation of slaves for twenty odd years. . . . His objections are . . . that such importations render the United States weaker, more vulnerable, and less capable of defence. To this I readily agree, and all good men wish the entire abolition of slavery, as soon as it can take place with safety to the public, and for the lasting good of the present wretched race of slaves. The only possible step that could be taken towards it by the convention was to fix a period after which they should not be imported. . . .

To make the objections the more plausible, they are called *The objections of the Hon. George Mason, etc.* — They may possibly be his, but be assured they were not those made in convention, and being directly against what he there supported in one instance ought to caution you against giving any credit to the rest; his violent opposition to the powers given congress to regulate trade, was an open decided preference of all the world to you. . . .

It may be asked how I came by my information respecting Col. Mason's conduct in convention, as the doors were shut? To this I answer, no delegate of the late convention will contradict my assertions, as I have repeatedly heard them made by others in presence of several of them, who could not deny their truth.

_____

CLII. James Wilson in the Pennsylvania Convention.[2]

December 11, 1787.

The singular unanimity that has attended the whole progress of their business will in the minds of those considerate men, who have not had opportunity to examine the general and particular interest of their country, prove to their satisfaction that it is an excellent

_____

[1] According to Mr. P. L. Ford: "The paragraph containing Mason's objection to the mere majority power of Congress to regulate commerce, was included in all the southern papers, but omitted in copies furnished to the papers north of Maryland." See also CLV below.

[2] McMaster and Stone, *Pennsylvania and the Federal Constitution*, 383–399.

constitution, and worthy to be adopted, ordained and established, by the people of the United States.

. . . We were told some days ago, by the honorable gentleman from Westmoreland (Mr. Findley,) when speaking of this system and its objects, that the convention, no doubt, thought they were forming a compact or contract of the greatest importance. Sir, I confess I was much surprised at so late a stage of the debate to hear such principles maintained. It was matter of surprise to see the great leading principle of this system still so very much misunderstood. "The convention, no doubt, thought they were forming 'a contract!'" I cannot answer for what every member thought; but I believe it cannot be said that they thought they were making a contract, because I cannot discover the least trace of a compact in that system.[1] There can be no compact unless there are more parties than one. It is a new doctrine that one can make a compact with himself. "The convention were forming compacts!" With whom? I know no bargains that were made there. I am unable to conceive who the parties could be. The State governments make a bargain with one another; that is the doctrine that is endeavored to be established by gentlemen in opposition; their State sovereignties wish to be represented! But far other were the ideas of this convention, and far other are those conveyed in the system itself.

. . . I do not think, that in the powers of the Senate, the distinction is marked with so much accuracy as I wished, and still wish; . . .

. . . Neither the President nor the Senate solely, can complete a treaty; they are checks upon each other, and are so balanced as to produce security to the people.

I might suggest other reasons, to add weight to what has already been offered, but I believe it is not necessary; yet let me, however, add one thing, the Senate is a favorite with many of the States, and it was with difficulty that these checks could be procured; it was one of the last exertions of conciliation, in the late convention, that obtained them.

. . . The manner of appointing the President of the United States, I find, is not objected to, therefore I shall say little on that point. But I think it well worth while to state to this house, how little the difficulties, even in the most difficult part of this system, appear to have been noticed by the honorable gentlemen in opposition. The Convention, Sir, were perplexed with no part of this plan so much as with the mode of choosing the President of the United States.

---

[1] Yet Wilson had said on November 24 (see CXLII above), "Providence has designed us for an united people, under one great political compact."

For my own part, I think the most unexceptionable mode, next after the one prescribed in this Constitution, would be that practised by the eastern States, and the State of New York; yet if gentlemen object, that an eighth part of our country forms a district too large for elections, how much more would they object, if it was extended to the whole Union! On this subject, it was the opinion of a great majority in Convention, that the thing was impracticable; other embarrassments presented themselves.

Was the president to be appointed by the legislature? Was he to continue a certain time in office, and afterwards was he to become ineligible?

. . . To avoid the inconveniences already enumerated, and many others that might be suggested, the mode before us was adopted. _____

CLIII. James Wilson in the Pennsylvania Convention.[1]

December 11, 1787. (afternoon).

We have been told, Sir, by the honorable member from Fayette (Mr. Smilie,) "that the trial by jury was *intended* to be given up, and the civil law was *intended* to be introduced into its place, in civil cases."

Before a sentiment of this kind was hazarded, I think, Sir, the gentleman ought to be prepared with better proofs in its support, than any he has yet attempted to produce. It is a charge, Sir, not only unwarrantable, but cruel; the idea of such a thing, I believe, never entered into the mind of a single member of that convention; and I believe further, that they never suspected there would be found within the United States, a single person that was capable of making such a charge. . . .

Let us apply these observations to the objects of the judicial department, under this constitution. I think it has been shewn already, that they all extend beyond the bounds of any particular State; but further, a great number of the civil causes there enumerated, depend either upon the law of nations, or the marine law, that is, the general law of mercantile countries. Now, Sir, in such cases, I presume it will not be pretended that this mode of decision ought to be adopted; for the law with regard to them is the same here as in every other country, and ought to be administered in the same manner. There are instances in which I think it highly probable, that the trial by jury will be found proper; and if it is highly probable that it will be found proper, is it not equally probable that it

_____

[1] McMaster and Stone, *Pennsylvania and the Federal Constitution*, pp. 403–405.

will be adopted? There may be causes depending between citizens of different States, and as trial by jury is known and regarded in all the States, they will certainly prefer that mode of trial before any other. The Congress will have the power of making proper regulations on this subject, but it was impossible for the convention to have gone minutely into it; but if they could, it must have been very improper, because alterations, as I observed before, might have been necessary; and whatever the convention might have done would have continued unaltered, unless by an alteration of the Constitution. Besides, there was another difficulty with regard to this subject. In some of the States they have courts of chancery and other appellate jurisdictions, and those States are as attached to that mode of distributing justice, as those that have none are to theirs.

_____

CLIV. The Landholder [Oliver Ellsworth], VII.[1]

I have often admired the spirit of candour, liberality, and justice, with which the Convention began and completed the important object of their mission. . . .

_____

CLV. James Madison to George Washington.[2]

New York Decr. 20. 1787.

Tricks of this sort are not uncommon with the Enemies of the new Constitution. Col. Mason's objections were as I am told published in Boston mutilated of that which pointed at the regulation of Commerce.[3] Docr Franklins concluding speech which you will meet with in one of the papers herewith inclosed, is both mutilated & adulterated so as to change both the form & the spirit of it.

_____

CLVI. Ezra Stiles: Diary.[4]

[December] 21. [1787]. Mr. Baldwin was one of the Continental Convention at Philada last Summer. He gave me an Acct of the whole Progress in Convention. It appeared that they were pretty unanimous in the followg Ideas, viz. 1. In a firm foederal Government. 2. That this shd be very popular or stand on the People at large. 3. That their Object shd comprehend all Things of common foederal Concern & wc individual States could not determine or enforce. 4. That the Jurisdictions & Govt of each State shd be

_____

[1] P. L. Ford, *Essays on the Constitution*, 167; first printed in the *Connecticut Courant*, December 17, 1787.

[2] *Documentary History of the Constitution*, IV, 416–417.

[3] See CLI and note 2 above.

[4] *Literary Diary of Ezra Stiles*, III, 293–295.

left intire & preserved as inviolate as possible consistent with the coercive Subordina for preservg the Union with Firmness. 5. That the present foederal Govt was inadequate to this End. 6. That a certain Portion or Deg. of Dominion as to *Laws* and *Revenue*, as well as to Treaties with foreign Nations, War & Armies, was necessy to be ceded by individual States to the Authory of the National Council. 7. That the National Council shd consist of two Branches viz, a Senate, & Representatives. That the last shd be a local Representa apportioned to the Property & Number of Inhabitants, as far as practicable. That this shd be the governg Idea. And yet that the Distinction of States shd be preserved in the House of Representa as well as in the Senate. 8. That the Senate stand on the Election & Distinction of States as at present in Congress, and tho' like the Representa be in some measure proportioned to the No of Inhab. yet that besides this the Vote in Senate shd be by States, tho' in the House of Representa the Vote shd be by Plurality of Members present indeed but not by States as States. Hereby two things are secured, one, that the People at large shall be efficaciously represented, the other that the States as separate States be as also efficaciously represented. 9. That these two Branches combined into one Republican Body be the supreme Legislature & become vested with the Sovereignty of the Confederacy; & have powers of Govt & Revenue adequate to these Ends. 10. As to a President, it appeared to the Opin. of Convention, that he shd be a Character respectable by the Nations as well as by the foederal Empire. To this End that as much Power shd be given him as could be consistently with guardg against all possibility of his ascending in a Tract of years or Ages to Despotism & absolute Monarchy: — of which all were cautious. Nor did it appear that any Members in Convention had the least Idea of insidiously layg the Founda of a future Monarchy like the European or Asiatic Monarchies either antient or modern. But were unanimously guarded & firm against every Thing of this ultimate Tendency. Accordinly they meant to give considerable Weight as Supreme Executive, but fixt him dependent on the States at large, and at all times impeachable. 10. They vested Congress thus modified with the Power of an adequate Revenue, by Customs on Trade, Excise and direct Taxation by Authory of Congress; as well as with the Army, Navy & makg War & Peace. These were delicate Things, on which all felt sollicitous & yet all were unanimously convinced that they were necessary. 11. They were unanimous also in the Expedy & Necessy of a supreme judiciary Tribunal of universal Jurisdiction — in Controversies of a legal Nature between States — Revenue — & appellate Causes between subjects of foreign or different States. 12. The Power of appointing Judges & Officers of the supreme Judiciary to be in the Senate.

These & other general & commandg Ideas the Members found themselves almost unanimous in. The Representa would feel for the Interests of their respective local Representations: and the Senate must feel, not for particular local Districts but a Majority of the States or the Universal Interest.

After some Discourses, it was proposed that any & all the Members shd. draught their Ideas. These were all bro't in & examd & as approved, entered, until all were satisfied they had gone through. Then they reduced these to one Sheet (written) of Articles or Members of the Constitution. These they considered afresh, sometimes in Committee of the Whole, & sometimes in Convention, with subjoyned Alterations & Additions until August; when they adjourned a few Weeks leavg all to be digested by a Committee of 5 Messrs Sherman, Elsworth,

On the Return of Adjournt the whole Digest was printed and every Member entered his Remarks, Altera & Corrections. These again were committed to a Committee of one Member of each State of wc Mr. Baldwin one. This maturated the whole. Finally a Committee of 5 viz, Mess. Dr Johnson, Governeur Morris. Wilson, ———   These reduced it to the form in which it was published. Messrs Morris & Wilson had the chief hand in the last Arrangt & Composition. This was completed in September. By this Time several Members were absent party Judge Yates of Albany, Mr. Wyth of Virginia, Judge Sherman & Elsworth. About 42 signed it. Messrs Mason of Virg. & Gerry of Boston & Gov. Randolph refused. Dr Franklin sd he did not entirely approve it but, tho't it a good one, did not know but he shd. hereafter think it the best, on the whole was ready to sign it & wished all would sign it, & wished all would sign it, & that it shd be adopted by all the States.

Dr Franklins Idea that the American Policy, be one Branch only or Representative Senate of one Order, proportioned to Number of Inhab. & Property — often elected —, with a President assisted with an executive Council: but this last have nothg to do in Legislation & Senatorial Government. Teste Mr. Baldwin..

CLVII. The Landholder [Oliver Ellsworth], VIII.[1]

To the Hon. Elbridge Gerry, Esquire.

  Sir,

  When a man in public life first deviates from the line of truth

---

[1] P. L. Ford, *Essays on the Constitution,* 172–175; first printed in the *Connecticut Courant,* December 24, 1787.

and rectitude, an uncommon degree of art and attention becomes necessary to secure him from detection . . . . his first leap into the region of treachery and falsehood is often as fatal to himself as it was designed to be to his country. Whether you and Mr. Mason may be ranked in this class of trangressors I pretend not to determine. Certain it is, that both your management and his for a short time before and after the rising of the foederal convention impress us with a favorable opinion, that you are great novices in the arts of dissimulation. A small degree of forethought would have taught you both a much more successful method of directing the rage of resentment which you caught at the close of the business at Philadelphia, than the one you took. . . .

It is evident that this mode of proceeding would have been well calculated for the security of Mr. Mason; he there might have vented . . . his sore mortification for the loss of his favorite motion respecting the navigation act. . . .

You will doubtless recollect the following state of facts — if you do not, every member of the convention will attest them — that almost the whole time during the setting of the convention, and until the constitution had received its present form, no man was more plausible and conciliating upon every subject than Mr. Gerry — he was willing to sacrifice every private feeling and opinion — to concede every state interest that should be in the least incompatible with the most substantial and permanent system of general government — that mutual concession and unanimity were the whole burden of his song; and although he originated no idea himself, yet there was nothing in the system as it now stands to which he had the least objection — indeed, Mr. Gerry's conduct was agreeably surprising to all his acquaintance, and very unlike that turbulent obstinacy of spirit which they had formerly affixed to his character. Thus stood Mr. Gerry, till, toward the close of the business, he introduced a motion respecting the redemption of the old Continental Money — that it should be placed upon a footing with other liquidated securities of the United States. As Mr. Gerry was supposed to be possessed of large quantities of this species of paper, his motion appeared to be founded in such barefaced selfishness and injustice, that it at once accounted for all his former plausibility and concession, while the rejection of it by the convention inspired its author with the utmost rage and intemperate opposition to the whole system he had formerly praised.[1] His resentment could no

---

[1] For Gerry's reply see CLXII below. The controversy may be followed farther in CLXXV, CLXXXIX–CXCII, and CXCIX.

more than embarrass and delay the completion of the business for a few days; when he refused signing the constitution and was called upon for his reasons. These reasons were committed to writing by one of his colleagues[1] and likewise by the Secretary, as Mr. Gerry delivered them. These reasons were totally different from those which he has published, neither was a single objection which is contained in his letter to the legislature of Massachusetts ever offered by him in convention.[2]

Now Mr. Gerry, as this is generally known to be the state of facts, and as neither the reasons which you publish nor those retained on the Secretary's files can be supposed to have the least affinity to truth, or to contain the real motives which induced you to withhold your name from the constitution, it appears to me that your plan was not judiciously contrived. ———————

CLVIII. Luther Martin: Genuine Information.[3]

The Genuine Information, delivered to the Legislature of the State of Maryland, relative to the Proceedings of the General Convention, held at Philadelphia, in 1787, by LUTHER MARTIN, Esquire, Attorney-General of Maryland, and one of the Delegates in the said Convention.

Mr. Martin, when called upon, addressed the House nearly as follows:

---

[1] Probably refers to King, see *Records* of September 15.

[2] Somewhat too sweeping an assertion although there are great differences between Gerry's objections in Convention on September 15 and those embodied in his letter to the Massachusetts legislature. See *Records* of September 15, and CXXXIII above.

[3] Martin's "Genuine Information" was delivered to the Maryland legislature November 29, 1787. It was first printed in Dunlap's *Maryland Gazette and Baltimore Advertiser*, December 28, 1787—February 8, 1788. It was prefaced by the following note: —

"Mr. Hayes,

It was the wish of many respectable characters both in the House of Assembly, and others, that the information received from the Delegates to the late Convention, should be made public — I have taken some pains, to collect together, the substance of the information, which was given on that occasion to the House of Delegates by Mr. Martin; by your inserting in your paper, you will oblige.
                                                            A Customer."

With the kind assistance of Mr. George W. McCreary, Assistant Secretary and Librarian of the Maryland Historical Society, the text of the present edition has been revised so as to correspond to the document as it was first printed.

It is quite evident that the speech delivered was revised before printing, and it is important, therefore, to compare this document with the speech as reported in the legislative proceedings (see above CXLVIb).

Because of the length of the document Arabic numerals are attached to the various paragraphs for convenience of reference. See also Appendix A, CCXXIII, CCCLVII, CCCLXV, CCCLXXVII, CCCXCII, CCCXCVII.

[1] Since I was notified of the resolve of this Honorable House, that we should attend this day, to give information with regard to the proceedings of the late convention, my time has necessarily been taken up with business, and I have also been obliged to make a journey to the Eastern Shore. These circumstances have prevented me from being as well prepared as I could wish, to give the information required. However, the few leisure moments I could spare, I have devoted to refreshing my memory, by looking over the papers and notes in my possession; and shall, with pleasure, to the best of my abilities, render an account of my conduct.

[2] It was not in my power to attend the convention immediately on my appointment. I took my seat, I believe, about the eighth or ninth of June. I found that Governor Randolph, of Virginia, had laid before the convention certain propositions for their consideration, which have been read to this House by my honorable colleague, and I believe he has very faithfully detailed the substance of the speech with which the business of the convention was opened; for, though I was not there at the time, I saw notes which had been taken of it.

[3] The members of the convention from the States, came there under different powers, The greatest number, I believe, under powers nearly the same as those of the delegates of this State. Some came to the convention under the former appointment, authorising the meeting of delegates merely to regulate trade. Those of Delaware *were expressly instructed to agree to no system, which should take away from the States that equality of suffrage secured by the original articles of confederation.* Before I arrived, a number of rules had been adopted to regulate the proceedings of the convention, by one of which, seven States might proceed to business, and consequently four States, the majority of that number, might eventually have agreed upon a system, which was to affect the whole Union. *By another, the doors were to be shut, and the whole proceedings were to be kept secret;* and so far did this rule extend, that we were thereby prevented from corresponding with gentlemen in the different States upon the subjects under our discussion; a circumstance, Sir, which, I confess, I greatly regretted. I had no idea, that all the wisdom, integrity, and virtue of this State, or of the others, were centred in the convention. I wished to have corresponded freely and confidentially with eminent political characters in my own and other States; not implicitly to be dictated to by them, but to give their sentiments due weight and consideration. *So extremely solicitous* were they, that their proceedings should not transpire, that the members *were prohibited even from taking copies of resolutions, on*

which the convention were deliberating, or extracts of any kind from the journals, without formally moving for, and obtaining permission, by a vote of the convention for that purpose.

[4] You have heard, Sir, the resolutions which were brought forward by the honorable member from Virginia; let me call the attention of this House to the conduct of Virginia, when our confederation was entered into — That State then proposed, and obstinately contended, *contrary to the sense of, and unsupported by the other States, for an inequality of suffrage* founded on *numbers,* or *some such scale,* which should give her,[1] and certain other States, influence in the Union over the rest. Pursuant to that spirit which then characterized *her,* and uniform in her conduct, the very second resolve, is calculated expressly for that purpose, *to give her a representation proportioned to her numbers,* as if the want of that was the *principal defect* in our original system, and this alteration the great means of remedying the evils we had experienced under our present government.

[5] The object of *Virginia,* and *other large States,* to *increase their power* and *influence over the others,* did not escape observation; the subject, however, was discussed with great coolness, in the committee of the whole House (for the convention had resolved itself into a committee of the whole, to deliberate upon the propositions delivered in by the honorable member from Virginia). Hopes were formed, that the farther we proceeded in the examination of the resolutions, the better the House might be satisfied of the impropriety of adopting them, and that they would finally be rejected by a majority of the committee; if, on the contrary, a majority should report in their favor, it was considered, that it would not preclude the members from bringing forward and submitting any other system to the consideration of the convention; and accordingly, while those resolves were the subject of discussion in the committee of the whole House, a number of the members, who disapproved them, were preparing *another system,* such as *they thought more conducive to the happiness and welfare of the States.* The propositions originally submitted to the convention having been debated, and undergone a variety of alterations in the course of our proceedings, the committee of the whole House, *by a small majority agreed* to a *report,* which I am happy, Sir, to have in my power to lay before you; it was as follows:

[6] "1. *Resolved,* That it is the opinion of this committee, that a *national* government ought to be established, consisting of a supreme legislative, judiciary, and executive.

---

[1] The two lines following were omitted in the original, evidently by inadvertance.

"2. That the legislative ought to consist of *two branches*.

"3. That the members of the first branch of the national legislature ought to be elected by the people of the several States, for the term of three years, to receive fixed stipends, by which they may be compensated for the devotion of their time to public service, to be paid out of the national treasury, to be ineligible to any office established by a particular State, or under the authority of the United States, except those particularly belonging to the functions of the first branch, during the term of service, and under the national government, for the space of one year after its expiration.

"4. That the members of the second branch of the legislature ought to be chosen by the individual legislatures; to be of the age of thirty years at least; to hold their offices for a term sufficient to insure their independency, namely, seven years, one third to go out biennially; to receive fixed stipends, by which they may be compensated for the devotion of their time to public service, to be paid out of the national treasury; to be ineligible to any office by a particular State, or under the authority of the United States, except those peculiarly belonging to the functions of the second branch, during the term of service, and under the national government, for the space of one year after its expiration.

"5. That each branch ought to possess the right of originating acts.

"6. That the national legislature ought to be empowered to enjoy the legislative rights vested in Congress by the confederation, and, *moreover, to legislate in all cases to which the separate States are incompetent,* or in which the *harmony of the United States may be interrupted, by the exercise of individual legislation;* to *negative* all laws passed by the *several States,* contravening, in the *opinion* of the *legislature* of the *United States,* the articles of union, or any treaties subsisting under the authority of the Union.

"7. That the *right of suffrage* in the first branch of the national legislature, *ought not to be according to the rule established in the articles of confederation,* but according to some equitable rate of representation, namely, *in proportion to the whole number of white, and other free citizens and inhabitants of every age, sex, and condition, including those bound to servitude for a term of years, and three-fifths of all other persons* not comprehended in the foregoing description, except Indians not paying taxes in each State.

"8. That the *right of suffrage in the second branch* of the national legislature, *ought to be according to the rule established in the first.*

"9. That a national executive be instituted, to consist of a single person, *to be chosen by the national legislature* for the term of seven years, with power to carry into execution the national laws, *to appoint to offices* in cases not otherwise provided for, to be ineligible a second time, and to be removable on impeachment and conviction of malpractice or neglect of duty; to receive a fixed stipend, by which he may be compensated for the devotion of his time to public service, to be paid out of the national treasury.

"10. That the national executive shall have a right to *negative any legislative act which shall not afterwards be passed, unless by two third parts of each branch of the national legislature.*

"11. That a national judiciary be established, to consist of one supreme tribunal, the judges of which, to be appointed by the *second branch* of the national legislature, to hold their offices during good behaviour, and to receive punctually, at stated times, a fixed compensation for their services, in which no increase or diminution shall be made, so as to affect the persons actually in office at the time of such increase or diminution.

"12. That the *national legislature* be empowered to *appoint inferior tribunals.*

"13. That the jurisdiction of the *national* judiciary shall extend to cases which respect the collection of the national revenue; cases arising under the laws of the United States; impeachments of any national officer, *and questions which involve the national peace and harmony.*

"14. *Resolved,* That provision ought to be made for the admission of States lawfully arising within the limits of the United States, whether from a voluntary junction of government, territory, or otherwise, with the consent of a number of voices in the national legislature less than the whole.

"15. *Resolved,* That provision ought to be made for the continuance of Congress, and their authority and privileges, until a given day after the reform of the articles of union shall be adopted, and for the completion of all their engagements.

"16. That a republican constitution, and its existing laws, ought to be guarantied to each State by the United States.

"17. That provision ought to be made for the amendment of the articles of union whensoever it shall seem necessary.

"18. That the legislative, executive, and judiciary powers, within the several States, ought to be bound by oath to support the articles of the Union.

"19. That the amendments which shall be offered to the confederation by this convention, ought, at a proper time or times, after the approbation of Congress, to be submitted to an assembly or assemblies, recommended by the legislatures, to be expressly chosen by the people, to consider and decide thereon.

[7] *These* propositions, Sir, *were acceded to* by a *majority of the members of the committee;* — a system by which the *large States were to have not only an inequality of suffrage in the first branch,* but also *the same inequality* in the *second branch,* or Senate.   However, it was not designed the second branch should consist of the same *number* as the first.   It was proposed that the Senate should consist of *twenty-eight members,* formed on the following scale; Virginia to send five, Pennsylvania and Massachusetts each four, South Carolina, North Carolina, Maryland, New York, and Connecticut *two* each, and the States of New Hampshire, Rhode Island, Jersey, Delaware, and Georgia each of them *one;* upon this plan, the three large States, Virginia, Pennsylvania, and Massachusetts, would have *thirteen senators* out of *twenty-eight,* almost *one half of the whole number.*   Fifteen senators were to be a quorum to proceed to business; those *three States* would, therefore, have *thirteen* out of that quorum.   Having this inequality *in each branch* of the legislature, it must be evident, Sir, that *they would make what laws they pleased, however injurious or disagreeable to the other States;* and that *they would always prevent the other States from making any laws, however necessary and proper, if not agreeeable to the views of those three States.* They were not only, Sir, by this system, to have such an undue superiority in making laws and regulations for the Union, but to have the same superiority in the *appointment* of the *President,* the *judges,* and all *other officers* of government.   Hence, these three States would in reality have the appointment of the President, judges, and all the other officers.   This President and these judges, so appointed, we may be morally certain would be citizens of one of those three States; and the President, as appointed by them, and a citizen of one of them, would espouse their interests and their views, when they came in competition with the views and interests of the other States.   This President, so appointed by the three large States, and so unduly under their influence, was to have a negative upon every law that should be passed, which, if negatived by him, was not to take effect, unless assented to by two thirds of each branch of the legislature, a provision which deprived ten States of even the faintest shadow of liberty; for if they, by a miraculous unanimity, having all their members present, should outvote the other three, and pass a law contrary to their wishes, those three large States need only procure the President to negative it, and thereby prevent a possibility of its ever taking effect, because the representatives of those three States would amount to much more than one third (almost one half) of the representatives in each branch. And, Sir, this government so organized, with all this undue superi-

ority in those three large States, was, as you see, to have a power
of negativing the laws passed by every State legislature in the Union.
Whether, therefore, laws passed by the legislature of Maryland,
New York, Connecticut, Georgia, or of any other of the ten States,
for the regulation of their internal police, should take effect and be
carried into execution, was to depend on the good pleasure of the
representatives of Virginia, Pennsylvania, and Massachusetts.

This system of slavery, which bound hand and foot ten States
in the Union, and placed them at the mercy of the other three, and
under the most abject and servile subjection to them, was approved
by a majority of the members of the convention, and reported by
the committee.

[8] On this occasion the House will recollect, that the convention was resolved into a committee of the whole; of this committee
Mr. Gorham was chairman. The honorable Mr. Washington was
then on the floor, in the same situation with the other members
of the convention at large, to oppose any system he thought injurious,
or to propose any alterations or amendments he thought beneficial.
To these propositions, so reported by the committee, no opposition
was given by that illustrious personage, or by the President of the
State of Pennsylvania. They both appeared cordially to approve
them, and to give them their hearty concurrence; yet this system
I am confident, Mr. Speaker, there is not a member in this House
would advocate, or who would hesitate one moment in saying it
ought to be rejected. I mention this circumstance, in compliance
with the duty I owe this honorable body, not with a view to lessen
those exalted characters, but to show how far the greatest and best
of men may be led to adopt very improper measures through error
in judgment, State influence, or by other causes, and to show, that
it is our duty not to suffer our eyes to be so far dazzled by the splendor of names, as to run blindfolded into what may be our destruction.

[9] Mr. Speaker, I revere those illustrious personages as much
as any man here. No man has a higher sense of the important services they have rendered this country. No member of the convention went there more disposed to pay a deference to their opinions;
but I should little have deserved the trust this State reposed in me,
if I could have sacrificed its dearest interests to my complaisance
for their sentiments.

[10] When, contrary to our hopes, it was found, that a majority
of the members of the convention had in the committee agreed to
the system I have laid before you, we then thought it necessary
to bring forward the propositions which such of us as had disapproved
the plan before had prepared. The members who prepared these

resolutions were principally of the Connecticut, New York, Jersey, Delaware, and Maryland delegations. The honorable Mr. Patterson, of the Jerseys, laid them before the convention; of these propositions * I am in possession of a copy, which I shall beg leave to read to you.

[11] These propositions were referred to a committee of the whole House; unfortunately the New Hampshire delegation had not yet arrived, and the sickness of a relation of the honorable Mr. McHenry obliged him still to be absent; a circumstance, Sir, which I considered much to be regretted, as Maryland thereby was represented by only two delegates, and they unhappily differed very widely in their sentiments.

[12] The result of the reference of these last propositions to a committee was a speedy and hasty determination to reject them. I doubt not, Sir, to those who consider them with attention, so sudden a rejection will appear surprising; but it may be proper to inform you, that, on our meeting in convention, it was soon found there were among us three parties, of very different sentiments and views.

[13] One party, whose object and wish it was to abolish and annihilate all State governments, and to bring forward one general government, over this extensive continent, of a monarchical nature, under certain restrictions and limitations. Those who openly avowed this sentiment were, it is true, but few; yet it is equally true, Sir, that there was a considerable number, who did not openly avow it, who were by myself, and many others of the convention, considered as being in reality favorers of that sentiment; and, acting upon those principles, covertly endeavouring to carry into effect what they well knew openly and avowedly could not be accomplished.

[14] The second party was not for the abolition of the State governments, nor for the introduction of a monarchical government under any form; but they wished to establish such a system, as could give their own States undue power and influence in the government over the other States.

[15] A third party was what I considered truly federal and republican; this party was nearly equal in number with the other two, and was composed of the delegations from Connecticut, New York, New Jersey, Delaware, and in part from Maryland; also of some individuals from other representations. This party, Sir, were for proceeding upon terms of *federal equality;* they were for taking our present *federal system* as the basis of their proceedings, and, as far as experience had shown us that there were defects, to remedy those defects; as far as experience had shown that other powers were

* These will be inserted in some future number with few remarks upon them.

necessary to the federal government, to give those powers. They considered this the object for which they were sent by their States, and what their States expected from them; they urged, that, if, after doing this, experience should show that there still were defects in the system (as no doubt there would be), the same good sense that induced this convention to be called, would cause the States, when they found it necessary, to call another; and, if that convention should act with the same moderation, the members of it would proceed to correct such errors and defects as experience should have brought to light. That, by proceeding in this train, we should have a prospect at length of obtaining as perfect a system of federal government, as the nature of things would admit. On the other hand, if we, contrary to the purpose for which we were intrusted, considering ourselves as master-builders, too proud to amend our original government, should demolish it entirely, and erect a new system of our own, a short time might show the new system as defective as the old, perhaps more so. Should a convention be found necessary again, if the members thereof, acting upon the same principles, instead of amending and correcting its defects, should demolish that entirely, and bring forward a third system, that also might soon be found no better than either of the former; and thus we might always remain young in government, and always suffering the inconveniences of an incorrect, imperfect system.

[16] But, Sir, the favorers of monarchy, and those who wished the total abolition of State governments, well knowing, that a government founded on *truly federal principles*, the basis of which were the *thirteen State governments, preserved in full force and energy*, would be destructive of their views; and knowing they were too weak in numbers openly to bring forward their system; conscious also that the people of America would reject it if proposed to them, — joined their interest with that party, who wished a system, giving *particular States* the *power* and *influence over the others*, procuring in return mutual sacrifices from them, in giving the government *great* and *undefined powers* as to its *legislative* and *executive;* well knowing, that, by *departing from a federal system*, they paved the way for their favorite object, the *destruction of the State governments*, and the *introduction of monarchy*. And hence, Mr. Speaker, I apprehend, in a great measure, arose the objections of those honorable members, Mr. Mason and Mr. Gerry. In every thing that tended to give the *large States* power over the *smaller*, the *first* of those gentlemen could not forget he belonged to the *Ancient Dominion*, nor could the latter forget, that he represented Old Massachusetts. That part of the system, which tended to give those States power over

the others, met with their *perfect approbation;* but, when they viewed
it charged with *such powers,* as would *destroy all State governments,*
their own as well as the rest, — when they saw a president so constituted as to differ from a monarch scarcely but in name, and having
it in his power to become such in reality when he pleased; they
being *republicans* and *federalists,* as far as an attachment to their
own States would permit them, they warmly and zealously opposed
those parts of the system. From these different sentiments, and
from this combination of interest, *I apprehend,* Sir, proceeded the
fate of what was called the Jersey resolutions, and the report made
by the committee of the whole House.

[17] The Jersey propositions being thus rejected, the convention
took up those reported by the committee, and proceeded to debate
them by paragraphs. It was now that they, who disapproved
the report, found it necessary to make a *warm* and *decided opposition,*
which took place upon the discussion of the seventh resolution,
which related to the *inequality* of representation in the *first* branch.
Those who advocated this inequality urged, that, when the articles
of confederation were formed, it was *only* from *necessity* and *expediency*
that the States were admitted *each* to have an *equal vote;* but that
our situation was *now altered,* and therefore those States who considered it contrary to their interest, would *no longer abide* by it.
They said, no State ought to wish to have influence in government,
except in proportion to what it contributes to it; that, if it contributes but little, it ought to have but a small vote; that taxation
and representation ought always to go together; that if one State
had *sixteen times as many inhabitants as another,* or was *sixteen times
as wealthy,* it ought to have *sixteen times as many votes;* that an inhabitant of Pennsylvania ought to have as much weight and consequence as an inhabitant of Jersey or Delaware; that it was contrary
to the feelings of the human mind; what the *large States* would *never*
submit to; that the *large States* would have *great objects* in view, in
which they would never permit the *smaller States* to thwart them;
that *equality of suffrage* was the rotten part of the constitution, and
that this was a happy time to get clear of it. In fine, that it was
the poison which contaminated our whole system, and the source
of all the evils we experienced.

[18] This, Sir, is the substance of the arguments, if arguments
they may be called, which were used in favor of *inequality of suffrage.*
Those who advocated the *equality of suffrage,* took the matter up
on the original principles of government; they urged, that all men,
considered in a state of nature, before any government is formed,
are equally free and independent, no one having any right or author-

ity to exercise power over another, and this *without any regard to difference in personal strength, understanding, or wealth.* That, when such individuals enter into government, they have *each* a right to an *equal voice* in its first formation, and afterwards have *each* a right to an *equal vote* in every matter which relates to their government. That, if it could be done conveniently, they have a right to exercise it in person. Where it cannot be done in person, but for convenience representatives are appointed, to act for them, *every person* has a right to an *equal vote* in choosing that representative; who is intrusted to do for the whole, that which the whole, if they could assemble, might do in person, and in the transaction of which, each would have an equal voice. That, if we were to admit, because a man was *more wise, more strong*, or *more wealthy*, he should be entitled to *more votes* than another, it would be *inconsistent with the freedom and liberty of that other*, and would reduce him to *slavery.* Suppose, for instance, ten individuals in a state of nature, about to enter into government, *nine* of whom are *equally wise, equally strong*, and *equally wealthy*, the *tenth is ten times as wise*, ten times *as strong*, or ten times as *rich;* if, for this reason, he is to have *ten votes* for *each vote of either of the others*, the *nine* might as well have *no vote at all;* since, though the *whole nine* might assent to a measure, yet the vote of *the tenth* would *countervail*, and *set aside all their votes.* If this *tenth* approved of what *they* wished to adopt, it would be well, but if he disapproved, he could prevent it; and in the same manner, he could carry into execution *any measure he wished, contrary to the opinion of all the others, he* having *ten votes*, and the other altogether *but nine.* It is evident, that, on these principles, *the nine* would have *no will or discretion of their own*, but must be *totally dependent* on the *will* and *discretion* of the *tenth;* to *him* they would be as *absolutely slaves*, as *any negro* is to his *master.* If he did not attempt to carry into execution any measures injurious to the *other nine*, it could only be said, that *they* had a *good master;* they would not be the *less slaves*, because *they* would be *totally dependent* on the *will* of *another*, and not on *their own will.* They might not *feel their chains*, but they would, notwithstanding, *wear them;* and whenever their *master* pleased, he might draw them so tight as to gall them to the bone. Hence it was urged, the *inequality of representation*, or giving to one man more votes than another, on account of his wealth, *&c.*, was *altogether inconsistent with the principles of liberty*, and in the *same proportion as it should be adopted*, in favor of *one* or *more*, in *that proportion are the others enslaved.* It was urged, that though every individual should have an equal voice in the government, yet, even the superior wealth, strength, or understanding, would give great and undue advantages to those who possessed them. That wealth attracts respect and attention; superior strength would cause the weaker and more feeble to be cautious how they offended, and to put up with small injuries rather than to engage in an unequal contest; in like manner, superior understanding would give its possessor many opportunities of profiting at the expense of the more ignorant.

[19] Having thus established these principles, with respect to the *rights of individuals* in a *state of nature*, and what is due to *each*, on entering into government, (principles established by every writer on liberty,) they proceeded to show, that *States*, when *once formed*, are considered, *with respect* to *each other*, as *individuals* in a state of nature; that, like individuals, each *State* is considered *equally free* and *equally independent*, the one having no right to exercise authority *over* the other, though more *strong, more wealthy*, or *abounding with more inhabitants*. That, when a number of *States* unite themselves under *a federal government*, the *same principles apply to them, as when a number of individual men* unite themselves under a *State government*. That every argument which shows *one man* ought not to have *more votes* than *another*, because he is *wiser, stronger*, or *wealthier*, proves that *one State* ought not to have *more votes* than *another*, because it is *stronger, richer*, or *more populous*. And, that by *giving one State*, or *one or two States, more votes* than the *others*, the *others* thereby are *enslaved to such State or States*, having the *greater number of votes*, in the *same manner* as in the case before put, of *individuals*, when one has *more votes than the others*. That the reason why each individual man in forming a State government should have an equal vote, is because each individual, before he enters into government, is *equally free* and *independent*. So *each State*, when *States enter* into a federal government, are entitled to an equal vote; because, before they entered into such federal government, *each State was equally free* and *equally independent*. That *adequate* representation of *men formed into a State government*, consists in *each man* having an *equal voice*, either personally, or, if by representatives, that he should have an equal voice in choosing the representatives. So, adequate representation of *States* in a *federal government*, consists in *each State* having an *equal voice*, either in person or by its representative, in every thing which relates to the federal government. That this *adequacy of representation is more important in a federal*, than in a *State* government, because the members of a State government, the *district* of which is *not very large*, have generally such a *common interest*, that laws can scarcely be made by *one* part, *oppressive* to *the others*, without their *suffering in common;* but the *different States*, composing an extensive federal empire, widely distant one from the other, may

have *interests so totally distinct,* that the one part might be *greatly benefited* by what would be *destructive to the other.*

[20] They were not satisfied by resting it on principles; they also appealed to history. They showed, that in the amphictyonic confederation of the Grecian cities, *each city,* however *different* in *wealth, strength,* and other *circumstances,* sent the same *number* of deputies, and had *each* an *equal voice* in every thing that related to the common concerns of Greece. It was shown, that in the seven provinces of the United Netherlands, and the confederated Cantons of Switzerland, *each Canton* and *each province* have an *equal vote,* although there are as great distinctions of wealth, strength, population, and extent of territory among those provinces and *those Cantons,* as among *these States.* It was said, that the maxim, that taxation and representation ought to go together, was true so far, that no person ought to be *taxed* who is not *represented,* but not in the extent insisted upon, to wit, that the *quantum* of *taxation* and *representation* ought to be the *same;* on the contrary, the *quantum* of *representation* depends upon the quantum of *freedom;* and therefore all, whether *individual States,* or individual *men,* who are *equally free,* have a right to *equal representation.* That to those who insist, that he who pays the greatest share of taxes ought to have the greatest number of votes, it is a sufficient answer to say, that *this rule* would be *destructive* of the *liberty* of the *others,* and would render *them slaves* to the *more rich* and *wealthy.* That if one man pays *more taxes* than another, it is because he has more wealth to be protected by government, and he receives greater benefits from the government. So if one State pays more to the federal government, it is because, as a State, she enjoys greater blessings from it; she has more wealth protected by it, or a greater number of inhabitants, whose rights are secured, and who share its advantages.

[21] It was urged, that, upon these principles, the Pennsylvanian, or inhabitant of a large State, was of as much consequence as the inhabitant of Jersey, Delaware, Maryland, or any other State. That *his consequence* was to be decided by his situation in his *own State;* that if he was *there* as *free,* if he had as great *share* in the forming of his own government, and in the making and executing its laws, as the inhabitants of those other States, then was he equally important, and of equal consequence. Suppose a confederation of States had never been adopted, but every State had remained absolutely in its independent situation, no person could, with propriety, say that the citizen of the large State was not as important as the citizen of the smaller; the confederation of the States cannot alter the case.

It was said, that in all transactions *between State and State*, the freedom, independence, importance, and consequence, even the individuality of each citizen of the different States, might with propriety be said to be swallowed up, or concentrated, in the independence, the freedom, and the individuality *of the State* of which they are citizens. That the *thirteen States* are *thirteen distinct political individual existences*, as to each other; that the *federal government* is, or *ought to be*, a government *over these thirteen political individual existences*, which form the members of that government; and that, as the *largest State*, is only a *single individual* of this government, it ought to have only *one vote;* the *smallest State*, also being *one individual member* of this government, ought also to have *one vote*. To those who urged, that for the States to have equal suffrage was contrary to the feelings of the human heart, it was answered, that it was admitted to be contrary to the feelings of *pride* and *ambition*, but those were feelings which ought not to be gratified at the expense of *freedom*.

[22] It was urged, that the position, that great States would have great objects in view, in which they would not suffer the less States to thwart them, was one of the strongest reasons why inequality of representation ought not to be admitted. If those great objects were not *inconsistent* with the *interest* of the *less States*, they would readily concur in them; but if they were *inconsistent* with the *interest* of a *majority of the States* composing the government, in that case *two or three States* ought not to have it in their power to *aggrandize themselves*, at the *expense of all the rest*. To those who alleged, that equality of suffrage in our federal government, was the poisonous source from which all our misfortunes flowed, it was answered, that the allegation was not founded in fact; that *equality of suffrage* had *never been complained of by the States, as a defect* in our federal system; that, among the eminent writers, foreigners and others, who had treated of the defects of our confederation, and proposed alterations, *none had proposed an alteration in this part of the system;* and members of the convention, both in and out of Congress, who advocated the equality of suffrage, called upon their opponents, both in and out of Congress, and challenged them to produce *one single instance* where a *bad measure* had been adopted, or a *good measure* had failed of adoption, in consequence of the States having an *equal vote;* on the contrary, they urged, that all our evils flowed from the *want of power* in the federal head, and that, let the *right of suffrage* in the States be *altered in any manner* whatever, if no *greater powers* were given to the government, the *same inconveniences would continue*.

[23] It was denied that the *equality of suffrage* was *originally*

agreed to on principles of *necessity* or *expediency;* on the contrary, that it was adopted on the principles of the *rights of men* and the *rights of States*, which were *then* well known, and which then influenced our conduct, although *now* they seem to be *forgotten.* For this, the Journals of Congress were appealed to; it was from them shown, that when the committee of Congress reported to that body the articles of confederation, the very first article, which became the subject of discussion, was that respecting equality of suffrage. That Virginia proposed divers modes of suffrage, all on the principle of inequality, which were *almost unanimously* rejected; that on the question for adopting the article, it passed, Virginia being the only State which voted in the *negative.* That, after the articles of confederation were submitted to the States, by them to be ratified, almost every State proposed certain amendments, which they instructed their delegates to endeavour to obtain before ratification, and that among all the amendments proposed, *not one State*, not even Virginia, proposed an amendment of that *article, securing the equality of suffrage,* — the most convincing proof it was agreed to and adopted, *not* from *necessity*, but *upon a full conviction*, that, according to the *principles of free governments*, the States *had a right to that equality of suffrage.*

[24] But, Sir, it was to no purpose that the futility of their objections were shown, when driven from the *pretence*, that the *equality of suffrage* had been originally agreed to on principles of *expediency* and *necessity;* the representatives of the *large States* persisting in a declaration, that they would never agree to admit the *smaller States* to an *equality* of suffrage. In answer to this, they were informed, and informed in terms the *most strong* and *energetic* that could *possibly be used*, that *we never would agree* to a system giving them the *undue influence* and *superiority* they proposed. That we would risk every possible consequence. That from anarchy and confusion, *order might arise.* That *slavery* was the *worst* that could ensue, and we considered the *system proposed* to be the *most complete, most abject* system of *slavery* that the wit of man ever devised, under the *pretence* of forming a government for free States. That we never would submit tamely and servilely, to a *present certain evil*, in dread of a *future*, which might be *imaginary;* that we were sensible the eyes of our country and the world were upon us. That we would not labor under the *imputation* of being *unwilling* to *form a strong* and *energetic federal government;* but we would publish the system which we *approved*, and also that which we *opposed*, and leave it to our country, and the world at large, to judge between us, who *best understood* the rights of *free men* and *free States*, and who

best advocated them; and to the same tribunal we would submit, who ought to be answerable for all the consequences, which might arise to the Union from the convention breaking up, without proposing any system to their constituents.   During this debate *we* were *threatened*, that if we did not agree to the system proposed, we *never* should have an *opportunity* of *meeting in convention* to deliberate on *another*, and this was frequently urged.   In *answer*, we called upon them to show *what was to prevent it*, and from what quarter was our danger to proceed; was it from a *foreign enemy?*   Our *distance* from Europe, and the *political situation* of that country, left us but little to fear.   Was there any *ambitious State or States*, who, in *violation of every sacred obligation*, was preparing to *enslave* the *other States*, and raise *itself* to *consequence* on the *ruin* of the *others?*   Or was there any such *ambitious individual?*   We did not apprehend it to be the case; but suppose it to be true, it rendered it the *more necessary*, that *we* should *sacredly guard against a system*, which might enable *all those ambitious views to be carried into effect, even under the sanction of the constitution and government.*   In fine, Sir, *all these threats* were treated with *contempt*, and they were told, that we apprehended but one *reason* to prevent the States meeting again in convention; that, when they discovered the part *this* convention had acted, and how much its members were *abusing the trust* reposed in them, the States would never trust *another* convention.   At length, Sir, after every argument had been exhausted by the advocates of equality of representation, the question was called, when a majority decided in favor of the inequality; Massachusetts, Pennsylvania, Virginia, North Carolina, South Carolina, and Georgia voting for it; Connecticut, New York, New Jersey, and Delaware against it; Maryland divided.   It may be thought surprising, Sir, that Georgia, a State *now small* and comparatively *trifling* in the Union, should advocate this system of *unequal representation*, giving up her *present* equality in the federal government, and sinking herself almost to total insignificance in the scale; but, Sir, it must be considered, that Georgia has the *most extensive* territory in the Union, being *larger* than the *whole island of Great Britain*, and *thirty* times as large as *Connecticut.* This system being designed to *preserve to the States their whole territory unbroken*, and to prevent the erection of new States within the territory of any of them, Georgia looked forward *when*, her *population* being increased in some measure *proportioned* to her *territory*, she should *rise* in the scale, and *give law* to the *other States*, and hence we found the delegation of Georgia warmly advocating the proposition of giving the States unequal representation.   Next day the question came on, with respect to the *inequality* of representation in the *second* branch, but little debate took place; the subject had been exhausted on the former question. On the votes being taken, Massachusetts, Pennsylvania, Virginia, North Carolina, and South Carolina, voted for the inequality. Connecticut, New York, New Jersey, Delaware, and Maryland * were in the negative. Georgia had only *two* representatives on the floor, *one* of whom (not, I believe, because he was against the measure, but from a conviction, that we would go home, and thereby dissolve the convention, before we would give up the question,) voted also in the negative, by which that State was divided. Thus, Sir, on this *great* and *important* part of the system, the convention being equally divided, five States for the measure, five against, and one divided, there was a tótal stand, and we did not seem very likely to proceed any further. At length, it was proposed, that a select committee should be balloted for, composed of a member from each State, which committee should endeavour to devise some mode of *conciliation* or *compromise.* I had the honor to be on that committee; we met, and discussed the subject of difference; the *one side* insisted on the *inequality* of suffrage in *both branches,* the *other* insisted on the *equality* in both; each party was tenacious of their sentiments, when it was found, that nothing could induce us to yield to the inequality in both *branches;* they at length proposed, by way of compromise, if *we* would *accede* to their wishes as to the *first* branch, *they* would *agree* to the equal representation in the *second* Branch. To this it was answered, that there was no merit in the proposal; it was only consenting, after they had struggled, to put *both their feet on our necks,* to take *one of them off,* provided we would consent to let them *keep* the *other on;* when they knew at the same time, that they could not put *one foot* on *our necks,* unless *we would consent to it* and that by being permitted to keep on that one foot, they should *afterwards be able to place the other foot on whenever they pleased.*

[25] They were also called on to inform us what security they could give us should we agree to this compromise, that they would *abide* by the plan of government formed upon it, *any longer* that it *suited their interests,* or they found it *expedient.* "The States have *a right* to an equality of representation. This is *secured* to *us* by our present articles of confederation; *we* are in *possession* of this privi-

* On this question, Mr. Martin was the only delegate for Maryland present, which circumstance secured the State a negative. Immediately after the question had been taken, and the President had declared the votes, Mr. Jenifer came into the convention, when Mr. King, from Massachusetts, valuing himself on Mr. Jenifer to divide the State of Maryland on this question, as he had on the former, requested of the President that the question might be put again; however, the motion was too extraordinary in its nature to meet with success.

lege — It is *now* to be *torn from us* — What security can you give us, that, when you get the *power* the *proposed system* will give you, when you have *men* and *money*, that you will not *force from* the States that *equality* of suffrage in the *second branch*, which you *now* deny to be their right, and *only give up* from *absolute necessity?*' Will you tell us we ought to trust you because you *now enter into a solemn compact with us?* This you have done *before*, and *now* treat with the *utmost contempt.* — Will you *now* make an appeal to the Supreme Being, and call on him to guarantee your observance of this compact? The *same* you have *formerly done*, for your observance of the articles of confederation, which you are *now violating* in the most *wanton* manner.

[26] "The same reasons, which you *now* urge for destroying our *present* federal government, may be urged for *abolishing the system*, which you now propose to adopt; and as the *method prescribed* by the *articles* of confederation is *now totally disregarded* by you, as *little regard* may be shown by you to the *rules prescribed* for the amendment of the *new system*, whenever, having obtained power by the government, you shall *hereafter* be pleased either to *discard it entirely*, or so to *alter* it as to give *yourselves* all that *superiority*, which *you* have *now contended* for, and *to obtain* which you have shown yourselves disposed to *hazard* the Union." — Such, Sir, was the language used on that occasion, and they were told, that, as we could not *possibly* have a *greater tie* on them for their observance of the new system than we had for their observance of the articles of confederation, which had proved *totally insufficient*, it would be *wrong* and *imprudent* to *confide in them.* — It was further observed, that the inequality of the representation would be *daily increasing.* — — — That many of the States, whose territory was confined and whose population was at the time large in proportion to their territory, would probably, twenty, thirty, or forty years hence, have no more representatives than at the introduction of the government; whereas, the States having extensive territory, where lands are to be procured cheap, would be daily increasing in the number of their inhabitants, not only from propagation, but from the *emigration* of the inhabitants of the *other States*, and would have soon double, or perhaps treble the number of representatives that they are to have at first, and thereby enormously *increase* their *influence* in the national councils. However, the *majority* of the select committee at length agreed to a series of propositions, by way of compromise, part of which related to the representation in the first branch, nearly as the system is now published: And part of them to the second branch, securing, in that, equal representation, and reported them as a com-

promise, upon the *express terms*, that they were *wholly* to be *adopted*, or *wholly* to be *rejected:* upon this compromise, a great number of the members so far engaged themselves, that, if the system was progressed upon agreeable to the terms of compromise, they would lend it their names, by signing it, and would not actively oppose it, if their States should appear inclined to adopt it. — Some, however, in which number was myself, who joined in the report, and agreed to proceed upon those principles, and see *what kind of a system* would *ultimately* be formed upon it, yet reserved to themselves, in the most *explicit manner*, the right of *finally* giving a *solemn dissent* to the system, if it was thought by them *inconsistent* with the *freedom* and *happiness* of their country. This, Sir, will account why the members of the convention so *generally* signed their names to the system; not because they thought it a *proper one;* not because they *thoroughly approved*, or were *unanimous* for it; but because they thought it *better* than the system attempted to be forced upon them. This report of the select committee was after long dissension, adopted by a majority of the convention, and the system was proceeded in accordingly. I believe near a fortnight, perhaps more, was spent in the discussion of this business, during which we were on the verge of dissolution, scarce held together by the strength of an hair, though the public papers were announcing our extreme unanimity.

[27] Mr. Speaker, I think it my duty to observe, that, during this *struggle* to prevent the *large* States from having *all power* in their hands, which had nearly terminated in a dissolution of the convention, it did not appear to me, that either of those illustrious characters, the honorable Mr. *Washington* or the President of the State of Pennsylvania, was disposed to favor the claims of the *smaller States*, against the *undue superiority* attempted by the large States; on the contrary, the Honorable President of Pennsylvania was a *member* of the *committee* of *compromise*, and there *advocated* the right of the *large States* to an *inequality* in *both branches*, and only *ultimately conceded* it in the *second branch* on the *principle of conciliation*, when it was found no other terms would be accepted. This, Sir, I think it my duty to mention, for the *consideration of those*, who endeavour to *prop up a dangerous* and *defective* system by *great names;* Soon after this period, the Honorable Mr. *Yates* and Mr. *Lansing*, of New York, left us — they had uniformly opposed the system, and, I *believe*, despairing of getting a *proper one* brought forward, or of *rendering any real service*, they returned no more.[1] The *propositions* reported by the committee of the *whole house* hav‑

---

[1] See Appendix A, CLXXXV.

ing been fully discussed by the convention, and, with many alterations having been agreed to by a majority, a committee of five, were
appointed to *detail* the system, according to the principles contained
in what had been agreed to by that majority — This was likely to
require some time, and the convention adjourned for eight or ten
days. — Before the adjournment, I moved for liberty to be given
to the different members to take *correct copies* of the *propositions*,
to which the convention had then agreed, in order that during the
recess of the convention, we might have an opportunity of *considering*
them, and, if it should be thought that any *alterations* or *amendments*
were *necessary*, that we might be *prepared* against the convention
met, to bring them forward for discussion. But, Sir, the *same
spirit*, which caused *our doors to be shut*, our *proceedings* to be *kept
secret*, — *our journals to be locked up*, — and *every avenue, as far as
possible, to be shut* to *public information*, prevailed also in this case;
and the proposal, so *reasonable* and *necessary*, was *rejected* by a *majority* of the convention; thereby *precluding even the members themselves from the necessary means of information and deliberation* on the
important business in which they were engaged.

[28] It has been observed, Mr. Speaker, by my honorable colleagues, that the debate respecting the mode of representation, was
productive of considerable warmth; this observation is true. But,
Sir, it is equally true, that, if we could have *tamely* and *servilely* consented to be *bound in chains*, and *meanly condescended* to *assist* in
riveting them fast, we might have avoided all that warmth, and have
proceeded with as much calmness and coolness as any Stoic could
have wished.

[29] Having thus, Sir, given the honorable members of this
house a short history of some interesting parts of our proceedings,
I shall beg leave to take up the *system published* by the *convention*,
and shall request your indulgence, while I make some observations
on different parts of it, and give you such further information as may
be in my power. (Here Mr. Martin read the *first section* of the *first
article*, and then proceeded.) With respect to this part of the system, Mr. Speaker, there was a diversity of sentiment; those who
were for *two* branches in the legislature, a House of Representatives
and a Senate, urged the necessity of a *second branch*, to serve as a
check upon the *first*, and used all those trite and common-place arguments which may be proper and just, when applied to the formation
of a *State government*, over *individuals* variously distinguished in
their habits and manners, fortune and rank; where a body chosen
in a select manner, respectable for their wealth and dignity, may be
necessary, frequently, to prevent the hasty and rash measures of a

representation more popular. But, on the other side, it was urged, that none of those arguments could with propriety be *applied* to the formation of a *federal government* over a number of *independent States;* that it is the *State governments* which are to watch over and protect the *rights* of the *individual,* whether *rich* or *poor,* or of *moderate circumstances,* and in which the *democratic* and *aristocratic influence* or principles are to be so *blended, modified,* and *checked,* as to prevent *oppression* and *injury;* that the federal government is to guard and protect the *States* and their *rights,* and to regulate *their common concerns;* that a *federal government* is formed by the *States,* as *States,* that is, in their *sovereign* capacities, in the same manner as *treaties* and *alliances* are formed; that *sovereignties,* considered as such, cannot be said to have jarring interests or principles, the one aristocratic, and the other democratic; but that the principles of a *sovereignty,* considered as a sovereignty, are the *same,* whether that sovereignty is monarchical, aristocratical, democratical, or mixed — That the *history of mankind* doth not furnish *an instance,* from its *earliest* period to the *present* time, of a *federal government* constituted of *two distinct branches;* that the *members* of the *federal* government, if appointed by the *States,* in their *State capacities* that is, by their *legislatures,* as they *ought,* would be *select in their choice,* and, coming from *different States,* having different *interests* and *views,* this *difference* of interests and views would always be a *sufficient check* over the *whole.* And it was shewn, that even Adams, who, the reviewers have justly observed, appears to be as fond of *checks* and *balances* as Lord Chesterfield of the *Graces,* even *he* declares, that a council consisting of *one* branch has always been found *sufficient* in a *federal* government.

[30] It was urged, that the government we were forming was not in reality a *federal,* but a *national* government; not founded on the principles of the *preservation,* but the abolition or consolidation of all *State governments;* that we appeared *totally to have forgot* the business for which we were sent, and the situation of the country for which we were preparing our system — That we had not been sent to form a government over the *inhabitants* of America, considered as *individuals;* that as individuals, they were all subject to their respective State governments, which governments would still remain, though the federal government should be dissolved; that the *system of government* we were *entrusted* to prepare, was a government over *these thirteen States;* but that, in our proceedings, we adopted principles which would be right and proper, *only* on the supposition that there were *no State governments at all,* but that *all the inhabitants* of this *extensive continent* were, in their *individual*

capacity, without government, and in a *state of nature;* that, accordingly, the system proposes the legislature to consist of *two branches,* the *one* to be drawn from the *people at large,* immediately in their *individual capacity,* the *other* to be chosen in a *more select manner,* as a *check* upon the *first.* It is, in its very *introduction,* declared to be a compact between the people of the United States, as individuals; and it is to be ratified by the *people* at large, in their capacity *as individuals;* all which it was said would be quite right and proper, if there were *no State governments,* if *all the people* of this continent were in a *state of nature,* and we were forming one *national government for them as individuals;* and is nearly the same as was done in most of the States when they formed their governments *over the people* who compose them.

[31] Whereas it was urged, that the principles on which a *federal* government over *States* ought to be *constructed* and *ratified,* are the *reverse;* that instead of the legislature consisting of *two* branches, *one* branch was sufficient, whether examined by the *dictates* of reason, or the *experience* of *ages;* that the *representation,* instead of being drawn from the *people* at large, as *individuals,* ought to be drawn from the *States as States,* in their *sovereign* capacity; that, in a *federal* government, the *parties* to the compact are not the *people,* as *individuals,* but the States, as States; and that it is by the *States* as States, in their *sovereign* capacity, that the system of government ought to be *ratified,* and not by the *people, as individuals.*

[32] It was further said, that, in a *federal* government over States *equally* free, sovereign, and independent, *every State* ought to have an equal share in *making* the *federal laws* or *regulations,* in deciding upon them, and in *carrying them into execution; neither* of which was the case in this system, but the *reverse;* the States not having an *equal voice* in the *legislature,* nor in the *appointment* of the *executive,* the *judges,* and the *other officers of government.* It was insisted, that, in the *whole* system, there was but *one federal* feature, — the appointment of the senators by the States in their sovereign capacity, that is, by their legislatures, and the equality of suffrage in that branch; but it was said, that *this feature* was only *federal* in *appearance.*

[33] To prove *this,* and the Senate *as constituted* could not be a *security* for the *protection* and *preservation* of the State governments, and that the *senators* could not be justly considered the *representatives* of the *States, as States,* it was observed, that upon *just principles* of *representation,* the *representative* ought to *speak* the sentiments of his *constituents,* and ought to *vote* in the *same manner* that his *constituents* would do, (as far as he can judge,) provided his constituents were acting in *person,* and had the same knowledge

and information with himself; and, therefore, that the *representative* ought to be *dependent* on his *constituents*, and *answerable* to them; that the connexion between the *representative* and the *represented* ought to be as *near* and as *close* as *possible*. According to these principles, Mr. Speaker, in this State it is provided by *its constitution*, that the representatives in Congress shall be chosen *annually*, shall be paid by the *State*, and shall be subject to *recall* even within the year; so *cautiously* has our *constitution* guarded against an *abuse* of the trust reposed in our representatives in the federal government; whereas, by the *third* and *sixth* section of the *first* article of this new system, the senators are to be chosen for *six* years, instead of being chosen *annually*; instead of being paid by *their States*, who send them, *they*, in conjunction with the other branch, are to *pay themselves*, out of the treasury of the United States; and are not liable to be *recalled* during the period for which they are chosen. Thus, Sir, for *six years* the senators are rendered totally and absolutely *independent* of *their States*, of *whom* they ought to be the *representatives*, without *any bond* or *tie* between them. During *that time*, they may join in measures *ruinous* and *destructive* to *their States*, even such as should *totally annihilate* their *State governments*, and their States *cannot recall* them, *nor exercise any control over them*.

[34] Another consideration, Mr. Speaker, it was thought ought to have *great weight*, to prove that the *smaller* States cannot *depend* on the *Senate* for the *preservation* of *their rights*, either against *large* and *ambitious States*, or against an *ambitious and aspiring President*. The Senate, Sir, is so constituted, that they are not only to compose one branch of the legislature, but, by the second section of the second article, they are to *compose a privy council for the President;* hence, it will be necessary, that they should be, in a great measure, a *permanent* body, *constantly residing* at the seat of government. *Seven* years are esteemed for the life of a man; it can hardly be supposed, that a senator, especially from the States remote from the seat of empire, will accept of an appointment which must *estrange* him for *six years from his State*, without giving up, to a great degree, his prospects in his *own State*. If he has a family, he will take his family with him to the place where the government shall be fixed; *that* will become his *home*, and there is every reason to expect, that his *future* views and prospects will *centre* in the *favors* and *emoluments* of the *general government*, or of the government of *that State* where the seat of empire is established. In *either* case, he is *lost* to his *own State*. If he places his future prospects in the favors and emoluments of the *general government*, he will become the *dependent* and

creature of the *President*, as the system *enables* a senator to be *appointed to offices*, and, without the *nomination* of the President, *no appointment can take place;* as *such*, he will favor the wishes of the President, and concur in his measures; who, if he has no *ambitious views of his own* to gratify, may be *too favorable* to the *ambitious views* of the *large States*, who will have an *undue share* in his *original appointment*, and *on whom* he will be *more dependent* afterwards than on the States which are smaller. If the senator places his future prospects in that *State* where the seat of empire is fixed, from that time he will be, in every question wherein its particular interest may be concerned, the *representative of that State*, not of *his own.*

[35] But even this provision, *apparently* for the *security* of the *State governments, inadequate* as it is, is *entirely left* at the *mercy* of the general government; for, by the fourth section of the first article, it is *expressly provided,* that the *Congress* shall have a power to *make and alter* all regulations concerning the *time* and manner of *holding elections for senators;* a provision *expressly looking forward to,* and, *I have no doubt designed* for, the *utter extinction* and *abolition of all State governments;* nor will this, I believe, be doubted by any person, when I inform you, that some of the warm advocates and patrons of the system, in convention, *strenuously opposed* the *choice of* the senators by the *State legislatures, insisting,* that *the State governments ought not to be introduced in any manner,* so as to be *component parts of,* or *instruments for carrying into execution,* the general government. Nay, so far were the friends of the system from pretending that they meant it, or considered it as a *federal* system, that on the question being proposed, "that a union of the States, merely federal, ought to be the sole object of the exercise of the powers vested in the convention," it was negatived by a majority of the members, and it was resolved "that a national government ought to be formed." Afterwards the word "*national*" was struck out by them, because they thought the *word* might tend to *alarm;* and although, *now,* they who *advocate* the system pretend to call themselves *federalists,* in convention the distinction was quite the reverse; those who *opposed* the system were *there* considered and styled the *federal party,* those who advocated it, the *antifederal.*

[36] Viewing it as a *national,* not a *federal* government, as calculated and designed not to *protect* and *preserve,* but to *abolish* and *annihilate* the *State governments,* it was opposed for the following reasons. It was said, that this continent was *much too extensive* for *one national* government, which should have sufficient *power* and *energy* to *pervade* and hold in *obedience* and subjection all its *parts,*

consistent with the *enjoyment* and *preservation* of *liberty* — that the
genius and habits of the people of America were opposed to such
a government. That during their connexion with Great Britain,
they had been accustomed to have all their concerns transacted
within a narrow circle, their *colonial district;* they had been accustomed to have their seats of government near them, to which they
might have access, without much inconvenience, when their business should require it — That, at *this time*, we find, if a *county* is
rather large, the people complain of the inconvenience, and clamor
for a division of their county, or for a removal of the place where
their courts are held, so as to render it more central and convenient.
That in those States, the territory of which is extensive, as soon as
the population increases remote from the seat of government, the
inhabitants are urgent for the removal of the seat of their government, or to be erected into a new State. As a proof of this, the
inhabitants of the western parts of Virginia and North Carolina, of
Vermont and the province of Maine, were instances; even the inhabitants of the western parts of Pennsylvania, who, it is said,
already seriously look forward to the time when they shall either
be erected into a new State, or have their seat of government removed
to the Susquehanna. If the inhabitants of the different States
consider it as a grievance to attend a *county court*, or the *seat* of *their
own government*, when a little inconvenient, can it be supposed they
would ever *submit* to have a *national government* established, the
seat of which would be *more than a thousand miles removed from
some of them?*

[37] It was insisted, that governments of a *republican nature* are
those *best* calculated to *preserve* the *freedom* and happiness of the
citizen; that governments of *this kind* are *only calculated* for a territory but *small* in its extent; that the *only* method by which an extensive continent like America could be *connected* and *united* together,
consistent with the principles of freedom, must be by having a *number* of *strong* and *energetic State governments* for securing and protecting the rights of *individuals* forming those governments, and
for regulating all *their* concerns; and a strong, energetic *federal*
government *over those States,* for the protection and preservation,
and for regulating the *common* concerns of the State. It was further
insisted, that, even if it was possible to effect a total abolition of
the State governments at this time, and to establish one general
government over the people of America, *it could not long subsist,*
but in a *little time* would again be broken into a *variety* of governments of a *smaller extent,* similar, in some manner, to the present
situation of this continent; the principal difference, in all proba-

bìlity, would be, that the governments *so established*, being affected by some *violent convulsion*, might not be formed on principles so *favorable* to *liberty* as those of our present State governments. That *this* ought to be an *important consideration* to such of the States as had *excellent* governments, which was the case with Maryland and most others, whatever it might be to persons who *disapproving* of their particular State government, would be willing to *hazard* every thing to overturn and *destroy* it. These reasons, Sir, influenced *me* to *vote* against *two* branches in the legislature, and against *every part* of the system which was *repugnant* to the principles of a *federal* government.[1] Nor was there a single argument urged, or reason assigned, which to my mind was satisfactory, to prove, that a good government on *federal* principles was unattainable; the whole of their arguments only proving, what none of us controverted, that our federal government *as originally formed*, was defective, and *wanted amendment*. However, a majority of the convention hastily and inconsiderately, without condescending to make a fair trial, in their great wisdom, decided that a kind of government, which a Montesquieu and a Price have declared the best calculated of any to preserve internal liberty, and to enjoy external strength and security, and the only one by which a large continent can be connected and united, consistently with the principles of liberty, was totally impracticable; and they acted accordingly.

[38] With respect to that part of the second section of the *first* article, which relates to the *apportionment of representation* and *direct taxation*, there were considerable objections made to it, besides the great objection of *inequality*. It was urged, that no principle could justify taking *slaves* into computation in *apportioning* the number of *representatives* a State should have in the government. That it involved the absurdity of *increasing* the power of a State in making laws for *freemen* in *proportion* as that State *violated* the *rights of freedom*. That it might be proper to take slaves into consideration, when *taxes* were to be apportioned, because it had a tendency to *discourage slavery;* but to take them into account in *giving representation* tended to *encourage* the *slave-trade*, and to make it the *interest* of the States to *continue* that *infamous traffic*. That slaves could not be taken into account *as men* or *citizens*, because they were not admitted to the *rights of citizens*, in the States which adopted or continued slavery. If they were to be taken into account as *property*, it was asked, what peculiar circumstance should render this property, (of *all others* the most *odious* in its nature,) entitled

---

[1] See Appendix A, CCXXIII.

to the *high privilege* of conferring *consequence* and *power* in the *government* to its possessors, rather than *any other property?* and why *slaves* should, as property, be taken into account, rather than *horses, cattle, mules,* or any *other species* — and it was observed by an honorable member from Massachusetts, that he considered it as dishonorable and humiliating to enter into compact with the *slaves* of the *Southern States,* as it would with the *horses* and *mules* of the *Eastern.* It was also objected, that the *numbers* of representatives appointed by this section, to be sent by the particular States to compose the *first legislature,* were not precisely *agreeable* to the *rule* of representation adopted by this system, and that the numbers in this section are *artfully lessened* for the *large* States, while the smaller States have their *full proportion,* in order to prevent the *undue influence* which the *large* States will have in the government from being *too apparent;* and I think, Mr. Speaker, that this objection is *well founded.* I have taken some pains to obtain information of the number of freemen and slaves in the different States, and I have reason to believe, that, if the estimate was now taken, which is directed, and one delegate to be sent for every thirty thousand inhabitants, Virginia would have at least *twelve* delegates, Massachusetts *eleven,* and Pennsylvania *ten,* instead of the number *stated* in *this section;* whereas the *other States,* I believe, would not have more than the number there allowed them, nor would Georgia, most probably, at present, send more than *two.* If I am right, Mr. Speaker, upon the enumeration being made, and the representation being apportioned according to the rule prescribed, the *whole number* of delegates would be *seventy-one, thirty-six* of which would be a *quorum* to do business; the delegates of Virginia, Massachusetts, and Pennsylvania, would amount to *thirty-three* of that quorum. Those three States will, therefore, have *much more* than *equal power* and influence in *making the* laws and regulations, which are to affect this continent, and will have a *moral certainty* of *preventing* any laws or regulations which *they disapprove,* although they might be thought *ever so necessary* by *a great majority* of the States. It was further objected, that even if the States who had most inhabitants ought to have a greater number of delegates, yet the *number of delegates* ought not to be in *exact proportion* to the *number of inhabitants,* because the influence and power of those States whose delegates are numerous, will be *greater,* when compared to the influence and power of the other States, than the *proportion* which the numbers of their delegates bear to each other; as, for instance, though Delaware has *one* delegate, and Virginia but *ten,* yet Virginia has *more* than *ten times* as much *power* and *influence* in the government as

Delaware; to prove this, it was observed, that *Virginia* would have a *much greater* chance to carry any measure, than *any number of States* whose delegates were altogether ten, (suppose the States of Delaware, Connecticut, Rhode Island, and New Hampshire,) since the *ten delegates* from Virginia, in every thing that related to the interest of that State, would *act in union,* and *move one solid and compact body;* whereas, the *delegates of these four States,* though collectively *equal* in number to those from Virginia, coming from *different* States, having different *interests,* will be *less likely* to harmonize and move in concert. As a further proof, it was said, that Virginia, as the system is now reported, by uniting with her the delegates of *four* other States, can carry a question *against* the sense and interest of *eight* States, by *sixty-four* different combinations; the *four States* voting with Virginia being every time *so far different,* as not to be composed of the *same four;* whereas, the State of Delaware can only, by uniting four other States with her, carry a measure against the sense of eight States, by *two* different combinations, — a mathematical proof, that the State of *Virginia* has *thirty-two* times greater chance of carrying a measure, against the sense of eight States, than *Delaware,* although Virginia has only *ten times* as many delegates.

[39] It was also shown, that the idea was totally fallacious, which was attempted to be maintained, that, if a State had *one thirteenth* part of the *numbers composing the delegation in this system,* such State would have *as much influence* as under the articles of confederation. To prove the fallacy of this idea, it was shown, that, under the articles of confederation, the State of Maryland had but *one vote in thirteen,* yet no measure could be carried against her interests without *seven States,* a majority of the whole, concurring in it; whereas in this system, though Maryland has *six* votes, which is more than the *proportion* of *one in thirteen,* yet *five* States may, in a *variety of combinations,* carry a question *against* her interest, though seven other States concur with her; and *six* States, by a *much greater* number of combinations, may carry a measure against *Maryland, united with six other States.* I shall here, Sir, just observe, that, as the committee of detail reported the system, the delegates from the different States were to be *one* for every *forty thousand* inhabitants; it *was* afterwards altered to one for every *thirty* thousand. This alteration was made after I left the convention, at the instance of whom I know not; but it is evident, that the alteration is in favor of *the States* which have large and *extensive* territory, to increase their power and influence in the government, and to the injury of the *smaller States,* — since it is the States of *extensive territory,* who

will *most speedily* increase the number of their *inhabitants*, as before
has been observed, and will, therefore, most speedily procure an increase to the number of *their* delegates. By this alteration, Virginia, North Carolina, or Georgia, by obtaining one hundred and
twenty thousand additional inhabitants, will be entitled to *four*
additional delegates; whereas, such State would only have been
entitled to *three*, if *forty thousand* had *remained* the number by which
to apportion the delegation. As to that part of this section that relates to direct taxation, there was also an objection, for the following
reasons. It was said, that a *large sum* of money was to be brought
into the national treasury by the *duties* on commerce, which would
be almost *wholly* paid by the *commercial States;* it would be *unequal*
and *unjust,* that the sum which was necessary to be raised by *direct
taxation,* should be apportioned *equally* upon all the States, obliging
the commercial States to pay as large a share of the revenue arising
therefrom, as the States from whom no revenue had been drawn by
imposts; since the wealth and industry of the inhabitants of the
commercial States will, in the first place, be severely taxed through
their commerce, and afterwards be *equally taxed* with the industry
and wealth of the inhabitants of the other States, *who have paid no
part* of that *revenue;* so that, by this provision, the inhabitants
of the commercial States are in this system obliged to bear an unreasonable and disproportionate share in the expenses of the Union,
and the payment of that foreign and domestic debt, which was
incurred not more for the benefit of the commercial than of the
other States.

[40] In the *sixth* section of the *first* article, it is provided, that
senators and representatives may be appointed to any civil office
under the authority of the United States, except such as shall have
been created, or the emoluments of which have been increased, during the time for which they were elected. Upon this subject, Sir,
there was a great diversity of sentiment among the members of the
convention. As the propositions were reported by the committee
of the whole House, a senator or representative could not be appointed
to *any office* under a *particular State,* or under the *United States,*
during the time for which they were chosen, nor to any office under
the United States, until one year after the expiration of that time.
It was said, and, in my opinion justly, that no good reason could
be assigned, why a senator or representative should be incapacitated
to hold an office in *his own* government, since it can only bind him
more closely to his State, and attach him the more to its interests,
which, as its representative, he is bound to consult and sacredly
guard, as far as is consistent with the welfare of the Union; and

therefore, at most, would only add the additional motive of gratitude for discharging his duty; and, according to this idea, the clause which prevented senators or delegates from holding offices in their own States, was rejected by a considerable majority. But, Sir, we sacredly endeavoured to preserve all that part of the resolution which prevented them from being *eligible* to *offices* under the *United States;* as we considered it *essentially necessary* to preserve the *integrity, independence,* and *dignity* of the legislature, and to secure its members from *corruption.*

[41] I was in the number of those who were extremely solicitous to preserve this part of the report; but there was a powerful opposition made by such as wished the members of the legislature to be eligible to offices under the United States. *Three* different times did they attempt to procure an alteration, and *as often* failed; a majority firmly adhering to the resolution as reported by the committee — However, an alteration was at length, by dint of perseverance, obtained, even within the last twelve days of the convention; for it happened after I left Philadelphia. As to the exception, that they cannot be appointed to offices created by themselves, or the emoluments of which are by themselves increased, it is certainly of little consequence, since they may easily evade it by creating new offices, to which may be appointed the persons who fill the offices before created, and thereby vacancies will be made, which may be filled by the members who, for that purpose, have created the new offices.

[42] It is true, the acceptance of an office vacates their seat, nor can they be reëlected during their continuance in office. But it was said, that the evil would first take place; that the price for the office would be paid before it was obtained; that vacating the seat of the person who was appointed to office, made way for the admission of a new member, who would come there as desirous to obtain an office as he whom he succeeded, and as ready to pay the price necessary to obtain it; in fine, that it would be only driving away the flies who were *filled,* to make room for those that were *hungry;* and as the system is now reported, the *President* having the power to *nominate* to *all offices,* it must be evident, that there is *no possible security* for the *integrity* and *independence* of the *legislature,* but that they are most *unduly* placed under the *influence* of the *President,* and exposed to *bribery* and *corruption.*

[43] The seventh *section* of this article was also the subject of contest. It was thought by many members of the convention, that it was very wrong to confine the origination of all revenue bills to the House of Representatives, since the members of the Senate

will be chosen by the people, as well as the members of the House of Delegates, if not *immediately*, yet *mediately*, being chosen by the members of the State legislature, which members are elected by the *people;* and that it makes no real difference, whether we do a thing in *person*, or by a *deputy* or agent *appointed* by *him* for *that purpose.*

[44] That no argument can be drawn from the House of Lords in the British constitution, since they are neither mediately nor immediately the representatives of the people, but are one of the *three estates* composing that kingdom, having *hereditary rights and privileges distinct* from, and *independent of*, the *people.*

[45] That it may, and probably will, be a future source of dispute and controversy between the two branches, what are or are not revenue bills, and the more so as they are not *defined* in the constitution; which controversies may be difficult to settle, and may become serious in their consequences, there being no power in the constitution to decide upon, or authorized, in cases of absolute necessity, to terminate them by a prorogation or dissolution of either of the branches; a remedy provided in the British constitution, where the King has that power, which has been found necessary at times to be exercised, in case of violent dissensions between the Lords and Commons on the subject of money bills.

[46] That every regulation of commerce, every law relative to excises, stamps, the post-office, the imposing of taxes and their collection, the creation of courts and offices; in fine, every law for the Union, if enforced by any pecuniary sanctions, as they would tend to bring money into the continental treasury, might, and no doubt would, be considered a revenue act; that, consequently, the Senate, the members of which will, it may be presumed, be the most select in their choice, and consist of men the most enlightened, and of the greatest abilities, who, from the duration of their appointment and the permanency of their body, will probably be best acquainted with the common concerns of the States, and with the means of providing for them, will be rendered almost useless as a part of the legislature; and that they will have but little to do in that capacity, except patiently to wait the proceedings of the House of Representatives, and afterwards examine and approve, or propose amendments.

[47] There were also objections to that part of this section which relates to the *negative* of the *President*. There were some who thought no good reason could be assigned for giving the President a negative of *any kind*. Upon the principle of a check to the proceedings of the legislature, it was said to be unnecessary; that the two branches having a control over each other's proceedings, and

the Senate being chosen by the State legislatures, and being composed of members from the *different States*, there would always be a sufficient guard against measures being *hastily* or *rashly* adopted; that the *President was* not likely to have *more wisdom* or *integrity* than the *senators*, or *any of them*, or to *better know* or *consult* the interest of the States, than *any member* of the Senate, so as to be entitled to a negative on that principle; and as to the precedent from the British constitution, (for we were eternally troubled with arguments and precedents from the British government,) it was said it would not apply. The King of Great Britain there composed *one* of the *three estates* of the kingdom; *he* was possessed of *rights* and *privileges* as such, *distinct from* the Lords and Commons; *rights* and *privileges* which *descended* to his *heirs*, and were inheritable by them; that, for the *preservation* of these, it was *necessary* he should have a negative, but that this was not the case with the President of the United States, who was no more than an *officer* of government, the *sovereignty* was not in *him*, but in the *legislature*. And it was further urged, even if he was allowed a negative, it ought not to be of so great extent as that given by the system, since *his single voice* is to countervail the *whole* of *either* branch, and any number *less* than *two thirds* of the other; however, a majority of the convention was of a different opinion, and adopted it as it now makes a part of the system.

[48] By the *eighth* section of this article, Congress is to have power to *lay* and *collect taxes, duties, imposts,* and *excises.* When we met in convention after our adjournment, to receive the report of the committee of detail, the members of that committee were requested to inform us, what powers were meant to be vested in Congress by the word *duties* in this section, since the word *imposts* extended to duties on goods *imported*, and by another part of the system no duties on *exports* were to be laid. In answer to this inquiry, we were informed, that it was meant to give the general government the power of laying *stamp* duties on paper, parchment, and vellum. We then proposed to have the power inserted in *express words*, lest disputes hereafter might arise on the subject, and that the meaning might be understood by *all* who were to be *affected* by it; but to this it was objected, because it was said, that the word stamp would probably sound *odiously* in the ears of many of the inhabitants, and be a cause of objection. By the power of imposing *stamp duties*, the Congress will have a *right* to declare, that no *wills, deeds,* or other *instruments* of writing shall be *good and valid*, without being *stamped;* that, without being reduced to *writing* and *being stamped*, no *bargain, sale, transfer of property*, or *contract* of any

kind or nature whatsoever, shall be *binding;* and also that no *exempli-fications of records, depositions,* or *probates* of any kind, shall be received in evidence, unless they have the same solemnity. They may likewise oblige all proceedings of a *judicial* nature to be *stamped,* to give them effect. Those stamp duties may be imposed to any amount they please; and, under the pretence of *securing* the *collection* of these duties, and to prevent the laws which imposed them from being evaded, the Congress may bring the *decision* of all *questions* relating to the *conveyance, disposition,* and *rights* of *property,* and *every question* relating to *contracts* between man and man, into the *courts* of the *general government* — Their inferior courts in the *first* instance, and the *superior* court by *appeal.* By the power to lay and collect imposts, they may impose duties on *any* or *every* article of *commerce* imported into these States, to what amount they please. By the power to lay *excises,* a power very *odious* in its nature, since it authorizes officers to go into your *houses,* your *kitchens,* your *cellars,* and to examine into your *private concerns,* the Congress may impose *duties* on every *article* of *use* or *consumption,* — on the *food* that we *eat,* on the *liquors* we *drink,* on the *clothes* that we *wear,* the *glass* which *enlightens* our *houses,* or the *hearths* necessary for our *warmth* and *comfort.* By the power to lay and collect taxes, they may proceed to *direct taxation* on *every individual,* either by a *capitation* tax on their *heads,* or an *assessment* on their *property.* By this part of the section therefore, the government has power to lay what duties they please on *goods imported;* to lay what duties they please, afterwards, on whatever we *use* or *consume;* to impose *stamp duties* to what amount they please, and in whatever case they please; afterwards to impose on the people *direct taxes,* by capitation tax, or by assessment, to what amount they choose; and thus to *sluice* them at *every vein,* as long as they have a *drop* of blood, without any control, limitation, or restraint; while *all the officers* for *collecting* these taxes, stamp duties, imposts, and excises, are to be appointed by the *general government,* under its directions, not accountable to the *States;* nor is there *even* a security, that they shall be *citizens* of the *respective States* in which they are to exercise their offices. At the same time, the construction of *every law imposing* any and all these taxes and duties, and *directing* the collection of them, and *every question* arising thereon, and on the *conduct* of the *officers* appointed to execute these laws and to collect *these taxes* and duties, so various in their kinds, *are taken away* from the courts of justice of the *different States,* and *confined* to the courts of the *general government,* there to be *heard* and *determined* by judges holding their offices under the appointment *not* of the *States,* but of the *general government.*

[49] Many of the members, and myself among the number, thought, that the *States* were much *better judges* of the circumstances of their citizens, and what sum of money could be collected from them by *direct taxation*, and of the manner in which it could be raised, with the *greatest ease* and *convenience* to their citizens, than the *general government* could be; and that the general government *ought* not to have the power of laying direct taxes in any case but in that of the *delinquency* of a State. Agreeably to this sentiment, I brought in a proposition, on which a vote of the convention was taken. The proposition was as follows: "And whenever the legislature of the United States shall find it necessary that *revenue* should be raised by *direct taxation*, having apportioned the same by the above rule, *requisitions* shall be made of the respective States to pay into the continental treasury their respective quotas, *within a time* in the said requisition to be specified; and in case of any of the States *failing* to comply with such requisition, then, and *then only*, to have power to devise and pass acts directing the mode and authorizing the collection of the same." Had this proposition been acceded to, the *dangerous* and *oppressive* power in the *general government*, of imposing *direct taxes* on the inhabitants, which it now enjoys *in all cases*, would have been only vested in it in case of the noncompliance of a State, as a *punishment* for its *delinquency*, and would have *ceased* the moment that the State *complied with the requisition*. But the proposition was rejected by a majority, consistently with their *aim* and *desire* of *increasing the power of the general government, as far as possible, and destroying the powers and influence of the States.* And, though there is a provision, that all duties, imposts, and excises shall be uniform, that is, to be laid to the same amount on the same articles in each State, yet this will not prevent Congress from having it in their power to cause them to fall *very unequal*, and *much heavier* on *some States* than *on others*, because these duties may be laid on articles but *little* or *not at all* used in some States, and of *absolute necessity* for the use and consumption of others; in which case, the *first* would pay *little* or *no part* of the revenue arising therefrom, while the *whole*, or nearly the whole of it, would be paid by the *last*, to wit, the States which use and consume the articles on which the imposts and excises are laid.

[50] By our original articles of confederation, the Congress have a power to borrow money and emit bills of credit, on the credit of the United States; agreeably to which, was the *report* on *this* system as *made* by the *committee of detail.* When we came to this part of the report, a motion was made to strike out the words "to emit bills of credit." Against the motion we urged, that it would

be improper to *deprive* the Congress of that *power;* that it would be a novelty unprecedented to establish a government which should not have such authority; that it was impossible to look forward into futurity so far as to decide, that events might not happen, that should render the *exercise* of such a power *absolutely* necessary; and that we doubted, whether, if a war should take place, it would be *possible* for this country to *defend* itself, without having recourse to *paper credit*, in which case, there would be a *necessity* of becoming a *prey* to our *enemies*, or *violating* the *constitution* of our government; and that, considering the administration of the government would be principally in the hands of the wealthy, there could be little reason to fear an *abuse* of the *power*, by an unnecessary or injurious exercise of it. But, Sir, a majority of the convention, being wise beyond every event, and being willing to risk any political evil, rather than admit the idea of a paper emission, in any *possible* event, refused to *trust* this authority to a government, to which they were *lavishing* the must *unlimited* powers of *taxation*, and to the *mercy* of which they were willing *blindly* to *trust* the *liberty* and *property* of the *citizens* of *every State* in the Union; and they *erased* that clause from the *system*. Among other powers given to this government in the eighth section, it has that of appointing tribunals *inferior* to the *Supreme Court*. To this power there was an opposition. It was urged, that there was no occasion for *inferior* courts of the *general government* to be appointed in the different States, and that such ought not to be admitted — That the different *State judiciaries* in the respective States would be *competent to*, and *sufficient for*, the cognizance, in the *first instance*, of all cases that should arise under the laws of the general government, which, being by this system made the supreme law of the States, would be binding on the different State judiciaries — That, by giving an *appeal* to the *Supreme* Court of the United States, the *general government* would have a *sufficient* check over their decisions, and security for the enforcing of their laws — That to have *inferior* courts appointed under the authority of Congress in the different States, would eventually *absorb* and *swallow* up the *State judiciaries*, by drawing all business from them to the courts of the general government, which the *extensive* and *undefined* powers, legislative and judicial, of which it is possessed, would *easily enable* it to do — That it would *unduly* and *dangerously* increase the *weight* and *influence* of Congress in the *several States*, be productive of a *prodigious number of officers*, and be attended with an *enormous* additional and unnecessary *expense* — That the judiciaries of the respective States, not having power to decide upon the laws of the general government, but the determination of those laws being *confined* to the judiciaries appointed under the authority of Congress, in the *first instance*, as well as on *appeal*, there would be a necessity for *judges* or magistrates of the general government, and those to a *considerable number*, in each county of *every State* — That there would be a necessity for courts to be holden by them in each county, and that these courts would stand in need of all the proper officers, such as *sheriffs*, *clerks*, and others, commissioned under the authority of the general government — In fine, that the administration of justice, as it will relate to the laws of the general government, would require in each State all the magistrates, courts, officers, and expense, which is now found necessary in the respective States, for the administration of justice as it relates to the laws of the State governments. But here, again, we were overruled by a majority, who, *assuming* it as a *principle*, that the general government and the State Governments (as long as they should exist) would be at *perpetual variance* and *enmity*, and that their *interests* would constantly be *opposed* to each other, insisted, for that reason, that the *State judges*, being citizens of their respective States, and holding their commissions under them, ought not, though *acting on oath*, to be *intrusted* with the administration of the laws of the general government.

[51] By the *eighth* section of the first article, the Congress have also the power given them to raise and support *armies*, without *any limitation* as to *numbers*, and without any restriction in *time of peace*. Thus, Sir, this plan of government, instead of *guarding against a standing army*, that *engine* of *arbitrary power*, which has so *often* and so *successfully* been used for the *subversion* of freedom, has in *its formation* given it an *express* and *constitutional sanction*, and hath *provided for its introduction*; nor could this be prevented. I took the sense of the convention on a proposition, by which the Congress should not have power, *in time of peace*, to keep embodied more than a certain number of regular troops *that number* to be ascertained by what should be considered a *respectable peace establishment*. This proposition was rejected by a majority; it being their determination, that the *power* of Congress to keep up a *standing army*, even in *peace*, should *only* be restrained by *their will* and *pleasure*.

[52] This section proceeds further to give a power to the Congress to provide for the calling forth the militia, to execute the laws of the Union, suppress insurrections, and repel invasions. As to *giving such a power*, there was no objection; but it was thought by some, that this power *ought* to be given with certain *restrictions*. It was thought, that not more than a certain part of the militia of any one State ought to be obliged to *march out* of the same, or be *employed*

out of the same, at any *one time*, without the consent of the legislature of such State. This *amendment* I endeavoured to obtain; but
it met with the same fate which attended almost every attempt to
limit the powers given to the general government, and *constitutionally* to guard against *their abuse*, it was not adopted. As it now
stands, the Congress will have the power, if they please, to march
the *whole* militia of Maryland to the *remotest* part of the Union, and
keep them in service as long as they think proper, without being
in any respect *dependent* upon the *Government of Maryland* for this
unlimited exercise of power over its citizens — — *All of whom*,
from the *lowest* to the *greatest*, may, during such service, be *subjected* to *military* law, and *tied up* and *whipped* at the *halbert*, like
the *meanest* of *slaves*.

[53] By the *next* paragraph, Congress is to have the power to
provide for *organizing*, *arming*, and *disciplining* the *militia*, and for
governing such part of them as may be *employed in the service* of the
United States.

[54] For this *extraordinary* provision, by which the *militia*, the
only defence and *protection* which the *State* can have for the security
of *their rights* against *arbitrary encroachments* of the *general government*, is taken entirely *out of the power* of their *respective States*, and
placed under the *power of Congress*, it was speciously assigned as
a reason, that the general government would cause the militia to
be better regulated and better disciplined than the State governments, and that it would be proper for the whole militia of the Union
to have a uniformity in their arms and exercise. To this it was
answered, that the reason, however *specious*, was *not just;* that it
would be absurd, the militia of the western settlements, who were
exposed to an Indian enemy, should either be confined to the *same
arms* or *exercise* as the militia of the eastern or middle States; that
the same penalties which would be sufficient to enforce an obedience to militia laws in some States, would be totally disregarded
in others; that, leaving the power to the several States, they would
respectively best know the situation and circumstances of their
citizens, and the regulations that would be necessary and sufficient
to effect a well-regulated militia in each; that we were satisfied the
militia had heretofore been as well disciplined as if they had been
under the regulations of Congress, and that the States would now
have an *additional* motive to keep their militia in proper order, and
fit for service, as it would be the *only chance* to preserve their *existence*
against a general government armed with powers *sufficient* to destroy
them.

[55] These observations, Sir, procured from some of the members

an open avowal of those reasons, by which we believed before that they were actuated. They said, that, as the States would be opposed to the general government, and at enmity with it, which, as I have already observed, they *assumed* as a *principle*, if the militia was under the control and the authority of the respective States, it would *enable* them to *thwart* and *oppose* the general government. They said, the States ought to be at the mercy of the general government, and, therefore, that the militia ought to be put under its power, and not suffered to remain under the power of the respective States. In answer to these declarations, it was urged, that, if after having retained to the general government the great powers already granted, and among those, that of *raising* and *keeping* up regular troops without limitations, the *power* over the *militia* should be *taken away* from *the States*, and also given to the general government, it ought to be considered as the last *coup de grace* to the *State governments;* that it must be the most convincing proof, the advocates of this system design the *destruction* of the State governments, and that no *professions* to the contrary ought to be *trusted;* and that every State in the Union ought to reject such a system with indignation, since, if the general government should attempt to oppress and enslave them, they could not have any possible means of self-defence; because, the proposed system taking away from the States the right of organizing, arming, and disciplining the militia, the *first attempt* made by a *State* to put the militia in a situation to counteract the arbitrary measures of the general government would be construed into an *act* of *rebellion* or *treason;* and Congress would *instantly march* their *troops* into the State. It was further observed that, when a government *wishes* to deprive its citizens of freedom, and reduce them to *slavery*, it *generally makes use of a standing army* for that purpose, and leaves the militia in a situation as contemptible as possible, lest they might oppose its arbitrary designs; that, in *this* system, we give the general government every provision it could wish for, and even *invite* it to subvert the *liberties* of the *States* and *their citizens;* since we give it the right to increase and keep up a standing army as numerous as it would wish, and, by placing the militia under its power, enable it to leave the militia *totally unorganized, undisciplined*, and even to disarm them; while the *citizens*, so far from complaining of this *neglect*, might even esteem it a favor in the general government, as thereby they would be freed from the burden of militia duties, and left to their own private occupations or pleasures. However, *all* arguments, and every reason that could be urged on this subject, as well as on many others, were obliged to yield to *one* that was *unanswerable*, — a *majority* upon the division.

[56] By the *ninth* section of this article, the importation of such persons as any of the States now existing shall think proper to admit, shall not be prohibited prior to the year one thousand eight hundred and eight; but a duty may be imposed on such importation, not exceeding ten dollars for each person.

[57] The design of this clause is to prevent the general government from prohibiting the importation of slaves; but the same reasons which caused them to strike out the word "national," and not admit the word "*stamps*," influenced them here to guard against the word "*slaves*." They anxiously sought to avoid the admission of expressions which might be odious in the ears of Americans, although they were willing to admit into their system those *things* which the *expressions* signified. And hence it is, that the clause is so worded, as really to authorize the general government to impose a duty of ten dollars on every foreigner who comes into a State to become a citizen, whether he comes *absolutely* free, or *qualifiedly* so, as a servant; although this is contrary to the design of the framers, and the duty was only meant to extend to the importation of *slaves*.

[58] This clause was the subject of a great diversity of sentiment in the convention. As the system was reported by the committee of detail, the provision was general, that such importation should not be prohibited, without confining it to any particular period. This was rejected by eight States, — Georgia, South Carolina, and, I think, North Carolina, voting for it.

[59] We were then told by the delegates of the two first of those States, that their States would never agree to a *system*, which put it in the power of the general government to prevent the importation of slaves, and that they, as delegates from those States, must withhold their assent from such a system.

[60] A committee of one member from each State was chosen by ballot, to take this part of the system under their consideration, and to endeavour to agree upon some report, which should reconcile those States. To this committee also was referred the following proposition, which had been reported by the committee of detail, to wit; "No *navigation* act shall be passed without the assent of *two thirds* of the members present in each House"; a proposition which the *staple* and *commercial States* were solicitous to *retain*, lest their *commerce* should be placed too much under the power of the *eastern* States; but which these last States were as anxious to *reject*. This committee, of which also I had the honor to be a member, met and took under their consideration the subjects committed to them. I found the *eastern* States, notwithstanding their *aversion to slavery*, were very willing to indulge the southern States, at least

with a temporary liberty to prosecute the *slave-trade*, provided the southern States would, in their turn, gratify them, by laying *no restriction on navigation acts;* and after a very little time the committee, by a great majority, agreed on a report, by which the general government was to be prohibited from preventing the importation of slaves for a limited time, and the restrictive clause relative to navigation acts was to be omitted.

[61] This report was adopted by a majority of the convention, but not without considerable opposition. It was said, that we had just assumed a place among independent nations, in consequence of our opposition to the attempts of Great Britain to *enslave us;* that this opposition was grounded upon the preservation of *those rights* to which God and nature had entitled *us*, not in *particular*, but in *common* with *all the rest of mankind;* that we had *appealed* to the *Supreme Being* for his *assistance*, as the *God of freedom*, who could not but *approve* our efforts to preserve the *rights* which he had thus *imparted to his creatures;* that now, when we scarcely had risen from our *knees*, from *supplicating* his *aid* and *protection*, in *forming our government* over a *free people*, a government formed pretendedly on the *principles* of *liberty* and for *its preservation*, — in *that* government, to have a provision not only putting it out of *its* power to *restrain* and *prevent* the *slave-trade*, but *even encouraging that most infamous traffic*, by giving the *States power* and *influence* in the *Union*, *in proportion* as they *cruelly and wantonly sport with the rights of their fellow creatures*, ought to be considered as a *solemn mockery of*, and *insult to that God* whose protection we had then implored, and could not fail to hold us up in *detestation*, and render us *contemptible* to every *true friend* of liberty in the world. It was said, it ought to be considered that national *crimes* can only be, and *frequently are punished* in this world, by national punishments; and that the *continuance* of the slave-trade, and thus giving it a *national sanction* and *encouragement*, ought to be considered as *justly exposing* us to the *displeasure* and *vengeance* of *Him*, who is equally Lord of all, and who views with equal eye the poor *African slave* and his *American master*.

[62] It was urged, that, by this system, we were giving the general government full and absolute power to regulate commerce, under which general power it would have a right to *restrain*, or *totally prohibit*, the *slave-trade*; it must, therefore, appear to the world absurd and disgraceful to the last degree, that we should *except* from the exercise of that power, the *only branch* of *commerce* which is *unjustifiable in its nature*, and *contrary* to the rights of *mankind;* that, on the contrary, we ought *rather to prohibit expressly* in our constitution, the *further importation of slaves;* and to *authorize* the

general government, from time to time, to make such regulations as should be thought most advantageous for the *gradual abolition of slavery*, and the *emancipation* of the *slaves* which are already in the States: That *slavery* is *inconsistent* with the *genius* of *republicanism*, and has a tendency to *destroy* those *principles* on which it is *supported*, as it *lessens* the *sense* of the *equal rights* of *mankind*, and habituates us to *tyranny* and *oppression*.

[63] It was further urged that, by this system of government, every State is to be protected both from *foreign invasion* and from *domestic insurrections;* that, from this consideration, it was of the *utmost importance* it should have a power to restrain the importation of slaves; since in *proportion* as the number of slaves are increased in any State, in the *same* proportion the State is *weakened*, and *exposed* to foreign invasion or domestic insurrection, and *by so much less* will it be able to protect itself against *either;* and, therefore, will by so much the more want aid from, and be a burden to the Union. It was further said, that as, in this system, we were giving the general government a power under the idea of national character, or national interest, to regulate even our *weights* and *measures*, and have prohibited all possibility of *emitting paper money*, and *passing instalment laws*, &c., it must appear still more extraordinary, that we should prohibit the government from interfering with the slave-trade, than which, *nothing* could so *materially affect* both our *national honor* and *interest*. These reasons influenced me, both on the committee and in convention, most decidedly to oppose and vote against the clause as it now makes a part of the system.

[64] You will perceive, Sir, not only that the general government is prohibited from interfering in the slave-trade *before* the year eighteen hundred and eight, but that there is no provision in the constitution that it shall *afterwards* be prohibited, nor any security that such prohibition will ever take place; and I think there is great reason to believe, that, if the importation of slaves is permitted until the year eighteen hundred and eight, it will not be prohibited afterwards. At *this time*, we do not generally hold this commerce in so great *abhorrence* as we have done. When our *own* liberties were at stake, we *warmly* felt for the *common rights of men*. The danger being thought to be past, which threatened ourselves, we are daily growing *more insensible* to those rights. In those States which have restrained or prohibited the importation of slaves, it is only done by legislative acts, which may be repealed. When those States find, that they must, in their *national character* and *connexion*, suffer in the *disgrace*, and share in the *inconveniences* attendant upon that detestable and iniquitous traffic, they may be desirous

also to share in the *benefits* arising from it; and the odium attending it will be greatly effaced by the sanction which is given to it in the general government.

[65] By the next paragraph, the general government is to have a *power* of *suspending* the *habeas corpus act,* in cases of *rebellion* or *invasion.*

[66] As the State governments have a power of suspending the *habeas corpus* act in those cases, it was said, there could be no reason for giving such a power to the general government; since whenever the State which is invaded, or in which an insurrection takes place, finds its safety requires it, it will make use of that power. And it was urged, that if we gave this power to the general government, it would be an engine of oppression in its hands; since, whenever a State should oppose its views, however arbitrary and unconstitutional, and refuse submission to them, the general government may declare it to be *an act of rebellion,* and, suspending the habeas corpus act, may *seize* upon the persons of those *advocates of freedom,* who have had *virtue* and *resolution* enough to excite the opposition, and may *imprison* them during its pleasure, in the *remotest* part of the Union; so that a citizen of Georgia might be *bastiled* in the furthest part of New Hampshire, or a citizen of New Hampshire in the furthest extreme to the south, cut off from their family, their friends, and their every connexion. These considerations induced me, Sir, to give my negative also to this clause.

[67] In this same section, there is a provision, that no preference should be given to the ports of one State over another, and that vessels bound to or from one State shall not be obliged to enter, clear, or pay duties in another. This provision, as well as that which relates to the uniformity of impost duties and excises, was introduced, Sir, by the delegation of this State. Without such a provision, it would have been in the power of the general government to have compelled all ships sailing into or out of the Chesapeake, to clear and enter at Norfolk, or some port in Virginia; a regulation which would be extremely injurious to our commerce, but which would, if considered merely as to the interest of the Union, perhaps not be thought unreasonable; since it would render the collection of the revenue arising from commerce more certain and less expensive.

[68] But, Sir, as the system is now reported, the general government have a *power* to *establish what ports they please in each State,* and to ascertain at what ports in every State ships shall clear and enter in such State; a power which may be so used as to *destroy* the *effect* of that provision; since by it may be established a port in such

a place, as shall be so *inconvenient* to the States, as to render it *more eligible* for their shipping to clear and enter in *another* than in their own States.   Suppose, for instance, the general government should determine, that all ships which cleared or entered in Maryland, should clear and enter at Georgetown, on the Potomac; it would oblige all the ships which sailed from or were bound to any other port of Maryland, to clear or enter in some port in *Virginia*.   To prevent such a use of the power which the general government now has, of *limiting the number of ports* in a State, and *fixing the place or places where they shall be*, we endeavoured to obtain a provision, that the general government should only, in the first instance, have authority to ascertain the *number* of ports proper to be established in each State, and transmit information thereof to the several States, the legislatures of which, respectively, should have the power to fix the *places* where those ports should be, according to their idea of what would be most *advantageous* to the *commerce* of their State, and most for the *ease and convenience* of their *citizens;* and that the general government should not interfere in the establishment of the *places*, unless the legislature of the State should neglect or refuse so to do; but we could not obtain this alteration.

[69] By the tenth section every State is *prohibited from emitting bills of credit*.   As it was reported by the committee of detail, the States were *only* prohibited from emitting them *without the consent of Congress*; but the convention was so *smitten* with the *paper money dread*, that they insisted the prohibition should be *absolute*.   It was my opinion, Sir, that the States ought not to be *totally deprived of the right to emit bills of credit*, and that, as we had *not given* an *authority* to the *general government* for that purpose, it was the *more necessary* to *retain* it in the *States*.   I considered that *this State*, and *some others*, had *formerly received great benefit* from paper emissions, and that, if public and private credit should once more be restored, such emissions might *hereafter be equally advantageous;* and, further, that it is impossible to foresee, that events may not take place, which shall render paper money of *absolute necessity*; and it was my opinion, if this power was not to be exercised by a State, without the permission of the general government, it ought to be satisfactory even to those who were the *most haunted* by the apprehensions of paper money.   I therefore thought it my duty to vote against this part of the system.

[70] The same section also puts it out of the power of the States to make any thing but gold and silver coin a tender in payment of debts, or to pass any law impairing the obligation of contracts.

[71] I considered, Sir, that there might be times of such *great*

public calamities and *distress*, and of such *extreme scarcity of specie*,
as should render it the *duty* of a government, for the *preservation*
of even the *most valuable part* of its citizens, in some measure to
interfere in their favor, by passing laws *totally or partially stopping*
the courts of justice, or authorizing the debtor to pay by *instalments*,
or by delivering up his property to his creditors at a *reasonable* and
honest valuation. The times have been such as to render regulations
of this kind necessary in most or all of the States, to prevent the
wealthy creditor and the *moneyed* man from *totally* destroying the *poor*,
though even *industrious* debtor. *Such times* may *again* arrive. I
therefore voted against depriving the States of this power, a power
which I am decided they ought to possess, but which, I admit, ought
only to be exercised on very important and urgent occasions. I
apprehend, Sir, the principal cause of complaint among the people
at large is, the public and private debt with which they are oppressed,
and which, in the present scarcity of cash, threatens them with
destruction, unless they can obtain so much indulgence in point
of time, that by industry and frugality they may extricate themselves.

[72] This government proposed, I apprehend, *so far from removing*, will greatly increase those complaints, since, grasping in its
all-powerful hand the citizens of the respective States, it will, by
the imposition of the variety of *taxes, imposts, stamps, excises*, and
other duties, squeeze from them the little money they may acquire,
the hard earnings of their industry, as you would squeeze the juice
from an orange, till not a drop more can be extracted, and then
let *loose* upon them their *private creditors*, to whose *mercy* it *consigns*
them, by *whom* their property is to be *seized upon* and *sold*, in this
scarcity of *specie, at a sheriff's sale*, where nothing but *ready cash*
can be received, for a *tenth part* of *its value*, and *themselves* and their
families, to be consigned to *indigence* and *distress*, without *their
governments* having a *power* to *give them a moment's indulgence*, however *necessary* it might be, and however *desirous* to grant them aid.

[73] By this same section, every State is also prohibited from
laying any imposts or duties on imports or exports, without the
permission of the general government. It was urged, that, as almost
all sources of taxation were given to Congress, it would be but reasonable to leave the States the power of bringing revenue into their
treasuries, by laying a duty on exports if they should think proper,
which might be so *light* as not to injure or discourage industry, and
yet might be productive of considerable revenue. Also, that there
might be cases in which it would be proper, for the purpose of encouraging manufactures, to lay duties to prohibit the exportation

of raw materials; and, even in addition to the duties laid by Congress on *imports* for the sake of *revenue*, to lay a duty to discourage the importation of particular articles into a State, or to enable the *manufacturer here* to supply us on as *good terms* as they could be obtained from a *foreign market;* However, the most we could obtain was, that this power might be exercised by the States with, and *only* with the consent of Congress, and subject to its control. And so anxious were they to seize on *every shilling* of our money, for the general government, that they insisted *even* the *little revenue* that might thus arise, should not be appropriated to the use of the respective States where it was collected, but should be paid into the treasury of the United States; and accordingly it is so determined.

[74] The second article, relates to the executive, — his mode of election, his powers, and the length of time he shall continue in office.

[75] On these subjects there was a great diversity of sentiment. Many of the members were desirous, that the President should be elected for seven years, and not to be eligible a second time; others proposed, that he should not be absolutely ineligible, but that he should not be capable of being chosen a second time, until the expiration of a certain number of years. The supporters of the above propositions went upon the idea, that the best security for liberty was a limited duration and a rotation of office in the chief executive department.

[76] There was a party who attempted to have the President appointed during good behaviour, without any limitation as to time; and, not being able to succeed in that attempt, they then endeavoured to have him reëligible without any restraint. It was objected, that the choice of a President to continue in office during good behaviour, would be at once rendering our system an elective monarchy; and, that if the President was to be reëligible without any interval of disqualification, it would amount nearly to the same thing; since with the powers that the President is to enjoy, and the interests and influence with which they will be attended, he will be almost absolutely certain of being reëlected, from time to time, as long as he lives. As the propositions were reported by the committee of the whole House, the President was to be chosen for seven years, and not to be eligible, at any time after. In the same manner the proposition was agreed to in convention, and so it was reported by the committee of detail, although a variety of attempts were made to alter that part of the system, by those who were of a contrary opinion, in which they repeatedly failed; but, Sir, by never losing sight of their object, and choosing a proper time for their purpose,

they succeeded at length in obtaining the alteration, which was not made until within the last twelve days before the convention adjourned.

[77] As the propositions were agreed to by the committee of the whole House, the President was to be appointed by the national legislature; and as it was reported by the committee of detail, the choice was to be made by ballot, in such a manner that the States should have an equal voice in the appointment of this officer, as they, of right, ought to have; but those who wished as far as possible to establish a *national* instead of a *federal* government, made repeated attempts to have the President chosen by the people at large. On this the sense of the convention was taken, I think, not less than three times while I was there, and as often rejected; but, within the last fortnight of their session, they obtained the alteration in the manner it now stands, by which the large States have a very undue influence in the appointment of the President. There is no case where the States will have an equal voice in the appointment of the President, except where two persons shall have an equal number of votes, and those a majority of the whole number of electors, (a case very unlikely to happen,) or where no person has a majority of the votes. In these instances the House of Representatives are to choose by ballot, each State having an equal voice; but they are confined, in the last instance, to the five who have the greatest number of votes, which gives the largest States a very unequal chance of having the President chosen under their nomination.

[78] As to the Vice-President, that great officer of government, who is, in case of death, resignation, removal, or inability of the President, to supply his place, and be vested with his powers, and who is officially to be the President of the Senate, there is no provision by which a majority of the voices of the electors are necessary for his appointment; but, after it is decided who is chosen President, that person who has the next greatest number of votes of the electors, is declared to be legally elected to the Vice-Presidency; so that by this system it is very possible, and not improbable, that he may be appointed by the electors of a *single large State*; and a very undue influence in the Senate is given to that State of which the Vice-President is a citizen, since, in every question where the Senate is divided, that State will have two votes, the President having on those occasions a casting voice. Every part of the system which relates to the Vice-President, as well as the present mode of electing the President, was introduced and agreed upon after I left Philadelphia.

[79] Objections were made to that part of this article, by which

the President is appointed Commander-in-chief of the army and navy of the United States, and of the militia of the several States, and it was wished to be so far restrained, that he should not command in person; but this could not be obtained. The power given to the President, of granting reprieves and pardons, was also thought extremely dangerous, and as such opposed. The President thereby has the power of pardoning those who are guilty of treason, as well as of other offences; it was said, that no treason was so likely to take place as that in which the President himself might be engaged, — the attempt to assume to himself powers not given by the constitution, and establish himself in regal authority; in which attempt a provision is made for him to secure from punishment the creatures of his ambition, the associates and abettors of his treasonable practices, by granting them pardons, should they be defeated in their attempts to subvert the Constitution.

[80] To that part of this article also, which gives the President a right to *nominate*, and, with the consent of the Senate, to appoint all the officers, civil and military, of the United States, there was considerable opposition. It was said, that the person who *nominates* will always in reality *appoint*, and that this was giving the President a power and influence, which, together with the other powers bestowed upon him, would place him above all restraint or control. In fine, it was urged, that the President, as here constituted, was a king, in every thing but the name; that, though he was to be chosen but for a limited time, yet at the expiration of that time, if he is not re-elected, it will depend entirely upon his own moderation whether he will resign that authority with which he has once been invested; that, from his having the appointment of all the variety of officers, in every part of the civil department for the Union, who will be very numerous, in them and their connexions, relations, friends, and dependents, he will have a formidable host, devoted to his interest, and ready to support his ambitious views. That the army and navy, which may be increased without restraint as to numbers, the officers of which, from the highest to the lowest, are all to be appointed by him, and dependent on his will and pleasure, and commanded by him in person, will, of course, be subservient to his wishes, and ready to execute his commands; in addition to which, the militia also are entirely subjected to his orders. That these circumstances, combined together, will enable him, when he pleases, to become a king in *name*, as well as in substance, and establish himself in office not only for his own life, but even, if he chooses, to have that authority perpetuated to his family.

[81] It was further observed, that the only appearance of respon-

sibility in the President, which the system holds up to our view, is the provision for impeachment; but that when we reflect that he cannot be impeached but by the House of Delegates, and that the members of this House are rendered dependent upon, and unduly under the influence of the President, by being appointable to offices of which he has the sole nomination, so that without his favor and approbation they cannot obtain them, there is little reason to believe, that a majority will ever concur in impeaching the President, let his conduct be ever so reprehensible; especially, too, as the final event of that impeachment will depend upon a different body, and the members of the House of Delegate will be certain, should the decision be ultimately in favor of the President, to become thereby the objects of his displeasure, and to bar to themselves every avenue to the emoluments of government.

[82] Should he, contrary to probability, be impeached, he is afterwards to be tried and adjudged by the Senate, and, without the concurrence of two thirds of the members who shall be present, he cannot be convicted. This Senate being constituted a privy council to the President, it is probable many of its leading and influential members may have advised or concurred in the very measures for which he may be impeached; the members of the Senate also are by the system, placed as unduly under the influence of, and dependent upon the President, as the members of the other branch, since they also are appointable to offices, and cannot obtain them but through the favor of the President. There will be great, important, and valuable offices under this government, should it take place, more than sufficient to enable him to hold out the expectation of one of them to *each* of the senators. Under these circumstances, will any person conceive it to be difficult for the President always to secure to himself more than one third of that body? Or, can it reasonably be believed, that a criminal will be convicted, who is constitutionally empowered to bribe his judges, at the head of whom is to preside on those occasions the Chief Justice, which officer, in his original appointment, must be *nominated* by the President, and will, therefore, probably, be appointed not so much for his eminence in legal knowledge and for his integrity, as from favoritism and influence; since the President, knowing that in case of impeachment the Chief Justice is to preside at his trial, will naturally wish to fill that office with a person of whose voice and influence he shall consider himself secure? These are reasons to induce a belief, that there will be but little probability of the President ever being either impeached or convicted; but it was also urged, that, vested with the powers which the system gives him, and with the influence attendant

upon those powers, to him it would be of little consequence whether he was impeached or convicted, since he will be able to set both at defiance. These considerations occasioned a part of the convention to give a negative to this part of the system establishing the executive, as it is now offered for our acceptance.

[83] By the *third article*, the judicial power of the United States is vested in *one supreme court*, and in such *inferior courts*, as the Congress may from time to time ordain and establish. These courts, and *these only*, will have a right to decide upon the laws of the United States, and all questions arising upon their construction, and in a judicial manner to carry those laws into execution; to which the courts, both superior and inferior, of the respective States, and their judges and other magistrates, are rendered incompetent. To the courts of the general government are also *confined* all cases in law or equity, arising under the proposed constitution, and treaties made under the authority of the United States; all cases affecting ambassadors, other public ministers, and consuls; all cases of admiralty and maritime jurisdiction; all controversies to which the United States are a party; all controversies between two or more States; between a State and citizens of another State; between citizens of the same State, claiming lands under grants of different States; and between a State, or the citizens thereof, and foreign States, citizens, or subjects. Whether therefore, any *laws* or *regulations* of the *Congress*, or any *acts* of its *President* or *other officers*, are *contrary to*, or not *warranted* by the constitution, rests *only* with the judges, who are *appointed* by Congress to *determine;* by whose determinations *every State* must be *bound*. Should any question arise between a foreign consul and any of the citizens of the United States, however remote from the seat of empire, it is to be heard before the judiciary of the general government, and in the *first* instance to be heard in the Supreme Court, however inconvenient to the parties, and however trifling the subject of dispute.

[84] Should the mariners of an American or foreign vessel, while in any American port, have occasion to sue for their wages, or in any other instance a controversy belonging to the admiralty jurisdiction should take place between them and their masters or owners, it is in the courts of the general government the suit must be instituted; and either party may carry it by appeal to its Supreme Court. The injury to commerce, and the oppression to individuals, which may thence arise, need not be enlarged upon. Should a citizen of Virginia, Pennsylvania, or any other of the United States, be indebted to, or have debts due from a citizen of this State, or any other claim be subsisting on one side or the other, in consequence

of commercial or other transactions, it is only in the courts of Congress that either can apply for redress. The case is the same should any claim subsist between citizens of this State and foreigners, merchants, mariners, and others, whether of a commercial or of any other nature; they must be prosecuted in the same courts; and though in the first instance they may be brought in the inferior, yet an appeal may be made to the supreme judiciary, even from the remotest State in the Union.

[85] The inquiry concerning, and trial of, every offence against, and breach of, the laws of Congress, are also *confined* to its courts; the same courts also have the *sole* right to inquire concerning and try every offence, from the lowest to the highest, committed by the citizens of any other State, or of a foreign nation, against the laws of this State, within its territory; and in *all these cases*, the decision may be ultimately brought before the supreme tribunal, since the *appellate jurisdiction* extends to *criminal* as well as to civil cases: And in all those cases where the general government has jurisdiction in civil questions, the proposed constitution *not only* makes *no provision for trial by jury* in the *first* instance, but, by its appellate jurisdiction, *absolutely takes away that inestimable privilege;* since it expressly declares the Supreme Court shall have appellate jurisdiction both as to law and *fact*. Should, therefore, a jury be adopted in the *inferior court*, it would only be a *needless expense*, since, on an appeal, the *determination* of that *jury, even on questions of fact*, however honest and upright, is to be of *no possible effect*. The Supreme Court is to take up *all questions of fact, to examine the evidence relative* thereto, to *decide upon them* in the *same manner* as if they had *never been tried by a jury*; nor is *trial by jury secured in criminal cases*. It is true, that, in the first instance, in the inferior court, the trial is to be by jury. In this, and in this only, is the difference between criminal and civil cases. But, Sir, the *appellate jurisdiction extends*, as I have observed, to cases *criminal* as well as to civil; and, on the *appeal*, the court is to *decide not only* on the law, but on the *fact*. If, therefore, *even* in *criminal* cases, the general government is not satisfied with the verdict of the jury, its officer may remove the prosecution to the Supreme Court, and *there* the *verdict of the jury is to be of no effect*, but the *judges of this court* are to *decide upon the fact* as well as the law, the *same as in civil cases*.

[86] Thus, Sir, *jury trials*, which have ever been the *boast* of the English constitution, which have been by our several *State constitutions* so *cautiously secured* to us, — *jury trials*, which have so long been considered the *surest barrier* against *arbitrary power*, and the *palladium of liberty*, with the *loss* of *which* the *loss* of our

freedom may be dated, are *taken away*, by the proposed form of government, not *only* in a *great variety* of questions between *individual* and *individual*, but in *every case*, whether *civil* or *criminal*, arising *under the laws* of the United States, or the *execution* of those laws. It is *taken away* in *those very cases*, where, of *all others*, it is *most essential for our liberty* to have it *sacredly guarded* and *preserved;* in *every case*, whether *civil* or *criminal*, between *government* and its *officers* on the one part, and the *subject or citizen* on the other. Nor was this the effect of inattention, nor did it arise from any real difficulty in establishing and securing jury trials by the proposed constitution, if the convention had wished so to do; but the *same reason* influenced *here* as in the case of the establishment of inferior courts; as they could not trust *State judges*, so would they not confide in *State juries*. They alleged, that the general government and the State governments would always be at variance; that the citizens of the different States would enter into the views and interests of their respective States, and therefore ought not to be trusted in determining causes in which the general government was any way interested, without giving the general government an opportunity, if it disapproved the verdict of the jury, to appeal, and to have the *facts examined* into *again*, and *decided upon* by *its own judges*, on whom it was thought a reliance might be had by the general government, they being appointed under its authority.

[87] Thus, Sir, in consequence of this *appellate jurisdiction*, and its *extension to facts* as well as to law, every *arbitrary act* of the general government, and every *oppression* of all that *variety of officers* appointed under its authority, for the *collection* of *taxes, duties, impost, excise*, and other *purposes*, must be *submitted* to by the *individual*, or must be *opposed* with *little prospect* of *success*, and *almost a certain prospect* of *ruin*, at least in those cases where the *middle* and *common class* of citizens are interested; since, to *avoid* that *oppression*, or to *obtain redress*, the application must be made to one of the courts of the United States. By good fortune should this application be in the *first* instance attended with success, and should damages be recovered equivalent to the injury sustained, an *appeal* lies to the *Supreme Court;* in which case, the citizen must at once give up his cause, or he must attend to it at the distance of perhaps more than a thousand miles from the place of his residence, and must take measures to procure before that court, on the appeal, all the evidence necessary to support his action, which, even if ultimately prosperous, must be attended with a *loss of time, a neglect of business,* and an *expense* which will be *greater* than the *original grievance*, and *to which* men in *moderate* circumstances would be *utterly unequal.*

[88] By the *third* section of this article, it is declared, that treason against the United States shall consist in levying war against them, or in adhering to their enemies, giving them aid or comfort.

[89] By the *principles* of the American revolution, *arbitrary power may* and *ought* to be resisted, even by *arms* if necessary. The time may come, when it shall be the *duty* of a *State*, in order to preserve itself from the oppression of the general government, to have recourse to the sword; in which case, the proposed form of government declares, that the *State* and every of *its citizens* who *act under its authority* are guilty of a direct act of treason; — reducing, by this provision, the different States to this alternative, that they must *tamely* and *passively yield* to *despotism*, or *their citizens* must *oppose it* at the *hazard* of the *halter* if unsuccessful: and reducing the citizens of the State which shall take arms, to a situation in which they must be *exposed* to *punishment*, let them *act as they will;* since, if they *obey* the authority of their *State government*, they will be *guilty of treason against the United States;* if they *join* the *general government*, they will be *guilty of treason* against *their own State.*

[90] To save the citizens of the respective States from this disagreeable dilemma, and to secure them from being punishable as *traitors* to the *United States*, when *acting* expressly in *obedience* to the *authority of their own State*, I wished to have obtained, as an amendment to the third section of this article, the following clause: "Provided, that no act or acts done by *one* or *more of the States* against the United States, or by *any citizen* of any *one* of the United States, *under the authority* of *one or more of the said States*, shall be deemed *treason*, or *punished as such;* but, in case of war being levied by one or more of the States against the United States, the conduct of each party towards the other, and their adherents respectively, shall be regulated by the *laws of war* and of *nations*."

[91] But this provision was not adopted, being too much opposed to the great object of many of the leading members of the convention, which was, by all means to *leave the States* at the *mercy* of the *general government*, since they could not succeed in their *immediate* and *entire* abolition.

[92] By the third section of the fourth article, no new State shall be formed or erected within the jurisdiction of any other State, without the consent of the legislature of such State.

[93] There are a number of States which are so circumstanced, with respect to themselves and to the other States, that every principle of justice and sound policy require their dismemberment or division into smaller States. Massachusetts is divided into two districts, totally separated from each other by the State of New

Hampshire, on the northeast side of which lie the Provinces of Maine and Sagadahock, more extensive in point of territory, but less populous than old Massachusetts, which lies on the other side of New Hampshire. No person can cast his eye on the map of that State but he must in a moment admit, that every argument drawn from convenience, interest, and justice, require, that the Provinces of Maine and Sagadahoc should be erected into a new State, and that they should not be compelled to remain connected with old Massachusetts under all the inconveniences of their situation.

[94] The State of Georgia is larger in extent than the whole island of Great Britain, extending from its sea-coast to the Mississippi, a distance of eight hundred miles or more; its breadth, for the most part, about three hundred miles. The States of North Carolina and Virginia, in the same manner, reach from the sea-coast unto the Mississippi.

[95] The hardship, the inconvenience, and the injustice of compelling the inhabitants of those States who may dwell on the western side of the mountains, and along the Ohio and Mississippi rivers, to remain connected with the inhabitants of those States respectively, on the Atlantic side of the mountains, and subject to the same State governments, would be such, as would, in my opinion, justify even recourse to arms, to free themselves from, and to shake off, so ignominious a yoke.

[96] This representation was made in convention, and it was further urged, that the territory of these States was too large, and that the inhabitants thereof would be too much disconnected for a *republican government* to extend to them its *benefits*, which is only suited to a small and compact territory. That a regard, also, for the peace and safety of the Union ought to excite a desire, that those States should become in time divided into separate States, since, when their population should become proportioned in any degree to their territory, they would, from their strength and power, become *dangerous members* of a *federal* government. It was further said, that, if the general government was not by its constitution to interfere, the inconvenience would soon remedy itself, for that, as the population increased in those States, their legislatures would be obliged to consent to the erection of new States to avoid the evils of a civil war; but as, by the proposed constitution, the general government is obliged to protect each State against domestic violence, and, consequently, will be obliged to assist in suppressing such commotions and insurrections, as may take place from the struggle to have new States erected, the general government ought to have a power to decide upon the propriety and necessity of estab-

lishing or erecting a new State, even without the approbation of
the legislature of such States, within whose jurisdiction the new State
should be erected; and for this purpose I submitted to the convention
the following proposition: "That, on the application of the inhabitants of any district of territory, within the limits of any of the States,
it shall be lawful for the legislature of the United States, if they shall
under all circumstances think it reasonable, to erect the same into
a new State, and admit it into the Union, *without the consent* of the
State of which the said district may be a part.". And it was said,
that we surely might trust the general government with *this power*
with *more propriety* than with *many others*, with which they were
proposed to be intrusted; and that, as the general government was
bound to suppress all insurrections and commotions, which might
arise on this subject, it ought to be in the power of the general government to decide upon it, and not in the power of the legislature
of a single State, by obstinately and unreasonably opposing the
erection of a new State, to prevent its taking effect, and thereby
extremely to *oppress* that part of its citizens which live remote from,
and inconvenient to, the seat of its government, and even to involve the Union in war to support its injustice and oppression.
But, upon the vote being taken, Georgia, South Carolina, North
Carolina, Virginia, Pennsylvania, and Massachusetts were in the
negative. New Hampshire, Connecticut, Jersey, Delaware, and
Maryland, were in the *affirmative*. New York was absent.

[97] That it was inconsistent with the rights of free and independent States, to have their territory dismembered without their
consent, was the principal argument used by the opponents of this
proposition. The truth of the objection we readily admitted, but
at the same time insisted, that it was not *more inconsistent* with the
rights of free and independent States, than that *inequality of suffrage*
and *power* which the *large States* had *extorted* from *the others;* and
that, if the *smaller States* yielded up *their rights* in *that instance*,
they were entitled to demand from the States of extensive territory
a *surrender* of their rights in this *instance;* and in a particular manner,
as it was *equally necessary* for the true interest and happiness of the
citizens of *their own States*, as of *the Union*. But, Sir, although,
when the large States demanded *undue* and *improper* sacrifices to
be made to their *pride* and *ambition*, they treated the rights of free
States with more contempt, than ever a British Parliament treated
the rights of her colonial establishments; yet, when a *reasonable*
and *necessary sacrifice* was asked *from them*, they spurned the idea
with ineffable disdain. They *then perfectly understood* the *full
value* and the *sacred obligation* of *State rights*, and at the least attempt

to infringe them, *where they were concerned*, they were tremblingly alive, and agonized at every pore.

[98] When we reflect how *obstinately* those States contended for that *unjust superiority* of power in the government, which they have *in part* obtained, and for the establishment of this superiority by the constitution; when we reflect that they appeared willing to hazard the existence of the Union, rather than not to succeed in their unjust attempt; that, should their legislatures consent to the erection of new States within their jurisdiction, it would be an immediate sacrifice of that power, to obtain which they appeared disposed to sacrifice every other consideration. When we further reflect that they *now* have a *motive* for desiring to preserve their territory entire and unbroken, which they *never had before, — the gratification of their ambition, in possessing and exercising superior power over their sister States,* — and that this constitution is to give them the *means* to *effect* this desire, *of which* they were *formerly destitute; the whole force of the United States pledged to them for restraining intestine commotions,* and *preserving to them the obedience and subjection of their citizens,* even in the *extremest part of their territory;* — I say, Sir when we consider these things, it would be too absurd and improbable to deserve a serious answer, should any person suggest, that *these States* mean ever to *give their consent* to the *erection of new States within their territory.* Some of them, it is true, have been for some time past *amusing* their inhabitants, in those districts that wished to be erected into new States; but, should this constitution be adopted, *armed with a sword and halter* to compel their obedience and subjection, they will no longer act with indecision; and the State of Maryland may, and probably will, be called upon to assist, with her wealth and her blood, in subduing the inhabitants of Franklin, Kentucky, Vermont, and the provinces of Maine and Sagadahoc, and in compelling them to continue in subjection to the States which respectively claim jurisdiction over them.

[99] Let it not be forgotten at the same time, that a great part of the territory of these large and extensive States, which they now hold in possession, and over which they now claim and exercise jurisdiction, were crown lands, unlocated and unsettled when the American revolution took place, — lands which were *acquired* by the *common blood and treasure*, and which *ought* to have been the *common stock*, and for the *common benefit* of the Union. Let it be remembered, that the State of Maryland was so deeply sensible of the injustice that these lands should be held by particular States for their own emolument, even at a time when no *superiority* of

authority or power was *annexed to extensive territory,* that, in the *midst of the late war* and all the *dangers* which *threatened* us, it withheld, for a long time, its assent to the articles of confederation for that reason; and, when it ratified those articles, it entered a *solemn protest* against what it considered so *flagrant injustice.* But, Sir, the question is not *now,* whether those States shall hold that territory unjustly to themselves, but whether, by *that act of injustice,* they shall *have superiority of power and influence over the other States,* and *have a constitutional right to domineer* and *lord it* over them. Nay, more, whether we will *agree* to a *form of government,* by which we *pledge* to *those States* the *whole force of the Union,* to *preserve* to them their *extensive territory entire* and *unbroken;* and, with our *blood and wealth, to assist them,* whenever they please to demand it, to *preserve the inhabitants thereof under their subjection,* for the *purpose of increasing their superiority over us,* — of *gratifying their unjust ambition,* — in a word, for the *purpose of giving ourselves masters,* and of *riveting our chains*!

[100] The part of the system which provides, that *no religious test* shall ever be required as a qualification to any office or public trust under the United States, was adopted by a great majority of the convention, and without much debate; however, there were some members *so unfashionable* as to think, that a *belief of the existence of a Deity,* and of a *state of future rewards and punishments* would be some security for the good conduct of our rulers, and that, in a Christian country, it would be *at least decent* to hold out some distinction between the professors of Christianity and downright infidelity or paganism.

[101] The seventh article declares, that the ratification of *nine States* shall be sufficient for the establishment of this constitution, between the States ratifying the same.

[102] It was attempted to obtain a resolve, that, if seven States, whose votes in the first branch should amount to a majority of the representation in that branch, concurred in the adoption of the system, it should be sufficient; and this attempt was supported on the principle, that a majority ought to govern the minority; but to this it was objected, that, although it was true, after a constitution and form of government is agreed on, in every act done under and consistent with that constitution and form of government, the act of the majority, unless otherwise agreed in the constitution, should bind the minority, yet it was directly the *reverse* in *originally forming* a constitution, or *dissolving it;* that, in originally forming a constitution, it was necessary that *every individual* should agree to it, to become bound thereby; and that, when *once adopted,* it

could not be *dissolved* by consent, unless with the consent of *every individual* who was *party* to the original agreement; that in forming our original federal government, *every member* of that government, that is, each State, expressly consented to it; that it is a *part* of the *compact* made and entered into, in the *most solemn* manner, that there should be no *dissolution* or *alteration* of that federal government, without the consent of *every State*, the members of, and parties to, the original compact; that, therefore, *no alteration* could be made by a consent of a *part* of these States, or by the consent of the *inhabitants* of a *part of the States*, which could either *release* the States so consenting from the obligation they are under to the other States, or which could in any manner become *obligatory* upon those States that should not ratify such alterations. Satisfied of the *truth* of these positions, and not holding ourselves at liberty to *violate* the *compact*, which this State had *solemnly entered into* with the others, by *altering* it in a *different* manner from that which by the same compact is provided and stipulated, a number of the members, and among those the *delegation* of *this State*, opposed the ratification of this system in *any other manner*, than by the *unanimous consent* and agreement of *all the States*.

[103] By our original articles of confederation, any alterations proposed are, in the first place, to be *approved* by Congress. Accordingly, as the resolutions were originally adopted by the convention, and as they were reported by the committee of detail, it was proposed that this system should be laid before Congress *for their approbation*. But, Sir, the warm advocates of this system, fearing it would not meet with the approbation of Congress, and determined, even though Congress and the respective State legislatures should disapprove the same, to force it upon them, if possible, through the intervention of the people at large, moved to strike out the words "for their approbation," and succeeded in their motion; to which, it being directly in violation of the mode prescribed by the articles of confederation for the alteration of our federal government, a part of the convention, and myself in the number, thought it a duty to give a decided negative.

[104] Agreeably to the articles of confederation, entered into in the most *solemn* manner, and for the *observance of which the States* pledged themselves to each other, and called upon the *Supreme Being* as a *witness* and *avenger* between them, no *alterations* are to be made in those articles, unless, after they are approved by Congress, they are agreed to and ratified by the *legislature* of every *State;* but, by the resolve of the convention, this constitution is not to be ratified by the legislatures of the respective States, but is to be submitted

to conventions chosen by the people, and, if ratified by them, is to be binding.

[105] This resolve was opposed, among others, by the delegation of Maryland. Your delegates were of opinion, that, as the form of government proposed was, if adopted, most essentially to *alter* the *constitution* of *this State*; and as our constitution had pointed out a mode by which, and by which *only*, alterations were to be made therein, a convention of the people could not be called to agree to and ratify the said form of government, without a *direct violation* of our constitution, which it is the duty of every individual in this State to protect and support. In this opinion, all your delegates who were attending were unanimous. I, Sir, opposed it also upon a more extensive ground, as being directly *contrary* to the mode of altering our federal government, *established* in our original compact; and, as such, being a *direct violation* of the mutual faith plighted by the States to each other, I gave it my negative.

[106] I was also of opinion, that the States, considered as States, in their political capacity, are the members of a federal government; that the States, in their political capacity, or as sovereignties, are entitled, and *only entitled* originally to agree upon the form of, and submit themselves to, a federal government, and afterwards, by mutual consent, to dissolve or alter it; that every thing which relates to the formation, the dissolution, or the alteration of a *federal* government over States equally free, sovereign, and independent, is the *peculiar* province of the *States*, in their *sovereign* or political capacity, in the same manner as what relates to forming alliances or treaties of peace, amity, or commerce; and that the people at large, in their individual capacity, have no more right to interfere in the one case than in the other. That according to these principles we originally acted, in forming our confederation; it was the States, as States, by their representatives in Congress, that formed the articles of confederation; it was the States, as States, by their legislatures, ratified those articles; and it was there established and provided, that the States, as States, that is, by their legislatures, should agree to any alterations that should hereafter be proposed in the federal government, before they should be binding; and any alterations agreed to in any other manner, cannot release the States from the obligation they are under to each other, by virtue of the original articles of confederation. The people of the different States never made any objection to the manner the articles of confederation were formed or ratified, or to the mode by which alterations were to be made in that government; with the rights of their respective States they wished not to interfere. Nor do I believe the people, in their

individual capacity, would ever have expected or desired to have been appealed to, on the present occasion, in violation of the rights of their respective States, if the favorers of the proposed constitution, imagining they had a better chance of forcing it to be adopted by a *hasty* appeal to the people at large, who could not be so good judges of the dangerous consequence, had not insisted upon this mode. Nor do these positions in the least interfere with the principle, that all power originates from the people; because, when once the people have *exercised their power in establishing and forming* themselves into a *State government*, it never *devolves back* to them, nor have they a *right* to *resume* or *again to exercise that power*, until such events take place as will amount to a *dissolution* of their *State government*. And it is an established principle, that a dissolution or alteration of a *federal* government doth not dissolve the *State* governments which compose it. It was also my opinion, that, upon *principles of sound policy*, the agreement or disagreement to the proposed system ought to have been by the State legislatures; in which case, let the event have been what it would, there would have been but little prospect of the *public peace* being *disturbed* thereby. Whereas, the attempt to force down this system, although Congress and the respective State legislatures should disapprove, by appealing to the people, and to procure its establishment in a manner totally unconstitutional, has a tendency to set the *State governments* and their *subjects* at *variance* with each other, to *lessen* the *obligations* of *government*, to *weaken* the *bands of society*, to introduce *anarchy* and *confusion*, and to *light* the *torch of discord and civil war* throughout this continent. All these considerations weighed with me most forcibly against giving my assent to the mode by which it is resolved this system is to be ratified, and were urged by me in opposition to the measure.

[107] I have now, Sir, in discharge of. the duty I owe to this House, given such information as hath occurred to me, which I consider most material for them to know; ' and you will easily perceive, from this detail, that a great portion of that time, which ought to have been devoted calmly and impartially to consider what alterations in our federal government would be most likely to procure and preserve the happiness of the Union, was employed in a *violent struggle* on the one side to obtain *all power* and *dominion* in their own hands, and on the other to prevent it; and that the *aggrandizement* of particular States and particular individuals, appears to have been much more the object sought after, than the welfare of our country.

[108] The interest of this State, not confined merely to itself,

abstracted from all others, but considered relatively, as far as was consistent with the common interest of the other States, I thought it my duty to pursue, according to the best opinion I could form of it.

[109] When I took my seat in the convention, I found it attempting to bring forward a system, which I was sure never had entered into the contemplation of those I had the honor to represent, and which, upon the fullest consideration, I considered not only injurious to the interest and the rights of this State, but also incompatible with the political happiness and freedom of the States in general. From that time until my business compelled me to leave the convention, I gave it every possible opposition, in every stage of its progression. I opposed the system there with the same explicit frankness with which I have here given you a history of our proceedings; an account of my own conduct, which in a particular manner I consider you as having a right to know. While there, I endeavoured to act as became a free man, and *the delegate* of a free State. Should my conduct obtain the approbation of those who appointed me, I will not deny it would afford me satisfaction; but to me that approbation was at most no more than a *secondary* consideration; my first was to deserve it. Left to myself, to act according to the best of my discretion, my conduct should have been the same, had I been even sure your censure would have been my only reward; since I hold it sacredly my duty to dash the cup of poison, if possible, from the hand of a State, or an individual, however anxious the one or the other might be to swallow it.

[110] Indulge, me Sir, in a single observation further. There are persons who endeavour to hold up the idea, that this system is only opposed by the officers of government — I, Sir, am in that predicament. I have the honor to hold an appointment in this State. Had it been considered any objection, I presume I should not have been appointed to the convention. If it could have had any effect on my mind, it would only be that of warming my heart with gratitude, and rendering me more anxious to promote the true interest of that State which has conferred on me the obligation, and to heighten my guilt had I joined in sacrificing its essential rights. But, Sir, it would be well to remember, that this system is not calculated to *diminish* the *number* or the *value* of *offices;* on the contrary, if adopted, it will be productive of an enormous increase in their number; many of them will be also of great honor and emoluments. Whether, Sir, in this variety of appointments, and in the scramble for them, I might not have as good a prospect to advantage myself as many others, is not for me to say; but this, Sir, I can say with truth, that, so far was I from being influenced in my con-

duct by interest, or the consideration of office, that I would cheerfully resign the appointment I now hold; I would bind myself never
to accept another, either under the general government or that
of my own State. I would do more, Sir; — so destructive do I
consider the present system to the happiness of my country, I would
cheerfully sacrifice that share of property with which Heaven has
blessed a life of industry; I would reduce myself to indigence and
poverty, and those who are dearer to me than my own existence
I would intrust to the care and protection of that Providence, who
hath so kindly protected myself, if on *those terms only* I could procure my country to reject those chains which are forged for it.

CLIX. LISTE DES MEMBRES ET OFFICIERS DU CONGRÉS. 1788.[1]

Avec des nottes sur les personnages les plus
intéressans des différens Etats.

New Hampshire.

Nich. Gillman. . . . Jeune homme à prétentions; peu aimé par
ses collègues; on l'appelle par dérision *le Congrès.* Il
a cependant l'avantage d'avoir représenté son Etat
dans la grande Convention de Philadelphie et
d'avoir signé la nouvelle Constitution. Cette cir-
constance prouve qu'il n'y a pas un grand choix à
faire dans cet Etat, on que du moins les hommes les
plus sensés et les plus habiles ne sont pas assés
riches pour accepter une place publique. M. G. a
servi pendant la guerre comme aide de camp. . . .

John Langdon. Un des hommes les plus intéressans et les plus
aimables des Etats Unis; ci devant gouverneur du
New Hampshire et à la tête d'un parti très puissant,
qui se trouve en opposition avec le Gal. Sullivan.*

---

*Cette opposition n'est que personelle et ne porte aucunement sur les sentimens
politiques. Ces deux antagonistes sont également attachés à leur patrie, à la révolution et à la France, mais Sullivan est l'homme du peuple et Langdon le protégé des
gentlemen. L'un a pour lui les gens de la campagne, l'autre les commerçans. Quelque soit le succès de leurs intrigues, la chose publique ne peut jamais y perdre et les
principes de gouvernement resteront les mêmes. Dans la société, M. Langdon l'em-
porte de beaucoup sur son adversaire. Mais il faut voir Sullivan au barreau ou à
la tête de la milice.

---

[1] French Archives: *Ministère des Affaires Etrangères. Archives. Etats–Unis.
Correspondance. Supplément,* 2e Série, Vol. XV, pp. 314 ff. Although this document
strictly does not belong to the records of the Federal Convention, it contains such
interesting characterizations of so many of the delegates to that body, that it has
seemed worth while to print it.

M. L. a fait une grande fortune dans le commerce, c'est le Rob. Morris de son Etat, faisant une grande dépense et s'attachant beaucoup de citoyens par ses libéralités. Il a été un des principaux membres de la convention de Philadelphie, mais il n'a siégé en Congrès que peu de jours, et quoique ses collègues lui ayent offert la présidence, il n'a pas voulu y rester, parce qu'il avoit en vue de se faire reélire Gouverneur dans le New Hampshire, et que ses affaires de commerce ne lui permettent pas de faire une longue absence. Il est sincèrement attaché à la France et même prévenu pour nos usages et nos manières. Pour répandre le goût de nos meubles, il en a fair venir de très beaux de Paris. On prétend qu'il est jaloux de sa femme, chose assés rare en Amérique. Plusieurs officiers françois ont vu avec chagrin que cette jalousie n'étoit guères fondée.

Massachusetts.

[*Elbridge Gerry*.]

. . . En Congrès, il [Nathan Dane] a toujours fait cause commune avec M. Gerry*, qui ne nous aime pas, et qui s'est principalement opposé a la ratification de notre Convention consulaire. Il a plus de talens que M. Gerry et moins de duplicité.

Connecticut.

[*Oliver Ellsworth*]

. . . M. Ellsworth, ci devant membre du Congrès, est un homme absolument de la même tournure et des mêmes dispositions.† On peut en dire

---

* M. Elb. Gerry est un petit homme, très intriguant et rempli de petites finesses, qui jusqu'ici lui ont assés bien réussi. C'est celui de tous les membres du Congrès qui ait été le plus longtems en activité. Il y a acquis une grande co[n]noissance des affaire publiques, dont il tire parti pour se faire valoir auprès de ses concitoyens. En 1782, il fit un assez beau discours dans la législature de Boston pour l'engager à ne pas permettre la ratification de la Convention consulaire. Il affecte d'aimer beaucoup M. le Chev. de La Luzerne, mais on doit se méfier de toutes ses belles protestations. Nous avons généralement très peu d'amis parmi les hommes puisans du Massachusetts, notre commerce ne les intéresse pas et nos pêcheries les gênent. M. Bowdoin, M. King, M. Sam. Adams etc. puisent toutes leurs notions politiques dans les écrits ou dans les conversations de Mrs. Jay et J. Adams. Le peuple en général aime les François, puisqu'il a vu souvent nos flottes et qu'il se souvient des services que nous lui avons rendus.

† That is, of Benjamin Huntington, of whom it has just been said: "C'est un homme simple dans ses manières, mais sage et infiniment raisonnable; n'ayant jamais suivi aucun parti et voulant le bien sans considérer des motifs personnels. Il nous a souvent donné des preuves d'attachement et de zèle."

autant de M. *Sherman.* — Les gens de cet Etat ont,
en général, un caractère national qu'on ne trouve
guères dans les autres parties de continent. Ils se
raprochent plus de la simplicité républicaine; ils
sont tous à leur aise sans connoître l'opulence.
L'économie rurale et l'industrie domestiques sont
poussées très loin dans le Connecticut; le peuple
y est heureux.

New York.

Alex. Hamilton. . . . Grand orateur; intrépide dans les débats
publics. Partisan zélé et même outré de la nouvelle
Constitution et ennemi déclare du gouv. Clinton,
qu'il a eu le courage d'attaquer publiquement dans
les Gazettes, sans aucune provocation. C est un
de ces hommes rares qui s'est distingué également
au champ de bataille et au barreau. Il doit tout
à ses talens. Une indiscrétion l'a brouillé avec le
gal. Washington, dont il était le secrétaire de confiance; d'autres indiscrétions l'ont obligé de quitter
le Congrès en 1783. Il a un peu trop de prèten-
tions et trop peu de prudence.

Voici ce que M. le chev[alier] de L[a] L[u-
zerne] dit de lui en 1780: "M. H[amilton], un des
"aides de camp du Gal. Wash[ington] a le plus
"d'ascendant sur lui; homme d'esprit, d'une
"médiocre probité; éloigné des Anglais parce
"qu'étant d'une très basse extraction dans une de
"leurs colonies, il craint de rentrer dans son ancien
"Etat. Ami particulier de M. de La Fayette. M.
"Conway pense qu' Hamilton haît les François,
"qu'il est absolument corrompu et que les liaisons
"qu'il paroitra avoir avec nous ne seront jamais
"que trompeuses."

M. Hamilton n'a rien fait qui puisse justifier
cette dernière opinion; il est seulement trop im-
pétueux, et à force de vouloir tout conduire, il manque
son but. Son éloquence est souvent hors de saison
dans les débats publics, ou l'on préfère la précision
et la clarté à une imagination brillante. On croit
que M. H[amilton] est l'auteur de pamphlet inti-
tulé le *Fédéraliste.* Il y a encore manqué son but.
Cet ouvrage n'est d'aucune utilité aux gens instruits,
et il est trop savant et trop long pour les ignorans.

Il lui a cependant donné une grande célébrité, et l'on a nommé le *Hamilton* une petite frégatte que, dans la grande procession fédérale on a trainé par les rues de New York. Mais ces parades ne sont ici comme ailleurs qu'une impression nomentanée et comme le parti des Antifédéralistes est le plus nombreux dans l'Etat, M. Hamilton a plutôt perdu que gagné par le zèle qu'il a déploye à cette occasion.

Etranger dans cet Etat, où il a été élevé par charité, M. Hamilton a trouvé moyen d'enlever la fille du Gal. Schuyler*, grand propriétaire et tres influent. Après s'être réconcilié avec la famille, il jouit dans ce moment ci du crédit de son beau père.

New Jersey.

Dayton.   . . . Peu connu; n'ayant d'autre mérite que d'être le fils d'un bon patriote et du bienfaiteur de M. d'Anteroches, ce qui fait présumer qu'il aime les François.

Il se trouve dans cet Etat plusieurs particuliers qu'il nous importe de ménager, parce qu'ils sont nos amis, et qu'ils jouissent d'une grande influence.

[*Livingston.*]   1. *William Livingston*, Esq., Gouverneur depuis le commencement de la révolution, très instruit, ferme, patriote, préférant le bien public à sa popularité et ayant souvent exposé sa place pour empêcher la legislature de passer de mauvaises lois. Quoiqu'il ne cesse de fronder le peuple, il est toujours réélu, puisque même ses ennemis conviennent qu'il est un des hommes les plus habiles et les plus vertueux du continent. Il est père de Made Jay et de M. Broc. Livingston. . . .

Pennsylvania.

[*Franklin.*]   Le *Dr. Franklin*, Président actuel de cet Etat, set trop bien connu pour avoir besoin des éloges que nous lui devons. Il sent, plus que tout autre Américain, que, pour être vraiment patriote, il faut être l'ami de la France. Malheureusement ce philoso-

---

* Les enlèvemens sont plus co[m]muns en Amérique qu'en France, les parens se fâchent d'abord, ils s'attendrissent et se réconcilient au bout de quelques mois. Tout le monde s'intéresse à ces sortes de mariage, puisqu'ils paroissent plus conformes à la première impulsion de la nature.

phe, qui a su braver les foudres du ciel et du Parlement d'Angleterre, ne luttera plus longtems contre les infirmités de l'âge. Nous devons regretter que l'immortalité n'appartienne qu'à son nom et a ses écrits.

[*Mifflin.*]   *Tho. Mifflin.* Ci devant Gal., Président du Congrès, orateur de l'assemblée, etc. Ami déclaré et éprouvé de la France. Très populaire et maniant avec une facilité étonnante le monstre à cent têtes apellé peuple. Bon avocat, bon officier, bon patriote, et d'une société agréable. Faisant bien tout se qu'il entreprend, par ce qu'il tient de la nature et qu'il ne peut que gagner en se montrant tel qu'il est.

[*R. Morris.*]   *Rob. Morris.* Surintendant des Finances pendant la guerre, négociant très puissant dans son Etat. Devant tout à sa bonne tête et à son expérience, peu à l'étude. Il s'est un peu refroidi sur le compte de la France depuis que M. de Marbois a pris avec tant de chaleur le parti de M. Hotker et qu'on a désapprouvé son contrat avec la ferme. Il sera cependant facile de la gagner par de bons procédés. C'est un homme du plus grand poids et dont l'amitié ne sauroit nous être indifférente.

[*G. Morris.*]   *Gouv. Morris.* Citoyen de l'Etat de New York, mais toujours en relation avec M. Rob. Morris et ayant représenté plusieurs fois la Pennsylvanie. Avocat célébre; une des têtes les mieux organisées du continent, mais sans moeurs, et, si l'on en croit ses ennemis, sans principes; infiniment intéressant dans le conversation et ayant étudié avec un soin particulier la partie des finances. Il travaille constamment avec M. Rob. Morris. On le craint encore plus ne l'admire, mais peu de gens l'estiment.

[*Wilson.*]   . . . *James Wilson.* Jurisconsulte distingué. C'est lui qui fut désigné par M. Gerard comme avocat de la nation françoise, place dont on a reconnu depuis l'inutilité. Homme altier, aristocrate intrépide, actif, éloquent, profond, dissimulé, connu sous le nom de *James the Caledonian*, que ses e[n]nemis lui ont donné. Ayant dérangé sa fortune par de grandes enterprises que les affaires publiques ne lui permettoient pas de suivre. Médiocrement attaché a la France.

[*Dickinson.*]   . . . *John Dickinson.* Auteur des lettres du fermier de Pensylvanie; homme très riche, étant au co[m]mencement de la révolution du parti anti anglican, sans cependant favoriser l'indépendance, contre laquelle il a même voté publiquement. Il est vieux, foible et sans influence. . . .

Maryland.

[*Martin.*]   . . . *M. Luther Martin.* Avocat distingué et qui a beaucoup écrti contre les résolutions de la Convention de Philadelphie, dont il a été membre.

Virginie.

James Madison   Instruit, sage, modéré, docile, studieux; peut être plus profond que M. Hamilton, mais moins brillant; ami intime de M. Jefferson et sincèrement attaché à la France. Il a été en Congrès fort jeune et il paroit s'être voué particulièrement aux affaires publiques. Il pourra être un jour gouverneur de son Etat, si sa modestie lui permet d'accepter cette place. Il a refusé en dernier lieu celle de président du Congrès. C'est un homme qu'il faut étudier longtemps pour s'en former une idée juste.

[*Randolph.*]   . . . *Edmund Randolph,* gouverneur actuel, est un des hommes les plus distingués en Amérique par ses talents et son influence; il a cependant perdu une partie de sa considération en s'opposant avec trop de violence à la ratification de la nouvelle Constitution. Il fut membre de Congrès en 1780 et 1781, et à en juger par toutes les difficultés qu'éprouva M. le Chev[alier] de la Luzerne en negociant avec lui notre convention consulaire, nous devons le considérer au moins comme très indifférent sur le compte de la France. Toutes les objections qui se trouvent dans le raport de M. Jay furent faites alors par M. Randolph et le ministre de France ne dut son succès qu'à la modération des autres membres du Committé. . . .

Caroline du Nord.

Hugh Williamson.   Médecin et ci-devant Professeur d'astronomie. Bizarre a l'excès, aimant à pérorer, mais parlant avec esprit. Il est difficile de bien connoître son caractère; il est même possible qu'il n'en ait pas; mais son activité lui a donné depuis quelque temps beaucoup d'influence au Congrès. . . .

Carolina du Sud.

[*Rutledge.*]   . . . *J. Rutledge.* Gouverneur pendant la guerre, membre du Congrès, de la Convention et en général employé dans toutes les grandes occasions. L'homme le plus éloquent, mais le plus fier et le plus impérieux des Etats-Unis. Il tire parti de sa grande influence et de ses co[n]noissances comme Avocat pour ne pas payer ses dettes, qui excèdent de beaucoup sa fortune. Son fils voyage en France pour s'instruire. . . .

Géorgie.

Abrah. Baldwin.   Raisonnable et bien intentionné, mais n'ayant jamais en l'occasion de sa distinguer. Le Congrès vient de lui en donner les moyens, en le no[m]mant parmi les Commissaires pour régler ses comptes avec les Etats.

William Few.   Sans être un grand génie, il a plus de connoissances que son nom et son extérieur ne paroissent indiquer. Quoique jeune encore, il a été constamment employé pendant la guerre. Ses collègues en ont une bonne opinion Il est très timide et embarassant dans la société, à moins qu'on ne lui parle d'affaires. _____

CLX. Hugh Williamson: Remarks on the New Plan of Government.[1]

It seems to be generally admitted, that the system of government which has been proposed by the late convention, is well calculated to relieve us from many of the grievances under which we have been laboring. If I might express my particular sentiments on this subject, I should describe it as more free and more perfect than any form of government that has ever been adopted by any nation; but I would not say it has no faults. Imperfection is inseparable from every device. Several objections were made to

_____

[1] P. L. Ford, *Essays on Constitution*, pp. 397–406; first printed in the *State Gazette of North Carolina*. No file of that paper is known to exist, so its date is doubtful. It probably appeared in 1788. Mr. Ford printed his copy from a clipping preserved by Williamson.

this system by two or three very respectable characters in the convention, which have been the subject of much conversation; . . .

When you refer the proposed system to the particular circumstances of North Carolina, and consider how she is to be affected by this plan, you must find the utmost reason to rejoice in the prospect of better times. This is a sentiment that I have ventured with the greater confidence, because it is the general opinion of my late-honourable colleagues, and I have the utmost reliance in their superior abilities. But if our constituents shall discover faults where we could not see any—or if they shall suppose that a plan is formed for abridging their liberties, when we imagined that we had been securing both liberty and property on a more stable foundation—if they perceive that they are to suffer a loss, where we thought they must rise from a misfortune—they will, at least do us the justice to charge those errors to the head, and not to the heart.

CLXI. The Federalist, No. XXXIII. [Hamilton.] [1]

But SUSPICION may ask, Why then was it [Art. I, Sect. 8, last paragraph] introduced? The answer is, that it could only have been done for greater caution, and to guard against all cavilling refinements in those who might hereafter feel a disposition to curtail and evade the legitimate authorities of the union. The convention probably foresaw, that it has been a principal aim of these papers to inculcate, that the danger which most threatens our political welfare is, that the state governments will finally sap the foundations of the union; and might therefore think it necessary, in so cardinal a point, to leave nothing to construction. Whatever may have been the inducement to it, the wisdom of the precaution is evident from the cry which has been raised against it; as that very cry betrays a disposition to question the great and essential truth which it is manifestly the object of that provision to declare.

CLXII. [Gerry:] Reply to a Landholder, I. [2]

Mr. Russell:

You are desired to inform the publick from good authority, that Mr. Gerry . . . never heard, in the Convention, a motion made, much less did make any, "for the redemption of the old continental

---

[1] Hallowell edition, 1837; first printed in the *Daily Advertiser*, January 3, 1788.

[2] P. L. Ford, *Essays on the Constitution*, 127-128; first printed in the *Massachusetts Centinel*, January 5, 1788. The article by "The Landholder" to which this a reply. will be found above, CLVII. The controversy may be followed farther in CLXXV, CLXXXIX-CXCII and CXCIX.

money;" but that he proposed the public debt should be made neither better nor worse by the new system, but stand precisely on the same ground by the Articles of Confederation; that had there been such a motion, he was not interested in it, as he did not then, neither does he now, own the value of ten pounds in continental money; that he neither was called on for his reasons for not signing, but stated them fully in the progress of the business. His objections are chiefly contained in his letter to the Legislature; that he believes his colleagues men of too much honour to assert what is not truth; that his reasons in the Convention "were totally different from those which he published," that his only motive for dissenting from the Constitution, was a firm persuasion that it would endanger the liberties of America; that if the people are of a different opinion, they have a right to adopt; but he was not authorized to an act, which appeared to him was a surrender of their liberties; that a representative of a free state, he was bound in honour to vote according to his idea of her true interest, and that he should do the same in similar circumstances.

CLXIII. Oliver Ellsworth in the Connecticut Convention.[1]

January 7, 1788.

Mr. President, this is a most important clause in the Constitution; and the gentlemen do well to offer all the objections which they have against it. Through the whole of this debate, I have attended to the objections which have been made against this clause; and I think them all to be unfounded. The clause is general; it gives the general legislature "power to lay and collect taxes, duties, imposts, and excises, to pay the debts and provide for the common defence and general welfare of the United States." There are three obejctions against this clause — first, that it is too extensive, as it extends to all the objects of taxation; secondly, that it is partial; thirdly, that Congress ought not to have power to lay taxes at all.

. . . The second objection is, that the impost is not a proper mode of taxation; that it is partial to the Southern States. I confess I am mortified when I find gentlemen supposing that their delegates in Convention were inattentive to their duty, and made a sacrifice of the interests of their constituents. . . .

This Constitution defines the extent of the powers of the general government. If the general legislature should at any time overleap their limits, the judicial department is a constitutional check. If

---

[1] Jonathan Elliot, *Debates in the several State Conventions on the Adoption of the Federal Constitution*, II, 190–197.

the United States go beyond their powers, if they make a law which the Constitution does not authorize, it is void; and the judicial power, the national judges, who to secure their impartiality, are to be made independent, will declare it to be void. On the other hand, if the states go beyond their limits, if they make a law which is a usurpation upon the federal government the law is void; and upright, independent judges will declare it to be so. Still, however, if the United States and the individual states will quarrel, if they want to fight, they may do it, and no frame of government can possibly prevent it. It is sufficient for this Constitution, that, so far from laying them under a necessity of contending, it provides every reasonable check against it. But perhaps, at some time or other, there will be a contest; the states may rise against the general government. If this do take place, if all the states combine, if all oppose, the whole will not eat up the members, but the measure which is opposed to the sense of the people will prove abortive. In republics, it is a fundamental principle that the majority govern and that the minority comply with the general voice. How contrary, then, to republican principles, how humiliating, is our present situation! A single state can rise up, and put a *veto* upon the most important public measures. We have seen this actually take place. A single state has controlled the general voice of the Union; a minority, a very small minority, has governed us. So far is this from being consistent with republican principles, that it is, in effect, the worst species of monarchy.

Hence we see how necessary for the Union is a coercive principle. No man pretends the contrary: we all see and feel this necessity. The only question is, Shall it be a coercion of law, or a coercion of arms? There is no other possible alternative. Where will those who oppose a coercion of law come out? Where will they end? A necessary consequence of their principles is a war of the states one against the other. I am for coercion by law — that coercion which acts only upon delinquent individuals. This Constitution does not attempt to coerce sovereign bodies, states, in their political capacity. No coercion is applicable to such bodies, but that of an armed force. If we should attempt to execute the laws of the Union by sending an armed force against a delinquent state, it would involve the good and bad, the innocent and guilty, in the same calamity.

But this legal coercion singles out the guilty individual, and punishes him for breaking the laws of the Union. All men will see the reasonableness of this; they will acquiesce, and say, Let the guilty suffer.

How have the morals of the people been depraved for the want of an efficient government, which might establish justice and righteousness! For the want of this, iniquity has come in upon us like an overflowing flood. If we wish to prevent this alarming evil, if we wish to protect the good citizen in his right, we must lift up the standard of justice; we must establish a national government, to be enforced by the equal decisions of law, and the peaceable arm of the magistrate. _____

CLXIV. George Washington to Edmund Randolph.[1]

Mount Vernon January 8th. 1788

The various passions and medium by which men are influenced are concomitants of falibility — engrafted into our nature for the purposes of unerring wisdom; but had I entertained a latent hope (at the time you moved to have the Constitution submitted to a second Convention) that a more perfect form would be agreed to — in a word that any Constitution would be adopted under the impressions and Instructions of the members, the publications which have taken place since would have eradicated every form of it. . . .

To my judgment, it is more clear than ever, that an attempt to amend the Constitution which is submitted, would be productive of more heat, & greater confusion than can well be conceived. There are somethings in the new form, I will readily acknowledge, wch. never did, and I am persuaded never will, obtain my *cordial* approbation; but I then did conceive, and now do most firmly believe, that, in the aggregate, it is the best Constitution that can be obtained at this Epocha; and that this, or a dissolution of the Union awaits our choice, & are the only alternatives before us — Thus believing, I had not, nor have I now any hesitation in deciding on which to lean.

I pray your forgiveness for the expression of these sentiments. In acknowledging the receipt of your Letter on this subject, it was hardly to be avoided, although I am well disposed to let the matter rest entirely on its own merits — and mens minds to their own workings. _____

CLXV. Robert Morris to a Friend.[2]

January, 1788.

This paper has been the subject of infinite investigation, disputation, and declamation. While some have boasted it as a work from Heaven, others have given it a less righteous origin. I have

---

[1] *Documentary History of the Constitution*, IV, 431–432.
[2] *Pennsylvania Magazine of History and Biography*, II, 191–192.

many reasons to believe that it is the work of plain, honest men, and such, I think, it will appear. Faulty it must be, for what is perfect? But if adopted, experience will, I believe, show that its faults are just the reverse of what they are supposed to be. As yet this paper is but a dead letter. Pennsylvania, Delaware, New Jersey, Connecticut, and Georgia have adopted it. We wait impatiently the result of their deliberations in Massachusetts. Should that State also adopt it, which I *hope and believe*, there will then be little doubt of a general acquiescence.

CLXVI. THE FEDERALIST, No. XXXVII. [MADISON].[1]

Among the difficulties encountered by the convention, a very important one must have lain, in combining the requisite stability and energy in government, with the inviolable attention due to liberty, and to the republican form. Without substantially accomplishing this part of their undertaking, they would have very imperfectly fulfilled the object of their appointment, or the expectation of the public: yet that it could not be easily accomplished, will be denied by no one who is unwilling to betray his ignorance of the subject. . . .

Here, then, are three sources of vague and incorrect definitions; indistinctness of the object, imperfection of the organ of perception, inadequateness of the vehicle of ideas. Any one of these must produce a certain degree of obscurity. The convention, in delineating the boundary between the federal and state jurisdictions, must have experienced the full effect of them all.

To the difficulties already mentioned, may be added the interfering pretensions of the larger and smaller states. We cannot err, in supposing that the former would contend for a participation in the government, fully proportioned to their superior wealth and importance; and that the latter would not be less tenacious of the equality at present enjoyed by them. We may well suppose, that neither side would entirely yield to the other, and consequently that the struggle could be terminated only by compromise. It is extremely probable also, that after the ratio of representation had been adjusted, this very compromise must have produced a fresh struggle between the same parties, to give such a turn to the organization of the government, and to the distribution of its powers, as would increase the importance of the branches, in forming which they had respectively obtained the greatest share of influence. There are features in the constitution which warrant each of these

---

[1] Hallowell edition, 1837; first printed in the *Daily Advertiser*, January 11, 1788.

suppositions; and as far as either of them is well founded, it shows that the convention must have been compelled to sacrifice theoretical propriety, to the force of extraneous considerations.

Nor could it have been the large and small states only, which would marshal themselves in opposition to each other on various points. Other combinations, resulting from a difference of local position and policy, must have created additional difficulties. As every state may be divided into different districts, and its citizens into different classes, which give birth to contending interests and local jealousies; so that different parts of the United States are distinguished from each other, by a variety of circumstances, which produce a like effect on a larger scale. And although this variety of interests, for reasons sufficiently explained in a former paper, may have a salutary influence on the administration of the government when formed; yet every one must be sensible of the contrary influence, which must have been experienced in the task of forming it.

Would it be wonderful, if under the pressure of all these difficulties, the convention should have been forced into some deviations from that artificial structure and regular symmetry, which an abstract view of the subject might lead an ingenious theorist to bestow on a constitution planned in his closet, or in his imagination? The real wonder is, that so many difficulties should have been surmounted; and surmounted with an unanimity almost as unprecedented, as it must have been unexpected. It is impossible for any man of candour to reflect on this circumstance, without partaking of the astonishment. It is impossible, for the man of pious reflection not to perceive in it a finger of that Almighty Hand, which has been so frequently and signally extended to our relief in the critical stages of the revolution.

CLXVII. Robert Yates and John Lansing, Jr. to the Governor of New York.[1]

Sir, We do ourselves the honor to advise your excellency, that in pursuance of concurrent resolutions of the honorable senate and assembly, we have, together with Mr. Hamilton, attended the convention, appointed for revising the articles of confederation, and reporting amendments to the same.

It is with the sincerest concern we observe, that, in the prosecution of the important objects of our mission, we have been reduced

---

[1] Yates, *Secret Proceedings and Debates* (Edit. 1821), 280–283. See also CLXXXV below.

to the disagreeable alternative, of either exceeding the powers delegated to us, and giving our assent to measures which we conceive
destructive to the political happiness of the citizens of the United
States, or opposing our opinions to that of a body of respectable
men, to whom those citizens had given the most unequivocal proofs
of confidence. — Thus circumstanced, under these impressions, to
have hesitated, would have been to be culpable; we, therefore, gave
the principles of the constitution, which has received the sanction
of a majority of the convention, our decided and unreserved dissent; but we must candidly confess, that we should have been
equally opposed to any system, however modified, which had in
object the consolidation of the United States into one government.

We beg leave, briefly, to state some cogent reasons, which,
among others, influenced us to decide against a consolidation of the
states. These are reducible into two heads.

1st. The limited and well-defined powers under which we acted,
and which could not, on any possible construction, embrace an idea
of such magnitude, as to assent to a general constitution, in subversion of that of the state.

2d. A conviction of the impracticability of establishing a general
government, pervading every part of the United States, and extending essential benefits to all.

Our powers were explicit, and confined to the sole and express
purpose of revising the articles of confederation, and reporting such
alterations and provisions therein, as should render the federal
constitution adequate to the exigencies of government, and the
preservation of the union.

From these expressions, we were led to believe, that a system
of consolidated government could not in the remotest degree, have
been in contemplation of the legislature of this state? for that so
important a trust, as the adopting measures which tended to deprive
the state government of its most essential rights of sovereignty,
and to place it in a dependent situation, could not have been confided
by implication; and the circumstance, that the acts of the convention were to receive a state approbation in the last resort, forcibly
corroborated the opinion, that our powers could not involve the subversion of a constitution, which being immediately derived from the
people, could only be abolished by their express consent, and not
by a legislature, possessing authority vested in them for its preseveration.
tion.   Nor could we suppose, that if it had been the intention of the
legislature, to abrogate the existing confederation, they would, in such
pointed terms, have directed the attention of their delegates to the
revision and amendment of it, in total exclusion of every other idea.

Reasoning in this manner, we were of opinion, that the leading feature of every amendment, ought to be the preservation of the individual states, in their uncontrouled constitutional rights, and that in reserving these, a mode might have been devised of granting to the confederacy, the monies arising from a general system of revenue; the power of regulating commerce, and enforcing the observance of foreign treaties, and other necessary matters of less moment.

Exclusive of our objections originating from the want of power, we entertained an opinion, that a general government, however guarded by declarations of rights, or cautionary provisions, must unavoidably, in a short time, be productive of the destruction of the civil liberty of such citizens who could be effectually coerced by it: by reason of the extensive territory of the United States, the dispersed situation of its inhabitants, and the insuperable difficulty of controuling or counteracting the views of a set of men (however unconstitutional and oppressive their acts might be) possessed of all the powers of government; and who from their remoteness from their constituents and necessary permanency of office, could not be supposed to be uniformly actuated by an attention to their welfare and happiness; that however wise and energetic the principles of the general government might be, the extremities of the United States could not be kept in due submission and obedience to its laws, at the distance of many hundred miles from the seat of government; that if the general legislature was composed of so numerous a body of men, as to represent the interests of all the inhabitants of the United States, in the usual and true ideas of representation, the expence of supporting it would become intolerably burdensome; and that if a few only were vested with a power of legislation, the interests of a great majority of the inhabitants of the United States, must necessarily be unknown; or if known, even in the first stages of the operations of the new government, unattended to.

These reasons were, in our opinion, conclusive against any system of consolidated government: to that recommended by the convention, we suppose most of them very forcibly apply.

It is not our intention to pursue this subject farther, than merely to explain our conduct in the discharge of the trust which the honorable the legislature reposed in us. — Interested, however, as we are, in common with our fellow citizens, in the result, we cannot forbear to declare, that we have the strongest apprehensions, that a government so organized, as that recommended by the convention, cannot afford that security to equal and permanent liberty, which we wished to make an invariable object of our pursuit.

We were not present at the completion of the new constitution; but before we left the convention, its principles were so well established, as to convince us, that no alteration was to be expected, to conform it to our ideas of expediency and safety. A persuasion, that our further attendance would be fruitless and unavailing, rendered us less solicitious to return.

We have thus explained our motives for opposing the adoption of the national constitution, which we conceived it our duty to communicate to your excellency, to be submitted to the consideration of the honorable legislature.

We have the honor to be, With the greatest respect, Your excellency's Most obedient, and Very humble servants,

ROBERT YATES,
JOHN LANSING, Jun.

His Excellency Governor Clinton.

CLXVIII. CALEB STRONG IN THE MASSACHUSETTS CONVENTION.[1]

January 15, 1788.

The Hon. Mr. Strong rose to reply to the inquiry of the Hon. Mr. Adams, why the alteration of elections from annual to biennial was made, and to correct an inaccuracy of the Hon. Mr. Gorham, who, the day before, had said that *that* alteration was made to gratify South Carolina. He said he should then have arisen to put his worthy colleague right; but his memory was not sufficiently retentive to enable him immediately to collect every circumstance. He had since recurred to the original plan. When the subject was at first discussed in convention, some gentlemen were for having the term extended to a considerable length of time; others were opposed to it, as it was contrary to the ideas and customs of the Eastern States; but a majority were in favor of three years, and it was, he said, urged by the Southern States, which are not so populous as the Eastern, that the expense of more frequent elections would be great. He concluded by saying that a general concession produced the term as it stood in the section, although it was agreeable to the practice of South Carolina. [From "Debates of Convention"]

Caleb Strong. Stated the grounds proceeded on in Federal Convention; determined at first to be triennial; afterwards reduced to biennial; South Carolina having at home biennial elections, and it was a compromise [From "Parson's Minutes"]

----

[1] *Debates and Proceedings in Convention of Massachusetts in 1788,* Edit. of 1856, pp. 103–104, 287,

CLXIX. Caleb Strong in the Massachusetts Convention.[1]

January 16, 1788.

The Hon. Mr. Strong . . . Gentlemen have said, the proposed Constitution was in some places ambiguous. I wish they would point out the particular instances of ambiguity; for my part I think the whole of it is expressed in the plain, common language of mankind. If any parts are not so explicit as they could be, it cannot be attributed to any design; for I believe a great majority of the men who formed it were sincere and honest men.[2]

CLXX. Debate in the South Carolina Legislature.[3]

House of Representatives.   In the Legislature,
Wednesday, January 16, 1788.

Hon. Charles Pinckney (one of the delegates of the Federal Convention) rose in his place, and said that, although the principles and expediency of the measures proposed by the late Convention will come more properly into discussion before another body, yet, as their appointment originated with them, and the legislatures must be the instrument of submitting the plan to the opinion of the people, it became a duty in their delegates to state with conciseness the motives which induced it. . . .

Under these momentous impressions the Convention met, when the first question that naturally presented itself to the view of almost every member, although, it was never formally brought forward, was the formation of a new, or the amendment of the existing system. Whatever might have been the opinions of a few speculative men, who either did, or pretended to, confide more in the virtue of the people than prudence warranted, Mr. Pinckney said he would venture to assert that the states were unanimous in preferring a change.

. . . It was sufficient to remark that the Convention saw and felt the necessity of establishing a government upon different principles, which, instead of requiring the intervention of thirteen different legislatures between the demand and the compliance, should operate upon the people in the first instance.

He repeated, that the necessity of having a government which should at once operate upon the people, and not upon the states,

---

[1] *Debates and Proceedings in Convention of Massachusetts in 1788.*   Edit. of 1856, p. 122.

[2] See below CCCIV, CCCXIV.

[3] Elliot, *Debates in State Conventions on adoption of the Federal Constitution,* IV, 253–267.

was conceived to be indispensable by every delegation present; that, however they may have differed with respect to the quantum of power, no objection was made to the system itself. They considered it, however, highly necessary that, in the establishment of a constitution possessing extensive national authorities, a proper distribution of its powers should be attended to. Sensible of the danger of a single body, and that to such a council the states ought not to intrust important rights, they considered it their duty to divide the legislature into two branches, and, by a limited revisionary power, to mingle, in some degree, the executive in their proceedings — a provision that he was pleased to find meets with universal approbation. The degree of weight which each state was to have in the federal council became a question of much agitation. The larger states contended that no government could long exist whose principles were founded in injustice; that one of the most serious and unanswerable objections to the present system was the injustice of its tendency in allowing each state an equal vote, notwithstanding their striking disparity. The small ones replied, and perhaps with reason, that, as the states were the pillars upon which the general government must ever rest, their state governments must remain; that, however they may vary in point of territory or population, as political associations they were equal; that upon these terms they formally confederated, and that no inducement whatsoever should tempt them to unite upon others; that, if they did, it would amount to nothing less than throwing the whole government of the Union into the hands of three or four of the largest states.

After much anxious discussion, — for, had the Convention separated without determining upon a plan, it would have been on this point, — a compromise was effected, by which it was determined that the first branch be so chosen as to represent in due proportion the people of the Union; that the Senate should be the representatives of the states, where each should have an equal weight. Though he was at first opposed to this compromise, yet he was far from thinking it an injudicious one. . . . The purpose of establishing different houses of legislation was to introduce the influence of different interests and principles. . . .

And the executive, he said, though not constructed upon those firm and permanent principles which he confessed would have been pleasing to him, is still as much so as the present temper and genius of the people will admit. . . .

He had been opposed to connecting the executive and the Senate in the discharge of those duties, because their union, in his opinion, destroyed that responsibility which the Constitution should, in this respect, have been careful to establish; but he had no apprehensions of an aristocracy.

. . . Though at first he considered some declaration on the subject of trial by jury in civil causes, and the freedom of the press, necessary, and still thinks it would have been as well to have had it inserted, yet he fully acquiesced in the reasoning which was used to show that the insertion of them was not essential. . . .

On the subject of juries, in civil cases, the Convention were anxious to make some declaration; but when they reflected that all courts of admiralty and appeals, being governed in their propriety by the civil law and the laws of nations, never had, or ought to have, juries, they found it impossible to make any precise declaration upon the subject; they therefore left it as it was, trusting that the good sense of their constituents would never induce them to suppose that it could be the interest or intention of the general government to abuse one of the most invaluable privileges a free country can boast; in the loss of which, themselves, their fortunes and connections, must be so materially involved, and to the deprivation of which, except in the cases alluded to, the people of this country would never submit. . . .

Judge Pendleton read a paragraph in the Constitution, which says "the Senate shall have the sole power of impeachment." . . .

Maj. Pierce Butler (one of the delegates of the Federal Convention) was one of a committee that drew up this clause, and would endeavor to recollect those reasons by which they were guided. It was at first proposed to vest the sole power of making peace or war in the Senate; but this was objected to as inimical to the genius of a republic, by destroying the necessary balance they were anxious to preserve. Some gentlemen were inclined to give this power to the President; but it was objected to, as throwing into his hands the influence of a monarch, having an opportunity of involving his country in a war whenever he wished to promote her destruction The House of Representatives was then named; but an insurmountable objection was made to this proposition — which was, that negotiations always required the greatest secrecy, which could not be expected in a large body. The honorable gentleman then gave a clear, concise opinion on the propriety of the proposed Constitution.

Gen. Charles Cotesworth Pinckney (one of the delegates of the Federal Convention) observed, that the honorable judge, from his great penetration, had hit upon one of those difficult points which for a long time occasioned much debate in the Convention. Indeed, this subject appeared to be of so much magnitude, that a committee consisting of one member from each state was appointed to consider and report upon it. His honorable friend (Major Butler) was on the committee for this state. Some members were for vesting the power for making treaties in the legislature; but the secrecy and despatch which are so frequently necessary in negotiations evinced the impropriety of vesting it there. The same reason showed the impropriety of placing it solely in the House of Representatives. A few members were desirous that the President alone might possess this power, and contended that it might safely be lodged with him, as he was to be responsible for his conduct, and therefore would not dare to make a treaty repugnant to the interest of his country and from his situation he was more interested in making a good treaty than any other man in the United States. This doctrine General Pinckney said he could not acquiesce in. Kings, he admitted, were in general more interested in th welfare of their country than any other individual in it, because the prosperity of the country tended to increase the lustre of the crown, and a king never could receive a sufficient compensation for the sale of his kingdoms; for he could not enjoy in any other country so advantageous a situation as he permanently possessed in his own. Hence kings are less liable to foreign bribery and corruption than any other set of men, because no bribe that could be given them could compensate the loss they must necessarily sustain for injuring their dominions; indeed, he did not at present recollect any instance of a king who had received a bribe from a foreign power, except Charles II., who sold Dunkirk to Louis XIV. But the situation of a President would be very different from that of a king: he might withdraw himself from the United States, so that the states could receive no advantage from his responsibility; his office is not to be permanent, but temporary; and he might receive a bribe which would enable him to live in greater splendor in another country than his own; and when out of office, he was no more interested in the prosperity of his country than any other patriotic citizen: and in framing a treaty, he might perhaps show an improper partiality for the state to which he particularly belonged. The different propositions made on this subject, the general observed, occasioned much debate. At last it was agreed to give the President a power of proposing treaties, as he was the ostensible head of the Union, and to vest the Senate (where each state had an equal voice) with the power of agreeing or disagreeing to the terms proposed. This, in some measure, took away their responsibility, but not totally; for, though the Senate were to be judges on impeachments, and the members of it would not probably condemn a measure they had agreed to confirm, yet, as they were not a permanent body, they might be tried hereafter by other senators, and condemned, if they deserved it. On the whole, a large majority of the Convention thought this power would be more safely lodged where they had finally vested it, than any where else. It was a power that must necessarily be lodged somewhere: political caution and republican jealousy rendered it improper for us to vest it in the President alone; the nature of negotiation, and the frequent recess of the House of Representatives, rendered that body an improper depository of this prerogative. The President and Senate joined were, therefore, after much deliberation, deemed the most eligible corps in whom we could with safety vest the diplomatic authority of the Union.

. . . Gen. Charles Cotesworth Pinckney rose to obviate some of the objections made by the honorable gentleman who sat down, . . . If we should not be represented in the Senate, it would be our own fault; the mode of voting in that body *per capita*, and not by states, as formerly, would be a strong inducement to us to keep up a full representation: the alteration was approved by every one of the Convention who had been a member of Congress. He then mentioned several instances of difficulties which he had been informed had occurred in Congress in determining questions of vast importance to the Union, on account of the members voting as states, and not individually. . . .   _____

CLXXI. C. C. Pinckney: Speech in South Carolina House of Representatives.[1]

Thursday, January, 1788.

. . . But now that the senators vote individually, and not by states, each state will be anxious to keep a full representation in the Senate; and the Senate has now power to compel the attendance of its own members. We shall thus have no delay, and business will be conducted in a fuller representation of the states than it hitherto has been. All the members of the Convention, who had served in Congress, were so sensible of the advantage attending this mode of voting, that the measure was adopted unanimously. For my own part, I think it infinitely preferable to the old method. . . .

. . . Every state in the Union, except Rhode Island, was so thoroughly convinced that our government was inadequate to our situation, that all, except her, sent members to the Convention at Philadelphia. General Pinckney said, it had been alleged that, when there, they exceeded their powers. He thought not. They had a right, he apprehended, to propose any thing which they imag-

[1] Elliot, *Debates in State Conventions on the Adoption of the Federal Constitution*, IV, 277–286.

ined would strengthen the Union, and be for the advantage of our country; but they did not pretend to a right to determine finally upon any thing.   . . .

Every member who attended the Convention, was, from the beginning, sensible of the necessity of giving greater powers to the federal government.   This was the very purpose for which they were convened.   The delegations of Jersey and Delaware were, at first, averse to this organization; but they afterwards acquiesced in it; and the conduct of their delegates has been so very agreeable to the people of these states, that their repsective conventions have unanimously adopted the Constitution.   As we have found it necessary to give very extensive powers to the federal government both over the persons and estates of the citizens, we thought it right to draw one branch of the legislature immediately from the people, and that both wealth and numbers should be considered in the representation. We were at a loss, for some time, for a rule to ascertain the proportionate wealth of the states.   At last we thought that the productive labor of the inhabitants was the best rule for ascertaining their wealth.   In conformity to this rule, joined to a spirit of concession, we determined that representatives should be apportioned among the several states, by adding to the whole number of free persons three fifths of the slaves.   We thus obtained a representation for our property; and I confess I did not expect that we had conceded too much to the Eastern States, when they allowed us a representation for a species of property which they have not among them.

The numbers in the different states, according to the most accurate accounts we could obtain, were —

In New Hampshire,	102,000
Massachusetts,	360,000
Rhode Island,	58,000
Connecticut,	202,000
New York,	233,000
New Jersey,	138,000
Pennsylvania,	360,000
Delaware,	37,000
Maryland, (including three fifths of 80,000 negroes,)	218,000
Virginia, (including three-fifths of 280,000 negroes,)	420,000
N. Carolina, (including three-fifths of 60,000 negroes,)	200,000
S. Carolina, (including three-fifths of 80,000 negroes,)	150,000
Georgia, (including three-fifths of 20,000 negroes,)	90,000

. . . The general then said he would make a few observations on the objections which the gentleman had thrown out on the restrictions that might be laid on the African trade after the year 1808. On this point your delegates had to contend with the religious and political prejudices of the Eastern and Middle States, and with the interested and inconsistent opinion of Virginia, who was warmly opposed to our importing more slaves. I am of the same opinion now as I was two years ago, when I used the expressions the gentleman has quoted — that, while there remained one acre of swampland uncleared of South Carolina, I would raise my voice against restricting the importation of negroes. I am as thoroughly convinced as that gentleman is, that the nature of our climate, and the flat, swampy situation of our country, obliges us to cultivate our lands with negroes, and that without them South Carolina would soon be a desert waste.

You have so frequently heard my sentiments on this subject, that I need not now repeat them. It was alleged, by some of the members who opposed an unlimited importation, that slaves increased the weakness of any state who admitted them; that they were a dangerous species of property, which an invading enemy could easily turn against ourselves and the neighboring states; and that, as we were allowed a representation for them in the House of Representatives, our influence in government would be increased in proportion as we were less able to defend ourselves. "Show some period," said the members from the Eastern States, "when it may be in our power to put a stop, if we please, to the importation of this weakness, and we will endeavor, for your convenience, to restrain the religious and political prejudices of our people on this subject." The Middle States and Virginia made us no such proposition; they were for an immediate and total prohibition. We endeavored to obviate the objections that were made in the best manner we could, and assigned reasons for our insisting on the importation, which there is no occasion to repeat, as they must occur to every gentleman in the house: a committee of the states was appointed in order to accommodate this matter, and, after a great deal of difficulty, it was settled on the footing recited in the Constitution.

By this settlement we have secured an unlimited importation of negroes for twenty years. Nor is it declared that the importation shall be then stopped; it may be continued. We have a security that the general government can never emancipate them, for no such authority is granted; and it is admitted, on all hands, that the general government has no powers but what are expressly granted by the Constitution, and that all rights not expressed were reserved by the several states. We have obtained a right to recover our slaves in whatever part of America they may take refuge, which is a right we had not before. In short, considering all circumstances, we have made the best terms for the security of this species of property it

was in our power to make.   We would have made better if we could;
but, on the whole, I do not think them bad.

CLXXII. RUFUS KING IN THE MASSACHUSETTS CONVENTION.[1]

January 17, 1788.

Mr. King said that gentlemen had made it a question, why a
qualification of property in a representative is omitted.   . . . Such
a qualification was proposed in Convention, but by the delegates
of Massachusetts, it was contested that it should not obtain.   . . .

The third paragraph of the second section being read,

Mr. King rose to explain it.   There has, says he, been much
misconception on this section.   It is a principle of this Constitution, that representation and taxation should go hand in hand.
This paragraph states that the number of free persons shall be determined, by adding to the whole number of free persons, including
those bound to service for a term of years, and excluding Indians
not taxed, three-fifths of all other persons.   These persons are the
slaves.   By this rule is representation and taxation to be apportioned.   And it was adopted, because it was the language of all
America.   According to the Confederation, ratified in 1781, the
sums for the general welfare and defence should be apportioned
according to the surveyed lands, and improvements thereon, in the
several States.   But it hath never been in the power of Congress to
follow that rule; the returns from the several States being so very
imperfect.   [From "Debates of Convention."]

Hon. Mr. King.   The principle on which this paragraph is
founded is, that taxation and representation should go hand in
hand.   By the Confederation, the apportionment is upon surveyed
land, the buildings and improvements.   The rule could never be
assessed.   A new rule has been proposed by Congress, similar to the
present rule, which has been adopted by eleven States — all but New
Hampshire and Rhode Island.   [From "Parsons's Minutes."]

CLXXIII. C. C. PINCKNEY: SPEECH IN SOUTH CAROLINA HOUSE
OF REPRESENTATIVES.[2]

Friday, January 18, 1788.

. . . He said, that the time for which the President should hold
his office, and whether he should be reëligible, had been fully dis-

---

[1] *Debates and Proceedings in Convention of Massachusetts in* 1788.   Edit. 1856,
pp. 133–134, 299.

[2] Elliot, *Debates in State Conventions on the Adoption of the Federal Constitution*,
IV, 315–316.

cussed in the Convention. It had been once agreed to by a majority, that he should hold his office for the term of seven years, but should not be reëlected a second time. But upon reconsidering that article, it was thought that to cut off all hopes from a man of serving again in that elevated station, might render him dangerous, or perhaps indifferent to the faithful discharge of his duty. His term of service might expire during the raging of war, when he might, perhaps, be the most capable man in America to conduct it; and would it be wise and prudent to declare in our Constitution that such a man should not again direct our military operations, though our success might be owing to his abilities? The mode of electing the President rendered undue influence almost impossible; and it would have been imprudent in us to have put it out of our power to reëlect a man whose talents, abilities, and integrity, were such as to render him the object of the general choice of his country. With regard to the liberty of the press, the discussion of that matter was not forgotten by the members of the Convention. It was fully debated, and the impropriety of saying any thing about it in the Constitution clearly evinced. The general government has no powers but what are expressly granted to it; it therefore has no power to take away the liberty of the press. That invaluable blessing, which deserves all the encomiums the gentleman has justly bestowed upon it, is secured by all our state constitutions; and to have mentioned it in our general Constitution would perhaps furnish an argument, hereafter, that the general government had a right to exercise powers not expressly delegated to it. For the same reason, we had no bill of rights inserted in our Constitution; for, as we might perhaps have omitted the enumeration of some of our rights, it might hereafter be said we had delegated to the general government a power to take away such of our rights as we had not enumerated; but by delegating express powers, we certainly reserve to ourselves every power and right not mentioned in the Constitution. Another reason weighed particularly, with the members from this state, against the insertion of a bill of rights. Such bills generally begin with declaring that all men are by nature born free. Now, we should make that declaration with a very bad grace, when a large part of our property consists in men who are actually born slaves. As to the clause guarantying to each state a republican form of government being inserted near the end of the Constitution, the general observed that it was as binding as if it had been inserted in the first article. The Constitution takes its effect from the ratification, and every part of it is to be ratified at the same time, and not one clause before the other; but he thought there was a peculiar propriety in inserting it where it was, as it was necessary to form the government before that government could guaranty any thing.

CLXXIV. THE FEDERALIST, No. XL. [MADISON.][1]

In one particular, it is admitted, that the convention have departed from the tenor of their commission. Instead of reporting a plan requiring the confirmation *of all the states*, they have reported a plan, which is to be confirmed, and may be carried into effect, by *nine states only*. It is worthy of remark, that this objection, though the most plausible, has been the least urged in the publications which have swarmed against the convention. The forbearance can only have proceeded from an irresistible conviction of the absurdity of subjecting the fate of twelve states to the perverseness or corruption of a thirteenth; from the example of inflexible opposition given by a *majority* of one sixtieth of the people of America, to a measure approved and called for by the voice of twelve states, comprising fifty-nine sixtieths of the people; an example still fresh in the memory and indignation of every citizen who has felt for the wounded honour and prosperity of his country. As this objection, therefore, has been in a manner waved by those who have criticised the powers of the convention, I dismiss it without further observation.

The *third* point to be inquired into is, how far considerations of duty arising out of the case itself, could have supplied any defect of regular authority.

In the preceding inquiries, the powers of the convention have been analyzed and tried with the same rigour, and by the same rules, as if they had been real and final powers, for the establishment of a constitution for the United States. We have seen, in what manner they have borne the trial, even on that supposition. It is time now to recollect, that the powers were merely advisory and recommendatory; that they were so meant by the states, and so understood by the convention; and that the latter have accordingly planned and proposed a constitution, which is to be of no more consequence than the paper on which it is written, unless it be stamped with the approbation of those to whom it is addressed. This reflection places the subject in a point of view altogether different, and will enable us to judge with propriety of the course taken by the convention.

Let us view the ground on which the convention stood. It may be collected from their proceedings, that they were deeply and unanimously impressed with the crisis, which had led their country, almost with one voice, to make so singular and solemn an experi-

---

[1] Hallowell edition, 1837; first printed in the *New York Packet*, January 18, 1788.

ment, for correcting the errors of a system, by which this crisis had been produced; that they were no less deeply and unanimously convinced, that such a reform as they have proposed, was absolutely necessary to effect the purposes of their appointment. It could not be unknown to them, that the hopes and expectations of the great body of citizens, throughout this great empire, were turned with the keenest anxiety, to the event of their deliberations. They had every reason to believe, that the contrary sentiments agitated the minds and bosoms of every external and internal foe to the liberty and prosperity of the United States. They had seen in the origin and progress of the experiment, the alacrity with which the *proposition*, made by a single state (Virginia) towards a partial amendment of the confederation had been attended to and promoted. They had seen the *liberty assumed* by *very few* deputies, from a *very few* states, convened at Annapolis, of recommending a great and critical object, wholly foreign to their commission, not only justified by the public opinion, but actually carried into effect, by twelve out of the thirteen states. They had seen, in a variety of instances, assumptions by congress, not only of recommendatory but of operative powers, warranted in the public estimation, by occasions and objects infinitely less urgent than those by which their conduct was to be governed. They must have reflected, that in all great changes of established governments, forms ought to give way to substance; that a rigid adherence in such cases to the former, would render nominal and nugatory the transcendent and precious right of the people to "abolish or alter their governments as to them shall seem most likely to affect their safety and happiness;"* since it is impossible for the people spontaneously and universally, to move in concert towards their object: and it is therefore essential, that such changes be instituted by some *informal and unauthorized propositions*, made by some patriotic and respectable citizen, or number of citizens. They must have recollected, that it was by this irregular and assumed privilege, of proposing to the people plans for their safety and happiness, that the states were first united against the danger with which they were threatened by their ancient government; that committees and congresses were formed for concentrating their efforts, and defending their rights; and that *conventions* were *elected* in *the several states*, for establishing the constitutions under which they are now governed. Nor could it have been forgotten, that no little ill-timed scruples, no zeal for adhering to ordinary forms, were anywhere seen, except in those who wished to indulge, under these masks, their secret enmity to the substance contended for. They

* Declaration of Independence.

must have borne in mind, that as the plan to be framed and proposed, was to be submitted *to the people themselves*, the disapprobation of this supreme authority would destroy it forever: its approbation blot out all antecedent errors and irregularities. It might even have occurred to them, that where a disposition to cavil prevailed, their neglect to execute the degree of power vested in them, and still more their recommendation of any measure whatever not warranted by their commission, would not less excite animadversion, than a recommendation at once of a measure fully commensurate to the national exigencies. ───────────

CLXXV. LUTHER MARTIN'S DEFENSE OF GERRY.[1]

I beg leave, through the channel of your Paper, to declare to the Public that from the time I took my seat in convention, which was early in June, until the fourth day of September, when I left Philadelphia, I am satisfied I was not ten minutes absent from convention while sitting (excepting only five days in the beginning of August, immediately after the committee of detail had reported, during which but little business was done.) That during my attendance I never heard Mr. Gerry or any other member introduce a proposition for the redemption of continental money according to its nominal or any other value, nor did I ever hear that such a proposition had been offered to consideration or had been thought of.[2] I was intimate with Mr. Gerry, and never heard him express, in private conversation or otherwise, a wish for the redemption of continental money, or assign the want of such a provision as a defect. Nor did I ever hear in Convention, or anywhere else, such a motive of conduct attributed to Mr. Gerry. I also declare to the Public that a considerable time before I left the convention Mr. Gerry's opposition to the System was warm and decided; that in a particular manner he strenuously opposed that provision by which the power and authority over the militia is taken away from the States and given to the general government; that in the debate he declared if that measure was adopted it would be the most convincing proof that the destruction of the State governments and the introduction of a king was designed, and that no declarations to the contrary ought to be credited, since it was giving the states the last coup de grace by taking from them the only means of self preservation. The conduct of the advocates and framers of this system towards the

─────────

[1] P. L. Ford, *Essays on the Constitution*, 341–343; first printed in the *Maryland Journal* of January 18, 1788.

[2] See CLVII above. Gerry's reply is in CLXII, the controversy is continued in CLXXXIX–CXCII and CXCIX.

thirteen States, in pretending that it was designed for their advantage, and gradually obtaining power after power to the general government, which could not but end in their slavery, he compared to the conduct of a number of jockeys who had thirteen young colts to break; they begin with the appearance of kindness, giving them a lock of hay, or a handful of oats, and stroaking them while they eat, until being rendered sufficiently gentle they suffer a halter to be put round their necks; obtaining a further degree of their confidence, the jockeys slip a curb bridle on their heads and the bit into their mouths, after which the saddle follows of course, and well booted and spurred, with good whips in their hands, they mount and ride them at their pleasure, and although they may kick and flounce a little at first, nor being able to get rid of their riders, they soon become as tame and passive as their masters could wish them. In the course of public debate in the convention Mr. Gerry applied to the system of government, as then under discussion, the words of Pope with respect to vice, "that it was a monster of such horrid mien, as to be hated need but to be seen." And some time before I left Philadelphia, he in the same public manner declared in convention that he should consider himself a traitor to his country if he did not oppose the system there, and also when he left the convention. These, sir, are facts which I do not fear being contradicted by any member of the convention, and will, I apprehend, satisfactorily shew that Mr. Gerry's opposition proceeded from a conviction in his own mind that the government, if adopted, would terminate in the destruction of the States and in the introduction of a kingly government.   _____

CLXXVI. Caleb Strong in the Massachusetts Convention.[1]

January 18, 1788.

Mr. Strong. This mode of census is not new. Our General Court have considered it, and the General Court have agreed. The southern States have their inconveniences; none but negroes can work there; the buildings are worth nothing. When the delegates were apportioned, forty-thousand was the number. Massachusetts had eight, and a fraction; New Hampshire two, and a large fraction. New Hampshire was allowed three; Georgia three, &c. Representation is large enough, because no private local interests are concerned. Very soon, as the country increases, it will be larger. He considered the increasing expense.

_____

[1] *Debates and Proceedings in Convention of Massachusetts in 1788.* Edit. 1856, p. 303.

CLXXVII. PROCEEDINGS IN THE MASSACHUSETTS CONVENTION.[1]

January 19, 1788.

The Hon. E. Gerry, Esq., answered the question proposed to him yesterday, as follows, viz: —

Saturday Morning, 19th January.

SIR: — I have no documents in Boston, and am uncertain whether I have any at home, to assist me in answering the question, "Why, in the last requisition of Congress, the portion required of this State was thirteen times as much as of Georgia, and yet we have but eight representatives in the general government, and Georgia has three?" but if my memory serves me, the reason assigned by the committee who made the apportionment for giving such a number to Georgia, was, that that State had of late greatly increased its numbers by migration, and if not then, would soon be entitled to the proportion assigned her. I think it was also said, that the apportionment was made, not by any fixed principle, but by a compromise. These reasons not being satisfactory, a motion was made on the part of Massachusetts, for increasing her number of representatives, but it did not take effect. [From "Journal of Convention."]

Hon. Mr. King. It so happened that I was both of the Convention and Congress at the same time, and if I recollect right, the answer of Mr. Gerry does not materially vary. . . .

The Hon. Mr. Strong mentioned the difficulty which attended the construction of the Senate in the Convention; and that a committee, consisting of one delegate from each State, was chosen to consider the subject, who reported as it now stands; and that Mr. Gerry was on the committee, from Massachusetts. [From "Debates of Convention."]

Mr. Gerry's answer, in writing, produced and filed — respecting Georgia having three representatives.

Mr. King will give the answer, which he does at large. The estimate by which the requisitions are made, was made in 1782; no alteration since. Georgia has great additions and emigration, and is now in an Indian war. Connecticut and New Hampshire have paid nothing. If I was for it now, it is improper, till we are more united. . . .

Hon. Mr. Strong. There were large debates on this subject in the Convention. The Convention would have broke up if it had

<hr>

[1] *Debates and Proceedings in Convention of Massachusetts in 1788.* Edit. 1856, pp 63, 144, 147, 306–307.

not been agreed to allow an equal representation in the Senate. It was an accommodation, reported by a Committee, of which Mr. Gerry was one. [From "Parsons's Minutes."]

CLXXVIII. KING AND STRONG IN THE MASSACHUSETTS CONVENTION.[1]

January 19, 1788.

Rufus King explained and enlarged on the same subject: said that no certain rule ever had been in the power of Congress, therefore laid their taxes as they found the States able; the judgment founded on conjecture; and the money paid considered as *so much loaned on credit* by each State, and to be settled hereafter. The case of Georgia was, before the war, small; much harrassed by it; since rapidly increasing; the number of representatives no more than what they had, or would have, a right to, considering their increasing population. . . .

Strong. — A detail of proceedings in Convention about Senate; that Gerry was of the Committee about proportioning the Senate; that the Committee was appointed because the small States were jealous of the large ones; and the Convention was nigh breaking up but for this.

CLXXIX. BELKNAP TO HAZARD.[2]

Boston, Jan. 20. 1788.

On Friday P. M., an honest member, who, I believe, is a Federalist, and I believe you know him, Major Fuller, of Newton, desired to know why Georgia had 3 representatives allowed in the new plan, and Massachusetts 8, when, in the *last* requisition for taxes, they were assessed but one thirteenth of what Massachusetts was. One of the Anti-feds. desired that Mr. G. might answer this question. It was put to vote, and passed in the affirmative. Mr. G. *himself* then asked the President to reduce the question to writing, which he did, and gave it to him. . . . A vote passed, desiring him to take his own time, and give his answer in writing. He delivered it yesterday A.M. It was to this purpose: That the mode of apportioning taxes in Congress was by a kind of compromise, and that Georgia had lately been increased by migration. R. K. then explained the matter at large, and much more to everybody's satisfaction.

---

[1] Belknap's Notes, printed in Massachusetts Historical Society, *Proceedings*, 1855–1858, pp. 297–298.

[2] Massachusetts Historical Society, *Collections*, Fifth Series, III, 7–8.

CLXXX. Benjamin Lincoln to George Washington.[1]

Boston, Jany 20, 1788

Having been detained from convention for a number of day I requested one of my friends to give me a general state of matters which statement I do myself the pleasure to inclose . . .

[Enclosure]

. . . when a question, for the first time, was proposed to Mr Gerry viz Why Georgia was entitled to three reps, under this Constitution, and Massts but to eight, when in former requisitions on Massts, she had been requir'd to pay thirteen times the amount Georgia was assess'd — a motion was made by Mr Dana, at the request of Mr G— as he declared in Convention, & Mr Gerry acceded to, that the question should be reduced to writing, & the answer in writing be laid on the table — this was complied with on saturday morning — a debate then ensued on the first paragraph in the 3d section — and an objection was raised against the equality of the representation of the states in the senate — Mr Strong stated that this was a matter of long debate in the fed-convention — & that a committee consisting of a member from each state in the Convention was appointed to consider the subject — that, in regard to an equality of representation of states in the senate the committee agreed[2] & so reported to Convention —

CLXXXI. Elbridge Gerry to the Vice President of the Convention of Massachusetts.[3]

Cambridge, 21st January, 1788.

After having, on Saturday morning, stated an answer to the question proposed the preceding evening, I perceived that your honourable body were considering a paragraph which respected an equal representation of the States in the Senate, and one of my honorable colleagues observed, that this was agreed to by a committee consisting of a member from each State, and that I was one of the number. This was a partial narrative of facts, which I conceived placed my conduct in an unfavorable point of light, probably without any such intention on the part of my colleague. . . .

I shall only add, Sir, that I have subjoined a state of facts,

---

[1] *Documentary History of the Constitution*, IV, 451–453.

[2] Crossed out "unanimously".

[3] *Debates and Proceedings in the Convention of Massachusetts in 1788*, pp. 65–71, note.

founded on documents relative to my consent that the lesser States should have an equal representation in the Senate.   . . .

A STATE OF FACTS, REFERRED TO IN THE PRECEDING LETTER.

The business of the Federal Convention having been opened by Governor Randolph, of Virginia, and the outlines of a plan of government having been proposed by him, they were referred to a Committee of the whole house, and after several weeks' debate, the committee reported general principles for forming a Constitution, amongst which were the following: —

'7th. That the right of suffrage in the first branch of the National Legislature' (by which was intended the House of Representatives) 'ought not to be according to the rule established in the Articles of Confederation, but according to some equitable ratio of representation, viz.: in proportion to the whole number of white and other free citizens and inhabitants, of every age, sex and condition, including those bound to servitude for a term of years, and three-fifths of all other persons not comprehended in the foregoing description, except Indians, not paying taxes, in each State.

'8th. That the right of suffrage in the second branch of the National Legislature' (meaning the senate) 'ought to be according to the rule established for the first.'

In the Committee of the Whole, the eighth article above recited, for which I voted, was carried, if my memory serves me, by six States against five; and when under consideration of the Convention, it produced a ferment, and a separate meeting, as I was informed, of most of the delegates of those five States, the result of which was, a firm determination on their part not to relinquish the right of equal representation in the Senate, confirmed as it was, to those States, by the Articles of Confederation. The matter at length became so serious as to threaten a dissolution of the Convention, and a Committee, consisting of a member from each State, was appointed, to meet (if possible) on the ground of accommodation. The members from the three large States of Virginia, Pennsylvania and Massachusetts, were Mr. Mason, Doctor Franklin and myself, and after debating the subject several days, during which time the Convention adjourned, the Committee agreed to the following Report: —

'That the subsequent propositions be recommended to the Convention, on condition that both shall be generally adopted: —

'First. That in the first branch of the Legislature, each of the States now in the Union be allowed one member for every forty thousand inhabitants, of the description reported in the seventh resolution of the Committee of the whole House — that each State not containing that number shall be allowed one member — that all writs for raising or appropriating money, and for fixing the salaries of the officers of government of the United States, shall originate in the first branch of the Legislature, and shall not be altered or amended by the second branch — and that no money shall be drawn from the treasury of the United States, but in pursuance of appropriations to be originated by the first branch.

'*Secondly.* That in the second branch of the Legislature each State shall have an equal vote.'

The number of forty thousand inhabitants to every member in the House of Representatives, was not a subject of much debate, or an object insisted on, as some of the Committee were opposed to it. Accordingly, on the 10th of July, a motion was made 'to double the number of representatives, being sixty-five,' and it passed in the negative.

The admission, however, of the smaller States to an equal representation in the Senate, never would have been agreed to by the Committee, or by myself, as a member of it, without the provision 'that all bills for raising or appropriating money, and for fixing the salaries of the officers of government,' should originate in the House of Representatives, and 'not be altered or amended' by the Senate, 'and that no money should be drawn from the treasury' 'but in pursuance of such appropriations.'

This provision was agreed to by the Convention, at the same time and by the same vote, as that which allows to each State an equal voice in the Senate, and was afterwards referred to the Committee of Detail, and reported by them as part of the Constitution, as will appear by documents in my possession. Nevertheless, the smaller States having attained their object of an equal voice in the Senate, a new provision, now in the Constitution, was substituted, whereby the Senate have a right to propose amendments to revenue bills, and the provision reported by the Committee was *effectually destroyed.*

It was conceived by the Committee to be highly unreasonable and unjust that a small State, which would contribute but one sixty-fifth part of any tax, should, nevertheless, have an equal right with a large State which would contribute eight or ten sixty-fifths of the same tax, to take money from the pockets of the latter, more especially as it was intended that the powers of the new legislature should extend to internal taxation. It was likewise conceived, that the right of expending should be in proportion to the ability of raising money — that the larger States would not have the least security

for their property if they had not the due command of their own
purses — that they would not have such command, if the lesser
States in either branch had an equal right with the larger to originate,
or even to alter, money bills — that if the Senate should have the
power of proposing amendments, they may propose that a bill,
originated by the House, to raise one thousand, should be increased
to one hundred thousand pounds — that although the House may
negative amendments proposed by the Senate, yet the giving them
power to propose amendments, would enable them to increase the
grants of the House, because the Senate (as well as the House)
would have a right to adhere to their votes, and would oblige the
House to consent to such an increase, on the principle of accommodation — that the lesser States would thus have nearly as much
command of the property of the greater, as they themselves — that
even if the representation in the Senate had been according to numbers, in each State, money bills should not be originated or altered
by that branch, because, by their appointments, the members would
be farther removed from the people, would have a greater and more
independent property in their offices, would be more extravagant,
and not being so easily removed, would be ever in favor of higher
salaries than members of the House — that it was not reasonable
to suppose the aristocratical branch would be as saving of the public
money as the democratical branch: — but that, on the other hand,
should the Senate have only the power of concurrence or non-con-
currence of such bills, they would pass them, although the grants
should not equal their wishes, whilst, with the power of amendment,
they would never be satisfied with the grants of the House — that
the Commons of Great Britain had ever strenuously and successfully contended for this important right, which the Lords had often,
but in vain, endeavored to exercise — that the preservation of this
right, the right of holding the purse-strings, was essential to the
preservation of liberty — and that to this right, perhaps, was principally owing the liberty that still remains in Great Britain.

These are the facts and reasons whereon was grounded the
admission of the smaller States to an equal representation in the
Senate, and it must appear that there is an essential difference between
an unqualified admission of them to an equal representation in the
Senate, and admitting them from necessity, on the express condition
provided in the recited report of the Committee; and it must also
appear, that had that provision been preserved in the Constitution,
and the Senate precluded from a right to alter or amend money or
revenue bills, agreeably to the said report, the lesser States would
not have that undue command of the property of the larger States

which they are now to have by the Constitution, and that I never
consented to an equal representation of the States in the Senate,
as it now stands, in the new system.

CLXXXII. RUFUS KING IN THE MASSACHUSETTS CONVENTION.[1]

January 21, 1788.

Hon. Mr. King rose to pursue the inquiry, why the *place and
manner* of holding elections were omitted in the section under debate.
It was to be observed, he said, that in the Constitution of Massachusetts, and other States, the manner and place of elections were
provided for; the manner was by ballot, and the places towns; for,
said he, we happened to settle originally in townships. But it was
different in the southern States. He would mention an instance.
In Virginia there are but fifteen or twenty towns, and seventy or
eighty counties; therefore no rule could be adopted to apply to the
whole. If it was practicable, he said, it would be necessary to have
a district the fixed place. But this is liable to exceptions; as a district that may now be fully settled, may in time be scarcely inhabited;
and the back country, now scarcely inhabited, may be fully settled.
Suppose this State thrown into eight districts, and a member apportioned to each: if the numbers increase, the representatives and
districts will be increased. The matter, therefore, must be left
subject to the regulation of the State legislature, or the general
government. Suppose the State legislature, the circumstance will
be the same. It is truly said, that our representatives are but a
part of the Union, and that they may be subject to the control of
the rest; but our representatives make a ninth part of the whole,
and if any authority is vested in Congress it must be in our favor.
But to the subject: in Connecticut they do not choose by numbers,
but by corporations. Hartford, one of their largest towns, sends
no more delegates than one of their smallest corporations, each
town sending two, except latterly, when a town was divided. The
same rule is about to be adopted in Rhode Island. The inequality
of such representation, where every corporation would have an equal
right to send an equal number of representatives, was apparent.
In the southern States, the inequality is greater. By the Constitution of South Carolina, the city of Charleston has a right to send
thirty representatives to the General Assembly, the whole number
of which amounts to two hundred. The back parts of Carolina
have increased greatly since the adoption of their Constitution,
and have frequently attempted an alteration of this unequal mode

---

[1] *Debates and Proceedings in Convention of Massachusetts in 1788*, pp. 149–150.

of representation; but the members from Charleston, having the balance so much in their favor, will not consent to an alteration; and we see that the delegates from Carolina in Congress have always been chosen from the delegates of that city. The representatives, therefore, from that State, will not be chosen by the people, but will be the representatives of a faction of that State. If the general government cannot control in this case, how are the people secure?

_____

CLXXXIII. Rufus King in the Massachusetts Convention.[1]

"Some of the powers of the Legis. are ambiguous and others indefinite and dangerous." This clause contains an imputation so very general that no reply in detail can be attempted without commenting on every sentence wh. forms the Grant of powers to Congress. Most of the sentences are transcribed from the present Confederation, and we can only observe that it was the intention and honest desire of the Convention to use those expressions that were most easy to be understood and least equivocal in their meaning; and we flatter ourselves they have not been entirely disappointed. We believe that the powers are closely defined, the expressions as free from ambiguity as the Convention could form them, and we never could have assented to the Report, had we supposed the Danger Mr. G. predicts.   _____

CLXXXIV. Rufus King in the Massachusetts Convention.[2]

Monday, 28th. — Mr. King, in speaking on the *Inspection Laws* (Sect. 10, 1st Article), said this was introduced on account of the State of Virginia, where it is the custom to lodge the tobacco in public warehouses for inspection and for safety; that the owner receives a certificate from the inspecting officer of the quantity of tobacco lodged there; that the State *insures* it, while there remaining, from fire and other accidents; that these certificates pass from one to another as bank-bills, and that the tobacco is delivered to the person who demands it, on presenting the certificate; that, on receiving it, he pays the charge of inspection and storage, and a premium of insurance, which goes into the public treasury, and amounts to a duty on exportation. . . .

_____

[1] MS. note in King's handwriting found among the King papers; printed in C. R. King, *Life and Correspondence of Rufus King*, I, 305–306. This MS. is undated, and if it embodies notes of a speech in the Massachusetts Convention, that speech probably was made on January 24. But the various points that are taken up are those made by Gerry in his "Objections" to the Constitution. See CXXXIII above.

[2] Belknap's Notes in Massachusetts Historical Society, *Proceedings*, 1855–1858, p. 301.

Mr. King stated the reasons for not appointing a Council, which were that the small States would insist on having one, at least; and that would make another body similar to the Senate. Therefore it was thought, if in some cases the Senate might answer, and in others the President might require the opinion of the officers of State, that, in this case, secrecy, despatch, and fidelity were more to be expected than where there is a multitudinous executive.

CLXXXV. LUTHER MARTIN TO T. C. DEYE.[1]

To the HON. THOMAS COCKEY DEYE, Speaker of the House of Delegates of Maryland.

SIR,

I FLATTER myself the subject of this letter will be a sufficient apology for thus publicly addressing it to you, and through you to the other members of the house of delegates. It cannot have escaped your or their recollection, that when called upon as the servant of a free state, to render an account of those transactions in which I had had a share, in consequence of the trust reposed in me by that state, among other things, I informed them, "that some time in July, the honorable Mr. Yates and Mr. Lansing of New-York, left the convention; that they had uniformly opposed the system, and that I believe, despairing of getting a proper one brought forward, or of rendering any real service, they returned no more." [2] — You cannot, sir, have forgot, for the incident was too remarkable not to have made some impression, that upon my giving this information, the zeal of one of my honorable colleagues, in favor of a system which I thought it my duty to oppose, impelled him to interrupt me, and in a manner which I am confident his zeal alone prevented him from being convinced was not the most delicate, to insinuate pretty strongly, that the statement which I had given of the conduct of those gentlemen, and their motives for not returning, were not candid.

Those honorable members have officially given information on this subject, by a joint letter to his excellency governor Clinton — it is published.[3] Indulge me, sir, in giving an extract from it, that it may stand contrasted in the same page with the information I gave, and may convict me of the want of candor of which I was charged, if the charge was just — if it will not do that, then let it silence my accusers.

"Thus circumstanced, under these impressions, to have hesitated

[1] Yates, *Secret Proceedings and Debates* (Albany, 1821), pp. 9-10; first printed in the *Maryland Gazette*, January 29, 1788.

[2] See CLVIII (27) above.   [3] See CLXVII above.

would have been to be culpable; — we therefore gave the principles of the constitution, which has received the sanction of a majority of the convention, our decided and unreserved dissent. We were not present at the completion of the new constitution; but before we left the convention, its principles were so well established as to convince us, that no alteration was to be expected to conform it to our ideas of expediency and safety. A persuasion that our further attendance would be fruitless and unavailing rendered us less solicitous to return."

These, sir, are their words; on this I shall make no comment; I wish not to wound the feelings of any person, I only wish to convince.

I have the honor to remain, With the utmost respect, Your very obedient servant,

LUTHER MARTIN.

BALTIMORE, *January* 27, 1788.

———

CLXXXVI. GEORGE WASHINGTON TO LA FAYETTE.[1]

Mount Vernon February 7th. 1788

It appears to me, then, little short of a miracle, that the Delegates from so many different States (which States you know are also different from each other in their manners, circumstances and prejudices) should unite in forming a system of national Government, so little liable to well founded objections.

. . . Had I but slightly suspected (at the time when the late Convention was in session) that another Convention would not be likely to agree upon a better form of Government, I should now be confirmed in the fixed belief that they would not be able to agree upon any system whatever. ———

CLXXXVII. BENJAMIN FRANKLIN TO M. LE VEILLARD.[2]

Philada Feby 17th. 1788

I sent you with my last a Copy of the new Constitution propos'd for the United States by the late General Convention. I sent one also to our excellent Friend the Duke de la Rochefoucault.

I attended the Business of the Convention faithfully for four Months. Enclos'd you have the last speech I made in it.

———

CLXXXVIII. THE FEDERALIST. No. LXII. [MADISON.][3]

2. It is equally unnecessary to dilate on the appointment of senators by the state legislatures. Among the various modes which

---

[1] *Documentary History of the Constitution*, IV, 484–486.
[2] *Documentary History of the Constitution*, IV, 506.
[3] Hallowell   edition, 1837; from the *Independent Journal*.

might have been devised for constituting this branch of the government, that which has been proposed by the convention is probably the most congenial with the public opinion. It is recommended by the double advantage of favouring a select appointment, and of giving to the state governments such an agency in the formation of the federal government, as must secure the authority of the former, and may form a convenient link between the two systems.

3. The equality of representation in the senate is another point, which, being evidently the result of compromise between the opposite pretensions of the large and the small states, does not call for much discussion. ─────────

CLXXXIX. The Landholder [Oliver Ellsworth], X.[1]

To the Honourable Luther Martin, Esq,

Sir,

I have just met with your performance in favour of the Honourable Mr. Gerry, published in the Maryland Journal of the 18th January, 1788.[2] As the Public may be ignorant of the Sacrifice you have made of your resentments on this occasion, you will excuse me for communicating what your extreme modesty must have induced you to conceal. You, no doubt, remember that you and Mr. Gerry never voted alike in Convention, except in the instances I shall hereafter enumerate. He uniformly opposed your principles, and so far did you carry your abhorrence of his politics, as to inform certain members to be on their guard against his wiles, so that, he and Mr. Mason held private meetings, where plans were concerted "to aggrandise, at the expence of the small States, Old Massachusetts and the Ancient Dominion." After having thus opposed him and accused him, to appear his Champion and intimate acquaintance, has placed you beyond the reach of ordinary panegyric. Having done this justice to your magnanimity, I cannot resist drawing the veil of the Convention a little farther aside; not, I assure you, with any intention to give pain to your Constituents, but merely to induce them to pity you for the many piercing mortifications you met with in the discharge of your duty. The day you took your seat must be long remembered by those who were present; nor will it be possible for you to forget the astonishment your behaviour almost instantaneously produced. You had scarcely time to read the propositions which had been agreed to after the

─────────

[1] P. L. Ford, *Essays on the Constitution*, pp. 182–188; first printed in the *Maryland Journal*, February 29, 1788.

[2] For the origin of this controversy see above, CLVII, CLXII, and CLXXV. It is continued in CXC–CXCII and CXCIX.

fullest investigation, when, without requesting information, or to be let into the reasons of the adoption of what you might not approve, you opened against them in a speech which held during two days, and which might have continued two months, but for those marks of fatigue and disgust you saw strongly expressed on whichever side of the house you turned your mortified eyes.   There needed no other display to fix your character and the rank of your abilities, which the Convention would have confirmed by the most distinguished silence, had not a certain similarity in genius provoked a sarcastic reply from the pleasant Mr. Gerry; in which he admired the strength of your lungs and your profound knowledge in the first principles of government; mixing and illustrating his little remarks with a profusion of those hems, that never fail to lengthen out and enliven his oratory.   This reply (from your intimate acquaintance), the match being so equal and the contrast so comic, had the happy effect to put the house in good humor, and leave you a prey to the most humiliating reflections.   But this did not teach you to bound your future speeches by the lines of moderation; for the very next day you exhibited without a blush another specimen of eternal volubility.   It was not, however, to the duration of your speeches you owed the perfection of your reputation.   You, alone, advocated the political heresy, that the people ought not to be trusted with the election of representatives.   You held the jargon, that notwithstanding each state had an equal number of votes in the Senate, yet the states were unequally represented in the Senate.   You espoused the tyrannic principle, that where a State refused to comply with a requisition of Congress for money, that an army should be marched into its bowels, to fall indiscriminately upon the property of the innocent and the guilty, instead of having it collected as the Constitution proposed, by the mild and equal operation of laws. One hour you sported the opinion that Congress, afraid of the militia resisting their measures, would neither arm nor organize them, and the next, as if men required no time to breathe between such contradictions, that they would harass them by long and unnecessary marches, till they wore down their spirit and rendered them fit subjects for despotism.   You, too, contended that the powers and authorities of the new Constitution must destroy the liberties of the people; but that the same powers and authorities might be safely trusted with the Old Congress.   You cannot have forgotten, that by such ignorance in politics and contradictory opinions, you exhausted the politeness of the Convention, which at length prepared to slumber when you rose to speak; nor can you have forgotten, you were only twice appointed a member of a committee, or that these appointments were merely made to avoid your endless garrulity, and if possible, lead you to reason, by the easy road of familiar conversation. But lest you should say that I am a record only of the bad, I shall faithfully recognize whatever occurred to your advantage. You originated that clause in the Constitution which enacts, that "This Constitution and the laws of the United States which shall be made in pursuance thereof, and all treaties made or which shall be made, under the authority of the United States, shall be the supreme law of the land, and the judges in every State shall be bound thereby, anything in the Constitution or the law of any State to the contrary notwithstanding." You voted that an appeal should lay to the Supreme Judiciary of the United States, for the correction of all errors, both in law and fact. You also agreed to the clause that declares nine States to be sufficient to put the government in motion. These are among the greater positive virtues you exhibited in the Convention; but it would be doing you injustice were I to omit those of a negative nature. Since the publication of the Constitution, every topic of vulgar declamation has been employed to persuade the people, that it will destroy the trial by jury, and is defective for being without a bill of rights. You, sir, had more candour in the Convention than we can allow to those declaimers out of it; there you never signified by any motion or expression whatever, that it stood in need of a bill of rights, or in any wise endangered the trial by jury. In these respects the Constitution met your entire approbation; for had you believed it defective in these essentials, you ought to have mentioned it in Convention, or had you thought it wanted further guards, it was your indispensable duty to have proposed them. I hope to hear that the same candour that influenced you on this occasion, has induced you to obviate any improper impressions such publications may have excited in your constituents, when you had the honor to appear before the General Assembly. From such high instances of your approbation (for every member, like you, had made objections to parts of the Constitution) the Convention were led to conclude that you would have honored it with your signature, had you not been called to Maryland upon some indispensable business; nor ought it to be withheld from you, that your colleagues informed many Gentlemen of the House, that you told them you intended to return before its completion. Durst I proceed beyond these facts, to which the whole Convention can witness, I would ask you why you changed your opinion of the Constitution after leaving Philadelphia. I have it from good authority that you complained to an intimate acquaintance, that nothing grieved you so much as the apprehension of being detained in Maryland longer than you could wish; for that you had rather lose one hundred guineas, than not have your name appear to the Constitution. But as this circumstance seems to have been overlooked when you composed your defence of Mr. Gerry, you may have your recollection of it revived by applying to Mr. Young, of Spruce street, Philadelphia, to whom you made your complaint. But leaving this curious piece of human vanity to such further investigation as you may think it deserves, let us come to those matters more particularly between us. You have said, that you "never heard Mr. Gerry, or any other member, introduce a proposition for the redemption of Continental money according to its nominal or any other value; nor did you ever hear that such a proposition had been offered to the Convention, or had been thought of." That the Public may clearly comprehend what degree of credit ought to be given to this kind of evidence, they should know the time you were absent from the Convention, as well as the time you attended. If it should appear that you were only a few days absent, when unimportant business was the object, they will conclude in your favor, provided they entertain a good opinion of your veracity; on the other hand, should it appear that you were absent nearly half the session, however your veracity may be esteemed, they must reject your evidence. As you have not stated this necessary information, I shall do it for you. The Session of Convention commenced the 14th of May, and ended the 17th of September, which makes 126 days. You took your seat the 10th of June, and left it the 4th of September, of which period you were absent at Baltimore ten days, and as many at New York, so that you attended only 66 days out of 126. Now, sir, is it to be presumed that you could have been minutely informed of all that happened in Convention, and committees of Convention, during the 60 days of your absence? or does it follow by any rule of reasoning or logic, that because a thing did not happen in the 66 days you were present, that it did not happen in the 60 days which you did not attend? Is it anywise likely that you could have heard what passed, especially during the last 13 days, within which period the Landholder has fixed the apostacy of Mr. Gerry? or if it is likely that your particular intimacy with Mr. Gerry would stimulate to inquiries respecting his conduct, why is it that we do not see Mr. McHenry's verification of your assertion, who was of the Committee for considering a proposition for the debts of the union? Your reply to my second charge against this gentleman may be soon dismissed. Compare his letter to the Legislature of his State with your defence, and you will find that you have put into his mouth objections different from anything it contains, so that if your representation be true, his must be false. But there is another circumstance which militates against your new friend. Though he was face to face with his colleagues at the State Convention of Massachusetts, he has not ventured to call upon them to clear him either of this charge, or that respecting the Continental money. But as the Public seemed to require that something should be said on this occasion, an anonymous writer denies that he made such a motion, and endeavours to abate the force of my second allegation, merely by supposing that "his colleagues were men of too much honor to assert that his reasons in Convention were totally different from those which he has published."

But alas, his colleagues would not acquit him in this way, and he was of too proud a spirit to ask them to do it in person.* Hence the charge remains on its original grounds, while you, for want of proper concert, have joined his accusers and reduced him to the humiliating necessity of endeavouring to stifle your justification. These points being dismissed, it remains only to reconcile the contradictory parts you have acted on the great political stage. You entered the convention without a sufficient knowledge in the science of government, where you committed a succession of memorable blunders, as the work advanced. Some rays of light penetrated your understanding, and enabled you (as has been shown) to assist in raising some of its pillars, when the desire of having your name enrolled with the other laborers drew from you that remarkable complaint so expressive of vanity and conviction. But self-interest soon gained the ascendant, you quickly comprehended the delicacy of your situation, and this restored your first impressions in all their original force. You thought the Deputy Attorney General of the United States for the state of Maryland, destined for a different character, and that inspired you with the hope that you might derive from a desperate opposition what you saw no prospect of gaining by a contrary conduct. But I will venture to predict, that though you were to double your efforts, you would fail in your object. I leave you now to your own reflections, under a promise, however, to give my name to the public, should you be able to procure any indifferent testimony to contradict a single fact I have stated.

* I will not say this writer makes a distinction between a thing done in convention and a thing done in committee. Be this as it may, he confesses more than Mr. Martin; for it seems that Mr. Gerry proposed that "the public debt should stand on the same ground it now stands on by the articles of confederation." He might have subjoined that Mr. Gerry prefaced this motion by observing that it was the same in substance as his first, in as much as it included his first. But notwithstanding this motion was readily agreed to without his explanation being contradicted, yet he never afterwards favoured the convention with a look of peace, or a word of reconcilement.

CXC. LUTHER MARTIN'S REPLY TO THE LANDHOLDER.[1]

Baltimore, March 3, 1788.

But the Landholder wishes it to be supposed, that though my veracity should not be doubted, yet my evidence ought to be rejected, and observes, that to comprehend what credit ought to be given to it, by which I suppose he means its sufficiency if credited, it ought to be known how long I was absent from Convention, as well as the time I attended. I believe Sir, whoever will read my former publication will in a moment perceive, that I there 'stated' all the 'information' on this subject that was necessary or material, and that I left no defect for the Landholder to supply. I there mentioned that 'I took my seat early in June, that I left Philadelphia on the fourth of September, and during that period was not absent from the convention while sitting, except only five days in the beginning of August, immediately after the Committee of Detail had reported.' I did not state the precise day of June when I took my seat — it was the ninth, not the tenth — a very inconsiderable mistake of the Landholder. But between that day and the fourth of September he says that I was absent ten days at Baltimore, and as many at New York, and thereby insinuates that an absence of twenty days from the Convention intervened during that period, in which time Mr. Gerry might have made and failed in his motion concerning continental money. A short state of facts is all that is necessary to shew the disingenuity of the Landholder, and that it is very possible to convey a falsehood, or something very much like it, almost in the words of truth. On the twenty-fifth of July the Convention adjourned, to meet again on the sixth of August. I embraced that opportunity to come to Baltimore, and left Philadelphia on the twenty-seventh; I returned on the fourth of August, and on the sixth attended the Convention, with such members as were in town, at which time the Committee of Detail made their report, and many of the members being yet absent, we adjourned to the next day. Mr. Gerry left Philadelphia to go to New York the day before I left there to come to Baltimore; he had not returned on Tuesday, the seventh of August, when I set out for New York, from whence I returned and took my seat in Convention on Monday, the thirteenth. It is true that from the twenty-fifth of July to the thirteenth of August eighteen (not twenty) days had elapsed, but on one of those days I attended, and on twelve of them the Convention did not meet.

---

[1] P. L. Ford, *Essays on the Constitution*, 345–351; first printed in the *Maryland Journal*, March 7, 1788. For the origin of this controversy see above CLVII, CLXI, CLXXV, and CLXXXIX. It is continued in CXCI, CXCII and CXCIX

I was, therefore, perfectly correct in my original statement that from early in June to the fourth of September I was absent but five days from the Convention while sitting, and in that statement omitted no 'necessary information'. It is also true that of those eighteen days Mr. Gerry was absent twelve or thirteen, and that one of those days when he was not absent was Sunday, on which day the Convention did not meet. Thus, Sir, by relating facts as they really occurred, we find the only time between early in June and the fourth of September when such a motion could have been made by Mr. Gerry without my being present is narrowed down to four, or at most five days, as I originally stated it, although Landholder wishes it should be supposed there were twenty days during that period when it might have taken place without my knowledge, to wit, ten while I was at Baltimore, and as many more while at New York. The Landholder also states that the Convention commenced the fourteenth day of May, and that I did not take my seat till the tenth day of June, by which, if he means anything, I presume he means to insinuate that within that portion of time Mr. Gerry's motion might have been made and rejected. He is here, Sir, equally unfortunate and disingenuous. Though the Convention was to have met by appointment on the fourteenth of May, yet no material business was entered upon till on or about the thirtieth of that month. It was on that day that the Convention, having had certain propositions laid before them by the Honourable Governor of Virginia, resolved to go into a consideration of these propositions. In this fact I am confident I am not mistaken, as I state the day not merely from my own recollection but from minutes which I believe to be very correct, in my possession, of the information given by the Honourable Mr. McHenry to the assembly. The truth is, Sir, that very little progress had been made by the Convention before I arrived, and that they had not been more than ten days, or about that time, seriously engaged in business. The first thing I did after I took my seat was carefully to examine the journals for information of what had already been done or proposed. I was also furnished with notes of the debates which had taken place, and can with truth say that I made myself 'minutely informed' of what had happened before that period. In the same manner, after my return from New York, I consulted the journals (for we were permitted to read them, although we were not always permitted to take copies). If the motion attributed to Mr. Gerry had been made and rejected, either before I first took my seat or while at New York, it would have there appeared, and that no such motion was made and rejected during either of these periods I appeal to the highest possible authority. I appeal to those very journals, which ought to have been published, and which we are informed are placed in the possession of our late Honourable President. But why, Sir, should I appeal to these journals, or to any other authority? Let the Landholder turn to his eighth number, addressed to the Honourable Mr. Gerry; let him blush, unless incapable of that sensation, while he reads the following passage: 'Almost the whole time during the sitting of the Convention, and until the Constitution had received its present form, no man was more plausible and conciliating on every subject than Mr. Gerry,' &c. Thus stood Mr. Gerry, till towards the close of the business he introduced a motion respecting the redemption of paper money. The whole time of the sitting of the Convention was not almost past. The Constitution had not received its present form, nor was the business drawing towards a close, until long after I took my seat in Convention. It is therefore proved by the Landholder himself that Mr. Gerry did not make this motion at any time before the ninth day of June. Nay more, in the paper now before me he acknowledges that in his eighth number he meant (and surely no one ought to know his meaning better than himself) to fix Mr. Gerry's apostacy to a period within the last thirteen days. Why then all this misrepresentation of my absence at Baltimore and New York? Why the attempt to induce a belief that the Convention had been engaged in business from the fourteenth of May, and the insinuation that it might have happened in those periods? And why the charge that in not stating those facts I had withheld from the public information necessary to its forming a right judgment of the credit which ought to be given to my evidence. But, Sir, I am really at a loss which most to admire — the depravity of this writer's heart, or the weakness of his head. Is it possible he should not perceive that the moment he fixes the time of Mr. Gerry's motion to the last thirteen days of the Convention, he proves incontestably the falsehood and malice of his charges against that gentleman — for he has expressly stated that this motion and the rejection it received was the cause, and the sole cause, of his apostacy; that 'before, there was nothing in the system, as it now stands, to which he had any objection, but that afterwards he was inspired with the utmost rage and intemperate opposition to the whole system he had formerly praised;' whereas I have shown to the clearest demonstration, that a considerable time before the last thirteen days, Mr. Gerry had given the most decided opposition to the system. I have shown this by recital of facts, which if credited, incontestibly prove it — facts which, I again repeat, will never be contradicted by any member of the Convention. I ground this

assertion upon the fullest conviction that it is impossible to find a
single person in that number so wicked, as publicly and deliberately
to prostitute his name in support of falsehood, and at the same time
so weak as to do this when he must be sure of detection. But the
Landholder is willing to have it supposed that Mr. Gerry might
have made the motion in a 'committee', and that there it might
have happened without my knowledge; to such wretched subterfuges is he driven. This evasion, however, will be equally unavailing. The business of the committees were not of a secret nnture,
nor were they conducted in a secret manner; I mean as to the members of the Convention. I am satisfied that there was no committee
while I was there, of whose proceedings I was not at least 'so minutely
informed', that an attempt of so extraordinary a nature as that
attributed to Mr. Gerry, and attended with such an immediate and
remarkable revolution in his conduct, could not have taken place
without my having heard something concerning it. The non-
adoption of a measure by a committee did not preclude its being
proposed to the Convention, and being there adopted. Can it be
presumed that a question in which Mr. Gerry is represented to have
been so deeply interested, and by the fate of which his conduct was
entirely influenced, would for want of success in a committee have
been totally relinquished by him, without a single effort to carry it
in Convention! If any other proof is wanting, I appeal again to the
Landholder himself. In his eighth number he states that the motion
was rejected 'by the Convention.' Let it be remembered also, as
I have before observed, in the paper now before me, he declares it
was his intention in that number to fix Mr. Gerry's apostacy to a
period within the last thirteen days; and in the same number he
observes that Mr. Gerry's resentment could only embarrass and
delay the completion of the business for a few days; all which equally
militate against every idea of the motion being made before he left
Philadelphia, whether in Committee or in Convention. The Landholder hath also asserted, that I have 'put into Mr. Gerry's mouth,
objections different from any thing his letter to the legislature of
his State contains, so that if my representation is true, his must
be false.' In this charge he is just as well founded as in those I
have already noticed. Mr. Gerry has more than once published
to the world, under the sanction of his name, that he opposed the
system from a firm persuasion that it would endanger the liberties of
America, and destroy the freedom of the States and their citizens.
Every word which I have stated as coming from his mouth, so far
from being inconsistent with those declarations, are perfectly cor-
respondent thereto and direct proofs of their truth. When the

Landholder informed us that Mr. Gerry was 'face to face with his colleagues in the Convention of Massachusetts,' why did he not, unless he wished to mislead the public, also inform us for what purpose he was there? that it was only to answer questions; that might be proposed to him, not himself to ask questions that he could not consistently interfere in any manner in the debates, and that he was even prohibited an opportunity of explaining such parts of his conduct as were censured in his presence? By the anonymous publication alluded to by the Landholder, and inserted in the note, Mr. Gerry's colleagues are not called upon to acquit him: it only declares 'that he believes them to be men of too much honour to assert that his reasons in Convention were totally different from those he published;' and in this I presume he was not disappointed for the Landholder otherwise would have published it with triumph; but if Mr. Gerry, as it is insinuated, was only prevented by pride, from, in person, requesting them to acquit him, it amounts to a proof of his consciousness that, as men of honour, they could not have refused it, had he made the request. No person who views the absurdities and inconsistencies of the Landholder, can I think, have a very respectable opinion of his understanding, but I who am not much prejudiced in his favour, could scarcely have conceived him so superlatively weak as to expect to deceive the public and obtain credit to himself by asking 'if charges against Mr. Gerry are not true why do not his colleagues contradict them?' and 'why is it that we do not see Mr. McHenry's verification of your assertions?" If these Gentlemen were to do Mr. Gerry that justice, he might as well inquire 'why is it we do not also see the verification of A, B, C, and D and so on to the last letter of the Conventional alphabet. When the Landholder in his eighth number addressed himself to Mr. Gerry he introduces his charges by saying 'you doubtless will recollect the following state of facts; if you do not every member of the Convention will attest them.' One member of the Convention has had firmness sufficient to contradict them with his name, although he was well apprised that he thereby exposed himself as a mark for the arrows of his political adversaries, and as to some of them, he was not unacquainted with what kind of men he had to deal. But of all the members who composed that body, not one has yet stepped forward to make good the Landholder's prediction; nor has one been found to 'attest' his statement of facts. Many reasons may be assigned why the members of the Convention should not think themselves under a moral obligations of involving themselves in controversy by giving their names in vindication of Mr. Gerry; and I do not believe any of those who signed the proposed Constitution

would consider themselves bound to do this by any political obligation: But, Sir I can hardly suppose that Mr. Gerry is so perfectly
esteemed and respected by every person who had a seat in that body,
that not a single individual could possibly be procured to give his
sanction to the Landholder's charges, if it could be done with justice and as to myself, I much question whether it would be easy to
convince any person, who was present at our information to the
assembly, that every one of my honourable colleagues, (to each of
whose merit I cordially subscribe, though compelled to differ from
them in political sentiments) would be prevented by motives of
personal delicacy to myself, from contradicting the facts I have stated
relative to Mr. Gerry, if it could be done consistent with truth. . . .

CXCI. LUTHER MARTIN'S REPLY TO THE LANDHOLDER.[1]

Baltimore, March 14, 1788.

I shall at this time beg your indulgence, while I make some
observations on a publication which the Landholder has done me
the honour to address to me, in the Maryland Journal of the 29th
of February last. In my controversy with that writer, on the subject of Mr. Gerry, I have already enabled you to decide, without
difficulty, on the credit which ought to be given to his most positive
assertions and should scarce think it worth my time to notice his
charges against myself, was it not for the opportunity it affords me
of stating certain facts and transactions, of which you ought to be
informed, some of which were undesignedly omitted by me when I
had the honour of being called before the House of Delegates. No
'extreme modesty' on my part was requisite to induce me to conceal
the 'sacrifice of resentments' against Mr. Gerry, since no such sacrifice had ever been made, nor had any such resentments ever existed.
The principal opposition in sentiment between Mr. Gerry and myself, was on the subject of representation; but even on that subject,
he was much more conceding than his colleagues, two of whom
obstinately persisted in voting against the equality of representation
in the senate, when the question was taken in Convention upon the
adoption of the conciliatory propositions, on the fate of which depended, I believe, the continuance of the Convention. In many
important questions we perfectly harmonized in opinion, and where
we differed, it never was attended with warmth or animosity, nor

---

[1] P. L. Ford. *Essays on the Constitution* pp 353-359; first printed in the
Maryland Journal, March 18, 1788. For the origin of this controversy see above
CLVII, CLXII, CLXXV, CLXXXIX. CXC. It is continued in CXCII and CXCIX.
below.

did it in any respect interfere with a friendly intercourse and interchange of attention and civilities. We both opposed the extraordinary powers over the militia, given to the general government.
We were both against the re-eligibility of the president. We both
concurred in the attempt to prevent members of each branch of the
legislature from being appointable to offices, and in many other
instances, although the Landholder, with his usual regard to truth
and his usual imposing effrontery, tells me, that I 'doubtless must
remember Mr. Gerry and myself never voted alike, except in the
instances' he has mentioned. As little foundation is there in his
assertion, that I 'cautioned certain members to be on their guard
against his wiles, for that he and Mr. Mason held private meetings,
where the plans were concerted to aggrandize, at the expence of the
small States, old Massachusetts and the ancient dominion.' I need
only state facts to refute the assertion. Some time in the month
of August, a number of members who considered the system, as
then under consideration and likely to be adopted, extremely exceptionable, and of a tendency to destroy the rights and liberties of the
United States, thought it advisable to meet together in the evenings,
in order to have a communication of sentiments, and to concert a
plan of conventional opposition to, and amendment of that system,
so as, if possible, to render it less dangerous. Mr. Gerry was the
first who proposed this measure to me, and that before any meeting
had taken place, and wished we might assemble at my lodgings, but
not having a room convenient, we fixed upon another place. There
Mr. Gerry and Mr. Mason did hold meetings, but with them also
met the Delegates from New Jersey and Connecticut, a part of the
Delegation from Delaware, an honorable member from South Carolina, one other from Georgia, and myself. These were the only
'private meetings' that ever I knew or heard to be held by Mr.
Gerry and Mr. Mason, meetings at which I myself attended until
I left the Convention, and of which the sole object was not to aggrandize the great at the expense of the small, but to protect and preserve, if possible, the existence and essential rights of all the states,
and the liberty and freedom of their citizens. Thus, my fellow
citizens, I am obliged, unless I could accept the compliment at an
expence of truth equal to the Landholder's, to give up all claim to
being 'placed beyond the reach of ordinary panegyrick,' and to that
'magnanimity' which he was so solicitous to bestow upon me, that
he has wandered [into] the regions of falsehood to seek the occasion.
When we find such disregard of truth, even in the introduction,
while only on the threshold, we may form judgment what respect
is to be paid to the information he shall give us of what passed in the

Convention when he 'draws aside the veil,' a veil which was inter-
posed between our proceedings and the Public, in my opinion, for
the most dangerous of purposes, and which was never designed by
the advocates of the system to be drawn aside, or if it was, not till
it should be too late for any beneficial purpose, which as far as it is
done, or pretended to be done, on the present occasion, is only for
the purpose of deception and misrepresentation. It was on Saturday
that I first took my seat. I obtained that day a copy of the propositions that had been laid before the Convention, and which were
then the subject of discussion in a committee of the whole. The
Secretary was so polite as, at my request, to wait upon me at the
State House the next day (being Sunday), and there gave me an
opportunity of examining the journals and making myself acquainted
with the little that had been done before my arrival. I was not a
little surprised at the system brought forward, and was solicitous
to learn the reasons which had been assigned in its support; for this
purpose the journals could be of no service; I therefore conversed
on the subject with different members of the Convention, and was
favoured with minutes of the debates which had taken place before
my arrival. I applied to history for what lights it could afford me,
and I procured everything the most valuable I could find in Philadelphia on the subject of governments in general, and on the American revolution and governments in particular. I devoted my whole
time and attention to the business in which we were engaged, and
made use of all the opportunities I had, and abilities I possessed,
conscientiously to decide what part I ought to adopt in the discharge
of that sacred duty I owed to my country, in the exercise of the trust
you had reposed in me. I attended the Convention many days
without taking any share in the debates, listening in silence to the
eloquence of others, and offering no other proof that I possessed the
powers of speech, than giving my yea or nay when a question was
taken, and notwithstanding my propensity to 'endless garrulity,'
should have been extremely happy if I could have continued that
line of conduct, without making a sacrifice of your rights and political happiness. The committee of the whole house had made but
small progress, at the time I arrived, in the discussion of the propositions which had been referred to them; they completed that discussion, and made their report. The propositions of the minority
were then brought forward and rejected. The Convention had
resumed the report of the committee, and had employed some days
in its consideration. Thirty days, I believe, or more, had elapsed
from my taking my seat before in the language of the Landholder,
I 'opened in a speech which held during two days.' Such, my fellow

citizens, is the true state of the conduct I pursued when I took my seat in Convention, and which the Landholder, to whom falsehood appears more familiar than truth, with his usual affrontery, has misrepresented by a positive declaration, that without obtaining or endeavoring to obtain any information on the subject, I hastily and insolently obtruded my sentiments on the Convention, and to the astonishment of every member present, on the very day I took my seat, began a speech, which continued two days, in opposition to those measures which, on mature deliberation, had been adopted by the Convention.   But I 'alone advocated the political heresy, that the people ought not to be trusted with the election of representatives.'   On this subject, as I would wish to be on every other, my fellow citizens, I have been perfectly explicit in the information I gave to the House of Delegates, and which has since been published.   In a state government, I consider all power flowing immediately from the people in their individual capacity, and that the people, in their individual capacity, have, and ought to have the right of choosing delegates in a state legislature, the business of which is to make laws, regulating their concerns, as individuals, and operating upon them as such; but in a federal government, formed over free states, the power flows from the people, and the right of choosing delegates belongs to them only mediately through their respective state governments which are the members composing the federal government, and from whom all its power immediately proceeds; to which state governments, the choice of the federal delegates immediately belongs.   I should blush indeed for my ignorance of the first elements of government, was I to entertain different sentiments on the subject; and if this is 'political heresy,' I have no ambition to be ranked with those who are orthodox. . . . As to the 'jargon' attributed to me of maintaining that notwithstanding each state had an equal number of votes in the senate, yet the states were unequally represented in the senate,' the Landholder has all the merit of its absurdity; nor can I conceive what sentiment it is that I ever have expressed, to which he, with his usual perversion and misrepresentation, could give such a colouring.   That I ever suggested the idea of letting loose an army indiscriminately on the innocent and guilty, in a state refusing to comply with the requisitions of Congress, or that such an idea ever had place in my mind, is a falsehood so groundless, so base and malignant, that it could only have originated or been devised by a heart which would dishonour the midnight assassin.   My sentiments on this subject are well known; it was only in the case where a state refused to comply with the requisitions of Congress, that I was willing to grant the general government those powers which the proposed constitution gives it in every case.* Had I been a greater friend to a standing army, and not quite so averse to expose your liberties to a soldiery, I do not believe the Landholder would have chose me for the object on whom to expend his artillery of falsehood.

That a system may enable government wantonly to exercise power over the militia, to call out an unreasonable number from any particular state without its permission, and to march them upon, and continue them in, remote and improper services; that the same system should enable the government totally to discard, render useless, and even disarm, the militia, when it would remove them out of the way of opposing its ambitious views, is by no means inconsistent, and is really the case in the proposed constitution. In both these respects it is, in my opinion, highly faulty, and ought to be amended. In the proposed system the general government has a power not only without the consent, but contrary to the will of the state government, to call out the whole of its militia, without regard to religious scruples, or any other consideration, and to continue them in service as long as it pleases, thereby subjecting the freemen of a whole state to martial law and reducing them to the situation of slaves. It has also, by another clause, the powers by which only the militia can be organized and armed, and by the neglect of which they may be rendered utterly useless and insignificant, when it suits the ambitious purposes of government. Nor is the suggestion unreasonable, even if it had been made, that the government might improperly oppress and harass the militia, the better to reconcile them to the idea of regular troops, who might relieve them from the burthen, and to render them less opposed to the measures it might be disposed to adopt for the purpose of reducing them to that state of insignificancy and uselessness. When the Landholder declared that 'I contended the powers and authorities of the new constitution must destroy the liberties of the people,' he for once stumbled on the truth, but even this he could not avoid coupling with an assertion utterly false. I never suggested that 'the same powers

* According to this idea, I endeavored to obtain as an amendment to the system the following clause: 'And whenever the legislature of the United States shall find it necessary that revenue shall be raised by direct taxation, having apportioned the same by the above rule, requisitions shall be made of the respective states to pay into the continental treasury their respective quotas within a time in the said requisition to be specified, and in case of any of the states failing to comply with such requisition, then, and then only, to have power to devise and pass acts directing the mode, and authorizing the same in the state failing therein.' This was rejected, and that power, which I wished to have given the government only in this particular instance, is given to it without any restraint or limitation in every case.

could be safely entrusted to the old Congress;' on the contrary, I opposed many of the powers as being of that nature that, in my opinion, they could not be entrusted to any government whatever consistent with the freedom of the states and their citizens, and I earnestly recommended, what I wish my fellow citizens deeply to impress on your minds, that in altering or amending our federal government no greater powers ought to be given than experience has shown to be necessary, since it will be easy to delegate further power when time shall dictate the expediency or necessity, but powers once bestowed upon a government, should they be found ever so dangerous or destructive to freedom, cannot be resumed or wrested from government but by another revolution.

CXCII. LUTHER MARTIN'S REPLY TO THE LANDHOLDER.[1]

Baltimore, March 19, 1788.

In the recognition which the Landholder professes to make 'of what occurred to my advantage,' he equally deals in the arts of misrepresentation, as while he was 'only the record of the bad,' and I am equally obliged from a regard to truth to disclaim his pretended approbation as his avowed censure. He declares that I originated the clause which enacts that 'this Constitution and the laws of the United States, which shall be made in pursuance thereof, and all treaties made, or which shall be made, under the authority of the United States, shall be the supreme law of the land, and the judges in every state shall be bound thereby, any thing in the Constitution or the laws of any state to the contrary notwithstanding.' To place this matter in a proper point of view, it will be necessary to state, that as the propositions were reported by the committee of the whole house, a power was given to the general government to negative the laws passed by the state legislatures, a power which I considered as totally inadmissible; in substitution of this I proposed the following clause, which you will find very materially different from the clause adopted by the Constitution, 'that the legislative acts of the United States, made by virtue and in pursuance of the articles of the union, and all treaties made and ratified under the authority of the United States, shall be the supreme law of the respective states, so far as those acts or treaties shall relate to the said states or their citizens, and that the judiciaries of the several states shall be bound thereby in their decisions, any thing in the respective laws of the individual

---

[1] P. L. Ford, *Essays on the Constitution*, 360–371; first printed in the *Maryland Journal*, March 21, 1788. For the origin of this controversy see above CLVII, CLXII, CLXXV, CLXXXIX–CXCI, see also CXCIX.

states to the contrary notwithstanding.' When this clause was introduced, it was not established that inferior continental courts should be appointed for trial of all questions arising on treaties and on the laws of the general government, and it was my wish and hope that every question of that kind would have been determined in the first instance in the courts of the respective states; had this been the case, the propriety and the necessity that treaties duly made and ratified, and the laws of the general government, should be binding on the state judiciaries which were to decide upon them, must be evident to every capacity, while at the same time, if such treaties or laws were inconsistent with our constitution and bill of rights, the judiciaries of this state would be bound to reject the first and abide by the last, since in the form I introduced the clause, notwithstanding treaties and the laws of the general government were intended to be superior to the laws of our state government, where they should be opposed to each other, yet that they were not proposed nor meant to be superior to our constitution and bill of rights. It was afterwards altered and amended (if it can be called an amendment) to the form in which it stands in the system now published, and as inferior continental, and not state courts, are originally to decide on those questions, it is now worse than useless, for being so altered as to render the treaties and laws made under the federal government superior to our constitution, if the system is adopted it will amount to a total and unconditional surrender to that government, by the citizens of this state, of every right and privilege secured to them by our constitution, and an express compact and stipulation with the general government that it may, at its discretion, make laws in direct violation of those rights. But on this subject I shall enlarge in a future number.

That I 'voted an appeal should lay to the supreme judiciary of the United States, for the correction of all errors both in law and fact,' in rendering judgment is most true, and it is equally true that if it had been so ordained by the Constitution, the supreme judiciary would only have had an appellate jurisdiction, of the same nature with that possessed by our high court of appeals, and could not in any respect intermeddle with any fact decided by a jury; but as the clause now stands, an appeal being given in general terms from the inferior courts, both as to law and fact, it not only doth, but is avowedly intended, to give a power very different from what our court of appeals, or any court of appeals in the United States or in England enjoys, a power of the most dangerous and alarming nature, that of setting at nought the verdict of a jury, and having the same facts which they had determined, without any regard or respect to their determination, examined and ultimately decided by the judges themselves, and that by judges immediately appointed by the government. But the Landholder also says that 'I agreed to the clause that declares nine states to be sufficient to put the government in motion.' I cannot take to myself the merit even of this without too great a sacrifice of truth. It was proposed that if seven states agreed that should be sufficient; by a rule of Convention in filling up blanks, if different numbers were mentioned, the question was always to be taken on the highest. It was my opinion, that to agree upon a ratification of the constitution by any less number than the whole thirteen states, is so directly repugnant to our present articles of confederation, and the mode therein prescribed for their alteration, and such a violation of the compact which the states, in the most solemn manner, have entered into with each other, that those who could advocate a contrary proposition, ought never to be confided in, and entrusted in public life. I availed myself of this rule, and had the question taken on thirteen, which was rejected. Twelve, eleven, ten and nine were proposed in succession; the last was adopted by a majority of the members. I voted successively for each of these members, to prevent a less number being agreed on. Had nine not been adopted, I should on the same principle have voted for eight. But so far was I from giving my approbation that the assent of a less number of states than thirteen should be sufficient to put the government in motion, that I most explicitly expressed my sentiments to the contrary, and always intended, had I been present when the ultimate vote was taken on the constitution, to have given it my decided negative, accompanied with a solemn protest against it, assigning this reason among others for my dissent. Thus, my fellow citizens, that candour with which I have conducted myself through the whole of this business obliges me, however reluctantly, and however 'mortifying it may be to my vanity,' to disavow all 'those greater positive virtues' which the Landholder has so obligingly attributed to me in Convention, and which he was so desirous of conferring upon me as to consider the guilt of misrepresentation and falsehood but a trifling sacrifice for that purpose, and to increase my mortification, you will find I am equally compelled to yield up every pretence even to those of a negative nature, which a regard to justice has, as he says, obliged him not to omit. These consist, as he tells us, in giving my entire approbation to the system as to those parts which are said to endanger a trial by jury, and as to its want of a bill of rights, and in having too much candour there to signify that I thought it deficient in either of these respects.

But how, I pray, can the Landholder be certain that I deserve this encomium? Is it not possible, as I so frequently exhausted the politeness of the Convention, that some of those marks of fatigue and disgust, with which he intimates I was mortified as oft as I attempted to speak, might at that time have taken place, and have been of such a nature as to attract his attention; or, perhaps, as the Convention was prepared to slumber whenever I rose, the Land-holder, among others, might have sunk into sleep, and at that very moment might have been feasting his imagination with the comple-tion of his ambitious views, and dreams of future greatness. But supposing I never did declare in Convention that I thought the sys-tem defective in those essential points, will it amount to a positive proof that I approved the system in those respects, or that I culpably neglected an indispensable duty? Is it not possible, whatever might have been my insolence and assurance when I first took my seat, and however fond I might be at that time of obtruding my sentiments, that the many rebuffs with which I met, the repeated mortifications I experienced, the marks of fatigue and disgust with which my eyes were sure to be assailed wherever I turned them — one gaping here, another yawning there, a third slumbering in this place, and a fourth snoring in that — might so effectually have put to flight all my original arrogance, that, as we are apt to run into extremes, having at length become convinced of my comparative nothingness, in so august an assembly and one in which the science of government was so perfectly understood, I might sink into such a state of modesty and diffidence as not to be able to muster up resolution enough to break the seal of silence and open my lips even after the rays of light had begun to penetrate my understanding, and in some measure to chase away those clouds of error and ignorance in which it was enveloped on my first arrival? Perhaps had I been treated with a more forbearing indulgence while committing those memorable blunders, for a want of a sufficient knowledge in the science of govern-ment, I might, after the rays of light had illuminated my mind, have rendered my country much more important services, and not only assisted in raising some of the pillars, but have furnished the edifice with a new roof of my own construction, rather better calculated for the convenience and security of those who might wish to take shelter beneath it, than that which it at present enjoys. Or even admitting I was not mortified, as I certainly ought to have been, from the Landholder's account of the matter, into a total loss of speech, was it in me, who considered the system, for a variety of reasons, absolutely inconsistent with your political welfare and hap-piness, a culpable neglect of duty in not endeavouring, and that against every chance of success, to remove one or two defects, when I had before ineffectually endeavoured to clear it of the others, which therefore, I knew must remain? But to be serious, as to what relates to the appellate jurisdiction in the extent given by the system proposed, I am positive there were objections made to it, and as far as my memory will serve me, I think I was in the number of those who actually objected; but I am sure that the objections met with my approbation. With respect to a bill of rights, had the government been formed upon principles truly federal, as I wished it, legislating over and acting upon the states only in their collective or political capacity, and not on individuals, there would have been no need of a bill of rights, as far as related to the rights of individuals, but only as to the rights of states. But the proposed constitution being intended and empowered to act not only on states, but also immediately on individuals, it renders a recognition and a stipulation in favour of the rights both of states and of men, not only proper, but in my opinion absolutely necessary. I endeavoured to obtain a restraint on the powers of the general government, as to standing armies, but it was rejected. It was my wish that the general government should not have the power of suspending the privilege of the writ of habeas corpus, as it appears to me altogether unnecessary, and that the power given to it may and will be used as a dangerous engine of oppression, but I could not succeed. An honorable member from South Carolina most anxiously sought to have a clause inserted securing the liberty of the Press, and repeatedly brought this subject before the Convention, but could not obtain it. I am almost positive he made the same attempt to have a stipulation in favour of liberty of conscience, but in vain. The more the system advanced the more was I impressed with the necessity of not merely attempting to secure a few rights, but of digesting and forming a complete bill of rights, including those of states and of individuals, which should be assented to, and prefixed to the Constitution, to serve as a barrier between the general government and the respective states and their citizens; because the more the system advanced the more clearly it appeared to me that the framers of it did not consider that either states or men had any rights at all, or that they meant to secure the enjoyment of any to either the one or the other; accordingly, I devoted a part of my time to the actually preparing and draughting such a bill of rights, and had it in readiness before I left the Convention, to have laid it before a committee. I conversed with several members on the subject; they agreed with me on the propriety of the measure, but at the same time expressed their sentiments that it would be impossible to procure its adoption if attempted. A very few days before I left the Convention, I shewed to an honorable member sitting by me a proposition, which I then had in my hand, couched in the following words; 'Resolved that a committee be appointed to prepare and report a bill of rights, to be prefixed to the proposed Constitution,' and I then would instantly have moved for the appointment of a committee for that purpose, if he would have agreed to second the motion, to do which he hesitated, not as I understand from any objection to the measure, but from a conviction in his own mind that the motion would be in vain.

Thus my fellow citizens, you see that so far from having no objections to the system on this account, while I was at Convention, I not only then thought a bill of rights necessary, but I took some pains to have the subject brought forward, which would have been done, had it not been for the difficulties I have stated. At the same time I declare that when I drew up the motion, and was about to have proposed it to the Convention, I had not the most distant hope it would meet with success. The rejection of the clauses attempted in favour of particular rights, and to check and restrain the dangerous and exorbitant powers of the general government from being abused, had sufficiently taught me what to expect. And from the best judgment I could form while in Convention, I then was, and yet remained, decidedly of the opinion that ambition and interest had so far blinded the understanding of some of the principal framers of the Constitution, that while they were labouring to erect a fabrick by which they themselves might be exalted and benefited, they were rendered insensible to the sacrifice of the freedom and happiness of the states and their citizens, which must, inevitably be the consequence. I most sacredly believe their object is the total abolition and destruction of all state governments, and the erection on their ruins of one great and extensive empire, calculated to aggrandize and elevate its rulers and chief officers far above the common herd of mankind, to enrich them with wealth, and to encircle them with honours and glory, and which according to my judgment on the maturest reflection, must inevitably be attended with the most humiliating and abject slavery of their fellow citizens, by the sweat of whose brows, and by the toil of whose bodies, it can only be effected. And so anxious were its zealous promoters to hasten to a birth this misshapened heterogenous monster of ambition and interest, that, for some time before the Convention rose, upon the least attempt to alter its form, or modify its powers, the most fretful impatience was shown, such as would not have done much honour to a State Assembly, had they been sitting as long a time, and their treasury empty; while it was repeatedly urged on the contrary, but urged in vain, that in so momentous an undertaking, in forming a system for such an extensive continent, on which the political happiness of so many millions, even to the latest ages, may depend, no time could be too long — no thoughts and reflections too great — and that if by continuing six months, or even as many years, we could free the system from all its errors and defects, it would be the best use to which we could possibly devote our time. Thus my fellow citizens am I under necessity of resigning again into the hands of the Landholder, all those virtues both of a positive and negative kind, which from an excess of goodness he bestowed upon me, and give him my full permission to dispose of them hereafter in favour of some other person, who may be more deserving, and to whom they will be more acceptable: at the same time, I must frankly acknowledge, however it may operate as a proof of my dullness and stupidity, that the "ignorance in the science of government" under which I laboured at first was not removed by more than two months close application under those august and enlightened masters of the science with which the Convention abounded, nor was I able to discover during that time, either by my own researches, or by any light borrowed from those luminaries, anything in the history of mankind or in the sentiments of those who have favoured the world with their ideas on government, to warrant or countenance the motley mixture of a system proposed: a system which is an innovation in government of the most extraordinary kind; a system neither wholly federal, nor wholly national — but a strange hotch-potch of both — just so much federal in appearance as to give its advocates in some measure, an opportunity of passing it as such upon the unsuspecting multitude, before they had time and opportunity to examine it, and yet so predominantly national as to put it in the power of its movers, whenever the machine shall be set agoing, to strike out every part that has the appearance of being federal, and to render it wholly and entirely a national government: And if the framing and approving the Constitution now offered to our acceptance, is a proof of knowledge in the science of government, I not only admit, but I glory in my ignorance; and if my rising to speak had such a somnific influence on the Convention as the Landholder represents, I nave no doubt the time will come, should this system be adopted, when my countrymen will ardently wish I had never left the Convention, but remained there to the last, daily administering to my associates the salutary opiate. Happy, thrice happy, would it have been for my country, if the whole of that time had been devoted to sleep, or been a blank in our lives, rather than employed in forging its chains. As I fully intended to have returned to the Convention before the completion of its business, my colleagues very probably might, and were certainly well warranted to, give that information the Landholder mentions; but whether the Convention was led to conclude that I 'would have honoured the Constitution with my signature had not indispensable business called me away,' may be easily determined after stating a few facts. The Landholder admits I was at first against the system — when the compromise took place on the subject of representation, I in the most explicit manner declared in Convention, that though I had concurred in the report, so far as to consent to proceed upon it that we might see what kind of a system might be formed, yet I disclaimed every idea of being bound to give it my assent, but reserved to myself the full liberty of finally giving it my negative, if it appeared to me inconsistent with the happiness of my country. In a desultory conversation which long after took place in Convention, one morning before our honourable president took the chair, he was observing how unhappy it would be should there be such a diversity of sentiment as to cause any of the members to oppose the system when they returned to their states; on that occasion I replied that I was confident no state in the union would more readily accede to a proper system of government than Maryland, but that the system under consideration was of such a nature, that I never could recommend it for acceptance; that I thought the state never ought to adopt it, and expressed my firm belief that it never would.

An honourable member from Pennsylvania objected against that part of the sixth article which requires an oath to be taken by the persons there mentioned, in support of the constitution, observing (as he justly might from the conduct the convention was then pursuing) how little such oaths were regarded. I immediately joined in the objection, but declared my reason to be, that I thought it such a constitution as no friend of his country ought to bind himself to support. And not more than two days before I left Philadelphia, another honourable member from the same state urged most strenuously that the Convention ought to hasten their deliberations to a conclusion, assigning as a reason that the Assembly of Pennsylvania was just then about to meet, and that it would be of the greatest importance to bring the system before that session of the legislature, in order that a Convention of the State might be immediately called to ratify it, before the enemies of the system should have an opportunity of making the people acquainted with their objections, at the same time declaring that if the matter should be delayed and the people have time to hear the variety of objections which would be made to it by its opposers, he thought it doubtful whether that

state or any other state in the union would adopt it. As soon as
the honourable member took his seat, I rose and observed, that
I was precisely of the same opinion, that the people of America never
would, nor did I think they ought to, adopt the system, if they had
time to consider and understand it; whereas a proneness for novelty
and change — a conviction that some alteration was necessary, and
a confidence in the members who composed the Convention — might
possibly procure its adoption, if brought hastily before them, but
that these sentiments induced me to wish that a very different line
of conduct should be pursued from that recommended by the honourable member. I wished the people to have every opportunity
of information, as I thought it much preferable that a bad system
should be rejected at first, than hastily adopted and afterwards be
unavailingly repented of. If these were instances of my "high
approbation," I gave them in abundance as all the Convention can
testify, and continued so to do till I left them. That I expressed
great regret at being obliged to leave Philadelphia, and a fixed determination to return if possible before the Convention rose, is certain. That I might declare that I had rather lose an hundred guineas
than not to be there at the close of the business is very probable —
and it is possible that some who heard me say this, not knowing my
reasons, which could not be expressed without a breach of that
secrecy to which we were enjoined, might erroneously have concluded
that my motive was the gratification of vanity, in having my name
enrolled with those of a Franklin and a Washington. As to the
first, I cordially join in the tribute of praise so justly paid to the
enlightened philosopher and statesman, while the polite, friendly
and affectionate treatment myself and family received from that
venerable sage and the worthy family in which he is embosomed,
will ever endear him to my heart. The name of Washington is far
above my praise. I would to Heaven that'on this occasion one more
wreath had been added to the number of those which are twined
around his amiable brow — that those with which it is already
surrounded may flourish with immortal verdure, nor wither or fade
till time shall be no more, is my fervent prayer, and may that glory
which encircles his head ever shine with undiminished rays. To
find myself under the necessity of opposing such illustrious characters, whom I venerated and loved, filled me with regret; but viewing the system in the light I then did, and yet do view it, to have
hesitated would have been criminal; complaisance would have been
guilt. If it was the idea of my state that whatever a Washington
or Franklin approved, was to be blindly adopted, she ought to have
spared herself the expence of sending any members to the Conven-

tion, or to have instructed them implicitly to follow where they led the way. It was not to have my 'name enrolled with the other labourers,' that I wished to return to Philadelphia — that sacrifice which I must have made of my principles by putting my name to the Constitution, could not have been effaced by any derivative lustre it could possibly receive from the bright constellation with which it would have been surrounded. My object was in truth the very reverse; as I had uniformly opposed the system in its progress, I wished to have been present at the conclusion, to have then given it my solemn negative, which I certainly should have done, even had I stood single and alone, being perfectly willing to leave it to the cool and impartial investigation both of the present and of future ages to decide who best understood the science of government — who best knew the rights of men and of states, who best consulted the true interest of America, and who most faithfully discharged the trust reposed in them, those who agreed to or those who opposed the new Constitution — and so fully have I made up my own mind on this subject, that as long as the history of mankind shall record the appointment of the late Convention, and the system which has been proposed by them, it is my highest ambition that my name may also be recorded as one who considered the system injurious to my country, and as such opposed it.

CXCIII. LUTHER MARTIN'S LETTER TO THE CITIZENS OF MARYLAND.[1]

Baltimore, March 25, 1788.

Those who would wish you to believe that the faults in the system proposed are wholly or principally owing to the difference of state interests, and proceed from that cause, are either imposed upon themselves, or mean to impose upon you. The principal questions, in which the state interests had any material effect, were those which related to representation, and the number in each branch of the legislature, whose concurrence should be necessary for passing navigation acts, or making commercial regulations. But what state is there in the union whose interest would prompt it to give the general government the extensive and unlimited powers it possesses in the executive, legislative and judicial departments, together with the powers over the militia, and the liberty of establishing a standing army without any restriction? What state in the union considers it advantageous to its interest that the President should be re-eligible

---

[1] P. L. Ford, *Essays on Constitution*, pp. 374–375; first printed in the *Maryland Journal*, March 28, 1788.

— the members of both houses appointable to offices,— the judges capable of holding other offices at the will and pleasure of the government, and that there should be no real responsibility either in the President or in the members of either branch of the Legislature? Or what state is there that would have been averse to a bill of rights, or that would have wished for the destruction of jury trial in a great variety of cases, and in a particular manner in every case without exception where the government itself is interested? These parts of the system, so far from promoting the interest of any state, or states, have an immediate tendency to annihilate all the state governments indiscriminately, and to subvert their rights and the rights of their citizens. To oppose these, and to procure their alteration, is equally the interest of every state in the union. The introduction of these parts of the system must not be attributed to the jarring interests of states, but to a very different source, the pride, the ambition and the interest of individuals.

CXCIV. GEORGE NICHOLAS TO JAMES MADISON.[1]

Charlottesville, April 5th. 88.

You know better than I do what was the conduct of Mr. Mason at the convention, immediately after his return, he declared, that notwithstanding his objections to particular parts of the plan, he would take it as it was rather than lose it altogether; since that I have reason to believe his sentiments are much changed which I attribute to two causes: first the irritation he feels from the hard things that have been said of him, and secondly to a vain opinion he entertains (which has industriously been supported by some particular characters) that he has influence enough to dictate a constitution to Virginia, and through her to the rest of the Union.

CXCV. BENJAMIN FRANKLIN TO THE EDITOR OF THE FEDERAL GAZETTE.[2]

To conclude, I beg I may not be understood to infer, that our general Convention was divinely inspired when it form'd the new federal Constitution, merely because that Constitution has been unreasonably and vehemently opposed; yet I must own I have so much Faith in the general Government of the World by PROVIDENCE, that I can hardly conceive a Transaction of such momentous Importance to the Welfare of Millions now existing, and to exist in the

---

[1] *Documentary History of the Constitution*, IV, 552.

[2] *Documentary History of the Constitution*, IV, 567–571; printed in the *Federal Gazette*, April 8, 1788.

Posterity of a great Nation, should be suffered to pass without being in some degree influenc'd, guided and governed by that omnipotent, omnipresent & beneficent Ruler, in whom all inferior Spirits live & move and have their Being. —

CXCVI. JAMES MADISON TO EDMUND RANDOLPH.[1]

Orange April 10th. 1788

I do not know of anything in the new Constitution that can change the obligations of the public with regard to the old money. The principle on which it is to be settled, seems to be equally in the power of that as of the existing one. The claim of the Indiana Company cannot I should suppose be any more validated by the new System, than that of all the creditors and others who have been aggrieved by unjust laws. You do not mention what part of the Constitution, could give colour to such a doctrine. The condemnation of retrospective laws, if that be the part, does not appear to me, to admit on any principle of such a retrospective construction. As to the religious test, I should conceive that it can imply at most nothing more than that without that exception, a power would have been given to impose an oath involving a religious test as a qualification for office. The constitution of necessary offices being given to the Congress, the proper qualifications seem to be evidently involved. I think too there are several other satisfactory points of view in which the exception might be placed. ———

CXCVII. BENJAMIN FRANKLIN TO M. LE VEILLARD.[2]

April 22. 1788.

It is very possible, as you suppose, that all the Articles of the propos'd new Government will not remain unchang'd after the first meeting of the Congress. I am of Opinion with You, that the *two* Chambers where not necessary, and I disliked some other Articles that are in, and wish'd for some that are not in the propos'd Plan: — I nevertheless hope it may be adopted, though I shall have nothing to do with the execution of it, being determined to quit all public Business with my present Employment, . . .

CXCVIII. GEORGE WASHINGTON TO LA FAYETTE.[3]

Mount Vernon April 28th. 1788

For example: there was not a member of the convention, I

---

[1] Hunt, *Writings of James Madison*, V, 118.
[2] *Documentary History of the Constitution*, IV, 584.
[3] *Documentary History of the Constitution*, IV, 599–602.

believe, who had the least objection to what is contended for by the Advocates for a *Bill of Rights* and *Tryal by Jury*. The first, where the people evidently retained every thing which they did not in express terms give up, was considered nugatory as you will find to have been more fully explained by Mr. Wilson and others:—And as to the second, it was only the difficulty of establishing a mode which should not interfere with the fixed modes of any of the States, that induced the Convention to leave it, as a matter of future adjustment.

There are other points on which opinions would be more likely to vary. As for instance, on the ineligibility of the same person for President, after he should have served a certain course of years. Guarded so effectually as the proposed Constitution is, in respect to the prevention of bribery and undue influence in the choice of President: I confess, I differ widely myself from Mr Jefferson and you, as to the necessity of expediency of rotation in that appointment. The matter was fairly discussed in the Convention, & to my full convictions; though I cannot have time or room to sum up the arguments in this letter. There cannot, in my judgment, be the least danger that the President will by any practicable intrigue ever be able to continue himself one moment in office, much less perpetuate himself in it — but in the last stage of corrupted morals and political depravity: and even then there is as much danger that any other species of domination would prevail. Though, when a people shall have become incapable of governing themselves and fit for a master, it is of little consequence from what quarter he comes.

CXCIX. [GERRY:] REPLY TO A LANDHOLDER, II.[1]

In a late address to the honorable Luther Martin, Esquire, the Landholder has asserted, that Mr. Gerry "uniformly opposed Mr. Martin's principles," but this is a circumstance wholly unknown to Mr. Gerry, until he was informed of it by the Connecticut Land holder; indeed Mr. Gerry from the first acquaintance with Mr. Martin, has "uniformly had a friendship for him."

This writer has also asserted, "that the day Mr. Martin took his seat in convention, without requesting information, or to be let into the reasons of the adoption of what he might not approve, he opened against them in a speech which held during two days." But the facts are, that Mr. Martin had been a considerable time in conven-

-----

[1] P. L. Ford, *Essays on the Constitution*, 129–133, where it is taken from the *New York Journal*, April 30, 1788. For the origin of this controversy see CLVII. It is continued in CLXII, CLXXV, CLXXXIX–CXCII.

tion before he spoke; that when he entered into the debates he appeared not to need "information," as he was fully possessed of the subject; and that his speech, if published, would do him great honor.

Another assertion of this famous writer is, that Mr. Gerry in "a sarcastical reply, admired the strength of Mr. Martin's lungs, and his profound knowledge in the first principles of government;" that "this reply" "left him a prey to the most humiliating reflections; but these did not teach him to bound his future speeches by the lines of moderation; for the very next day he exhibited, without a blush, another specimen of eternal volubility." This is so remote from the truth, that no such reply was made by Mr. Gerry to Mr. Martin, or to any member of the convention; on the contrary, Mr. Martin, on the first day he spoke, about the time of adjournment, signified to the convention that the heat of the season, and his indisposition prevented his proceeding, and the house adjourned without further debate, or a reply to Mr. Martin from any member whatever.

Again, the Landholder has asserted that Mr. Martin voted "an appeal should lay to the supreme judiciary of the United States for the correction of all errors both in law and fact," and "agreed to the clause that declares nine states to be sufficient to put the government in motion:" and in a note says, "Mr. Gerry agreed with Mr. Martin on these questions." Whether there is any truth in the assertions as they relate to Mr. Martin, he can best determine; but as they respect Mr. Gerry, they reverse the facts; for he not only voted against the first proposition (which is not stated by the Landholder, with the accuracy requisite for a writer on government) but contended for jury trials in civil cases, and declared his opinion, that a federal judiciary with the powers above mentioned, would be as oppressive and dangerous, as the establishment of a star-chamber, and as to the clause that "declares nine states to be sufficient to put the government in motion," Mr. Gerry was so much opposed to it, as to vote against it in the first instance, and afterwards to move for a reconsideration of it.

The Landholder having in a former publication asserted "that Mr. Gerry introduced a motion, respecting the redemption of old continental money" and the public having been informed by a paragraph in the Massachusetts Centinel, No. 32, of vol. 8, as well as by the honorable Mr. Martin, that neither Mr. Gerry, or any other member, had introduced such a proposition, the Landholder now says that "out of 126 days, Mr. Martin attended only 66," and then enquires "whether it is to be presumed that Mr. Martin could have been minutely informed, of all that happened in convention, and committees of convention, during the sixty days of absence?" and

"Why is it that we do not see Mr. McHenry's verification of his assertion, who was of the committee for considering a provision for the debts of the union?" But if these enquiries were intended for subterfuges, unfortunately for the Landholder, they will not avail him: for, had Mr. Martin not been present at the debates on this subject, the fact is, that Mr. Gerry was not on a committee with Mr. McHenry, or with any other person, for considering a provision for the debts of the union, or any provision that related to the subject of old continental money; neither did he make any proposition, in convention, committee, or on any occasion, to any member of convention or other person, respecting the redemption of such money; and the assertions of the Landholder to the contrary, are altogether destitute of the shadow of truth.

The Landholder addressing Mr. Martin, further says, "Your reply to my second charge against Mr. Gerry, may be soon dismissed: compare his letter to the legislature of his state, with your defence, and you will find, that you have put into his mouth, objections different from anything it contains, so that if your representation be true, his must be false." The objections referred to, are those mentioned by Mr. Martin, as being made by Mr. Gerry, against the supreme power of Congress over the militia. Mr. Gerry, in his letter to the legislature, states as an objection, "That some of the powers of the federal legislature are ambiguous, and others (meaning the unlimited power of Congress, to keep up a standing army, in time of peace, and their entire controul of the militia) are indefinite and dangerous." Against both these did Mr. Gerry warmly contend, and why his representations must be false, if Mr. Martin's are true, which particularized what Mr. Gerry's stated generally, can only be discovered by such a profound reasoner, as the Connecticut Landholder. _____

CC. Charles Pinckney: Letter in State Gazette of South Carolina.[1]

Charleston, May 2d, 1788.

Mr. Martin's long mischievous detail of the opinions and proceedings of the late general convention, . . . with all his colourings and uncandid insinuations, in regard to General Washington and Doct. Franklin, . . .

What pity the salutary caution of Doct. Franklin, just previous to his signing the constitution recommended by the convention, had not been strictly attended to! If we split, it will in all probability happen in running headlong on the dangerous rock he so

_____

[1] P. L. Ford, *Essays on Constitution*, p. 412.

prophetically (as it were) warded us from, "That the opinions of the errors of the constitution born within the walls of the convention, should die there, and not a syllable be whispered abroad." This Hint is full of that foresight and penetration the Doctor has always been remarkable for.

When the general convention met, no citizen of the United States could expect less from it than I did, so many jarring interests and prejudices to reconcile! The variety of pressing dangers at our doors, even during the war, were barely sufficient to force us to act in concert and necessarily give way at times to each other. But when the great work was done and published, I was not only most agreeably disappointed, but struck with amazement. Nothing less than that superintending hand of Providence, that so miraculously carried us through the war (in my humble opinion), could have brought it about so complete, upon the whole.

CCa. PIERCE BUTLER TO WEEDON BUTLER.[1]

Mary Villa, May ye 5th. 1788.

I am not only much obliged, but much flattered by your opinion of the result of Our Deliberations last Summer, because I had a small hand in the formation. It is a subject that formerly for me I have for some Years past turned my thoughts to; yet still I am sensible I am unequal to the magnitude of it. I therefore previous to the Election declined serving; but as I was Elected I would not refuse going. It is truly an Important Era to the United States; and they now seem sensible of it. The Constitution I think will be agreed to, and be adopted tho' it has some few opponents. Where is that work of man that pleases everybody! Pains and attention were not spared to form such a Constitution as woud preserve to the individual as large a share of natural right as coud be left consistent with the good of the whole — to balance the powers of the three Branches, so that no one shoud too greatly perponderate. We had before us all the Ancient and modern Constitutions on record, and none of them was more influential on Our Judgements than the British in Its Original purity. Let you and I compare the two for a moment — yet if I begin I shall tire you. I will be as concise as possible, indeed I am ill able to write at present, and much less to think. You have a King, House of Lords and House of Commons. We have a President, Senate and House of Representatives. Their powers in some general points are similar; but when we attentively

---

[1] British Museum, Additional MSS. 16,603. Copy furnished through the courtesy of the Department of Historical Research of the Carnegie Institution of Washington.

compare the total of the two Governments, we shall find, I think, a material difference. In One, the People at large have little to say, and less to do; the other is much more of a popular Government — the whole is Elective. In the King of G.B. not only all Executive power is lodged, but he is himself also a very important and essential branch of the Legislature. Without him there can be no Parliament, and in him is the sole power of Dissolving it. No Law can be passed without His Consent. He can put a Negative upon any Bill tho' it may previously have met with the Unanimous approbation of the People. He can Alone form Treaties, which shall bind the Nation. He has the sole Right of declaring War or making Peace, so that the lives of thousands of His Subjects are at His will. He has the sole Power of Conferring honors and Titles. It is truly observed by one of Your Law Writers that "the House of Lords seems politically Constituted for the support of the rights of the Crown". He is the head of the Church. All your Dignities flow from him. He may by a Re Exeat Regnum prevent any person from leaving the Kingdom. He alone has the right of Erecting Courts of Judicature; the Court of King's Bench — I mean the Officers of it, are created by Letters Patent from Him. The Crown is Hereditary. A weak man, or a madman, may as Heir ascend to it. He is not Responsible — *the King can do no wrong.* His person is sacred, even tho' the measure pursued in His Reign be arbitrary, for no Earthly Jurisdiction has power to try Him in a Criminal way. The President of the United States is the Supreme Executive Officer. He has no separate legislative power whatever. He can't prevent a Bill from passing into a Law. In making Treaties two thirds of the Senate must concur. In the Appointment of Ambassadors, Judges of the Supreme Court, &ca., He must have the concurrence of the Senate. He is responsible to His Constituents for the use of his power. He is Impeachable. His Election, the mode of which I had the honor of proposing in the Committee in my weak judgment precludes Corruption and tumult. Yet after all, My Dear Sir, I am free to acknowledge that His Powers are full great, and greater than I was disposed to make them. Nor, Entre Nous, do I believe they would have been so great had not many of the members cast their eyes towards General Washington as President; and shaped their Ideas of the Powers to be given to a President, by their opinions of his Virtue. So that the Man, who by his Patriotism and Virtue, Contributed largely to the Emancipation of his Country, may be the Innocent means of its being, when He is lay'd low, oppress'd.

I am free to confess that after all our Endeavours, Our System is little better than matter of Experiment; and that much must depend on the morals and manners of the People at large. It is a large and wide Extended Empire, let then the System be ever so perfect, good Order and Obedience must greatly depend on the Patriotism of the Citizen. I am not insensible that the Constitution we have Ventured to recommend to the States has its faults; but the Circumstances under which it was framed are some Alleviation of them. It is probable there were Abilities in the Convention to bring forward a more perfect System of Government for a Country better adapted to the reception of it than America ever can be. Was America, or rather the States, more compact It is possible our system woud have been more perfect. Besides our Labours required the unanimous Consent of the States in Convention to Insure success from abroad. We were therefore in prudence obliged to Accomodate ourselves to Interests not only opposite but in some measure as you observe, Clashing. I will just mention one Object, and that an Important One, in which there appeared a Clashing of Interests — I mean Commerce — When we withdrew from G. Britain the Eastern States were deprived of a benefit they long enjoyd on a large participation of the Carrying Trade; with many other benefits that they had in Common with the British, under your Navigation Laws and wise Commercial System — that lucrative Branch of Trade the fishing on the Banks was neither enlarged nor better secured by withdrawing from Britain. What then did Our Brethren of the Eastern States gain by a long and bloody contest? Why nothing but the honor of calling themselves Independent States. Let us turn Our Eyes for a moment to the Southern or Staple States, and we shall see how they stood before the War and wherein they have benefited by Independence. While they were Colonies they were in a great measure Confined to One market for the Sale of their Produce — they were restricted to ship in British Bottoms. By Independence a Variety of markets were thrown open to them — the Ships of every Nation may come into their Ports — thus an Emulation is Created in the Carrying Trade, which of course lowers Freights and raises the Price of Staple Articles — thus Circumstanced we were obliged to Accomodate ourselves to the Interests of the Whole; and Our System shoud be considered as the result of a Spirit of Accomodation, and not as the most perfect System, that under the Circumstances coud be devised by the Convention. When you consider, my Dear Sir, the Great Extent of Territory, the various Climates & products, the differing manners and, as I before observed, the Contending Commercial Interests, You will agree with me that it required a pretty General Spirit of Accomodation in the members of the Convention to bring forward such a system as woud be agreed to and approved of by all. In this light then are You to View the Product of Our Joint Endeavours. The Convention saw, I think justly, the Critical Situation of the United States — Slighted from abroad and totering on the brink of Confusion at home; they therefore thought it wise to bring forward such a system as bid fairest for general approbation and adoption so as to be brought soon into operation. _____

CCI. John Dickinson: Letters of Fabius.[1]

There is another improvement equally deserving regard, and that is, the varied representation of sovereignties and people in the constitution now proposed.

It has been said, that this representation was a mere compromise.

It was not a mere compromise. *The equal representation of each state in one branch of the legislature,* was an original substantive proposition, made in convention, very soon after the draft offered by Virginia, to which last mentioned state United America is much indebted not only in other respects, but for her merit in the origination and prosecution of this momentous business.

The proposition was expressly made upon this principle, that a territory of such extent as that of United America, could not be safely and advantageously governed, but by a combination of republics, each retaining all the rights of supreme sovereignty, excepting such as ought to be contributed to the union; that for the securer preservation of these sovereignties, they ought to be represented in a body by themselves, and with equal suffrage; and that they would be annihilated, if both branches of the legislature were to be formed of representatives of the people, in proportion to the number of inhabitants in each state.

_____

CCII. George Mason to Thomas Jefferson.[2]

Virginia, Gunston-Hall May 26th. 1788.

I make no Doubt that You have long ago received Copys of the new Constitution of Government, framed last Summer, by the Delegates of the several States, in general Convention, at Philadelphia. Upon the most mature consideration I was capable of, and from Motives of sincere Patriotism, I was under the Necessity of refusing my Signature, as one of the Virginia Delegates; and drew

_____

[1] P. L. Ford, *Pamphlets on the Constitution,* pp. 206–207; first printed early in 1788, this number probably appeared early in May.

[2] *Documentary History of the Constitution,* IV, 629–630.

up some general Objections; which I intended to offer, by way of Protest; but was discouraged from doing so, by the precipitate, & intemperate, not to say indecent Manner, in which the Business was conducted, during the last week of the Convention, after the Patrons of this new Plan found they had a decided Majority in their Favour; which was obtained by a Compromise between the Eastern & the two Southern States, to permit the latter to continue the Importation of Slaves for twenty odd Years; a more favourite Object with them, than the Liberty and Happiness of the People.

CCIII. Daniel Carroll to James Madison.[1]

May 28th. 1788.

The people were alarm'd at their possitive assertions, and I am assurd when they attended the Polls, a wildness appeard in many which show'd they were realy frightend by what they had just heard — I am sorry to add on this occasion to yrself only, or such as you can entirely confide in, without my names being mentiond that it is probable Mr Mercer's assertions contributed in no small degree to this effect — Among other things take the following. A few men had long before projected the propos'd plan of Govt Mr Morris' report to Congress proposing certain specific funds, & the mode of collection which you may remember were read if not debated in Congress, was made out to be part of this plan, & some thing from the French Minister in Support of it — Hence was a Juncto with a French Interest infer'd — This was to be disclosd to our Convention and be opend in yrs, and some of the then members of Congress were to be call'd on as evidences to the truth of it. What do you say to this wonderfull plot? Extraordinary as the assertion was in itself, it became more effectual for the purposes intended by some of the hearers, confounding the time, and takeing up the Idea that the French Minister was actually concernd in promoting that scheme at the federal Convention — Again, a Member from N. Hampshire (I believe Langdon) declar'd in Convention that rather than the States shou'd have the power of emitting paper money he woud consent to make General Washington despot of America — further that it was the declar'd sense of the Convention that Tryales by jurys in civil cases were taken away. &ca.

. . . Among other matters which have been circulated, there is one which had the effect my Enemies (if I may so call any persons) wishd. I was on a ballot last winter for members of Congress left out by the difference of 2 or 3. — It was imputed to the Majority of the Delegates being Anti-federal; but I find from some Members another matter operated for that purpose — It has come to light that Luther Martin in his Tavern harangues among the members during the sitting of that Assembly had informd many of them that more than 20 Members of the Convention were in favor of a Kingly Government, and that he receivd the information from Mr McHenry who had a list of their names on the 1st printed report of the Committee of Detail — This positive assertion under the weight of Mr McHenrys name had the effect I have mentioned — Some time after the breaking up of the Assembly being informd of what Martin had said, I wrote to Mr McHenry who gave for answer, that seeing a list of names on Mr Mercers report, he copied it & ask'd him what the words *for* and *against* meant, who replied, *for* a Kingly governmt. *against* it.   I wrote to Mr McHenry that as I had been injurd by his names being mentiond   I desird he wou'd take a proper occasion whilst the Convention was sitting of having justice done me — He has answerd that on speaking to Mercer, on the Subject, he told him that he meant a National Govt. to which McHenry says I do not know what you meant, but you said a Kingly Govert.' — This Mercer denies and has given from under his hand that he neither said Kingly or National Govt. — I have a letter from Luther Martin wherein he says he had the information from McHenry without Mercer being mentioned who told him he might rely on ye persons being as markd for a Kingly Govt. — Thus this matter rests at present — it is to be setteld between McHenry & Martin on one point, & him & Mercer on another — [1]

CCIV. HUGH WILLIAMSON TO JAMES MADISON.[2]

New York June 2nd 1788

By the Time this comes to Hand you will be pretty well engaged in discussing the new Constitution & attempting to convince men who came forward with the Resolution not to be convinced.   Of all the wrong heads who have started in opposition none have been mentioned who appear to be so palpably wrong as the People of Kentucke.   It is said that some antifed in Maryland on the last Winter fastened on the Ear of Genl Wilkinson who was accidentally there and persuaded him that in case of a new Govt. the Navigation of the Mississippi would infallibly be given up.   Your Recollection must certainly enable you to say that there is a Proviso in the new Sistem which was inserted for the express purpose of preventing a majority of the Senate or of the States which is considered

---

[1] See CCXI below.   [2] *Documentary History of the Constitution*, IV, 677–678.

as the same thing from giving up the Mississippi It is provided that two thirds of the Members present in the senate shall be required to concur in making Treaties and if the southern states attend to their Duty, this will imply $\frac{2}{3}$. of the States in the Union together with the President, a security rather better than the present 9 States especially as Vermont & the Province of Main may be added to the Eastern Interest and you may recollect that when a Member, Mr Willson objected to this Proviso, saying that in all Govts. the Majority should govern it was replyed that the Navigation of the Mississippi after what had already happened in Congress was not to be risqued in the Hands of a meer Majority and the Objection was withdrawn. _____

CCV. EDMUND RANDOLPH IN THE VIRGINIA CONVENTION.[1]

June 4, 1788.

I refused to sign, and if the same were to return, again would I refuse. Wholly to adopt or wholly to reject, as proposed by the convention, seemed too hard an alternative to the citizens of America, whose servants we were, and whose pretensions amply to discuss the means of their happiness, were undeniable. . . . When I withheld my subscription, I had not even the glimpse of the genius of America, relative to the principles of the new constitution. Who, arguing from the preceding history of Virginia, could have divined that she was prepared for the important change? In former times indeed, she transcended every colony in professions and practices of loyalty; but she opened a perilous war, under a democracy almost as pure as representation would admit: she supported it under a constitution which subjects all rule, authority and power, to the legislature: every attempt to alter it had been baffled: the increase of congressional power, had always excited an alarm. I therefore would not bind myself to uphold the new constitution, before I had tried it by the true touchstone; especially too, when I foresaw, that even the members of the general convention, might be instructed by the comments of those who were without doors. But I had moreover objections to the constitution, the most material of which, too lengthy in detail, I have as yet barely stated to the public, but shall explain when we arrive at the proper points. Amendments were consequently my wish; these were the grounds of my repugnance to subscribe, and were perfectly reconcileable with my unalterable resolution, to be regulated by the spirit of America, if after our best efforts for amendments, they could not be removed. . . .

---

[1] Robertson, *Debates of the Convention of Virginia, 1788* (2d ed., 1805), pp. 29-32.

. . . The members of the general convention were particularly deputed to meliorate the confederation. On a thorough contemplation of the subject, they found it impossible to amend that system: what was to be done? The dangers of America, which will be shewn at another time by particular enumeration, suggested the expedient of forming a new plan: . . . after meeting in convention the deputies from the states communicated their information to one another: on a review of our critical situation, and of the impossibility of introducing any degree of improvement into the old system; what ought they to have done? Would it not have been treason to have returned without proposing some scheme to relieve their distressed country? The honorable gentleman asks, why we should adopt a system, that shall annihilate and destroy our treaties with France, and other nations? I think, the misfortune is, that these treaties are violated already, under the honorable gentleman's favorite system. I conceive that our engagements with foreign nations are not all affected by this system, for the sixth article expressly provides, that 'all debts contracted, and engagements entered into, before the adoption of this constitution, shall be as valid against the United States under this constitution, as under the confederation,' Does this system then, cancel debts due to or from the continent? Is it not a well known maxim that no change of situation can alter an obligation once rightly entered into? He also objects because nine states are sufficient to put the government in motion: what number of states ought we to have said? Ought we to have required the concurrence of all the thirteen? Rhode-Island, in rebellion against integrity; Rhode-Island plundered all the world by her paper money, and notorious for her uniform opposition to every federal duty, would then have it in her power to defeat the union; and may we not judge with absolute certainty from her past conduct, that she would do so? Therefore, to have required the ratification of all the thirteen states would have been tantamount to returning without having done any thing. What other number would have been proper? Twelve? The same spirit that has actuated me in the whole progress of the business, would have prevented me from leaving it in the power of any one state to dissolve the union: for would it not be lamentable, that nothing could be done for the defection of one state? A majority of the whole would have been two few. Nine states therefore seem to be a most proper number. . . . In the whole of this business, I have acted in the strictest obedience to the dictates of my conscience, in discharging what I conceive to be my duty to my country. I refused my signature, and if the same reasons operated on my mind, I would still refuse;

but as I think that those eight states which have adopted the constitution will not recede, I am a friend to the union.

CCVI. EDMUND RANDOLPH IN THE VIRGINIA CONVENTION.[1]

June 6, 1788.

The trial by jury in criminal cases is secured — in civil cases it is not so expressly secured, as I could wish it; but it does not follow, that congress has the power of taking away this privilege which is secured by the constitution of each state, and not given away by this constitution — I have no fear on this subject — congress must regulate it so as to suit every state. I will risk my property on the certainty, that they will institute the trial by jury in such manner as shall accommodate the conveniences of the inhabitants in every state: the difficulty of ascertaining this accommodation, was the principal cause of its not being provided for.

CCVII. EDMUND RANDOLPH IN THE VIRGINIA CONVENTION.[2]

June 7, 1788.

The system under consideration is objected to in an unconnected and irregular manner: detached parts are attacked without considering the whole: this, sir, is disingenuous and unreasonable. Ask if the powers be unnecessary. If the end proposed can be obtained by any other means, the powers may be unnecessary. Infallibility was not arrogated by the convention; they included in the system those powers they thought necessary . . .

As to the mode of paying taxes, little need be said — it is immaterial which way they are to be paid; for they are to be paid only once. I had an objection which pressed heavily on my mind — I was solicitous to know the objects of taxation. I wished to make some discrimination with regard to the demands of congress, and of the states, on the same object. As neither can restrain the other in this case; as the power of both is unlimited, it will be their interest mutually to avoid interferences. It will most certainly be the interest of either to avoid imposing a tax on an article, which shall have been previously taxed by the other. This consideration, and the structure of the government satisfy me.

---

[1] Robertson, *Debates of the Convention of Virginia, 1788* (2d edit., 1805), p. 59.
[2] Robertson, *Debates of the Convention of Virginia, 1788* (2d edit., 1805), pp. 95-99.

CCVIII. Edmund Randolph in the Virginia Convention.[1]

June 10. 1788.

Freedom of religion is said to be in danger. I will candidly say, I once thought that it was, and felt great repugnance to the constitution for that reason. I am willing to acknowledge my apprehensions removed — and I will inform you by what process of reasoning I did remove them. The constitution provides, that "the senators "and representatives before mentioned, and the members of the "several state legislatures, and all executive and judicial officers, "both of the United States and of the several states, shall be bound "by oath, or affirmation, to support this constitution; but no re- "ligious test shall ever be required as a qualification to any office "or public trust under the United States." It has been said, that if the exclusion of the religious test were an exception from the general power of congress, the power over religion would remain. I inform those who are of this opinion, that no power is given expressly to congress over religion. The senators and representatives, members of the state legislatures, and executive and judicial officers, are bound by oath, or affirmation, to support this constitution. This only binds them to support it in the exercise of the powers constitutionally given it. The exclusion of religious tests is an exception from this general provision, with respect to oaths, or affirmations. Although officers, &c. are to swear that they will support this constitution, yet they are not bound to support one mode of worship, or to adhere to one particular sect. It puts all sects on the same footing. A man of abilities and character, of any sect whatever, may be admitted to any office or public trust under the United States. I am a friend to a variety of sects, because they keep one another in order. How many different sects are we composed of throughout the United States? How many different sects will be in congress? We cannot enumerate the sects that may be in congress. And there are so many now in the United States that they will prevent the establishment of any one sect in prejudice to the rest, and will forever oppose all attempts to infringe religious liberty. If such an attempt be made, will not the alarm be sounded throughout America? If congress be as wicked as we are foretold they will, they would not run the risk of exciting the resentment of all, or most of the religious sects in America.

The judiciary is drawn up in terror — here I have an objection of a different nature. I object to the appellate jurisdiction as the greatest evil in it.

---

[1] Robertson, *Debates of the Convention of Virginia, 1788* (2d edit., 1805), pp. 151–152.

CCIX. James Madison in the Virginia Convention.[1]

June 12, 1788.

The congressional proceedings are to be occasionally published, including *all receipts and expenditures* of public money, of which no part can be used, but in consequence of appropriations made by law. This is a security which we do not enjoy under the existing system. That part which authorises the government to withhold from the public knowledge what in their judgment may require secrecy, is imitated from the confederation — that very system which the gentleman advocates. _____

CCX. Debate in the Virginia Convention.[2]

June 14, 1788.

(*The 4th and 5th sections read.*)

Mr. *Monroe* wished that the honorable gentleman, who had been in the federal convention, would give information respecting the clause concerning elections. He wished to know why congress had an ultimate controul over the time, place, and manner of elections of representatives, and the time and manner of that of senators; and also why there was an exception as to the *place* of electing senators.

Mr. *Madison.* — Mr. Chairman, — The reason of the exception was, that if congress could fix the *place* of choosing the senators, it might compel the state legislatures to elect them in a different place from that of their usual sessions, which would produce some inconvenience, and was not necessary for the object of regulating elections. But it was necessary to give the general government a controul over the time and manner of choosing the senators, to prevent its own dissolution.

With respect to the other point, it was thought that the regulation of time, place, and manner of electing the representatives, should be uniform throughout the continent. Some states might regulate the elections on the principles of equality, and others might regulate them otherwise. This diversity would be obviously unjust. Elections are regulated now unequally in some states, particularly South Carolina, with respect to *Charleston*, which is represented by 30 members. — Should the people of any state, by any means be deprived of the right of suffrage, it was judged proper that it should be remedied by the general government. It was found impossible to fix the time, place, and manner, of the election of representatives in the constitu-

---

[1] Robertson, *Debates of the Convention of Virginia, 1788* (2d edit., 1805), p. 236.

[2] Robertson, *Debates of the Convention of Virginia, 1788* (2d edit., 1805), pp. 261-290.

tion. It was found necessary to leave the regulation of these, in the first place, to the state governments, as being best acquainted with the situation of the people, subject to the controul of the general government, in order to enable it to produce uniformity, and prevent its own dissolution. And considerng the state governments and general government as distinct bodies, acting in different and independent capacities for the people, it was thought the particular regulations should be submitted to the former, and the general regulations to the latter. Were they exclusively under the controul of the state governments, the general government might easily be dissolved. But if they be regulated properly by the state legislatures, the congressional controul will very probably never be exercised. The power appears to me satisfactory, and as unlikely to be abused as any part of the constitution.

Mr. *Monroe* wished to hear an explanation of the clause which prohibits either house, during the session of congress, from adjourning for more than three days without the consent of the other. He asked if it was proper or right, that the members of the lower house should be dependent on the senate? He considered that it rendered them in some respect dependent on the senators, as it prevented them from returning home, or adjourning, without their consent, and as this might encrease their influence unduly, he thought it improper.

Mr. *Madison* wondered that this clause should meet with a shadow of objection. It was possible, he observed, that the two branches might not agree concerning the time of adjourning, and that this possibility suggested the power given the president of adjourning both houses to such time as he should think proper, in case of their disagreement. — That it would be very exceptionable to allow the senators, or even the representatives, to adjourn without the consent of the other house, at *any* season whatsoever, without any regard to the situation of public exigencies. That it was possible, in the nature of things, that some inconvenience might result from it; but that it was as well secured as possible.

Governor *Randolph* observed, that the constitution of Massachusetts was produced as an example, in the grand convention, in favor of this power given to the president. If, said his excellency, he be honest, he will do what is right. — If dishonest, the representatives of the people will have power of impeaching him.

(*The 6th section read.*)

Mr. *Henry.* — Mr. Chairman — Our burden should, if possible, be rendered more light. I was in hopes some other gentleman would have objected to this part. The pay of the members is, by the constitution, to be fixed by themselves, without limitation or restraint. They may therefore indulge themselves in the fullest extent. They may make their compensations as high as they please. I suppose, if they be good men, their own delicacy will lead them to be satisfied with moderate salaries. But there is no security for this, should they be otherwise inclined. I really believe that if the state legislatures were to fix their pay, no inconvenience would result from it, and the public mind would be better satisfied. But in the same section there is a defect of much greater consequence. There is no restraint on corruption. They may be appointed to offices without any material restriction, and the principal source of corruption in representatives, is the hopes and expectations of offices and emoluments. After the first organization of offices, and the government is put in motion, they may be appointed to any existing offices which become vacant, and they may create a multiplicity of offices, in order thereafter to be appointed to them. What says the clause? "No senator or representative, shall, during the time for which he was elected, be appointed to any civil office under the authority of the United States, which shall have been created, or the emoluments whereof shall have been increased, during such time." This is an idea strangely expressed. He shall not accept of any office created during the time he is elected for, or to any office whereof the emoluments have been increased in that time! Does not this plainly say, that if an office be not created during the time for which he is elected, or if its emoluments be not increased during such time, that he may accept of it? I can see it in no other light. If we wish to preclude the inticement to getting offices, there is a clear way of expressing it. If it be better that congress should go out of their representative offices, by accepting other offices, then it ought to be so. If not, we require an amendment in the clause, that it shall not be so. I may be wrong. Perhaps the honorable member may be able to give a satisfactory answer on this subject.

Mr. Madison. — Mr. Chairman. — I most sincerely wish to give a proper explanation on this subject, in such a manner as may be to the satisfaction of every one. I shall suggest such considerations as led the convention to approve of this clause. With respect to the right of ascertaining their own pay, I will acknowledge, that their compensations, if practicable, should be fixed in the constitution itself, so as not to be dependent on congress itself, or on the state legislatures. The various vicissitudes, or rather the gradual diminution of the value of all coins and circulating medium, is one reason against ascertaining them immutably; as what may be now an adequate compensation, might, by the progressive reduction of the value of our circulating medium, be extremely inadequate at a period not far distant.

It was thought improper to leave it to the state legislatures, because it is improper that one government should be dependent on another: and the great inconveniences experienced under the old confederation, shew, that the states would be operated upon by local considerations, as contradistinguished from general and national interests. — Experience shews us, that they have been governed by such heretofore, and reason instructs us, that they would be influenced by them again. This theoretic inconvenience of leaving to congress the fixing their compensations, is more than counterbalanced by this in the confederation; that the state legislatures had a right to determine the pay of the members of congress, which enabled the states to destroy the general government. There is no instance where this power has been abused. In America, legislative bodies have reduced their own wages lower rather than augmented them. This is a power which cannot be abused without rousing universal attention and indignation. What would be the consequence of the Virginia legislature raising their pay to four or five pounds each per day? The universal indignation of the people. Should the general congress annex wages disproportionate to their service, or repugnant to the sense of the community, they would be universally execrated. The certainty of incurring the general detestation of the people will prevent abuse. It was conceived that the great danger was in creating new offices, which would increase the burdens of the people: and not in an uniform admission of all meritorious characters to serve their country in the old offices. There is no instance of any state constitution which goes as far as this. It was thought to be a mean between two extremes. It guards against abuse by taking away the inducement to create new offices, or increase the emoluments of old offices. And it gives them an opportunity of enjoying, in common with other citizens, any of the existing offices which they may be capable of executing. To have precluded them from this, would have been to exclude them from a common privilege to which every citizen is entitled, and to prevent those who had served their country with the greatest fidelity and ability from being on a par with their fellow-citizens. I think it as well guarded as reason requires: More so than the constitution of any other nation. . . .

Mr. *Madison.* — Mr. Chairman — Let me ask those who oppose this part of the system, whether any alteration would not make it equally, or more liable to objections? Would it be better to fix their compensations? Would not this produce inconveniencies? What authorises us to conclude, that the value of coins will continue always the same? Would it be prudent to make them dependent on the state governments for their salaries — on those who watch them with jealous eyes, and who consider them as encroaching, not on the people, but on themselves? But the worthy member supposes, that congress will fix their wages so low, that only the rich can fill the offices of senators and representatives. Who are to appoint them? The rich? No, sir, the people are to choose them. If the members of the general government were to reduce their compensations to a trifle, before the evil suggested could happen, the people could elect other members in their stead, who would alter that regulation. The people do not choose them for their wealth. If the state legislatures choose such men as senators, it does not influence the people at large in their election of representatives. They can choose those who have the most merit and least wealth. If congress reduce their wages to a trifle, what shall prevent the states from giving a man of merit, so much as will be an adequate compensation? I think the evil very remote, and if it were now to happen, the remedy is in our own hands, and may by ourselves be applied.

Another gentleman seems to apprehend infinite mischief from a possibility that any member of congress may be appointed to an office, although he ceases to be a member the moment he accepts it! What will be the consequence of precluding them from being so appointed? If you have in your country one man whom you could in time of danger trust above all others, with an office of high importance, he cannot undertake it till the two years expire if he be a representative; or till the six years elapse, if a senator. Suppose America was engaged in war; and the man of the greatest military talents and approved fidelity, was a member of either house — would it be right that this man who could lead us to conquer, and who could save his country from destruction, could not be made general till the term of his election expired? Before that time we might be conquered by our enemies. This will apply to civil as well as military offices. It is impolitic to exclude from the service of his country, in any office, the man who may be most capable of discharging its duties, when they are most wanting.

The honorable gentleman said, that those who go to congress will look forward to offices as a compensation for their services, rather than salaries. Does he recollect that they shall not fill offices created by themselves? When they go to congress the old offices will be filled. They cannot make any probable calculation that the men in office will die, or forfeit their offices. As they cannot get any new offices, one of these contingencies must happen before they can get any office at all. The chance of getting an office is therefore so remote, and so very distant, that it cannot be considered as a sufficient reason to operate on their minds to deviate from their duty.

Let any man calculate in his own mind, the improbability of a member of the general government getting into an office, when he cannot fill any office newly created, and when he finds all the old offices filled at the time he enters into congress. Let him view the danger and impolicy of precluding a member of congress from holding existing offices, and the danger of making one government dependent on another, and he will find that both clauses deserve applause.

The observations made by several honorable members illustrate my opinion, that it is impossible to devise any system agreeable to all. — When objections so contradictory are brought against it, how shall we decide? Some gentlemen object to it, because they may make their wages too high — Others object to it, because they may make them too low! If it is to be perpetually attacked by principles so repugnant, we may cease to discuss. For what is the object of our discussion? — Truth, sir. To draw a true and just conclusion. Can this be done without rational premises and syllogistic reasoning.

As to the British parliament, it is nearly as he says. But how does it apply to this case? Suppose their compensations had been appointed by the state governments, or fixed in the constitution — Would it be a safe government for the union, if its members depended on receiving their salaries from other political bodies at a distance, and fully competent to withhold them? Its existence would at best be but precarious. If they were fixed in the constitution, they might become extremely inadequate, and produce the very evil which gentlemen seem to fear. For then a man of the highest merit could not act unless he were wealthy. This is the most delicate part in the organization of a republican government. It is the most difficult to establish on unexceptionable grounds. It appears to me most eligible as it is. The constitution has taken a medium between the two extremes, and perhaps with more wisdom than either the British or the state governments, with respect to their eligibility to offices. They can fill no new offices created by themselves, nor old ones of which they encreased the salaries. If they were excluded altogether, it is possible that other disadvantages might accrue from it, besides the impolicy and injustice of depriving them of a common privilege. They will not relinquish their legislative in order to accept other offices. They will more probably confer them on their friends and connections. If this be an inconvenience, it is incident to all governments. After having heard a variety of principles developed, I thought that on which it is established the least exceptionable, and it appears to me sufficiently well guarded. . . .

(The 7th section read.)

Mr. *Grayson* objected to the power of the senate to propose or concur with amendments to money bills. He looked upon the power of proposing amendments to be equal in principle to that of originating, and that they were in fact the same. As this was, in his opinion, a departure from that great principle which required that the immediate representatives of the people only should interfere with money bills; he wished to know the reasons on which it was founded. The lords in England had never been allowed to intermeddle with money bills. He knew not why the senate should. In the lower house, said he, the people are represented according to their numbers. In the upper house, the states are represented in their political capacities. Delaware or Rhode-Island has as many representatives here as Massachusetts. Why should the senate have a right to intermeddle with money, when the representation is neither equal or just?

Mr. *Madison.* — Mr. Chairman — The criticism made by the honorable member, is, that there is an ambiguity in the words, and that it is not clearly ascertained where the origination of money bills may take place. I suppose the first part of the clause is sufficiently expressed to exclude all doubts. The gentlemen who composed the convention divided in opinion, concerning the utility of confining this to any particular branch. Whatever it be in Great-Britain, there is a sufficient difference between us and them to render it inapplicable to this country. It always appeared to me to be a matter of no great consequence, whether the senate had a right of originating, or proposing amendments to money bills or not. To withhold it from them would create disagreeable disputes. Some American constitutions make no difference. Virginia and South-Carolina, are, I think, the only states where this power is restrained. In Massachusetts, and other states, the power of proposing amendments is vested unquestionably in their senates. No inconvenience has resulted from it. On the contrary, with respect to South-Carolina, this clause is continually a source of disputes. When a bill comes from the other house, the senate entirely rejects it, and this causes contentions. When you send a bill to the senate, without the power of making any alteration you force them to reject the bill altogether, when it would be necessary and advantageous that it should pass. The power of proposing alterations removes this inconvenience, and does not appear to me at all objectionable. I should have no objection to their having a right of originating such bills. People would see what was done, and it would add the intelligence of one house to that of the other. It would be still in the power of the other house to obstruct any injudicious measure proposed by them. There is no land-mark or constitutional provision in Great-Britain, which prohibits the house of lords from intermeddling with money bills; but the house of commons have established this rule. Yet the lords insist on their having a right to originate them, as they possess great property, as well as the commons, and are taxed like them. The house of commons object to their claim, least they should too lavishly make grants to the crown, and increase the taxes. The honorable member says, that there is no difference between the right of originating bills, and proposing amendments. There is some difference, though not considerable. If any grievances should happen in consequence of unwise regulations in revenue matters, the odium would be divided, which will now be thrown on the house of representatives. But you may safely lodge this power of amending with the senate. When a bill is sent with proposed amendments to the house of representatives, if they find the alterations defective, they are not conclusive. The house of representatives are the judges of their propriety, and the recommendation of the senate is nothing. The experience of this state justifies this clause. — The house of delegates has employed weeks in forming a money bill; and because the senate had no power of proposing amendments, the bill was lost altogether; and a new bill obliged to be again introduced, when the insertion of one line by the senate would have done. Those gentlemen who oppose this clause will not object to it, when they recollect that the senators are appointed by the states, as the present members of congress are appointed. For, as they will guard the political interests of the states in other respects, they will attend to them very probably in their amendments to money bills. I think this power, for these considerations, is useful and necessary. . . .

(The 8th section read.)

Mr. *Clay* wished to be informed, why the congress were to have power to provide for calling forth the militia, to put the laws of the union in execution.

Mr. *Madison* supposed the reasons of this power to be so obvious that they would occur to most gentlemen. If resistance should be made to the execution of the laws, he said, it ought to be overcome. This could be done only two ways; either by regular forces, or by the people. By one or the other it must unquestionably be done.

If insurrections should arise, or invasions should take place, the people ought unquestionably to be employed to suppress and repel them, rather than a standing army. The best way to do these things, was to put the militia on a good and sure footing, and enable the government to make use of their services when necessary. . . .

Governor *Randolph*. . . . With respect to a standing army, I believe there was not a member in the federal convention who did not feel indignation at such an institution. What remedy then could be provided? — Leave the country defenceless? In order to provide for our defence, and exclude the dangers of a standing army, the general defence is left to those who are the objects of defence. It is left to the militia who will suffer if they become the instruments of tyranny. The general government must have power to call them forth when the general defence requires it. In order to produce greater security, the state governments are to appoint the officers. The president, who commands them when in the actual service of the union, is appointed secondarily by the people. — This is a further security. It is not incredible that men who are interested in the happiness of their country, whose friends, relations, and connections, must be involved in the fate of their country, should turn against their country? I appeal to every man, whether, if any of our own officers were called upon to destroy the liberty of their country, he believes they would assent to such an act of suicide? The state governments having the power of appointing them, may elect men who are the most remarkable for their virtue & attachment to their country. . . .

Mr. *Madison*. . . . The power of regulating the time, place, and manner of elections, must be vested some where. It could not be fixed in the constitution without involving great inconveniences. — They could then have no authority to adjust the regulations to the changes of circumstances. The question then is, whether it ought to be fixed unalterably in the state governments, or subject to the controul of the general government. Is it not obvious that the general government would be destroyed without this controul? It has already been demonstrated that it will produce many inconveniences.

CCXI. DANIEL CARROLL: NOTES AND CORRESPONDENCE.[1]

Copy of what Col. Mercer gave me [Daniel Carroll] at Annapolis during the sitting of the Assembly.

---

[1] These papers in the handwriting of Daniel Carroll were found among the McHenry MSS. They are reprinted here from the *American Historical Review*, XI, 619–624. They are put here under the date of the last two items, — the letters of McHenry — in order to bring them all together. See also CCIII above.

Mr. Mercer had during the sitting of the Convention at Pha. a list of the members of that body taken down on the printed Constitution, and against their names, these words — for and against. Mr. McHenry seeing it (without its being shewn to him) at the table where the Members from the State sat copied it without the leave or interference of Mr. Mercer and added Mr. Mercers name with those of Mr. Martin and himself — as against. Mr Mercer askd him what authority he had for setting him down against. Mr. McHenry made some reply rather in a light manner — that he had left Mr. Mercer room to change side, or to that effect. Some conversation took place but not of so serious a nature, as to make any impression on Mr. Mercers memory, but he is persuaded that he entered into no explanation of the list to authorize Mr. McHenry to say the members were markd as for a *Kingly* or *national* Government, and the list being on the Constitution with the words for and against and nothing else, Mr. McHenry cou'd have no authority from that. Mr. Mercer and Mr. McHenry were not in the habit of Confidential communication — nor has Mr. Mercer ever mentioned any political opinion as the opinion of Mr. D. Carroll to any one. In a variety of private conversations it is probable he receiv'd the opinions of almost every Member in Convention, but he has never related more than what came from them in debate. At that moment the Cant expression was *high toned* Government which superceeded the usual descriptions of Monarchy, Aristocracy, or Democracy and which perswades Mr. Mercer that the word Kingly coud never have been used by him.

But as Mr. Martins information to Mr. Mercer of what passd between him and Mr. McHenry fixes it, that Mr. McHenry told him, that he knew it of his own knowledge and from his acquaintance with the Characters, Mr. Mercer thinks that Mr. McHenry has very improperly introduc'd him into the business.

Extracts from Mr. McHenrys Letter to me [Daniel Carroll] dated the 9th of Jan'y 88

Nothing that Mr. Martin can say can make me uneasy, or give me any Surprize. I will tell you in a few words the ground of his misrepresentation. I observ'd Mr. Mercer one day in Convention taking down the names of the members on a blank side of his report and affixing to most of them the word for or against. I askd him what question occasioned his being so particular, upon which he told me, it was no question, but those marked with a for were in favor of Monarchy. How do you learn that? No matter said he the thing is so. I then ask'd him to let me copy it, and Mr. Martin took a copy from mine, which was also on a blank page of my report. This is the whole history, and you may make what use of it you please.

The following is a copy Mr. Martins letter to me [Daniel Carroll] in consequence of what passd between us on Col. Mercer's calling him to me, at the time we were in conversation —

May 20th. 1788

Agreeable to your request I here present you the Substance of our this days conversation —

Sometime after Mr. McHenrys return to Convention conversing on the System then under discussion, and of the object and views of the Members of the Convention, Mr. McHenry told me that a very considerable Number of them were in favour of a Monarchical Government (under certain limitations and restrictions as I concluded) and shewed me a list of the then attending Members from each State marked with the words *for* and *against,* to distinguish such as were for or against such a Government; this list was written on a blank page of his printed report of the Committee of detail, and I copied it on a blank page of mine with the same distinctive marks — more than twenty were noted in the list as being in favour of a Monarchy, among those was yr name.

I observ'd to Mr McHenry that as to many of them I perfectly concurd in opinion, but as to some, I thought he was mistaken — he replied I might depend upon it, he was better informed on the Subject, and better knew their sentiments than I did, and that every one who was there distinguisd in favor of a King was so in reality; Mr McHenry did not mention to me particularly whom he drew the inference or how he had obtained the Knowledge or the belief which he express'd, but I naturally concluded that it proceeded from the Sentiments he had heard them express, — from information which had been given to him by others or from their Conduct in Convention, or from all these Sources combin'd. I have no possible recollection that Col. Mercers name was mentiond to me on that or any other occasion by Mr McHenry as having given him any information on the Subject, on the contrary, I well remember that I was surprizd when I heard Col Mercers name lately mentioned on the occasion, as being totally unacquainted with his sentiments on that Subject, and as being ignorant that he had ever expressed such Sentiments. And I am well convinc'd from the fullest recollection and reflection that Mr. McHenry did not mention to me any person in particular from whom he had receiv'd the information or who had impressd on his mind the opinion he at that time entertaind.

At the time we were before the Assembly to give information Mr. McHenry's report of the Committee with other papers were laying on the Table, at that time the list I have mention'd was upon it; And as Mr. McHenry endeavour'd to impress an Idea that there cou'd be no foundation for my Sentiment, that tho' but few members openly avowed their being for a Monarchical Government, yet there were a much greater number who secretly favord that System, I with difficulty restraind myself from laying my hands upon it. and producing it to the Assembly as a proof that he had himself once entertaind Similar Sentiments, altho' he might since be convincd of his error. —

The foregoing is a just State of what passd between Mr McHenry and myself on the Subject concerning which you expressed a desire that I wou'd give you information, and you have my full permission to make any use of it which you may think proper.

I am sr. yr. Obt Sert.

Copy.   LUTHER MARTIN

The following is from a Scrip of paper sent me [Daniel Carroll] by my Brother from Mr McHenry —

I mentioned to Mr Mercer, at the Governors that Mr Danl. Carroll had been made very uneasy by Mr Martins having reported, that when in Convention he had been for a Kingly Government, and related the Substance of what I had written to Mr. Carroll on that Subject. Mr Mercer replied that he had put down no such thing opposite the names, and that he only meant that those which had *for* annex'd to them were for a national Government. I said I did not know what he meant, but that he told me in Convention when I copied the names from his paper that those mark'd for were for a King. He spoke of Mr Martins having acted improperly on this occasion and some others.

DANIEL CARROLL TO REVEREND JOHN CARROLL.

June 11th. 1788

Dear Brother,

The inclosd[1] is for Mr. McHenry. During a long course of Public Service, I have never before heard of any imputation being cast on my conduct. This is of a nature which woud deservedly deprive me of the confidence of the Public, at least. My character I hold dear, and will maintain it against attempts to injure it. Where the blame is, I will not undertake to determine. I did not conceive it probable, that such a paper as is mentiond in Mr. McHenrys

---

[1] Apparently the items printed above.

Letter of the 9th of Jany. coud have been circulated among some of the deputies from Maryland without my privity, much less, that Mr McHenry woud furnish Mr. Martin with one with my name to it. Until lately I woud not believe that my name was on the list.

Dear Brother

Yrs etca—

[Address:] The Revd. Mr. John Carroll.   DANL CARROLL.

JAMES McHENRY TO REVEREND JOHN CARROLL.[1]

BALTIMORE 16 June 1788.

I have read Mr. Martins and Mr. Mercers information to Mr. D. Carroll. With respect to their statements, I can only subjoin, to what I have already written to Mr. Carroll, that I copied the list in question with Mr. Mercers permission, without adding any thing of my own or altering any thing of his, which may be ascertained by comparing the two together; and that on Mr Merc[e]rs changing his seat to another part of the house, Mr. Martin asked me, what I had been copying, and without waiting for an answer took up my report and read over the list. I told him, I had copied it from a list made out by Mr. Mercer, and that the names having *for* annexed to them, Mr. Mercer said, were for a king. Mr. Martin asked me to let him take a copy, and I permitted it, and this was *all* the conversation I held then or at any other time with Mr. Martin on that subject.

This relation is copied in substance from my note book of the transactions of the convention, which I wrote down daily,[2] and is besides fresh in my memory so that there can be no mistake upon my part. I did not shew the list to Mr. Carroll or Mr Jenifer or any other person (except Martin who got it by surprise), because I took it only with a view to relate the circumstances attending its origin in case it should ever be brought forward to answer improper purposes; nor have I at any time since mentioned any thing respecting either the list or its object, to any person whatever but Mr. D. Carroll and his brother.

Mr. D. Carroll has my consent to make what use he may think proper of the above.

JAMES McHENRY.

---

[1] The following documents are rough drafts of two letters in McHenry's handwriting.

[2] By reference to McHenry's notes of August 6, it will be seen that the item in question is an insertion.

James McHenry to Reverend John Carroll.

BALTIMORE 16 June 1788.

Dr. Sir.

You have been so kind as to put your brothers letter into my hand. I have read it attentively and cannot help thinking that he has looked for an illustration where his own experience might have taught him it could not possibly be found. He doubts where the blame lays. When did Mr. Martin and Mr. Mercer become authorities? He suggests also that I should have made him acquainted with the list. If I had shewn it to him, I must have shewn it to others who were equally affected by it, with some of whom I have been for these thirteen years past in the closest habits of intimacy and friendship. Such a step, he must be aware, would have brought on immediate personal altercations (at a most critical time) with a man prone to anger, and excessively captious. I did what I thought much safer and more decisive. I reserved myself to expose it publicly in case a public use had been made of it. This has never been done tho' the fairest opportunity in the world was offred for doing it. Can any one who witnessed that occasion, who heard me charge Mr. Martin with uttering falsehoods, entertain a belief that his representation to Mr. Carroll is true, or that he would have remained silent and condemned before the general assembly, if he could have given me as an evidence of what he there asserts? As to Mr. Mercer, I wish your brother had mentioned what he has recently done or said that has induced him to think more favorably of his veracity.

I have only to regret in this affair that my anxiety for the public good and your brothers quiet, for whom I have the most sincere friendship, should have occasioned him a moments uneasiness, and am only surprised that he has not treated this as he has the other fictions which have been gravely reported to the world for truths.

I am very respectfully

Sir Your obt. and hble st.

JAMES McHENRY

[Address:] Revd. John Carroll Esqr.

CCXII. DEBATE IN THE VIRGINIA CONVENTION.[1]

June 17, 1788.

(The first clause, of the ninth section, read.)

. . . Mr. *Madison.* — Mr. Chairman — I should conceive this clause to be impolitic, if it were one of those things which could be excluded without encountering greater evils. — The southern

---

[1] Robertson, *Debates of the Convention of Virginia, 1788* (2d edit., 1805), pp. 321–345.

states would not have entered into the union of America, without the temporary permission of that trade. And if they were excluded from the union, the consequences might be dreadful to them and to us. We are not in a worse situation than before. That traffic is prohibited by our laws, and we may continue the prohibition. The union in general is not in a worse situation. Under the articles of confederation, it might be continued forever: But by this clause an end may be put to it after twenty years. There is therefore an amelioration of our circumstances. A tax may be laid in the mean time; but it is limited, otherwise congress might lay such a tax as would amount to a prohibition. From the mode of representation and taxation, congress cannot lay such a tax on slaves as will amount to manumission. Another clause secures us that property which we now possess. At present, if any slave elopes to any of those states where slaves are free, he becomes emancipated by their laws. For the laws of the states are uncharitable to one another in this respect. But in this constitution, "no person held to service, or labor, in one state, under the laws thereof, escaping into another, shall in consequence of any law or regulation therein, be discharged from such service or labor; but shall be delivered up on claim of the party to whom such service or labor may be due." — This clause was expressly inserted to enable owners of slaves to reclaim them. This is a better security than any that now exists. No power is given to the general government to interpose with respect to the property in slaves now held by the states. The taxation of this state being equal only to its representation, such a tax cannot be laid as he supposes. They cannot prevent the importation of slaves for twenty years; but after that period they can. The gentlemen from South-Carolina and Georgia argued in this manner: — "We have now liberty to import this species of property, and much of the property now possessed, has been purchased, or otherwise acquired, in contemplation of improving it by the assistance of imported slaves. What would be the consequence of hindering us from it? The slaves of Virginia would rise in value, and we would be obliged to go to your markets." I need not expatiate on this subject. Great as the evil is, a dismemberment of the union would be worse. If those states should disunite from the other states, for not indulging them in the temporary continuance of this traffic, they might solicit and obtain aid from foreign powers. . . .

(The 2d, 3d, and 4th clauses read.)

. . . Mr. *Madison* replied, that even the southern states, who were most affected, were perfectly satisfied with this provision, and dreaded no danger to the property they now hold. It appeared to him, that the general government would not intermeddle with that property for twenty years, but to lay a tax on every slave imported, not exceeding ten dollars; and that after the expiration of that period they might prohibit the traffic altogether. The census in the constitution was intended to introduce equality in the burdens to be laid on the community.—No gentleman objected to laying duties, imposts, and excises, uniformly. But uniformity of taxes would be subversive of the principles of equality: For that it was not possible to select any article which would be easy for one state, but what would be heavy for another. — . . .

(The 5th and 6th clauses read.)

Mr. *George Mason,* apprehended the loose expression of "publication from time to time," was applicable to any time. It was equally applicable to monthly and septennial periods. It might be extended ever so much. The reasons urged in favor of this ambiguous expression, was, that there might be some matters which might require secrecy. In matters relative to military operations, and foreign negotiations, secrecy was necessary sometimes. But he did not conceive that the receipts and expenditures of the public money ought ever to be concealed. The people, he affirmed, had a right to know the expenditures of their money. But that this expression was so loose, it might be concealed forever from them, and might afford opportunities of misapplying the public money, and sheltering those who did it. He concluded it to be as exceptionable as any clause in so few words could be. . . .

Mr. *Madison* thought it much better than if it had mentioned any specified period. Because if the accounts of the public receipts and expenditures were to be published at short stated periods, they would not be so full and connected as would be necessary for a thorough comprehension of them, and detection of any errors. But by giving them an opportunity of publishing them from time to time, as might be found easy and convenient, they would be more full and satisfactory to the public, and would be sufficiently frequent. He thought, after all, that this provision went farther than the constitution of any state in the union, or perhaps in the world.

Mr. *Mason* replied, that in the confederation the public proceedings were to be published monthly, which was infinitely better than depending on men's virtue to publish them or not, as they might please. If there was no such provision in the constitution of Virginia, gentlemen ought to consider the difference between such a full representation, dispersed and mingled with every part of the community, as the state representation was, and such an inadequate representation as this was. One might be safely trusted, but not the other.

Mr. *Madison* replied, that the inconveniences which had been experienced from the confederation in that respect, had their weight with him in recommending this in preference to it; for that it was impossible, in such short intervals, to adjust the public accounts in any satisfactory manner. . . .

Governor *Randolph*. . . . The next restriction is, that no titles of nobility shall be granted by the United States. If we cast our eyes to the manner in which titles of nobility first orginated, we shall find this restriction founded on the same principles. These sprung from military and civil offices; Both are put in the hands of the united states, and therfore I presume it to be an exception to that power.

The last restriction restrains any persons in office from accepting of any present or emolument, title or office, from any foreign prince or state. It must have been observed before, that though the confederation had restricted congress from exercising any powers not given them, yet they inserted it, not from any apprehension of usurpation, but for greater security. This restriction is provided to prevent corruption. All men have a natural inherent right of receiving emoluments from any one, unless they be restrained by the regulations of the community. An accident which actually happened, operated in producing the restriction. A box was presented to our ambassador by the king of our allies.[1] It was thought proper, in order to exclude corruption and foreign influence, to prohibit any one in office from receiving or holding any emoluments from foreign states. I believe, that if at that moment, when we were in harmony with the king of France, we had supposed that he was corrupting our ambassador, it might have disturbed that confidence, and diminished that mutual friendship, which contributed to carry us through the war. . . .

(*The first clause, of the tenth section, read.*)

. . . Mr. *Madison* . . . The first clause of the sixth article, provides, that " All debts contracted, and engagements entered into before

---

[1] "Dr. Franklin is the person alluded to by Randolph. In the winter of 1856, in Philadelphia, under the roof of a venerable granddaughter of Dr. Franklin, I saw the beautiful portrait of Louis XVI, snuff-box size, presented by that king to the doctor. As the portrait is exactly such as is contained in the snuff-boxes presented by Crowned heads, one of which I have seen, it is probable this portrait of Louis was originally attached to the box in question, which has in the lapse of years been lost or given away by Dr. Franklin." H. B. Grigsby, *History of the Virginia Federal Convention of 1788* (Virginia Historical Society *Collections*, vols. 9–10), p. 264.

the adoption of this constitution, shall be as valid against the U. States under this constitution, as under the confederation." He affirmed that it was meant there should be no change with respect to claims by this political alteration; and that the public would stand, with respect to their creditors, as before. He thought that the validity of claims ought not to diminish by the adoption of the constitution. But however, it could not increase the demands on the public.

. . . Governor *Randolph.* — Mr. Chairman — This clause in spite of the invective of the gentleman, is a great favourite of mine; . . . He says, this clause will be injurious, and that no scale can be made, because there is a prohibition on congress of passing *ex post facto* laws. . . . *Ex post facto* laws, if taken technically, relate solely to criminal cases; and my honorable colleague tells you that it was so interpreted in convention. What greater security can we have against arbitrary proceedings in criminal jurisprudence than this? In addition to the interpretation of the convention, let me shew him still greater authority. The same clause provides, that no bill of attainder shall be passed. It shews that the attention of the convention was drawn to criminal matters alone. . . .

Governor *Randolph* could not coincide with the construction put by the honorable gentleman on *ex post facto* laws. The technical meaning which confined such laws solely to criminal cases, was followed in the interpretation of treaties between nations, and was concurred in by all civilians. The prohibition of bills of attainder, he thought a sufficient proof, that *ex post facto* laws related to criminal cases only, and that such was the idea of the convention.

(The next clause read.)

. . . Mr. *Madison.* — Mr. Chairman — Let us take a view of the relative situation of the states. Some states export the produce of other states. Virginia exports the produce of North-Carolina; Pennsylvania those of Jersey and Delaware; and Rhode-Island those of Connecticut and Massachusetts. The exporting states wished to retain the power of laying duties on exports, to enable them to pay the expences incurred. The states whose produce is exported by other states, were extremely jealous, lest a contribution should be raised of them by the exporting states, by laying heavy duties on their commodities. If this clause be fully considered, it will be found to be more consistent with justice and equity than any other practicable mode: For if the states had the exclusive imposition of duties on exports, they might raise a heavy contribution of the other states, for their own exclusive emoluments. The hon-

orable member who spoke in defence of the clause, has fairly represented it. As to the reimbursement of the loss that may be sustained
by individuals, a tax may be laid on tobacco when brought to the
warehouses, for that purpose. The sum arising therefrom may be
appropriated to it consistently with the clause. For it only says,
that "the *nett* produce of all duties and imposts, laid by any state
on imports or exports, shall be for the use of the treasury of the
United States," which necessarily implies that all contingent charges
shall have been previously paid.

(The 1st section, of the 2d article, read.)

. . . Governor *Randolph.* . . . I will acknowledge that at one
stage of this business, I had embraced the idea of the honorable gentleman, that the re-eligibility of the president was improper. But I
will acknowledge, that on a further consideration of the subject,
and attention to the lights which were thrown upon it by others,
I altered my opinion of the limitation of his eligibility. When we
consider the advantages arising to us from it, we cannot object to it.
That which has produced my opinion against the limitation of his
eligibility, is this — that it renders him more independent in his
place, and more solicitous of promoting the interest of his constituents. For, unless you put it in his power to be re-elected, instead
of being attentive to their interests, he will lean to the augmentation
of his private emoluments.

CCXIII. James Madison in the Virginia Convention.[1]

June 18, 1788.

(The 1st section, of the 2d article, still under consideration.)

. . . Mr. *Madison.* — Mr. Chairman — I will take the liberty of
making a few observations which may place this in such a light as
may obviate objections. It is observable, that none of the honorable
members objecting to this, have pointed out the right mode of election. It was found difficult in the convention, and will be found
so by any Gentleman who will take the liberty of delineating a mode
of electing the president, that would exclude those inconveniences
which they apprehend. I would not contend against some of the
principles laid down by some gentlemen if the interests of some
states only were to be consulted. But there is a great diversity of
interests. The choice of the people ought to be attended to. I have
found no better way of selecting the man in whom they place the

---

[1] Robertson, *Debates of the Convention of Virginia, 1788* (2d edit., 1805), p. 351.

highest confidence, than that delineated in the plan of the convention — nor has the gentleman told us. Perhaps it will be found impracticable to elect him by the immediate suffrages of the people. Difficulties would arise from the extent and population of the states. Instead of this the people choose the electors. — This can be done with ease and convenience, and will render the choice more judicious. As to the eventual voting by states, it has my approbation. The lesser states, and some large states, will be generally pleased by that mode. The deputies from the small states argued, (and their is some force in their reasoning) that when the people voted, the large states evidently had the advantage over the rest, and without varying the mode, the interests of the little states might be neglected or sacrificed. Here is a compromise. — For in the eventual election, the small states will have the advantage.

CCXIV. Debate in the Virginia Convention.[1]

June 19, 1788.

(The 1st and 2d sections, of the 3d article, were read.)

. . . Mr. *George Mason.* . . . The principle itself goes to the destruction of the legislation of the states, whether or not it was intended. As to my own opinion, I most religiously and conscientiously believe, that it was intended, though I am not absolutely certain. But I think it will destroy the state governments, whatever may have been the intention. There are many gentlemen in the United States who think it right, that we should have one great national consolidated government, and that it was better to bring it about slowly and imperceptibly, rather than all at once. This is no reflection on any man, for I mean none. To those who think that one national consolidated government would be best for America, this extensive judicial authority will be agreeable; but I hope there are many in this convention of a different opinion, and who see their political happiness resting on their state governments. I know, from my own knowledge, many worthy gentlemen of the former opinion. — (Here Mr. *Madison* interrupted Mr. *Mason,* and demanded an unequivocal explanation. As those insinuations might create a belief, that every member of the late federal convention was of that opinion, he wished him to tell who the gentlemen were to whom he alluded.) — Mr. *Mason* then replied — I shall never refuse to explain myself. It is notorious that this is a prevailing principle. — It was at least the opinion of many gentlemen in con-

---

[1] Robertson, *Debates of the Convention of Virginia, 1788* (2d edit., 1805), pp. 371–372.

vention, and many in the United States. I do not know what explanation the honorable gentleman asks. I can say with great truth, that the honorable gentleman, in private conversation with me, expressed himself against it: Neither did I ever hear any of the delegates from this state advocate it.

Mr. *Madison* declared himself satisfied with this, unless the committee thought themselves entitled to ask a further explanation.

After some desultory remarks, Mr. *Mason* continued. — I have heard that opinion advocated by gentlemen, for whose abilities, judgment, and knowledge, I have the highest reverence and respect. . . . The last clause is still more improper. To give them cognizance in disputes between a state and the citizens thereof, is utterly inconsistent with reason or good policy.

Here Mr. *Nicholas* arose, and informed Mr. *Mason*, that his interpretation of this part was not warranted by the words.

Mr. *Mason* replied, that if he recollected rightly, the propriety of the power as explained by him, had been contended for; but that as his memory had never been good, and was now much impaired from his age, he would not insist on that interpretation.

CCXV. JAMES MADISON IN THE VIRGINIA CONVENTION.[1]

June 20, 1788.

(The 1st and 2d sections, of the 3d article, still under consideration.)

Mr. *Madison.* — . . . It may be proper to remark, that the organization of the general government for the United States, was, in all its parts, very difficult. — There was a peculiar difficulty in that of the Executive. — Every thing incident to it, must have participated of that difficulty. — That mode which was judged most expedient was adopted, till experience should point out one more eligible. — This part was also attended with difficulties. It claims the indulgence of a fair and liberal interpretation. I will not deny that, according to my view of the subject, a more accurate attention might place it in terms which would exclude some of the objections now made to it. But if we take a liberal construction, I think we shall find nothing dangerous or inadmissible in it. In compositions of this kind, it is difficult to avoid technical terms which have the same meaning. An attention to this may satisfy gentlemen, that precision was not so easily obtained as may be imagined. I will illustrate this by one thing in the constitution. — There is a general

---

[1] Robertson, *Debates of the Convention of Virginia, 1788* (2d edit., 1805), pp. 377-382.

power to provide courts to try felonies and piracies committed on the high seas.— *Piracy* is a word which may be considered as a term of the law of nations. — Felony is a word unknown to the law of nations, and is to be found in the British laws, and from thence adopted in the laws of these states. It was thought dishonorable to have recourse to that standard. A technical term of the law of nations is therefore used, that we should find ourselves authorized to introduce it into the laws of the United States. . . .

. . . His criticism is that the judiciary, has not been guarded from an increase of the salary of the judges. I wished myself, to insert a restraint on the augmentation as well as diminution of their compensation; and supported it in the convention. — But I was over-ruled. I must state the reasons which were urged. — They had great weight. — The business must increase. If there was no power to increase their pay, according to the increase of business, during the life of the judges, it might happen, that there would be such an accumulation of business, as would reduce the pay to a most trivial consideration. This reason does not hold as to the president. For in the short period which he presides, this cannot happen. His salary ought not therefore to be increased. It was objected yesterday, that there was no provision for a jury from the vicinage. If it could have been done with safety, it would not have been opposed. It might so happen that a trial would be impracticable in the county. Suppose a rebellion in a whole district, would it not be impossible to get a jury? The trial by jury is held as sacred in England as in America. There are deviations of it in England: yet greater deviations have happened here since we established our independence, than have taken place there for a long time, though it be left to the legislative discretion. It is a misfortune in any case that this trial should be departed from, yet in some cases it is necessary. It must be therefore left to the discretion of the legislature to modify it according to circumstances. This is a complete and satisfactory answer.

CCXVI. Alexander Hamilton in the New York Convention.[1]

June 20, 1788.

In order that the committee may understand clearly the principles on which the general Convention acted, I think it necessary to explain some preliminary circumstances. Sir, the natural situation of this country seems to divide its interests into different classes. There are navigating and non-navigating states. The

---

[1] Elliot, *Debates in State Conventions on the Adoption of the Federal Constitution*, II, 235–237.

Northern are properly navigating states: the Southern appear to possess neither the means nor the spirit of navigation. This difference of situation naturally produces a dissimilarity of interests and views respecting foreign commerce. It was the interest of the Northern States that there should be no restraints on their navigation, and they should have full power, by a majority in Congress, to make commercial regulations in favor of their own, and in restraint of the navigation of foreigners. The Southern States wish to impose a restraint on the Northern, by requiring that two thirds in Congress should be requisite to pass an act in regulation of commerce. They were apprehensive that the restraints of a navigation law would discourage foreigners, and, by obliging them to employ the shipping of the Northern States, would probably enhance their freight. This being the case, they insisted strenuously on having this provision ingrafted in the Constitution; and the Northern States were as anxious in opposing it. On the other hand, the small states, seeing themselves embraced by the Confederation upon equal terms, wished to retain the advantages which they already possessed. The large states, on the contrary, thought it improper that Rhode Island and Delaware should enjoy an equal suffrage with themselves. From these sources a delicate and difficult contest arose. It became necessary, therefore, to compromise, or the Convention must have dissolved without effecting any thing. Would it have been wise and prudent in that body, in this critical situation, to have deserted their country? No. Every man who hears me, every wise man in the United States, would have condemned them. The Convention were obliged to appoint a committee for accommodation. In this committee, the arrangement was formed as it now stands, and their report was accepted. It was a delicate point, and it was necessary that all parties should be indulged. Gentlemen will see that, if there had not been a unanimity, nothing could have been done; for the Convention had no power to establish, but only to recommend, a government. Any other system would have been impracticable. Let a convention be called to-morrow; let them meet twenty times, — nay, twenty thousand times; they will have the same difficulties to encounter, the same clashing interests to reconcile. . . .

The first thing objected to is that clause which allows a representation for three fifths of the negroes. . . . The regulation complained of was one result of the spirit of accommodation which governed the Convention; and without this indulgence no union could possibly have been formed.

CCXVII. DEBATE IN THE VIRGINIA CONVENTION.[1]

June 21, 1788.

. . . Governor *Randolph.* where is the part that has a tendency to the abolition of slavery? Is it the clause which says, that "the migration or importation of such persons as any of the states now existing, shall think proper to admit, shall not be prohibited by congress prior to the year 1808?" This is an exception from the power of regulating commerce, and the restriction is only to continue till 1808. Then congress can, by the exercise of that power, prevent future importations; but does it affect the existing state of slavery? Were it right here to mention what passed in convention on the occasion, I might tell you that the southern states, even South-Carolina herself, conceived this property to be secure by these words. I believe, whatever we may think here, that there was not a member of the Virginia delegation who had the smallest suspicion of the abolition of slavery. . . .

I have never hesitated to acknowledge, that I wished the regulation of commerce had been put in the hands of a greater body than it is in the sense of the constitution. But I appeal to my colleagues in the federal convention, whether this was not a *sine qua non* of the union. . . .

Mr. *George Mason.* — Mr. Chairman — With respect to commerce and navigation, he has given it as his opinion, that their regulation, as it now stands, was a *sine qua non* of the union, and that without it, the states in convention would never concur. I differ from him. It never was, nor in my opinion ever will be, a *sine qua non* of the union. I will give you, to the best of my recollection, the history of that affair. This business was discussed at Philadelphia for four months, during which time the subject of commerce and navigation was often under consideration; and I assert, that eight states out of twelve, for more than three months, voted for requiring two-thirds of the members present in each house to pass commercial and navigation laws. True it is, that afterwards it was carried by a majority, as it stands. If I am right, there was a great majority for requiring two-thirds of the states in this business, till a compromise took place between the northern and southern states; the northern states agreeing to the temporary importation of slaves, and the southern states conceding, in return, that navigation and commercial laws should be on the footing on which they now stand. If I am mistaken, let me be put right. These are my reasons for saying that

---

[1] Robertson, *Debates of the Convention of Virginia, 1788* (2d edit., 1805), pp. 428–444.

this was not a *sine qua non* of their concurrence. The Newfoundland fisheries will require that kind of security which we are now in want of: The eastern states therefore agreed at length, that treaties should require the consent of two-thirds of the members present in the senate.

Mr. *Madison.* . . . It is worthy of our consideration, that those who prepared the paper on the table, found difficulties not to be described, in its formation — mutual deference and concession were absolutely necessary. Had they been inflexibly tenacious of their individual opinions, they would never have concurred. Under what circumstances was it formed? When no party was formed, or particular proposition made, and men's minds were calm and dispassionate. Yet under these circumstances, it was difficult, extremely difficult to agree to any general system. . . .

The state of New-York has been adduced. Many in that state are opposed to it from local views. The two who opposed it in the general convention from that state, are in the state convention. Every step of this system was opposed by those two gentlemen. They were unwilling to part with the old confederation. . . .

The regulation of commerce, he further proposes, should depend on two-thirds of both houses. I wish I could recollect the history of this matter, but I cannot call it to mind with sufficient exactness. But I well recollect the reasoning of some gentlemen on that subject. It was said, and I believe with truth, that every part of America, does not stand in equal need of security. It was observed that the northern states were most competent to their own safety. Was it reasonable, asked they, that they should bind themselves to the defence of the southern states; and still be left at the mercy of the the minority for commercial advantages? Should it be in the power of the minority to deprive them of this and other advantages, when they were bound to defend the whole union, it might be a disadvantage for them to confederate. These were their arguments. ———————

CCXVIII. Debate in the New York Convention.[1]

June 23, 1788.

The Hon. Mr. Lansing. I do not rise, Mr. Chairman, to answer any of the arguments of the gentlemen, but to mention a few facts. In this debate, much reliance has been placed on an accommodation which took place in the *general Convention*. I will state the progress

---

[1] Elliot, *Debates in State Conventions on the Adoption of the Federal Constitution*, II, 272–274.

of that business. When the subject of the apportionment of representatives came forward, the large states insisted that the equality of suffrage should be abolished. This the small states opposed contending that it would reduce them to a state of subordination There was such a division that a dissolution of the Convention appeared unavoidable, unless some conciliatory measure was adopted. A committee of the states was then appointed, to agree upon some plan for removing the embarrassment. They recommended, in their report, the inequality of representation, which is the groundwork of the section under debate. With respect to the ratio of representation, it was at first determined that it should be one for forty thousand. In this situation the subject stood when I left the Convention. The objection to a numerous representation, on account of the expense, was not considered as a matter of importance: other objections to it, however, were fully discussed; but no question was taken.   . . .

Hon. Mr. Hamilton. It is not my design, Mr. Chairman, to extend this debate by any new arguments on the general subject. . . . I only rise to state a fact with respect to the motives which operated in the general Convention. I had the honor to state to the committee the diversity of interests which prevailed between the navigating and non-navigating, the large and the small states, and the influence which those states had upon the conduct of each. It is true, a difference did take place between the large and the small states, the latter insisting on equal advantages in the House of Representatives. Some private business calling me to New York, I left the Convention for a few days: on my return, I found a plan, reported by the committee of details; and soon after, a motion was made to increase the number of representatives. On this occasion, the members rose from one side and the other, and declared that the plan reported was entirely a work of accommodation, and that to make any alterations in it would destroy the Constitution. I discovered that several of the states, particularly New Hampshire, Connecticut, and New Jersey, thought it would be difficult to send a great number of delegates from the extremes of the continent to the national government; they apprehended their constituents would be displeased with a very expensive government; and they considered it as a formidable objection. After some debate on this motion, it was withdrawn. Many of the facts stated by the gentleman and myself are not substantially different. The truth is, the plan, in all its parts, was a plan of accommodation.

Mr. Lansing. I will enter no further into a discussion of the motives of the Convention; but there is one point in which the gentleman and myself do not agree.   The committee of details recommend an equality in the Senate.   In addition to this, it was proposed that every forty thousand should send one representative to the general legislature.   Sir, if it was a system of accommodation, and to remain untouched, how came that number afterwards to be reduced to thirty thousand?

Mr. Hamilton.   I recollect well the alteration which the gentleman alludes to; but it by no means militates against my idea of the principles on which the Convention acted, at the time the report of the committee was under deliberation.   This alteration did not take place till the Convention was near rising, and the business completed; when his excellency, the president, expressing a wish that the number should be reduced to thirty thousand, it was agreed to without opposition.   _____

CCXIX. Debate in the New York Convention.[1]

June 24, 1788.

Hon. Mr. Lansing . . . I believe it was undoubtedly the intention of the framers of this Constitution to make the lower house the proper, peculiar representative of the interests of the people; the Senate, of the sovereignty of the states. . . . Now, if it was the design of the plan to make the Senate a kind of bulwark to the independence of the states, and a check to the encroachments of the general government, certainly the members of this body ought to be peculiarly under the control, and in strict subordination to the state who delegated them. . . . The idea of rotation has been taken from the articles of the old Confederation. . . .

Hon. Mr. Hamilton . . . Sir, the main design of the Convention, in forming the Senate, was to prevent fluctuations and cabals.   With this view, they made that body small, and to exist for a considerable period.   _____

CCXX. Edmund Randolph in the Virginia Convention.[2]

June 25, 1788.

Governor *Randolph.* — Mr. Chairman — One parting word I humbly supplicate.

The suffrage which I shall give in favor of the constitution, will be ascribed by malice to motives unknown to my breast,   But although for every other act of my life, I shall seek refuge in the *mercy*

_____

[1] Elliot, *Debates in State Conventions on the Adoption of the Federal Constitution,* II, pp. 289, 305.

[2] Robertson, *Debates of the Convention of Virginia, 1788* (2d edit., 1805), pp. 465–466.

of God — for this I request his *justice* only.   Lest however some future annalist should in the spirit of party vengeance, deign to mention my name, let him recite these truths, — that I went to the federal convention with the strongest affection for the union; that I acted there in full conformity with this affection; that I refused to subscribe because I had, as I still have, objections to the constitution, and wished a free enquiry into its merits; and that the accession of eight states reduced our deliberations to the single question of union or no union.

CCXXI.   Debate in the New York Convention.[1]

June 28, 1788.

Hon. Mr. Lansing.   . . . It has been admitted by an honorable gentleman from New York, (Mr. Hamilton,) that the state governments are necessary to secure the liberties of the people.   He has urged several forcible reasons why they ought to be preserved under the new system; and he has treated the idea of the general and state governments being hostile to each other as chimerical.   I am, however, firmly persuaded that an hostility between them will exist. This was a received opinion in the late Convention at Philadelphia. That honorable gentleman was then fully convinced that it would exist, and argued, with much decision and great plausibility, that the state governments ought to be subverted, at least so far as to leave them only corporate rights, and that, even in that situation, they would endanger the existence of the general government.   But the honorable gentleman's reflections have probably induced him to correct that sentiment.

(Mr. Hamilton here interrupted Mr. Lansing, and contradicted, in the most positive terms, the charge of inconsistency included in the preceding observations.   This produced a warm personal altercation between those gentlemen, which engrossed the remainder of the day.)

CCXXII.   Mr. Smith in the New York Convention.[2]

Mr. Smith   4 July 1788

"Resolved as the Opinion of this Committee that the President "of the United States shall hold his Office during the Term of seven "Years & that he shall not be eligible a second Time."

---

[1] Elliot, *Debates in State Conventions on the Adoption of the Federal Constitution*, II, 376.

[2] *Documentary History of the Constitution*, IV, 734; taken from the Hamilton Papers.

(

This he says was at one Time a Resolution of the grand Convention — — (& I suppose we must adhere to that Idea which upon more mature Consideration appeared to them improper.)

CCXXIII. J. B. Cutting to Thomas Jefferson.[1]

London July 11. 1788

Mr Martin, the attorney general, who was primarily appointed to that office by Mr Chase — was by the same influence deputed to represent the state — after Mesrs Carrol, Johnson &c &c the first choice of the legislature declined quitting Maryland even upon the important business of new-framing the national government. Mr Chase having just before menaced the Senate for rejecting a wide emission of paper money — and appealed to the people against them — they had joined in that general issue — and cou'd not venture to relinquish to a violent and headstrong party their active influence in the senate as well as in the lower house — at the very moment — when it was so essentially needed to stem the torrent of the populace for the paper. Those Gentlemen therefore remained at home — convinced their fellow citizen of their superior rectitude and wisdom — and defeated that favourite measure of Mr Chase: meanwhile Mr Martin and Mr John F. Mercer — a young gentleman whom you well know —went to the general Convention — opposed the great leading features of the plan which was afterwards promulged — withdrew themselves from any signature of it: — and from the moment when it was proposed for ratification — in conjunction with Mr Chase and his sure coadjutor Mr Paca — exerted every effort to hinder its adoption. So far did Mr Martin proceed in his avowed hostility, as even to detail in the face of decency — before the assembled Legislature of Maryland — the petty dialogues and paltry anecdotes of every description — that came to his knowledge in conventional committees and private conversations with the respective members of the Convention — when at Philadelphia. I blush'd in my own bed-chamber when I read his speech on this side of the Atlantic.

CCXXIV. George Washington to Sir Edward Newenham.[2]

Mount Vernon July 20th. 1788

Although there were some few things in the Constitution recommended by the fœderal Convention to the determination of the People, which did not fully accord with my wishes; yet, having

---

[1] *Documentary History of the Constitution*, IV, 772–773.
[2] *Documentary History of the Constitution*, IV, 807.

taken every circumstance seriously into consideration, I was convinced it approached nearer to perfection than any government hitherto instituted among men. I was also convinced, that nothing but a genuine spirit of amity and accomodation could have induced the members to make those mutual concessions and to sacrifice (at the shrine of enlightened Liberty) those local prejudices, which seemed to oppose an insurmountable barrier, to prevent them from harmonising in any System whatsoever.

CCXXV. Debate in the North Carolina Convention.[1]

July 24, 1788.

Mr. Davie . . . These are some of the leading causes which brought forward this new Constitution. It was evidently necessary to infuse a greater portion of strength into the national government. But Congress were but a single body, with whom it was dangerous to lodge additional powers. Hence arose the necessity of a different organization. In order to form some balance, the departments of government were separated, and as a necessary check, the legislative body was composed of *two branches*. Steadiness and wisdom are better insured when there is a second branch, to balance and check the first The stability of the laws will be greater when the popular branch, which might be influenced by local views, or the violence of party, is checked by another, whose longer continuance in office will render them more experienced, more temperate, and more competent to decide rightly.

The Confederation derived its sole support from the state legislatures. This rendered it weak and ineffectual. It was therefore necessary that the foundations of this government should be laid on the broad basis of the people. Yet the state governments are the pillars upon which this government is extended over such an immense territory, and are essential to its existence. The House of Representatives are immediately elected by the people. The senators represent the sovereignty of the states; they are directly chosen by the state legislatures, and no legislative act can be done without their concurrence. The election of the executive is in some measure under the control of the legislatures of the states, the electors being appointed under their direction.

The difference, in point of magnitude and importance, in the members of the confederacy, was an additional reason for the division of the legislature into two branches, and for establishing an

---

[1] Elliot, *Debates in State Conventions on the Adoption of the Federal Constitution*, IV, 20–32.

equality of suffrage in the Senate. The protection of the small states against the ambition and influence of the larger members, could only be effected by arming them with an equal power in one branch of the legislature. On a contemplation of this matter, we shall find that the jealousies of the states could not be reconciled any other way. The lesser states would never have concurred unless this check had been given them, as a security for their political existence, against the power and encroachments of the great states. It may be also proper to observe, that the executive is separated in its functions from the legislature, as well as the nature of the case would admit, and the judiciary from both. . . .

In the formation of this system, many difficulties presented themselves to the Convention.

Every member saw that the existing system would ever be ineffectual, unless its laws operated on individuals, as military coercion was neither eligible nor practicable. Their own experience was fortified by their knowledge of the inherent weakness of all confederate governments. They knew that all governments merely federal had been short-lived, or had existed from principles extraneous from their constitutions, or from external causes which had no dependence on the nature of their governments. These considerations determined the Convention to depart from that solecism in politics — the principle of legislation for states in their political capacities.

The great extent of country appeared to some a formidable difficulty; but a confederate government appears, at least in theory, capable of embracing the various interests of the most extensive territory. Founded on the state governments solely, as I have said before, it would be tottering and inefficient. It became, therefore, necessary to bottom it on the people themselves, by giving them an immediate interest and agency in the government. There was, however, some real difficulty in conciliating a number of jarring interests, arising from the incidental but unalterable difference in the states in point of territory, situation, climate, and rivalship in commerce. Some of the states are very extensive, others very limited: some are manufacturing states, others merely agricultural: some of these are exporting states, while the carrying and navigation business are in possession of others. It was not easy to reconcile such a multiplicity of discordant and clashing interests. Mutual concessions were necessary to come to any concurrence. A plan that would promote the exclusive interests of a few states would be injurious to others. Had each state obstinately insisted on the security of its particular local advantages, we should never have come to a conclusion. Each, therefore, amicably and wisely relinquished its particular views. The Federal Convention have told you, that the Constitution which they formed "was the result of a spirit of amity, and of that mutual deference and concession which the peculiarity of their political situation rendered indispensable." I hope the same laudable spirit will govern this Convention in their decision on this important question.

The business of the Convention was to amend the Confederation by giving it additional powers. The present form of Congress being a single body, it was thought unsafe to augment its powers, without altering its organization. The act of the Convention is but a mere proposal, similar to the production of a private pen. . . .

Mr. Lenoir. Mr. Chairman, I have a greater objection on this ground than that which has just been mentioned. I mean, sir, the legislative power given to the President himself. It may be admired by some, but not by me. He, sir, with the Senate, is to make treaties, which are to be the supreme law of the land. This is a legislative power given to the President, and implies a contradiction to that part which says that all legislative power is vested in the two houses.

Mr. Spaight answered, that it was thought better to put that power into the hands of the senators as representatives of the states — that thereby the interest of every state was equally attended to in the formation of treaties — but that it was not considered as a legislative act at all. . . .

Mr. Davie. . . . The gentleman "does not wish to be represented with negroes." This, sir, is an unhappy species of population; but we cannot at present alter their situation. The Eastern States had great jealousies on this subject. They insisted that their cows and horses were equally entitled to representation; that the one was property as well as the other. It became our duty, on the other hand, to acquire as much weight as possible in the legislation of the Union; and, as the Northern States were more populous in whites, this only could be done by insisting that a certain proportion of our slaves should make a part of the computed population. It was attempted to form a rule of representation from a compound ratio of wealth and population; but, on consideration, it was found impracticable to determine the comparative value of lands and other property, in so extensive a territory, with any degree of accuracy; and population alone was adopted as the only practicable rule or criterion of representation. It was urged by the deputies of the Eastern States, that a representation of two fifths would be of little utility and that their entire representation would be unequal and burdensome — that, in a time of war, slaves rendered a country more vulnerable, while its defence devolved upon its free inhabitants. On the other hand, we insisted that, in time of peace, they contributed, by their labor, to the general wealth, as well as other members of the community — that, as rational beings, they had a right of representation, and, in some instances, might be highly useful in war. On these principles the Eastern States gave the matter up, and consented to the regulation as it has been read. I hope these reasons will appear satisfactory. It is the same rule or principle which was proposed some years ago by Congress, and assented to by twelve of the states. . . .

Mr. James Galloway said, that he did not object to the representation of negroes, so much as he did to the fewness of the number of representatives. He was surprised how we came to have but five, including those intended to represent negroes. That, in his humble opinion, North Carolina was entitled to that number independent of the negroes.

Mr. Spaight endeavored to satisfy him, that the Convention had no rule to go by in this case — that they could not proceed upon the ratio mentioned in the Constitution till the enumeration of the people was made — that some states had made a return to Congress of their numbers, and others had not — that it was mentioned that we had had time, but made no return — that the present number was only temporary — that in three years the actual census would be taken, and our number of representatives regulated accordingly.

CCXXVI. WILLIAM R. DAVIE IN THE NORTH CAROLINA CONVENTION.[1]

July 25, 1788.

Mr. Chairman, I will state to the committee the reasons upon which this officer was introduced. I had the honor to observe to the committee, before, the causes of the particular formation of the Senate — that it was owing, with other reasons, to the *jealousy* of the states, and, particularly, to the extreme jealousy of the lesser states of the power and influence of the larger members of the confederacy. It was in the Senate that the several political interests of the states were to be preserved, and where all their powers were to be perfectly balanced. The commercial jealousy between the Eastern and Southern States had a principal share in this business. It might happen, in important cases, that the voices would be equally divided. Indecision might be dangerous and inconvenient to the

----

[1] Elliot, *Debates in State Conventions on the Adoption of the Federal Constitution*, IV, 42–60.

public. It would then be necessary to have some person who should determine the question as impartially as possible. Had the Vice-President been taken from the representation of any of the states, the vote of that state would have been under local influence in the second. It is true he must be chosen from some state; but, from the nature of his election and office, he represents no one state in particular, but all the states. It is impossible that any officer could be chosen more impartially. He is, in consequence of his election, the creature of no particular district or state, but the officer and representative of the Union. He must possess the confidence of the states in a very great degree, and consequently be the most proper person to decide in cases of this kind. These, I believe, are the principles upon which the Convention formed this officer. . . .

The 1st clause of the 4th section read.

. . . Mr. Davie. Mr. Chairman, a consolidation of the states is said by some gentlemen to have been intended. They insinuate that this was the cause of their giving this power of elections. If there were any seeds in this Constitution which might, one day, produce a consolidation, it would, sir, with me, be an insuperable objection, I am so perfectly convinced that so extensive a country as this can never be managed by one consolidated government. The Federal Convention were as well convinced as the members of this house, that the state governments were absolutely necessary to the existence of the federal government. They considered them as the great massy pillars on which this political fabric was to be extended and supported; and were fully persuaded that, when they were removed, or should moulder down by time, the general government must tumble into ruin. A very little reflection will show that no department of it can exist without the state governments.

. . . The gentleman from Edenton (Mr. Iredell) has pointed out the reasons of giving this control over elections to Congress, the principal of which was, to prevent a dissolution of the government by designing states. If all the states were equally possessed of absolute power over their elections, without any control of Congress, danger might be justly apprehended where one state possesses as much territory as four or five others; and some of them, being thinly peopled now, will daily become more numerous and formidable. Without this control in Congress, those large states might successfully combine to destroy the general government. It was therefore necessary to control any combination of this kind.

Another principal reason was, that it would operate, in favor of the people, against the ambitious designs of the federal Senate.

I will illustrate this by matter of fact. The history of the little state of Rhode Island is well known. An abandoned faction have seized on the reins of government, and frequently refused to have any representation in Congress. If Congress had the power of making the law of elections operate throughout the United States, no state could withdraw itself from the national councils, without the consent of a majority of the members of Congress. Had this been the case, that trifling state would not have withheld its representation. What once happened may happen again; and it was necessary to give Congress this power, to keep the government in full operation. This being a federal government, and involving the interests of several states, and some acts requiring the assent of more than a majority, they ought to be able to keep their representation full. It would have been a solecism, to have a government without *any means* of self-preservation. The Confederation is the only instance of a government without such means, and is a nerveless system, as inadequate to every purpose of government as it is to the security of the liberties of the people of America. When the councils of America have this power over elections, they can, in spite of any faction in any particular state, give the people a representation.

CCXXVII. Debate in the North Carolina Convention.[1]

The 5th section of the 1st article read.   July 26, 1788.

. . . Mr. Graham wished to hear an explanation of the words "from time to time," whether it was a short or a long time, or how often they should be obliged to publish their proceedings.

Mr. Davie answered, that they would be probably published after the rising of Congress, every year — that if they sat two or three times, or oftener, in the year, they might be published every time they rose — that there could be no doubt of their publishing them as often as it would be convenient and proper, and that they would conceal nothing but what it would be unsafe to publish. He further observed, that some states had proposed an amendment, that they should be published annually; but he thought it very safe and proper as it stood — that it was the sense of the Convention that they should be published at the end of every session. . . .

Mr. Spaight. Mr. Chairman, it was thought absolutely necessary for the support of the general government to give it power to raise taxes. Government cannot exist without certain and adequate

[1] Elliot, *Debates in State Conventions on the Adoption of the Federal Constitution,* IV, 72-104.

funds. Requisitions cannot be depended upon. For my part, I think it indifferent whether I pay the tax to the officers of the continent or to those of the state. I would prefer paying to the Continental officers, because it will be less expensive. . . .

1st clause of the 9th section read.

Mr. J. M'Dowall wished to hear the reasons of this restriction.

Mr. Spaight answered, that there was a contest between the Northern and Southern States; that the Southern States, whose principal support depended on the labor of slaves, would not consent to the desire of the Northern States to exclude the importation of slaves absolutely; that South Carolina and Georgia insisted on this clause, as they were now in want of hands to cultivate their lands; that in the course of twenty years they would be fully supplied; that the trade would be abolished then, and that, in the mean time, some tax or duty might be laid on. . . .

Mr. Spaight further explained the clause. That the limitation of this trade to the term of twenty years was a compromise between the Eastern States and the Southern States. South Carolina and Georgia wished to extend the term. The Eastern States insisted on the entire abolition of the trade. That the state of North Carolina had not thought proper to pass any law prohibiting the importation of slaves, and therefore its delegation in the Convention did not think themselves authorized to contend for an immediate prohibition of it. . . .

Article 2d, section 1st.

Mr. Davie. . . . The clause meets my entire approbation. I only rise to show the principle on which it was formed. The principle is, the separation of the executive from the legislative — a principle which pervades all free governments. A dispute arose in the Convention concerning the reëligibility of the President. It was the opinion of the deputation from this state, that he should be elected for five or seven years, and be afterwards ineligible. It was urged, in support of this opinion, that the return of public officers into the common mass of the people, where they would feel the tone they had given to the administration of the laws, was the best security the public had for their good behavior; that it would operate as a limitation to his ambition, at the same time that it rendered him more independent; that when once in possession of that office, he would move heaven and earth to secure his reëlection, and perhaps become the cringing dependant of influential men; that our opinion was supported by some experience of the effects of this principle in several of the states. A large and very respectable majority were of the contrary opinion. It was said that such an exclusion would be improper for many reasons; that if an enlightened, upright man had discharged the duties of the office ably and faithfully, it would be depriving the people of the benefit of his ability and experience, though they highly approved of him; that it would render the President less ardent in his endeavors to acquire the esteem and approbation of his country, if he knew that he would be absolutely excluded after a given period; and that it would be depriving a man of singular merit even of the rights of citizenship. It was also said, that the day might come, when the confidence of America would be put in one man, and that it might be dangerous to exclude such a man from the service of his country. It was urged, likewise, that no undue influence could take place in his election; that, as he was to be elected on the same day throughout the United States, no man could say to himself, *I am to be the man.* Under these considerations, a large, respectable majority voted for it as it now stands. With respect to the unity of the executive, the superior energy and secrecy wherewith one person can act, was one of the principles on which the Convention went. But a more predominant principle was, the more obvious responsibility of one person. It was observed that, if there were a plurality of persons, and a crime should be committed, when their conduct came to be examined, it would be impossible to fix the fact on any one of them, but that the public were never at a loss when there was but one man. For these reasons, a great majority concurred in the unity, and reëligibility also, of the executive. I thought proper to show the spirit of the deputation from this state. However, I heartily concur in it as it now stands, and the mode of his election precludes every possibility of corruption or improper influence of any kind.

CCXXVIII. Debate in the North Carolina Convention.[1]

July 28, 1788.

Mr. Davie. Mr. Chairman, although treaties are mere conventional acts between the contracting parties, yet, by the law of nations, they are the supreme law of the land to their respective citizens or subjects. All civilized nations have concurred in considering them as paramount to an ordinary act of legislation. This concurrence is founded on the reciprocal convenience and solid advantages arising from it. A due observance of treaties makes nations more friendly to each other, and is the only means of rendering less frequent those mutual hostilities which tend to depopulate

---

[1] Elliot, *Debates in State Conventions on the Adoption of the Federal Constitution,* IV, pp. 119–144.

and ruin contending nations. It extends and facilitates that commercial intercourse, which, founded on the universal protection of private property, has, in a measure, made the world one nation.

The power of making treaties has, in all countries and governments, been placed in the executive departments. This has not only been grounded on the necessity and reason arising from that degree of secrecy, design, and despatch, which is always necessary in negotiations between nations, but to prevent their being impeded, or carried into effect, by the violence, animosity, and heat of parties, which too often infect numerous bodies. Both of these reasons preponderated in the foundation of this part of the system. . . .

On the principle of the propriety of vesting this power in the executive department, it would seem that the whole power of making treaties ought to be left to the President, who, being elected by the people of the United States at large, will have their general interest at heart. But that jealousy of executive power which has shown itself so strongly in all the American governments, would not admit this improvement. Interest, sir, has a most powerful influence over the human mind, and is the basis on which all the transactions of mankind are built. It was mentioned before that the extreme jealousy of the little states, and between the commercial states and the non-importing states, produced the necessity of giving an equality of suffrage to the Senate. The same causes made it indispensable to give to the senators, as representatives of states, the power of making, or rather ratifying, treaties. Although it militates against every idea of just proportion that the little state of Rhode Island should have the same suffrage with Virginia, or the great commonwealth of Massachusetts, yet the small states would not consent to confederate without an equal voice in the formation of treaties. Without the equality, they apprehended that their interest would be neglected or sacrificed in negotiations. This difficulty could not be got over. It arose from the unalterable nature of things. Every man was convinced of the inflexibility of the little states in this point. It therefore became necessary to give them an absolute equality in making treaties.

. . . The gentleman from Anson has said that the Senate destroys the independence of the President, because they must confirm the nomination of officers. The necessity of their interfering in the appointment of officers resulted from the same reason which produced the equality of suffrage. In other countries, the executive or chief magistrate, alone, nominates and appoints officers. The small states would not agree that the House of Representatives should have a voice in the appointment to offices; and the extreme jealousy of all the states would not give it to the President alone.

. . . I have only to add the principle upon which the General Convention went — that the power of making treaties could nowhere be so safely lodged as in the President and Senate; and the extreme jealousy subsisting between some of the states would not admit of it elsewhere. If any man will examine the operation of that jealousy, in his own breast, as a citizen of North Carolina, he will soon feel the inflexibility that results from it, and perhaps be induced to acknowledge the propriety of this arrangement. . . .

Mr. Spaight. Mr. Chairman, the gentleman insinuates that differences existed in the Federal Convention respecting the clauses which he objects to. Whoever told him so was wrong; for I declare that, in that Convention, the unanimous desire of all was to keep separate and distinct the objects of the jurisdiction of the federal from that of the state judiciary. They wished to separate them as judiciously as possible, and to consult the ease and convenience of the people. . . .

Mr. Spaight. Mr. Chairman, the trial by jury was not forgotten in the Convention; the subject took up a considerable time to investigate it. It was impossible to make any one uniform regulation for all the states, or that would include all cases where it would be necessary. It was impossible, by one expression, to embrace the whole. There are a number of equity and maritime cases, in some of the states, in which jury trials are not used. Had the Convention said that all causes should be tried by a jury, equity and maritime cases would have been included. It was therefore left to the legislature to say in what cases it should be used; and as the trial by jury is in full force in the state courts, we have the fullest security.

CCXXIX. W. R. Davie in the North Carolina Convention.[1]

July 29, 1788.

The Federal Convention knew that several states had large sums of paper money in circulation, and that it was an interesting property, and they were sensible that those states would never consent to its immediate destruction, or ratify any system that would have that operation. The mischief already done could not be repaired: all that could be done was, to form some limitation to this great political evil. As the paper money had become private property, and the object of numberless contracts, it could not be destroyed

---

[1] Elliot, *Debates in State Conventions on the Adoption of the Federal Constitution,* IV, 183–184, 191.

or intermeddled with in that situation, although its baneful tendency was obvious and undeniable. It was, however, effecting an important object to put bounds to this growing mischief. If the states had been compelled to sink the paper money instantly, the remedy might be worse than the disease. As we could not put an immediate end to it, we were content with prohibiting its future increase, looking forward to its entire extinguishment when the states that had an emission circulating should be able to call it in by a gradual redemption.

In Pennsylvania, their paper money was not a tender in discharge of private contracts. In South Carolina, their bills became eventually a tender; and in Rhode Island, New York, New Jersey, and North Carolina, the paper money was made a legal tender in all cases whatsoever. The other states were sensible that the destruction of the circulating paper would be a violation of the rights of private property, and that such a measure would render the accession of those states to the system absolutely impracticable. The injustice and pernicious tendency of this disgraceful policy were viewed with great indignation by the states which adhered to the principles of justice. In Rhode Island, the paper money had depreciated to eight for one, and a hundred per cent. with us. The people of Massachusetts and Connecticut had been great sufferers by the dishonesty of Rhode Island, and similar complaints existed against this state. This clause became in some measure a preliminary with the gentlemen who represented the other states. "You have," said they, "by your iniquitous laws and paper emissions shamefully defrauded our citizens. The Confederation prevented our compelling you to do them justice; but before we confederate with you again, you must not only agree to be honest, but put it out of your power to be otherwise." Sir, a member from Rhode Island itself could not have set his face against such language. The clause was, I believe, unanimously assented to: it has only a future aspect, and can by no means have a retrospective operation; and I trust the principles upon which the Convention proceeded will meet the approbation of every honest man. . . .

Mr. Chairman, I believe neither the 10th section, cited by the gentleman, nor any other part of the Constitution, has vested the general government with power to interfere with the public securities of any state. I will venture to say that the last thing which the general government will attempt to do will be this. They have nothing to do with it. The clause refers merely to contracts between individuals. That section is the best in the Constitution. It is founded on the strongest principles of justice. It is a section, in short, which I thought would have endeared the Constitution to this country. When the worthy gentleman comes to consider, he will find that the general government cannot possibly interfere with such securities. How can it? It has no negative clause to that effect. Where is there a negative clause, operating negatively on the states themselves? It cannot operate retrospectively, for this would be repugnant to its own express provisions. It will be left to ourselves to redeem them as we please. We wished we could put it on the shoulders of Congress, but could not. Securities may be higher, but never less. I conceive, sir, that this is a very plain case, and that it must appear perfectly clear to the committee that the gentleman's alarms are groundless.

CCXXX. R. D. Spaight in the North Carolina Convention.[1]

July 30, 1788.

Mr. Chairman, I am one of those who formed this Constitution. The gentleman says, we exceeded our powers. I deny the charge. We were sent with a full power to amend the existing system. This involved every power to make every alteration necessary to meliorate and render it perfect. It cannot be said that we arrogated powers altogether inconsistent with the object of our delegation. There is a clause which expressly provides for future amendments, and it is still in your power. What the Convention has done is a mere proposal. It was found impossible to improve the old system without changing its very form; for by that system the three great branches of government are blended together. All will agree that the concession of a power to a government so constructed is dangerous. The proposing a new system, to be established by the assent and ratification of nine states, arose from the necessity of the case. It was thought extremely hard that one state, or even three or four states, should be able to prevent necessary alterations. The very refractory conduct of Rhode Island, in uniformly opposing every wise and judicious measure, taught us how impolitic it would be to put the general welfare in the power of a few members of the Union. It was, therefore, thought by the Convention, that, if so great a majority as nine states should adopt it, it would be right to establish it. It was recommended by Congress to the state legislatures to refer it to the people of their different states. Our Assembly has confirmed what they have done, by proposing it to the consideration of the people. It was there, and not here, that

---

[1] Elliot, *Debates in State Conventions on the Adoption of the Federal Constitution*, IV, 206–210.

the objection should have been made. This Convention is therefore to consider the Constitution, and whether it be proper for the
government of the people of America; and had it been proposed
by any one individual, under these circumstances, it would be right
to consider whether it be good or bad. The gentleman has insinuated that this Constitution, instead of securing our liberties, is a
scheme to enslave us. He has produced no proof, but rests it on
his bare assertion — an assertion which I am astonished to hear,
after the ability with which every objection has been fully and
clearly refuted in the course of our debates. I am, for my part,
conscious of having had nothing in view but the liberty and happiness of my country; and I believe every member of that Convention
was actuated by motives equally sincere and patriotic.

. . . The gentleman has again brought on the trial by jury. The
Federal Convention, sir, had no wish to destroy the trial by jury.
It was three or four days before them. There were a variety of
objections to any one mode. It was thought impossible to fall
upon one any mode but what would produce some inconveniences.
I cannot now recollect all the reasons given. Most of them have
been amply detailed by other gentlemen here. I should suppose
that, if the representatives of twelve states, with many able lawyers
among them, could not form any unexceptionable mode, this Convention could hardly be able to do it.

. . . He has made another objection, that land might not be
taxed, and the other taxes might fall heavily on the poor people.
Congress has a power to lay taxes, and no article is exempted or
excluded. The proportion of each state may be raised in the most
convenient manner. The census or enumeration provided is meant
for the salvation and benefit of the Southern States. It was mentioned that land ought to be the only object of taxation. As an
acre of land in the Northern States is worth many acres in the Southern States, this would have greatly oppressed the latter. It was then
judged that the number of people, as therein provided, was the best
criterion for fixing the proportion of each state, and that proportion
in each state to be raised in the most easy manner for the people.

CCXXXI. John Lansing to Abraham Yates and Melancton
Smith.[1]

Octb. 3d 1788.

I take the Liberty to transmit you enclosed the State of Mr.
Hamilton's & my observations respecting his sentiments delivered

---

[1] New York Historical Society, Lamb and Tillinghast MSS.

in the general Convention & Judge Yates's Information on that subject.[1]

I have confined myself to the Revisal of my own observations, leaving Mr. Hamilton & Mr. Jay to do the like with theirs — Some of the observations of the former are not accurately stated & some omitted, but I suppose he will correct them.

In the paper enclosed wherever it is divided into Columns the first Column contains the sentiments of Judge Yates or myself as revised — the second is a Copy of Mr. Child's verbatim — in the other parts my sentiments are of my own stating — those of the others of Mr Childs — without the least Alteration.

It would have been my wish that this Business might have been represented by Child's after subjecting the Revisions of both parties to the perusal of the other — but tho' I intimated this to Mr. Childs he never signified any assent & I would not repeat it. — Mr. Hamilton may therefore give such an Account of it as he thinks proper — I shall only reserve the Right if I suppose it is not accurate to contradict it.

CCXXXII. James Madison to Philip Mazzei.[2]

New York, Octr. 8th. 1788.

You ask me why I agreed to the constitution proposed by the Convention of Philada. I answer because I thought it safe to the liberties of the people, and the best that could be obtained from the jarring interests of States, and the miscellaneous opinions of Politicians; and because experience has proved that the real danger to America & to liberty lies in the defect of *energy* & *stability* in the present establishments of the United States. — Had you been a member of that assembly and been impressed with the truths which our situation discloses, you would have concurred in the necessity which was felt by the other members. . . .

CCXXXIII. Lord Dorchester to Lord Sydney.[3]

It is generally admitted that the federal convention which assembled at Philadelphia in 1787, was composed of many of the ablest men in the states; after much previous discussion, three plans were submitted to their consideration and debated:

1st. That of New Jersey, supposed to be the production of

---

[1] This interesting document is unfortunately missing.

[2] G. Hunt, *Writings of James Madison*, V, 267.

[3] Communication enclosed by Lord Dorchester in a letter to Lord Sydney, October 14, 1788; printed in *Report on Canadian Archives*, 1890, p. 101.

Governor Livingston, which went merely to the increase of the powers of the present congress; it was judged insufficient.

2nd. Colonel Hamilton's, that had in view the establishment of a monarchy, and the placing the crown upon the head of a foreign prince, which was overruled, although supported by some of the ablest members of the convention.

3rd. That of Virginia which was adopted.

CCXXXIV. Benjamin Franklin to the Duc de La Roche-
foucauld.[1]

Philada. [Oct. 22, 1788].

That which you mention did not pass unnoticed in the Convention. Many, if I remember right, were for making the President incapable of being chosen after the first four Years; but a Majority were for leaving the Election free to chuse whom they pleas'd; and it was alledged that such Incapability might tend to make the President less attentive to the duties of his Office, and to the Interests of the People, than he would be if a second Choice depended on their good opinion of them.

CCXXXV. James Madison to G. L. Turberville.[2]

New York, Novr. 2, 1788.

I am not of the number if there be any such, who think the Constitution lately adopted a faultless work. On the contrary there are amendments wch I wished it to have received before it issued from the place in which it was formed. . . .

Having witnessed the difficulties and dangers experienced by the first Convention, which assembled under every propitious circumstance, I should tremble for the result of a Second, meeting in present temper of America and under all the disadvantages I have mentioned.

CCXXXVI. A Citizen of New Haven [Roger Sherman], I.[3]

It is proposed that members of congress be rendered ineligible to any other office during the time for which they are elected members of that body.

This is an objection that will admit of something plausible to be said on both sides, and it was settled in convention on full discussion and deliberation. There are some offices which a member

[1] Smyth, *Writings of Franklin*, IX, 666.

[2] G. Hunt, *Writings of James Madison*, V, 298, 300.

[3] P. L. Ford, *Essays on the Constitution*, p. 234; printed in the *New Haven Gazette*, December 4, 1788.

of congress may be best qualified to fill, from his knowledge of public affairs acquired by being a member, such as minister to foreign courts, &c., and on accepting any other office his seat in congress will be vacated, and no member is eligible to any office that shall have been instituted or the emoluments increased while he was a member. ——————

CCXXXVII. Charles Pinckney to Rufus King.[1]

Charleston, January 26, 1789.

You know I always preferred the election by the legislature, to that of the people, & I will now venture to pronounce that the mode which you & Madison & some others so thoroughly contended for & ultimately carried is the greatest blot in the constitution [2] — of this however more hereafter.

CCXXXVIII. Charles Pinckney to James Madison.[3]

Charleston March 28: 1789.

Are you not, to use a full expression, abundantly convinced that the theoretical nonsense of an election of the members of Congress by the people in the first instance, is clearly and practically wrong.[4] — that it will in the end be the means of bringing our councils into contempt & that the legislature are the only proper judges of who ought to be elected? — —

Are you not fully convinced that the Senate ought at least to be double their number to make them of consequence & to prevent their falling into the same comparative state of insignificance that the state Senates have, merely from their smallness? —

CCXXXIX. James Madison in the House of Representatives.[5]

May 13, 1789.

I conceive the constitution, in this particular, was formed in order that the Government, whilst it was restrained from laying a total prohibition, might be able to give some testimony of the sense of America with respect to the African trade. We have liberty to impose a tax or duty upon the importation of such persons, as any of the States now existing shall think proper to admit; and this liberty was granted, I presume, upon two considerations: The first

----

[1] C. R. King, *Life and Correspondence of Rufus King*, I, 359.
[2] See CCXXXVIII below.
[3] *Documentary History of the Constitution*, V, 168–169.
[4] See CCXXXVII above.
[5] *Annals of Congress*, First Congress, I, 339–340.

was, that until the time arrived when they might abolish the importation of slaves, they might have an opportunity of evidencing their sentiments on the policy and humanity of such a trade. The other was, that they might be taxed in due proportion with other articles imported; for if the possessor will consider them as property, of course they are of value, and ought to be paid for.

CCXL. James Madison in the House of Representatives.[1]

May 15, 1789.

The constitution, as had already been observed, places the power in the House of originating money bills. The principal reason why the constitution had made this distinction was, because they were chosen by the People, and supposed to be best acquainted with their interests, and ability. In order to make them more particularly acquainted with these objects, the democratic branch of the Legislature consisted of a greater number, and were chosen for a shorter period, so that they might revert more frequently to the mass of the People.

CCXLI. Debate in the House of Representatives.[2]

May 19, 1789.

Mr. Smith said, he had doubts whether the officer could be removed by the President. He apprehended he could only be removed by an impeachment before the Senate, and that, being once in office, he must remain there until convicted upon impeachment. . . .

Mr. Madison did not concur with the gentleman in his interpretation of the constitution. What, said he, would be the consequence of such construction? It would in effect establish every officer of the Government on the firm tenure of good behaviour; not the heads of departments only, but all the inferior officers of those departments, would hold their offices during good behavior, and that to be judged of by one branch of the Legislature only on the impeachment of the other. . . .

It is very possible that an officer who may not incur the displeasure of the President, may be guilty of actions that ought to forfeit his place. The power of this House may reach him by the means of an impeachment, and he may be removed even against the will of the President; so that the declaration in the constitution, was intended as a supplemental security for the good behavior of the public officers. . . .

---

[1] *Annals of Congress*, First Congress, I, 347.
[2] *Annals of Congress*, First Congress, I, 372, 380.

But why, it may be asked, was the Senate joined with the President in appointing to office, if they have no responsibility? I answer, merely for the sake of advising, being supposed, from their nature, better acquainted with the characters of the candidates than an individual; ————

CCXLII. DEBATE IN HOUSE OF REPRESENTATIVES.[1]

June 8, 1789.

Mr. Madison. The first of these amendments relates to what may be called a bill of rights. I will own that I never considered this provision so essential to the federal constitution, to make it improper to ratify it, until such an amendment was added; at the same time, I always conceived, that in a certain form, and to a certain extent, such a provision was neither improper nor altogether useless. . . .

Mr. Sherman. — I do not suppose the constitution to be perfect, nor do I imagine if Congress and all the Legislatures on the continent were to revise it, that their united labors would make it perfect. I do not expect any perfection on this side the grave in the works of man; but my opinion is, that we are not at present in circumstances to make it better. It is at wonder that there has been such unanimity in adopting it, considering the ordeal it had to undergo; and the unanimity which prevailed at its formation is equally astonishing; amidst all the members from the twelve States present at the federal convention, there were only three who did not sign the instrument to attest their opinion of its goodness.

CCXLIII. ROGER SHERMAN IN THE HOUSE OF REPRESENTATIVES.[2]

June 18, 1789.

The convention, who formed this constitution, thought it would tend to secure the liberties of the people, if they prohibited the President from the sole appointment of all officers. They knew that the Crown of Great Britain, by having that prerogative has been enabled to swallow up the whole administration; the influence of the Crown upon the Legislature subjects both Houses to its will and pleasure. Perhaps it may be thought, by the people of that kingdom, that it is best for the Executive Magistrate to have such kind of influence; if so, it is very well, and we have no right to complain that it is injurious to them, while they themselves consider it beneficial. But this Government is different, and intended by the people to be different.

---

[1] *Annals of Congress,* First Congress, I, 436, 448.
[2] *Annals of Congress,* First Congress, I, 537.

CCXLIV. Abraham Baldwin in the House of Representatives.[1]

June 19, 1789.

I am well authorized to say, that the mingling the powers of the President and Senate was strongly opposed in the convention which had the honor to submit to the consideration of the United States, and the different States, the present system for the Government of the Union. Some gentlemen opposed it to the last; and finally, it was the principal ground on which they refused to give it their signature and assent. One gentleman called it a monstrous and unnatural connexion, and did not hesitate to affirm it would bring on convulsions in the Government.

CCXLV. Sherman to John Adams.[2]

July 20, 1789.

Wherever the chief magistrate may appoint to office without control, his government may become absolute, or at least aggressive; therefore the concurrence of the senate is made requisite by our constitution.

CCXLVI. Roger Sherman in the House of Representatives.[3]

August 14. 1789.

Mr. Sherman said, if they were now forming a constitution, he should be in favor of one representative for forty thousand, rather than thirty thousand. The proportion by which the several States are now represented in this House was founded on the former calculation. In the convention that framed the constitution, there was a majority in favor of forty thousand, and though there were some in favor of thirty thousand, yet that proposition did not obtain until after the constitution was agreed to, when the President had expressed a wish that thirty thousand should be inserted, as more favorable to the public interest; during the contest between thirty and forty thousand, he believed there were not more than nine States who voted in favor of the former.

CCXLVII. James Madison to Edmund Randolph.[4]

N. Y. Aug. 21. 89.

I find in looking over the notes of your introductory discourse in the Convention at Philada that it is not possible for me to do

---

[1] *Annals of Congress*, First Congress, I, 557.

[2] *Life and Works of John Adams*, VI, 439.

[3] *Annals of Congress*, First Congress, I, 725.

[4] *Documentary History of the Constitution*, V, 191-192.

justice to the substance of it. I am anxious for particular reasons, to be furnished with the means of preserving this as well as the other arguments in that body, and must beg that you will make out & forward me the scope of your reasoning. You have your notes I know & from these you can easily deduce the argument on a condensed plan. I make this request with an earnestness wch. will not permit you either to refuse or delay a compliance.

CCXLVIII. ROGER SHERMAN IN THE HOUSE OF REPRESENTATIVES.[1]

August 21, 1789.

[On motion] to add to the articles of amendment the following: "Congress shall not alter, modify, or interfere in the times, places, or manner of holding elections of Senators, or Representatives, except when any State shall refuse or neglect, or be unable, by invasion or rebellion, to make such election." . . .

Mr. Sherman observed, that the Convention were very unanimous in passing this clause; that it was an important provision, and if it was resigned it would tend to subvert the Government.

CCXLIX. ANECDOTE OF WASHINGTON AND JEFFERSON.[2]

There is a tradition that, on his return from France, Jefferson called Washington to account at the breakfast-table for having agreed to a second chamber. 'Why,' asked Washington, 'did you pour that coffee into your saucer?' 'To cool it,' quoth Jefferson. 'Even so,' said Washington, 'we pour legislation into the senatorial saucer to cool it.'

CCL. ROGER SHERMAN IN THE HOUSE OF REPRESENTATIVES.[3]

February 3, 1790.

Mr. Sherman thought that the interests of the State where the emigrant intended to reside ought to be consulted, as well as the interests of the General Government. He presumed it was intended by the Convention, who framed the Constitution, that Congress should have the power of naturalization, in order to prevent particular States receiving citizens, and forcing them upon others who would not have received them in any other manner. It was therefore meant to guard against an improper mode of naturalization, rather than foreigners should be received upon easier terms than those adopted by the several States.

---

[1] *Annals of Congress*, First Congress, I, 768, 770.
[2] M. D. Conway, *Omitted Chapters of History*, p. 91.
[3] *Annals of Congress*, First Congress, I, 1110.

CCLI. Abraham Baldwin in the House of Representatives.[1]

February 12, 1790.

Mr. Baldwin was sorry the subject had ever been brought before Congress, because it was of a delicate nature as it respected some of the States. Gentlemen who had been present at the formation of this Constitution could not avoid the recollection of the pain and difficulty which the subject caused in that body. The members from the Southern States were so tender upon this point, that they had well nigh broken up without coming to any determination; however, from the extreme desire of preserving the Union, and obtaining an efficient Government, they were induced mutually to concede, and the Constitution jealously guarded what they agreed to. If gentlemen look over the footsteps of that body, they will find the greatest degree of caution used to imprint them, so as not to be easily eradicated; but the moment we go to jostle on that ground, I fear we shall feel it tremble under our feet. Congress have no power to interfere with the importation of slaves beyond what is given in the ninth section of the 1st article of the Constitution; everything else is interdicted to them in the strongest terms. If we examine the constitution, we shall find the expressions relative to this subject cautiously expressed, and more punctiliously guarded than any other part, "The migration or importation of such persons shall not be prohibited by Congress." But least this should not have secured the object sufficiently, it is declared, in the same section, "That no capitation or direct tax shall be laid, unless in proportion to the census;" this was intended to prevent Congress from laying any special tax upon negro slaves, as they might, in this way, so burthen the possessors of them as to induce a general emancipation. If we go on to the fifth article, we shall find the first and fifth clauses of the ninth section of the first article restrained from being altered before the year 1808.

CCLII. Elbridge Gerry in the House of Representatives.[2]

February 25, 1790.

Gentlemen have said, that it never was in contemplation to assume the State debts. When the present Constitution was under consideration in the General Convention, a proposition was brought forward, that the General Government should assume and provide for the State debts, as well as the debts of the Union. It was opposed on this ground, that it did not extend to the repayment of that part

---

[1] *Annals of Congress*, First Congress, II, 1200–1201.
[2] *Annals of Congress*, First Congress, II, 1360–1361.

which the States had sunk, as well as that which remained unpaid; had it not been for this objection, I believe that the very provision which gentlemen say was never expected, would have been incorporated in the Constitution itself. If I recollect rightly, it was also contended, in Convention, that the proposition would be useless, as Congress were authorized, under other parts of the Constitution, to make full provision on this head. From this circumstance, gentlemen will see that the assumption of the State debts was in contemplation from the very commencement of the new Government. ─────────

CCLIII. Tench Coxe to James Madison.[1]

Philada. March 31, 1790 —

I will mention to you *confidentially* that great pains have been heretofore taken to restrain Applications to the general Government on the subject of the slave trade. A very strong paper was drawn & put into my hands to procure the signature of Dr. Franklin to be presented to the federal convention — I enclosed to the Dr. with my opinion that it would be a very improper season & place to hazard the Application considering it as an over zealous act of honest men.

─────────

CCLIV. James Madison in the House of Representatives.[2]

April 22, 1790.

One of my colleagues has asked a very proper question — If, as we have been told, the assumption originated in the Convention, why were not words inserted that would have incorporated and made the State debts part of the debts of the United States? Sir, if there was a majority who disapproved of the measure, certainly no argument can be drawn from this source; if there was a majority who approved of it, but thought it inexpedient to make it a part of the Constitution, they must have been restrained by a fear that it might produce dissensions and render the success of their plan doubtful. I do recollect that such a measure was proposed; and, if my memory does not deceive me, the very gentleman [3] who now appeals to the Constitution in support of his argument, disrelished the measure at that time, and assigned for a reason, that it would administer relief perhaps exactly in proportion as the States had been deficient in making exertions.

─────────

[1] *Documentary History of the Constitution*, V, 239.
[2] *Annals of Congress*, First Congress, II, 1538.
[3] Gerry, see CCLII above.

CCLV. ROGER SHERMAN IN THE HOUSE OF REPRESENTATIVES.[1]

May 3, 1790.

Mr. Sherman said, that a proposition to vest Congress with power to establish a National University was made in the General Convention; but it was negatived. It was thought sufficient that this power should be exercised by the States in their separate capacity.

CCLVI. ROGER SHERMAN IN THE HOUSE OF REPRESENTATIVES.[2]

May 25, 1790.

It is objected that this is a new project — and not mentioned in the Constitution. The novelty of it is no just objection against adopting it — if the measure be just. It was mentioned in the general convention — but it was not thought necessary or proper to insert it in the Constitution, for Congress would have sufficient power to adopt it if they should judge it expedient.

CCLVII. JAMES MADISON IN THE HOUSE OF REPRESENTATIVES.[3]

February 2, 1791.

In making these remarks on the merits of the bill, he had reserved to himself the right to deny the authority of Congress to pass it. He had entertained this opinion from the date of the Constitution. His impression might, perhaps, be the stronger, because he well recollected that a power to grant charters of incorporation had been proposed in the General Convention and rejected.

CCLVIII. ELBRIDGE GERRY IN THE HOUSE OF REPRESENTATIVES.[4]

February 7, 1791.

The gentleman from Virginia has endeavored to support his interpretation of the Constitution by the sense of the Federal Convention; but how is this to be obtained? By applying proper rules of interpretation? If so, the sense of the Convention is in favor of the bill; or are we to depend on the memory of the gentleman for a history of their debates, and from thence to collect their sense? This would be improper, because the memories of different gentlemen would probably vary, as they had already done, with respect to those facts; and if not, the opinions of the individual members who debated are not to be considered as the opinions of the Conven-

---

[1] *Annals of Congress*, First Congress, II, 1551.
[2] L. H. Boutell, *Life of Roger Sherman*, p. 244.
[3] *Annals of Congress*, First Congress, II, 1896.
[4] *Annals of Congress*, First Congress, II, 1952.

tion. Indeed, if they were, no motion was made in that Convention, and therefore none could be rejected for establishing a National Bank; and the measure which the gentleman has referred to was a proposition merely to enable Congress to erect commercial corporations, which was, and always ought to be, negatived.

_____

CCLIX. Thomas Jefferson: on the Constitutionality of a National Bank.[1]

February 15, 1791.

It is an established rule of construction where a phrase will bear either of two meanings, to give it that which will allow some meaning to the other parts of the instrument, and not that which would render all the others useless. Certainly no such universal power was meant to be given them. It was intended to lace them up straitly within the enumerated powers, and those without which, as means, these powers could not be carried into effect. It is known that the very power now proposed *as a means* was rejected as *an end* by the Convention which formed the Constitution. A proposition was made to them to authorize Congress to open canals, and an amendatory one to empower them to incorporate. But the whole was rejected, and one of the reasons for rejection urged in debate was, that then they would have a power to erect a bank, which would render the great cities, where there were prejudices and jealousies on the subject, adverse to the reception of the Constitution.

_____

CCLX. Alexander Hamilton: On the Constitutionality of a National Bank.[2]

February 23, 1791.

Another argument made use of by the Secretary of State is, the rejection of a proposition by the Convention to empower Congress to make corporations, either generally, or for some special purpose.

What was the precise nature or extent of this proposition, or what the reasons for refusing it, is not ascertained by any authentic document, or even by accurate recollection. As far as any such document exists, it specifies only canals. If this was the amount of it, it would, at most, only prove that it was thought inexpedient to give a power to incorporate for the purpose of opening canals, for which purpose a special power would have been necessary, except with regard to the western territory, there being nothing in any

_____

[1] P. L. Ford, *Writings of Thomas Jefferson*, V, 286–287.
[2] H. C. Lodge, *Works of Alexander Hamilton* (Federal Edition) 462–463.

part of the Constitution respecting the regulation of canals. It must be confessed, however, that very different accounts are given the import of the proposition, and of the motives for rejecting it. Some affirm that it was confined to the opening of canals and obstructions in rivers; others, that it embraced banks; and others, that it extended to the power of incorporating generally. Some, again, allege that it was disagreed to because it was thought improper to vest in Congress a power of erecting corporations. Others, because it was thought unnecessary to *specify* the power, and inexpedient to furnish an additional topic of objection to the Constitution. In this state of the matter, no inference whatever can be drawn from it.

CCLXI. ABRAHAM BALDWIN IN THE HOUSE OF REPRESENTATIVES.[1]

November 10, 1791.

It had not been found practicable to ground representation in the Federal Constitution upon any other principle than that of numbers; but extent of territory is unquestionably one of the natural principles on which it rests, and should if possible be regarded.

CCLXII. ELBRIDGE GERRY IN THE HOUSE OF REPRESENTATIVES.[2]

November 21, 1791.

Mr. Gerry contended that the Constitution was misconstrued by the gentleman from North Carolina; and in reply to the gentleman from New Jersey, he said he was surprised to hear the remarks which he made, when he recollected his being a member of the Convention — in which, it must be remembered by that gentleman, the larger States consented to placing the small States on a par with them in the Senate, to obviate the difficulty which the smaller States objected against the larger representations from the larger States.

CCLXIII. JONATHAN DAYTON IN THE HOUSE OF REPRESENTATIVES.[3]

December 22, 1791.

Mr. Dayton also objected to the motion; he thought fourteen days would be a more proper time; it was the design of the Constitution, though it is not expressed, that the President should not know the characters to whom he is indebted for his election.

---

[1] *Annals of Congress*, Second Congress, 173.
[2] *Annals of Congress*, Second Congress, 203.
[3] *Annals of Congress*, Second Congress, 279.

CCLXIV. Hugh Williamson in the House of Representatives.[1]

January 24, 1792.

Mr. Williamson observed, that although some complaints were
made of the fractional parts not being represented, he never could
conceive that the framers of the Constitution entertained an idea
of a representation of the people distinct from the States, but contemplated the representation of the people of each State, according
to some given ratio.

CCLXV. Hugh Williamson in the House of Representatives.[2]

February 3, 1792.

In the Constitution of this Government there are two or three
remarkable provisions, which seem to be in point. It is provided,
that direct taxes shall be apportioned among the several States
according to their respective numbers. It is also provided, that
all duties, imposts, and excises, shall be uniform throughout the
United States; and it is provided, that no preference shall be given,
by any regulation of commerce or revenue, to the ports of one
State over those of another. The clear and obvious intention of
the articles mentioned was, that Congress might not have the power
of imposing unequal burdens; that it might not be in their power
to gratify one part of the Union by oppressing another. It appeared
possible, and not very improbable, that the time might come, when,
by greater cohesion, by more unanimity, by more address, the Representatives of one part of the Union might attempt to impose unequal taxes, or to relieve their constituents at the expense of other
people. To prevent the possibility of such a combination, the articles that I have mentioned were inserted in the Constitution. . . .

Perhaps the case I have put is too strong — Congress can never
do a thing that is so palpably unjust — but this, sir, is the very
mark at which the theory of bounties seems to point. The certain
operation of that measure is the oppression of the Southern States,
by superior numbers in the Northern interest. This was to be
feared at the formation of this Government, and you find many
articles in the Constitution, besides those I have quoted, which were
certainly intended to guard us against the dangerous bias of interest,
and the power of numbers. Wherefore was it provided that no duty
should be laid on exports? Was it not to defend the great staples
of the Southern States — tobacco, rice and indigo — from the opera-

---

[1] *Annals of Congress*, Second Congress, 333.
[2] *Annals of Congress*, Second Congress, 378–380.

tion of unequal regulations of commerce, or unequal indirect taxes, as another article had defended us from unequal direct taxes?

I do not hazard much in saying, that the present Constitution had never been adopted without those preliminary guards in it.

CCLXVI. JAMES MADISON IN THE HOUSE OF REPRESENTATIVES.[1]

February 6, 1792.

I, sir, have always conceived — I believe those who proposed the Constitution conceived, and it is still more fully known, and more material to observe that those who ratified the Constitution conceived — that this is not an indefinite Government, deriving its powers from the general terms prefixed to the specified powers, but a limited Government, tied down to the specified powers which explain and define the general terms.

CCLXVII. THOMAS JEFFERSON: ANAS.[2]

April the 6th [1792.] The President called on me before breakfast, and first introduced some other matter, then fell on the representation bill, which he had now in his possession for the tenth day. I had before given him my opinion in writing, that the method of apportionment was contrary to the constitution. He agreed that it was contrary to the common understanding of that instrument, and to what was understood at the time by the makers of it: that yet it would bear the construction which the bill put, and he observed that the vote for and against the bill was perfectly geographical, a northern against a southern vote, and he feared he should be thought to be taking side with a southern party. . . .

Written this the 9th of April.

CCLXVIII. ALEXANDER HAMILTON TO EDWARD CARRINGTON.[3]

May 26, 1792.

As to the third point, the question of an assumption of the State debts by the United States was in discussion when the convention that framed the present government was sitting at Philadelphia, and in a long conversation which I had with Mr. Madison in an afternoon's walk, I well remember that we were perfectly agreed in the expediency and propriety of such a measure; though we were both of opinion that it would be more advisable to make it a measure

---

[1] *Annals of Congress*, Second Congress, 386.
[2] T. J. Randolph, *Memoir, Correspondence, . . . of Thomas Jefferson*, IV, 466–467.
[3] H. C. Lodge, *Works of Alexander Hamilton* (Federal Edition), IX, 515.

of administration than an article of Constitution, from the impolicy of multiplying obstacles to its reception on collateral details.

CCLXIX. GEORGE MASON'S ACCOUNT OF CERTAIN PROCEEDINGS IN CONVENTION.[1]

Gunston hall. Sep. 30. 92. ex relatione G. Mason

The constn as agreed to till a fortnight before the convention rose was such a one as he wd have set his hand & heart to. 1. the presidt was to be elected for 7. years, then ineligible for 7. more. 2. rotation in the senate. 3. a vote of ⅔ in the legislature on particular subjects, & expressly on that of navign. the 3. new Engld. states were constantly with us in all questions (Rho. isld. not there, & N. York seldom) so that it was these 3. states with the 5. Southern ones against Pennsva Jersey & Delaware. with respect to the importn of slaves it was left to Congress. this disturbed the 2 Southernmost states who knew that Congress would immediately suppress the importn of slaves. those 2 states therefore struck up a bargain with the 3. N. Engld. states, if they would join to admit slaves for some years, the 2 Southernmost states wd join in changing the clause which required ⅔ of the legislature in any vote. it was done. these articles were changed accordingly, & from that moment the two S. states and the 3 Northern ones joined Pen. Jers. & Del. & made the majority 8. to 3. against us instead of 8. to 3. for us as it had been thro' the whole Convention. under this coalition the great principles of the Constn were changed in the last days of the Convention.

Anecdote. Yates Lansing & Hamilton represented N. Y. Yates & Lansing never voted *in one single instance* with Ham. who was so much mortified at it that he went home. when the season for courts came on, Yates a judge & Lansing a lawyer went to attend their courts. then Ham. returned.

Anecdote. the constn as agreed at first was that amendments might be proposed either by Congr. or the legislatures a commee was appointed to digest & redraw. Gov. Morris & King were of the commee. one morng. Gov. M. moved an instrn for certain alterns (not ½ the members yet come in) in a hurry & without understanding it was agreed to. the Commee reported so that Congr. shd have the exclusve. power of proposg. amendmts. G. Mason observd it on the report & opposed it. King denied the constrn. Mason demonstrated it, & asked the Commee by what authority they had varied what had been agreed. G. Morris then impudently

---

[1] From the Jefferson Papers and in the handwriting of Jefferson. Printed in *Documentary History of the Constitution*, V, 246–247.

got up & said by authority of the convention & produced the blind instruction beforementd. which was unknown by ½ of the house & not till then understood by the other. they then restored it as it stood originally.[1] ⸺⸺⸺

CCLXX. Alexander Hamilton: Reply to Anonymous Charges.[2]

In reference to it, a reply, published by Hamilton in seventeen hundred and ninety-two, to anonymous charges,[3] containing a misrepresentation of his course in the convention, and stated by him "to be of a nature to speak the malignity and turpitude of the accuser, denoting clearly the personal enemy in the garb of the political opponent," mentions "that the deliberations of the convention, which were carried on in private, were to *remain unmolested*. And every prudent man," he observed, "must be convinced of the propriety of the one and the other. Had the deliberations been open while going on, the clamours of faction would have prevented any satisfactory result. Had they *been afterwards disclosed*, much food would have been afforded to inflammatory declamation. Propositions, made without due reflection, and perhaps abandoned by the proposers themselves on more mature reflection, would have been handles for a profusion of ill-natured accusation. . . .

In the reply previously referred to, made by Hamilton to an anonymous attack in the year seventeen hundred and ninety-two, at the seat of government, when nearly all the members of the convention were living, to a charge that he "*opposed* the constitution in the grand convention, because it was too republican," he remarked, "This I affirm to be a gross misrepresentation. To prove it so, it were sufficient to appeal to a single fact, namely, that the gentleman alluded to was the only member from the state to which he belonged who signed the constitution, and, it is notorious, against the prevailing weight of the official influence of the state, and against what would probably be the opinion of a large majority of his fellow-citizens, till better information should correct their first impressions. How, then, can he be believed to have opposed a thing which he actually agreed to, and that in so unsupported a situation and under circumstances of such peculiar responsibility? To this, I shall add two more facts: — One, that the member in question never made a proposition to the convention which was not conformable to the republican theory. The other, that the highest toned of any of the propositions made by him, was actually voted for by the

---

[1] See CCLXXXI below.
[2] J. C. Hamilton, *History of the Republic of the United States*, III, 256, 339-340.
[3] In the *National Gazette*, established by Jefferson and Madison.

representatives of several states, including some of the principal ones, and including individuals who, in the estimation of those who deem themselves the only republicans, are pre-eminent for republican character. More than this I am not at liberty to say."

CCLXXI. Anonymous Letter to Alexander Hamilton.[1]

New York Augt. 30th. 1793

A publication appeared some time since in Greenleaf's paper, charging you with having moved in Convention that the Goverment of the United States should be by a *King, Lords* & Commons — I took some pains to discover the author of that piece, but without success — Bùt a conversation lately happened between Comodore Nicholson & Mr. Leonard Bleeker, in the hearing of others, in which the Commodore said; he had read the piece before alluded to, but doubted the truth of it untill it was lately confirmed by Mr. Abraham Baldwin, who was also a member of the Convention — This Mr. Baldwin did publicly in a pretty large company at the Commodores own Table. He said your motion was seconded by Mr. Gover Morris & that you was so chagrined when it failed that you left the House in disgust; That you returned however on a subsequent day, delivered your sentiments in writing, & Came off to New york, declaring you intermeddle no farther in the matter — Notwithstanding you returned, & assented to the Constitution as it is — This writing he suggested contained your Ideas of the kind of Government proper to be adopted — In repeating from other persons, words are often changed; but the foregoing is the substance of what the Commodore reports Mr. Baldwin to have said — I leave to yourself the expediency of taking any notice of it.

CCLXXII. Abraham Baldwin in the House of Representatives.[2]

March 14, 1796.

He would begin it by the assertion, that those few words in the Constitution on this subject,[3] were not those apt, precise, definite expressions, which irresistibly brought upon them the meaning which he had been above considering. He said it was not to disparage the instrument, to say that it had not definitely, and with precision, absolutely settled everything on which it had spoke. He

---

[1] *Documentary History of the Constitution*, V, 249–250.

[2] *Annals of Congress*, Fourth Congress, First Session, 537.

[3] Power of making treaties vested in the President and Senate, and that treaties were to be "the supreme law of the land."

had sufficient evidence to satisfy his own mind that it was not supposed by the makers of it at the time, but that some subjects were left a little ambiguous and uncertain. It was a great thing to get so many difficult subjects definitely settled at once. If they could all be agreed in, it would compact the Government. The few that were left a little unsettled might, without any great risk, be settled by practice or by amendments in the progress of the Government. He believed this subject of the rival powers of legislation and Treaty was one of them; the subject of the Militia was another, and some question respecting the Judiciary another. When he reflected on the immense difficulties and dangers of that trying occasion — the old Government prostrated, and a chance whether a new one could be agreed in — the recollection recalled to him nothing but the most joyful sensations that so many things had been so well settled, and that experience had shown there was very little difficulty or danger in settling the rest.

CCLXXIII. SECRETARY OF STATE: CONVENTION PAPERS RECEIVED
FROM PRESIDENT WASHINGTON.[1]

Department of State March 19. 1796.
Received from the President of the U. States this journal of the general or fœderal convention, in one hundred & fifty three pages; together with a journal of the proceedings of the Committee of the Whole House; a book exhibiting on eight pages a detail of yeas & nays on questions taken in the Convention & two loose sheets & a half sheet, containing nine pages of the like yeas and nays; a printed draught of the Constitution; a sheet marked No 1. exhibiting the state of the resolutions submitted to the consideration of the House by Mr Randolph, as agreed to in a Committee of the whole house; another sheet, marked No 2. exhibiting the state of those resolutions as *altered*, *amended* & agreed to in a Committee of the whole House; and seven other papers, marked No 3. No 4. No 5. No 6. No 7. No 8. & No 9. of no consequence in relation to the proceedings of the Convention, but which are on file with the printed draught of the Constitution and the papers marked No 1. & No 2.

The leaf containing the pages of this journal numbered 151 & 152, was loose; it had plainly been torn from the place where it is now inserted following page 150. —

TIMOTHY PICKERING,
Secy of State.

---

[1] *Documentary History of the Constitution*, I, 47.

CCLXXIV. President Washington: Message to House of Representatives on Jay's Treaty.[1]

March 30, 1796

Having been a member of the General Convention, and knowing the principles on which the Constitution was formed, I have ever entertained but one opinion on this subject, and from the first establishment of the Government to this moment, my conduct has exemplified that opinion, that the power of making Treaties is exclusively vested in the President, by and with the advice and consent of the Senate, provided two-thirds of the Senators present concur; and that every Treaty so made, and promulgated, thenceforward becomes the law of the land. . . .

It is a fact, declared by the General Convention, and universally understood, that the Constitution of the United States was the result of a spirit of amity and mutual concession. And it is well known that, under this influence, the smaller States were admitted to an equal representation in the Senate, with the larger States; and that this branch of the Government was invested with great powers; for, on the equal participation of those powers, the sovereignty and political safety of the smaller States were deemed essentially to depend.

If other proofs than these, and the plain letter of the Constitution itself, be necessary to ascertain the point under consideration, they may be found in the Journals of the General Convention, which I have deposited in the office of the Department of State. In those Journals it will appear, that a proposition was made, 'that no Treaty should be binding on the United States which was not ratified by a law,' and that the proposition was explicitly rejected.[2]

As, therefore, it is perfectly clear to my understanding, that the assent of the House of Representatives is not necessary to the validity of a Treaty; . . .[3]

---

[1] *Annals of Congress*, Fourth Congress, First Session, 761.

[2] See CCLXXV and CCLXXVI below.

[3] The following note, dated January 25, 1826, is found among the Madison Papers: —

"In the Richmond Enquirer of the 21st is an extract from the Report of Secretary Hamilton on the constitutionality of the Bank, in which he opposes a resort, in expounding the Constitution, to the rejection of a proposition in the Convention, or to any evidence extrinsic to the text. Did he not advise, if not draw up, the message refusing to the House of Representatives the papers relating to Jay's treaty, in which President Washington combats the right of their call by appealing to his personal knowledge of the intention of the Convention, having been himself a member of it, to the authority of a rejected proposition appearing on the journals of the Convention, and to the opinion's entertained in the State Conventions?" (*Letters and Other Writings of James Madison*, III, 515.)

CCLXXV. James Madison to Thomas Jefferson.[1]

Philada, April 4, 1796.

The Newspapers will inform you that the call for the Treaty papers was carried by 62 agst 37. You will find the answer of the President herewith inclosed.[2] The absolute refusal was as unexpected as the tone & tenor of the message are improper & indelicate. If you do not at once perceive the drift of the appeal to the Genl Convention & its journal, recollect one of Camillus' last numbers, & read the latter part of Murray's speech. . . .

According to my memory & that of others, the Journal of the Convention was, by a vote deposited with the P., to be kept sacred until called for by some competent authority. How can this be reconciled with the use he has made of it? Examine my notes if you please at the close of the business, & let me know what is said on the subject. — You will perceive that the quotation is nothing to the purpose. Most of the majority wd decide as the Convention did because they think there may be some Treaties, as a Mere Treaty of peace that would not require the Legislative power — a ratification by law also expressed a different idea from that entertained by the House of its agency.[3] _____

CCLXXVI. James Madison in the House of Representatives.[4]

April 6, 1796.

He proceeded to review the several topics on which the Message relied. First. The intention of the body which framed the Constitution. . . .

1. When the members on the floor, who were members of the General Convention, particularly a member from Georgia and himself, were called on in a former debate for the sense of that body on the Constitutional question, it was a matter of some surprise, which was much increased by the peculiar stress laid on the information expected. He acknowledged his surprise, also, at seeing the Message of the Executive appealing to the same proceedings in the General Convention, as a clue to the meaning of the Constitution.

It had been his purpose, during the late debate, to make some observations on what had fallen from the gentlemen from Connecticut and Maryland, if the sudden termination of the debate had not cut him off from the opportunity. He should have reminded them that this was the ninth year since the Convention executed

---

[1] Hunt, *Writings of James Madison*, VI, 264-5.
[2] See CCLXXIV above.   [3] See CCLXXVI below.
[4] *Annals of Congress*, Fourth Congress, First Session, 774-780.

their trust, and that he had not a single note in this place to assist his memory. He should have remarked, that neither himself nor the other members who had belonged to the Federal Convention, could be under any particular obligation to rise in answer to a few gentlemen, with information, not merely of their own ideas of that period, but of the intention of the whole body; many members of which, too, had probably never entered into the discussions of the subject. He might have further remarked, that there would not be much delicacy in the undertaking, as it appeared that a sense had been put on the Constitution by some who were members of the Convention, different from that which must have been entertained by others, who had concurred in ratifying the Treaty. . . .

It would have been proper for him, also, to have recollected what had, on a former occasion, happened to himself during a debate in the House of Representatives. When the bill for establishing a National Bank was under Consideration, he had opposed it, as not warranted by the Constitution, and incidentally remarked, that his impression might be stronger, as he remembered that, in the Convention, a motion was made and negatived, for giving Congress a power to grant charters of incorporation. This slight reference to the Convention, he said, was animadverted on by several, in the course of the debate, and particularly by a gentleman from Massachusetts, who had himself been a member of the Convention, and whose remarks were not unworthy the attention of the Committee. Here Mr. M. read a paragraph from Mr. Gerry's speech, from the Gazette of the United States, page 814, protesting, in strong terms, against arguments drawn from that source.[1]

Mr. M. said, he did not believe a single instance could be cited in which the sense of the Convention had been required or admitted as material in any Constitutional question. In the case of the Bank, the Committee had seen how a glance at that authority had been treated in this House. When the question on the suability of the States was depending in the Supreme Court, he asked, whether it had ever been understood that the members of the Bench, who had been members of the Convention, were called on for the meaning of the Convention on that very important point, although no Constitutional question would be presumed more susceptible of elucidation from that source?

He then adverted to that part of the Message which contained an extract from the Journal of the Convention, showing that a proposition 'that no Treaty should be binding on the United States, which

---

[1] See CCLVII—CCLVIII above.

was not ratified by law,' was explicitly rejected.   He allowed this to be much more precise than any evidence drawn from the debates in the Convention, or resting on the memory of individuals.   But admitting the case to be as stated, of which he had no doubt, although he had no recollection of it, and admitting the record of the Convention to be the oracle that ought to decide the true meaning of the Constitution, what did this abstract vote amount to? Did it condemn the doctrine of the majority? So far from it, that, as he understood their doctrine, they must have voted as the Convention did; for they do not contend that no Treaty shall be operative without a law to sanction it; on the contrary, they admit that some Treaties will operate without this sanction; and that it is no further applicable in any case than where Legislative objects are embraced by Treaties.   The term 'ratify' also deserved some attention; for, although of loose signification in general, it had a technical meaning different from the agency claimed by the House on the subject of Treaties.[1]

But, after all, whatever veneration might be entertained for the body of men who formed our Constitution, the sense of that body could never be regarded as the oracular guide in expounding the Constitution.   As the instrument came from them it was nothing more than the draft of a plan, nothing but a dead letter, until life and validity were breathed into it by the voice of the people, speaking through the several State Conventions.   If we were to look, therefore, for the meaning of the instrument beyond the face of the instrument, we must look for it, not in the General Convention, which proposed, but in the State Conventions, which accepted and ratified the Constitution.

. . . He should limit himself, therefore, to two observations. The first was, that if the spirit of amity and mutual concession from which the Constitution resulted was to be consulted on expounding it, that construction ought to be favored which would preserve the mutual control between the Senate and House of Representatives, rather than that which gave powers to the Senate not controllable by, and paramount over those of the House of Representatives, whilst the House of Representatives could in no instance exercise their powers without the participation and control of the Senate. The second observation was, that, whatever jealousy might unhappily have prevailed between the smaller and larger States, as they had most weight in one or the other branch of Government, it was a fact, for which he appealed to the Journals of the old Congress,

---

[1] See CCLXXIV above.

from its birth to its dissolution, and to those of the Congress under the present Government, that in no instance would it appear, from the yeas and nays, that a question had been decided by a division of the votes according to the size of the States. He considered this truth as affording the most pleasing and consoling reflection, and as one that ought to have the most conciliating and happy influence on the temper of all the States.

CCLXXVII. WILLIAM FINDLEY IN THE HOUSE OF REPRESENTA-TIVES.[1]

January 23, 1798.

When the Constitution of the United States was under considera-tion, it was well known to those members of the committee [of the whole] who were present at that time, (and some he saw,) that this [President's power of appointing to office] was an important question. It was thrown into different shapes, until at last it was adopted, as it appeared in the Constitution. This regulation was adopted upon principle, and was not a mere arbitrary thing. The power of appoint-ing to office was brought down by placing a part of it in the Legis-lature. It was further restrained by prohibiting any member of the Legislature from enjoying, during the period for which he was elected, any office which should have been created, or the emoluments of which should have been increased, during that time. Thus, hold-ing up to view the avenues by which corruption was most likely to enter.

CCLXXVIII. BALDWIN: INCIDENT IN HOUSE OF REPRESENTATIVES.[2]

1798 March the 11th. . . . Baldwin mentions at table the following fact. When the bank bill was under discussion in the House of Representatives, Judge Wilson came in, and was stand-ing by Baldwin. Baldwin reminded him of the following fact which passed in the grand convention. Among the enumerated powers given to Congress, was one to erect corporations. It was, on debate, struck out. Several particular powers were then pro-posed. Among others, Robert Morris proposed to give Congress a power to establish a national bank. Gouverneur Morris opposed it, observing that it was extremely doubtful whether the consti-tution they were framing could ever be passed at all by the people of America; that to give it its best chance, however, they should make it as palatable as possible, and put nothing into

---

[1] *Annals of Congress*, Fifth Congress, Vol. I, p. 905.

[2] Jefferson's Anas in T. J. Randolph, *Memoir, Correspondence . . . of Thomas Jefferson*, IV, 506–507.

it not very essential, which might raise up enemies; that his colleague (Robert Morris) well knew that 'a bank' was, in their State (Pennsylvania) the very watch-word of party; that *a bank* had been the great bone of contention between the two parties of the State, from the establishment of their constitution, having been erected, put down, and erected again, as either party preponderated; that therefore, to insert this power, would instantly enlist against the whole instrument, the whole of the anti-bank party in Pennsylvania. Whereupon it was rejected, as was every other special power, except that of giving copyrights to authors, and patents to inventors; the general power of incorporating being whittled down to this shred. Wilson agreed to the fact.

CCLXXIX. Charles Pinckney in the House of Representatives.[1]

May 10, 1798.

The gentleman from Pennsylvania had said, with great truth, that it was the object of those who formed the Constitution, that the powers of Government should be distributed among the different departments, and that they ought not to be assigned or relinquished. ————

CCLXXX. Debate in the House of Representatives.[2]

June 16–20, 1798.

Mr. B[aldwin]. thought the 9th section, forbidding Congress to prohibit the migration, &c., was directly opposed to the principle of this bill. He recollected very well that when the 9th section of the Constitution was under consideration in the Convention, the delegates from some of the Southern States insisted that the prohibition of the introduction of slaves should be left to the State Governments; it was found expedient to make this provision in the Constitution; there was an objection to the use of the word slaves, as Congress by none of their acts had ever acknowledged the existence of such a condition. It was at length settled on the words as they now stand, 'that the migration or importation of such persons as the several States shall think proper to admit, should not be prohibited till the year 1808.' It was observed by some gentlemen present that this expression would extend to other persons besides slaves,[3] which was not denied, but this did not produce any alteration of it. . . .

---

[1] *Annals of Congress*, Fifth Congress, 2d and 3d Session, II, 1660.
[2] *Annals of Congress*, Fifth Congress, 2d and 3d Session, II, 1968–2005.
[3] See CCCXXXI below.

Mr. Dayton (the Speaker) commenced his observations with declaring that he should not have risen on this occasion, if no allusion had been made to the proceedings in the Federal Convention which framed the Constitution of the United States, or if the representation which was given of what passed in that body, had been a perfectly correct and candid one.   He expressed his surprise at what had fallen from the gentleman from Georgia (Mr. Baldwin) relatively to that part of the Constitution, which had been selected as the text of opposition to the bill under consideration, viz: 'The migration 'or importation of such persons as any of the States now existing 'shall think proper to admit, shall not be prohibited by Congress, 'prior to the year 1808.'   He could only ascribe either to absolute forgetfulness, or to wilful misrepresentation, the assertion of the member from Georgia, that it was understood and intended by the General Convention that the article in question should extend to the importation or introduction of citizens from foreign countries. As that gentleman and himself were the only two members of the House of Representatives who had the honor of a seat in that body, he deemed it his indispensable duty to correct the misstatement that had thus been made.   He did not therefore, hesitate to say, in direct contradiction to this novel construction of the article (made as it would seem to suit the particular purposes of the opponents of the Alien bill) that the proposition itself was originally drawn up and moved in the Convention, by the deputies from South Carolina, for the express purpose of preventing Congress from interfering with the introduction of slaves into the United States, within the time specified.   He recollected also, that in the discussion of its merits, no question arose, or was agitated respecting the admission of foreigners, but, on the contrary, that it was confined simply to slaves, and was first voted upon and carried with that word expressed in it, which was afterwards upon reconsideration changed for '*such persons*,' as it now stands, upon the suggestion of one of the Deputies from Connecticut.   The sole reason assigned for changing it was, that it would be better not to stain the Constitutional code with such a term, since it could be avoided by the introduction of other equally intelligible words, as had been done in the former part of the same instrument, where the same sense was conveyed by the circuitous expression of 'three fifths of all other persons.'   Mr. Dayton said that at that time he was far from believing, and that indeed until the present debate arose, he had never heard, that any one member supposed that the simple change of the term would enlarge the construction of this prohibitory provision, as it was now contended for.   If it could have been conceived to be really liable to such interpretation, he was convinced that it would not have been adopted, for it would then carry with it a strong injunction upon Congress to prohibit the introduction of foreigners into newly erected States immediately, and into the then existing States after the year 1808, as it undoubtedly does, that of slaves after that period. . . .

Mr. Baldwin . . . observed that he was yesterday obliged to leave the House a little before adjournment, and he had understood that, in his absence, the remarks which he had made on that point, a few days ago, in Committee of the Whole, had been controverted, and that it had been done with some degree of harshness and personal disrespect. What he had before asserted was, that the clause respecting migration and importation was not considered at the time when it passed in the Convention as confined entirely to the subject of slaves. He spoke with the more confidence on this point, as there was scarcely one to which his attention had been so particularly called at the time. In making the Federal Constitution, when it was determined that it should be a Government possessing Legislative powers, the delegates from the two Southern States, of which he was one, were so fully persuaded that those powers would be used to the destruction of their property in slaves, that for some time they thought it would not be possible for them to be members of it: to that interesting state of the subject he had before alluded. In the progress of the business, other obstacles occurring, which he need not repeat, it was concluded to give to the delegates of those States the offer of preparing a clause to their own minds, to secure that species of property. He well remembered that when the clause was first prepared, it differed in two respects from the form in which it now stands. It used the word "slaves" instead of "migration," or "importation," of persons, and instead of "ten dollars," it was expressed "five per cent. ad valorem on their importation," which it was supposed would be about the average rate of duties under this Government. Several persons had objections to the use of the word 'slaves,' as Congress had hitherto avoided the use of it in their acts, and not acknowledged the existence of such a condition. It was expressly observed at the time, that making use of the form of expression as it now stands, instead of the word slaves, would make the meaning more general, and include what we now consider as included; this did not appear to be denied, but still it was preferred in its present form. He had more confidence than common in his recollection on this point, for the reasons which he had before stated. He gave it as the result of his very clear recollection. Any other member of that body was doubtless at liberty to say he did not recollect it. Still that would not diminish the confidence he felt on this occasion. . . .

The Speaker rose from the Chair and said, that there was something so unmanly and improper in the opportunity which had been sought by the member from Georgia of replying to the observations he had made yesterday, that he felt himself irresistibly impelled to break through the rigid form, and to express, in a single word, his sense of it. It could not have escaped the general observation, that, although they had been for some time in Committee of the Whole, when the Speaker was on the floor, and had a right in common with the other members to join in any discussion, yet that member had thought proper in that situation to maintain a perfect silence, and to permit the committee to rise, that he might take advantage of the injunction imposed upon the Chair of never entering into the debate, not even to defend himself. This advantage had been eagerly seized, and the House were witnesses of the manner of his doing it. As to the matter contained in the reply, it was not of such importance, nor so worthy of notice, the Speaker said, as to justify his requesting the House to go again into a committee, merely to give him an opportunity of directly and positively contradicting the member from Georgia, as he should most assuredly and positively do, so far as respected the proceedings of the Federal Convention in 1787. _____

CCLXXXI. Albert Gallatin in the House of Representatives.[1]

June 19, 1798.

Mr. G[allatin] said he was well informed that those words had originally been inserted in the Constitution as a limitation to the power of laying taxes. After the limitation had been agreed to, and the Constitution was completed, a member of the Convention, (he was one of the members who represented the State of Pennsylvania) being one of a committee of revisal and arrangement, attempted to throw these words into a distinct paragraph, so as to create not a limitation, but a distinct power. The trick, however, was discovered by a member from Connecticut, now deceased, and the words restored as they now stand.[2]

---

[1] *Annals of Congress*, Fifth Congress, 2d and 3d Session, II, 1976.

CCLXXXII. Abraham Baldwin in the House of Representatives.[1]

January 11, 1799.

All society showed that there was in the human character a foundation for radical different opinions on political subjects; there is not a place in which it does not show itself. . . . There was no doubt but that it showed itself early in this country; . . .

It also showed itself soon after the peace, in repeated attempts to jostle the pillars of the old Government, and that in defiance and without the consent of those who were administering it. After they consented to recommend a Convention to make alterations, it is well known to have shown itself in that assembly; the greatness of the occasion unexpectedly called forth such a portion of the oldest and most venerable statesmen of our country as effectually to correct and control the councils on those subjects; they kept the same ground as the Revolution had taken, and which was seen in all the State Governments. They took their principles from that set of political economists and philosophers now generally denominated in the English language Whigs, and consecrated them as a Constitution for the government of the Country. Though this was a very great and decided majority, yet it is equally well known that there were some who entertained very different opinions; they no doubt still entertain them, and they who expect to find any time when this will not be the case, expect too much of human nature, they will be sure to be disappointed. _____

CCLXXXIII. Abraham Baldwin in the House of Representatives.[2]

January 15, 1799.

But it is insisted on, said Mr. B., by some gentlemen, that as the power to pass uniform laws on the subject of bankruptcy is expressly given to Congress by the Constitution, it is their duty to do it; and some go as far as to say that it is not proper for the States to legislate on that subject. He thought there was no great weight in that argument. Congress not having passed such a law for these ten years past, and the States having legislated upon it in their own way, is a sufficient proof that that has not been the understanding of the Constitution. . . .

Many other instances might be adduced to prove the same thing, if necessary. The fact is, the powers given to Congress as well as to all other Legislatures, are in general submitted to their

---

[1] *Annals of Congress*, Fifth Congress, III, 2630-2631.
[2] *Annals of Congress*, Fifth Congress, III, 2670-2671.

discretion to use them as the circumstances of the country should require. He had no doubt in saying, as well from the perusal of the instrument as from his own recollection, that many of them must have been considered as of very difficult execution, and that it must have been supposed that the existence of the power in Congress would effect the control which they desired, would check the abuses which might otherwise have taken place, and prevent the necessity of using it. Any other view of that instrument, he thought, would lead to great perplexity and embarrassment. He was sure it was the one which its best friends had originally indulged, and had made the administration of the Government much more practicable and successful than it otherwise could have been.

CCLXXXIV. James Madison to Thomas Jefferson.[1]

Feby 8, 1799.

The idea of publishing the Debates of the Convention ought to be well weighed before the expediency of it, in a public as well as personal view be decided on. Besides the intimate connection between them the whole volume ought to be examined with an eye to the use of which every part is susceptible. In the Despotism at present exercised over the rules of construction, and [illegible] reports of the proceedings that would perhaps be made out & mustered for the occasion, it is a problem what turn might be given to the impression on the public mind. But I shall be better able to form & explain my opinion by the time, which now approaches when I shall have the pleasure of seeing you. And you will have the advantage of looking into the sheets attentively before you finally make up your own. _____

CCLXXXV. Gouverneur Morris: Oration upon Washington.[2]

It is a question, previous to the first meeting, what course shall be pursued. Men of decided temper, who, devoted to the public, overlooked prudential considerations, thought a form of government should be framed entirely new. But cautious men, with whom popularity was an object, deemed it fit to consult and comply with the wishes of the people. AMERICANS! — let the opinion then delivered by the greatest and best of men, be ever present to your remembrance. He was collected within himself. His countenance had more than usual solemnity — His eye was fixed, and seemed to

---

[1] Hunt, *Writings, of Madison*, VI, 329–330.
[2] G. Morris, *An Oration upon the Death of General Washington*, p. 20–21; delivered in New York, December 31, 1799.

look into futurity. 'It is (said he)too probable that no plan we propose will be adopted. Perhaps another dreadful conflict is to be
sustained. If to please the people, we offer what we ourselves disapprove, how can we afterwards defend our work? Let us raise a
standard to which the wise and the honest can repair. The event
is in the hand of God.' — this was the patriot voice of WASHING-
TON; and this the constant tenor of his conduct.

CCLXXXVI. Debate in the United States Senate.[1]

January 23, 1800.

Mr. C. Pinckney, of South Carolina, . . . remembered very
well that in the Federal Convention great care was used to provide
for the election of the President of the United States, independently
of Congress; to take the business as far as possible out of their hands.
The votes are to be given by Electors appointed for that express
purpose, the Electors are to be *appointed* by each State, and the
whole direction as to the manner of their appointment is given to
the State Legislatures. Nothing was more clear to him than that
Congress had no right to meddle with it at all; as the whole was
entrusted to the State Legislatures, they must make provision for
all questions arising on the occasion.

Mr. Baldwin, of Georgia . . . must say, for himself, that he
did not agree that the present provisions on this subject were
so defective and absurd as had been represented. His general
respect for those who had gone before him in this House, and
especially for the venerable assembly of the most experienced
statesmen of the country by whom the Constitution had been
formed, forbade him to entertain the belief that this subject, which
is the strong feature that characterizes this as an Elective Government, could have been till now so entirely out of sight and
neglected. Gentlemen appeared to him, from their observations,
to forget that the Constitution in directing *Electors* to be appointed
throughout the United States equal to the whole number of the
Senators and Representatives in Congress, for the express purpose
of entrusting this Constitutional branch of power to them, had provided for the existence of as respectable a body as Congress, and in
whom the Constitution on this business has more confidence than
in Congress. Experience had proved that a more venerable selection of characters could not be made in this country than usually
composed that electoral body. And what are the questions which
can arise on the subject entrusted to them to which they are incom-

petent, or to which Congress is so much more competent? The questions which present themselves seem to be:

1. Those which relate to the elections, returns and qualifications, of their own members. Shall these be taken away from that body, and submitted to the superior decision and control of Congress, without a particle of authority for it from the Constitution?

2. The legality or constitutionality of the different steps of their own proceedings, as, whether they vote for two persons both of the same state; whether they receive votes for a person under thirty-five years of age, or one who has not been fourteen years a citizen of the United States &c. It is true they, as well as any other Constitutional branch of this Government acting under that instrument, may be guilty of taking unconstitutional or corrupt steps, but they do it at their peril. Suppose either of the other branches of the Government, the Executive or the Judiciary, or even Congress, should be guilty of taking steps which are unconstitutional, to whom it is submitted, or who has control over it, except by impeachment? The Constitution seems to have equal confidence in all the branches on their own proper ground, and for either to arrogate superiority, or a claim to greater confidence, shows them in particular to be unworthy of it, as it is in itself directly unconstitutional.

3. The authentication of their own acts. This would seem to be as complete in them, as in either of the other branches of the Government. Their own authentication of their act finishes the business entrusted to them. It is true this must be judged of by the persons who are concerned in carrying it into execution; as in all laws and official acts under this Government, they to whom they are directed, and who are to be bound by them, must judge, and judge at their peril, whether they are duly authenticated or whether they are only a forgery.

If this be the just view of the subject, (and he could see no other which did not involve inextricable difficulties,) it leaves no possible question for the Senators and Representatives, when met together to count the votes agreeably to the Constitution, but to judge of the authentication of the act of the Electors, and then to proceed and count the votes as directed. If this body of the Electors of all the States had been directed by the Constitution to assemble in one place, instead of being formed into different Electoral colleges, he took it for granted none of the questions on which this resolution had been brought forward, would have occurred; every one would have acknowledged that they were to be settled in that assembly. It having been deemed more safe by the Constitution to form them into different Electoral colleges, to be assembled in the several

States, does not at all alter the nature or distinctness of their powers, or subject them any more to the control of the other departments of the Government.

He observed further, on the other points to which gentlemen had spoken, that if such radical and important changes were to be made on this subject, as seemed to be in contemplation under this resolution, he thought they must be made by proposing an amendment to the Constitution to that effect; and that they could not be made by law, without violating the Constitution. He did not agree with the gentleman from Massachusetts, (Mr. Dexter,) that the clause at the close of the 8th section of the Constitution, which gives to Congress power to pass all laws necessary and proper to carry into effect the foregoing powers of that section, and all other powers vested by the Constitution in the Government of the United States, or in any department or officer thereof, could be extended to this case; that speaks of the use of the powers vested by the Constitution — this resolution relates to the formation of a competent and essential part of the Government itself: that speaks of the movements of the Government after it is organized; this relates to the organization of the Executive branch, and is therefore clearly a Constitutional work, and to be done, if at all, in the manner pointed out by the Constitution, by proposing an article of amendment to the Constitution on that subject. His own opinion, however, was, what he had before stated, that the provisions on this subject were already sufficient; that all the questions which had been suggested were as safely left to the decision of the assemblies of Electors, as of any body of men that could be devised; and that the members of the Senate and of the House of Representatives, when met together in one room, should receive the act of the Electors as they would the act of any other Constitutional branch of the Government, to judge only of its authentication, and then to proceed to count the votes, as directed in the second article of the Constitution.

CCLXXXVII. CHARLES PINCKNEY IN THE UNITED STATES SEN-ATE.[1]

March 5, 1800.

The remainder of the clause respecting privilege is so express on the subjects of privilege from arrest, government of members, and expulsion, that every civil officer in the United States, and every man who has the least knowledge, cannot misunderstand them. I assert, that it was the design of the Constitution, and that not only

---

[1] *Annals of Congress*, Sixth Congress, 72, 74, 97, 101.

its spirit, but letter, warrant me in the assertion, that it never was intended to give Congress, or either branch, any but specified, and those very limited, privileges indeed. They well knew how oppressively the power of undefined privileges had been exercised in Great Britain, and were determined no such authority should ever be exercised here. They knew that in free countries very few privileges were necessary to the undisturbed exercise of legislative duties, and those few only they determined that Congress should possess; they never meant that the body who ought to be the purest, and the least in want of shelter from the operation of laws equally affecting all their fellow citizens, should be able to avoid them; they therefore not only intended, but did confine their privileges within the narrow limits mentioned in the Constitution.

. . . Let us inquire, why the Constitution should have been so attentive to each branch of Congress, so jealous of their privileges, and have shewn so little to the President of the United States in this respect. . . . No privilege of this kind was intended for your Executive, nor any except that which I have mentioned for your Legislature. The Convention which formed the Constitution well knew that this was an important point, and no subject had been more abused than privilege. They therefore determined to set the example, in merely limiting privilege to what was necessary, and no more.

. . . If the opinions of the Federal Convention ought to have weight, they so strongly insisted upon it [the separation of the three departments of government] as even to refuse after repeated trials, associating the Judges with the President in the exercise of his revisionary power.

. . . I have always been of opinion, that it was wrong to give the nomination of Judges to the President.

CCLXXXVIII. CHARLES PINCKNEY IN THE UNITED STATES SENATE.[1]

March 28, 1800.

It was intended to give your President the command of your forces, the disposal of all the honors and offices of your Government, the management of your foreign concerns, and the revision of your laws. Invested with these important powers, it was easily to be seen that the honor and interest of your Government required he should execute them with firmness and impartiality; that, to do this, he must be independent of the Legislature; that they must

---

[1] *Annals of Congress*, Sixth Congress, 129–139.

have no control over his election; that the only mode to prevent this was to give the exclusive direction to the State Legislatures in the mode of choosing Electors, who should be obliged to vote secretly; and that the vote should be taken in such manner, and on the same day, as to make it impossible for the different States to know who the Electors are for, or for improper domestic, or, what is of much more consequence, foreign influence and gold to interfere; that by doing this the President would really hold his office independent of the Legislature; that instead of being the creature, he would be the man of the people; that he would have to look to them, and to the confidence which he felt his own meritorious actions would inspire, for applause or subsequent appointments. . . .

Knowing that it was the intention of the Constitution to make the President completely independent of the Federal Legislature, I well remember it was the object, as it is at present not only the spirit but the letter of that instrument, to give to Congress no interference in, or control over the election of a President. It is made their duty to count over the votes in a convention of both Houses, and for the President of the Senate to declare who has the majority of the votes of the Electors so transmitted. It never was intended, nor could it have been safe, in the Constitution, to have given to Congress thus assembled in convention, the right to object to any vote, or even to question whether they were constitutionally or properly given. This right of determining on the manner in which the Electors shall vote; the inquiry into the qualifications, and the guards necessary to prevent disqualified or improper men voting, and to insure the votes being legally given, rests and is exclusively vested in the State Legislatures. If it is necessary to have guards against improper elections of Electors, and to institute tribunals to inquire into their qualifications, with the State Legislatures, and with them alone, rests the power to institute them, and they must exercise it. To give to Congress, even when assembled in convention, a right to reject or admit the votes of States, would have been so gross and dangerous an absurdity, as the framers of the Constitution never could have been guilty of. How could they expect, that in deciding on the election of a President, particularly where such election was strongly contested, that party spirit would not prevail, and govern every decision? Did they not know how easy it was to raise objections against the votes of particular elections, and that in determining upon these, it was more than probable, the members would recollect their *sides*, their favorite candidate, and sometimes their own interests? Or must they not have supposed, that, in putting the ultimate and final decision of the Electors in

Congress, who were to decide irrevocably and without appeal, they would render the President their creature, and prevent his assuming and exercising that independence in the performance of his duties upon which the safety and honor of the Government must forever rest? . . .

The disqualifications against any citizen being an Elector, are very few indeed; they are two. The first, that no officer of the United States shall be an Elector; and the other, that no member of Congress shall. The first, an indispensable one, because every officer of the United States is nominated by the President, and (except Judges) removable at his pleasure. The latter, that no member of Congress shall, is a provision which goes unanswerably to prove the solidity of my objections to this bill, and to show how extremely guarded the Constitution is in preventing the members of Congress from having any agency in the election, except merely in counting the votes.

They well knew, that to give to the members of Congress a right to give votes in this election, or to decide upon them when given, was to destroy the independence of the Executive, and make him the creature of the Legislature. This therefore they have guarded against, and to insure experience and attachment to the country, they have determined that no man who is not a natural born citizen, or citizen at the adoption of the Constitution, of fourteen years residence, and thirty-five years of age, shall be eligible. . . .

In 1792, being the first time the exercise of this power was necessary, Congress passed a law, entitled "An act relative to the election of President and Vice President," &c., directing how the States should appoint Electors for the election; when they should meet and vote; that they should sign three certificates of all the votes given; directing how the votes should be disposed of; detailing the duty of the Executive of each State in certifying the lists of Electors chosen; of the Secretary of State on the non-receipt of votes; that Congress shall always be in session on the second Wednesday in February in every fourth year, for the purpose of opening and counting the votes, and declaring a President elected agreeably to the Constitution; ascertaining the duties, allowances to, and penalties on persons sent with the votes; and making provision in case of the death of both President and Vice President, or their refusal to serve, and fixing the time when their service commences.

It is very important in deciding on the bill before you, to peruse this act with great attention; to recollect by whom, and when, and under what circumstances, it was made. This law was passed in 1792, when a number of able and well informed men, who have been since appointed to some of your most respectable situations at home and abroad, and many who have voluntarily retired with deserved and well-earned honor to private life, filled the seats of both Houses of Congress: when the Executive authority was held by Gen. WASHINGTON, for whom your whole nation at present mourns; by him who had no rival in the public affection, whose honors no man envied, and whose re-election to office as long as he pleased, he well knew, would always have been without contest; in him was placed the revision of your laws. And here, sir, let me ask, whether from a Congress thus ably formed, and from an Executive thus discerning and independent, as much knowledge of the Constitution, its precise directions, and the agency it intended Congress to have in the counting the votes and declaring the President, were not to have been expected, as from the present? Were not the then Executive, and a number of the members of both Houses, members of the Convention which framed the Constitution; and if it intended to give to Congress, or to authorize them to delegate to a committee of their body, powers contemplated by this bill, could the Congress or the President of 1792, have been so extremely uninformed, and indeed ignorant of its meaning and of their duty, as not to have known it?

. . . By viewing the 1st section of the 2d article of the Constitution, it is to be seen, that on the day fixed by law, which is the second Wednesday in February, the President of the Senate shall, in the presence of the Senate and House of Representatives, open all the certificates, and the votes shall then be counted; the person having the greatest number of votes shall be President, if such number be a majority of the whole number of Electors appointed; and if there be more than one who have such majority, and have an equal number of votes, then, the House of Representatives *shall immediately* choose by ballot one of them for President; and if no person have a majority, then, from the five highest on the list, the said House shall *in like manner* choose the President. From this part of the Constitution it is evident that no power or authority is given to Congress, even when both houses are assembled in convention, further than to open and count the votes, and declare who are the President and Vice President, if an election has been made; but that in case no election is made by the Electors, or no candidate has a majority, then the House of Representatives are (voting by States) *immediately* to choose, out of the five highest on the list, the President, &c.

In order that every man may understand what is here meant by the Constitution, and what is its express *directions* and *letter* as to this election, let us examine what is the literal meaning of the word *immediately*, and why it was introduced here. The best and most generally admired expounders of the English language, give this explanation of the word *immediately;* they say it means "instantly" — at the present time — without delay. This is the meaning the framers of the Constitution intended to give it, and it admits of no other. The plain, express, literal direction of that instrument therefore is, that in case of no election, the House of Representatives, voting by States, are *immediately*, that is instantly, and on the spot, without leaving the House in which they are then assembled, and without adjournment, to choose, out of the five highest candidates that have been voted for by the Electors, the one who is to be the Executive.

The reasons for this immediate election are, in my judgment, unanswerable; they show very clearly the foresight and caution of the Convention, and, if not strictly attended to, may be productive of the most serious calamities to our country. The reasons are these: that from our rapidly increasing strength and commerce, from the enterprise of our citizens, and our particular maritime situation as it respects the West Indies, South America, and the Powers having possessions in both, it was easily to be seen, that in any conflict between these Powers, our friendship or hospitality must be of the greatest importance; that they therefore would never cease to interfere in our politics and endeavor to direct them in the manner most suitable to their own interests; that from the difficulty of influencing so large a body as Congress, and from the immense power of the President, not only over the laws, but foreign connexions of the Union, that their principal effort would be always to have one of their own friends chosen; and to effect this, no influence would be left untried. To prevent this therefore, and to make the Executive independent of Congress, the election has been given exclusively to the States, under the direction of the State Legislatures. If an election is made by the Electors, and subject to no future control or revision on the part of Congress, then the end intended by the Constitution, of preventing the interference of foreign influence, is completely answered: for, elected as they are, and voting as the Electors must, the interference of foreign gold, or influence, is impossible. But it was to be supposed, that instances would occur, where two candidates, having a majority, may be equal in their number of votes; or where no candidate had a majority of the whole of the Electors appointed, and an election must take place by the National Legislature, or a branch of it; the question then arose, how was this election to be guarded to prevent, as far as human prudence could, improper domestic combinations, or, what is infinitely worse, foreign interference? It was a difficult thing, and required much deliberation. The Constitution directs that the Electors shall vote *by ballot*, and seal up and transmit their votes to the President of the Senate. It is expected and required by the Constitution, that the votes shall be secret and unknown, until opened in the presence of both Houses. To suffer them to be known, as heretofore, has been the practice, is unconstitutional and dangerous, and goes to defeat in some measure, the wise provisions of that instrument, in declaring, that when the House of Representatives are to elect, that it shall be done immediately. The Electors, therefore, ought never to divulge their votes. . . .

It is to be remembered, that around the seat of Congress will be placed all the open and accredited Ministers, as well as secret emissaries, of foreign Powers. Here too will be assembled the concealed leaders of domestic faction; all the arts and intrigues that have been used in Elective Governments in the Old World, will soon find their way among us; and if the Electors do not conceal their votes until the day appointed by law for opening them, and in case of no election by them, an immediate one by the House of Representatives does not take place, we shall soon have the scenes of Polish Diets and elections re-acted here, and in not many years the fate of Poland may be that of United America.

Wisely foreseeing this, the Constitution expressly orders that the Electors shall vote by ballot; and we all know, that to vote by ballot is to vote secretly; that the votes shall be sealed up, and not opened until the day appointed by law, and that if no election has been made by the Electors, an immediate one shall take place by the House of Representatives; that so far from appointing committees to receive memorials or petitions respecting the election, or decide upon it, or so far from having any right to delegate an authority on this subject, that Congress shall not themselves, even when in convention, have the smallest power to decide on a single vote; that they shall not have authority to adjourn for one moment, but shall instantly and on the spot, in case of no election by the Electors, proceed to the choice of a President, and not separate until it is determined. ————————

CCLXXXIX. Gouverneur Morris in the United States Senate.[1]

January 8, 1802.

There are some honorable gentlemen now present, who sat in

————————
[1] *Annals of Congress*, Seventh Congress, First Session, I, 40.

the Convention which formed this Constitution. I appeal to their recollection, if they have not seen the time when the fate of America was suspended by a hair? my life for it, if another convention be assembled, they will part without doing anything. Never, in the flow of time, was there a moment so propitious, as that in which the Convention assembled. The States had been convinced, by melancholy experience, how inadequate they were to the management of our national concerns. The passions of the people were lulled to sleep; State pride slumbered; the Constitution was promulgated; and then it awoke, and opposition was formed; but it was in vain. The people of America bound the States down by this compact. ⸻

CCXC. Gouverneur Morris in the United States Senate.[1]

January 14, 1802.

To form, therefore, a more perfect union, and to insure domestic tranquillity, the Constitution has said there shall be courts of the Union to try causes, by the wrongful decision of which the Union might be endangered or domestic tranquillity be disturbed. And what courts? Look again at the cases designated. The Supreme Court has no original jurisdiction. The Constitution has said that the judicial powers shall be vested in the supreme and inferior courts. It has declared that the judicial power so vested shall extend to the cases mentioned, and that the Supreme Court shall not have original jurisdiction in those cases. Evidently, therefore, it has declared that they shall (in the first instance) be tried by inferior courts, with appeal to the Supreme Court. This, therefore, amounts to a declaration, that the inferior courts shall exist. Since, without them, the citizen is deprived of those rights for which he stipulated, or rather those rights verbally granted would be actually withheld; and that great security of our Union, that necessary guard of our tranquillity, be completely paralyzed, if not destroyed. In declaring then that these tribunals shall exist, it equally declares that the Congress shall ordain and establish them. I say they shall; this is the evident intention, if not the express words, of the Constitution. The Convention in framing, the American people in adopting, that compact, did not, could not presume, that the Congress would omit to do what they were thus bound to do. They could not presume, that the Legislature would hesitate one moment, in establishing the organs necessary to carry into effect those wholesome, those important provisions. . . .

---

[1] *Annals of Congress,* Seventh Congress, First Session, I, 78–79, 86–87.

The Constitution says, the judicial power shall be vested in one Supreme Court, and in inferior courts. The Legislature can therefore only organize one Supreme Court, but they may establish as many inferior courts as they shall think proper. The designation made of them by the Constitution is, such inferior courts as the Congress may from time to time ordain and establish. But why, say gentlemen, fix precisely one Supreme Court, and leave the rest to Legislative discretion? The answer is simple: It results from the nature of things from the existent and probable state of our country. There was no difficulty in deciding that one and only one Supreme Court would be proper or necessary, to which should lie appeals from inferior tribunals. Not so as to these. The United States were advancing in rapid progression. Their population of three millions was soon to become five, then ten, afterwards twenty millions. This was well known, as far as the future can become an object of human comprehension. In this increase of numbers, with a still greater increase of wealth, with the extension of our commerce and the progress of the arts, it was evident that although a great many tribunals would become necessary, it was impossible to determine either on the precise number or the most convenient form. The Convention did not pretend to this prescience; but had they possessed it, would it have been proper to have established, then, all the tribunals necessary for all future times? Would it have been wise to have planted courts among the Chickasaws, the Choctaws, the Cherokees, the Tuscaroras, and God knows how many more, because at some future day the regions over which they roam might be cultivated by polished men? Was it not proper, wise, and necessary, to leave in the discretion of Congress the number and the kind of courts which they might find it proper to establish for the purpose designated by the Constitution? This simple statement of facts — facts of public notoriety — is alone a sufficient comment on, and explanation of, the word on which gentlemen have so much relied. The Convention in framing, the people in adopting, this compact, say the judicial power shall extend to many cases, the original cognizance whereof shall be by the inferior courts; but it is neither necessary, nor even possible, now to determine their number or their form; that essential power, therefore, shall vest in such inferior courts as the Congress may from time to time, in the progression of time, and according to the indication of circumstances, establish; not provide, or determine, but establish. Not a mere temporary provision, but an establishment. If, after this, it had said in general terms, that judges should hold their offices during good behaviour, could a doubt have existed on the interpretation of this act, under all its attending circumstances, that the judges of the inferior courts were intended as well as those of the Supreme Court? But did the framers of the Constitution stop here? Is there then nothing more? Did they risk on these grammatical niceties the fate of America? Did they rest here the most important branch of our Government? Little important, indeed, as to foreign danger; but infinitely valuable to our domestic peace, and to personal protection against the oppression of our rulers. No; lest a doubt should be raised, they have carefully connected the judges of both courts in the same sentence; they have said, 'the judges both of the supreme and inferior courts' thus coupling them inseparably together. You may cut the bands, but you can never untie them. With salutary caution they devised this clause to arrest the overbearing temper which they knew belonged to Legislative bodies. They do not say the judges, simply, but the judges of the supreme and inferior courts shall hold their offices during good behaviour. They say, therefore, to the Legislature, you may judge of the propriety, the utility, the necessity, of organizing these courts; but when established, you have done your duty. Anticipating the course of passion in future times, they say to the Legislature, you shall not disgrace yourselves by exhibiting the indecent spectacle of judges established by one Legislature removed by another. We will save you also from yourselves. We say these judges shall hold their offices; and surely, sir, to pretend that they can hold their office after the office is destroyed, is contemptible.

The framers of this Constitution had seen much, read much, and deeply reflected. They knew by experience the violence of popular bodies, and let it be remembered, that since that day many of the States, taught by experience, have found it necessary to change their forms of government to avoid the effects of that violence. The Convention contemplated the very act you now attempt. They knew also the jealousy and the power of the States; and they established for your and for their protection this most important department. I beg gentlemen to hear and remember what I say: It is this department alone, and it is the independence of this department, which can save you from civil war.

CCXCI. GOUVERNEUR MORRIS TO THE PRESIDENT OF THE NEW YORK SENATE.[1]

Washington, December 25th, 1802.

When this article was under consideration in the National Con-

---

[1] Jared Sparks, *Life of Gouverneur Morris*, III, 174–175.

vention it was observed, that every mode of electing the chief magistrate of a powerful nation hitherto adopted is liable to objection. The instances where violence has been used, and murders committed, are numerous; those, in which artifice and fraud have succeeded against the general wish and will, are innumerable. And hence it was inferred, that the mode least favorable to intrigue and corruption, that in which the unbiassed voice of the people will be most attended to, and that which is least likely to terminate in violence and usurpation, ought to be adopted. To impress conviction on this subject, the case of Poland was not unaptly cited. Great and ambitious Princes took part in the election of a Polish King. Money, threats, and force were employed; violence, bloodshed, and oppression ensued; and now that country is parcelled out among the neighboring Potentates, one of whom was but a petty Prince two centuries ago.

The evils, which have been felt in the present mode of election, were pointed out to the Convention; but, after due advisement, the other mode appeared more exceptionable. Indeed, if the present be changed, it might be better to abolish the office of Vice President, and leave to legislative provision the case of a vacancy in the seat of the first magistrate.

The Convention was aware, that every species of trick and contrivance would be practised by the ambitious and unprincipled. It was, therefore, conceived, that if in elections the President and Vice President were distinctly designated, there would generally be a vote given for one of only two rival Presidents, while there would be numerous candidates for the other office; because he, who wished to become President, would naturally connect himself with some popular man of each particular district, for the sake of his local influence, so that the Vice Presidency would be but as a bait to catch state gudgeons. The person chosen would have only a partial vote, be perhaps unknown to the greater part of the community, and probably unfit for those duties, which the death of a President might call on him to perform.

The Convention not only foresaw, that a scene might take place similar to that of the last presidential election, but even supposed it not impossible, that at some time or other a person admirably fitted for the office of President might have an equal vote with one totally unqualified, and that, by the predominance of faction in the House of Representatives, the latter might be preferred. This, which is the greatest supposable evil of the present mode, was calmly examined, and it appeared that, however prejudicial it might be at the present moment, a useful lesson would result from it for the future, to teach contending parties the importance of giving both votes to men fit for the first office.

CCXCII. ALEXANDER HAMILTON'S PROPOSALS IN THE FEDERAL CONVENTION.[1]

A subsequent misstatement of his course in the convention, drew forth a voluntary publication from Luther Martin. "That Hamilton in a most able and eloquent address, did express his general ideas upon the subject of government, and of that government which would in all human probability be most advantageous for the United States, I admit; but, in thus expressing his sentiments, he did not suggest a wish that any one officer of the government should derive his power from any other source than the people; that there should be in any instance an hereditary succession to office, nor that any person should continue longer than during good behaviour."

Another publication appeared, charging him with having proposed a monarchy to the convention. This was denied, and it was replied, that "he proposed a system composed of three branches, an assembly, a senate, and a governor. That the assembly should be elected by the people for three years, and that the senate and governor should be likewise elected by the people during good behaviour."

In answer to this publication, Hamilton published a full explanatory view of the propositions made by him.

"Thus the charge," he said, "is at length reduced to specific terms. Before it can be decided, however, whether this would be a *monarchy* or a *republic*, it seems necessary to settle the meaning of those terms. . . .

Were we to attempt a correct definition of a republican government, we should say, 'That is a republican government, in which both the executive and legislative organs are appointed by a popular election, and hold their offices upon a responsible and defeasible tenure.' If this be not so, then the tenure of good behavior for the judicial department is anti-republican, and the government of this state is not a republic; if the contrary, then a government would not cease to be republican because a branch of the legislature, or even the executive, held their offices during good behaviour. In this case the two *essential criteria* would still concur — the creation of the officer by a popular election, and the possibility of his removal in the course of law, by accusation before, and conviction by, a competent tribunal.

---

[1] J. C. Hamilton, *History of the Republic of the United States*, III, 341–343.

How far it may be expedient to go, even within the bounds of the theory, in framing a constitution, is a different question, upon which we pretend not to give our opinion. It is enough for the purpose of our assertion, if it be *in principle* correct. For even then, upon the statement of the 'citizen' himself, General Hamilton did not propose *a monarchy.*

Thus much too we will add, that whether General Hamilton at any stage of the deliberations of the convention did, or did not make the proposition ascribed to him, it is certain that his more deliberate and final opinion, adopted a moderate term of years for the duration of the office of president; as also appears by a plan of a constitution, *in writing now in this city*, drawn up by that gentleman in detail.

Whether the *first* system presented by Mr. Hamilton, was the one to which he gave a decided preference, it would be difficult to say, since we find him adopting and proposing *a different one* in the course of the sitting of the convention. It may have been that his opinion was nearly balanced between the two; nay, it is possible he may have really preferred the *one last proposed*, and that the former, like many others, was brought forward to make it the subject of discussion, and see what would be the opinions of different gentlemen on so momentous a subject. And, it is now repeated with confidence, that the *Virginia* delegation did vote for the most energetic form of government, and that Mr. Maddison was of the number. But we desire to be distinctly understood, that it was never intended, by mentioning this circumstance, to impeach the purity of Mr. Maddison's motives. To arraign the morals of any man, because he entertains a speculative opinion on government different from ourselves, is worse than arrogance. He who does so, must entertain notions in ethics extremely crude, and certainly unfavourable to virtue."

CCXCIII. OLIVER ELLSWORTH WOOD TO GEORGE BANCROFT.[1]

March 6th, 1880.

Oliver Ellsworth, Jr., Judge E's son, was his private secretary. In a manuscript of his,[2] O. E. Jr., about the early history of Windsor occurs the following:

"He, Judge E., told me one day as I was reading a Newspaper to him containing Eulogiums upon the late General Washington, which among other things ascribed to him the founding of the American Government to which Judge Ellsworth objected, saying President

---

[1] Bancroft MS., "Papers of Ellsworth," in Lenox Library, New York City.
[2] Stiles' *History of Ancient Windsor*, Vol. I, pp. 142–143, refers to the MS. of Oliver Ellsworth, Jr., as "written in 1802."

Washington's influence while in the Convention was not very great, at least not much as to the forming of the present Constitution of the United States in 1787, which Judge Ellsworth said was drawn by himself and five others, viz — General Alexander Hamilton, Gorham of Mass, deceased, James Wilson of Pennsylvania, Rutledge of South Carolina and Madison of Virginia."

CCXCIV. Timothy Pickering to Alexander Hamilton.[1]

Salem Massachusetts April 5th. 1803

The assertion of the Jacobins, that you are an aristocrat and a Monarchist, is not new: But at a late meeting of the *sect* in this town, one of their leaders declared "That Genl. Hamilton proposed (and it was understood, advocated) in the General Convention, that the President of the United States, and the Senators, should be chosen for life: that this was intended as an introduction to Monarchy: And that the Federalists of this county (Essex) had adopted Genl Hamiltons plan." Your friends here (who are the real friends of their country) are very desirous of knowing the fact — If you did not make and advocate that proposition, it will be useful to have it known and the Jacobin lie contradicted: If the proposition was offered in the Convention, your friends will know to what motives to ascribe it; and that, whatever form of Government you may have suggested for consideration, the public welfare, and the permanent liberty of your Country were not less the objects of pursuit with you, than with the other members of the Convention. Your answer will gratify me and your numerous friends here.[2] Such use only shall be made of it as you shall prescribe —

CCXCV. Alexander Hamilton to Timothy Pickering.[3]

New York Septr. 16th. 1803

I will make no apology for my delay in answering your inquiry some time since made,[4] because I could offer none which would satisfy myself. I pray you only to believe that it proceeded from any thing rather than want of respect or regard. I shall now comply with your request — The highest toned propositions, which I made in the Convention, were for a President, Senate and Judges during good behaviour — a house of representatives for three years. Though I would have enlarged the Legislative power of the General Govern-

---

[1] *Documentary History of the Constitution*, V, 268–269.
[2] For Hamilton's reply see CCXCV below.
[3] *Documentary History of the Constitution*, V, 284–286.
[4] See CCXCIV above.

ment, yet I never contemplated the abolition of the state Governments; but on the contrary, they were, in some particulars, constituent parts of my plan — This plan was in my conception conformable with the strict theory of a Government purely republican; the essential criteria of which are that the principal organs of the Executive and Legislative departments be elected by the people and hold their offices by a *responsible* and temporary or *defeasible* tenure — A vote was taken on the proposition respecting the Executive — Five states were in favour of it; among these Virginia; and though from the manner of voting, by delegations, individuals were not distinguished, it was morally certain, from the known situation of the Virginia members (six in number, two of them *Mason* and *Randolph* professing popular doctrines) that *Madison* must have concurred in the vote of Virginia — Thus, if I sinned against *Republicanism*, Mr. Madison was not less guilty — I may truly then say, that I never proposed either a President, or Senate for life, and that I neither recommended nor meditated the annihilation of the State Governments — And I may add, that in the course of the discussions in the Convention, neither the propositions thrown out for debate, nor even those voted in the earlier stages of deliberation were considered as evidences of a definitive opinion in the proposer or voter.   It appeared to me to be in some sort understood, that with a view to free investigation, experimental propositions might be made, which were to be received merely as suggestions for consideration — Accordingly, it is a fact, that my final opinion was against an Executive during good behaviour, on account of the increased danger to the public tranquilly incident to the election of a Magistrate of this degree of permanency.   In the plan of a Constitution, which I drew up while the convention was sitting, and which I communicated to Mr Madison about the close of it, perhaps a day or two after, the office of President has no greater duration than for three years — This plan was predicated upon these bases — 1.   That the political principles of the people of this country would endure nothing but republican government — 2. That in the actual situation of the country, it was in itself right and proper that the republican theory should have a fair and full trial — 3. That to such a trial it was essential that the Government should be so constructed as to give all the energy and stability reconcileable with the principles of that theory.   These were the genuine sentiments of my heart, and upon them I acted. I sincerely hope, that it may not hereafter be discovered, that through want of sufficient attention to the last idea, the experiment of Republican Government, even in this country, has not been as com·plete, as satisfactory and as decisive as could be wished —

CCXCVI. Timothy Pickering to General Hamilton.[1]

City of Washington Oct. 18. 1803

I duly received your letter of Septr. 16th. relative to the propositions you made in the General Convention.[2] It was obvious, that those, with the propositions of others, were presented for consideration and discussion, to be adopted or rejected, as a sense of the public safety should require; and by no means as the definitive opinions of the movers.

Dining in company with General Pinckney, as he passed thro' Salem, in September, I was asked, by one of the guests, some question concerning the nature of the propositions you made in the General Convention. I referred the enquirer to the General, who was a member. — He answered, That you proposed, that the Governors of the several states should be appointed by the President of the U States: But that Mr. Madison moved, and was seconded by his cousin Charles Pinckney, That all the laws of the individual states should be subject to the negative of the Chief Executive of the U. States. The General added, That he did not know which would be deemed the strongest measure.

CCXCVII. Jonathan Dayton in the United States Senate.[3]

October 24, 1803.

Mr. Dayton . . . said the great inducements of the framers of the Constitution to admit the office of Vice President was, that, by the mode of choice, the best and most respectable man should be designated; and that the Electors of each State should vote for one person at least, living in a different State from themselves.

CCXCVIII. Rufus King to Colonel Pickering [?].[4]

New York, Nov. 4, 1803.

Congress may admit new States, but can the Executive by treaty admit them, or, what is equivalent, enter into engagements binding Congress to do so? As by the Louisiana Treaty, the ceded territory must be formed into States, & admitted into the Union, is it understood that Congress can annex any condition to their admission? if not, as Slavery is authorized & exists in Louisiana, and the treaty engages to protect the property of the inhabitants, will not the present inequality, arising from the Representation of Slaves, be increased?

------

[1] *Documentary History of the Constitution*, V, 288–289.
[2] See above CCXCV.
[3] *Annals of Congress*, Eighth Congress, First Session, p. 21.
[4] C. R. King, *Life and Correspondence of Rufus King*, IV, 324–325.

As the provision of the Constitution on this subject may be regarded as one of its greatest blemishes, it would be with reluctance that one could consent to its being extended to the Louisiana States; and provided any act of Congress or of the several states should be deemed requisite to give validity to the stipulation of the treaty on this subject, ought not an effort to be made to limit the Representation to the free inhabitants only? Had it been foreseen that we could raise revenue to the extent we have done, from indirect taxes, the Representation of Slaves wd. never have been admitted; but going upon the maxim that taxation and Representation are inseparable, and that the Genl. Govt. must resort to direct taxes, the States in which Slavery does not exist, were injudiciously led to concede to this unreasonable provision of the Constitution.

CCXCIX.   Pierce Butler in the United States Senate.[1]

November, 23, 1803.

It never was intended by the Constitution that the Vice President should have a vote in altering the Constitution.

CCC.   Jonathan Dayton in the United States Senate.[2]

November 24, 1803.

Mr. Dayton believed it would come to this, that when the question came to be discussed, and the rights of the small States maintained, the large States would threaten us with their power. The same threats had been heard in the old Congress, but they were laughed at, for the votes of the States were equal; they were heard in the Convention, but they were spurned at, for the votes were equal there also; the large States must be cautious here, for in this body, too, the votes are equal. The gentleman had talked of a classification of States as a novelty, but he would ask if that gentleman pretended to be wiser than the Constitution? Look through that instrument from beginning to end, and you will not find an article which is not founded on the presumption of a clashing of interests. Was this fine process instituted for nothing? Was developing the election in particular circumstances in the House of Representatives intended for nothing? Was nothing meant by the provision of the Constitution, that no amendment should ever deprive the States of the equality of votes in this House? Yet, it was that jealous caution which foresaw the necessity of guarding against the encroachments of large States. The States, whatever was their relative magnitude,

---

[1] *Annals of Congress*, Eighth Congress, First Session, 82.
[2] *Annals of Congress*, Eighth Congress, First Session, 100–101.

were equal under the old Confederation, and the small States gave up a part of their rights as a compromise for a better form of government and security; but they cautiously preserved their equal rights in the Senate and in the choice of a Chief Magistrate. The same voice that now addresses you made the solemn claim, and declared there was no safety in association unless the small States were protected here. The warning was taken and you find in that part, as in all others, a classification governs every line of the Constitution.

CCCI. Gouverneur Morris to Henry W. Livingston.[1]

Morrisania, November 25th, 1803.

It is not possible for me to recollect with precision all that passed in the Convention, while we were framing the Constitution; and if I could, it is most probable, that a meaning may have been conceived from incidental expressions, different from that which they were intended to convey, and very different from the fixed opinions of the speaker. This happens daily.

I am very certain that I had it not in contemplation to insert a decree *de coercendo imperio* in the Constitution of America. Without examining whether a limitation of territory be or be not essential to the preservation of republican government, I am certain that the country between the Mississippi and the Atlantic exceeds by far the limits, which prudence would assign, if in effect any limitation be required. Another reason of equal weight must have prevented me from thinking of such a clause. I knew as well then, as I do now, that all North America must at length be annexed to us. Happy, indeed, if the lust of dominion stop there. It would, therefore, have been perfectly Utopian to oppose a paper restriction to the violence of popular sentiment in a popular government.[2]

CCCII. Jonathan Dayton in the United States Senate.[3]

November 29, 1803.

Every member who had spoken on this subject seemed to have admitted, by the very course and pointing of their arguments, even though they may have denied it in words, that this was really a question between great and small States, and disguise it as they would the question would be so considered out of doors. The privilege given by the Constitution extended to five, out of which the choice of President should be made; and why should the smaller,

---

[1] Jared Sparks, *Life of Gouverneur Morris*, III, 185.
[2] See CCCIV below.
[3] *Annals of Congress*, Eighth Congress, First Session, 109.

for whose benefit and security that number was given, now wantonly throw it away without an equivalent? As to the Vice President, his election had no influence upon the number, because the choice of President in the House of Representatives was as free and unqualified as if that subordinate office did not exist. Nay, he said, he would venture to assert that, even if the number five were continued, and the Vice Presidency entirely abolished, there would not be as great a latitude of choice as under the present mode, because those five out of whom the choice must eventually be made, were much more likely hereafter to be nominated by the great States, inasmuch as their electors would no longer be compelled to vote for a man of a different State. The honorable gentleman from Maryland (Mr. Smith) has said, he was not surprised that those who had seats in the old Congress, should perplex themselves with the distinctions; but he could tell that gentleman, that it was not in the old Congress he had learnt them, for there he had seen all the votes of the States equal, and had known the comparatively little State of Maryland controlling the will of the *Ancient Dominion*. It was in the Federal Convention that distinction was made and acknowledged; and he defied that member to do, what had been before requested of the honorable gentleman from Virginia, viz: to open the Constitution, and point out a single article, if he could, that had not evidently been framed upon a presumption of diversity (he had almost said, adversity) of interest between the great and small States.

CCCIII. Debate in the United States Senate.[1]

December 2, 1803.

Mr. Dayton . . . Although, however, no arguments can avail to prevent the adoption of an amendment of the Constitution so fatal to the interests of a great portion of the community, yet, as a member of one of the small States, I claim a right to mourn over our fallen honors and dignity, and as a Representative from New Jersey, I deem it my duty to enter my solemn protest against the injury done to our interests and our sovereignty. But a few years ago we were equal in votes and influence, though inferior in size and population, to the largest States. We consented to give up a certain portion of that influence for the general good, expressly retaining the other portion for our own protection and security. This instrument, the Constitution, which we have sworn to support, and are now about to deface, is the new compact which that temper produced. It is the

---

great plan of compromise between the jarring and contending interests of the great and small States. . . .

Through the whole course of this discussion great art has been used by some of the most zealous advocates of the measure, to divert us from the real ground of distinction upon which it rests, and to lull into a fatal repose the jealousies of the small States for their rights and sovereignty. A remark of the honorable gentleman from Maryland (Mr. Smith) tending to that object, ought not to escape animadversion. He averred that no law could be found in our statute book that was produced by a combination of States, and hence inferred that no such combination ought to be apprehended. The fact admitted, said Mr. D., and what does it prove? Not what the gentleman from Maryland would infer; not what he ought to prove, before the assertion and the argument can be worth anything to him on this occasion; not that such combination may not be feared if you alter the Constitution, but that it is impracticable as it now stands. The refined process established for electing a President was calculated to guard against that very danger, but if altered and destroyed, we shall soon be subject to that evil. Why is it, sir, that none of our laws are the result of any combination of States? The reason is to be found in the checks provided against it in the Constitution. Any project founded upon a coalition of the small states, originating as it must in the Senate, would be checked in the House of Representatives; and, on the other hand, any one resulting from any concert among the great States in the other branch, would and must be defeated in this. But if these wholesome checks could be done away, where could be found a security against so great a temptation? I thank God that the Convention were so enlightened as to place the equality of States in the Senate beyond the reach of amendment. . . .

Mr. Pickering . . . believed that one of the most embarrassing questions before the General Convention, respected the choice of the chief Executive officer. He had been informed by a member of that convention, the gentleman from Georgia on his left, (Mr. Baldwin), that it had been proposed and concluded that the President of the United States should be elected by Congress for seven years, and be ever after ineligible to that office; but that late in their session the present complex mode of electing the President and Vice President was proposed; that the mode was perfectly novel, and therefore occasioned a pause; but when explained and fully considered was universally admired, and viewed as the most pleasing feature in the Constitution. . . .

Mr. Butler . . . Whatever may be the sentiments or wishes of the individuals who vote, he could take upon him to say what was the intention of the Constitution; the framers of that instrument were apprehensive of an elective Chief Magistrate; and their views were directed to prevent the putting up of any powerful man; that for this end the States should choose two, and that as public suffrage would be common to both, that either would be alike eligible, and as it was totally immaterial which — he feared that the election of a single individual might exhibit all the evils which afflicted Poland.

. . . He thought that after a contention of seven years, with a party who he had thought abused their power, the time was come when a better course would have been pursued; he had conceived that principles would have prevailed, and that men would not absorb every consideration; but, with a member of the Convention, he would say, I hoped after so long a course of pork that our diet would be changed, but I find it is pork still with only a change of sauce.

CCCIV. Gouverneur Morris to Henry W. Livingston.[1]

Morrisania, December 4th, 1803.

A circumstance, which turned up in conversation yesterday, has led me again to read over your letter of the third of November, and my answer of the twenty-eighth.[2] I perceive now, that I mistook the drift of your inquiry, which is substantially whether the Congress can admit, as a new State, territory, which did not belong to the United States when the Constitution was made. In my opinion they cannot.

I always thought that, when we should acquire Canada and Louisiana it would be proper to govern them as provinces, and allow them no voice in our councils. In wording the third section of the fourth article, I went as far as circumstances would permit to establish the exclusion. Candor obliges me to add my belief, that, had it been more pointedly expressed, a strong opposition would have been made.

CCCV. Gouverneur Morris to Lewis R. Morris.[3]

Morrisania, December 10th, 1803.

That if, in the new legislature, as in the old Congress, each had been equally represented, and each preserved an equal vote, the sacrifice of rights would have been equal. But when it was admitted, that, in the National Legislature, the Representatives should be

---

[1] Jared Sparks, *Life of Gouverneur Morris*, III, 192.
[2] See CCCI above.
[3] Jared Sparks, *Life of Gouverneur Morris*, III, 193–194.

appointed according to the number of citizens, the sacrifice of rights was great, in proportion as the States were small. Thus Delaware, which had but one Representative out of sixty-five, retained only one sixty-fifth part of the nation's authority; and Virginia, which had ten Representatives, obtained two thirteenths. Wherefore, since each had previously enjoyed one thirteenth, Delaware lost four fifths of its power, and that of Virginia was doubled, so that Delaware, compared to Virginia, was reduced under the new establishment from equality to one tenth. It was moreover evident, that the course of population would daily increase this decided superiority of the great States. That, of course, if the whole power of the union had been *expressly* vested in the House of Representatives, the smaller States would never have adopted the Constitution. But in the Senate they retained an equal representation, and to the Senate was given a considerable share of those powers exercised by the old Congress. One important point, however, that of making war, was divided between the Senate and House of Representatives.

That the legislative authority, being thus disposed of, in a manner which appeared reasonable, care was taken to preserve to the Senate a feeble share of the ancient executive power of Congress, by their negative on their appointments to office.

That it was, however, certain the President and Vice President would be taken from the larger States, unless the smaller had some proportion of their original right preserved, and therefore the number of electors is compounded of the number of Senators, who represent States, and of the number of members who represent the people. Still, however, the chance was, from the superiority of numbers, so greatly in favor of the large States, that a farther right was reserved to the smaller ones by the particular mode of election. The necessity of voting for two persons as President, one of whom should not be of the State voting, and the right of choosing a President out of the five highest on the list, where no absolute choice was made by the electors, is perhaps the most valuable provision in favor of the small States, which can be found in the Constitution. By the former, the chance of an absolute choice is greatly diminished, and by the latter, the decision among five candidates is preserved to the States in their political capacity. It will, of course, under such circumstances, be always in the power of the smaller States to judge of the personal character of the parties presented for choice, and though natives and citizens of large States, one of them may possess such attachment to the country at large, and such a sense of justice, that from his administration there would be no danger of encroachment on their political rights.

CCCVI. Trial of Impeachment of Judge Chase before the
United States Senate.[1]

February 23, 1804.

Luther Martin, [attorney for the defence]:   . . . We have
been told by an honorable Manager, (Mr. Campbell,) that the
power of trying impeachments was lodged in the Senate with
the most perfect propriety; for two reasons — the one, that
the person impeached would be tried before those who had given
their approbation to his appointment to office. This certainly was
not the reason by which the framers of the Constitution were influenced, when they gave this power to the Senate. Who are the officers
liable to impeachment? The President, the Vice President, and all
civil officers of Government. In the election of the two first, the
Senate have no control, either as to nomination or approbation. As
to other civil officers, who hold their appointments during good
behavior, it is extremely probable that, though they were approved
by one Senate, yet from lapse of time, and the fluctuations of that
body, an officer may be impeached before a Senate, not one of whom
had sanctioned his appointment, not one of whom, perhaps, had he
been nominated after their election, would have given him their
sanction.

This, then, could not have been one of the reasons for thus
placing the power over *these* officers. But as a second reason, he
assigned, that, if any other inferior tribunal had been entrusted with
the trial of impeachments, the members might have an interest in
the conviction of an officer, thereby to have him removed in order
to obtain his place; but, that no Senator could have such inducement.   . . .

I see two honorable members of this Court, (Messrs. Dayton
and Baldwin,) who were with me in Convention, in 1787, who as
well as myself, perfectly knew why this power was invested in the
Senate. It was because, among all our speculative systems, it was
thought this power could no where be more properly placed, or
where it would be less likely to be abused. A sentiment, sir, in which
I perfectly concurred, and I have no doubt but the event of this
trial will show that we could not have better disposed of that power.

. . . Will it be pretended, for I have heard such a suggestion,
that the House of Representatives have a right to impeach *every citizen
indiscriminately*? For *what* shall they impeach them? For *any*
criminal act? Is the House of Representatives, then, to constitute
a grand jury to receive information of a criminal nature against all

---

[1] *Annals of Congress*, Eighth Congress, Second Session, 429–432, 436, 501–502.

our citizens, and *thereby to deprive them of a trial by jury?* This was never intended by the Constitution?

The President, Vice President, and other civil officers, can only be impeached. They only in that case are deprived of a trial by jury; they, when they accept their offices, accept them on those terms, and, as far as relates to the tenure of their offices, relinquish that privilege; they, therefore, cannot complain. Here, it appears to me, the framers of the Constitution have so expressed themselves as to leave not a single doubt on this subject.

In the first article, section the third, of the Constitution, it is declared that, judgment in all cases of impeachment, shall not extend further than removal from office, and disqualification to hold any office of honor, trust, or profit, under the United States. This clearly evinces, that no persons but those *who hold offices* are liable to impeachment. They are to lose their offices; and, having misbehaved themselves in such manner as to lose their offices, are, with propriety, to be rendered ineligible thereafter. . . .

The truth is, the framers of the Constitution, for many reasons, which influenced them, did not think proper to place the officers of Government in the power of the two branches of the Legislature, further than the tenure of their office. Nor did they choose to permit the tenure of their offices to depend upon the passions or prejudices of jurors. The very clause in the Constitution, of itself, shows that it was intended the persons impeached and removed from office might still be indicted and punished for the same offence, else the provision would have been not only nugatory, but a reflection on the enlightened body who framed the Constitution; since no person ever could have dreamed that a conviction on impeachment and a removal from office, in consequence, for one offence, could prevent the same person from being indicted and punished for another and different offence. . . .

I again repeat, that as the framers of the Constitution of the United States did not insert in their Constitution such a clause as is inserted in the constitution of Pennsylvania, it is the strongest proof that they did not mean a judge or other officer should be displaced by an address of any portion of the Legislature, but only according to the Constitutional provisions. . . .

February 25, [1804.]

Before I conclude, let me add one other proof that the framers of the Constitution never intended that juries should have any power to decide the law contrary to the instructions of the court, much less to decide upon the *constitutionality* of a law. By the 2d section of the 3d article of the Constitution of the United States, it is pro-

vided, that in all cases to which the judicial power applies, except
cases affecting Ambassadors, other public Ministers and Consuls,
and those in which a State is a party, "the Supreme Court shall
have '*appellate jurisdiction,* both as to law and fact, with such exceptions and under such regulations as Congress shall make.'"

Thus, therefore, it is in the power of Congress to authorize, in
all such cases, an *appeal* to the Supreme Court, *even as to the fact,*
from the *verdict of a jury,* and empower the Supreme Court to control the jury if they appear to have erred.   And such was the intention of the framers of the Constitution.

They assumed as a principle, that the interests of the State
governments and of the General Government would often be at
variance; that laws passed by the United States, the most wise and
salutary, might be very obnoxious to and unpopular in, some of the
states; judges holding their commissions under the respective States,
that is, the State judges, the framers of the Constitution would not,
therefore, entrust with the execution of the laws of the United States.
They also considered that, as far as juries were introduced, the jurors
would be citizens of the respective States wherein the trials should
be had, that they would, in consequence, probably partake of the
interests, the prejudices, and the passions prevailing in the State,
and therefore might decide contrary to the direction of the judges
appointed by the United States, and thereby prevent the due execution of their laws.   To obviate this, the Constitution has a provision for an appeal to the Supreme Court, even from the verdict
of such a jury.   Judge then whether the framers of the Constitution ever contemplated giving power to counsel to argue to jurors
*against the opinions of their judges, or juries to decide against such
opinions.*

————————

CCCVII. Jonathan Dayton in the United States Senate.[1]

March 19, 1804.

The provision of the Constitution had arisen from an experience of the necessity of establishing a permanent seat for the Government.   To avert the evils arising from a perpetual state of mutation,
and from the agitation of the public mind whenever it is discussed,
the Constitution had wisely provided for the establishment of a
permanent seat, vesting in Congress exclusive legislation over it.

—————

[1] *Annals of Congress,* Eighth Congress, First Session, 284.

CCCVIII. James Madison to Noah Webster.[1]

Washington, Oct. 12, 1804.

When the convention as recommended at Annapolis took place at Philadelphia, the deputies from Virginia supposed, that as that state had been first in the successive steps leading to a revision of the federal system, some introductory propositions might be expected from them. They accordingly entered into consultation on the subject, immediately on their arrival in Philadelphia, and having agreed among themselves on the outline of a plan, it was laid before the convention by Mr. Randolph, at that time governor of the state, as well as member of the convention. This project was the basis of its deliberations; and after passing through a variety of changes in its important as well as its lesser features, was developed and amended into the form finally agreed to.

CCCIX. Governor Lewis to —— .[2]

I will conclude this long epistle by a concise account of a conversation had with Hamilton, which may not be deemed uninteresting, since it exhibits him as a statesman who looked beyond the present to the far future interests of his country. It is well known that he never was in the habit of concealing or disguising his sentiments on the subject of government.

Openly denouncing, on all occasions, the assertion 'that the best administered was best', as a political heresy, maintaining the superior aptitude to a good administration of some systems over others, and giving the preference, abstractedly considered, to a well-balanced and limited monarchy, he was at the same time undeviating from the opinion that such a government could not be established in the United States, because a necessary ingredient in its composition, a privileged order, would be sought for in vain among a people whose favourite motto was 'Liberty and Equality.' When, therefore, the paragraphists of the day announced that he had proposed in the convention of the states a monarchic form of government, I was satisfied it was the effect of misconception or designed misrepresentation.

A second version, that he proposed a presidency for life, I thought more probable, but determined to suspend my opinion until I should have an interview with him. This was afforded to me soon after his return to the city of New-York. The monarchic proposition, as I expected, he explicitly denied. The other he admitted, with

[1] Hunt, *Writings of James Madison*, VII, 166.
[2] J. C. Hamilton, *History of the Republic of the United States*, III, 345–347.

the qualification, a president during good behaviour, or for a competent period, subject to impeachment, with an ineligibility forever thereafter.

"My reasons," he said, "were, an exclusion, as far as possible, of the influence of executive patronage in the choice of a chief magistrate, and a desire to avoid the incalculable mischief which must result from the too frequent elections of that officer." In conclusion, he made the following prophetic observation: "You nor I, my friend, may not live to see the day, but most assuredly it will come, when every vital interest of the state will be merged in the all-absorbing question of *who shall be the next* PRESIDENT?"

CCCX. EXTRACTS FROM YATES' SECRET PROCEEDINGS.[1]

"The representatives from the different states having met on the 25th of May, 1787, at the state-house in Philadelphia, General Washington having been unanimously placed in the chair, and Major Jackson, by the votes of all the states, except Pennsylvania, appointed secretary; the convention proceeded to read the powers given by the different states to their delegates, among which were particularly noticed the power of Delaware, which restrained its delegates from assenting to an abolition of the fifth article of the confederation, by which it is declared 'that each state shall have one vote.'

"The 28th, his excellency Governour Randolph, a member from Virginia, got up, and in a long and elaborate speech, showed the defects existing in the federal government then in existence, as totally inadequate to the peace, safety, and security of the confederacy, and the absolute necessity of a more energetick government.

"He closed these remarks with a set of resolutions, fifteen in number, which he proposed to the convention for their adoption, and as leading principles whereon to form a new government. He candidly confessed, they were not calculated for a federal government. He meant a strong consolidated union, in which the idea of states should be nearly annihilated.

---

[1] *A Letter to the Electors of President and Vice-President of the United States.* By a Citizen of New York [E. C. E. Genet] Accompanied with an extract of the secret debates of the Federal Convention, held in Philadelphia, in the year 1787, taken by Chief Justice Yates. New York Printed by Henry C. Southwick, No. 2 Wall Street, 1808.

These same extracts were reprinted in Hall's *American Law Journal*, 1813, IV, 563–570, from which the copy in the text is taken.

The interest attaching to this document is due to the garbling of the extracts in such a way as to make Madison responsible for an attempt to annihilate the state governments.

"Mr. C. Pinckney, a member from South Carolina, added, that he had reduced his ideas of a new government to a system which he read, and confessed that it was grounded on the same principle as those resolutions.

"The 2d of June, 1787, Mr. Randolph displayed the views of the plan of Virginia, with respect to the executive branch of the union. He proposed the establishment of a directory of three — dividing the states in three divisions, and taking an executive from each, chosen by the people and invested with extensive power. The idea was rejected by almost all the other delegates, and the principle of a single executive adopted.

"Mr. Madison, from Virginia, endeavoured to support the plan of that state in all its branches, and after a speech pronounced by Mr. Reed, to prove that the state-governments must sooner or later be at an end, and that therefore it was the duty of the convention to make the new national government as perfect as possible; he gave it as his opinion that when the convention agreed to the first resolve of having a national government it was then intended to *operate to the exclusion of federal government*, and that the more extensive the basis was made the greater would be the probability of duration, happiness and good order.

"Mr. James Wilson, from Pennsylvania, opposed the annihilation of the state-governments, and he represented that the freedom of the people and their local and internal good police depended on their existence in full vigour, and that it was not possible that a general government as despotick even as that of the Roman emperours, could be adequate to the government of North America.

"Mr. King, in the course of these debates, did not show himself averse to the state governments, but on the contrary, in opposition to Mr. Madison, who wanted the new constitution to be accepted by the people at large, he observed that as the people in every state, had tacitly agreed to a federal government, the legislature in every state had a right to confirm any alteration or amendment in it, and he supposed that the most eligible mode of approving the constitution would be a convention in every state.

"The 8th of June, Mr. C. Pinckney having moved that the National Legislature should have the power of negativing all the laws passed by the state legislatures, which they may deem improper, he was warmly supported by Mr. Madison, who insisted that the unlimited power in the general government of negativing the laws passed by the state-governments was absolutely necessary — that it was the only attractive principle which would retain the centrifugal force, and that without it planets will fly from their orbits.

"Mr. Gerry observed ironically, that he was not willing to take such a leap in the dark, and recommended to designate the power of the National Legislature, to which the negative ought to apply. Mr. Madison insisted, that nothing but the proposed system could restore the peace and harmony of the country. — Mr. Pinckney's motion was lost, seven states against, and Virginia, Pennsylvania, and Massachusetts for it.

"The 9th of June, the convention being engaged in the discussion of the right of suffrage by the number of inhabitants and not by states, Mr. Wilson having moved that the mode of representation of each ·of the states, ought to be from the number of its free inhabitants, and of every other description three-fifths to one free inhabitant, Mr. Madison agreed to fix accordingly, the standard of representation.

"On the question to fill up the blank of the duration of the first branch of the National Legislature, Mr. Madison was for three years, though Mr. Gerry was afraid that the people would be alarmed at that clause savouring of despotism.

"On the motion to fill up the blank of the duration of the second branch of the National Legislature, Mr. Madison was for seven years — and declared, that considering this branch *as a check on democracy*, it could not be too strong.

"A plan opposed to the Virginia plan supported by Mr. Madison, having been presented by Mr. Patterson, the purpose of which was merely to amend the old confederacy, Mr. Madison attempted to have it rejected in toto; but Mr. Hamilton prevented it, and said, that he was not in sentiment with either plan — that he supposed both might again be considered as federal plans, and being both fairly in committee be contracted so as to make a comparative estimate of the two.

"The 16th of June, Messrs. Lansing and Patterson, exposed all the inconveniences of the Virginia plan, and its dangerous tendency, after which Mr. Wilson stated as follows the two plans:

VIRGINIA

Proposes two branches in the Legislature.
The Legislative power derived from the people.
A directory first, and by amendment a single executive.
The legislature to legislate on all national concerns.
The legislature to have the power of negativing all the state-laws.

JERSEY

A single legislative body.
Legislative power derived from the state.

No provision for the executive.

The legislature to legislate only on limited objects.

The executive to have the power to compel obedience.

"Mr. Hamilton's ideas were materially dissimilar to those two plans, and in an eloquent speech stigmatized them both. He did not approve the total abolition of the state-governments, but he wanted to reduce them to simple corporations, with very limited powers. He did not think that a federal government could suit this country; but still he pretended that he was at a loss to know what could be substituted for it; a republican form of government could not be perfect. But he would hold it, however, unwise to change it, though he considered the British form of government as the best model that the world ever produced. He wished that the convention could go the utmost length of republican principles, and thought that they would not deviate from it if they made the chief magistrate of the republick elective for life, and gave him the power of negativing all laws, of making war and peace with the advice of the Senate, and the sole direction of all military operations, &c. &c. He proposed also to appoint in each state an officer, to have a negative on all state-laws. He confessed that his plan and that from Virginia were very remote from the ideas of the people, and he admitted explicitly, that the Jersey plan was nearest to their expectations. He described the Virginia plan as being nothing but democracy, checked by democracy, or *pork still, with a little change of the sauce!*

"Mr. Madison did not relish at all the criticism of Mr. Hamilton, and in a long speech vindicated the Virginia system, and attempted to demonstrate its superiority over the Jersey plan.

"On a motion of Mr. King, the Jersey plan was rejected as inadmissible, seven states against it and four for it, including New York.

"The Committee then rose and reported again the Virginia plan.

"Mr. Wilson, on the first clause, represented, that it was not a desirable object to annihilate the state-governments.

"Mr. Hamilton corrected what he had said against those governments; but intimated that they ought to be reduced to a smaller scale.

"Mr. King observed, that none of the states could properly be called sovereign, being deprived of several sovereign rights, such as making peace and war; and that in reality the consolidation had already taken place by the articles of confederation.

"To compromise matters between the Virginia and the Jersey plan, Dr. Johnson, proposed, that the state-governments should be preserved, with some modification; and that the states, in their legislative capacity, should have the right to appoint the second branch of the National Legislature, in order to unite them with the general government.

"Messrs. Ellsworth and Johnson, spoke in favour of that modification, and observed that the state-legislature were more competent to make a judicious choice than the people at large for the second branch, where wisdom and firmness were wanted.

"Mr. Madison opposed that idea, and for his part, he persisted to apprehend the greatest danger from the state-governments; and he declared, that he was always inclined for a general government emanating from the people at large, and independent of any local authority. Finding, however, that the majority was against him, he proposed a postponement; but it was negatived, and the clause proposed by Dr. Johnson adopted.

"Mr. Madison, on the sub-question relative to the organization of the Senate, and the rotation in that branch, said, we are acting in the same manner as the confederation; and by the vote already taken, the temper of the state-legislatures will transfuse into the Senate.

The 26th of June, on the question of the continuance of the senators in office, the same Mr. Madison gave it as his opinion that the longer the senators remain in office, the better it will be for the stability and permanency of the government. Several members thought differently on that question, and proved that the longer the senators resided at the seat of government, the more they would become naturalized to its climate and habits; that they might even settle there, and forget their own state and its interest.

"The 26th, on a motion to strike out the clause declaring, that the senators of the union should be ineligible to any state office; Mr. Madison opposed it, and observed, that Congress had heretofore depended on state-interest, and that the convention was now pursuing the same plan. He was contradicted by Messrs. Pinckney and Butler, who observed, that the state and general governments must act together; that the Senate, or second branch, was the aristocratick part of our government, and that they must be controled by the states — The motion for striking out was carried.

"The following motion was made by Mr. Lansing, of New York: — That the representation of the second branch be according to the articles of confederation, that is to say, on federal principles of equality. A debate took place, in which Mr. Madison, supporting the Virginia plan, declared that the representation must not be on federal principles, but relative to the number of inhabitants. He was answered by several members, but particularly by Dr. Johnson, who observed, that the idea of destroying the state-governments having been over-ruled, the convention was to frame a government, not for the people of America, but for the political societies called states, which compose the union; and that they must, therefore, have a voice in the second branch, if it was meant to preserve their existence, the people composing already the first branch.

"Mr. Madison rose up against Dr. Johnson in defence of the Virginia plan, and supported the following dogmas; "that there is a gradation of power in all societies, from the lowest corporation to the highest sovereign; that the states never possessed the right of sovereignty; that they were only corporations having the power of making by-laws; that they ought to be still more under the control of the general government, at least as much as they were under the King and British government.

"Mr. Hamilton, without adopting the ideas of Mr. Madison, spoke against the motion of Mr. Lansing, which was lost, four states for and six against it.

"Judge Ellsworth then moved, as an amendment to the plan of Virginia, that in the second branch each state should have an equal vote: equality of votes being the principle on which all confederacies are formed.

"Mr. Madison refused to compromise, and exclaimed that the greatest danger for the general government would arise from the opposition of the northern interest of the continent to the southern interest: alluding to certain expressions of several members leaning towards a division of the union, if Mr. Madison's plan was not modified.

"Dr. Franklin recommended a compromise on that subject, and made, in his usual way, the following comparison: "when a joiner wants to fit two boards, he takes off with his plane the uneven parts from each side, and thus they fit: let us do the same, said he, and as an expedient he proposed, that the Senate be elected by the states equally." But Mr. Madison, considering, that by his plan the Senate was to be the greatest engine by which all the state-laws could be reversed and annulled, would consent to no arrangement that would deprive the large states of having in both branches a weight proportioned to their population.

"Mr. King recommended moderation, and was in sentiment with those who wished the preservation of the state-governments. The general government, in his opinion, could be constructed so as to effect that object. The new constitution must be considered as a commission under which the general government is to act, and as such be the guardian of the state-rights. Five states voted for the amendment, and five against it, and one state was divided, and the amendment proposed by Mr. Elsworth was lost.

"The 2d of July, General Pinckney moved for a select committee, to take into consideration both branches of the legislature. Divers opinions were presented, among which Gouverneur Morris suggested the propriety of rendering the Senate an absolute aristocracy, representing large property combined with distinguished talents.

"Mr. Madison opposed the appointment of a committee — he thought it would delay the business; and if appointed from each state, would contain the whole strength of state-prejudices. A committee notwithstanding was appointed from each state.

"The 3d of July the committee met, and agreed on the following report, on condition that both propositions should generally be adopted:

1st. That in the first branch of the legislature, each of the states be allowed one member for every 40,000 inhabitants, of the description reported in the seventh resolution of the committee of the whole house — that each state not containing that number shall be allowed one member — That all bills for raising or apportioning money and for fixing salaries of the officers of government of the United States, shall originate in the first branch, and shall not be altered or amended by the second branch — and that no money shall be drawn from the publick treasury but in pursuance of appropriation to be originated by the first branch.

"2dly. That in the second branch of the legislature of states, each state shall have an equal vote.

"Mr. Madison said he restrained himself from animadverting on the report from the respect alone which he bore to the members of the committee."

Here end the notes of Mr. Yates. He left at that period, with Mr. Lansing, the convention. They had both uniformly opposed the Virginia system, and despairing of rendering any real service to their country, and to the state who had sent them, they left the convention and returned no more.

CCCXI. James Madison to Thomas Jefferson.[1]

Montpelier July 17. 1810.

Among the papers relating to the Convention of 1787. communicated to you, that copies in your hands might double the security agst. destructive casualties, was a delineation of Hamilton's plan of a Constitution in his own writing. On looking for it among the Debates &c, which were returned to me, this particular paper does not appear. I conclude therefore, that it had not then been copied, or was at the time in some separate situation. I am very sorry to trouble you on such a subject, but being under an engagement to furnish a Copy of that project, I must ask the favor of you to see whether it be not among your papers; & if so, to forward it by the mail. ————

CCCXII. John W. Eppes to James Madison.[1]

Cumberland Near Ca-Ira Nov. 1. 1810

My absence from Chesterfield prevented my receiving your letter until a few days since —

When the papers relating to the proceedings of the convention were put into my hands for the purpose of being copied Mr. Jefferson was very particular in his charge — I understood from him perfectly that it was a trust entirely confidential — The particular and confidential manner in which he entrusted them to me prevented my making the smallest extract from any part of them — and so careful was I of preserving sacred a document the importance of which to posterity I could not but feel, that I never suffered the papers to mix either with my own or any others entrusted to my care — They were kept in a Trunk in which whenever I ceased writing they were replaced and each original as copied was returned with the copy to Mr. Jefferson —

I remember among the papers one headed "plan of a constitution by Colo: Hamilton" — it was on smaller paper than your copy and fastened with a pin to one of the leaves of the original — Whether it was in your hand writing or Colo: Hamiltons I do not remember — I remember its features & that after copying it I fastened it again with the same pin — I still think that by turning carefully over the original you will find the paper fastened with a pin to one of the sheets —

I have but few papers remaining of those I possessed in Philadelphia — As you requested it I have carefully gone through them — I was certain however prior to the search that it was utterly impossible from the precautions I took in consequence of Mr Jeffersons charge that any paper belonging to your manuscript could be mixed with mine — For years after the copy was taken so far did I consider the whole transaction on my part confidential that I did not even consider myself at liberty to mention that a copy of the

[1] *Documentary History of the Constitution*, V, 294–296.

debates of the convention existed — It was not until within a few years since when I found the fact known to others through yourself and Mr. Jefferson that I thought it unnecessary to impose on myself the same rigid silence — I should as a member of the community deeply deplore the loss of the paper as it contains proof clear as holy writ that the idol of the Federal party was not a Monarchist in Theory merely, but the open zealous and unreserved advocate for the adoption of the monarchical system in this Country — Your evidence however of the fact will be sufficient with posterity; and that you will find among the originals a paper headed in the way I mention containing his plan of Government as suggested to you I have no doubt —   ⸺

CCCXIII. Gouverneur Morris to Robert Walsh.[1]

Morrisania, February 5th, 1811.

General Hamilton had little share in forming the Constitution. He disliked it, believing all Republican government to be radically defective. . . .

Those, who formed our Constitution, were not blind to its defects. They believed a monarchial form to be neither solid nor durable. They conceived it to be vigorous or feeble, active or slothful, wise or foolish, mild or cruel, just or unjust, according to the personal character of the Prince. . . .

Fond, however, as the framers of our national Constitution were of Republican government, they were not so much blinded by their attachment, as not to discern the difficulty, perhaps impracticability, of raising a durable edifice from crumbling materials. History, the parent of political science, had told them, that it was almost as vain to expect permanency from democracy, as to construct a palace on the surface of the sea.

But it would have been foolish to fold their arms, and sink into despondency, because they could neither form nor establish the best of all possible systems. They tell us in their President's letter of the seventeenth of September, 1787; 'The Constitution, which we now present, is the result of a spirit of amity, and of that mutual deference and concession, which the peculiarity of our political situation rendered indispensable.' It is not easy to be wise for all times; not even for the present, much less for the future; and those, who judge of the past, must recollect that when it was present, the present was future.

. . . It is necessary here to anticipate one of your subsequent

---

[1] Jared Sparks, *Life of Gouverneur Morris*, III, 260–265.

questions, 'What has been, and what is now the influence of the State governments on the Federal system? To obtain anything like a check on the rashness of democracy, it was necessary not only to organize the legislature into different bodies, (for that alone is a poor expedient,) but to endeavor that these bodies should be animated by a different spirit. To this end the States in their corporate capacity were made electors of the Senate; and so long as the State governments had considerable influence, and the consciousness of dignity, which that influence imparts, the Senate felt something of the desired sentiment, and answered in some degree the end of its institution. But that day is past.

This opens to our view a dilemma, which was not unperceived when the Constitution was formed. If the State influence should continue, the union could not last; and, if it did not, the utility of the Senate would cease. It was observed in the Convention at an early day, by one who had afterwards a considerable share of the business, when the necessity of drawing a line between national sovereignty and State independence was insisted on, 'that, if Aaron's rod could not swallow the rods of the Magicians, their rods would swallow his.' But it is one thing to perceive a dilemma, and another thing to get out of it. In the option between two evils, that which appeared to be the least was preferred, and the power of the union provided for. At present the influence of the general government has so thoroughly pervaded every State, that all the little wheels are obliged to turn according to the great one.

CCCXIV. Gouverneur Morris to Timothy Pickering.[1]

Morrisania, December 22d, 1814.

While I sat in the Convention, my mind was too much occupied by the interests of our country to keep notes of what we had done. Some gentlemen, I was told, passed their evenings in transcribing speeches from shorthand minutes of the day. They can speak positively on matters, of which I have little recollection. My faculties were on the stretch to further our business, remove impediments, obviate objections, and conciliate jarring opinions. All which I can now do is to ask myself what I should do were questions stated anew; for, in all probability, what I should now do would be what I then did, my sentiments and opinions having undergone no essential change in forty years.

Propositions to countenance the issue of paper money, and the consequent violation of contracts, must have met with all the oppo-

---

[1] Jared Sparks, *Life of Gouverneur Morris*, III, 322–323.

sition I could make. But, my dear Sir, what can a history of the Constitution avail towards interpreting its provisions. This must be done by comparing the plain import of the words, with the general tenor and object of the instrument. That instrument was written by the fingers, which write this letter. Having rejected redundant and equivocal terms, I believed it to be as clear as our language would permit; excepting, nevertheless, a part of what relates to the judiciary. On that subject, conflicting opinions had been maintained with so much professional astuteness, that it became necessary to select phrases, which expressing my own notions would not alarm others, nor shock their selflove, and to the best of my recollection, this was the only part which passed without cavil.

CCCXV. GOUVERNEUR MORRIS TO MOSS KENT.[1]

Morrisania, January 12th, 1815.

When, in framing the Constitution, we restricted so closely the power of government over our fellow citizens of the militia, it was not because we supposed there would ever be a Congress so mad as to attempt tyrannizing over the people or militia, by the militia. The danger we meant chiefly to provide against was, the hazarding of the national safety by a reliance on that expensive and inefficient force. An overweening vanity leads the fond many, each man against the conviction of his own heart, to believe or affect to believe, that militia can beat veteran troops in the open field and even play of battle. This idle notion, fed by vaunting demagogues, alarmed us for our country, when in the course of that time and chance, which happen to all, she should be at war with a great power.

Those, who, during the Revolutionary storm, had confidential acquaintance with the conduct of affairs, knew well that to rely on militia was to lean on a broken reed. We knew, also, that to coop up in a camp those habituated to the freedom and comforts of social life, without subjecting them to the strict observation and severe control of officers regularly bred, would expose them to such fell disease, that pestilence would make more havoc than the sword. We knew that when militia were of necessity called out, and nothing but necessity can justify the call, mercy as well as policy requires, that they be led immediately to attack their foe. This gives them a tolerable chance; and when superior in number, possessing, as they must, a correct knowledge of the country, it is not improbable that their efforts may be crowned with success. To that end, never-

---

[1] Jared Sparks, *Life of Gouverneur Morris*, III, 328-329.

theless, it is proper to maintain in them a good opinion of themselves, for despondency is not the road to victory.

But to rely on undisciplined, ill-officered men, though each were individually as brave as Caesar, to resist the well-directed impulse of veterans, is to act in defiance of reason and experience. We flattered ourselves, that the constitutional restriction on the use of militia, combined with the just apprehension of danger to liberty from a standing army, would force those entrusted with the conduct of national affairs, to make seasonable provision for a naval force. We were not ignorant of the puerile notions entertained by some on that subject, but we hoped, alas! we vainly hoped, that our councils would not be swayed by chattering boys, nor become the sport of senseless declamation. _____

CCCXVI. Thomas Jefferson to John Adams.[1]

Monticello, August 10, 1815.

Do you know that there exists in manuscript the ablest work of this kind ever yet executed, of the debates of the constitutional convention of Philadelphia in 1788? The whole of every thing said and done there was taken down by Mr. Madison, with a labor and exactness beyond comprehension.

CCCXVII. Gouverneur Morris to W. H. Wells.[2]

Morrisania, February 24th, 1815.

The Constitution, I think, intended that certain offices should be held at the President's pleasure. It is unquestionably an abuse to *create* a vacancy in the recess of the Senate, by turning a man out of office, and then filling it as a vacancy that has *happened*. . . . Shortly after the Convention met, there was a serious discussion on the importance of arranging a national system of sufficient strength to operate, in despite of State opposition, and yet not strong enough to break down State authority. I delivered on that occasion this short speech. 'Mr President; if the rod of Aaron do not swallow the rods of the Magicians, the rods of the Magicians will swallow the rod of Aaron.'

You will ask, perhaps, how, under such impressions, I could be an advocate of the Federal Constitution. To this I answer, first, that I was warmly pressed by Hamilton to assist in writing the Federalist, which I declined. Secondly, that nothing human can be perfect. Thirdly, that the obstacles to a less imperfect system were

---

[1] T. J. Randolph, *Memoir, Correspondence, etc., of Thomas Jefferson*, IV, 268.
[2] Jared Sparks, *Life of Gouverneur Morris*, III, 338–339.

insurmountable. Fourthly, that the Old Confederation was worse. And, fifthly, that there was no reason, at that time, to suppose our public morals would be so soon and so entirely corrupted. Mr. Mason, a delegate from Virginia, constantly inveighing against Aristocracy, labored to introduce Aristocratic provisions. Some of them might have been wholesome, but they would have been rejected by public feeling, in the form proposed, and if modified to render them acceptable, by detracting proportionately from executive authority, which was his plan, we should have risked less indeed from the whelming flood of Democracy, but we should have had a President unable to perform the duties of his office. Surrounded by difficulties, we did the best we could; leaving it with those who should come after us to take counsel from experience, and exercise prudently the power of amendment, which we had provided.

CCCXVIII. Rufus King in the United States Senate.[1]

March 20, 1816.

The States may now severally direct the manner of choosing their own Electors; it is proposed that the manner shall be prescribed by the Constitution. This, Mr. K[ing] thought would be an important change, and the only change suggested in the Constitution which he deemed an improvement. He thought he might venture to say, that if there was any part of the Constitution deemed by its framers and advocates to be better secured than any other against the enterprises which have since occurred, it was the very provision on the subject of elections to the Presidency. The idea was, that the action of that particular agency which has since controlled it, was as much displaced by the Constitutional plan of election of President and Vice President, as could possibly be devised. The opinion had been that all undue agency or influence was entirely guarded against; that the men selected by the people from their own body would give their votes in such a manner as that no opportunity would be afforded for a combination, to change the freedom and popular character which naturally belonged to the electoral bodies. Such had been the idea of the nation at the time of the adoption of the Constitution. We all know, said he, the course which this thing has taken. The election of a President of the United States is no longer that process which the Constitution contemplated. In conformity with the original view of the authors of that instrument, I would restore, as thoroughly as possible, the freedom of election to the people . . . It was with the people the Con-

------

[1] *Annals of Congress*, Fourteenth Congress, First Session, 216.

stitution meant to place the election of the Chief Magistrate, that being the source least liable to be corrupt.

CCCXIX. AUTOBIOGRAPHY OF WILLIAM FEW.[1]

At the time appointed for the meeting of the Convention at Philadelphia, a full representation of all the States convened in the State House, and chose G. Washington for their President, and commenced their business, but they had to encounter incalculable difficulties. The modification of the State Rights, the different interests and diversity of opinions seemed for some time to present obstacles that could not be surmounted. After about three weeks deliberation and debating, the Convention had serious thoughts of adjourning without doing anything. All human efforts seemed to fail. Doctor Franklin proposed to appoint a chaplain and implore Divine assistance, but his motion did not prevail. It was an awful and critical moment. If the Convention had then adjourned, the dissolution of the union of the States seemed inevitable. This consideration no doubt had its weight in reconciling clashing opinions and interests. It was believed to be of the utmost importance to concede to different opinions so far as to endeavor to meet opposition on middle ground, and to form a Constitution that might preserve the union of the States. On that principle of accommodations the business progressed, and after about three months' arduous labor, a plan of Constitution was formed on principles which did not altogether please anybody, but it was agreed to be the most expedient that could be devised and agreed to.

CCCXX. JAMES MADISON TO JOHN QUINCY ADAMS.[2]

Montpelier Decr. 23. 1817

The best answer I can give to your communication on the subject of his wish for a copy of the Journal of the Convention, is to state the circumstance, that at the close of the Convention, the question having arisen what was to be done with the Journal & other papers, and it being suggested that they ought to be either destroyed or deposited in the Custody of the Presidt. it was determined that they should remain in his hands subject only to the orders of the

---

[1] Printed in *Magazine of American History*, VII, 352–353, from MS. in the possession of William Few Chrystie. There is no date ascribed to the MS. The last date in it is October, 1816. In the opening paragraph he refers to the "approach of age." As he was born in 1748, he would have been sixty-eight years old in 1816, so the MS. is probably of about that date.

[2] *Documentary History of the Constitution*, V, 298–299.

National Legislature. — Whether a publication of them ought to be promoted, as having a useful tendency, you will probably be better able to decide, on a perusal of the document than one who can not take the same abstract view of the subject.

CCCXXI. JAMES MADISON TO JAMES MONROE.[1]

Montpellier, Dec. 27, 1817.

These considerations remind me of the attempts in the Convention to vest in the Judiciary Dept. a qualified negative on Legislative *bills*. Such a Controul, restricted to Constitutional points, besides giving greater stability & system to the rules of expounding the Instrument, would have precluded the question of a Judiciary annulment of Legislative *Acts*.

CCCXXII. RUFUS KING IN THE UNITED STATES SENATE.[2]

January 12, 1818.

Without adverting to the several branches of the executive power, for the purpose of distinguishing the cases in which it is exclusively vested in the President, from those in which it is vested in him jointly with the Senate, it will suffice on this occasion to observe that, in respect to foreign affairs, the President has no exclusive binding power, except that of receiving the Ambassadors and other foreign Ministers, which, as it involves the decision of the competence of the power which sends them, may be an act of this character; to the validity of all other definitive proceedings in the management of the foreign affairs, the Constitutional advice and consent of the Senate are indispensable.

In these concerns the Senate are the Constitutional and the only responsible counsellors of the President. And in this capacity the Senate may, and ought to, look into and watch over every branch of the foreign affairs of the nation; they may, therefore, at any time call for full and exact information respecting the foreign affairs, and express their opinion and advice to the President respecting the same, when, and under whatever other circumstances, they may think such advice expedient.

There is a peculiar jealousy manifested in the Constitution concerning the power which shall manage the foreign affairs, and make treaties with foreign nations. Hence the provision which requires the consent of two-thirds of the Senators to confirm any compact with a foreign nation that shall bind the United States;

---

[1] G. Hunt, *Writings of James Madison*, VIII, 406.
[2] *Annals of Congress*, Fifteenth Congress, First Session, I, 106–107.

thus putting it in the power of a minority of the Senators, or States to control the President and a majority of the Senate: a check on the Executive power to be found in no other case.

To make a treaty includes all the proceedings by which it is made; and the advice and consent of the Senate being necessary in the making of treaties, must necessarily be so, touching the measures employed in making the same. The Constitution does not say that treaties shall be concluded, but that they shall be made, by and with the advice and consent of the Senate: none therefore can be made without such advice and consent; and the objections against the agency of the Senate in making treaties, or in advising the President to make the same, cannot be sustained, but by giving to the Constitution an interpretation different from its obvious and most salutary meaning.

To support the objection, this gloss must be given to the Constitution, "that the President shall make treaties, and by and with the advice and consent of the Senate ratify the same." That this is, or could have been intended to be the interpretation of the Constitution, one observation will disprove. If the President alone has power to make a treaty, and the same be made pursuant to the powers and instructions given to his Minister, its ratification follows as a matter of course, and to refuse the same would be a violation of good faith; to call in the Senate to deliberate, to advise, and to consent to an act which it would be binding on them to approve and ratify, will, it is presumed, be deemed too trivial to satisfy the extraordinary provision of the Constitution, that has been cited.

_____

CCCXXIII. RESOLUTION OF CONGRESS.[1]

Resolved by the Senate and House of Representatives of the United States of America, in Congress assembled, That the journal of the convention which formed the present constitution of the United States, now remaining in the office of the Secretary of State, and all acts and proceedings of that convention, which are in the possession of the government of the United States, be published under the direction of the President of the United States, . . . And that one thousand copies thereof be printed, of which one copy shall be furnished to each member of the present Congress, and the residue shall remain subject to the future disposition of Congress.

APPROVED, March 27, 1818.

_____

[1] United States, *Statutes at Large,* III, 475.

CCCXXIV. James Madison to John Quincy Adams.[1]

Montpellier, Novr. 2, 1818.

I have received your letter of the 22 ult: and enclose such extracts from my notes relating to the two last days of the Convention, as may fill the chasm in the Journals, according to the mode in which the proceedings are recorded.[2]

Col. Hamilton did not propose in the Convention any plan of a Constitution. He had sketched an outline which he read as part of a speech; observing that he did not mean it as a proposition, but only to give a more correct view of his ideas.

Mr. Patterson regularly proposed a plan which was discussed & voted on.

I do not find the plan of Mr. Charles Pinkney among my papers.

CCCXXV. John Quincy Adams: Memoirs.[3]

[1818, November] 19th.   Major William Jackson, of Philadelphia, called upon me; . . . As he was the Secretary of the Convention of 1787, which formed the Constitution of the United States, I asked him to call again at my office this day, to look at the journals and papers deposited by President Washington in the Department of State, 19th March, 1796, and, if he could, to explain the condition in which they are. He did accordingly call, and looked over the papers, but he had no recollection of them which could remove the difficulties arising from their disorderly state, nor any papers to supply the deficiency of the missing papers. He told me that he had taken extensive minutes of the debates in the Convention, but, at the request of President Washington, had promised they should never be published during his own life, which he supposed had been a loss to him of many thousand dollars. He told me how he had been chosen Secretary to the Convention, for which place W. T. Franklin and Beckley were his competitors, and said that by far the most efficient member of the Convention was Mr. Madison; that Mr. Hamilton took no active part in it, and made only one remarkable speech. He also said Mr. King had told him he could perhaps supply some papers relating to the Convention, of which he was a member.

---

[1] G. Hunt, *Writings of James Madison*, VIII, 416.
[2] Omitted here as containing nothing new.
[3] Vol. IV, pp. 174–175.

CCCXXVI. Charles Pinckney to John Quincy Adams.[1]

In Charleston, Dec. 30th 1818.

Sir

On my return to this City as I promised I examined carefully all the numerous notes & papers which I had retained relating to the federal Convention — among them I found several rough draughts of the Constitution I proposed to the Convention — although they differed in some measure from each other in the wording & arrangement of the articles — yet they were all substantially the same — they all proceeded upon the idea of throwing out of View the attempt to amend the existing Confederation (then a very favourite idea of a number) & proceeding de novo — of a Division of the Powers of Government into legislative executive & judicial & of making the Government to operate directly upon the People & not upon the States — — My Plan was substantially adopted in the sequel except as to the Senate & giving more power to the Executive than I intended — the force of Vote which the small & middling states had in the Convention prevented our obtaining a proportional representation in more than one branch & the great power given to the President was never intended to have been given to him while the Convention continued in that patient & coolly deliberative situation in which they had been for nearly the whole of the preceding five months of their session,[2] nor was it until within the last week or ten days that almost the whole of the Executive Department was altered — I can assure you as a fact that for more than Four months & a half out of Five The power of exclusively making treaties, appointing public Ministers & judges of the supreme Court was given to the Senate after numerous debates & considerations of the subject both in Committee of the whole & in the house — this I not only aver but can prove by printed Documents in my possession to have been the case — & should I ever have the pleasure to see you & converse on this subject will state to you some things relative to this business that may be new and perhaps surprising to you — the Veil of secrecy from the Proceedings of the Convention being removed by Congress & but very few of the members alive would make disclosures now of the scenes there acted less improper than before — With the aid of the journal & the numerous notes & memorandums I have preserved should now be in my power to give a View of the almost insuperable difficulties the Convention had to encounter & of the conflicting opinions of the members & I believe I should have at-

---

[1] *Documentary History of the Constitution*, I, 309–311.

[2] For Madison's criticism of this and the following statements see CCCLXXXII and CCCLXXXIII below.

tempted it had I not always understood Mr Madison intended it — he alone I believed possessed & retained more numerous & particular notes of their proceedings than myself — I will thank you sir to do me the honour to send me or to get the President to direct a copy of the Journal of the Convention to be sent me as also of the Secret Journals of Congress should it be considered not improper in me to make the request — —

I have already informed you I have several rough draughts of the Constitution I proposed & that they are all substantially the same differing only in words & the arrangement of the Articles — at the distance of nearly thirty two Years it is impossible for me now to say which of the 4 or 5 draughts I have was the one but enclosed I send you the one I believe was it — I repeat however that they are substantially the same differing only in form & unessentials — — It may be necessary to remark that very soon after the Convention met I changed & avowed candidly the change of my opinion on giving the power to Congress to revise the State Laws in certain cases & in giving the exclusive Power to the Senate to declare War thinking it safer to refuse the first altogether & to vest the latter in Congress —

[Endorsed:] Pinckney Charles, December 30. 1818.
Recd January 6 1819.

with a Copy of the Dft of his Constitutions proposed in the federal Convention.

_____

CCCXXVII. Rufus King in the Senate of the United States.[1]

By the articles of confederation the common treasury was to be supplied by the several states, according to the value of the lands, with the houses and improvements thereon, within the respective states. From the difficulty in making this valuation, the old congress were unable to apportion the requisitions for the supply of the general treasury, and were obliged to propose to the states an alteration of the articles of confederation, by which the whole number of free persons, with three-fifths of the slaves contained in the respective states, should become the rule of such apportionment of the taxes. A majority of the states approved of this alteration, but some of them disagreed to the same; and for want of a practicable rule of apportionment, the whole of the requisitions of taxes made by congress during the revolutionary war, and afterwards, up to the establishment of the constitution of the United States, were merely provisional, and subject to the revision and correction

_____

[1] C. R. King, *Life and Correspondence of Rufus King*, VI, 697–700. No date is attached to this document, but it is probably a speech of March, 1819.

as soon as such rules should be adopted. The several states were credited for their supplies, and charged for the advances made to them by congress; but no settlement of their accounts could be made for the want of a rule of appointment, until the establishment of the constitution.

When the general convention that formed the constitution took this subject into their consideration, the whole question was once more examined, and while it was agreed that all contributions to the common treasury should be made according to the ability of the several states, to furnish the same, the old difficulty recurred in agreeing upon a rule whereby such ability should be ascertained, there being no simple standard by which the ability of individuals to pay taxes, can be ascertained. A diversity in the selection of taxes has been deemed requisite to their equalization: between communities, this difficulty is less considerable, and although the rule of relative numbers would not accurately measure the relative wealth of nations, in states, in the circumstances of the United States, whose institutions, laws and employments are so much alike, the rule of number is probably as nearly equal as any other simple and practical rule can be expected to be, (though between the old and new states its equity is defective,) these considerations, added to the approbation which had already been given to the rule, by a majority of the states, induced the convention to agree, that direct taxes should be apportioned among the states, according to the whole number of free persons, and three-fifths of the slaves which they might respectively contain. . . .

The present House of Representatives consists of 181 members, which are apportioned among the states in a ratio of one representative for every thirty-five thousand federal numbers, which are ascertained by adding to the whole number of free persons, three-fifths of the slaves. . . . Thus while 35,000 free persons are requisite to elect one representative in a state where slavery is prohibited, 25,559 free persons in Virginia may and do elect a representative — so that five free persons in Virginia have as much power in the choice of representatives to Congress, and in the appointment of presidential electors, as seven free persons in any of the states in which slavery does not exist.

This inequality in the appointment of representatives was not misunderstood at the adoption of the constitution; but as no one anticipated the fact that the whole of the revenue of the United States would be derived from indirect taxes (which cannot be supposed to spread themselves over the several states according to the rule for the apportionment of direct taxes), but it was believed that

a part of the contribution to the common treasury would be apportioned among the states by the rule for the apportionment of representatives — the states in which slavery is prohibited, ultimately,
though with reluctance, acquiesced in the disproportionate number
of representatives and electors that was secured to the slave-holding
states.   The concession was, at the time, believed to be a great one,
and has proved to have been the greatest which was made to secure
the adoption of the constitution.

Great, however, as this concession was, it was definite, and its
full extent was comprehended.   It was a settlement between the
original thirteen states.   The considerations arising out of their
actual condition, their past connection, and the obligation which
all felt to promote a reformation in the federal government, were
peculiar to the time and to the parties; and are not applicable to
the new states which congress may now be willing to admit into the
Union.

The equality of rights, which includes an equality of burdens, is
a vital principle in our theory of government, and its jealous preservation is the best security of public and individual freedom; the departure from this principle in the disproportionate power and influence
allowed to the slave-holding states, was a necessary sacrifice to the
establishment of the constitution.   The effect of this concession
has been obvious in the preponderance which it has given to the
slave-holding states, over the other states.   Nevertheless, it is an
ancient settlement, and faith and honor stand pledged not to disturb it.   But the extension of this disproportionate power to the new
states would be unjust and odious.   The states whose power would
be abridged, and whose burdens would be increased by the measure,
cannot be expected to consent to it; and we may hope that the other
states are too magnanimous to insist on it.

CCCXXVIII.   John Quincy Adams: Memoirs.[1]

[1819, May] 13th, IV. 30.   Four hours of this morning again
engaged in examining the journals of the Convention of 1787, and
the sheets of yeas and nays, which I compared with the questions in
the journals.   This comparison has led me to the conclusion that
the journals ought to be published with notes.   The journals were
loosely kept, and the yeas and nays only show the votes of States,
and not of individual members.   There are some questions on the
face of the journals, and which were evidently taken by yeas and
nays, but which are omitted in the sheets, and some on the sheets

---

of yeas and nays which were not entered upon the journals. The journal never mentions by whom a motion was made, but it often appears upon the sheets of yeas and nays. I must revise and superintend the publication of this volume myself. . . .

16th. The remainder of the day I was employed in delving into the Convention journals and papers. They are to be printed by T. Wait, at Boston, which I now find to be the cause of some inconvenience. From the examination of all the papers that I have collected, it is apparent that the usefulness of the publication will depend altogether upon their arrangement. When the Convention adjourned, they passed a resolution that their journals and papers, which had been kept by Major William Jackson, their Secretary, should be delivered to their President, Washington, to be kept by him, subject to the future order of Congress, after the Constitution should go into operation. Washington kept them until the 19th day of March, 1796, when he deposited them in the Department of State, where they have remained till this time. A resolution of Congress of 27th March, 1818, directed that they, together with the secret journals of the old Congress, and their foreign correspondence to the Peace of 1783, except such parts of it as the President may think it improper now to publish, should be printed under the direction of the President. He devolved this duty upon me; but the books and papers deposited by President Washington were so imperfect, and in such disorder, that to have published them, as they were, would have given to the public a book useless and in many respects inexplicable.

It happened that General Bloomfield, a member of Congress from New Jersey, as executor of the will of David Brearley, one of the members of the Convention, had come to the possession of his papers, among which were several very important ones relating to the proceedings of the Convention. He sent them all to me. The journal itself was imperfect, and the journal of the last two days was wanting. I wrote to President Madison, and obtained from him the means of completing it.[1] There was a plan of Constitution mentioned on the journals as having been proposed by Mr. Charles Pinckney, of South Carolina. I wrote to him and obtained a copy of that.[2] With all these papers suitably arranged, a correct and tolerably clear view of the proceedings of the Convention may be presented; but there is one great and irreparable defect. In the printed journals of the old Congress the yeas and nays appear nominally as well as

---

[1] See CCCXXIII above, and also CCCXXIX below.
[2] See CCCXXVI above.

by States, although the votes were taken by States. So they were in the Convention; but the yeas and nays show only the votes of the States, and not of the individual members.[1] Copies of the journals, and of most of the papers, were sent last autumn to Wait, at Boston, but I had not time to examine and collate the whole, and I did not dare trust the task to any one else. I have now nearly gone through it, and have settled the mode of publication, but to carry it into effect I must have again all the papers that have been sent to Wait. There is also one paper wanting, to be collected from the resolutions scattered over the journal from 19th June to 23d July, 1787. I began this day to prepare it.

17th. Wrote to Wait, and continued plodding upon the journals and papers of the Convention. Proceeded with the draft of the supplementary paper, and made out a list of the members who attended. . . .

20th. Continued at home the preparations for the publication of the Convention journals. . . .

22d. Still occupied upon the journals of the Convention, upon which I begin to think I shall spend too much time and descend too much to minutiae. . . .

26th. Finished the first draft of an advertisement to be prefixed to the publication of the journals of the Convention of 1787, and the list of the members. . . .

31st. Resumed the task of arranging the Convention journals and papers for publication. Among the papers transmitted to me by General Bloomfield was a plan of the Constitution proposed by Alexander Hamilton, of New York. At the time when the Constitution was offered to the people, the principal objections against it were that it had too many features of, or, as Patrick Henry expressed it with more energy than elegance, "an awful squinting towards," monarchy. This objection was much urged during the whole Administration of President Washington and that of his immediate successor, my father. When Hamilton, as Secretary of the Treasury, came in conflict with Jefferson, as Secretary of State, and consequently with Virginia, this plan of his was often alluded to in party discussions as a proof of his propensities to monarchy. As it has never yet been published, it became a subject of extraordinary curiosity, and will again excite some public attention on the publication of the journals. The only remarkable facts in it are, that he proposes the tenure of office of the Chief Executive Magis-

---

[1] Hamilton stated that in voting "individuals were not distinguished." See CCXCV above

trate and of the members of the Senate should be during good behavior, which of course, in ordinary cases, is a tenure for life,   It
seems Hamilton did not formally propose this as a plan for discussion, but read it as part of a speech.   I wrote this evening to Mr.
Madison and enquired on what debate, and when, the speech was
delivered, with a view to printing the paper immediately after the
journal of the day.[1] . . .

[June] 2d.   After the journal of yesterday, I resumed the arrangement and preparation of the Convention journals for the press.   It
is truly 'in tenui labor' — the longer I brood upon it the more pro-
tracted and unprofitable the toil becomes.   The journals and papers
were very loosely and imperfectly kept.   They were no better than
the daily minutes from which the regular journal ought to have
been, but never was, made out.   I find, on close inspection, a great
number of questions, some of them important, entered on the loose
sheets of yeas and nays, and not entered at all in the journal.   I
intend to have them all inserted at their respective places on the
journal.   There was one loose page of yeas and nays of which I
had been able to make nothing until this morning, when I found it
must have been the Secretary's first expedient for taking down the
yeas and nays.   The page is divided into thirteen columns, with
the initials of the names of the States, from New Hampshire to
Georgia, numbered from 1 to 13, at the head of the page; but no
space is left on the page either to enter the question upon which the
yeas and nays were taken, or the sum of the votes on either side.
There are five successive sets of the yeas and nays taken, not summed
up, and with nothing to indicate upon what questions they were
taken.   After these, the New Hampshire column is divided into
two, upon which the sum of the yeas and nays on each question is
entered, to the bottom of the page; and in eight instances, at intervals, the question upon which the question was taken is crowded into
the square of the Rhode Island column.   New Hampshire and
Rhode Island were the two States not then represented, and their
columns of course remained in blank after the yeas and nays were
taken and entered.   There are twenty-eight questions, the result of
which appears upon this page; on the other side of which is the name
of Mr. Gorham, with seven strokes of the pen, and that of Mr.
Rutledge, with one, by their side.   This is obviously the noting down
of the vote by ballot for a Chairman to the committee of the whole.
The vote for Rutledge was probably Gorham's.   He was at that time
President of the old Congress.   Before Jackson, the Secretary, had

[1] See CCCXXIX below.

got half down this page, he found the want of spaces to enter the questions upon which the votes were taken, and the sums of the yeas, nays, and divided votes. The sheets that he afterwards used were divided accordingly; but he entered upon them only a part of the questions that he had already taken down on the first experimental page. He began with the question of a "Single Executive," which is the seventeenth on the experimental page. He entered it the first, on his book of yeas and nays, and then resorted again to loose sheets, after filling two of which he returned to his book, leaving blank pages apparently to have the contents of the loose sheets copied upon them. The single Executive question, being the first entered upon the book, was the first with which I found the corresponding question in the journal of the committee of the whole; and from that time I traced the questions in the journals and collated them with the questions on the sheets of yeas and nays. This left, however, a number of questions on the journal of the committee of the whole, taken before that of the single Executive, but not noted either on the book or on the loose sheets of yeas and nays, and the yeas and nays upon which I had hitherto been unable to trace. This morning I first noticed the coincidence of the "Single Executive" question, the first entered upon the book and the seventeenth upon the experimental page; and immediately inferred that the sixteen preceding votes entered upon the page must have been upon the questions taken in the committee of the whole before that upon the single Executive. But to which question each set of the yeas and nays applied was yet to be traced out, the ninth and fifteenth of the questions being the only two entered upon the Rhode Island square. I traced the questions on the journal to the first taken in the committee of the whole, apparently by yeas and nays, and was collating it with the first vote on the experimental page of yeas and nays, when the consumption of time in this petty research brought it to past noon, and I was obliged to break it off and go to my office.

CCCXXIX. JAMES MADISON TO JOHN QUINCY ADAMS.[1]

Montpellier June 7, 1819.

I have duly received your letter of the 1st: instant. On recurring to my papers for the information it requests, I find that the speech of Col: Hamilton in the Convention of 1787, in the course of which he read a sketch of a plan of Government for the U. States, was delivered on the 18th of June; the subject of debate being a resolu-

---

[1] G. Hunt, *Writings of James Madison*, VIII, 438.

tion proposed by Mr. Dickinson "that the Articles of Confederation ought to be revised and amended so as to render the Government of the U. States adequate to the exigencies, the preservation, and the prosperity of the Union." _____

CCCXXX. James Madison to John Quincy Adams.[1]

Montpellier June 27, 1819

I return the list of yeas and nays in the Convention with the blanks filled according to your request, as far as I could do it, by tracing the order of the yeas and nays and their coincidences with those belonging to successive questions in my papers. In some instances, the yeas and nays in the list, corresponding with those on more questions than one did not designate the particular question on which they were taken; and of course did not enable me to fill the blanks. In other instances, as you will find by the paper formerly sent you, there are questions noted by me, for which the list does not contain yeas and nays. I have taken the liberty as you will see of correcting one or two slips in the original list or in the copy: and I have distinguished the days on which the several votes passed.[2]

_____

CCCXXXI. James Madison to Judge Roane.[3]

September 2, 1819.

It could not but happen, and was foreseen at the birth of the Constitution, that difficulties and differences of opinion might occasionally arise in expounding terms and phrases necessarily used in such a charter; more especially those which divide legislation between the general and local governments; and that it might require a regular course of practice to liquidate and settle the meaning of some of them. But it was anticipated, I believe, by few, if any, of the friends of the Constitution, that a rule of construction would be introduced as broad and pliant as what has occurred.[4] And those who recollect, and, still more, those who shared in what passed in the State conventions, through which the people ratified the Constitution, with respect to the extent of the powers vested in Congress, cannot easily be persuaded that the avowal of such a rule would not have prevented its ratification.

---

[1] Library of Congress, Madison Papers.
[2] [Endorsed:] To J. Q. Adams Secy of State answering his of June 18.
[3] *Letters and other Writings of James Madison*, III, 145.
[4] Decision of Supreme Court in McCulloch *vs.* Maryland.

CCCXXXII. James Madison to Robert Walsh.[1]

Montpellier Novr. 27—1819

Your letter of the 11th was duly recd, and I should have given it a less tardy answer, but for a succession of particular demands on my attention, and a wish to assist my recollections, by consulting both manuscript & printed sources of information on the subjects of your enquiry. Of these, however, I have not been able to avail myself, but very partially.

As to the intention of the framers of the Constitution in the clause relating to "the migration and importation of persons &c" the best key may perhaps be found in the case which produced it. The African trade in slaves had long been odious to most of the States, and the importation of slaves into them had been prohibited. Particular States however continued the importion, and were extremely averse to any restriction on their power to do so. In the Convention the former States were anxious, in framing a new constitution, to insert a provision for an immediate and absolute stop to the trade. The latter were not only averse to any interference on the subject; but solemnly declared that their constituents would never accede to a constitution containing such an article. Out of this conflict grew the middle measure providing that Congress should not interfere until the year 1808; with an implication, that after that date, they might prohibit the importation of slaves into the States then existing, & previous thereto, into the States not then existing. Such was the tone of opposition in the States of S. Carolina & Georgia, & such the desire to gain their acquiescence in a prohibitory power, that on a question between the epochs of 1800 & 1808, the States of N. Hampshire, Massatts. & Connecticut, (all the eastern States in the convention); joined in the vote for the latter, influenced however by the collateral motive of reconciling those particular States to the power over commerce & navigation; against which they felt, as did some other States, a very strong repugnance. The earnestness of S. Carolina & Georgia was further manifested by their insisting on the security in the V. article, against any amendment to the Constitution affecting the right reserved to them, & their uniting with the small states who insisted on a like security for their equality in the Senate.

But some of the States were not only anxious for a constitutional provision against the introduction of Slaves. They had scruples against admitting the term "Slaves" into the Instrument. Hence the descriptive phrase "migration or importation of persons"; the term migration allowing those who were scrupulous of acknowledg-

---

[1] *Documentary History of the Constitution*, V, 303–306.

ing expressly a property in human beings, to view *imported* persons as a species of emigrants, whilst others might apply the term to foreign malefactors sent or coming into the country. It is possible tho' not recollected, that some might have had an eye to the case of freed blacks, as well as malefactors.

But whatever may have been intended by the term "migration" or the term "persons", it is most certain, that they referred, exclusively, to a migration or importation from other countries into the U. States; and not to a removal, voluntary or involuntary, of Slaves or freemen, from one to another part of the U. States. Nothing appears or is recollected that warrants this latter intention. Nothing in the proceedings of the State conventions indicates such a construction there.* Had such been the construction it is easy to imagine the figure it would have made in many of the states, among the objections to the constitution, and among the numerous amendments to it proposed by the state conventions,† not one of which amendments refers to the clause in question. . . .

* The debates of the Pennsylvania convention contain a speech of Mr. Wilson (Dec. 3— 1787) who had been a member of the general convention, in which, alluding to the clause tolerating for a time, the further importation of Slaves, he consoles himself "with the hope that in a few years it would be prohibited altogether; observing that in the mean time, the new "States which were to be formed would be under the controul of Congress *in this particular,* and slaves would never be introduced among them." In another speech on the day following and alluding to the same clause, his words are "yet the lapse of a few years & Congress will have power to *exterminate* slavery within our borders." How far the language of Mr. W. may have been accurately reported is not known. The expressions used, are more vague & less consistent than would be readily ascribed to him. But as they stand, the fairest construction would be, that he considered the power given to Congress, to arrest the importation of Slaves as "laying a foundation for banishing slavery out of the country; & tho at a period more distant than might be wished, producing the same kind of gradual change which was pursued in Pennsylvania" (see his Speech page 90 of the Debates). By this "change" after the example of Pennsylvania, he must have meant a change by the other States influenced by that example, & yielding to the general way of thinking & feeling, produced by the policy of putting an end to the importation of slaves. He could not mean by "banishing slavery," more than by a power "to exterminate it," that Congress were authorized to do what is literally expressed.[1]

† In the Convention of Virga. the opposition to the Constitution comprized a number of the ablest men in the State. Among them were Mr Henry & Col Mason, both of them distinguished by their acuteness, and anxious to display unpopular constructions. One of them Col Mason had been a member of the general convention, and entered freely into accounts of what passed within it. Yet neither of them, nor indeed any of the other opponents, among the multitude of their objections, and far fetched interpretations, ever hinted, in the debates on the 9th Sect of Ar. 1. at a power given by it, to prohibit an interior migration of any sort. The meaning of the Secn. as levelled against migrations or importations from abroad was not contested.

[1] See CCCXXXIII below.

It falls within the scope of your enquiry, to state the fact, that there was a proposition in the convention, to discriminate between the old and new States, by an article in the Constitution declaring that the aggregate number of representatives from the states thereafter to be admitted, should never exceed that of the states originally adopting the Constitution. The proposition happily was rejected. The effect of such a descrimination, is sufficiently evident.

CCCXXXIII. James Madison to Robert Walsh.[1]

Montpr. Jany 11. 1820.

It is far from my purpose to resume a subject on which I have perhaps already exceeded the proper limits. But having spoken with so confident a recollection of the meaning attached by the Convention to the term "migration" which seems to be an important hinge in the argument, I may be permitted merely to remark that Mr. Wilson,* with the proceedings of that assembly fresh on his mind, distinctly applies the term to persons coming to the U. S. *from abroad*, (see his printed speech p. 59): and that a consistency of the passage cited from the Federalist with my recollections, is preserved by the discriminating term "*beneficial*" added to "voluntary emigrations from Europe to America"

* See letter of J. M. to Mr. Walsh of Novr. 27. 1819 [CCCXXXII above.]

CCCXXXIV. Walter Lowrie of Pennsylvania in the United States Senate.[2]

January 20, 1820.

In the Constitution it is provided that "the migration or importation of such persons as any of the States now existing shall think proper to admit, shall not be prohibited by the Congress prior to the year 1808, but a tax," etc. In this debate it seems generally to be admitted, by gentlemen on the opposite side, that these two words are not synonomous; but what their meaning is, they are not so well agreed. One gentlemen tells us, it was intended to prevent slaves from being brought in by land; another gentleman says, it was intended to restrain Congress from interfering with emigration from Europe.

These constructions cannot both be right. The gentlemen who have preceded me on the same side, have advanced a number of pertinent arguments to settle the proper meaning of these words.

---

[1] *Documentary History of the Constitution*, V, 306.
[2] *Annals of Congress*, Sixteenth Congress, First Session, I, 202–203.

I, sir, shall not repeat them. Indeed, to me, there is nothing more dry and uninteresting, than discussions to explain the meaning of single words. In the present case, I will only refer to the authority of Mr. Madison and Judge Wilson, who were both members of the Convention, and who gave their construction to these words, long before this question was agitated. Mr. Madison observes, that, to say this clause was intended to prevent emigration does not deserve an answer. And Judge Wilson says, expressly, it was intended to place the new States under the control of Congress, as to the introduction of slaves. The opinion of this latter gentleman is entitled to peculiar weight. After the Convention had labored for weeks on the subject of representation and direct taxes — when those great men were like to separate without obtaining their object, Judge Wilson submitted the provision on this subject, which now stands as a part of your Constitution. Sir, there is no man, from any part of the nation, who understood the system of our Government better than him; not even excepting Virginia, from whence the gentleman from Georgia (Mr. Walker) tells us we have all our great men.

CCCXXXV. James Madison to President Monroe.[1]

Monpr. Feby. 10. 1820.

I have been truly astonished at some of the doctrines and declarations to which the Missouri question has led; and particularly so at the interpretation put on the terms "migration or importation &c". Judging from my own impressions I shd. deem it impossible that the memory of any one who was a member of the Genl. Convention, could favor an opinion that the terms did not *exclusively* refer to migration & importation, *into the U. S.* Had they been understood in that Body in the sense now put on them, it is easy to conceive the alienation they would have there created in certain States: and no one can decide better than yourself the effect they would had in the State conventions, if such a meaning had been avowed by the advocates of the Constitution. If a suspicion had existed of such a construction, it wd. at least have made a conspicuous figure among the amendments proposed to the Instrument.

CCCXXXVI. Charles Pinckney in the House of Representatives.[2]

February 14, 1820.

Among the reasons which have induced me to rise, one is to ex-

---

[1] *Documentary History of the Constitution*, V, 307.
[2] *Annals of Congress*, Sixteenth Congress, First Session II, 1311–1318.

press my surprise. Surprise, did I say? I ought rather to have said, my extreme astonishment, at the assertion I heard made on both floors of Congress, that, in forming the Constitution of the United States, and particularly that part of it which respects the representation on this floor, the Northern and Eastern States, or, as they are now called, the non-slaveholding States, have made a great concession to the Southern, in granting to them a representation of three-fifths of their slaves; that they saw the concession was a very great and important one at the time, but that they had no idea it would so soon have proved itself of such consequence; that it would so soon have proved itself to be by far the most important concession that had been made. They say, that it was wrung from them by their affection to the Union, and their wish to preserve it from dissolution or disunion; that they had, for a long time, lamented they had made it; and that, if it was to do over, no earthly consideration should again tempt them to agree to so unequal and so ruinous a compromise. . . .

It was, sir, for the purpose of correcting this great and unpardonable error; unpardonable, because it is a wilful one, and the error of it is well known to the ablest of those who make it; of denying the assertion, and proving that the contrary is the fact, and that the concession, on that occasion, was from the Southern and the Northern States, that, among others, I have risen.

It is of the greatest consequence that the proof I am about to give should be laid before this nation; for, as the inequality of representation is the great ground on which the Northern and Eastern States have always, and now more particularly and forcibly than ever, raised all their complaints on this subject, if I can show and prove that they have not even a shadow of right to make pretences or complaints; that they are as fully represented as they ought to be; while we, the Southern members, are unjustly deprived of any representation for a large and important part of our population, more valuable to the Union, as can be shown, than any equal number of inhabitants in the Northern and Eastern States can, from their situation, climate, and productions, possibly be. If I can prove this, I think I shall be able to show most clearly the true motives which have given rise to this measure; to strip the thin, the cobweb veil from it, as well as the pretended ones of religion, humanity, and love of liberty; and to show, to use the soft terms the decorum of debate oblige me to use, the extreme want of modesty in those who are already as fully represented here as they can be, to go the great lengths they do in endeavoring, by every effort in their power, public and private, to take from the Southern and Western States, which are already so greatly and unjustly deprived of an important part of the representation, a still greater share; to endeavor to establish the first precedent, which extreme rashness and temerity have ever presumed, that Congress has a right to touch the question and legislate on slavery; thereby shaking the property in them, in the Southern and Western States, to its very foundation, and making an attack which, if successful, must convince them that the Northern and Eastern States are their greatest enemies; that they are preparing measures for them which even Great Britain in the heat of the Revolutionary War, and when all her passions were roused by hatred and revenge to the highest pitch never ventured to inflict upon them. Instead of a course like this, they ought, in my judgment, sir, to be highly pleased with their present situation; that they are fully represented, while we have lost so great a share of our representation; they ought, sir, to be highly pleased at the dexterity and management of their members in the Convention, who obtained for them this great advantage; and, above all, with the moderation and forbearance with which the Southern and Western States have always borne their many bitter provocations on this subject, and now bear the open, avowed, and, by many of the ablest men among them, undisguised attack on our most valuable rights and properties. . . .

The revolt of New Jersey and Pennsylvania accelerated the new Constitution. On a motion from Virginia the Convention met at Philadelphia, where, as you will find from the Journals, we were repeatedly in danger of dissolving without doing any thing; that body being equally divided as to large and small States, and each having a vote, and the small States insisting most pertinaciously, for near six weeks, on equal power in both branches — nothing but the prudence and forbearance of the large States saved the Union. A compromise was made, that the small States and large should be equally represented in the Senate, and proportionally in the House of Representatives. I am now arrived at the reason for which I have, sir, taken the liberty to make these preliminary remarks. For, as the true motive for all this dreadful clamor throughout the Union, this serious and eventful attack on our most sacred and valuable rights and properties, is, to gain a fixed ascendency in the representation in Congress; and, as the only flimsy excuse under which the Northern and Eastern States shelter themselves, is, that they have been hardly treated in the representation of this House, and that they have lost the benefit of the compromise they pretend was made, and which I shall most positively deny, and show that nothing like a compromise was ever intended.

By all the public expenses being borne by indirect taxes, and not direct, as was expected; if I can show that all their pretensions and claims are wholly untrue and unfounded, and that while they are fully represented, they did, by force, or something like it, deprive us of a rightful part of our representation, I shall then be able to take the mask from all their pretended reasons and excuses, and show this unpardonable attack, this monster, in its true and uncovered hideousness. . . .

If, as no doubt, you will in future confine your imports to the amount of your exports of native products, and all your revenue is to be, as it is now, raised by taxes or duties on your imports, I ask you who pays the expense, and who, in fact, enables you to go on with your Government at all, and prevents its wheels from stopping? I will show you by the papers which I hold in my hand. This, sir, is your Secretary of the Treasury's report, made a few weeks ago, by which it appears that all the exports of native products, from Maine to Pennsylvania, inclusive, for the last year, amounted to only about eighteen millions of dollars; while those among the slave-holding States, to the Southward of Pennsylvania, amounted to thirty-two millions or thereabouts, thereby enabling themselves, or acquiring the right, to import double as much as the others, and furnishing the Treasury with double the amount the Northern and Eastern States do. And here let me ask, from whence do these exports arise? By whose hands are they made? I answer, entirely by the slaves; and yet these valuable inhabitants, without whom your very government could not go on, and the labor of two or three of whom in the Southern States is more valuable to it than the labor of five of their inhabitants in the Eastern States, the States owning and possessing them are denied a representation but for three-fifths on this floor, while the whole of the comparatively un-productive inhabitants of the Northern and Eastern States are fully represented here. Is it just — is it equal? And yet they have the modesty to complain of the representation, as unjust and unequal; and that they have not the return made them that they expected, by taxing the slaves, and making them bear a proportion of the public burdens. . . .

Before I proceed to the other parts of this question, I have thus endeavored to give a new view of the subject of representation in this House; to show how much more the Eastern and Northern States are represented than the Southern and Western; . . .

The supporters of the amendment contend that Congress have the right to insist on the prevention of involuntary servitude in Missouri; and found the right on the ninth section of the first article, which says, "the migration or importation of such persons as the

States now existing may think proper to admit, shall not be prohibited by the Congress prior to the year 1808, but a tax or duty may be imposed on such importation not exceeding ten dollars."

In considering this article, I will detail, as far as at this distant period is possible, what was the intention of the Convention that formed the Constitution in this article. The intention was, to give Congress a power, after the year 1808, to prevent the importation of slaves either by land or water from other countries. The word *import*, includes both, and applies wholly to slaves. Without this limitation, Congress might have stopped it sooner under their general power to regulate commerce; and it was an agreed point, a solemnly understood compact, that, on the Southern States consenting to shut their ports against the importation of Africans, no power was to be delegated to Congress, nor were they ever to be authorized to touch the question of slavery; that the property of the Southern States in slaves was to be as sacredly preserved, and protected to them, as that of land, or any other kind of property in the Eastern States were to be to their citizens.

The term, or word, migration, applies wholly to free whites; in its Constitutional sense, as intended by the Convention, it means "voluntary change of servitude", from one country to another. The reasons of its being adopted and used in the Constitution, as far as I can recollect, were these; that the Constitution being a frame of government, consisting wholly of delegated powers, all power, not expressly delegated, being reserved to the people or the States, it was supposed, that, without some express grant to them of power on the subject, Congress would not be authorized ever to touch the question of migration hither, or emigration to this country, however pressing or urgent the necessity for such a measure might be; that they could derive no such power from the usages of nations, or even the laws of war; that the latter would only enable them to make prisoners of alien enemies, which would not be sufficient, as spies or other dangerous emigrants, who were not alien enemies, might enter the country for treasonable purposes, and do great injury; that, as all governments possessed this power, it was necessary to give it to our own, which could alone exercise it, and where, on other and much greater points, we had placed unlimited confidence; it was, therefore, agreed that, in the same article, the word migration should be placed; and that, from the year 1808, Congress should possess the complete power to stop either or both, as they might suppose the public interest required; the article, therefore, is a *negative pregnant*, restraining for twenty years, and giving the power after.

The reasons for restraining the power to prevent migration hither for twenty years, were, to the best of my recollection, these: That, as at this time, we had immense and almost immeasurable territory, peopled by not more than two millions and a half of inhabitants, it was of very great consequence to encourage the emigration of able, skilful, and industrious Europeans. The wise conduct of William Penn, and the unexampled growth of Pennsylvania, were cited. It was said, that the portals of the only temple of true freedom now existing on earth should be thrown open to all mankind; that all foreigners of industrious habits should be welcome, and none more so than men of science, and such as may bring to us arts we are unacquainted with, or the means of perfecting those in which we are not yet sufficiently skilled — capitalists whose wealth may add to our commerce or domestic improvements; let the door be ever and most affectionately open to illustrious exiles and sufferers in the cause of liberty; in short, open it liberally to science, to merit, and talents, wherever found, and receive and make them your own. That the safest mode would be to pursue the course for twenty years, and not, before that period, put it at all into the power of Congress to shut it; that, by that time, the Union would be so settled, and our population would be so much increased, we could proceed on our own stock, without the farther accession of foreigners; that, as Congress were to be prohibited from stopping the importation of slaves to settle the Southern States, as no obstacle was to be thrown in the way of their increase and settlement for that period, let it be so with the Northern and Eastern, to which, particularly New York and Philadelphia, it was expected most of the emigrants would go from Europe: and it so happened, for, previous to the year 1808, more than double as many Europeans emigrated to these States, as of Africans were imported into the Southern States.

. . . I will only mention here, as it is perfectly within my recollection, that the power was given to Congress to regulate the commerce by water between the States, and it being feared, by the Southern, that the Eastern would, whenever they could, do so to the disadvantage of the Southern States, you will find, in the 6th section of the 1st article, Congress are prevented from taxing exports, or giving preference to the ports of one State over another, or obliging vessels bound from one State to clear, enter, or pay duties in another; which restrictions, more clearly than any thing else, prove what the power to regulate commerce among the several States means.

CCCXXXVII. James Madison to John Quincy Adams.[1]

Montpr. June 13 1820

I have recd. & return my thanks for your polite favor accompanying the Copy of the printed Journal of the Federal Convention transmitted in pursuance of a late Resolution of Congress.

In turning over a few pages of the Journal, which is all I have done a casual glance caught a passage which erroneously prefixes my name, to ye proposition made on the 7th. day of Sepr. for making a Council of six members a part of the Executive branch of the Govt. The proposition was made by Col: George Mason one of the Virga. delegates, & seconded by Dr. Franklin. I cannot be mistaken in the fact: For besides my recollection which is sufficiently distinct on the subject, my notes contain the observations of each in support of the proposition.[2]

As the original journal according to my extract from it, does not name the mover of ye propn the error, I presume must have had its source in some of the extrinsic communications to you; unless indeed it was found in some of the separate papers of the Secretary of the Convention: or is to be ascribed to a copying pen. The degree of symphony in the two names Madison & Mason may possibly have contributed to the substitution of the one for the other.

This explanation having a reference to others as well as myself, I have thought it wd. be neither improper nor unacceptable.

CCCXXXVIII. Charles Pinckney in the House of Representatives.[3]

February 13, 1821.

Mr. Speaker, there are many reasons which make it incumbent on me not to suffer this question, which I consider the final one on the acceptance or rejection of the constitution of Missouri, and her admission into the Union, to pass without presenting my views on the subject to the House. These reasons are, the importance of the question itself, the great interest the State I represent, in part, has in it, and, not among the least, the frequent calls made upon me in this House, and references in the other, as to the true meaning of the second section of the fourth article of the Constitution of the United States, which it appears, from the Journal of the General Convention that formed the Constitution, I first proposed in that body. . . .

---

[1] *Documentary History of the Constitution*, V, 307–308

[2] Crossed out: "The only part I bore in it, was merely that of promoting a fair consideration of the object of my colleague."

[3] *Annals of Congress*, Sixteenth Congress, Second Session, pp. 1129, 1134.

I say it is not, in my judgment, unconstitutional, for the following reasons, in which I mean briefly to answer to the call that has been made upon me: It appears by the Journal of the Convention that formed the Constitution of the United States, that I was the only member of that body that ever submitted the plan of a constitution completely drawn in articles and sections; and this having been done at a very early state of their proceedings, the article on which now so much stress is laid, and on the meaning of which the whole of this question is made to turn, and which is in these words: "the citizens of each State shall be entitled to all privileges and immunities in every State," having been made by me, it is supposed I must know, or perfectly recollect, what I meant by it. In answer, I say, that, at the time I drew that constitution, I perfectly knew that there did not then exist such a thing in the Union as a black or colored citizen, nor could I then have conceived it possible such a thing could have ever existed in it; nor, notwithstanding all that has been said on the subject, do I now believe one does exist in it.

CCCXXXIX. James Madison to Joseph Gales.[1]

Montpr. Aug. 26. 1821

I thank you for your friendly letter of the 20th. inclosing an extract from notes by Judge Yates, of debates in the Convention of 1787, as published in a N. Y. paper.* The letter did not come to hand till yesterday.

If the extract be a fair sample, the work about to be published will not have the value claimed for it. Who can believe that so palpable a mistatement was made on the floor of the Convention, as that the several States were political Societies, *varying* from the *lowest* Corporation to the *highest Sovereign;* or that the States had vested *all* the essential rights of sovereignty in the Old Congress? This intrinsic evidence alone ought to satisfy every candid reader of the extreme incorrectness of the passage in question. As to the remark that the States ought to be under the controul of the Genl. Govt. at least as much as they formerly were under the King & B. parliament, it amounts as it stands when taken in its presumable meaning, to nothing more than what actually makes a part of the Constitution; the powers of Congs. being much greater, especially on the great points of taxation & trade than the B. Legislature were ever permitted to exercise.

* Commercial Advertizer, Aug: 18, 1821

---

[1] *Documentary History of the Constitution*, V, 308–309.

Whatever may have been the personal worth of the 2 delegates from whom the materials in this case were derived, it cannot be unknown that they represented the strong prejudices in N. Y. agst. the object of the Convention which was among other things to take from that State the important power over its commerce and that they manifested, untill they withdrew from the Convention, the strongest feelings of dissatisfaction agst. the contemplated change in the federal system and as may be supposed, agst. those most active in promoting it. Besides misapprehensions of the ear therefore, the attention of the note taker wd naturally be warped, as far at least as, an upright mind could be warped, to an unfavorable understanding of what was said in opposition to the prejudices felt.

CCCXL. James Madison to Thomas Ritchie.[1]

Montpelr. Sepr. 15 1821.
(Confidential)

I have recd. yours of the 8th. instant on the subject of the proceedings of the convention of 1787.

It is true as the public has been led to understand, that I possess materials for a pretty ample view of what passed in that Assembly. It is true also that it has not been my intention that they should for ever remain under the veil of secresy. Of the time when it might be not improper for them to see the light, I had formed no particular determination. In general it had appeared to me that it might be best to let the work be a posthumous one; or at least that its publication should be delayed till the Constitution should be well settled by practice, & till a knowledge of the controversial part of the proceedings of its framers could be turned to no improper account. Delicacy also seemed to require some respect to the rule by which the Convention "prohibited a promulgation without leave of what was spoken in it;" so long as the policy of that rule could be regarded as in any degree unexpired. As a guide in expounding and applying the provisions of the Constitution, the debates and incidental decisions of the Convention can have no authoritative character. However desirable it be that they should be preserved as a gratification to the laudable curiosity felt by every people to trace the origin and progress of their political Insitutions, & as a source parhaps of some lights on the Science of Govt. the legitimate meaning of the Instrument must be derived from the text itself; or if a key is to be sought elsewhere, it must be not in the opinions or intentions of the Body which planned & proposed the Constitution, but in the sense attached

---

[1] *Documentary History of the Constitution*, V, 310–312.

to it by the people in their respective State Conventions where it recd. all the authority which it possesses.

Such being the course of my reflections I have suffered a concurrence & continuance of particular inconveniences for the time past, to prevent me from giving to my notes the fair & full preparation due to the subject of them. Of late, being aware of the growing hazards of postponement, I have taken the incipient steps for executing the task; and the expediency of not risking an ultimate failure is suggested by the Albany publication from the notes of a N. York member of the Convention. I have not seen more of the volume than has been extracted into the newspapers, but it may be inferred from these samples, that it not only a very mutilated [1] but a very erroneous edition of the matter to which it relates. There must be an entire omission also of the proceedings of the latter period of the Session from which Mr. Yates & Mr. Lansing withdrew in the temper manifested by their report to their Constituents: the period during which the variant & variable opinions, converged & centered in the modifications seen in the final act of the Body.

It is my purpose now to devote a portion of my time to an exact digest of the voluminous materials in my hands. How long a time it will require, under the interruptions & avocations which are probable I can not easily conjecture. Not a little will be necessary for the mere labour of making fair transcripts. By the time I get the whole into a due form for preservation, I shall be better able to decide on the question of publication.

CCCXLI. JAMES MADISON TO J. G. JACKSON.[2]

Montpr. Decr. 27–1821.

With respect to that portion of the mass, which contains the voluminous proceedings of the Convention, it has always been my intention that they should some day or other see the light. But I have always felt at the same time the delicacy attending such a use of them; especially at an early season. In general I have leaned to the expediency of letting the publication be a posthumous one. The result of my latest reflections on the subject, I cannot more conveniently explain, than by the inclosed extract from a letter * confidentially written since the appearance of the proceedings of the Convention as taken from the Notes of Chf: Juste Yates.

Of this work I have not yet seen a copy. From the scraps thrown

---

* See letter of the   of Sepr. 1821. to Ths. Ritchie [CCCXL].

[1] Crossed out "deficient".

[2] *Documentary History of the Constitution*, V, 312–315.

into the Newspapers I cannot doubt that the prejudices of the author guided his pen, and that he has committed egregious errors at least, in relation to others as well as to myself.

That most of us carried into the Convention a profound impression produced by the experienced inadequacy of the old Confederation, and by the monitory examples of all similar ones ancient & modern, as to the necessity of binding the States together by a strong Constitution, is certain. The necessity of such a Constitution was enforced by the gross and disreputable inequalities which had been prominent in the internal administrations of most of the States. Nor was The recent & alarming insurrection headed by Shays, in Massachusetts without a very sensible effect on the pub: mind. Such indeed was the aspect of things, that in the eyes of all the best friends of liberty a crisis had arrived which was to decide whether the Amn. Experiment was to be a blessing to the world, or to blast for ever the hopes which the republican cause had enspired; and what is not to be overlooked the disposition to give to a new System all the vigour consistent with Republican principles, was not a little stimulated by a backwardness in some quarters towards a Convention for the purpose, which was ascribed to a secret dislike to popular Govt. and a hope that delay would bring it more into disgrace, and pave the way for a form of Govt. more congenial with Monarchical or aristocratical predilections.

This view of the crisis made it natural for many in the Convention to lean more than was perhaps in strictness warranted by a proper distinction between causes temporary as some of them doubtless were, and causes permanently inherent in popular frames of Govt. It is true also, as has been sometimes suggested that in the course of discussions in the Convention, where so much depended on compromise, the patrons of different opinions often set out on negociating grounds more remote from each other, than, the real opinions of either were from the point at which they finally met.

For myself, having from the first moment of maturing a political opinion, down to the present one, never ceased to be a votary of the principle of self-Govt: I was among those most anxious to rescue it from the danger which seemed to threaten it; and with that view was willing to give to a Govt. resting on that foundation, as much energy as would ensure the requisite stability and efficacy. It is possible that in some instances this consideration may have been allowed a weight greater than subsequent reflection within the Convention, or the actual operation of the Govt. would sanction. It may be remarked also that it sometimes happened that opinions as to a particular modification or a particular power of the Govt. had a conditional reference to others which combined therewith would vary the character of the whole.

But whatever might have been the opinions entertained in forming the Constitution, it was the duty of all to support it in its true meaning as understood *by the Nation* at the time of its ratification. No one felt this obligation more than I have done; and there are few perhaps whose ultimate & deliberate opinions on the merits of the Constitution, accord in a greater degree with that obligation.

CCCXLII. James Madison: Note to his Speech on the Right of Suffrage.[1]

Note[2] to the Speech of J. M. on the   day of

These observations (in the speech of J. M.   See debates in the Convention of 1787. on the   day of   ) do not convey the speaker's more full & matured view of the subject, which is subjoined.   He felt too much at the time the example of Virginia

The right of suffrage is a fundamental Article in Republican Constitutions.   The regulation of it is, at the same time, a task of peculiar delicacy.   Allow the right exclusively to property, and the rights of persons may be oppressed.   The feudal polity alone sufficiently proves it.   Extend it equally to all, and the rights of property or the claims of justice may be overruled by a majority without property, or interested in measures of injustice.   Of this abundant proof is afforded by other popular Govts. and is not without examples in our own, particularly in the laws impairing the obligation of contracts.

In civilized communities, property as well as personal rights is an essential object of the laws, which encourage industry by securing the enjoyment of its fruits: that industry from which property results, & that enjoyment which consists not merely in its immediate use, but in its posthumous destination to objects of choice and of kindred affection.

In a just & a free, Government, therefore, the rights both of property & of persons ought to be effectually guarded.   Will the former be so in case of a universal & equal suffrage?   Will the latter be so in case of a suffrage confined to the holders of property?

As the holders of property have at stake all the other rights common to those without property, they may be the more restrained from infringing, as well as the less tempted to infringe the rights of

---

[1] *Documentary History of the Constitution*, V. 440–449.

[2] This note seems to have been written about 1821, when Madison was preparing his Debates for publication.

the latter. It is nevertheless certain, that there are various ways in which the rich may oppress the poor; in which property may oppress liberty; and that the world is filled with examples. It is necessary that the poor should have a defence against the danger.

On the other hand, the danger to the holders of property can not be disguised, if they be undefended against a majority without property. Bodies of men are not less swayed by interest than individuals, and are less controlled by the dread of reproach and the other motives felt by individuals. Hence the liability of the rights of property, and of the impartiality of laws affecting it, to be violated by Legislative majorities having an interest real or supposed in the injustice: Hence agrarian laws, and other leveling schemes: Hence the cancelling or evading of debts, and other violations of contracts. We must not shut our eyes to the nature of man, nor to the light of experience. Who would rely on a fair decision from three individuals if two had an interest in the case opposed to the rights of the third? Make the number as great as you please, the impartiality will not be increased, nor any further security against justice be obtained, than what may result from the greater difficulty of uniting the wills of a greater number.

In all Govts. there is a power which is capable of oppressive exercise. In Monarchies and Aristocracies oppression proceeds from a want of sympathy & responsibility in the Govt. towards the people. In popular Governments the danger lies in an undue sympathy among individuals composing a majority, and a want of responsibility in the majority to the minority. The characteristic excellence of the political System of the U. S. arises from a distribution and organization of its powers, which at the same time that they secure the dependence of the Govt. on the will of the nation, provides better guards than are found in any other popular Govt. against interested combinations of a Majority against the rights of a Minority.

The U. States have a precious advantage also in the actual distribution of property particularly the landed property; and in the universal hope of acquiring property. This latter peculiarity is among the happiest contrasts in 'their situation to that of the old world, where no anticipated change in this respect, can generally inspire a like sympathy with the rights of property. There may be at present, a Majority of the Nation, who are even freeholders, or the heirs, or aspirants to Freeholds. And the day may not be very near when such will cease to make up a Majority of the community. But they cannot always so continue. With every admissible subdivision of the Arable lands, a populousness not greater than that of England or France, will reduce the holders to a Minority. And whenever the Majority shall be without landed or other equivalent property and without the means or hope of acquiring it, what is to secure the rights of property agst. the danger from an equality & universality of suffrage, vesting compleat power over property in hands without a share in it: not to speak of a danger in the mean time from a dependence of an increasing number on the wealth of a few? In other Countries this dependence results in some from the relations between Landlords & Tenants in other both from that source, & from the relations between wealthy capitalists & indigent labourers. In the U. S. the occurrence must happen from the last source; from the connection between the great Capitalists in Manufactures & Commerce and the members employed by them. Nor will accumulations of Capital for a certain time be precluded by our laws of descent & of distribution; such being the enterprize inspired by free Institutions, that great wealth in the hands of individuals and associations, may not be unfrequent. But it may be observed, that the opportunities, may be diminished, and the permanency defeated by the equalizing tendency of the laws.

No free Country has ever been without parties, which are a natural offspring of Freedom. An obvious and permanent division of every people is into the owners of the Soil, and the other inhabitants. In a certain sense the Country may be said to belong to the former. If each landholder has an exclusive property in his share, the Body of Landholders have an exclusive property in the whole. As the Soil becomes subdivided, and actually cultivated by the owners, this view of the subject derives force from the principle of natural law, which vests in individuals an exclusive right to the portions of ground with which he has incorporated his labour & improvements. Whatever may be the rights of others derived from their birth in the Country, from their interest in the high ways & other parcels left open for common use as well, as in the national Edifices and monuments; from their share in the public defence, and from their concurrent support of the Govt., it would seem unreasonable to extend the right so far as to give them when become the majority, a power of Legislation over the landed property without the consent of the proprietors. Some barrier agst the invasion of their rights would not be out of place in a just & provident System of Govt. The principle of such an arrangement has prevailed in all Govts. where peculiar privileges or interests held by a part were to be secured agst. violation, and in the various associations where pecuniary or other property forms the stake. In the former case a defensive right has been allowed; and if the arrangement be wrong, it is not in the defense, but in the kind of privilege to be defended.

In the latter case, the shares of suffrage allotted to individuals, have been with acknowledged justice apportioned more or less to their respective interests in the Common Stock.

These reflections suggest the expediency of such a modification of Govt. as would give security to the part of the Society having most at stake and being most exposed to danger. Three modifications present themselves.

1. *Confining* the right of suffrage to freeholders, & to such as hold an equivalent property, convertible of course into freeholds. The objection to this regulation is obvious. It violates the vital principle of free Govt. that those who are to be bound by laws, ought to have a voice in making them. And the violation wd. be more strikingly unjust as the lawmakers become the minority: The regulation would be as unpropitious also as it would be unjust. It would engage the numerical & physical force in a constant struggle agst. the public authority; unless kept down by a standing army fatal to all parties.

2. Confining the right of suffrage for one Branch to the holders of property, and for the other Branch to those without property. This arrangement which wd. give a mutual defence, where there might be mutual danger of encroachment, has an aspect of equality & fairness. But it wd. not be in fact either equal or fair, because the rights to be defended would be unequal, being on one side those of property as well as of persons, and on the other those of persons only. The temptation also to encroach tho' in a certain degree mutual, wd. be felt more strongly on one side than on the other; It wd. be more likely to beget an abuse of the Legislative Negative in extorting concessions at the expence of property, than the reverse. The division of the State into the two Classes, with distinct & independt. Organs of power, and without any intermingled Agency whatever, might lead to contests & antipathies not dissimilar to those between the Patricians & Plebeians at Rome.

3. Confining the right of electing one Branch of the Legislature to freeholders, and admitting all others to a common right with holders of property, in electing the other Branch. This wd. give a defensive power to holders of property, and to the class also without property when becoming a majority of electors, without depriving them in the mean time of a participation in the public Councils. If the holders of property would thus have a twofold share of representation, they wd. have at the same time a twofold stake in it, the rights of property as well as of persons the twofold object of political Institutions. And if no exact & safe equilibrium can be introduced, it is more reasonable that a preponderating weight shd.

be allowed to the greater interest than to the lesser. Experience alone can decide how far the practice in this case would correspond with the Theory. Such a distribution of the right of suffrage was tried in N. York and has been abandoned whether from experienced evils, or party calculations, may possibly be a question. It is still on trial in N. Carolina, with what practical indications is not known. It is certain that the trial, to be satisfactory ought to be continued for no inconsiderable period; untill in fact the non freeholders should be the majority.

4 Should Experience or public opinion require an equal & universal suffrage for each branch of the Govt., such as prevails generally in the U. S., a resource favorable to the rights of landed & other property, when its possessors become the Minority, may be found in an enlargement of the Election Districts for one branch of the Legislature, and an extension of its period of service. Large districts are manifestly favorable to the election of persons of general respectability, and of probable attachment to the rights of property, over competitors depending on the personal solicitations practicable on a contracted theatre. And altho' an ambitious candidate, of personal distinction, might occasionally recommend himself to popular choice by espousing a popular though unjust object it might rarely happen to many districts at the same time. The tendency of a longer period of service would be, to render the Body more stable in its policy, and more capable of stemming popular currents taking a wrong direction, till reason & justice could regain their ascendancy.

5. Should even such a modification as the last be deemed inadmissible, and universal suffrage and very short periods of elections within contracted spheres be required for each branch of the Govt., the security for the holders of property when the minority, can only be derived from the ordinary influence possessed by property, & the superior information incident to its holders; from the popular sense of justice enlightened & enlarged by a diffusive education; and from the difficulty of combining & effectuating unjust purposes throughout an extensive country; a difficulty essentially distinguishing the U. S. and even most of the individual States, from the small communities where a mistaken interest or contagious passion, could readily unite a majority of the whole under a factious leader, in trampling on the rights of the Minor party.

Under every view of the subject, it seems indispensable that the Mass of Citizens should not be without a voice, in making the laws which they are to obey, & in chusing the Magistrates, who are to administer them, and if the only alternative be between an equal

& universal right of suffrage for each branch of the Govt. and a confinement of the *entire* right to a part of the Citizens, it is better that those having the greater interest at stake namely that of property & persons both, should be deprived of half their share in the Govt.; than, that those having the lesser interest, that of personal rights only, should be deprived of the whole.

CCCXLIII. JAMES MADISON: "GENL. REMARKS ON THE CONVENTION." [1]

For case of suffrage see Deb.: Aug. 7.

1. Its Members of the most select kind & possessing particularly the confidence of yr. Constituents

2. do- generally of mature age & much political experience.

3. Disinterestedness & candor demonstrated by mutual concessions, & frequent changes of opinion

4. Few who did not change in the progress of discussions the opinions on important points which they carried into the Convention

5. Few who, at the close of the Convention, were not ready to admit this change as the enlightening effect of the discusions —

6. And how few, whose opinions at the close of the Convention, have not undergone changes on some points, under the more enlightening influence of experience.

7. Yet how much fewer still who, if now living, with the recollection of the difficulties in the Convention, of overcoming or reconciling honest differences of opinion, political biasses, and local interests; and with due attention to the varieties & discords of opinion, the vicisitudes of parties, and the collisions real or imagined of local interests, witnessed on the face of the Nation, would not felicitate their Country on the happy result of the original Convention, and deprecate the experiment of another with general power to revise its work.

8. The restraining influence of the Constin on the aberrations of the States of great importance tho' invisible. It stifles wishes & inclinations which wd otherwise ripen into overt & pernicious acts. The States themselves are unconscious of the effect. Were these Constitul. and insuperable obstacles out of the way — how many political ills might not have sprung up where not suspected. The propensities in some cases, as Mas: Kenty. &c have not been altogether contrould, and but for foreseen difficulties might have been followd. by greater

---

[1] *Documentary History of the Constitution*, V, 465–466. It seems as if this document may have been intended as an introduction to CCCXLII.

CCCXLIV. John Quincy Adams: Memoirs.[1]

[1823, January] 9th. . . . I received a letter from General Alexander Smyth, asking the inspection of Mr. Brearley's printed draft of a constitution, reported to the Federal Convention on the 12th of September, 1787. I see at once his object, which is a new device to trump up a charge before the public against me. My first impression was to send him the paper itself, requesting him to return it at his convenience, and I wrote him an answer accordingly. But, reflecting upon the insidious character, as well as the malignity, of his first attack upon me, and on the evident portion of the same ingredients in this application, I thought it not safe to trust the paper with him. I therefore wrote him that the paper would be submitted to his inspection at the office whenever it would suit his convenience to call. . . .

11th. When I came to my own office, I found General Alexander Smyth there, with Mr. E. B. Jackson, another member of the House of Representatives, from Virginia. They were in my room with Mr. Brent, and Mr. Smyth was inspecting Mr. Brearley's copy of the draft of a Constitution — was taking a copy of a passage in it, and writing a certificate under the copy that he made which certificate he desired Mr. Brent to sign. The journal of the Federal Convention was published by a resolution of Congress under my direction, in the year 1819. In the section and paragraph enumerating the powers of Congress there are errors of *punctuation* — errors of the press, which had escaped my attention. Mr. Smyth now came with the intention of trumping up a charge against me of having intentionally falsified that publication, by introducing a false *punctuation*. Smyth was comparing Brearley's printed draft with the copy of it printed in the journal of the Convention, and eagerly seeking for variations between them. He found on Brearley's paper a manuscript minute, "Brought into the Convention 13th of September, 1787." "The book says on the 12th," said Smyth, and, charmed with his imaginary detection of a new blunder, wrote his certificate for Brent to sign, that it was a true copy from the Constitution reported on the 13th of September, showing the punctuation, obliteration, and amendments. He had written the copy in two different hands, one, it seems, intended to represent the printed, and the other the manuscript part of the copy.

Mr. Brent showed me the certificate, asking if he should sign it. I said the certificate, as written, was not correct. Smyth said, "It's not true. It is correct." I said the certificate purported to show

---

the punctuation, obliteration, and amendments, but did not specify what part was in print and what part in manuscript. It also stated the Constitution to have been reported on the 13th, while the journal showed that it had been reported on the 12th of September. He said he had taken the date from what was written on the Brearley paper itself. I then showed by the journal that the report had been made on the 12th, and ordered to be printed for the use of the members, so that Brearley's manuscript minute, "Brought into the Convention 13th September," had reference to the printed paper, and not to the report itself, which had been brought in the day before.

Smyth then struck out of his projected certificate the 13th and inserted 12th; but I still objected that as the copy did not specify what part was print and what part manuscript, it was not fair for comparison with the printed journal of the Convention, which professedly gave only the printed part of Brearley's paper.

Smyth then cut off his proposed certificate from his copy and threw the certificate away. I immediately picked it up, and asked him to let me have the copy itself — which he refused. He said he meant to keep that himself. I might have a fac-simile of it. A fac-simile of the paper was what he wanted.

I then said that the book had not been printed from the printed paper, but from a copy of it made at this office, and which had been returned to it from the printers, and was still in the office. Smyth said he had what he wanted — the copy from the original paper.

I then said I was ready to explain any variation which there might be between the original paper and the printed book, and, turning to Jackson, I desired him to notice that Smyth had refused to let me have the copy which he had made; adding that I might perhaps be under a necessity of requiring his testimony hereafter.

This at length brought Smyth to; Jackson having repeated to him that I had said I should hereafter need his testimony. I then showed to Jackson the copy of Brearley's paper, which was sent to the printers at Boston, and from which the book was printed. In this copy the punctuation was not precisely the same as in Brearley's printed paper, from which it was copied, but it was the same at the passage upon which Smyth wished to fix the charge of falsification. Jackson asked how it was in the copy of the Constitution printed in the first volume of Bioren's edition of the laws, published under direction of Mr. Monroe when Secretary of State, and Mr. Rush, Attorney-General. Smyth said there were some differences of punctuation in that. I sent for the original roll of the Constitution itself, and for a copy printed from it in 1820 by my direction and then collated with the roll. The punctuation in no two of the copies was exactly the same. But the proof was complete that, in the only passage at which the punctuation could affect the sense, the copy made at the office and sent to Boston to be printed agreed precisely with the original printed paper of Mr. Brearley.

After a long and pertinacious examination of all the papers, which were taken for the purpose from my chamber into that of Mr. Brent, Smyth declared himself satisfied that he had been mistaken in his suspicions, and that the error of punctuation in the volume of the journal of the Convention, consisting in the substitution of a colon for a semicolon —: instead of ; — and a capital *T* instead of a small *t*, was not a deliberate and wilful forgery of mine to falsify the Constitution and vest absolute and arbitrary powers in Congress, but a mere error of the press. He took, however, a certified copy from Mr. Brent of the passage as printed in Brearley's paper, with the punctuation, obliteration, and manuscript interlineations.

───────────

CCCXLV. JAMES MADISON TO GEORGE HAY.[1]

Montpellier Aug 23. 1823.

I have recd. your letter of the 11th with the Newspapers containing your remarks on the present mode of electing a President, and your proposed remedy for its defects. I am glad to find you have not abandoned your attention to great Constitutional topics.

The difficulty of finding an unexceptionable process for appointing the Executive Organ of a Government such as that of the U. S., was deeply felt by the Convention; and as the final arrangement of it took place in the latter stage of the Session, it was not exempt from a degree of the hurrying influence produced by fatigue and impatience in all such Bodies: tho' the degree was much less than usually prevails in them.

The part of the arrangement which casts the eventual appointment on the House of Reps. voting by States, was, as you presume, an accomodation to the anxiety of the smaller States for their sovereign equality, and to the jealousy of the larger towards the cumulative functions of the Senate. The Agency of the H. of Reps. was thought safer also than that of the Senate, on account of the greater number of its members. It might indeed happen that the event would turn on one or two States having one or two Reps. only; but even in that case, the Representations of most of the States being numerous, the House would present greater obstacles to corruption than the Senate with its paucity of Members. It may be observed

───────────────────────────

[1] *Documentary History of the Constitution*, V, 315–317.

also, that altho' for a certain period the evil of State votes given by one or two individuals, would be extended by the introduction of new States, it would be rapidly diminished by growing populations within extensive territories. At the present period, the evil is at its maximum. . . .

I agree entirely with you in thinking that the election of Presidential Electors by districts, is an amendment very proper to be brought forward at the same time with that relating to the eventual choice of President by the H. of Reps. The district mode was mostly, if not exclusively, in view when the Constitution was framed and adopted; & was exchanged for the general ticket & the legislative election, as the only expedient for baffling the policy of the particular States which had set the example.

CCCXLVI. Rufus King to C. King.[1]

Monday Evening, Sept. 29, 1823.

To prove that your construction of the Constitution respecting the appointment of Electors is correct, it may be observed that according to the printed Journal of the Convention, it is evident that the choice of the President was a subject of great difficulty; and the more so, as the practice of the States was at that period dissimilar in the elections of Governor, or the state executive. In all the States except N. Jersey, east of Maryland, the choice of Govr. was made by the people; in New Jersey and the five southern States, the Gov. was chosen by the several State Legislatures. The members of the Convention in settling the manner of electing the Executive of the U. S. seem to have been prejudiced in favor of the manner, to which they were accustomed, in the election of the Governor of their respective States.

According to the Journal, on the 19th. of July, the Convention resolved that the Pr. shd. be chosen by Electors appointed "*by the Legislatures of the States*": on the 23. of July, they reconsidered this vote, and on the next day resolved that the President should be chosen "*by the national Legislature.*"

This appears to have been unsatisfactory, and to have given occasion to much discussion and to different projects; the subject was referred to a large Committee, which rejected the choice by the national legislature, and reported the provision which is contained in the Constitution, viz that the President shall be chosen by Electors to be appointed "*in such manner as the Legislature of each State may direct.*"

---

[1] C. R. King, *Life and Correspondence of Rufus King*, VI, 532–534.

Comparing this established mode of choosing the Pr. with that which was adopted on the 19th. of July, recollecting the immediate reconsideration of that mode, and the deliberate adoption of the mode of choosing wh. is provided by the Constitution, it is reasonable to infer, that the power to direct the manner in which Electors may be chosen, does not give to the Legislature of each State, the power by which they themselves may make such appointment of the Electors.

Again the Constitution provides that Representatives shall be chosen *by the People;* Senators *by the Legislature* of each State and Electors *in such manner as the Legislature of each State may direct.* The Legislature may direct that Electors may be chosen by the people, by a genl. ticket in each State, or by districts; they may authorize the persons qualified to vote for the most numerous branch of the State Legislature, to vote for the Electors; or they may confine the choice to free-holders, as is the case in Virginia; or they may direct that the people shall in the several States, by ballot, or vivā voce, choose Electors, with power to appoint the Electors of the President; in this way the Senate of Maryland is appointed; and it appears by the printed Journal of the Convention, that General Hamilton proposed this very mode of choosing the Electors of the President. As the language of the Constitution on this subject differs from the language of the first Resolution, wh. gave the appointment of Electors to the State Legislatures, in like manner as the Constitution gives the power to appoint Senators, it is not only reasonable, but almost necessary to give the provision of the Constitution a different interpretation, and to limit the same, so that the State Legislature may by law designate those who may appoint the Electors altho' they themselves may not appoint them.

This course of thinking has occurred to me, I suggest it to you; the facts are correct as I state them.

CCCXLVII. JAMES MADISON TO THOMAS JEFFERSON.[1]

Montpellier, Jany 14, 1824.

An appeal from an abortive ballot in the first meeting of the Electors to a reassembling of them, a part of the several plans, has something plausible, and, in comparison with the existing arrangement, might not be inadmissible. But it is not free from material objections. It relinquishes, particularly, the policy of the Constitution in allowing as little time as possible for the Electors to be known and tampered with. And beside the opportunities for in-

----

[1] *Letters and other Writings of James Madison,* III, 361.

trigue furnished by the interval between the first and second meeting, the danger of having one electoral body played off against another, by artful misrepresentations rapidly transmitted, a danger not to be avoided, would be at least doubled.

CCCXLVIII. Rufus King in the Senate of the United States.[1]

March 18, 1824.

The dangers to which experience had shown that the election of Executive Chiefs are liable; dangers which had led other nations to prefer hereditary to elective Executives, were, without doubt, well considered by the members of the General Convention, who, nevertheless, did indulge the hope, by apportioning, limiting, and confining the Electors within their respective States, and by the guarded manner of giving and transmitting the ballots of the Electors to the Seat of Government, that intrigue, combination, and corruption, would be effectually shut out, and a free and pure election of the President of the United States made perpetual. . . .

The House of Representatives is composed on the basis of the numbers of the respective States, the small States here yielding to the large ones, and the Senate is composed on the basis of the equality of the States, the larger States here, in turn, deferring to the small ones. The Executive is chosen by neither rule, but by the influence of both rules united; it is well known that the small States would not have consented to the choice by Electors, a mode favorable to the large States; but, upon the consent of the large States, on the failure of the choice of the President by the Electors on the first trial, that the House of Representatives voting by States, the representation from each State having one vote, shall choose the President, not from those they deem the most worthy, but from the persons having the highest numbers, not exceeding three, on the list of those voted for by the Electors, thereby restricting the choice of the House of Representatives to the three highest candidates nominated by the large States. To this adjustment, which was brought about by compromise between the States, no objections were made at the period when the Constitution was afterwards under the discussion of the several States. Though great difficulties occurred in the debates of the State conventions on other portions of the Constitution of the United States, no opposition appeared to the provisions of the Constitution respecting the manner of electing the President, and no such objection occurred until the fourth

---

[1] *Annals of Congress*, Eighteenth Congress, First Session, I, 355–356, 370.

election of the President, which was made by the House of Representatives; since that period, five Presidential elections have taken place, and, in eight of the nine elections, the President has been chosen by the Electors; the fourth election is the only instance in which the President, not being chosen by the Electors, the election devolved on the House of Representatives. The compromise, on the subject of the Presidential election, which has been always binding in honor and good faith, seems of late to have been forgotten; and dissatisfaction and complaint have appeared at the seat of government in Virginia, New York, and other States, that the influence of the great States was unreasonably impaired by the provision of the Constitution, that, after the failure to choose the President by the Electors, the election should devolve upon the House of Representatives, although the House of Representatives is restricted to the choice of the President from three candidates, nominated by the Electors, a majority of whom are appointed by the large States. Hence it has happened, from year to year, that attempts have been made by certain States, to alter the Constitution on the subject of the Presidential election, notwithstanding this election is matter of compromise and compact between the States, without which no Constitution or Union could have been formed.

. . . The power of choosing the President is given to the Colleges of Electors — the election, in the first instance, is in their hands; and, to prevent the possibility of combination, they are chosen only about thirty days before their office is to be performed. The election is directed to be made in all the different States on the same day, and the Electors are permitted to make but one attempt at a choice. These provisions of the Constitution were adopted for the express purpose of preventing combinations — an effect which, Mr. B. [K?] thought, was greatly to be dreaded from the practice of nomination by Congressional caucuses.

CCCXLIX. Rufus King to C. King.[1]

Senate Chamber, 23 March, 1824.

The election of the Pr., as it is one of the most important, so it is one of the most intricate provisions of the Constitution, and in its object, except in the first stage of the process, is assigned to the States acting in their federal equal capacity. For this reason, measures which may be employed in the several States, under regulations and provisions of simple, and single sovereignties, could not be adopted in the balanced system of the Constitution of the U. S.

---

[1] C. R. King, *Life and Correspondence of Rufus King*, VI, 557–558.

— a compact between the States, wh. contains special provisions whereby the executive, legislative and judicial officers must be appointed.

Because Conventions may be, and are, held to nominate State officers it does not hence result that they may be held in order to concentrate the opinion, of the States, relative to the election of any officer of the U. S. _____

CCCL. JAMES MADISON TO EDWARD LIVINGSTON.[1]

Montpellier April 17. 1824.

I have read your observations with a due perception of the ability which pervades and the eloquence which adorns them; and I must add, not without the pleasure of noticing that you have pruned from the doctrine of some of your fellow labourers, its most luxuriant branches — I cannot but think at the same time, that you have left the root in too much vigour. This appears particularly in the question of Canals. My impression with respect to the authority to make them may be the stronger perhaps, (as I had occasion to remark as to the Bank on its original discussion,) from my recollection that the authority had been repeatedly proposed in the Convention, and negatived, either as improper to be vested in Congress, or as a power not likely to be yielded by the States. My impression is also very decided, that if the construction which brings Canals within the scope of commercial regulations, had been advanced or admitted by the advocates of the constitution in the State Conventions, it would have been impossible to overcome the opposition to it. It is remarkable that Mr. Hamilton himself, the strenuous patron of an expansive meaning in the text of the Constitution, with the views of the Convention fresh in his memory, and in a Report contending for the most liberal rules of interpretation, was obliged by his candour to admit that they could not embrace the case of canals. . . .

It cannot be denied without forgetting what belongs to human nature, that in consulting the cotemporary writings, which vindicated and recommended the Constitution, it is fair to keep in mind that the authors might be sometimes influenced by the zeal of advocates: But in expounding it now, — is the danger of bias less, from the influence of local interests, of popular currents, and even from an estimate of national utility.

---

[1] *Documentary History of the Constitution*, V, 329–330.

CCCLI. James Madison to Henry Lee.[1]

Montpellier, June 25, 1824.

What a metamorphosis would be produced in the code of law if all its ancient phraseology were to be taken in its modern sense! And that the language of our Constitution is already undergoing interpretations unknown to its founders will, I believe, appear to all unbiased inquirers into the history of its origin and adoption. Not to look farther for an example, take the word "consolidate," in the Address of the convention prefixed to the Constitution. It there and then meant to give strength and solidity to the union of the States. In its current and controversial application, it means a destruction of the States by transfusing their powers into the government of the Union.

CCCLII. James Madison to Henry Lee.[2]

Montpellier, January 14, 1825.

In our complex system of polity, the public will, as a source of authority, may be the will of the people as composing one nation; or the will of the States in their distinct and independent capacities; or the federal will, as viewed, for example, through the Presidential electors, representing, in a certain proportion, both the nation and the States. If, in the eventual choice of a President, the same proportional rule had been preferred, a joint ballot by the two houses of Congress would have been substituted for the mode which gives an equal vote to every State, however unequal in size. As the Constitution stands, and is regarded as the result of a compromise between the larger and smaller States, giving to the latter the advantage in selecting a President from the candidates, in consideration of the advantage possessed by the former in selecting the candidates from the people, it cannot be denied, whatever may be thought of the constitutional provision, that there is, in making the eventual choice, no other control on the votes to be given, whether by the representatives of the smaller or larger States, but their attention to the views of their respective constituents and their regard for the public good.

CCCLIII. T. W. Cobb in the United States Senate.[3]

February 23, 1825.

Having said thus much concerning the nature of the Federal Government, the limitations of its powers, the rule by which the

---

[1] Letters and other Writings of James Madison, III, 442–443.

[2] Letters and other Writings of James Madison, III, 479.

[3] Register of Debates in Congress, I, 1824–1825, 652–653.

Constitution should be expounded, I proceed to the inquiry, From what clause in that instrument can the power to construct roads and canals be derived? I admit there is no clause prohibiting the exercise of such a power — but it is equally plain that there is no clause containing an express grant of the right, as a distinct and independent power. May we not go somewhat farther, and say, that, in addition to the fact of no such express grant of power being found in the Constitution, there is a strong presumption that such a grant was intended to be denied to the General Government? This presumption is established from the Journal of the Convention, as I will read: On the 14th Sept. (Journal of Convention, p. 376,) it was proposed to add to the enumeration of powers contained in the 8th sec, 1st. art. the following: "To grant letters of incorporation for canals," &c. It was rejected, three states only voting for it, viz: Pennsylvania, Virginia, and Georgia. There is a slight difference in words, between the amendment thus rejected, and the bill under consideration. The amendment proposed to invest Congress with power to "grant letters of incorporation for canals," &c. The bill presupposes that Congress possesses the power to construct roads and canals. But every one will at once see that there is no difference in principle. For if the power to grant letters of incorporation for canals, &c, had been conferred on Congress, it would have carried with it a grant of power to Congress itself, to construct them, inasmuch as the letters of incorporation could confer only such powers as vested in the person or body politic by whom they were to be granted. What, then, is the presumption to be drawn from the refusal by the Convention to confer this power? It can be only one of two: 1st, That the Convention intended to deny the power to Congress, and if so, the question as to our power to pass the bill under consideration is settled: we can have no such power. 2d, The other presumption is, that the Convention refused to adopt the amendment, because they believed the power was conferred in some other clause or grant. If this last presumption were correct, we should have had some evidence, somewhere, of its truth. We should have had some hint, either from the early expositors of the Constitution, or from the declarations of some member of the Convention, that such was the opinion entertained by that body. Consult the Letters of Publius, published under the title of the Federalist — that work was principally written by two distinguished members of the convention, one of whom* was at his post when the vote was taken on the amendment. Does that work any where insinuate that such power was vested expressly or impliedly, in Congress, by

* Mr. Madison.

the Constitution? Nay, has not the distinguished individual alluded to, when subsequently President of the United States, in a solemn message to Congress, denied that any such power was conferred by the Constitution? Surely it would not have been unknown to him, if the Convention had ever intended to delegate the power. Consult, also, the work recently published by Mr. Yates, another member of the Convention, and nothing will be found favorable to the presumption. At the present moment, we have in this very body a distinguished member of that Convention.* He was present, and voted on the amendment I have read from the Journal. Doubtless he will be able to inform us whether the rejection of the amendment proceeded from a belief in the Convention that the power was conferred in some other clause of the Constitution.† This second presumption, then, is fallacious, and, consequently, Congress have no power, either express or implied, over the subject of roads and canals.

* Hon. Rufus King, of New York.

† In this part of his remarks, Mr. C. addressed himself to Mr. K. who, shaking his head, is understood to have said, "Such a thing was not thought of." Mr. K. voted against the bill.

CCCLIV. T. H. Benton on Retiring of Rufus King from the United States Senate.[1]

In one of our conversations, and upon the formation of the constitution in the federal convention of 1787, he said some things to me which, I think ought to be remembered by future generations, to enable them to appreciate justly those founders of our government who were in favor of a stronger organization than was adopted. He said: "You young men who have been born since the Revolution, look with horror upon the name of a King, and upon all propositions for a strong government. It was not so with us. We were born the subjects of a King, and were accustomed to subscribe ourselves 'His Majesty's most faithful subjects;' and we began the quarrel which ended in the Revolution, not against the King, but against his parliament; and in making the new government many propositions were submitted which would not bear discussion; and ought not to be quoted against their authors, being offered for consideration, and to bring out opinions, and which, though behind the opinions of this day, were in advance of those of that day." — These things were said chiefly in relation to General Hamilton, who had submitted propositions stronger than those adopted, but nothing like those which party spirit attributed to him.

---

[1] T. H. Benton, *Thirty Years' View*, I, 58.

CCCLV. William Steele to Jonathan D. Steele.[1]

Painted Post, September, 1825.

My dear Son: —

I some time ago repeated to you an historical anecdote, in which you felt so much interested that you extorted from me a promise, that I would at some moment of leisure commit it to paper for you. I am now seated for that purpose, and shall relate it as nearly as I can recollect, in the words of General Jonathan Dayton, one of the members of the General Convention, who framed the Constitution, and afterwards Speaker of the House of Representatives, in the Congress of the United States.

I was (said General Dayton) a delegate from New Jersey, in the General Convention which assembled in Philadelphia for the purpose of digesting a constitution for the United States, and I believe I was the youngest member of that body. The great and good Washington was chosen our president, and Dr. Franklin, among other great men, was a delegate from Pennsylvania. A disposition was soon discovered in some members to *display* themselves in oratorical flourishes; but the good sense and discretion of the majority put down all such attempts. We had convened to deliberate upon, and if possible effect, a great national object — to search for political *wisdom* and *truth;* these we meant to pursue with simplicity, and to avoid everything which would have a tendency to divert our attention, or perplex our scheme.

A great variety of projects were proposed, all republican in their general outlines, but differing in their details. It was, therefore, determined that certain *elementary principles* should at first be established, in each branch of the intended constitution, and afterwards the *details* should be debated and filled up.

There was little or no difficulty in determining upon the *elementary principles* — such as, for instance, that the government should be a *republican-representative* government — that it should be divided into three branches, that is, *legislative, executive,* and *judicial,* &c. But when the organization of the respective branches of the legis-

---

[1] Littell's *Living Age*, 25 May, 1850. The *National Intelligencer* of August 26, 1826, had printed this with the following introduction from the *New York Gazette:*

"A friend has favored us with an interesting Manuscript, relating to a most important period of our history. The circumstances here detailed are new to us, and we believe they have never before been published. The narrative is in the words of General ——, one of the members of the General Convention which framed the Constitution. It was committed to paper by the gentleman to whom General —— detailed the facts, and we now have the satisfaction of laying it before our readers."

For Madison's comment on this anecdote see CCCLXXIX and CCCXCIII below.

lature came under consideration, it was easy to be perceived that the eastern and southern states had *distinct interests*, which it was difficult to reconcile; and that the larger states were disposed to form a constitution, in which the smaller states would be mere appendages and satellites to the larger ones. On the first of these subjects, much animated and somewhat *angry* debate had taken place, when the *ratio* of representation in the lower house of Congress was before us — the southern states claiming for themselves the *whole* number of their black population, while the eastern states were for confining the elective franchise to *freemen* only, without respect to color.

As the different parties adhered pertinaciously to their different positions, it was feared that this would prove an insurmountable obstacle; — but as the members were already generally satisfied that no constitution could be formed, which would meet the views and subserve the interests of each individual state, it was evident that it must be a matter of *compromise* and mutual *concession*. Under these impressions, and with these views, it was agreed at length that each state should be entitled to one delegate in the House of Representatives for every 30,000 of its inhabitants — in which number should be included *three fifths* of the whole number of their *slaves*.

When the details of the House of Representatives were disposed of, a more knotty point presented itself in the organization of the Senate.   The larger states contended that the same *ratio*, as to states, should be common to both branches of the legislature; or, in other words, that each state should be entitled to a representation in the Senate, (whatever might be the number fixed on,) in proportion to its population, as in the House of Representatives.   The smaller states, on the other hand, contended that the House of Representatives might be considered as the guardian of the liberties of the *people*, and therefore ought to bear a just proportion to *their* numbers; but that the Senate represented the *sovereignty of the States*, and that as each state, whether great or small, was equally an independent and sovereign state, it ought, in this branch of the legislature, to have *equal* weight and authority; without this, they said, there could be no security for their equal rights — and they would, by such a distribution of power, be merged and lost in the larger states.

This reasoning, however plain and powerful, had but little influence on the minds of delegates from the larger states — and as they formed a large majority of the Convention, the question, after passing through the forms of debate, was decided that 'each state should be represented in the Senate in proportion to its population.'

When the Convention had adjourned over to the next day, the delegates of the four smallest states, i.e., Rhode Island, Connecticut, New Jersey, and Delaware, convened to consult what course was to be pursued in the important crisis at which we had arrived. After serious investigation, it was solemnly determined to ask for a *reconsideration* the next morning; and if it was not granted, or if, when granted, that offensive feature of the Constitution could not be expunged, and the smaller states put upon an *equal footing* with the largest, we would secede from the Convention, and, returning to our constituents, inform them that no compact could be formed with the large states, but one which would sacrifice our sovereignty and independence.

I was deputed to be the organ through which this communication should be made — I know not why, unless it be that *young* men are generally chosen to perform *rash* actions. Accordingly, when the Convention had assembled, and as soon as the minutes of the last sitting were read, I arose and stated the view we had taken of the organization of the Senate — our desire to obtain a *reconsideration* and suitable *modification* of that article; and, in failure thereof, our determination to secede from the Convention, and return to our constituents.

This disclosure, it may readily be supposed, produced an immediate and great excitement in every part of the house! Several members were immediately on the floor to express their surprise, or indignation! They represented that the question had received a full and fair investigation, and had been definitively settled by a very large majority. That it was altogether unparliamentary and unreasonable, for one of the *minority* to propose a reconsideration, at the moment their act had become a matter of *record*, and without pretending that any new light could be thrown on the subject. That if such a precedent should be established, it would in future be impossible to say when any one point was definitively settled; as a small minority might at any moment, again and again, move and obtain a reconsideration. They therefore hoped the Convention would express its decided disapprobation by passing silently to the business before them.

There was much warm and some *acrimonious* feeling exhibited by a number of the speeches — a *rupture* appeared almost inevitable, and the bosom of Washington seemed to labor with the most anxious solicitude for its issue. Happily for the United States, the Convention contained some individuals possessed of talents and virtues of the highest order, whose hearts were deeply interested in the establishment of a new and efficient form of government; and whose penetrating minds had already deplored the evils which would spring up in our newly established republic, should the present attempt to consolidate it prove abortive. Among those personages, the most prominent was Dr. Franklin. He was esteemed the *Mentor* of our body. To a mind naturally *strong* and *capacious*, enriched by much reading and the experience of many years, he added a manner of communicating his thoughts peculiarly his own — in which simplicity, beauty, and strength were equally conspicuous. As soon as the angry orators, who preceded him had left him an opening, the doctor rose, evidently impressed with the weight of the subject before them, and the difficulty of managing it successfully.

" We have arrived, Mr. President," said he, " at a very momentous and interesting crisis in our deliberations. Hitherto our views have been as harmonious, and our progress as great, as could reasonably have been expected. But now an unlooked for and formidable obstacle is thrown in our way, which threatens to arrest our course, and, if not skilfully removed, to render all our fond hopes of a constitution abortive. The ground which has been taken by the delegates of the four smallest states, was as unexpected by me, and as repugnant to my feelings, as it can be to any other member of this Convention. After what I thought a full and impartial investigation of the subject, I recorded my vote in the affirmative side of the question, and I have not yet heard anything whch induces me to change my opinion. But I will not, therefore, conclude that it is *impossible* for me to be wrong! I will not say that those gentlemen who differ from me are under a delusion — much less will I charge them with an intention of needlessly embarrassing our deliberations. It is *possible* some change in our late proceedings ought to take place upon principles of *political justice;* or that, all things considered, the *majority* may see cause to recede from some of their just pretensions, as a matter of *prudence* and *expediency.* For my own part, there is nothing I so much dread, as a failure to devise and establish some efficient and equal form of government for our infant republic. The present effort has been made under the happiest auspices, and has promised the most favorable results; but should this effort prove vain, it will be long ere another can be made with any prospect of success. Our *strength* and our *prosperity* will depend on our *unity;* and the secession of even *four* of the smallest states, interspersed as they are, would, in my mind, paralyze and render useless, any plan which the majority could devise. I should therefore be grieved, Mr. President, to see matters brought to the test, which has been, perhaps too *rashly* threatened on the one hand, and which some of my honored colleagues have treated too *lightly* on the other. I am convinced that it is a subject which should be approached with *caution*, treated with *tenderness*, and decided on with *candor* and *liberality*.

" It is, however, to be feared that the members of this Convention are not in a temper, at this moment, to approach the subject in which we differ, in this spirit. I would, therefore, propose, Mr. President, that, without proceeding further in this business at this time, the Convention shall adjourn for *three days*, in order to let the present ferment pass off, and to afford time for a more full, free, and dispassionate investigation of the subject; and I would earnestly recommend to the members of this Convention, that they spend the time of this recess, not in associating with their *own* party, and devising *new arguments* to fortify themselves in their *old opinions*, but that they mix with members of *opposite* sentiments, lend a patient ear to their reasonings, and candidly allow them all the weight to which they may be entitled; and when we assemble again, I hope it will be with a determination to form a constitution, if not such an one as we can individually, and in all respects, approve, yet the best, which, under existing circumstances, can be obtained." (Here the countenance of Washington brightened, and a cheering ray seemed to break in upon the gloom which had recently covered our political horizon.) The doctor continued: " Before I sit down, Mr. President, I will suggest *another matter;* and I am really surprised that it has not been proposed by some other member at an earlier period of our deliberations. I will suggest, Mr. President, the propriety of nominating and appointing, before we separate, a *chaplain* to this Convention, whose duty it shall be uniformly to assemble with us, and introduce the business of each day by an *address to the Creator of the universe*, and the Governor of all nations, beseeching Him to preside in our council, enlighten our minds with a portion of heavenly wisdom, influence our hearts with a love of truth and justice, and crown our labors with complete and abundant success!"

The doctor sat down, and never (said Gen. D.) did I behold a countenance at once so *dignified* and *delighted* as was that of Washington, at the close of this address! Nor were the members of the Convention, generally less affected. The words of the venerable Franklin fell upon our ears with a weight and authority, even greater than we may suppose an oracle to have had in a Roman senate! A silent admiration superseded, for a moment, the expression of that assent and approbation which was strongly marked on almost every countenance; i say *almost*, for *one* man was found in the Convention, Mr. H——, from ——, who rose and said, with regard to the first motion of the honorable gentleman, for an *adjournment*, he would yield his assent; but he protested against the second motion, for the appointment of a chaplain. He then commenced a high-strained eulogium on the assemblage of *wisdom, talent,* and *experience,* which the Convention embraced; declared the high sense he entertained of the honor which his constituents had conferred upon *him,* in making him a member of that respectable body; said he was confidently of opinion that *they were competent* to transact the business which had been entrusted to their care — that they were equal to every exigence which might occur; and concluded by saying, that therefore he did not see the necessity of calling in *foreign aid!*

Washington fixed his eye upon the speaker, with a mixture of *surprise* and *indignation,* while he uttered this impertinent and impious speech, and then looked around to ascertain in what manner it affected others. They did not leave him a moment to *doubt;* no one deigned to *reply,* or take the smallest notice of the speaker, but the motion for appointing a chaplain was instantly seconded and carried; whether under the *silent disapprobation* of Mr. H——, or his *solitary negative,* I do not recollect. The motion for an adjournment was then put and carried unanimously, and the Convention adjourned accordingly.

The three days of recess were spent in the manner advised by Doctor Franklin; the opposite parties mixed with each other, and a free and frank interchange of sentiments took place. On the fourth day we assembled again, and if great additional *light* had not been thrown on the subject, every *unfriendly feeling* had been expelled; and a spirit of conciliation had been cultivated, which promised, at least, a *calm* and *dispassionate reconsideration* of the subject.

As soon as the chaplain had closed his prayer, and the minutes of the last sitting were read, all eyes were turned to the doctor. He rose, and in a few words stated, that during the recess he had listened attentively to all the arguments pro and con, which had been urged by both sides of the house; that he had himself said much, and thought more on the subject; he saw difficulties and objections, which might be urged by individual states, against every scheme which had been proposed; and he was now, more than ever, convinced that the constitution which they were about to form, in order to be *just* and *equal,* must be formed on the basis of *compromise* and *mutual concession.* With such views and feelings, he would now move a *reconsideration* of the vote last taken on the organization of the Senate. The motion was seconded, the vote carried, the former vote rescinded, and by a successive motion and resolution, the Senate was organized on the present plan.

Thus, my dear son, I have detailed, as far as my memory serves me, the information which I received personally from General Dayton. It has been done from a recollection of ten years, and I may have differed much from General Dayton in his phraseology, but I am confident I have faithfully stated the *facts*. I have related this anecdote at different times to gentlemen of information, to all of whom it was entirely *new*. Some of them requested me to furnish them a written copy, but I deemed that improper without the permission of General Dayton; and I intended, the first opportunity I should have, to make the same request of *him* — but the hand of death has removed him.

In committing this anecdote to paper, I have been actuated not only by a wish to gratify *you*, but by a desire to *perpetuate the facts*, if, as I fear, they are not elsewhere recorded. As they relate to a very important feature in our republican institutions, and to some of the most celebrated individuals who achieved our independence and framed our national government, they will, I am persuaded, be interesting to every lover of this happy country.

I am, very affectionately,
Your father,

To Jonathan D. Steele. ——————   WM. STEELE.

CCCLVI. JAMES MADISON TO ANDREW STEVENSON.[1]

Montpellier Mar. 25. 26

Will you pardon me for pointing out an error of fact into which you have fallen, as others have done, by supposing that the term, *national* applied to the contemplated Government, in the early stage of the Convention, particularly in the propositions of Mr. Randolph, was equivalent to *unlimited* or consolidated. This was not the case. The term was used, not in contradistinction to a limited, but to a *federal* Government. As the latter operated within the extent of its authority thro' requisitions on the confederated States, and rested on the sanction of State Legislatures, the Government to take its place, was to operate within the extent of its powers directly & coercively on individuals, and to receive the higher sanction of the people of the States. And there being no technical or appropriate denomination applicable to the new and unique System, the term national was used, with a confidence that it would not be taken in a wrong sense, especially as a right one could be readily suggested if not sufficiently implied by some of the propositions themselves. Certain it is that not more than two or three members of the Body and they rather theoretically than practically, were in

---

[1] *Documentary History of the Constitution*, V, 332–334.

favor of an unlimited Govt. founded on a consolidation of the States; and that neither Mr. Randolph, nor any one of his colleagues was of the number. His propositions were the result of a meeting of the whole Deputation, and concurred or acquiesced in unanimously, merely as a general introduction of the business; such as might be expected from the part Virginia had in bringing about the Convention, and as might be detailed, and defined in the progress of the work. The Journal shews that this was done.

I cannot but highly approve the industry with which you have searched for a key to the sense of the Constitution, where alone the true one can be found; in the proceedings of the Convention, the cotemporary expositions, and above all in the ratifying Conventions of the States. If the instrument be interpreted by criticisms which lose sight of the intention of the parties to it, in the fascinating pursuit of objects of public advantage or conveniency, the purest motives can be no security against innovations materially changing the features of the Government.

CCCLVII. James Madison to Thomas Cooper.[1]

Montpellier Decr. 26. 1826—
The mail has furnished me with a copy of your Lectures on Civil Government, & on the constitution of the U. S.   I find in them much in which I concur; parts on which I might say — non liquet — & others from which I should dissent; but none, of which interesting veiws are not presented.   What alone I mean to notice is a passage in which you have been misled by the authorities before you, & by a misunderstanding of the term "National" used in the early proceedings of the Convention of 1787.   Both Mr. Yates & Mr. Martin brought to the Convention predispositions agt. its object, the one from Maryland representing the party of Mr. Chase opposed to federal restraints on the State Legislation; the other from New York, the party unwilling to lose the power over trade through which the State levied a tribute on the consumption of its neighbours. Both of them left the Convention long before it compleated its work; & appear to have reported in angry terms, what they had observed with jaundiced eyes.   Mr. Martin is said to have recanted at a later day; & Mr. Yates to have changed his politics & joined the party adverse to that which sent him to the Convention. —— With respect to the term "National" as contradistinguished from the term "federal," it was not meant to express the *extent* of power, but the *mode* of *its operation*, which was to be not like the power of the

---

[1] *Documentary History of the Constitution*, V, 338–339.

old Confederation operating on *States;* but like that of ordinary Governments operating on individuals; & the substitution of "United States" for "National" noted in the journal, was not designed to change the meaning of the latter, but to guard agt. a mistake or misrepresentation of what was intended. The term "National" was used in the original propositions offered on the part of the Virga. Deputies, not one of whom attached to it any other meaning than that here explained. Mr. Randolph himself the organ of the Deputation, on the occasion, was a strenuous advocate for the federal quality of limited & specified powers; & finally refused to sign the constitution because its powers were not sufficiently limited & dedefined.

————————

CCCLVIII. James Madison to S. H. Smith.[1]

Montpr. Feby. 2. 1827.

I have great respect for your suggestion with respect to the season for making public what I have preserved of the proceedings of the Revolutionary Congress, and of the General Convention of 1787. But I have not yet ceased to think, that publications of them, posthumous as to others as well as myself, may be most delicate and most useful also, if to be so at all. As no personal or party views can then be imputed, they will be read with less of personal or party feelings, and consequently, with whatever profit, may be promised by them. It is true also that after a certain date, the older such things grow, the more they are relished as new; the distance of time like that of space from which they are received, giving them that attractive character

It cannot be very long however before the living obstacles to the forthcomings in question, will be removed. Of the members of Congress during the period embraced, the lamps of all are extinct, with the exception I believe of 2. Rd. Peters, & myself; and of the signers of the Constitution, of all but 3. R. King, Wm. Few and myself; and of the lamps still burning, none can now be far from the Socket.

————————

CCCLIX. James Madison to Edward Everett.[2]

Montpellier June 3d. 1827 —

I offer for your brother and yourself the thanks I owe for the copy of his work on "America". . . . One error into which the author has been led, will I am sure be gladly corrected. In page 109.

————————————————————

[1] *Documentary History of the Constitution*, V, 339–340.
[2] *Documentary History of the Constitution*, V, 341.

it is said of Washington that he "appears to have wavered for a moment in making up his mind upon the constitution". I can testify from my personal knowledge, that no member of the Convention appeared to sign the Instrument with more cordiality than he did, nor to be more anxious for its ratification. I have indeed the most thorough conviction from the best evidence, that he never wavered in the part he took in giving it his sanction and support. The error may perhaps have arisen from his backwardness in accepting his appointment to the Convention, occasioned by peculiar considerations which may be seen in the 5th. volume of his Biographer (Marshall).

_____

CCCLX. Timothy Pickering to William Jackson.[1]

Philadelphia, Septr. 2, 1827.

Permit me also to urge your preparing those speeches in the General Convention which formed the Constitution of the U. States, of which you took abbreviated notes, and which yourself alone can write out at full length.   _____

CCCLXI. James Madison to George Mason.[2]

Montpellier, Decr 29, 1827.

The public situation in which I had the best opportunity of being acquainted with the genius, the opinions, and the public labours of Col. Mason, was that of our co-service in the Convention of 1787, which formed the Constitution of the United States. The objections which led him to withhold his name from it have been explained by himself. But none who differed from him on some points will deny that he sustained throughout the proceedings of the body the high character of a powerful reasoner, a profound statesmen, and a devoted Republican.   _____

CCCLXII. Timothy Pitkin: on Signing the Constitution.[3]

Of the fifty-five members who attended this convention, thirty-nine signed the constitution: of the remaining sixteen, some in favor of it were obliged from particular business to leave the convention before it was ready for signing. (This, we are assured, was the case with Caleb Strong, of Massachusetts, Oliver Ellsworth of Connecticut, and Mr. Davie of North Carolina.)

---

[1] Massachusetts Historical Society, Pickering MSS., 16, 214.
[2] *Letters and other Writings of James Madison*, III, 607.
[3] Timothy Pitkin, *Political and Civil History of the United States* (Copyright, January, 1828), II, 262, note.

CCCLXIII. James Madison to Martin Van Buren.[1]

May 13 1828.

You will not I am sure, take it amiss if I here point to an *error of fact*, in your "observations on Mr. Foot's amendment." It struck me when first reading them, but escaped my attention –when thanking you for the copy with which you favored me.—The *threatning contest*, in the Convention of 1787. did not, as you supposed, turn on the degree of power to be granted to the Federal Govt: but on the rule by which the States should be represented and vote in the Govt: the smaller States insisting on the rule of equality in all respects; the larger on the rule of proportion to inhabitants: and the Compromize which ensued was that which established an equality in the Senate, and an inequality in the House of Representatives.

The contests & compromises, turning on the grants of power, tho' very important in some instances, were Knots of a less "Gordian" character. _____

CCCLXIV. James Madison to J. C. Cabell.[2]

Montpr. Sepr. 18 1828.

8 That the encouragement of Manufactures, was an object of the power to regulate trade, is proved by the use made of the power for that object, in the first session of the first Congress under the Constitution; when among the members present were so many who had been members of the federal Convention which framed the Constitution, and of the State Conventions which ratified it; each of these classes consisting also of members who had opposed & who had espoused, the Constitution in its actual form. It does not appear from the printed proceedings of Congress on that occasion that the power was denied by any of them. And it may be remarked that members from Virga. in particular, as well of the antifederal as the federal party, the names then distinguishing those who had opposed and those who had approved the Constitution, did not hesitate to propose duties, & to suggest even prohibition in favor of several articles of her production; _____

CCCLXV. James Madison to J. C. Cabell.[3]

Montpellier Feby. 2. 1829—

What the extract is to be from Yates account of the Convention, which convicts me of inconsistency, I cannot divine — If

[1] *Documentary History of the Constitution*, V, 343–344.
[2] *Documentary History of the Constitution*, V, 346–348.
[3] *Documentary History of the Constitution*, V, 349–350.

any thing stated by him has that tendency, it must be among the many errors in his crude & broken notes of what passed in that Body. When I looked over them some years ago, I was struck with a number of instances in which he had totally mistaken what was said by me, or given it in scraps & terms, which, taken without the developments or qualifications accompanying them, had an import essentially different from what was intended. Mr. Yates bore the character of an honest man, & I do not impute to him wilful misrepresentation. But beside the fallible & faulty mode in which he noted down what passed, the prejudices he felt on the occasion, with those of which he was a Representative, were such as to give every tincture & warp to his mind of which an honest one could be susceptible. It is to be recollected too that he was present during the early discussions only, which were of a more loose & general cast; having withdrawn to make his welcome Report, before the rough materials were reduced to the size & shape proper for the contemplated Edifice. Certain it is that I shall never admit his report as a test of my opinions, when not in accordance with those which have been repeatedly explained & authenticated by myself. The Report of Luther Martin is as little to be relied on for accuracy & fairness.

CCCLXVI. JAMES MADISON TO J. C. CABELL.[1]

Montpellier, February 13, 1829.

For a like reason, I made no reference to the "power to regulate commerce among the several States." I always foresaw that difficulties might be started in relation to that power which could not be fully explained without recurring to views of it, which, however just, might give birth to specious though unsound objections. Being in the same terms with the power over foreign commerce, the same extent, if taken literally, would belong to it. Yet it is very certain that it grew out of the abuse of the power by the importing States in taxing the non-importing, and was intended as a negative and preventive provision against injustice among the States themselves, rather than as a power to be used for the positive purposes of the General Government, in which alone, however, the remedial power could be lodged.

CCCLXVII. JARED SPARKS: JOURNAL.[2]

[1830], *April 19th.* It was necessary for the old Congress to sit with closed doors, because it was the executive as well as legislative

---

[1] *Letters and other Writings of James Madison,* IV, 14–15.
[2] H. B. Adams, *Life and Writings of Jared Sparks,* I, 560–564; II, 31–36. Notes of a visit to James Madison.

body; names of persons and characters came perpetually before
them; and much business was constantly on hand which would
have been embarassed if it had gone to the public before it was
finished. It was likewise best for the convention for forming the Constitution to sit with closed doors, because opinions were so various
and at first so crude that it was necessary they should be long debated
before any uniform system of opinion could be formed. Meantime
the minds of the members were changing, and much was to be gained
by a yielding and accommodating spirit. Had the members committed themselves publicly at first, they would have afterwards
supposed consistency required them to maintain their ground,
whereas by secret discussion no man felt himself obliged to retain
his opinions any longer than he was satisfied of their propriety and
truth, and was open to the force of argument. Mr. Madison thinks
no Constitution would ever have been adopted by the convention
if the debates had been public. No chaplain was chosen for the
convention at any period of its session, although Dr. Franklin proposed one, as has been reported, after the convention had been some
time sitting. . . .

In the recent "History of the Convention for Framing the Constitution," published by order of the government in connection with
the "Secret Journal," there is a draft of a Constitution said to have
been presented by Charles Pinckney. It is remarkable for containing several important features in exact accordance with the Constitution as it was passed. This is the more strange, as some of these
very points grew out of the long debates which followed the presentation of the draft.

Mr. Madison seems a good deal perplexed on the subject. He
says Charles Pinckney presented a draft at the beginning of the session, that it went to a committee with other papers, and was no more
heard of during the convention. It was not preserved among the
papers on the files of the convention. When the above-mentioned
history was published, Mr. J. Q. Adams was Secretary of State, and
prepared the manuscript for the press. He wrote to Mr. Pinckney
for a copy of his draft, and received from him that which was printed.
How it happened that it should contain such particulars as it does,
Mr. Madison cannot tell; but he is perfectly confident that they
could not have been contained in the original draft as presented by
Mr. Pinckney, because some of them were the results of subsequent
discussions. Mr. Madison supposes that Mr. Pinckney must at
the time have added certain points as the convention proceeded,
particularly such as he approved, and as he thought would make his
draft more perfect, and that this altered draft had lain by him till

he had forgotten what parts were changed or improved; and thus he copied the whole. But however this may be explained, says Mr. Madison, it certainly is not the draft originally presented to the convention by Mr. Pinckney. It is obvious that Mr. Madison feels some embarrassment on the subject, because in his papers on the convention he has probably ascribed several of these particulars to the Virginia delegates, from whom they originated; and when his papers shall be made public, there will be found a discrepancy between them and Pinckney's draft. After the draft was printed, he intended to write to Mr. Pinckney asking, and even requiring, an explanation; but Mr. Pinckney died, and the opportunity was lost. It is known that Mr. Madison took down sketches of the debates of the convention, and preserved copies of all the important proceedings. He told me that nothing of his would come out till after his death. . . .

April 25th, Wednesday.—. . . Rode thence to Mr. Madison's, . . . where I spent the day most agreeably. . . .

The following anecdote he also mentioned as a remarkable instance of the failure of memory: —

It is well known that Hamilton inclined to a less democratical form of government than the one that was adopted, although he was a zealous friend of the Constitution in its present shape after it had received the sanction of the Convention. He considered it less perfect than it might have been, yet he thought it an immense improvement on the old confederation. He drew up a plan in accordance with his own views, which he put into the hands of Mr. Madison, who took a copy of it, and returned the original to the author, telling him at the same time that he had preserved a copy. Mr. Madison says he knew not Hamilton's motive for doing this, unless it was for the purpose of securing a written record of his views, which might afford a ready confutation of any future false statements respecting them.

Some time after the Convention a report went abroad that Hamilton was in favor of a system approaching a monarchy, and particularly that he wished the President to be elected for life. Mr. Pickering wrote to Hamilton asking if this report was true; to which he replied in the negative, and added, moreover, that, so far from its being true, he proposed the presidential office to continue for three years only, as would he seen by his plan of a Constitution put by him into the hands of Mr. Madison. Now it is remarkable that, on this very plan, the duration of the presidential office is fixed during good behavior. Mr. Madison expressed his belief very decidedly that this mistake arose from a want of recollection, for it was impossible that he should make the statement, and refer to the only source where it could be confuted, if he meant to deceive. . . .

In the Convention Dr. Franklin seldom spoke. As he was too feeble to stand long at a time, his speeches were generally written. He would arise and ask the favor of one of his colleagues to read what he had written. Occasionally, however, he would make short extemporaneous speeches with great pertinency and effect. . . .

It was Mr. Madison's custom, after he entered Congress, to take memoranda of the debates, rough sketches and copies of all the principal papers. The debates and proceedings of the Convention for adopting the Constitution he took much pains to record at the time, and has preserved the whole. Yate's book he speaks of as extremely imperfect, the author having been absent a good deal of the time, and both he and Lansing strenuously opposed to the Constitution. . . .

May 4th, Tuesday. — I mentioned to Mr. Adams (J. Q.) what Mr. Madison had said to me respecting Charles Pinckney's draft of a Constitution. Mr. Adams said that he prepared the manuscript of the history of the convention published by order of Congress, that the materials in the Department of State were very defective; that Pinckney's draft was not there; that he wrote to him for a copy, and received from him the one that is printed, together with a letter, in which he claimed to himself great merit for the part he took in framing the Constitution. Mr. Adams said he spoke once to Mr. Rufus King on the subject of the draft, who replied that Mr. Pinckney presented a draft, or a sketch of some sort, at the beginning of the convention, which went with other papers to a committee, and was never afterwards heard of. This accords with what Mr. Madison told me.

_____

CCCLXVIII. JOHN QUINCY ADAMS: MEMOIRS.[1]

[1830, May] 4th. Mr. Sparks called . . . Sparks said he had been spending a week at Mr. Madison's, who spoke to him much of the proceedings and published Journal of the Convention of 1787. He said he knew not what to make of the plan of Constitution in that volume purporting to have been presented by Charles Pinckney, of South Carolina. He said there was a paper presented by that person to the Convention, but it was nothing like the paper now in the book. It was referred to the committee who drafted the plan of the Constitution, and was never afterwards in any manner referred to or noticed. In the book it has the appearance as if it was the orig-

_____

[1] Vol. VIII, 224–225.

inal draft of the Constitution itself, and as if that which was finally adopted was Pinckney's plan, with a very few slight alterations. I told Mr. Sparks that Rufus King had spoken to me of C. Pinckney's paper precisely in the same manner as he says Mr. Madison now does; that it was a paper to which no sort of attention was paid by the Convention, except that of referring it to the committee, but when I compiled the Journal of the Convention, Charles Pinckney himself sent me the plan now in the book, as the paper which he had presented to the Convention; and with it he wrote me a letter, which obviously held the pretension that the whole plan of Constitution was his, and that the Convention had done nothing more than to deteriorate his work by altering some of his favorite provisions. Sparks said Mr. Madison added that this plan now in the book contained several things which could not possibly have been in Pinckney's paper, but which rose out of the debates upon the plan of Constitution reported by the committee. He conjectured that Mr. Pinckney's memory failed him, and that, instead of a copy of the paper which he did present, he had found a copy of the plan reported by the committee with interlined amendments, perhaps proposed by him, and, at a distance of more than thirty years, had imagined it was his own plan.

CCCLXIX. Jared Sparks to James Madison.[1]

Washington, May 5th. 1830

Since my return I have conversed with Mr Adams concerning Charles Pinckney's draft of a constitution. He says it was furnished by Mr. Pinckney, and that he has never been able to hear of another copy. It was accompanied by a long letter (written in 1819) now in the Department of State, in which Mr Pinckney claims to himself great merit for the part he took in framing the constitution. A copy of this letter may doubtless be procured from Mr Brent, should you desire to see it. Mr Adams mentioned the draft once to Mr Rufus King, who said he remembered such a draft, but that it went to a committee with other papers, and was never heard of afterwards. Mr King's views of the subject, as far as I could collect them from Mr Adams, were precisely such as you expressed.

CCCLXX. James Madison to M. L. Hurlbert.[2]

Montpellier, May, 1830.

And if I am to answer your appeal to me as a witness, I must say

---

[1] *Documentary History of the Constitution*, V, 350–351.
[2] *Letters and other Writings of James Madison*, IV, 74.

that the real measure of the powers meant to be granted to Congress by the Convention, as I understood and believe, is to be sought in the specifications, to be expounded, indeed, not with the strictness applied to an ordinary statute by a court of law, nor, on the other hand, with a latitude that, under the name of means for carrying into execution a limited Government, would transform it into a Government without limits. _____

CCCLXXI. JAMES MADISON TO JAMES HILLHOUSE.[1]

Montpellier, May —, 1830.

The difficulty of reconciling the larger States to the equality in the Senate, is known to have been the most threatening that was encountered in framing the Constitution. It is known, also, that the powers committed to that body, comprehending, as they do, Legislative, Executive, and Judicial functions, was among the most serious objections, with many, to the adoption of the Constitution.

_____

CCCLXXII. JAMES MADISON TO ANDREW STEVENSON.[2]

Montpr. Novr. 17. 1830

I have recd. your very friendly favor of the 20th instant, referring to a conversation when I had lately the pleasure of a visit from you, in which you mentioned your belief that the terms "common defence & general welfare" in the 8th. Section of the first Article of the Constitution of the U. S. were still regarded by some as conveying to Congress a substantive & indefinite power; and in which I communicated my views of the introduction and occasion of the terms, as precluding that comment on them; and you express a wish that I would repeat those views in the answer to your letter.

However disinclined to the discussion of such topics at a time when it is so difficult to separate in the minds of many, questions purely Constitutional from the party polemics of the day, I yield to the precedents which you think I have imposed on myself, & to the consideration that without relying on my personal recollections, which your partiality overvalues, I shall derive my construction of the passage in question, from sources of information & evidence known or accessible to all who feel the importance of the subject, and are disposed to give it a patient examination.

In tracing the history & determining the import of the terms "Common defence & general welfare" as found in the text of the

_____

[1] *Letters and other Writings of James Madison*, IV, 77.
[2] *Documentary History of the Constitution*, V, 352–365.

Constitution the following lights are furnished by the printed Journal of the Convention which formed it.

The terms appear in the general propositions offered May 29 as a basis for the incipient deliberations, the first of which "Resolved that the Articles of the Confederation ought to be so corrected & enlarged as to accomplish the objects proposed by their institution, namely — common defence, security of liberty, and general welfare". On the day following, the proposition was exchanged for Resolved "that an Union of the States merely federal will not accomplish the objects proposed by the Articles of Confederation; namely, common defence, security of liberty and general welfare".

The inference from the use here made of the terms, & from the proceedings on the subsequent propositions is, that altho' Common defence & general welfare were objects of the Confederation, they were limited objects, which ought to be enlarged by an enlargement of the particular powers to which they were limited — and to be accomplished by a change in the structure of the Union from a form merely federal to one partly national, and as these general terms are prefixed in the like relation to the several Legislative powers in the new Charter, as they were in the Old, they must be understood to be under like limitations in the new as in the Old.

In the course of the proceedings between the 30th. of May & the 6th. of Augt. the terms Common defence & General welfare as well as other equivalent terms must have been dropped: for they do not appear in the Draft of a Constitution, reported on that day, by a Committee appointed to prepare one in detail; the clause in which those terms were afterwards inserted, being, simply in the Draft "The Legislature of the U. S. shall have power to lay & collect taxes duties, imposts & excises".

The manner in which the terms became transplanted from the Old into the new System of Government, is explained by a course somewhat adventitiously given to the proceedings of the Convention.

On the 18th. of Augt. among other propositions referred to the Committee which had reported the draft was one "to *secure* the payment of the Public debt.", and,

On the same day, was appointed a Committee of Eleven members, (one from each State) "to consider the necessity & expediency of *the debts of the several States,* being assumed by the U. States"

On the 21st. of Augt. this last Committee reported a clause in the words following "The Legislature of the U. States *shall have power* to fulfil the engagements, *which have been* entered into by Congress, and to discharge as well the debts of the U. States, as the debts incurred by the *several* States, *during the late war,* for the *common* *defence* and *general welfare"; conforming herein to the 8th. of the Articles of Confederation, the language of which is, that "all charges of war and all other expences that shall be incurred for the common defence and general welfare, and allowed by the U. S in Congress assembled, shall be defrayed out of a common treasury" &c.

On the 22d. of Augst. the Committee of five reported among other additions to the clause *giving power* "to lay and collect taxes imposts & excises," a clause in the words following "for payment of the debts and necessary expences", with a proviso qualifying the duration of Revenue laws.

This Report being taken up, it was moved, as an amendment, that the clause should read "the Legislature *shall* fulfil the engagements and discharge the debts of the U. States"

It was then moved to strike out "discharge the debts", and insert "liquidate the claims"; which being rejected, the amendment was agreed to as proposed viz "the Legislature *shall* fulfil the engagements & discharge the debts of the U. States".

On the 23d. of Augst. the clause was made to read "the Legislature shall fulfil the engagements and discharge the debts of the U. States, and shall have the power to lay & collect taxes duties imposts & excises" the two powers relating to taxes & debts being merely transposed.

On the 25th. of August, the clause was again altered so as to read "all debts contracted and engagements entered into by or under the authority of Congress (the Revolutionary Congress) shall be as valid under this Constitution as under the Confederation"

This amendment was followed by a proposition (referring to the powers to lay & collect taxes &c — and to discharge the debts (*old* debts) to add "for payment of *said* debts, and for defraying the *expences that shall be* incurred *for the common defence & general welfare"*. The propostion was disagreed to, one State only voting for it.

Sepr. 4. The Committee of eleven reported the following modification — "The Legislature shall have power to lay & collect taxes duties imposts and excises, to pay the debts and provide for the common defence & general welfare"; thus retaining the terms of the Articles of Confederation, & covering by the general term "debts", those of the Old Congress.

A special provision in this mode could not have been necessary for the debts of the New Congress: For a power to provide money, and a power to perform certain acts of which money is the ordinary & appropriate means, must of course carry with them a power to pay the expence of performing the acts. Nor was any special provision for debts proposed, till the case of the Revolutionary debts was brought into view, and it is a fair presumption from the course of the varied propositions which have been noticed, that but for the old debts, and their association with the terms "common defence & general welfare", the clause would have remained as reported in the first Draft of a Constitution, expressing generally a "power in Congress to lay and collect taxes duties imposts & excises"; without any addition of the phrase "to provide for the common defence & general welfare". With this addition indeed the language of the clause being, in conformity with that of the clause in the Articles of Confederation, it would be qualified, as in those Articles, by the specification of powers subjoined to it.   But there is sufficient reason to suppose that the terms in question would not have been introduced but for the introduction of the old debts, with which they happened to stand in a familiar tho' inoperative relation.   Thus introduced however, they passed undisturbed thro' the subsequent stages of the Constitution.

If it be asked why the terms "common defence & general welfare", if not meant to convey the comprehensive power, which taken literally they express, were not qualified & explained by some reference to the particular powers subjoined, the answer is at hand, that altho' it might easily have been done, and experience shews it might be well if it had been done, yet the omission is accounted for by an inattention to the phraseology, occasioned, doubtless, by its identity with the harmless character attached to it in the Instrument from which it was borrowed

But may it not be asked with infinitely more propriety, and without the possibility of a satisfactory answer, why, if the terms were meant to embrace not only all the powers particularly expressed, but the indefinite power which has been claimed under them, the intention was not so declared; why on that supposition, so much critical labor was employed in enumerating the particular powers; and in defining and limiting their extent?

The variations & vicissitudes in the modifation of the clause in which the terms, "common defence & general welfare" appear, are remarkable; and to be no otherwise explained, than by differences of opinion concerning the necessity or the form, of a constitutional provision for the debts of the Revolution; some of the members, apprehending improper claims for losses, by depreciated emissions of bills of credit; others an evasion of proper claims if not positively brought within the authorized functions of the new Govt; and others again considering the past debts of the U. States as sufficiently secured by the principle that no change in the Govt. could change the obligations of the nation.   Besides the indications in the Journal, the history of the period sanctions this explanation.

But it is to be emphatically remarked, that in the multitude of motions, propositions, and amendments, there is not a single one having reference to the terms "common defence & general welfare", unless we were so to understand the proposition containing them, made on Aug. 25. which was disagreed to by all the States except one.[1]

The obvious conclusion to which we are brought is, that these terms copied from the Articles of Confederation, were regarded in the new as in the old Instrument merely as general terms, explained & limited by the subjoined specifications; and therefore requiring no critical attention or studied precaution

If the *practice* of the Revolutionary Congress be pleaded in opposition to this view of the case, the plea is met by the notoriety that on several accounts the practice of that Body is not the expositor of the "Articles of Confederation". These Articles were not in force till they were finally ratified by Maryland in 1781. Prior to that event the power of Congress was measured by the exigencies of the war, and derived its sanction from the acquiescence of the States. After that event, habit and a continued expediency, amounting often to a real or apparent necessity, prolonged the exercise of an undefined authority; which was the more readily overlooked; as the members of the Body held their seats during pleasure, as its Acts, particularly after the failure of the Bills of Credit, depended for their efficacy on the will of the States; and as its general impotency became manifest. Examples of departure from the prescribed rule, are too well known to require proof. The case of the old Bank of N. America might be cited as a memorable one. The incorporating Ordinance grew out of the inferred necessity of such an Institution to carry on the war, by aiding the finances which were starving under the neglect or inability of the States to furnish their assessed quotas. Congress was at the time so much aware of the deficient authority, that they recommended it to the State Legislatures to pass laws giving due effect to the Ordinance: which was done by Pennsylvania and several other States. In a little time, however, so much dissatisfaction arose in Pennsylvania where the Bank was located, that it was proposed to repeal the law of the State in support of it. This brought on attempts to vindicate the adequacy of the power of Congress, to incorporate such an Institution. Mr. Wilson, justly distinguished for his intellectual powers, being deeply impressed with the importance of a Bank at such a Crisis, published

---

[1] Crossed out: "The disagreement however was probably the result of some other consideration."

a small pamphlet, entitled "Considerations on the Bank of N. America", in which he endeavored to derive the power from the *nature* of the *Union*, in which the Colonies were declared & became Independent States; and also from the tenor of the "Articles of Confederation" themselves.   But what is particularly worthy of notice is, that with all his anxious search in those Articles for such a power, he never glanced at the terms "Common Defence & general Welfare" as a source of it.   He rather chose to rest the claim on a recital in the text, "that for the more convenient management of the *general* interests of the *United* States, Delegates shall be annually appointed to meet in Congress, which he said implied that the *United* States had *general* rights, *general* powers, and *general* obligations; not derived from *any* particular State, nor from *all* the particular States, taken separately; but "*resulting* from the *Union* of the whole" these *general* powers, not being controuled by the Article declaring that each State retained *all* powers not granted by the Articles, because "the *individual* States *never* possessed & could not *retain* a *general* power over the others"

The authority & argument here resorted to, if proving the ingenuity & patriotic anxiety of the author on one hand, shew sufficiently on the other, that the terms "common defence & general welfare cd. not according to the known acceptation of them avail his object.

That the terms in question were not suspected, in the Convention which formed the Constitution of any such meaning as has been constructively applied to them, may be pronounced with entire confidence.   For it exceeds the possibility of belief, that the known advocates in the Convention for a jealous grant & cautious definition of federal powers, should have silently permitted the introduction of words or phrases in a sense rendering fruitless the restrictions & definitions elaborated by them.

Consider for a moment the immeasurable difference between the Constitution limited in its powers to the enumerated objects; and expanded as it would be by the import claimed for the phraseology in question.   The difference is equivalent to two Constitutions, of characters essentially contrasted with each other; the one possessing powers confined to certain specified cases; the other extended to all cases whatsoever: For what is the case that would not be embraced by a general power to raise money, a power to provide for the general welfare, and a power to pass all laws necessary & proper to carry these powers into execution; all such provisions and laws superseding, at the same times, all local laws & constitutions at variance with them.   Can less be said with the evidence before us furnished by the Journal of the Convention itself, than that it is impossible that such a Constitution as the latter would have been recommended to the States by all the members of that Body whose names were subscribed to the Instrument.

Passing from this view of the sense in which the terms common defence & general welfare were used by the Framers of the Constitution, let us look for that in which they must have been understood by the Conventions, or rather by the people who thro' their Conventions, accepted & ratified it. And here the evidence is if possible still more irresistible, that the terms could not have been regarded as giving a scope to federal Legislation, infinitely more objectionable, than any of the specified powers which produced such strenuous opposition, and calls for amendments which might be safeguards against the dangers apprehended from them.

Without recurring to the published debates of those Conventions, which as far as they can be relied on for accuracy, would it is believed not impair the evidence furnished by their recorded proceedings, it will suffice to consult the lists of amendments proposed by such of the Conventions as considered the powers granted to the new Government too extensive or not safely defined.

Besides the restrictive & explanatory amendments to the text of the constitution it may be observed, that a long list was premised under the name & in the nature of "Declarations of Rights"; all of them indicating a jealousy of the federal powers, and an anxiety to multiply securities against a constructive enlargement of them. But the appeal is more particularly made to the number & nature of the amendments proposed to be made specific & integral parts of the Constitutional text.

No less than seven States, it appears, concurred in adding to their ratifications, a series of amendments, wch they deemed requisite. Of these amendments *nine* were proposed by the Convention of Massachusetts; *five* by that of S. Carolina; *twelve* by that of N. Hampshire; *twenty* by that of Virginia; *thirty three* by that of N. York; *twenty six* by that of N. Carolina; *twenty one* by that of R. Island.

Here are a majority of the States, proposing amendments, in one instance thirty three by a single State; all of them intended to circumscribe the powers granted to the General Government by explanations restrictions or prohibitions, without including a single proposition from a single State, referring to the terms, common defence & general welfare; which if understood to convey the asserted power, could not have failed to be the power most strenuously aimed at because evidently more alarming in its range, than all the powers objected to put together. And that the terms should have passed altogether unnoticed by the many eyes wch saw danger in terms & phrases employed in some of the most minute & limited of the enumerated powers, must be regarded as a demonstration, that it was taken for granted that the terms were harmless, because explained & limited, as in the "Articles of Confederation", by the enumerated powers which followed them.

A like demonstration, that these terms were not understood in any sense that could invest Congress with powers not otherwise bestowed by the Constitutional Charter may be found in what passed in the first Session of the first Congress, when the subject of Amendments was taken up, with the conciliatory view of freeing the Constitution from objections which had been made to the extent of its powers, or to the unguarded terms employed in describing them. Not only were the terms "common defence and general welfare", unnoticed in the long list of amendments brought forward in the outset; but the Journals of Congs. shew that in the progress of the discussions, not a single proposition was made in either branch of the Legislature which referred to the phrase as admitting a constructive enlargement of the granted powers, and requiring an amendment guarding against it. Such a forbearance & silence on such an occasion, and among so many members who belonged to the part of the nation, which called for explanatory & restrictive amendments, and who had been elected as known advocates for them, can not be accounted for without supposing that the terms "common defence & general welfare", were not at that time deemed susceptible of any such construction as has since been applied to them.

It may be thought perhaps, due to the subject, to advert to a letter of Octr. 5. 1787 to Samuel Adams and another of Ocr. 16 of the same year to the Governor of Virginia, from R. H. Lee, in both which, it is seen that the terms had attracted his notice, and were apprehended by him "to submit to Congress every object of human Legislation". But it is particularly worthy of Remark, that altho' a member of the Senate of the U. States, when Amendments to the Constitution were before that House, and sundry additions & alterations were there made to the list sent from the other, no notice was taken of those terms as pregnant with danger. It must be inferred that the opinion formed by the distinguished member at the first view of the Constitution, & before it had been fully discussed, & elucidated, had been changed into a conviction that the terms did not fairly admit the construction he had originally put on them: and therefore needed no explanatory precaution agst. it. . . .

Memorandum not used in Letter to Mr. Stevenson.[1]

These observations will be concluded with a notice of the argument in favor of the grant of a full power to provide for common defence and general welfare, drawn from the punctuation in some editions of the Constitution.

According to one mode of presenting the text, it reads as follows: "Congress shall have power — To lay and collect taxes, duties, imposts, and excises; to pay the debts and provide for the common defence and general welfare of the United States; but all duties, imposts, and excises, shall be uniform." To another mode, the same with commas *vice* semicolons.

According to the other mode, the text stands thus: "Congress shall have power; To lay and collect taxes, duties, imposts, and excises: To pay the debts and provide for the common defence and general welfare of the United States; but all duties, imposts, and excises shall be uniform throughout the United States."

And from this view of the text, it is inferred that the latter sentence conveys a distinct substantive power to provide for the common defence and general welfare.[2]

Without inquiring how far the text in this form would convey the power in question; or admitting that any mode of presenting or distributing the terms could invalidate the evidence which has been exhibited, that it was not the intention of the general or of the State Conventions to express, by the use of the terms common defence and general welfare, a substantive and indefinite power; or to imply that the general terms were not to be explained and limited by the specified powers succeeding them, in like manner as they were explained and limited in the former Articles of Confederation from which the terms were taken; it happens that the authenticity of the punctuation which preserves the unity of the clause can be as

---

[1] *Letters and other Writings of James Madison*, IV, 131–133.

[2] G. Hunt, *Writings of James Madison*, IX (1910), 413, reproduces this passage as follows:

"According to one mode of presenting the text: it reads as follows: Congress shall have power To lay & collect taxes duties-imposts & excises; to pay the debts & provide for the C. D. & G. W. of the U. S. but all duties imposts & excises shall be uniform; to another mode the same with commas — vice semicolons.

"According to the other mode the text stands thus: Congress shall have power,
 To lay & col. tax, ds. imp. & excises;
 To pay the debts & provide for the Com. d. & G. W. of the U. S.;
 but all ds. imp. & excs. shall be uniform throug: the U. S.
and from this view of the text, it is inferred that the latter sentence conveys a distinct substantive power to provide for the C. D. & G. W."

satisfactorily shown, as the true intention of the parties to the Constitution has been shown in the language used by them.

The only instance of a division of the clause afforded by the journal of the Convention is in the draught of a Constitution reported by a committee of five members, and entered on the 12th of September.

But that this must have been an erratum of the pen or of the press, may be inferred from the circumstance, that, in a copy of that report, printed at the time for the use of the members, and now in my possession, the text is so printed as to unite the parts in one substantive clause; an inference favoured also by a previous report of September 4, by a committee of eleven, in which the parts of the clause are united, not separated.

And that the true reading of the Constitution, as it passed, is that which unites the parts, is abundantly attested by the following facts:

1. Such is the form of the text in the Constitution printed at the close of the Convention, after being signed by the members, of which a copy is also now in my possession.

2. The case is the same in the Constitution from the Convention to the old Congress, as printed on their journal of September 28, 1787, and transmitted by that body to the Legislatures of the several States.

3. The case is the same in the copies of the transmitted Constitution, as printed by the ratifying States, several of which have been examined; and it is a presumption that there is no variation in the others.

The text is in the same form in an edition of the Constitution published in 1814, by order of the Senate; as also in the Constitution as prefixed to the edition of the United States; in fact, the proviso for uniformity is itself a proof of identity of them.

It might, indeed, be added, that in the journal of September 14, the clause to which the proviso was annexed, now a part of the Constitution, viz: "but all duties, imposts, and excises, shall be uniform throughout the United States," is called the "first," of course a "single" clause. And it is obvious that the uniformity required by the proviso implies that what it referred to was a part of the same clause with the proviso, not an antecedent clause altogether separated from it.

Should it be not contested that the original Constitution, in its engrossed and enrolled state, with the names of the subscribing members affixed thereto, presents the text in the same form, that alone must extinguish the argument in question.

If, contrary to every ground of confidence, the text, in its original enrolled document, should not coincide with these multiplied examples, the first question would be of comparative probability of error, even in the enrolled document, and in the number and variety of the concurring examples in opposition to it.

And a second question, whether the construction put on the text, in any of its forms or punctuations, ought to have the weight of a feather against the solid and diversified proofs which have been pointed out, of the meaning of the parties to the Constitution.

Supplement to the letter of November 27, 1830, to A. Stevenson, on the phrase "common defence and general welfare." — On the power of indefinite appropriation of money by Congress.[1]

It is not to be forgotten, that a distinction has been introduced between a power merely to appropriate money to the common defence and general welfare, and a power to employ all the means of giving full effect to objects embraced by the terms.

1. The first observation to be here made is, that an *express* power to appropriate money authorized to be raised, to objects authorized to be provided for, could not, as seems to have been supposed, be at all necessary; and that the insertion of the power "to pay the debts," &c., is not to be referred to that cause.   It has been seen, that the particular expresssion of the power originated in a cautious regard to debts of the United States antecedent to the radical change in the Federal Government; and that, but for that consideration, no particular expression of an appropriating power would probably have been thought of.   An express power to raise money, and an express power (for example) to raise an army, would surely imply a power to use the money for that purpose.   And if a doubt could possibly arise as to the implication, it would be completely removed by the express power to pass all laws necessary and proper in such cases.   . . .

The peculiar structure of the Government, which combines an equal representation of unequal numbers in one branch of the Legislature, with an equal representation of equal numbers in the other, and the peculiarity which invests the Government with selected powers only, not intrusting it even with every power withdrawn from the local governments, prove not only an apprehension of abuse from ambition or corruption in those administering the Government, but of oppression or injustice from the separate interests or views of the constituent bodies themselves, taking effect through the admin-

---

[1] *Letters and other Writings of James Madison*, IV, 134-137.

istration of the Government. These peculiarities were thought to be safeguards due to minorities having peculiar interests or institutions at stake, against majorities who might be tempted by interest or other motives to invade them. . . .

The result of this investigation is, that the terms "common defence and general welfare" owed their induction into the text of the Constitution to their connexion in the "Articles of Confederation," from which they were copied, with the debts contracted by the old Congress, and to be provided for by the new Congress; and are used in the one instrument as in the other, as general terms, limited and explained by the particular clauses subjoined to the clause containing them; that in this light they were viewed throughout the recorded proceedings of the Convention which framed the Constitution; that the same was the light in which they were viewed by the State Conventions which ratified the Constitution, as is shown by the records of their proceedings; and that such was the case also in the first Congress under the Constitution, according to the evidence of their journals, when digesting the amendments afterward made to the Constitution.

_____

CCCLXXIII. James Madison to I. K. Tefft.[1]

December 3d, 1830.

In the year 1828 I received from J. V. Bevan sundry numbers of the "Savannah Georgian," containing continuations of the notes of Major Pierce in the Federal Convention of 1787. They were probably sent on account of a marginal suggestion of inconsistency between language held by me in the Convention with regard to the Executive veto, and the use made of the power by myself, when in the Executive Administration.[2] The inconsistency is done away by the distinction, not adverted to, between an *absolute* veto, to which the language was applied, and the *qualified* veto which was exercised.

_____

CCCLXXIV. James Madison to Reynolds Chapman.[3]

January 6, 1831.

Perhaps I ought not to omit the remark, that although I concur in the defect of powers in Congress on the subject of internal improvements, my abstract opinion has been, that, in the case of canals particularly, the power would have been properly vested in Con-

_____

[1] *Letters and other Writings of James Madison*, IV, 139–140.
[2] The marginal note in the *Savannah Georgian* reads: "This same Mr. Madison did so when President. Eds. Geo." (*American Historical Review*, III, p. 322 note 4).
[3] *Letters and other Writings of James Madison*, IV, 149.

gress. It was more than once proposed in the Convention of 1787, and rejected from an apprehension, chiefly, that it might prove an obstacle to the adoption of the Constitution. Such an addition to the Federal powers was thought to be strongly recommended by several considerations: 1. As Congress would possess, exclusively, the sources of revenue most productive and least unpopular, that body ought to provide and apply the means for the greatest and most costly works. 2. There would be cases where canals would be highly important in a national view, and not so in a local view. 3. Cases where, though highly important in a national view, they might violate the interest, real or supposed, of the State through which they would pass, of which an example might now be cited in the Chesapeake and Delaware canal, known to have been viewed in an unfavourable light by the State of Delaware. 4. There might be cases where canals, or a chain of canals, would pass through sundry States, and create a channel and outlet for their foreign commerce, forming at the same time a ligament for the Union, and extending the profitable intercourse of its members, and yet be of hopeless attainment if left to the limited faculties and joint exertions of the States possessing the authority.

CCCLXXV. James Madison to C. J. Ingersoll.[1]

Montpellier, February 2, 1831.

The evil which produced the prohibitory clause in the Constitution of the United States was the practice of the States in making bills of credit, and in some instances appraised property, "a legal tender." If the notes of the State Banks, therefore, whether chartered or unchartered, be made a legal tender, they are prohibited; if not made a legal tender, they do not fall within the prohibitory clause. The No. of the "Federalist" referred to (44) was written with that view of the subject; and this, with probably other contemporary expositions, and the uninterrupted practice of the States in creating and permitting banks without making their notes a legal tender, would seem to be a bar to the question, if it were not inexpedient now to agitate it.

A virtual and incidental enforcement of the depreciated notes of the State Banks, by their crowding out a sound medium, though a great evil, was not foreseen; and if it had been apprehended, it is questionable whether the Constitution of the United States, which had many obstacles to encounter, would have ventured to guard against it by an additional obstacle.

---

[1] *Letters and other Writings of James Madison*, IV, 160.

CCCLXXVI. James Madison to Theodore Sedgwick, Jr.[1]

Montpr. Feb. 12, 1831

You ask whether Mr Livingston (formerly Governor of N. Jersey) took an active part in the debates (of the Fedl Convention of 1787) and whether he was considered as having a leaning towards the federal Party and principles; adding that you will be obliged by any further information it may be in my power to give you.

Mr Livingston did not take his seat in the Convention till some progress had been made in the task committed to it, and he did not take an active part in its debates; but he was placed on important Committees, where it may be presumed he had an agency and a due influence. He was personally unknown to many, perhaps most of the members, but there was a predisposition in all to manifest the respect due to the celebrity of his name.

I am at a loss for a precise answer to the question whether he had a leaning to the federal party and principles. Presuming that by the party alluded to, is meant those in the Convention who favored a more enlarged, in contradistinction to those who favored a more restricted grant of powers to the Fedl Govt, I can only refer to the recorded votes which are now before the public; and these being by States not by heads, the individual opinions are not disclosed by them. The votes of N. Jersey corresponded generally with the Plan offered by Mr. Patterson; but the main object of that being to secure to the smaller States an equality with the larger in the structure of the Govt, in opposition to the outline previously introduced, which had reversed the object, it is difficult to say what was the degree of power to which there might be an abstract leaning. The two subjects, the structure of the Govt and the question of power entrusted to it were more or less inseparable in the minds of all, as depending a good deal, the one on the other, after the compromise wch gave the small States an equality in one branch of the Legislature, and the large States an inequality in the other branch, the abstract leaning of opinions would better appear. With those however who did not enter with debate, and whose votes could not be distinguished from those of their State colleagues, their opinions could only be known among themselves, or to their particular friends.

I know not Sir that I can give you any of the further information you wish, that is not attainable with more authenticity and particularity from other sources. My acquaintance with Gov Livingston was limited to an exchange of the common civilities, and these to the period of the Convention.

---

[1] Library of Congress, Madison Papers, Draft.

CCCLXXVII. James Madison to James Robertson.[1]

March 27, 1831.

The journals of the State Legislatures, with the journal and debates of the State Conventions, and the journal and other printed accounts of the proceedings of the Federal Convention of 1787, are, of course, the primary sources of information. Some sketches of what passed in that Convention have found their way to the public, particularly those of Judge Yates and of Mr. Luther Martin. But the Judge, though a highly respectable man, was a zealous partizan, and has committed gross errors in his desultory notes. He left the Convention also before it had reached the stages of its deliberations in which the character of the body and the views of individuals were sufficiently developed. Mr. Martin, who was also present but a part of the time, betrays, in his communication to the Legislature of Maryland, feelings which had a discolouring effect on his statements. As it has become known that I was at much pains to preserve an account of what passed in the Convention, I ought perhaps to observe, that I have thought it becoming, in several views, that a publication of it should be at least of a posthumous date.

CCCLXXVIII. Jared Sparks to James Madison.[2]

New York, March 30th. 1831

Having recently engaged to write a life of Gouvernieur Morris, which is to be published with a selection from his writings, I take the liberty to apply to you for a few hints respecting the part he acted in the convention of 1787. From several quarters I have understood, that he was an active member, and had a good deal of weight and influence, but the published account of that convention is so meagre, such a very skeleton of dry bones with hardly a sinew, muscle, or ligature, to tell that it was a living thing, that it is impossible to ascertain from it the relative standing or prevailing views of any member.

Was Morris with Hamilton on the prominent doctrines of the constitution, or did he incline to the more democratic side? Was he a frequent speaker, and an efficient member? Was he the author of any of the important features of the constitution? Did he set forth any particular views, which he labored to enforce & establish?

I have been told by several persons, who professed to know the fact, that the constitution in its present form and language is from his pen; that is, after all debates were finished, and each particular

---

[1] *Letters and Other Writings of James Madison*, IV, 167.
[2] *Documentary History of the Constitution*, V, 365–367.

had been adopted in substance, the instrument was then put into his hands to be wrought into proper phraseology & style. His friends here are in the habit of thinking, that much is due to him for the clear, simple, & expressive language in which the constitution is clothed.

The following anecdote is also current among those, who suppose themselves well informed on the point. During the sitting of the convention G. Morris was absent several days to attend the funeral of his mother. On his return he called at the house of Robert Morris, where he found Washington, who, with R. Morris, was much dejected at what they deemed the deplorable state of things in the convention. Debates had run high, conflicting opinions were obstinately adhered to, animosities were kindling, some of the members were threatening to go home, and at this alarming crisis a dissolution of the convention was hourly to be apprehended. Instructed in these particulars, G. Morris went into the convention on the day following, and spoke with such eloquence and power on the necessity of union, of partial sacrifices, & temperate discussion, that he effected a change in the feelings of the members, which was the means of restoring harmony, and ultimately of effecting the objects of the convention. It is added, that, as his absence had prevented his partaking of the warmth, which had grown out of the previous discussions, his counsel & apparent disinterestedness had the greater effect. Do you recollect any incident of this sort? [1]

You will doubtless excuse me for troubling you with the above questions, since there is no other source, written or unwritten, to which I can apply for information, and since the world is become so curious to know all that pertains to the origin & history of the Constitution. Whatever you may think proper to communicate on this subject, I trust will be used with discretion. In touching on that part of Mr Morris's life, I shall take an opportunity to speak of the convention according to such light as I shall possess.

CCCLXXIX. James Madison to Jared Sparks.[2]

Montpellier, April 8, 1831.

I have duly received your letter of March 30th.[3] In answer to your inquiries, "respecting the part acted by Gouverneur Morris in the Federal Convention of 1787, and the political doctrines maintained by him," it may be justly said, that he was an able, an elo-

---

[1] See CCCLXXIX below.
[2] Jared Sparks, *Life of Gouverneur Morris*, I, 284–286.
[3] See CCCLXXVIII above.

quent, and an active member, and shared largely in the discussions succeeding the 1st of July, previous to which, with the exception of a few of the early days, he was absent.

Whether he accorded precisely with the "political doctrines of Hamilton," I cannot say. He certainly did not "incline to the democratic side," and was very frank in avowing his opinions, when most at variance with those prevailing in the Convention. He did not propose any outline of a constitution, as was done by Hamilton; but he contended for certain articles, (a Senate for life particularly) which he held essential to the stability and energy of a government, capable of protecting the rights of property against the spirit of democracy. He wished to make the weight of wealth balance that of numbers, which he pronounced to be the only effectual security to each, against the encroachments of the other.

The *finish* given to the style and arrangement of the Constitution fairly belongs to the pen of Mr Morris; the task having, probably, been handed over to him by the chairman of the Committee, himself a highly respectable member, and with the ready concurrence of the others. A better choice could not have been made, as the performance of the task proved. It is true, that the state of the materials, consisting of a reported draft in detail, and subsequent resolutions accurately penned, and falling easily into their proper places, was a good preparation for the symmetry and phraseology of the instrument, but there was sufficient room for the talents and taste stamped by the author on the face of it. The alterations made by the Committee are not recollected. They were not such, as to impair the merit of the composition. Those, verbal and others made in the Convention, may be gathered from the Journal, and will be found also to leave that merit altogether unimpaired.

The anecdote you mention may not be without a foundation, but not in the extent supposed. It is certain, that the return of Mr Morris to the Convention was at a critical stage of its proceedings. The knot, felt as the Gordian one, was the question between the larger and the smaller States, on the rule of voting in the senatorial branch of the legislature; the latter claiming, the former opposing, the rule of equality. Great zeal and pertinacity had been shown on both sides, and an equal division of votes on the question had been reiterated and prolonged, till it had become not only distressing, but seriously alarming. It was during that period of gloom, that Dr. Franklin made the proposition for a religious service in the Convention, an account of which was so erroneously given, with every semblance of authenticity, through the National Intelligencer,

several years ago.[1] The crisis was not over, when Mr Morris is
said to have had an interview and conversation with General Washington and Mr Robert Morris, such as may well have occurred.
But it appears that, on the day of his re-entering the Convention,
a proposition had been made from another quarter to refer the knotty
question to a Committee, with a view to some compromise, the indications being manifest, that sundry members from the larger States
were relaxing in their opposition, and that some ground of compromise was contemplated, such as finally took place, and as may be
seen in the printed Journal. Mr Morris was in the deputation from
the large State of Pennsylvania, and combated the compromise
throughout. The tradition is, however, correct, that, on the day
of his resuming his seat, he entered with anxious feelings into the
debate, and, in one of his speeches painted the consequences of an
abortive result to the Convention, in all the deep colors suited to
the occasion. But it is not believed, that any material influence
on the turn, which things took, could be ascribed to his efforts. For,
besides the mingling with them some of his most disrelished ideas,
the topics of his eloquent appeals to the members had been exhausted
during his absence, and their minds were too much made up, to be
susceptible of new impressions.

It is but due to Mr Morris to remark, that, to the brilliancy of
his genius, he added, what is too rare, a candid surrender of his opinions, when the lights of discussion satisfied him, that they had been
too hastily formed, and a readiness to aid in making the best of
measures in which he had been overruled.

CCCLXXX. James Madison to J. K. Paulding.[2]

Montpellier, Apl —, 1831.

Of Franklin I had no personal knowledge till we served together
in the Federal Convention of 1787, and the part he took there has
found its way to the public, with the exception of a few anecdotes
which belong to the unveiled part of the proceedings of that Assembly.

. . . As a proof of the fallability to which the memory of Mr.
Hamilton was occasionally subject, a case may be referred to so
decisive as to dispense with every other. In the year —— Mr.
Hamilton, in a letter answering an inquiry of Col. Pickering concerning the plan of Government which he had espoused in the Convention of 1787, states, that at the close of the Convention he put into

------

[1] See CCCLV above, and CCCXCIII below.
[2] *Letters and other Writings of James Madison*, IV, 174-175, 177.

my hands a draught of a Constitution; and in that draught he had proposed a "President for three years." Now, the fact is, that in that plan, the original of which I ascertained several years ago to be among his papers, *the tenure of office* for the President is not *three years, but during good behavior.*

CCCLXXXI. JAMES MADISON TO J. K. PAULDING.[1]

Apl. 1831.

Much curiosity & some comment have been excited by the marvellous identities in a "Plan of Govt. proposed by Chs. Pinckney in the Convn. of 1787, as published in the Journals with the text of the Constitution as finally agreed to. I find among my pamphlets a copy of a small one "entitled "Observations on the Plan of Govt submitted to the Fedl Convention in Phila on the 28th. of May by Mr. C. P. a Delegate from S. C. delivered at different times in the Convention"

My Copy is so defaced & mutilated that it is impossible to make out eno' of the Plan as referred to in the Observation, for a due comparison of it, with that printed in the Journal. The pamphlet was printed in N. Y. by Francis Childs. The year is effaced: It must have been not very long after the close of the Convention; and with the sanction at least of Mr. P. himself. It has occurred that a copy may be attainable at the Printing office if still kept up, or examined in some of the Libraries, or Historical Collections in the City. When you can snatch a moment in yr walks with other views; for a call at such places, you will promote an object of some little interest as well as *delicacy*, by ascertaining whether the article in question can be met with. I have among my manuscript papers, lights on the subject, The pamphlet of Mr. P. could not fail to add to them

CCCLXXXII. JAMES MADISON TO J. K. PAULDING.[2]

June 6. 1831.

Since my letter answering yours of Apl. 6, in which I requested you to make an enquiry concerning a small pamphlet of Charles Pinckney printed at the close of the Fedl Convention of 1787, it has occurred to me that the pamphlet might not have been put in circulation, but only presented to his friends &c. In that way I may have become possessed of the copy to which I referred as in damaged state. On this supposition the only chance of success must be among the Books &c. of individuals on the list of Mr. P–'s political associates

---

[1] *Documentary History of the Constitution*, V, 367–368.
[2] *Documentary History of the Constitution*, V, 371.

& personal friends. Of those who belonged to N. Y. I recollect no one so likely to have recd. a Copy as Rufus King. If that was the case, it may remain with his Representative– and I would suggest an informal resort to that quarter, with a hope that you will pardon this further tax on your kindness.

CCCLXXXIII. James Madison to Jared Sparks.[1]

June 27, 1831.

I have received your letter of the 16th. inst., inclosing a copy of the letter of Mr. Charles Pinckney to Mr. Adams, accompanying the draft of a Constitution for the United States, and describing it as essentially the draft proposed by him to the Federal Convention of 1787.[2] The letter to Mr. Adams was new to me.

Abundant evidence I find exists of material variance between the two drafts, and I am sorry that the letter of Mr. Pinckney is far from explaining them. It does not appear, as you inferred, that the draft sent to Mr. Adams was compiled from his notes and papers; but that it was one of the several drafts found amongst them, and the very one, he believed, that he had presented to the Convention, all the drafts, however, being substantially the same.

Some of the variances may be deduced from the printed journal of the Convention. You will notice, for example, that on the 6th or 7th of June, very shortly after his draft was presented, he proposed to take from the *people* the election of the Federal House of Representatives, and assign it to the *legislatures of the States*, a violent presumption that the latter, not the former, was the mode contained in his draft.

It is true, as Mr. Pinckney observes and as the journal shows, that the Executive was the last department of the government that received its full and final discussion; but I am not sure that he is free from error in the view his letter gives of what passed on the occasion, or that the error, with several others, may not be traced by a review of the journal.

I am at a loss for the ground of his contrast between the latter period of the Convention and the cool and patient deliberation for more than four and a half months preceding. The whole term of the Convention, from its appointed commencement, was short of that period; and its actual session, from the date of a quorum, but four months, three days. And the occasion on which the most serious and threatening excitement prevailed (the struggle between the

-----

[1] H. B. Adams, *Life and Writings of Jared Sparks*, II, 227–229.
[2] See CCCXXVI above.

larger and smaller States in relation to the representation in the Senate) occurred, as the journal will show, during the period noted as the cool and patient one. After the compromise which allowed an equality of votes in the Senate, that consideration, with the smaller number and longer tenure of its members, will account for the abridgment of its powers by associating the Executive in the exercise of them.

Among the instances in which the memory of Mr. Pinckney failed him is the remark in his letter that, very soon after the Convention met, he had avowed a change of opinion in giving Congress a power to revise the state laws, thinking it safer to refuse the power *altogether*. It appears from the journal that as late as the 23rd. of August the proposition was renewed, with a change only, requiring two thirds instead of a majority of each house. The journal does not name the mover, but satisfactory information exists that it was Mr. Pinckney.

Mr. Adams was probably restrained from printing the letter of Mr. Pinckney by the vague charges in it against the Convention, and a scruple of publishing a part only.

I have been suffering for some time a severe attack of rheumatism, and I offer this brief compliance with your request of my view of Mr. Pinckney's letter under an unabated continuance of it. This alone would be a reason for desiring that nothing in the communication should be referred to as resting upon my authority. But there are others, drawn from my relation to the subject and the relation which subsisted between Mr. Pinckney and myself, which must always require that I should not be a party to an exposure of the strange incongruities into which he has fallen, without a fuller view of the proofs, and the obligation not to withhold them, than the present occasion would permit.

CCCLXXXIV. James Madison to J. K. Paulding.[1]

June 27, 1831.

With your favor of the 20th instant I received the volume of pamphlets containing that of Mr. Charles Pinckney, for which I am indebted to your obliging researches. The volume shall be duly returned, and in the meantime duly taken care of. I have not sufficiently examined the pamphlet in question, but have no doubt that it throws light on the object to which it has relation.

---

[1] *Letters and other Writings of James Madison*, IV, 182–183.

CCCLXXXV. James Madison on the Pinckney Plan.[1]

The length of the Document laid before the Convention, and other circumstances having prevented the taking of a copy at the time, that which is here inserted [2] was taken from the paper furnished to the Secretary of State, and contained in the Journal of the Convention published in 1819 which it being taken for granted was a true copy was not then examined. The coincidence in several instances between that and the Constitution as adopted, having attracted the notice of others was at length suggested to mine. On comparing the paper with the Constitution in its final form, or in some of its Stages; and with the propositions, and speeches of Mr. Pinckney in the Convention, it would seem [3] that considerable errour must have [4] crept into the paper; occasioned possibly by the loss of the Document laid before the Convention, (neither that nor the Resolutions offered by Mr Patterson being among the preserved papers) and by a consequent resort for a copy to the rough draught, in which erasures and interlineations following what passed in the Convention, might be confounded in part at least with the original text, and after a lapse of more than thirty years, confounded also in the memory of the Author.

There is in the paper a similarity in some cases, and an identity in others, with details, expressions, and definitions, the results of critical discussions and modifications in the Convention that can not be ascribed to accident or anticipation.[5]

Examples may be noticed in Article VIII of the paper; which is remarkable also for the circumstance, that whilst it specifies the functions of the President, no provision is contained in the paper for the election of such an officer, nor indeed for the appointment of any Executive Magistracy: notwithstanding the evident purpose of the Author to provide an *entire* plan of a Federal Government.

Again, in several instances where the paper corresponds with the Constitution, it is at variance with the ideas of Mr. Pinckney, as decidedly expressed in his propositions, and in his arguments, the former in the Journal of the Convention, the latter in the report of its debates: Thus in Art: VIII of the paper, provision is made for removing the President by impeachment; when it appears that

---

[1] *Documentary History of the Constitution*, V, 417–432. This document was evidently intended as a note to the proceedings of May 29 in Madison's Debates. It was probably written before 1835, but as the "Editorial note" which is attached to it is the more important of the two, it is inserted here.

[2] Interlined "inserted in the debates".

[3] Interlined "it was apparent".   [4] Interlined "had".

[5] Interlined "could not have been anticipated".

in the Convention, July 20. he was opposed to any impeachability of the Executive Magistrate: In Art: III, it is required that all money-bills shall originate in the first Branch of the Legislature; which he strenuously opposed Aug: 8 and again Aug: 11: In Art: V members of each House are made ineligible to, as well as incapable of holding, any office under the Union &c, as was the case at one Stage of the Constitution; a disqualification highly disapproved and opposed by him Aug: 14.

A still more conclusive evidence of errour in the paper is seen in Art: III, which provides, as the Constitution does, that the first Branch of the Legislature shall be chosen by the people of the several States; whilst it appears, that on the 6th. of June, according to previous notice too, a few days only, after the Draft was laid before the Convention, its Author opposed that mode of choice, urging & proposing in place of it, an election by the Legislatures of the several States.

The remarks here made, tho' not material in themselves, were due to the authenticity and accuracy aimed at, in this Record of the proceedings of a Publick Body, so much an object, sometimes, of curious research, as at all times, of profound interest

As an Editorial note to the paper in the hand writing of Mr. M.
beginning "The length &c.-" [1]

Striking discrepancies will be found on a comparison of his plan, as furnished to Mr. Adams, and the view given of that which was laid before the Convention, in a pamphlet published by Francis Childs at New York shortly after the close of the Convention. The title of the pamphlet is "Observations on the plan of Government submitted to the Federal Convention on the 28th. of May 1787 by Charles Pinckney &ca."

But what conclusively proves that the choice of the H. of Reps. *by the people* could not have been the choice in the lost paper is a letter from Mr. Pinkney to J. M. of *March 28. 1789*, now on his files, in which he emphatically [shows] adherence to a choice by the *State Legres.* The following is an extract — "Are you not, to use a full expression, abundantly convinced that the theoretical nonsense of an election of the members of Congress by the people in the first instance, is clearly and practically wrong. — that it will in the end be the means of bringing our Councils into contempt and that the Legislatures (of the States) are the only proper judges of who ought to be elected." — —

---

[1] From letters to J. K. Paulding, see CCCLXXXI and CCCLXXXIV above, it is probable that this note was prepared about June, 1831.

Observations on Mr. Pinkney's plan &c. &c

In the plan of Mr. Pinkney as presented to Mr. Adams & published in the Journal of the Convention.	The plan according to his comments in the pamphlet printed by Francis Childs in New York.
The House of Representatives to be chosen.[1] No council of Revision.	No provision for electing the House of Representatives. A Council of Revision consisting of the Executive and principal officers of government. "This, I consider as an improvement in legislation, and have therefore incorporated it as a part of the system."
The President to be elected for years —	The Executive to be appointed septennially
not in the plan.	— "have a right to convene and prorogue the Legislature upon special occasions, when they cannot agree as to the time of their adjournment;
"and, except as to Ambassadors, other Ministers, and Judges of the Supreme Court, he shall nominate, and *with the consent of the Senate*, apppoint all other officers of the U. S."	and appoint all officers except Judges and Foreign Ministers."
The 7th Article gives the Senate the exclusive power to regulate the manner of deciding all disputes and controversies now subsisting, or which may arise, between the States, respecting jurisdiction or territory:	"The 9th article respecting the appointment of Federal Courts for deciding territorial controversies between different States, is the same with that in the Confederation; but this may with propriety be left to the Supreme Judicial."
Article 6th. "all laws regulating commerce shall require the assent	"In all those important questions where the present Confed-

---

[1] Crossed out: "by the people; with details similar to the 2d. section 1. article of the Constitution of the U. S."

of two thirds of the members present in each House."

eration has made the assent of nine States necessary, I have made the assent of ⅔ds. of both Houses, when assembled in Congress, and added to the number the regulation of trade and acts for levying an Impost and raising a revenue".

The 14th article gives the Legislature power to admit new States into the Union on the same terms with the original States by ⅔ of both Houses. — nothing further

"I have also added an article authorising the United States, upon petition from the majority of the Citizens of any State, or Convention authorised for that purpose, and of the Legislature of the State to which they wish to be annexed, or of the States among which they are willing to be divided, to consent to such junction or division, on the terms mentioned in the article." [1]

Plan.

Pamphlet.

no such provision.

page 25. "a provision respecting the attendance of the members of both Houses; the penalties under which their attendance is required, are such as to insure it, as we are to suppose no man

---

[1] The two paragraphs following were crossed out:

A number of important articles are referred to in the pamphlet & not found in the plan — for example " the provision respecting the attendance of the members of both Houses; the penalties under which their attendance is required, are such as to insure it, as we are to suppose no man would willingly expose himself to the ignominy of a disqualification (pa 25) providing for the writ of Habeas Corpus & trial by Jury in Civil cases (page 26) — " to secure to authors the exclusive right to their performances and discoveries " page 26.

So also In the plan presented the powers of the Senate are given in Article 7th. tho' ⟨The mode of appointment on the rotative principles each   mode of appointment class for 4 years,⟩ the mode of appointment of that body it is silent   The latter is given in the pamphlet but its powers are not enumerated.   The restriction on members of both Houses from holding any office under the union is not adverted to in the pamphlet — nor the power of the Legislature to appoint a Treasurer, to establish post and military roads &c.

"All criminal offences (except in cases of impeachment) shall be tried in the State where they shall be committed. The trials shall be open & public, & be by Jury."

        silent.

would willingly expose himself to the ignominy of a disqualification".

Trial by Jury is provided for "in all cases, criminal as well as *Civil*".

"to secure to authors the exclusive right to their performances and discoveries".

Powers of the Senate enumerated Article 7th. vizt. "to declare war, make treaties, & appoint ambassadors and Judges of the Supreme Court.[1]

silent.

"Every bill, which shall have passed the Legislature, shall be presented to the President for his revision; if he approves it he shall sign it; but if he does not approve it, he shall return it with his objections &a. &a. — The Legislature shall have power

    To subdue a rebellion in any State, on application of its Legislature;

    To provide such dockyards & arsenals, and erect such fortifications as may be necessary for the U. S. and to exercise exclusive jurisdiction therein;

    To establish post & military roads;

    To declare the law & punishment of counterfeiting coin.

The Executive "is not a branch of the Legislature, farther than as a part of the Council of Revision".

---

[1] In the left hand column under "Plan", were crossed out four paragraphs on: (1) ineligibility of members of legislature to hold office; (2) "Legislature to appoint a Treasurer"; (3) Legislature "to establish post & military roads"; and (4) members of both houses to be paid by their states. Opposite each paragraph in the right hand column, "silent" was crossed out.

To declare the punishment of treason, which shall consist only in levying war against the U. S., or any of them, or in adhering to their enemies. No person shall be convicted of treason but by the testimony of two witnesses.

The prohibition of any tax on exports — —

These and other important powers and are unnoticed in his remarks.

There is no numerical correspondence between the articles contained in the plan & those treated of in the pamphlet & the latter alludes to several more than are included in the former.

In Mr. Pinkney's letter to Mr. Adams, accompanying his plan, he states that "very soon after the Convention met, I changed and avowed candidly the change of my opinion on giving the power to Congress to revise the State laws in certain cases, and in giving the exclusive power to the Senate to declare war, thinking it safer to refuse the first altogether, and to vest the latter in Congress."

In his pamphlet he concludes the 5th. page of his argument in favor of the first power with these remarks — "In short, from their example, (other republics) and from our own experience, there can be no truth more evident than this, that, unless our Government is consolidated, as far as is practicable, by retrenching the State authorities, and concentering as much force & vigor in the Union, as are adequate to its exigencies, we shall soon be a divided, and consequently an unhappy people. I shall ever consider the revision and negative of the State laws, as one great and leading step to this reform, and have therefore conceived it proper to bring it into view."

On the 23. August He moved a proposition to vest this power in the Legislature, provided ⅔ of each House assented.

He does not designate the depository of the power to declare war & consequently avows no change of opinion on that subject in the pamphlet, altho' it was printed after the adjournment of the Convention and is stated to embrace the "observations he delivered at different times in the course of their discussions"

J. M. has a copy of the pamphlet much mutilated by dampness; but one in complete preservation is bound up with "Select Tracts Vol. 2." belonging to the New York Historical Society, numbered 2687.

Title

Observations on the plan of Government submitted to the Federal Convention, in Philadelphia, on the 28th. of May 1787, By Mr. Charles Pinkney, Delegate from the State of South Carolina — delivered at different times in the course of their discussions —
New York: — Printed by Francis Childs.

In the plan of Mr. Pinkney as presented to Mr. Adams and published in Journal	Plan as commented on in Pamphlet
Article 1. Style —	Not adverted to
Article 2. Division of Legislative power in two Houses.	recommended as essential page 8.
Article 3. Members of H. of D. to be chosen by the people. &a.	silent.
Article 4. Senate to be elected by the H. of Del. &c. . .	recommended page 9. but the 4th. article relates to extending rights of citizens of each State throughout U S. the delivery of fugitives from justice, on demand; & the giving faith & credit to records & proceedings of each — vide Art. 12 & 13.
Article 5 — relates to the mode of electing the H. of Del. by the people & rules &a. Every bill to be presented to the *President* for his revision.	This article declares that Individual states shall not exercise certain powers, founded on the principles of the 6th. of the Confederation. A *Council* of revision is stated to be incorporated in his plan page 9. vide Art 11. for prohibitions — empowers Congress to raise troops; & to levy taxes according to number of whites & ⅗ of other descriptions.
Article 6. powers of the Legislature enumerated & all constitutional acts thereof, and treaties declared to be the	This article is stated to be an important alteration in the fedl. system, giving to Congress not only a revision but a negative

supreme law & the judges bound thereby.

Article 7. Senate alone to declare war– make treaties & appoint ministers & Judges of Sup. Court — To regulate the manner of deciding disputes now subsisting, or which may arise, between States respecting jurisdiction or territory —

Article 8. The Executive power — H. E. President U. S. for ——— years & re-eligible– To give information to the Legislature of the state of the Union & recommend measures to their consideration — To take care that the laws be executed — To commission all officers of the U. S. and except ministers & Judges of Sup. Court, nominate & *with consent of Senate* appoint all other officers — to receive ministers & may correspond with Ex. of different States. To grant pardon except in impeachments. To be commander in chief — to receive a fixed compensation — to take an oath — removable on impeachment by H. of D. and conviction in Supreme Court of bribery or corruption. The President of Senate to act as Prest. in case of death &a and the Speaker of H. of D. in case of death of Pres. of Senate —

on the State laws. The States to retain only local legislation limited to concerns affecting each only. vide Art. 11th. Article 8. like same in Confed. & gives power to exact postage for expense of office & for revenue. The 7th. article invests the U. S. with the compleat power of regulating trade & levying imposts & duties. (The regulation of commerce is given in the powers enumerated article 6th. of plan.)

Page 9. The Executive should be appointed septennially, but his eligibility should not be limited — Not a branch of the Legislature further than as part of the Council of revision – His duties to attend to the execution of the acts of Congress, by the several States; to correspond with them on the subject; to prepare and digest, in concert with the great departments, business that will come before the Legislature. To acquire a perfect knowledge of the situation of the Union, and to be charged wth the business of the Home Deptmt. — To inspect the Departments. To consider their Heads as a Cabinet Council & to require their advice. To be Commander in Chief — to convene the legislature on special occasions & to appoint all officers but Judges & Foreign ministers — removable by impeachment — salary to be fixed permanently by the Legislature.

Article 9. gives the legislature power to establish Courts of law, equity & admiralty & relates to the appointment tenure & compensation of judges — one to be the Supreme Court — its jurisdiction over all cases under the laws of U. S. or affecting Ambassadors &c, to the trial of impeachment of officers of U. S.; cases of admiralty & maritime jurisdiction — cases where original & where appellate —

The 9th article respecting the appointment of Federal Courts, for deciding controversies between different States, is the same with the Confederation; but this may with propriety be left to the Supreme Judicial (*Article 7th. of the plan gives the power to the Senate* of regulating the manner of decision)

Article 10. after first census the H. of D– shall apportion the Senate by electing one Senator for every for every —— members each State shall have in H. of D– each State to have at least one member.

The 10th article gives Congress a right to institute such offices as are necessary; of erecting a Federal Judicial Court; and of appointing Courts of Admiralty.

page 19. The exclusive right of coining money &ca is essential to assuring the federal funds — &a.

page 20. In all important questions where the Confederation made the assent of 9 States necessary I have made ⅔ of both Houses — and have added to them the regulation of trade and acts for levying Impost & raising revenue —

page 20. The exclusive right of making regulations for the government of the Militia ought to be vested in the Federal Councils &a

page 22. The article empowering the U. S. to admit new States indispensable — vide Article 14.

see article 6th.

To establish uniform rules of naturalization in Article 6.

page 23. The Fed. Govt. should possess the exclusive right of declaring on what terms the privileges of citizenship & naturalization should be extended to foreigners —

Article 16. provides the same by ⅔ — —

page 23. Article 16. provides that alterations may be made by a given number of the Legislature —

Nothing of it —————

page 25. There is also in the articles, a provision respecting the attendance of members of both Houses — the penalties under which their attendance is required are such as to insure it &ca

It is provided in Art. 9. that "All criminal offenses (except in cases of impeachment) shall be tried in the State where committed. The trials shall be open & public, and be by Jury." nothing as to the rest —

page 26. The next article provides for the privilege of the writ of Habeas Corpus — the trial by Jury in all cases, criminal as well as civil — the freedom of the press, and the prevention of religious tests as qualifications for offices of trust &a

Article 6. provides for a seat of Govt. & a National University thereat — but no protection for authors is provided —

page 26. There is also an authority to the National legislature, permanently to fix the seat of the Genl. Govt., to secure to authors the exclusive right to their performances & discoveries & to establish a federal university.

Not in the plan — ———

There are other articles of subordinate consideration.

CCCLXXXVI. Jared Sparks to James Madison.[1]

November 14, 1831.

"Gouverneur Morris" is in press . . . It will be in three volumes, the first a memoir, and the other two selections from his writings, all of which I hope to send you in January. He has left

----

[1] H. B. Adams, *Life and Writings of Jared Sparks*, II, 230–231.

hardly a scrap of paper on the subject of the Convention, and I shall consequently have very little to say of that matter.

. . . I doubt whether any clear light can be gained till Pinckney's original draft shall be found, which is probably among the papers of one of the committee. It seems to me that your secretary of the Convention was a very stupid secretary, not to take care of those things better, and to make a better journal than the dry bones which now go by that name.

CCCLXXXVII. James Madison to Jared Sparks.[1]

Montpellier, November 25, 1831.

I have received your favor of the 14th instant. The simple question is, whether the draught sent by Mr. Pinckney to Mr. Adams, and printed in the Journal of the Convention, could be the same with that presented by him to the Convention on the 29th day of May, 1787; and I regret to say that the evidence that that was not the case is irresistible. Take, as a sufficient example, the important article constituting the House of Representatives, which, in the draught sent to Mr. Adams, besides being too minute in its details to be a possible anticipation of the result of the discussion, &c., of the Convention on that subject, makes the House of Representatives *the choice of the people.* Now, the known opinion of Mr. Pinckney was, that that branch of Congress ought to be chosen by the *State Legislatures*, and not immediately by the people. Accordingly, on the 6th day of June, not many days after presenting his draught, Mr. Pinckney, agreeably to previous notice, moved that, as an amendment to the Resolution of Mr. Randolph, the term "people" should be struck out and the word "Legislatures" inserted; so as to read, "Resolved, That the members of the first branch of the National Legislature ought to be elected by the Legislatures of the several States." But what decides the point is the following extract from him to me, dated March 28, 1789:

"Are you not, to use a full expression, abundantly convinced that the theoretic nonsense of an election of the members of Congress by the people, in the first instance, is clearly and practically wrong; that it will, in the end, be the means of bringing our Councils into contempt, and that the Legislatures are the only proper judges of who ought to be elected?"

Other proofs against the identity of the two draughts may be found in Article VIII of the Draught, which, whilst it specifies the functions of the President, contains no provision for the election

---

[1] *Letters and other Writings of James Madison*, IV, 201–203.

of such an officer, nor, indeed, for the appointment of any Executive Magistracy, notwithstanding the evident purpose of the author to provide an *entire* plan of a Federal Government.

Again, in several instances where the Draught corresponds with the Constitution, it is at variance with the ideas of Mr. Pinckney, as decidedly expressed in his votes on the Journal of the Convention. Thus, in Article VIII of the Draught, provision is made for removing the President by impeachment, when it appears that in the Convention, July 20, he was opposed to any impeachability of the Executive Magistrate. In Article III, it is required that all money-bills shall originate in the first branch of the Legislature; and yet he voted, on the 8th August, for striking out that provision in the Draught reported by the Committee on the 6th. In Article V, members of each House are made ineligible, as well as incapable, of holding any office under the Union, &c., as was the case at one stage of the Constitution; a disqualification disapproved and opposed by him August 14th.

Further discrepancies might be found in the observations of Mr. Pinckney, printed in a pamphlet by Francis Childs, in New York, shortly after the close of the Convention. I have a copy, too mutilated for use, but it may probably be preserved in some of your historical repositories.

It is probable that in some instances, where the Committee which reported the Draught of Augt 6th might be supposed to have borrowed from Mr. Pinckney's Draught, they followed details previously settled by the Convention, and ascertainable, perhaps, by the Journal. Still there may have been room for a passing respect for Mr. Pinckney's plan by adopting, in some cases, his arrangement; in others, his language. A certain analogy of outlines may be well accounted for. All who regard the object of the Convention to be a real and regular Government, as contradistinguished from the old Federal system, looked to a division of it into Legislative, Executive, and Judiciary branches, and of course would accommodate their plans to their organization. This was the view of the subject generally taken and familiar in conversation, when Mr. Pinckney was preparing his plan. I lodged in the same house with him, and he was fond of conversing on the subject. As you will have less occasion than you expected to speak of the Convention of 1787, may it not be best to say nothing of this delicate topic relating to Mr. Pinckney, on which you cannot use all the lights that exist and that may be added?

CCCLXXXVIII. James Madison to N. P. Trist.[1]

Decr. 1831.

I return with my thanks the printed speech of Col. Hayne on the 4th. of July last. It is blotted with many strange errors, some of a kind not to have been looked for from a mind like that of the author. . . .

But I find that by a sweeping charge, my inconsistency is extended to "my opinions on almost every important question which has divided the public into parties". In supporting this charge, an appeal is made to "Yates' secret Debates in the Federal Convention of 1787", as proving that I originally entertained opinions adverse to the Rights of the States; and to the writings of Col. Taylor of Caroline, as proving that I was in that convention, "an advocate for a *consolidated national Government.*

Of the Debates, it is certain that they abound in errors, some of them very material in relation to myself. Of the passages quoted, it may be remarked that they do not warrant the inference drawn from them. They import "that I was disposed to give Congress a power to repeal State laws", and "that the States ought to be *placed under the controul of the Genl. Government,* at least as much as they were formerly when under the British King & Parliament".

The obvious necessity of a controul on the laws of the States, so far as they might violate the Constn. & laws of the U. S. left no option but as to the mode. The modes presenting themselves, were 1. a Veto on the passage of the State laws. 2. a Congressional repeal of them, 3 a Judicial annulment of them. The first tho extensively favord, at the outset, was found on discussion, liable to insuperable objections, arising from the extent of Country, and the multiplicity of State laws. The second was not free from such as gave a preference to the *third* as now provided by the Constitution. The opinion that the States ought to be placed not less under the Govt. of the U. S. than they were under that of G. B, can provoke no censure from those who approve the Constitution as it stands with powers exceeding those ever allowed by the Colonies to G. B., particularly the vital power of taxation, which is so indefinitely vested in Congs. and to the claim of which by G. B. a bloody war, and final separation was preferred.

The author of the "Secret Debates", tho highly respectable in his general character, was the representative of the portion of the State of New York, which was strenuously opposed to the object of the Convention, and was himself a zealous partizan. His notes carry on their face proofs that they were taken in a very desultory manner, by which parts of sentences explaining or qualifying other parts, might often escape the ear. He left the Convention also on the 5th. of July before it had reached the midway of its Session, and before the opinions of the members were fully developed into their matured & practical shapes. Nor did he conceal the feelings of discontent & disgust, which he carried away with him. These considerations may account for errors; some of which are self-condemned. Who can believe that so crude and untenable a statement could have been intentionally made on the floor of the Convention as "that the *several States* were political Societies, *varying* from the *lowest Corporations*, to the *highest sovereigns*" or "that the States had vested *all* the *essential rights* of Government in the *old* Congress."

On recurring to the writings of Col. Taylor,* it will be seen that he founds his imputation agst. myself and Govr. Randolph, of favoring a Consolidated National Governt on the Resolutions introduced into the Convention by the latter, in behalf of the Virga. Delegates, from a consultation among whom they were the result. The Resolutions imported that a Govt. consisting of a *National* Legislre. Executive & Judiciary, ought to be substituted for the Existing Congs. Assuming for the term *National* a meaning coextensive with a Single Consolidated Govt. he filled a number of pages, in deriving from that source, a support of his imputation. The whole course of proceedings on those Resolutions ought to have satisfied him that the term *National* as contradistinguished from *Federal*, was not meant to express more than that the powers to be vested in the new Govt. were to operate as in a Natl. Govt. directly on the people, & not as in the Old Confedcy. on the States only. The extent of the powers to be vested, also tho' expressed in loose terms, evidently had reference to limitations & definitions, to be made in the progress of the work, distinguishing it from a plenary & Consolidated Govt.

It ought to have occurred that the Govt. of the U. S being a novelty & a compound, had no technical terms or phrases appropriate to it; and that old terms were to be used in new senses, explained by the context or by the facts of the case.

Some exulting inferences have been drawn from the change noted in the Journal of the Convention, of the word *National* into "*United States.*" The change may be accounted for by a desire to avoid a misconception of the former, the latter being preferred as a familiar caption. That the change could have no effect on the real character of the Govt. was & is obvious; this being necessarily

* See "New Views," written *after* the Journal of Convn. was printed.

deduced from the actual structure of the Govt. and the quantum of its powers. . . .

Another error has been in ascribing to the *intention* of the *Convention* which formed the Constitution, an undue ascendency in expounding it. Apart from the difficulty of verifying that intention it is clear, that if the meaning of the Constitution is to be sought out of itself, it is not in the proceedings of the Body that proposed it, but in those of the State Conventions which gave it all the validity & authority it possesses. ⸺⸺⸺

CCCLXXXIX. James Madison to James T. Austin.[1]

Montpellier Feby 6 1832

I have recd your letter of 19th ulto requesting "a communication of any facts connected with the services of the late V. President Gerry in the Convention of 1787" The letter was retarded by its address to Charlottesville instead of Orange City. It would give me pleasure to make any useful contribution to a biography of Mr. Gerry for whom I had a very high esteem and a very warm regard. But I know not that I could furnish any particular facts of that character separable from his general course in the Convention, especially without some indicating reference to them. I may say in general, that Mr. G. was an active an able, and interesting member of that assembly, and that the part he bore in its discussions and proceedings was important and continued to the close of them. The grounds on which he dissented from some of the results are well known. ⸺⸺⸺

CCCXC. James Madison to Professor Davis.[2]

Montpellier, 1832.

It deserves particular attention, that the Congress which first met contained sixteen members, eight of them in the House of Representatives,* fresh from the Convention which framed the Constitution, and a considerable number who had been members of the State Conventions which had adopted it, taken as well from the party which opposed as from those who had espoused its adoption. Yet it appears from the debates in the House of Representatives, (those in the Senate not having been taken,) that not a doubt was started of the power of Congress to impose duties on imports for the encouragement of domestic manufactures. . . .

* Nicholas Gilman, Elbridge Gerry, Roger Sherman, George Clymer, Thomas Fitzsimmons, Daniel Carroll, James Madison, Jr., Abraham Baldwin.

---

[1] Library of Congress, Madison Papers.
[2] *Letters and other Writings of James Madison*, IV, 247, 251–254.

The incapacity of the States separately to regulate their foreign commerce was fully illustrated by an experience which was well known to the Federal Convention when forming the Constitution. It was well known that the incapacity gave a primary and powerful impulse to the transfer of the power to a common authority capable of exercising it with effect. . . .

New York, Pennsylvania, Rhode Island, and Virginia, previous to the establishment of the present Constitution, had opportunities of taxing the consumption of their neighbours, and the exasperating effect on them formed a conspicuous chapter in the history of the period. The grievance would now be extended to the inland States, which necessarily receive their foreign supplies through the maritime States, and would be heard in a voice to which a deaf ear could not be turned.

The condition of the inland States is of itself a sufficient proof that it could not be the intention of those who framed the Constitution to *substitute* for a power in Congress to impose a protective tariff, a power merely to permit the States individually to do it. Although the present inland States were not then in existence, it could not escape foresight that it would soon, and from time to time, be the case. Kentucky was then known to be making ready to be an independent State, and to become a member of the Confederacy. What is now Tennessee was marked by decided circumstances for the same distinction. On the north side of the Ohio new States were in embryo under the arrangements and auspices of the Revolutionary Congress, and it was manifest, that within the Federal domain others would be added to the Federal family.

As the anticipated States would be without ports for foreign commerce, it would be a mockery to provide for them a permit to impose duties on imports or exports in favor of manufactures, and the mockery would be the greater as the obstructions and difficulties in the way of their bulky exports might the sooner require domestic substitutes for imports; and a protection for the substitutes, by commercial regulations, which could not avail if not general in their operation and enforced by a general authority. . . .

But those who regard the permission grantable in section ten, article one, to the States to impose duties on foreign commerce, as an intended substitute for a general power in Congress, do not reflect that the object of the permission, qualified as it is, might be less inconsistently explained by supposing it a concurrent or supplemental power, than by supposing it a substituted power.

Finally, it cannot be alleged that the encouragement of manufactures permissible to the States by duties on foreign commerce, is to be regarded as an incident to duties imposed for revenue. Such a view of the section is barred by the fact that revenue cannot be the object of the State, the duties accruing, not to the State, but to the United States. The duties also would even diminish, not increase, the gain of the federal treasury, by diminishing the consumption of imports within the States imposing the duties, and, of course, the aggregate revenue of the United States. The revenue, whatever it might be, could only be regarded as an incident to the manfacturing object, not this to the revenue. . . .

Attempts have been made to show, from the journal of the Convention of 1787, that it was intended to withhold from Congress a power to protect manufactures by commercial regulations. The intention is inferred from the rejection or not adopting of particular propositions which embraced a power to encourage them. But, without knowing the reasons for the votes in those cases, no such inference can be sustained. The propositions might be disapproved because they were in a bad form or not in order; because they blended other powers with the particular power in question; or because the object had been, or would be, elsewhere provided for. No one acquainted with the proceedings of deliberative bodies can have failed to notice the frequent uncertainty of inferences from a record of naked votes. It has been with some surprise, that a failure or final omission of a proposition "to establish public institutions, rewards, and immunities for the promotion of agriculture, commerce, and manufactures," should have led to the conclusion that the Convention meant to exclude from the federal power over commerce regulations encouraging domestic manufactures. (See Mr. Crawford's letter to Mr. Dickerson, in the National Intelligencer of ———.) Surely no disregard of a proposition embracing *public institutions, rewards,* and *immunities* for the *promotion* of *agriculture, commerce,* and *manufactures,* could be an evidence of a refusal to encourage the particular object of manufactures, by the particular mode of duties or restrictions on rival imports. In expounding the Constitution and deducing the intention of its framers, it should never be forgotten, that the great object of the Convention was to provide, by a new Constitution, a remedy for the defects of the existing one; that among these defects was that of a power to regulate foreign commerce; that in all nations this regulating power embraced the protection of domestic manufactures by duties and restrictions on imports; that the States had tried in vain to make use of the power, while it remained with them; and that, if taken from them and transferred to the Federal Government, with an exception of the power to encourage domestic manufactures, the American people, let it be repeated, present the solitary and strange spectacle of a nation disarming itself of a power exercised by every nation as a shield against the effect of the power as used by other nations. Who will say that such considerations as these are not among the best keys that can be applied to the text of the Constitution? and infinitely better keys than unexplained votes cited from the records of the Convention.   _____

CCCXCI. James Madison to W. C. Rives.[1]

Montpr. Ocr. 21 — 33.

As the charges of M——s.[2] are founded in the main, on "Yates debates in the federal Convention of 1787", it may be remarked without impeaching the integrity of the Reporter, that he was the representative in that Body of the party in N. York which was warmly opposed to the Convention, and to any change in the principles of the "articles of confederation"; that he was doubtless himself at the time, under all the political bias which an honest mind could feel; that he left the Convention, as the Journals shew, before the middle of the Session, and before the opinions or views of the members might have been developed into their precise & practical application; that the notes he took, are on the face of them, remarkably crude & desultory, having often the appearance of scraps & expressions as the ear hastily caught them, with a liability to omit the sequel of an observation or an argument which might qualify or explain it.

With respect to inferences from votes in the Journal of the Convention, it may be remarked, that being unaccompanied by the reasons for them, they may often have a meaning quite uncertain, and sometimes contrary to the apparent one. A proposition may be voted for, with a view to an expected qualification of it; or voted agst. as wrong in time or place, or as blended with other matter of objectionable import.

Although such was the imperfection of Mr Yates Notes of what passed in the Convention, it is on that authority alone that J. M. is charged with having said "that the States never possessed the essential *rights of sovereignty;* that these were always vested *in Congress*"

It must not be overlooked that this language is applied to the Condition of the States, and to that of Congress, under "the Articles of Confederation". Now can it be believed that Mr. Yates did not misunderstand J. M in making him say, that the States had *then*

_____

[1] *Documentary History of the Constitution*, V, 390–395.   [2] Mutius.

never possessed *the essential rights of sovereignty*" and that "*these* had always been vested in the *Congress then* existing. The charge is incredible, when it is recollected that the *second* of the Articles of Confederation emphatically declares "that each State *retains* its *sovereignty* freedom & independence and every power &c, which is not expressly delegated to the U. S. in Congs. assembled"

It is quite possible that J. M. might have remarked that certain powers attributes of sovereignty had been vested in Congs; for that was true as to the powers of war, peace, treaties &c" But that he should have held the language ascribed to him in the notes of Mr. Yates, is so far from being credible, that it suggests a distrust of their correctness in other cases where a strong presumptive evidence is opposed to it.

Again, J M. is made to say "that the States were only great political corporations having the power of making by-laws, and these are effectual only if they were not contradictory to the general confederation"

Without admitting the correctness of this statement in the sense it seems meant to convey, it may be observed that according to the *theory* of the old confederation, the laws of the States contradictory thereto would be ineffectual. That they were not so in *practice* is certain, and this practical inefficacy is well known to have been the primary inducement to the exchange of the old for the new system of Govt. for the U. S.

Another charge agst. J. M. is an "opinion that the States ought to be placed under the controul of the General Govt. at least as much as they formerly were under the King & Parliament of G. B."

The British power over the Colonies, as admitted by them, consisted mainly of 1. the Royal prerogatives of war & peace, treaties coinage &c. with a veto on the Colonial laws as a guard agst. laws interfering with the General law, and with each other: 2 the parliamentary power of regulating commerce, as necessary to be lodged somewhere, and more conveniently there than elsewhere. These powers are actually vested in the Federal Govt. with the difference, that for the veto power is substituted the general provision that the Constitution & laws of the U. S. shall be paramount to the Constitutions & laws of the States; and the further difference that no tax whatever should be levied by the British Parliament, even as a regulation of commerce; whereas an *indefinite* power of taxation is allowed to Congress, with the exception of a tax on exports, a tax the least likely to be resorted to. When it is considered that the power of taxation is the most commanding of powers, the one for which G. Britain contended for, and the Colonies resisted by a war of seven years, and when it is considered that the British Govt. was, in every branch, irresponsible to the American people, whilst every branch of the Federal Government is responsible to the States and the people as their Constituents, it might well occur on a general view of the subject, that in an effectual reform of the Federal system, as much power might be safely instrusted to the new Govt. as was allowed to G. B. in the old one.

An early idea taken up by J. M. with a view to the security of a Govt. for the Union, and the harmony of the State Governments, without allowing to the former an unlimited and consolidated power, appears to have been a negative on the State laws, to be vested in the Senatorial branch of the Govt; but under what modifications does not appear. This again is made a special charge against him. That he became sensible of the obstacles to such an arrangement, presented in the extent of the Country, the number of the States and the multiplicity of their laws, can not be questioned. But is it wonderful that among the early thoughts on a subject so complicated and full of difficulty, one should have been turned to a provision in the compound and on this point analogous system of which this Country had made a part; substituting for the distant, the independent & irresponsible authority of a King which had rendered the provision justly odius, an elective and responsible authority within ourselves.

It must be kept in mind that the radical defect of the old confederation lay in the power of the States to comply with to disregard or to counteract the authorisd requisitions & regulations of Congress that a radical cure for this fatal defect, was the essential object for which the reform was instituted; that all the friends of the reform looked for such a cure; that there could therefore be no question but as to the mode of effecting it. The deputies of Virga. to the Convention, consisting of G. W. Govr. R. &c appear to have proposed a power in Congs. to repeal the unconstitutional and interfering laws of the States. The proposed negative on them, as the Journals shew, produced an equal division of the Votes. In every proceeding of the Convention where the question of paramountship in the laws of the Union could be involved, the necessity of it appears to have been taken for granted. The mode of controuling the legislation of the States which was finally preferred has been already noticed. Whether it be the best mode, experience is to decide. But the necessity of some adequate mode of preventing the States in their individual characters, from defeating the Constitutional authority of the States in their united character, and from collisions among themselves, had been decided by a past experience. (It may be thought not unworthy of notice that Col. Taylor regarded the controul of the Fedl. Judiciary over the State laws as more objectionable than a Legislative negative on them. See New Views &c. p. 18. contra see Mr. Jefferson-vol. 2. p. 163)

M — s asks "If the States possessed no sovereignty, how could J. M. "demonstrate that the States retained a *residuary sovereignty*", and calls for a solution of the problem. He will himself solve it, by answering the question, which is most to be believed, that J M. should have been guilty of such an absurdity, or that Mr. Yates should have erred in ascribing it to him.

Mr. Y. himself says "that J. M. expressed as much attachment to the rights of the States as to the trial by Jury."

By associating J. M. with Mr. Hamilton who entertained peculiar opinions, M—s would fain infer that J. M. concurred with those opinions. The inference would have been as good, if he had made Mr. H. concur in all the opinions of J. M. That they agreed to a certain extent, as the body of the Convention manifestly did, in the expediency of an energetic Govt. adequate to the exigencies of the Union, is true. But when M — s adds "that Mr. H. & Mr. M. advocated a system, not only independent of the States, but which would have reduced them to the meanest municipalities", he failed to consult the recorded differences of opinion between the two individuals

_____

CCCXCII. James Madison to John Tyler.[1]

This letter it appears was not sent to Mr. Tyler — tho' it seems a fair vindication of the parties assailed.

In your speech of February 6th. 1833 you say "He (Edmund Randolph) proposed (in the Federal Convention of 1787) a Supreme National Government, with a Supreme Executive, a Supreme Legislature, and a Supreme Judiciary, and a power in Congress to veto State laws. Mr. Madison I believe, Sir, was also an advocate of this plan of govt. If I run into error on this point, I can easily be put right. The design of this plan, it is obvious, was to render the States nothing more than the provinces of a great government to rear upon the ruins of the old Confederacy a consolidated Government, one and indivisible."

I readily do you the justice to believe that it was far from your intention to do injustice to the Virginia Deputies to the Convention of 1787. But it is not the less certain that it has been done to all of them, and particularly to Mr Edmond Randolph.

_____

[1] *Documentary History of the Constitution*, V, 379-390.

The Resolutions proposed by him, were the result of a Consultation among the Deputies, the whole number, seven being present. The part which Virga. had borne in bringg. abt. the Convention, suggested the Idea that some such initiative step might be expected from her Deputation; and Mr. Randolph was designated for the task. It was perfectly understood, that the Propositions committed no one to their precise tenor or form; and that the members of the Deputation wd. be as free in discussing and shaping them as the other members of the Convention. Mr. R. was made the organ on the occasion, being then the Governor of the State, of distinguished talents, and in the habit of public speaking. Genl. Washington, tho' at the head of the list was, for obvious reasons disinclined to take the lead. It was also foreseen that he would be immediately called to the presiding station

Now what was the plan sketched in the Propositions?

They proposed that "the Articles of Confederation shd. be so corrected and enlarged as to accomplish the objects of their Institution — namely common defence, security of liberty, and general welfare,": (the words of the Confederation)

That a national Legislature, a national Executive and a national Judiciary should be established: (this organization of Departments the same as in the adopted Constitution)

That the right of suffrage in the Legislature shd be (not equal among ye States as in the Confederation but) proportioned to quotas of contribution or numbers of free inhabitants, as might seem best in different cases"; (the same principle corresponding with the mixed rule adopted)

"That it should consist of two branches: the first elected by the people of the several States, the second by the first of a number nominated by the State Legislatures", (a mode of forming a Senate regarded as more just to the large States, than the equality which was yielded to the small States by the compromise with them but not material in any other view. In reference to the practicable equilibrium between the General & the State authorities, the comparative influence of the two modes will depend on the question whether the small States, will incline most, to the former or to the latter scale.)

That a national Executive, with a Council of Revision consisting of a number of the Judiciary, (wch. Mr Jefferson wd. have approved) and a qualified negative on the laws, be instituted, to be chosen by the Legislature for the term of   years, to be ineligible a second time, and with a compensation to be neither increased nor diminished so as to affect the existing magistracy. (there is nothing in this Ex. modification, materially different in its Constitutional bearing from that finally adopted in the Constitution of the U. S.)

That a national Judiciary be established, consisting of a Supreme appellate and inferior, Tribunals, to hold their offices during good behavior, and with compensations, not to be *increased* or diminished, so as to affect persons in office (there can be nothing here subjecting it to unfavorable comparison with the article in the Constitution existing)

"That provision ought to be made for the admission of new States lawfully arising within the limits of the U. S. wth. the consent of a number of votes in the natl. Legislature less than the whole". (This is not at variance wth. the existing provision)

"That a Republican Govt. ought to be guaranteed by the U. S. to each State. (this is among the existing provisions)

"That provision ought to be made for amending the articles of Union, without requiring the assent of the National Legislature (this is done in the Constn.)

"That the Legisl: Ex. & Judiciary powers of the several States ought to be bound by oath to support the Articles of Union (this was provided with the emphatic addition of — "any thing in the Constn. or laws of the States notwithstanding)

"That the Act of the Convention, after the approbation of the (then) Congs. be submitted to an assembly or assemblies of Representatives recommended by the several Legislatures, to be expressly chosen by the people to decide thereon (This was the course pursued)

So much for the structure of the Govt. as proposed by Mr. Randolph, & for a few miscellaneous provisions. When compared with the Constn: as it stands what is there of a consolidating aspect that can be offensive to those who applaud approve or are satisfied with the Constn:

Let it next be seen what were the powers proposed to be lodged in the Govt. as distributed among its several Departments.

The Legislature, each branch possessing a right to originate acts, was to enjoy 1. the *Legislative* rights vested in the Congs. of the Confederation, (This must be free from objection, especially as the powers of that description were left to the selection of the Convention.

2. cases to which the separate States, would be incompetent or in which the harmony of the U. S. might be intercepted by individual Legislation. (It can not be supposed that these descriptive phrases were to be left in their indefinite extent to Legislative discretion. A selection & definition of the cases embraced by them was to be the task of the Convention. If there could be any doubt that this

was intended, & so understood by the Convention, it would be removed by the course of proceeding on them as recorded, in its Journal. many of the propositions made in the Convention, fall within this remark: being, as is not unusual general in their phrase, but if adopted to be reduced to their proper shape & specification.

3. to negative all laws passed by the several States contravening, in the opinion of the national Legislature, the Articles of Union or any Treaty subsisting under their Authority. (The necessity of some constitutional and effective provision guarding the Constn. & laws of the Union, agst. violations of them by the laws of the States, was felt and taken for granted by all from the commencement, to the conclusion of the work performed by the Convention. Every vote in the Journal involving the opinion, proves a unanimity among the Deputations, on this point. A voluntary & unvaried concurrence of so many, (then 13 with a prospect of continued increase), distinct & independent authorities, in expounding & acting on a rule of Conduct, which must be the same for all, or in force in none, was a calculation, forbidden by a knowledge of human nature, and especially so by the experience of the Confederacy, the defects of which were to be supplied by the Convention.)

With this view of the subject, the only question was the mode of controul on the Individual Legislatures. This might be either preventive or corrective; The former by a negative on the State laws; the latter by a Legislative repeal by a Judicial supersedeas, or by an administrative arrest of them. The preventive mode as the best if equally practicable with the corrective, was brought by Mr. R. to the consideration of the Convention. It was, tho' not a little favored as appears by the votes in the Journal finally abandoned, as not reducible to practice. Had the negative been assigned to the Senatorial branch of the Govt. representedg the State Legislatures, thus giving to the whole a controul of these over each, the expedient would probably have been still more favorably recd; tho' even in that form, subject to insuperable objections, in the distance of many of the State Legislatures, and the multiplicity of the laws of each.

Of the corrective modes, a repeal by the National Legislature was pregnant with inconveniences rendering it inadmissible.

The only remaining safeguard to the Constitution and laws of the Union, agst. the encroachment of its members and anarchy among themselves, is that which was adopted, in the Declaration that the Constitution laws & Treaties of the U. S should be the supreme law of the Land, and as such be obligatory on the Authorities of the States as well as those of the U. S.

The last of the proposed Legislative powers was "to call forth the force of the Union agst. any member failing to fulfil its duty under the Articles of Union"

The evident object of this provision was not to enlarge the powers of the proposed Govt. but to secure their efficiency. It was doubtless suggested by the inefficiency of the Confederate system, from the want of such a sanction; none such being expressed in its Articles; and if as Mr. Jefferson * argued, necessarily implied, having never been actually employed. The proposition as offered by Mr. R. was in general terms. It might have been taken into Consideration, as a substitute for, or as a supplement to the ordinary mode of enforcing the laws by Civil process; or it might have been referred to cases of territorial or other controversies between States and a refusal of the defeated party to abide by the decision; leaving the alternative of a Coercive interposition by the Govt. of the Union, or a war between its members, and within its bowels. Neither of these readings nor any other, which the language wd. bear, could countenance a just charge on the Deputation or on Mr. Randolph, of contemplating a consolidated Govt. with unlimited powers.

The Executive powers do not cover more ground, than those inserted by the Convention to whose discretion, the task of enumerating them was submitted. The proposed association with the Executive of a Council of Revision, could not give a consolidating feature to the plan.

The Judicial power in the plan, is more limited than the Jurisdiction described in the Constn; with the exception of cases of "impeachment of any national officer", and questions which involve the national peace & harmony."

The trial of Impeachts. is known to be one of the most difficult of Constl. arrangemts. The reference of it to the Judical Dept. may be presumed to have been suggested by the example in the Constitution of Virga. The option seemed to lie between that & the other Depts. of the Govt., no example of an organization excluding all the Departs. presenting itself. Whether the Judl mode proposed, was preferable to that inserted in the Const: or not, the difference cannot affect the question of a Consolidating aspect or tendency.

By questions involving "the Natl. peace and harmony", no one can suppose more was meant than might be *specified*, by the Convention as proper to be referred to the Judiciary either, by the Constn: or the Constl authority of the Legislature. They could be no rule, in that latitude, to a Court, nor even to a Legislature with limited powers.

That the Convention understood the entire Resolutions of Mr. R

* See his published letter of Aug. 4. 1787 to Edd. Carrington.

to be a mere sketch in which omitted details were to be supplied and the general terms and phrases to be reduced to their proper details, is demonstrated by the use made of them in the Convention. They were taken up & referred to a Come. of the whole in that sense; discussed one by one; referred occasionally to special Coms., to Comes. of detail on special points, at length to a Come. to digest & report the draft of a Constn: and finally to a Come. of arrangement and diction.

On this review of the whole subject, candour discovers no ground for the charge, that the Resolns. contemplated a Govt. materially different from or more national than that in which they terminated, and certainly no ground for the charge of consolidating views in those from whom the Resolns. proceeded.

What then is the ground on which the charge rests? It cd. not be on a plea that the plan of Mr. R. gave unlimited powers to the proposed Governt: for the plan expressly aimed at a specification, & of course a limitation of the powers.

It cd. not be on the supremacy of the general authority over the separate authorities, for that supremacy, as already noticed, is more fully & emphatically established by the text of the Constitution?

It cd. not be on the proposed ratification, by the people instead of the States for that is the ratification on wch. the Constn. is founded.

The Charge must rest on the term "National" prefixed to the organized Depts. in the propositions of Mr. R. yet how easy is it to acct. for the use of the term witht taking it in a consolidating sense?

In the 1st. place. It contradistinguished the proposed Govt from the Confederacy which it was to supersede.

2. As the System was to be a new & compound one a nondescript without a technical appellation for it, the term "National" was very naturally suggested by its national features. 1. in being estabd. not by the authority of State Legs but by the original authy. of the people 2. in its organization into Legisl. Ex. & Judy. Departs.: and 3. in its action on the people of the States immediately, and not on the Govts. of the States, as in a Confederacy.

But what alone would justify & acct. for the application of the term National to the proposed Govt. is that it wd. possess, exclusively all the attributes of a natl. Govt. in its relations with other nations including the most essential one, of regulating foreign Commerce; with an effective means of fulfilling the obligs. & responsiby of the U. S. to other nations.[2] Hence it was that the term natl. was at once

---

[2] Crossed out: "Even under the Confedy the States in their U. Character were considered and called a nation; altho their Treaties & transactions with foreign nations depended for their execution on the will of the several States, & altho the regulation of foreign commerce even remained with the States."

so readily applied to the new Govt. and that it has become so universal & familiar. It may safely be affirmed that the same wd. have been the case, whatever name might have been given to it by the props. of Mr. R. or by the Convention. A Govt: which alone is known & acknowledged by all foreign nations, and alone charged with the international relations, could not fail to be deemed & called at home, a Natl. Govt.

After all, in discussing & expounding the character & import of a Constn., let candor decide whether it be not more reasonable & just, to interpret the name or title by facts on the face of it, than to make the title torture the facts by a bed of Procrustes into a fitness to the title.

I must leave it to yourself to judge whether this exposition of the Resolns. in question be not sufficiently reasonable to protect them from the imputation of a consolidating tendency, and still more the Virga Deputies from having that for their object.

With respect to Mr. R. particularly, is not some respect due to his public letter to the Speaker of ye. H. of D. in which he gives for his refusal to sign the Constn: reasons irreconcileable with the supposition that he cd. have proposed the Resolns. in a meaning charged on them? Of Col. Mason who also refused, it may be inferred from his avowed reasons that he cd. not have acquiesced in the propositions, if understood or intended to effect a Consol. Gov.

So much use has been made of Judge Yates' minutes of debates in the Convention, that I must be allowed to remark that they abound in inaccuracies, and are not free from gross errors some of which do much injustice to the arguments & opinions of particular members. All this may be explained without a charge of wilful misrepresentation by the very desultory manner in which his notes appear to have been taken his ear catching particular expressions & losing qualifications of them; and by prejudices giving to his mind, all the bias which an honest one could feel. He & his colleague were the Representatives of the dominant party in N. York, which was opposed to the Convention & the object of it, which was averse to any essential change in the Articles of Confederation, which had inflexibly refused to grant even a duty of 5 per Ct. on imports for the urgent debt of the Revolution, which was availing itself, of the peculiar situation of New York, for taxing the consumption of her neighbours, and which foresaw that a primary aim of the Convention wd. be to transfer from the States to the Common authority, the entire regulation of foreign Commerce. Such were the feelings of the two Deputies, that on finding the Convention bent on radical reform of the Federal system, they left it in the midst of its discussions and before the opinions & views of many of the members were drawn out to their final shape & practical application.

Without impeaching the integrity of Luther Martin, it may be observed of him also, that his report of the proceedings of the Convention during his stay in it, shews by its colouring that his feelings were but too much mingled with his statements and inferences. There is good ground for believing that Mr. M. himself, became sensible and made no secret of his regret, that in his address to the Legislature of his State, he had been betrayed by the irritated state of his mind, into a picture that might do injustice both to the Body and to particular members. ————

CCCXCIII. JAMES MADISON TO THOMAS S. GRIMKE.[1]

Montpr. Jany, 6. 1834.

You wish to be informed of the errors in your pamphlet alluded to in my last. The first related to the proposition of Doctor Franklin in favor of a religious service in the Federal Convention. The proposition was received & treated with the respect due to it; but the lapse of time which had preceded, with considerations growing out of it, had the effect of limiting what was done, to a reference of the proposition to a highly respectable Committee. This issue of it may be traced in the printed Journal. The Quaker usage, never discontinued in the State & the place where the Convention held its sittings, might not have been without an influence as might also, the discord of religious opinions within the Convention, as well as among the Clergy of the Spot. The error into which you had fallen may have been confirmed by a communication in the National Intelligencer [2] some years ago, said to have been received through a respectable channel from a member of the Convention. That the communication was erroneous is certain; whether from misapprehension or misrecollection, uncertain.

The other error lies in the view which your note for the 18th. page, gives of Mr. Pinckney's draft of a Constitution for the U. S, and its conformity to that adopted by the Convention. It appears that the Draft laid by Mr. P. before the Convention, was like some other important Documents, not among its preserved proceedings. And you are not aware that *insuperable* evidence exists, that the Draft in the published Journal, could not, in a number of instances, material as well as minute, be the same with that laid before the Convention. Take for an example of the former, the Article relating to the House

---

[1] *Documentary History of the Constitution*, V, 395-398.
[2] See CCCLV and CCCLXXIX above.

of Representatives, more than any, the cornerstone of the Fabric. That the election of it by the *people*, as proposed by the printed draft in the Journal, could not be the mode of Election proposed in the lost Draft, must be inferred from the face of the Journal itself: For on the 6th. of June, but a few days after the lost Draft was presented to the Convention, Mr. P. moved to strike the word *"people"* out of Mr. Randolphs proposition; and to "Resolve that the members of the *first branch* of the national Legislature ought to be *elected* by the *Legislatures* of the *several States*." But there is other and most conclusive proof, that an election of the House of Representatives, by the *people*, could not have been the mode proposed by him. There are a number of other points in the published Draft some conforming most *literally*, to the adopted Constitution, which it is *ascertainable*, could not have been the same in the Draft laid before the Convention. The Conformity & even identity of the Draft in the Journal, with the adopted Constitution, on points & details the result of conflicts & compromizes of opinion apparent in the Journal, have excited an embarrassing curiosity often expressed to myself, or in my presence. The subject is in several respects a delicate one, and it is my wish that what is now said of it may be understood as yielded to your earnest request, and as entirely confined to yourself. I knew Mr. P. well, and was always on a footing of friendship with him. But this consideration ought not to weigh against justice to others, as well as against truth on a subject like that of the Constitution of the U. S.

The propositions of Mr. Randolph were the result of a consultation among the seven Virginia Deputies, of which he, being at the time Governor of the State, was the organ. The propositions were prepared on the supposition that, considering the prominent agency of Virga. in bringg. about the Convention some initiative step might be expected from that quarter. It was meant that they should sketch a real and adequate Govt. for the Union, but without committing the parties agst. a freedom in discussing & deciding on any of them. The Journal shews that they were in fact the basis of the deliberations & proceedings of the Convention. And I am persuaded that altho' not in a developed & organized form, they sufficiently contemplated it; and moreover that they embraced a fuller outline of an adequate System, than the plan laid before the Convention, variant as that, ascertainably, must have been from the Draft now in print.

Memor. No provision in the Draft of Mr. P. printed in the Journal for the mode of Electing the President of U. S.

CCCXCIV. James Madison to William Cogswell.[1]

Montpr Mar 10, 1834

You give me a credit to which I have no claim, in calling me "*The* writer of the Constitution of the U. S." This was not like the fabled Goddess of Wisdom, the offspring of a single brain. It ought to be regarded as the work of many heads and many hands.

CCCXCV. N. P. Trist: Memoranda.[2]

Montpellier, Sept. 27th, 1834.

"*Hamilton's Life* (the forthcoming volumes) I (N. P. T.) mentioned to Mr. M. [Madison], without telling him the *source*, what I had heard with regard to the bearing of the work upon him. His report of Hamilton's speech (in the convention which formed the Constitution), of which report I knew Mr. M. had furnished a copy to the son of A. H., was to be proved to be incorrect, and he was to be represented as having deserted Colonel Hamilton. Mr. M., 'I can't believe it.' Thereupon, I (N. P. T.) told him that my information as to the bearing of the forthcoming book upon him, came from the son of Colonel Hamilton himself — the son engaged in writing the life of his father, who had had a conversation on the subject with Professor Tucker of the University of Virginia, who has just returned from a trip to New York. Professor Tucker had mentioned it to Professor Davies, and the latter to me. I added, what I had heard, that there was nothing like unkind feeling towards him (Mr. Madison) manifested by young Mr. Hamilton, but the reverse. Such, however, was to be the complexion of the work as to himself.

"Mr. M., 'Sorry for it.' After a pause: 'I can't conceive on what ground the fidelity of my report of Colonel H.'s speech can be impugned, unless it should proceed from the error of confounding together his *first* speech and his *second*. The first, I reported at length. It was a very able and methodical one, containing a lucid expression of his views: *views which he made no secret of at the time or subsequently*, particularly with persons on a footing of the ordinary confidence among gentlemen thrown into political relations with each other on subjects of great moment. The *second* speech was little else than a repetition of the other, or parts of the other, with amplifications. *That* I did not report, for the reason just stated, and because he had told me of his intention to write it out himself, and

---

[1] Library of Congress, Madison Papers, Draft.

[2] H. S. Randall, *Life of Thomas Jefferson*, III, 594–595. Nicholas P. Trist resided at Monticello the last two or three years of Jefferson's life and kept daily memoranda of conversations with him.

had promised me a copy. The promised copy he never gave me; whether he ever executed his intention to write it out, even, I don't know. Yates has blended these two speeches together in his account of the proceedings.'

"I (N. P. T.) here reminded Mr. Madison of his having given me, some years ago, an account of these speeches, and those of others (of which I made a memorandum at the time, which is among my papers in Washington), and his having told me that he read to Colonel Hamilton and to Gouverneur Morris his reports of their speeches. That Col. H. acknowledged the accuracy of his, suggesting only one or two verbal alterations, and that G. M. laughed and said 'yes, it is all right.'

"Mr. M., 'Yes, Gouverneur Morris's speech was a very extravagant one. It displayed his usual talent, and also in a striking degree, his usual fondness for saying things and advancing doctrines that no one else would. At the moment, he was not perhaps himself conscious how far he went; and when the thing *stared him in the face* (this was Mr. M.'s exact expression), as written down by me, it caused him to laugh, while he acknowledged its truth.'

"Mr. M., 'As to the other branch of the subject, I deserted Colonel Hamilton, or rather Colonel H. deserted me; in a word, the divergence between us took place — from his wishing to *administration*, or rather to administer the Government (these were Mr. M.'s very words), into what he thought it ought to be; while, on my part, I endeavored to make it conform to the Constitution as understood by the Convention that produced and recommended it, and particularly by the State conventions that *adopted* it.'"

CCCXCVI. James Madison to Edward Coles.[1]

October 15, 1834.

It is well known that the large States, in both the Federal and State Conventions, regarded the aggregate powers of the Senate as the most objectionable feature of the Constitution.

CCCXCVII. James Madison to W. A. Duer.[2]

Montpellier, June 5th, 1835.

I have received your letter of April 25th, and with the aid of a friend and amanuensis, have made out the following answer:

On the subject of Mr. Pinckney's proposed plan of a Constitution, it is to be observed that the plan printed in the Journal was not

---

[1] *Letters and other Writings of James Madison*, IV, 369.
[2] *Letters and other Writings of James Madison*, IV, 378–381.

the document actually presented by him to the Convention. That document was no otherwise noticed in the proceedings of the Convention than by a reference of it, with Mr. Randolph's plan, to a committee of the whole, and afterwards to a committee of detail, with others; and not being found among the papers left with President Washington, and finally deposited in the Department of State, Mr. Adams, charged with the publication of them, obtained from Mr. Pinckney the document in the printed Journals as a copy supplying the place of the missing one. In this there must be error, there being sufficient evidence, even on the face of the Journals, that the copy sent to Mr. Adams could not be the same with the document laid before the Convention. Take, for example, the article constituting the House of Representatives the corner-stone of the fabric, the identity, even verbal, of which, with the adopted Constitution, has attracted so much notice. In the first place, the details and phraseology of the Constitution appear to have been anticipated. In the next place, it appears that within a few days after Mr. Pinckney presented his plan to the Convention, he moved to strike out from the resolution of Mr. Randolph the provision for the election of the House of Representatives by the people, and to refer the choice of that House to the Legislatures of the States, and to this preference it appears he adhered in the subsequent proceedings of the Convention. Other discrepancies will be found in a source also within your reach, in a pamphlet* published by Mr. Pinckney soon after the close of the Convention, in which he refers to parts of his plan which are at variance with the document in the printed Journal. A friend who had examined and compared the two documents has pointed out the discrepancies noted below.† Further

---

* Observations on the plan of Government submitted to the Federal Convention on the 28th of May, 1787, by C. Pinckney, &c. See Select Tracts, Vol. II, in the Library of the Historical Society of New York.

† Discrepancies noted between the plan of Mr. C. Pinckney as furnished by him to Mr. Adams, and the plan presented to the Convention as described in his pamphlet.

The pamphlet refers to the following provisions which are not found in the plan furnished to Mr. Adams as forming a part of the plan presented to the Convention: 1. The Executive term of service 7 years. 2. A council of revision. 3. A power to convene and prorogue the Legislature. 4. For the junction or division of States. 5. For enforcing the attendance of members of the Legislature. 6. For securing exclusive right of authors and discoverers.

The plan, according to the pamphlet, provided for the appointment of all officers, except judges and ministers, by the Executive, omitting the consent of the Senate required in the plan sent to Mr. Adams. Article numbered 9, according to the pamphlet, refers the decision of disputes between the States to the mode prescribed under the Confederation. Article numbered 7, in the plan sent to Mr. Adams, gives to the senate the regulating of the mode. There is no numerical correspondence

evidence* on this subject, not within your own reach, must await a future, perhaps a posthumous disclosure.

One conjecture explaining the phenomenon has been, that Mr. Pinckney interwove with the draught sent to Mr. Adams passages as agreed to in the Convention in the progress of the work, and which, after a lapse of more than thirty years, were not separated by his recollection.

The resolutions of Mr. Randolph, the basis on which the deliberations of the Convention proceeded, were the result of a consultation among the Virginia Deputies, who thought it possible that, as Virginia had taken so leading a part† in reference to the Federal Convention, some initiative propositions might be expected from them. They were understood not to commit any of the members absolutely or definitively on the tenor of them. The resolutions will be seen to present the characteristic provisions and features of a Government as complete (in some respects, perhaps, more so) as the plan of Mr. Pinckney, though without being thrown into a formal shape. The

between the articles as placed in the plan sent to Mr. Adams, and as noted in the pamphlet, and the latter refers numerically to more than are contained in the former.

It is remarkable, that although the plan furnished to Mr. Adams enumerates, with such close resemblance to the language of the Constitution as adopted, the following provisions, and among them the fundamental article relating to the constitution of the House of Representatives, they are unnoticed in his observations on the plan of Government submitted by him to the Convention, while minor provisions, as that enforcing the attendance of members of the Legislature are commented on. I cite the following, though others might be added: 3. To subdue a rebellion in any State on application of its Legislature. 2. To provide such dock-yards and arsenals, and erect such fortifications, as may be necessary for the U. States, and to exercise exclusive jurisdiction therein. 4. To establish post and military roads. 5. To declare the punishment of treason, which shall consist only in levying war against the United States, or any of them, or in adhering to their enemies. No person shall be convicted of treason but by the testimony of two witnesses. 6. No tax shall be laid on articles exported from the States.

   1. Election by the people of the House of Representatives.[a]
   2. The Executive veto on the laws. See the succeeding numbers as above.

   [a] Not improbably unnoticed, because the plan presented by him to the Convention contained his favourite mode of electing the House of Representatives by the State Legislatures, so essentially different from that of an election by the people, as in the Constitution recommended for adoption.

   ----

   * Alluding particularly to the debates in the Convention and the letter of Mr. Pinckney of March 28th, 1789, to Mr. Madison. (This note not included in the letter sent to Mr. Duer.)

   † Virginia proposed, in 1786, the Convention at Annapolis, which recommended the Convention at Philadelphia, of 1787, and was the first of the States that acted on, and complied with, the recommendation from Annapolis. (This note not included in the letter sent to Mr. Duer.)

moment, indeed, a real Constitution was looked for as a substitute for the Confederacy, the distribution of the Government into the usual departments became a matter of course with all who speculated on the prospective change, and the form of general resolutions was adopted as the most convenient for discussion. It may be observed, that in reference to the powers to be given to the General Government the resolutions comprehended as well the powers contained in the articles of Confederation, without enumerating them, as others not overlooked in the resolutions, but left to be developed and defined by the Convention.

With regard to the plan proposed by Mr. Hamilton, I may say to you, that a Constitution such as you describe was never proposed in the Convention, but was communicated to me by him at the close of it. It corresponds with the outline published in the Journal. The original draught being in possession of his family and their property, I have considered any publicity of it as lying with them.

Mr. Yates's notes, as you observe, are very inaccurate; they are, also, in some respects, grossly erroneous. The desultory manner in which he took them, catching sometimes but half the language, may, in part, account for it. Though said to be a respectable and honorable man, he brought with him to the Convention the strongest prejudices against the existence and object of the body, in which he was strengthened by the course taken in its deliberations. He left the Convention, also, long before the opinions and views of many members were finally developed into their practical application. The passion and prejudice of Mr. L. Martin betrayed in his published letter could not fail to discolour his representations. He also left the Convention before the completion of their work. I have heard, but will not vouch for the fact, that he became sensible of, and admitted his error. Certain it is, that he joined the party who favored the Constitution in its most liberal construction.

CCCXCVIII. James Madison on Nullification.[1]

1835-'6.

A political system which does not contain an effective provision for a peaceable decision of all controversies arising within itself, would be a government in name only. Such a provision is obviously essential; and it is equally obvious that it cannot be either peaceable or effective by making every part an authoritative empire. The final appeal in such cases must be to the authority of the whole, not to that of the parts separately and independently. This was

---

[1] *Letters and other Writings of James Madison*, IV, 425.

the view taken of the subject while the Constitution was under the consideration of the people. It was this view of it which dictated the clause declaring that the Constitution and laws of the United States should be the supreme law of the land, anything in the constitution or laws of any of the States to the contrary notwithstanding.*
It was the same view which specially prohibited certain powers and acts to the States, among them any laws violating the obligation of contracts, and which dictated the appellate provision in the judicial act passed by the first Congress under the Constitution.†

* See Article vi.   † See Article i.

CCCXCIX. James Madison to Joseph Wood.[1]

Feby 27, 1836.

I have received, sir, your letter of the 16th instant, requesting such information as I might be able to give pertaining to a biography of your father-in-law, the late Chief Justice Ellsworth.

. . . In the Convention which framed the Constitution of the U. States he bore an interesting part, and signed the instrument in its final shape, with the cordiality verified by the support he gave to its ratification.

CCCC. James Madison to ———— ————[2]

March, 1836.

It is well known that the equality of the States in the Federal Senate was a compromise between the larger and the smaller States, the former claiming a proportional representation in both branches of the Legislature, as due to their superior population; the latter an equality in both, as a safeguard to the reserved sovereignty of the States, an object which obtained the concurrence of members from the larger States. But it is equally true, though but little reverted to as an instance of miscalculating speculation, that, as soon as the smaller States had secured more than a proportional share in the proposed Government, they became favourable to augmentations of its powers, and that, under the administration of the Government, they have generally, in contests between it and the State governments, leaned to the former. . . .

Nothing is more certain than that the tenure of the Senate was meant as an obstacle to the instability, which not only history, but the experience of our country, had shown to be the besetting infirmity of popular governments. . . .

---

[1] *Letters and Other Writings of James Madison*, IV, 427–428.
[2] *Letters and Other Writings of James Madison*, IV, 429–430.

CCCCI. James Madison: Preface to Debates in the Convention of 1787.[1]

A sketch never finished nor applied.

As the weakness and wants of man naturally lead to an association of individuals, under a common authority, whereby each may have the protection of the whole against danger from without, and enjoy in safety within, the advantages of social intercourse, and an exchange of the necessaries & comforts of life: in like manner feeble communities, independent of each other, have resorted to a Union, less intimate, but with common Councils, for the common safety agst. powerful neighbors, and for the preservation of justice and peace among themselves. Ancient history furnishes examples of these confederacies, tho' with a very imperfect account, of their structure, and of the attributes and functions of the presiding Authority. There are examples of modern date also, some of them still existing, the modifications and transactions of which are sufficiently known.

It remained for the British Colonies, now United States, of North America, to add to those examples, one of a more interesting character than any of them: which led to a system without a precedent ancient or modern, a system founded on popular rights, and so combing. a federal form with the forms of indivual Republics, as may enable each to supply the defects of the other and obtain the advantages of both —

Whilst the Colonies enjoyed the protection of the parent country as it was called, against foreign danger; and were secured by its superintending controul, against conflicts among themselves, they continued independente of each other, under a common, tho' limited dependence, on the parental Authority. When the growth of the offspring in strength and in wealth, awakened the jealousy and tempted the avidity of the parent, into schemes of usurpation & exaction, the obligation was felt by the former of uniting their counsels, and efforts to avert the impending calamity.

As early as the year 1754, indications having been given of a design in the Brittish Government to levy contributions on the Col-

---

[1] The heading was crossed out by Madison, but it forms a good title to the paper. This document is a rough draft, evidently written by Madison near the close of his life (see the next to the last paragraph). There are many interlineations and double readings, which would have been removed by the final revision Madison was never able to give it. The editor has accordingly treated this document more freely than any other in this work in the attempt to render it serviceable. The text here printed is taken from the *Documentary History of the Constitution*, III, 1-7, 796 *et seq.;* some of the notes have been lost since Gilpin first printed it in 1840, and those gaps have been filled from the Gilpin edition.

onies, without their consent; a meeting of Colonial deputies took place at Albany, which attempted to introduce a compromising substitute that might at once satisfy the British requisitions and save their own rights from violation. The attempt had no other effect, than by bringing these rights into a more conspicuous view, to invigorate the attachment to them on one side; and to nourish the haughty encroaching spirit on the other.[1]

In 1774. The progress made by G. B. in the open assertion of her pretensions, and in the apprended purpose of otherwise maintaining them by Legislative enactments and declarations had been such that the Colonies did not hesitate to assemble, by their deputies, in a formal Congress, authorized to oppose to the British innovations whatever measures might be found best adapted to the occasion; without however losing sight of an eventual reconciliation.

The dissuasive measures of that Congress, being without effect, another Congress was held in 1775, whose pacific efforts to bring about a change in the views of the other party, being equally unavailing, and the commencement of actual hostilities having at length put an end to all hope of reconciliation; The Congress finding moreover that the popular voice began to call for an entire & perpetual dissolution of the political ties which had connected them with G. B., proceeded on the memorable 4th of July, 1776, to declare the 13 Colonies, independent States

During the discussions of this solemn Act, a Committee consisting of a Member from each colony had been appointed to prepare & digest a form of Confederation, for the future management of the common interests, which had hitherto been left to the discretion of Congress, guided by the exigences of the contest, and by the known intentions or occasional instructions of the Colonial Legislatures.

It appears that as early as the 21st of July 1775, A plan entitled "Articles of Confederation & *perpetual* Union of the Colonies" had been sketched by Docr Franklin, The plan being on that day submitted by him to Congress; and tho' not copied into their Journals remaining on their files in his handwriting. But notwithstanding

---

[1] Crossed out: "see the masterly letter of Dr. Franklin to Governour Shirly in 1754, in which at that early day the argumentative vindication of America against the claim of the British parliament is afterwards expanded into volumes, is brought seen within the compass of a nut shell few pages short letter which is fated with the greatest possible is triumphantly repelled, by reasoning, repelled with the greatest possible force, within the smallest possible compass. The letter short as it is comprises the germ, of which all the succeeding arguments, are but arguments of succeeding patriots are but a development."

the term "perpetual" observed in the title, the articles provided expressly for the event of a return of the Colonies to a connection with G. Britain.

This sketch became a basis for the plan reported by the Come. on the 12 of July, now also remaining on the files of Congress, in the handwriting of Mr. Dickinson. The plan, tho' dated after the Declaration of Independence, was probaly drawn up before that event; since the name of *Colonies*, and not *States* is used throughout the draught. The plan reported, was debated and amended from time to time till the 17th of November 1777, when it was agreed to by Congress, and proposed to the Legislatures of the States, with an explanatory and recommendatory letter. The ratifications of these by their Delegates in Congs. duly authorized took place at successive dates; but were not compleated till March 1, 1781. when Maryland who had made it a prerequisite that the vacant lands acquired from the British Crown should be a Common fund, yielded to the persuasion that a final & formal establishment of the federal Union & Govt. would make a favorable impression not only on other foreign nations, but on G. B. herself.

The great difficulty experienced in so framing the fedl. system as to obtain the unanimity required for its due sanction, may be inferred from the long interval, and recurring discussions, between the commencement and completion of the work; [1] from the changes made during its progress; from the language of Congs. when proposing it to the States, wch. dwelt on the impracticability of devising a system acceptable to all of them; from the reluctant assent given by some; and the various alterations proposed by others; and by a tardiness in others again which produced a special address to them from Congs. enforcing the duty of sacrificing local considerations and favorite opinions to the public safety, and the necessary harmony; nor was the assent of some of the States finally yielded without strong protests against particular articles, and a reliance on future amendments removing their objections.

It is to be recollected, no doubt, that these delays might be occasioned in some degree, by an occupation of the public Councils both general & local, with the deliberations and measures, essential to a Revolutionary struggle; But there must have been a balance for these causes, in the obvious motives to hasten the establishment of a regular and efficient Govt.; and in the tendency of the crisis to repress opinions and pretensions, which might be inflexible in another state of things.

---

[1] Crossed out: "see Jefferson's manuscript debates on the rules of voting and of taxing " and "see History of the confederation annexed to the Secret-Journal".

The principal difficulties which embarrassed the progress, and retarded the completion of the plan of Confederation, may be traced to 1. the natural reluctance of the parties to a relinquishment of power: 2 a natural jealousy of its abuse in other hands than their own: 3 the rule of suffrage among parties unequal in size, but equal in sovereignty.   4. The ratio of contributions in money and in troops, among parties, whose inequality in size did not correspond with that of their wealth, or of their military or free population.   5. The selection and definition of the powers, at once necessary to the federal head, and safe to the several members.

To these sources of difficulty, incident to the formation of all such confederacies, were added two others one of a temporary, the other of a permanent nature.   The first was the Case of the Crown lands, so called because they had been held by the British Crown, and being ungranted to individuals when, its authority ceased, were considered by the States within whose charters or asserted limits they lay, as devolving on them; whilst it was contended by the others, that being wrested from the dethroned authority by the equal exertion of all, they resulted of right and in equity to the benefit of all.   The lands being of vast extent and of growing value, were the occasion of much discussion & heart-burning; & proved the most obstinate of the impediments to an earlier consummation of the plan of federal Govt.   The State of Maryland the last that acceded to it held out as already noticed till March 1. 1781. and then yielded only to the hope that by giving a Stable & authoritative character to the Confederation, a successful termination of the contest might be accelerated.   The dispute was happily compromised by successive surrenders of portions of the territory by the States having exclusive claims to it, and acceptances of them by Congress.

The other source of dissatisfaction was the peculiar situation of some of the States, which having no convenient ports for foreign commerce, were subject to be taxed by their neighbors, thro whose ports, their commerce was carried on.   New Jersey, placed between Phila. & N. York, was likened to a Cask tapped at both ends: and N. Carolina between Virga. & S. Carolina to a patient bleeding at both Arms.   The Articles of Confederation provided no remedy for the complaint: which produced a strong protest on the part of N. Jersey; and never ceased to be a source of dissatisfaction & discord, until the new Constitution, superseded the old.

But the radical infirmity of "the arts. of Confederation." was the dependance of Congs, on the voluntary and simultaneous compliance with its Requisitions, by so many independant communities, each consulting more or less its particular interests & convenience and distrusting the compliance of the others. Whilst the paper emissions of Congs. continued to circulate they were employed as a sinew of war, like gold & silver. When that ceased to be the case, the fatal defect of the political System was felt in its alarming force. The war was merely kept alive and brought to a successful conclusion by such foreign aids and temporary expedients as could be applied; a hope prevailing with many, and a wish with all, that a state of peace, and the sources of prosperity opened by it, would give to the Confederacy in practice, the efficiency which had been inferred from its theory.

The close of the war however brought no-cure for the public embarrasments. The States relieved from the pressure of foreign danger, and flushed with the enjoyment of independent and sovereign power; (instead of a diminished disposition to part with it,) persevered in omissions and in measures incompatible with their relations to the Federal Govt. and with those among themselves;[1]

Having served as a member of Congs. through the period between Mar. 1780 & the arrival of peice in 1783, I had become intimately acquainted with the public distresses and the causes of them. I had observed the successful — opposition to every attempt to procure a remedy by new grants of power to Congs. I had found moreover that despair of success hung over the compromising provision for the public necessities of April 1783 which had been so elaborately planned and so impressively recommended to the States.* Sympathizing, under this aspect of affairs, in the alarm of the friends of free Govt, at the threatened danger of an abortive result to the great & perhaps last experiment in its favour, I could not be insensible to the obligation to co-operate as far as I could in averting the calamity. With this view I acceded to the desire of my fellow Citizens of the County that I should be one of its representitives in the Legislature, hoping that I might there best contribute to inculcate the critical posture to which the Revolutionary cause was reduced, and the merit of a leading agency of the State in bringing about a rescue of the Union and the blessings of liberty staked on it, from an impending catastrophe.

It required but little time after taking my seat in the House of Delegates in May 1784. to discover that however favorable the general disposition of the State might be towards the Confederacy the Legislature retained the aversion of its predecessors to transfers

* See address of Congress.

[1] Crossed out: "(notwithstanding, the urgency of the national engagements, and the increasing anarchy and collisions which threatened the Union itself)."

of power from the State to the Govt. of the Union; notwithstanding
the urgent demands of the Federal Treasury; the glaring inadequacy of the authorized mode of supplying it, the rapid growth of
anarchy in the Fedl. System, and the animosity kindled among its
members by their conflicting regulations.

The temper of the Legislature & the wayward course of its
proceedings may be gathered from the Journals of its Sessions in
the years 1784 & 1785.

The failure however of the varied propositions in the Legislature
for enlarging the powers of Congress, the continued failure of the
efforts of Congs. to obtain from them the means of providing for
the debts of the Revolution; and of countervailing the commercial
laws of G. B, a source of much irritation & agst. which the separate
efforts of the States were found worse than abortive; these Considerations with the lights thrown on the whole subject, by the free &
full discussion it had undergone led to a general acquiescence in
the Resoln. passed. on the 21. of Jany. 1786. which proposed &
invited a meeting of Deputies from all the States to insert the Resol
(See Journal.) 1.

The resolution had been brought forward some weeks before on
the failure of a proposed grant of power to Congress to collect a
revenue from commerce, which had been abandoned by its friends
in consequence of material alterations made in the grant by a Committee of the whole. The Resolution tho introduced by Mr. Tyler
an influencial member, who having never served in Congress, had
more the ear of the House than those whose services there exposed
them to an imputable bias, was so little acceptable that it was not
then persisted in. Being now revived by him, on the last day of
the Session, and being the alternative of adjourning without any
effort for the crisis in the affairs of the Union, it obtained a general
vote; less however with some of its friends from a confidence in the
success of the experiment than from a hope that it might prove a
step to a more comprehensive & adequate provision for the wants
of the Confederacy

It happened also that Commissioners who had been appointed by
Virga. & Maryd. to settle the jusisdiction on waters dividing the two
States had, apart from their official reports, recomended a uniformity in the regulations of the 2 States on several subjects & particularly on those having relation to foreign trade. It apeared at
the same time that Maryd. had deemed a concurrence of her neighbors Pena — & Delaware indispensable in such a case, who for like
reasons would require that of their neighbors. So apt and forceable
an illustration of the necessity of a uniformity throughout all the

States, could not but favour the passage of a Resolution which proposed a Convention having that for its object.

The comissioners appointed by the Legisl: & who attended the Convention were E. Randolph the Attorney of the State, St. Geo: Tucker & J. M. The designation of the time & place for its meeting to be proposed and communicated to the States having been left to the Comrs: they named for the time early September and for the place the City of Annapolis avoiding the residence of Congs. and large Commercial Cities as liable to suspicions of an extraneous influence.

Altho the invited Meeting appeared to be generally favored, five States only assembled; some failing to make appointments, and some of the individuals appointed not hastening their attendance, the result in both cases being ascribed mainly, to a belief that the time had not arrived for such a political reform, as might be expected from a further experience of its necessity.

But in the interval between the proposal of the Convention and the time of its meeting such had been the advance of public opinion in the desired direction, stimulated as it had been by the effect of the contemplated object of the meeting, in turning the general attention to the Critical State of things, and in calling forth the sentiments and exertions of the most enlightened & influencial patriots, that the Convention thin as it was did not scruple to decline the limited task assigned to it, and to recommend to the States a Convention with powers adequate to the occasion; nor was it unnoticed that the commission of the N. Jersey Deputation, had extended its object to a general provision for the exigencies of the Union. A recommendation for this enlarged purpose was accordingly reported by a Come. to whom the subject had been referred. It was drafted by Col: H. and finally agreed to unanimously in the following form. Insert it.

The recommendation was well recd. by the Legislature of Virga. which happened to be the *first* that *acted* on it, and [1] the example of her compliance was made as conciliatory and impressive as possible. The Legislatures were unanimous or very nearly so on the occasion, and as a proof of the magnitude & solemnity attached to it, they placed Genl. W. at the head of the Deputation from the State; and as a proof of the deep interest he felt in the case he overstepped the obstacles to his acceptance of the appointment.

The act complying with the recommendation from Annapolis was in the terms following.

A resort to a General Convention to remodel the Confederacy

---

[1] Crossed out: "as the preparation of the bill fell on me, it was my study to make".

was not a new idea. It had entered at an early date into the conversations and speculations of the most reflecting & foreseeing observers of the inadequacy of the powers allowed to Congress. In a pamphlet published in May–81 at the Seat of Congs Peletiah Webster an able tho' not conspicuous Citizen, after discussing the fiscal system of the U. States, and suggesting among other remedial provisions [one] including a national Bank remarks that "The Authority of Congs. at present is very inadequate to the performance of their duties; and this indicates the necessity of their calling a *Continental Convention* for the express purpose of ascertaining, defining, enlarging, and limiting the duties & powers of their Constitution."

On the 1. day of Apl. 1783, Col. Hamilton, in a debate in Congs. observed that: — [1]

He alluded probably to (see Life of Schuyler in Longacre) [2]

It does not appear however that his expectation had been fulfilled

In a letter to J. M. from R. H. Lee then President of Congs. dated Novr. 26 1784 He says: — [3]

The answer of J. M. remarks: — [4]

In 1785, Noah Webster whose pol. & other valuable writings had made him known to the public, in one of his publications of American policy brought into view the same resort for supplying the defects of the Fedl. System. (see his life in Longacre)

The proposed & expected Convention at Annapolis, the first of a general character that appears to have been realized, & the state of the public mind awakened by it, had attracted the particular attention of Congs. and favored the idea there of a Convention with fuller powers for amending the Confederacy.

It does not appear that in any of these cases, the reformed system was to be otherwise sanctioned than by the Legislative authy of the States; nor whether or how far a change was to be made in the structure of the Depository of Federal powers.

The act of Virga. providing for the Convention at Philada, was succeeded by appointments from other States as their Legislatures were assembled, the appointments being selections from the most experienced & highest standing Citizens. Rh. I. was the only exception to a compliance with the recommendation from Annapolis,

---

[1] "He wished . . . to see a general Convention take place" (Gilpin, 707).

[2] "Resolutions . . . by Schuyler in the Senate . . . of New York, . . . to recommend to the States to call a general Convention." (Gilpin, 707.)

[3] That a general convention is suggested by members of Congress. (Gilpin, 708).

[4] Question is only as to the mode. (Gilpin, 708).

well known to have been swayed by an obdurate adherence to an advantage which her position gave her of taxing her neighbors thro' their consumption of imported supplies, an advantage which it was foreseen would be taken from her by a revisal of the Articles of Confederation.

As the pub. mind had been ripened for a salutary Reform of the pol. System, in the interval between the proposal & the meeting, of Comrs. at Annapolis, the interval between the last event, and the meeting of Deps. at Phila. had continued to develop more & more the necessity & the extent of a Systematic provision for the preservation and Govt. of the Union; among the ripening incidents was the Insurrection of Shays in Massts. against her Govt; which was with difficulty suppressed, notwithstanding the influence on the insurgents of an apprehended interposition of the Fedl. troops.

At the date of the Convention, the aspect & retrospect of the pol: condition of the U. S. could not but fill the pub. mind with a gloom which was relieved only by a hope that so select a Body would devise an adequate remedy for the existing and prospective evils so impressively demanding it

It was seen that the public debt rendered so sacred by the cause in which it had been incurred remained without any provision for its payment. The reiterated and elaborate efforts of Cong. to procure from the States a more adequate power to raise the means of payment had failed. The effect of the ordinary requisitions of Congress had only displayed the inefficiency of the authy. making them; none of the States having duly complied with them, some having failed altogether or nearly so; and in one instance, that of N. Jersey, a compliance was expressly refused; nor was more yielded to the expostulations of members of Congs. deputed to her Legislature than a mere repeal of the law, without a compliance. (see letter of Grayson to J. M.)

The want of authy. in Congs. to regulate Commerce had produced in Foreign nations particularly G. B. a monopolizing policy injurious to the trade of the U. S. and destructive to their navigation; the imbecility and anticipated dissolution of the Confederacy extinguishg. all apprehensions of a Countervailing policy on the part of the U. States.

The same want of a general power over Commerce led to an exercise of this power separately, by the States, wch not only proved abortive, but engendered rival, conflicting and angry regulations. Besides the vain attempts to supply their respective treasuries by imposts, which turned their commerce into the neighbouring ports, and to co-erce a relaxation of the British monopoly of the W. Indn.

navigation, which was attemted by Virga. (see the Journal of   )
the States having ports for foreign commerce, taxed & irritated the
adjoining States, trading thro' them, as N. Y. Pena. Virga. & S–
Carolina. Some of the States, as Connecticut, taxed imports as
from Massts higher than imports even from G. B. of wch Massts.
complained to Virga. and doubtless to other States (see letter of
J. M.) In sundry instances of as N. Y. N. J. Pa. & Maryd. (see
) the navigation laws treated the Citizens of other States as
aliens.

In certain cases the authy. of the Confederacy was disregarded,
as in violations not only of the Treaty of peace; but of Treaties with
France & Holland, which were complained of to Congs.

In other cases the Fedl authy was violated by Treaties & wars
with Indians, as by Geo: by troops, raised & kept up. witht. the consent of Congs. as by Massts by compacts witht. the consent of Congs.
as between Pena. and N. Jersey. and between Virga. & Maryd.
From the Legisl: Journals of Virga. it appears, that a vote to apply
for a sanction of Congs. was followed by a vote agst. a communication of the Compact to Congs.

In the internal administration of the States a violations of Contracts had become familiar in the form of depreciated paper made
a legal tender, of property substituted for money, of Instalment
laws, and of the occlusions of the Courts of Justice; although evident that all such interferences affected the rights of other States,
relatively Creditor, as well as Citizens Creditors within the State

Among the defects which had been severely felt was that of
a uniformity in cases requiring it, as laws of naturalization,
bankruptcy, a Coercive authority opperating on individuals and a
guaranty of the internal tranquility of the States;

As a natural consequence of this distracted and disheartening
condition of the Union, the Fedl. authy had ceased to be respected
abroad, and dispositions shewn there, particularly in G. B. to take
advantage of its imbecility, and to speculate on its approaching
downfall; at home it had lost all confidence & credit. The unstable
and unjust career of the States had also forfeited the respect &
confidence essential· to order and good Govt., involving a general
decay of confidence & credit between man & man. It was found
moreover, that those least partial to popular Govt. or most distrust-
ful of its efficacy were yielding to anticipations that from an increase
of the confusion a Govt. might result more congenial with their
taste or their opinions; whilst those most devoted to the principles
and forms of Republics. were alarmed for the cause of liberty itself,
at stake in the American Experiment, and anxious for a System that

wd avoid the inefficacy of a mere Confederacy without passing into the opposite extreme of a Consolidated govt. It was known that there were individuals who had betrayed a bias towards Monarchy (see Knox to G. W. & him to Jay), and there had always been some not unfavorable to a partition of the Union into several Confederacies (Marshall's life); either from a better chanc of figuring on a Sectional Theatre, or that the Sections would require stronger Govts. or by their hostile conflicts lead to a monarchical consolidation. The idea of a dismemberment had recently made its appearance in the Newspapers.

Such were the defects, the deformities, the diseases and the ominous prospects, for which the Convention were to provide a remedy, and which ought never to be overlooked in expounding & appreciating the Constitutional Charter the remedy that was provided.

As a sketch the earliest perhaps on paper, of a Constitutional Govt. for the Union (organized into the regular Departments with physical means operating on individuals) to be sanctioned by *the people of the States*, acting in their original & sovereign character, was contained in a letter of Apl. 8. 1787 from J. M. to Govr. Randolph, a copy of the letter is here inserted.

The feature in the letter which vested in the general Authy a negative on the laws of the States, was suggested by the negative in the head of the British Empire, which prevented collisions between the parts & the whole, and between the parts themselves. It was supposed that the substitution, of an elective and responsible authority for an hereditary and irresponsible one, would avoid the appearance even of a departure from the principle of Republicanism. But altho' the subject was so viewed in the Convention, and the votes on it more than once equally divided, it was finally & justly abandoned, as, apart from other objections, it was not practicable among so many States, increasing in number, and enacting, each of them, so many laws. Instead of the proposed negative, the objects of it were left as finally provided for in the Constitution.

On the arrival of the Virginia Deputies at Philada. it occurred to them that from the early and prominent part taken by that State in bringing about the Convention some initiative step might be expected from them. The Resolutions introduced by Governor Randolph were the result of a Consolidation on the subject; with an understanding that they left all the Deputies entirely open to the lights of discussion, and free to concur in any alterations or modifications which their reflections and judgements might approve. The Resolutions as the Journals shew became the basis on which the proceedings of the Convention commenced, and to the developments,

variations and modifications of which the plan of Govt. proposed
by the Convention may be traced.

The curiosity I had felt during my researches into the History
of the most distinguished Confederacies, particularly those of antiq-
uity, and the deficiency I found in the means of satisfying it more
especially in what related to the process, the principles — the reasons, & the anticipations, which prevailed in the formation of them,
determined me to preserve as far as I could an exact account of what
might pass in the Convention whilst executing its trust, with the
magnitude of which I was duly impressed, as I was with the gratification promised to future curiosity by an authentic exhibition of
the objects, the opinions & the reasonings from which the new System of Govt. was to receive its peculiar structure & organization.
Nor was I unaware of the value of such a contribution to the fund
of materials for the History of a Constitution on which would be
staked the happiness of a young people great even in its infancy,
and possibly the cause of Liberty throught the world.

In pursuance of the task I had assumed I chose a seat in front
of the presiding member with the other members, on my right &
left hand.   In this favorable position for hearing all that passed, I
noted in terms legible & in abreviations & marks intelligible to
myself what was read from the Chair or spoken by the members; and
losing not a moment unnecessarily between the adjournment &
reassembling of the Convention I was enabled to write out my daily
notes during the seesion or within a few finishing days after its
close in the extent and form preserved in my own hand on my files.[1]

In the labor and correctness of this I was not a little aided by
practice, and by a familiarity with the style and the train of observation and reasoning which characterized the principal speakers.
It happened, also, that I was not absent a single day, nor more than
a casual fraction of an hour in any day, so that I could not have lost
a single speech, unless a very short one.

It may be proper to remark, that, with a very few exceptions,
the speeches were neither furnished, nor revised, nor sanctioned,
by the speakers, but written out from my notes, aided by the fresh-
ness of my recollections.   A further remark may be proper, that
views of the subject might occasionally be presented, in the speeches
and proceedings, with a latent reference to a compromise on some

---

[1] "Mr. Madison told Governor Edward Coles that the labor of writing out the
debates, added to the confinement to which his attendance in Convention subjected
him, almost killed him; but that having undertaken the task, he was determined to
accomplish it."   H. B. Grigsby, *History of Virginia Federal Convention of 1788*, I, 95
note.

middle ground, by mutual concessions. The exceptions alluded to were, — first, the sketch furnished by Mr. Randolph of his speech on the introduction of his propositions, on the twenty-ninth day of May; secondly, the speech of Mr. Hamilton, who happened to call on me when putting the last hand to it, and who acknowledged its fidelity, without suggesting more than a very few verbal alterations which were made; thirdly, the speech of Gouverneur Morris on the second day of May [July], which was communicated to him on a like occasion, and who acquiesced in it without even a verbal change. The correctness of his language and the distinctness of his enunciation were particularly favorable to a reporter. The speeches of Doctor Franklin, excepting a few brief ones, were copied from the written ones read to the Convention by his colleague, Mr. Wilson, it being inconvenient to the Doctor to remain long on his feet.

Of the ability and intelligence of those who composed the Convention the debates and proceedings may be a test; as the character of the work which was the offspring of their deliberations must be tested by the experience of the future, added to that of nearly half a century which has passed.

But whatever may be the judgment pronounced on the competency of the architects of the Constitution, or whatever may be the destiny of the edifice prepared by them, I feel it a duty to express my profound and solemn conviction, derived from my intimate opportunity of observing and appreciating the views of the Convention, collectively and individually, that there never was an assembly of men, charged with a great and arduous trust, who were more pure in their motives, or more exclusively or anxiously devoted to the object committed to them, than were the members of the Federal Convention of 1787, to the object of devising and proposing a constitutional system which should best supply the defects of that which it was to replace, and best secure the permanent liberty and happiness of their country.

SUPPLEMENT

CCCCII. WILLIAM SAMUEL JOHNSON: DIARY, 1787.[1]

AD 1787   Memoranda   New York, &c.

June 1st. Rain & Fair   Came to Philadelphia at 7 O'clock, & Lodged at Dickenson's.   . . .

2d. Made Visits. Took a Seat in Convention. . . . In eveng. took Lodgs. at City Tavern.   . . .

4th. Cold. At Convention.   . . .

5th. Fair. Cold. Rain. In Convention. Not well.   . . .

6th. Very Rainy. In Conventn. Dined Dr. Franklins.   . . .

7th. Showry. In Conventn. Dined Mr. Clymer's.   . . .

8th. Fair. In Conventn.   . . .

9th. Warm. At Conven.   . . .

11th. Hot. At Conventn. Dind. Mr. Morris's.   . . .

12th. Do. In Conventn.   . . .

13th. Do. In Conventn. Dind. Ingersolls.   . . .

14th. Do. In Conventn. but adj.   . . .

15th. Do. In Conventn. Do.   . . .

16th. Cool. In Conventn.   . . .

18th. Hot. In Conventn. Hamiltn.   . . .

19th. Do. In Conventn.   . . .

20th. Do. In Conventn.   . . .

21st. Do. In   Do.   Argt.   . . .

22d. Cool. In   Do.   . . .

23d. Do. In   Do.   . . .

25th. Cool. In Conventn.   . . .

26th. Hot. In Conventn.   . . .

27th. Do. In Conventn.   . . .

28th. Cool. In Conventn.   . . .

29th. Do. In Conventn.   . . .

30th. Hot. In Convention.   . . .

July 2d. Hot. In Conventn. Commee.   . . .

3d. Hot. No. Conventn.   . . .

4th. Do.   Do.   Independence. Heard Campbells Oration.   . . .

---

[1] After the manuscript of this work was in the printers' hands, the editor was privileged, through the courtesy of Mrs. S. E. Johnson Hudson of Stratford, Connecticut, to examine the diary of her great-grandfather, William Samuel Johnson. The "memoranda" amount to little more than a line each day. Though it was too late to incorporate them in the text, the extracts here given seemed to be of sufficient importance to warrant their insertion as a supplement to this appendix.

July 5th. Hot In Conventn. . . .

6th. Do. In Convention. Dined G. Washington. . . .

7th. Do. In Conventn. . . .

9th. Do. In Conventn. . . .

10th. Do. In Conventn. . . .

11th. Do. In Conventn. . . .

12th. Do. In Conventn. . . .

13th. Cool. In Conventn. . . .

14th. Do. In Conventn. . . .

16th. Do. In Conventn. . . .

17th. Do. In Conventn. . . .

18th. Do. In Conventn. . . .

19th. Do. In Conventn. . . .

20th. Set out at 8 O'clock in the Mail Stage with Judge Sherman &c. . . .

Augt. 6th. Rain. . . . Did not arrive till 7. in Eveng. . . .
In eveng. came to Mr. Lewis's met Coln. Johnston &c. . . .

7th. Hot. In Convention. . . .

8th. Do. In Conventn. . . .

9th. Do. In Conventn. . . .

10th. Do. Rain. In Do. . . .

11th. Cool. In Conventn. Dind. Pinckneys. . . .

13th. Hot. In Conventn. . . .

14th. Do. In Conventn. . . .

15th. Do. In Conventn. . . .

16th. Cool. In Conventn. . . .

17th. Do. In Conventn. . . .

18th. Do. In Conventn. . . .

20th. Rain. In Conventn. . . .

21st. Do. In Conventn. . . .

22d. Fine. In Conventn. . . . Fitchs Steam Boat. . . .

23d. Warm. In Conventn. . . .

24th. Hot. In Conventn. . . .

25th. Do. In Do. Dined with Gerry. . . .

27th. Cold. Rain. In Conventn. . . .

28th. Rain. In Convention. . . .

29th. Do. In Conventn. . . .

30th. Do. In Conventn. . . .

31st. Cool. In Conventn. . . .

Septemr. 1st. Rain. In Convention. . . .

3d. Cool. In Conventn. . . .

4th. Do. In Conventn. . . .

Septemr. 5th. Cool. In Conventn. . . .
     6th. Do. In Conventn. . . .
     7th. Do. In Conventn. . . .
     8th. Do. In Conventn. Dind. Mifflins. Eveng.
         Comee. . . .
     10th. Warm. In Convention. & Commee. . . .
     11th. Very hot. Do. Do. . . .
     12th. Do. Do. Do. Dind. Jack-
         sons . . . .
     13th. Rain. Do. Do. . . .
     14th. Do. Do. Do. . . . .
     15th. Cloudy. Do. Do. . . .
     17th. Cold. In Convention. Ended. . . .
     18th. Set out at 10 O'clock in the Stage. Gov. Living-
         ston, Few, Baldwin, Jackson &c in Company.

CCCCIII. John Dickinson: Extract of letter.[1]

In the Convention at Philadelphia in 1787,* I proposed the establishment of that Branch,‡ with an equal Representation therein of every State — assenting, in Consideration of such a provision to the Establishment of the other Branch, on another Principle.

Letter of my Father.

S. N. Dickinson.

* For the formation of the Federal Constitution.
‡ The Senate.

---

[1] This scrap of MS. in the handwriting of John Dickinson, with footnotes in the handwriting of his daughter, Sarah Norris Dickinson, is in the possession of Mr. William Redwood Wright of Philadelphia. It was furnished to the editor through the kindness of Mr. Albert Cook Myers.

While this volume is in press, the ninth and last volume of Gaillard Hunt's *Writings of James Madison* has appeared with three items which the editor would gladly have incorporated in the present work. The omission is of little real consequence, however, as the substance of all of these items is embodied in other letters of Madison included in this appendix. The significant portion of one item, a matter of punctuation, has been inserted in a foot-note to CCCLXXII.

These items have now been included in Volume IV.

APPENDIX B

THE DELEGATES TO THE FEDERAL CONVENTION,
THEIR CREDENTIALS, AND ATTENDANCE.

LIST OF DELEGATES.[1]

NEW HAMPSHIRE	John Langdon
	(John Pickering)
	Nicholas Gilman
	(Benjamin West)[1a]
MASSACHUSETTS	(Francis Dana)
	Elbridge Gerry
	Nathaniel Gorham
	Rufus King
	Caleb Strong
RHODE ISLAND	No appointment
CONNECTICUT	William Samuel Johnson
	Roger Sherman
	Oliver Ellsworth
	[Erastus Wolcott was elected but declined to serve.]
NEW YORK	Robert Yates
	Alexander Hamilton
	John Lansing, Junior
NEW JERSEY	David Brearley
	William Churchill Houston
	William Paterson
	(John Neilson)
	William Livingston
	(Abraham Clark)
	Jonathan Dayton
PENNSYLVANIA	Thomas Mifflin
	Robert Morris

---

[1] Those whose names are in parentheses did not attend. An alphabetical list of the delegates with the dates of attendance, etc., will be found at the end of this appendix.

[1a] Philadelphia newspapers of May 19, 1787, in their lists of delegates included the names of John Sparhawk and Pierce Long from New Hampshire.

PENNSYLVANIA (*continued*)	George Clymer Jared Ingersoll Thomas Fitzsimons James Wilson Gouverneur Morris Benjamin Franklin
DELAWARE	George Read Gunning Bedford, Junior John Dickinson Richard Bassett Jacob Broom
MARYLAND	James McHenry Daniel of St. Thomas Jenifer Daniel Carroll John Francis Mercer Luther Martin [Charles Carroll of Carrollton, Gabriel Duvall, Robert Hanson Harrison, Thomas Sim Lee, and Thomas Stone were elected but declined to serve.]
VIRGINIA	George Washington Edmund Randolph John Blair James Madison, Junior George Mason George Wythe James McClurg [Patrick Henry,[2] Richard Henry Lee, and Thomas Nelson were elected but declined to serve.]

---

[2] "There was a passage at arms between the Rev. John Blair Smith, president of Hampden-Sydney College in Prince Edward county, and Patrick Henry, who represented that county in the Convention. Henry had inveighed with great severity against the Constitution, and was responded to by Dr. Smith, who pressed the question upon Henry, why he had not taken his seat in the Convention and lent his aid in making a good Constitution, instead of staying at home and abusing the work of his patriotic compeers? Henry, with that magical power of acting in which he excelled all his contemporaries, and which before a popular assembly was irresistible, replied: 'I smelt a Rat.'" (H. B. Grigsby, *History of the Virginia Federal Convention of 1788*, I, 32.)

NORTH CAROLINA	Alexander Martin
	William Richardson Davie
	Richard Dobbs Spaight
	William Blount
	Hugh Williamson
	[Richard Caswell and Willie Jones were elected but declined to serve.]
SOUTH CAROLINA	John Rutledge
	Charles Pinckney
	Charles Cotesworth Pinckney
	Pierce Butler
	(Henry Laurens)
GEORGIA	William Few
	Abraham Baldwin
	William Pierce
	(George Walton)
	William Houstoun
	(Nathaniel Pendleton)

CREDENTIALS

[Arranged according to the date of legislative action, — VIRGINIA, NEW JERSEY, PENNSYLVANIA, NORTH CAROLINA, NEW HAMPSHIRE, DELAWARE, GEORGIA, NEW YORK, SOUTH CAROLINA, MASSACHUSETTS, CONNECTICUT, MARYLAND.]

VIRGINIA

Virginia

GENERAL ASSEMBLY begun and held at the Public Buildings in the City of Richmond on Monday the sixteenth day of October in the Year of our Lord one thousand seven hundred and Eighty six

AN ACT for appointing Deputies from this Commonwealth to a Convention proposed to be held in the City of Philadelphia in May next for the purpose of revising the federal Constitution.

WHEREAS the Commissioners who assembled at Annapolis on the fourteenth day of September last for the purpose of devising and reporting the means of enabling Congress to provide effectually for the Commercial Interests of the United States have represented the necessity of extending the revision of the fœderal System to all it's defects and have recommended that Deputies for that purpose be appointed by the several Legislatures to meet in Convention in the City of Philadelphia on the second day of May next a provision which was preferable to a discussion of the subject in Congress where it might be too much interrupted by the ordinary business before them and where it would besides be deprived of the valuable Counsels of sundry Individuals who are disqualified by the Constitution or Laws of particular States or restrained by peculiar circumstances from a Seat in that Assembly: AND WHEREAS the General Assembly of this Commonwealth taking into view the actual situation of the Confederacy as well as reflecting on the alarming representations made from time to time by the United States in Congress particularly in their Act of the fifteenth day of February last can no longer doubt that the Crisis is arrived at which the good People of America are to decide the solemn question whether they will by wise and magnanimous Efforts reap the just fruits of that Independence which they have so gloriously acquired and of that Union which they have cemented with so much of their common Blood, or whether by giving way to unmanly Jealousies and Prejudices or to partial and transitory Interests they will renounce the auspicious blessings prepared for them by the Revolution, and furnish to its Enemies an eventual Triumph over those by whose virtue and valor it has been accomplished: AND WHEREAS the same noble and extended policy and the same fraternal and affectionate Sentiments which originally determined the Citizens of this Commonwealth to unite with their Bretheren of the other States in establishing a Fœderal Government cannot but be Felt with equal force now as motives to lay aside every inferior consideration and to concur in such farther concessions and Provisions as may be necessary to secure the great Objects for which that Government was instituted and to render the *United States* as happy in peace as they have been glorious in War   BE IT THEREFORE ENACTED by the General Assembly of the Commonwealth of Virginia that seven Commissioners be appointed by joint Ballot of both Houses of Assembly who or any three of them are hereby authorized as Deputies from this Commonwealth to meet such Deputies as may be appointed and authorized by other States to assemble in Convention at Philadelphia as above recommended and to join with them in devising and discussing all such Alterations and farther Provisions as may be necessary to render the Fœderal Constitution adequate to the Exigencies of the Union and in reporting such an Act for that purpose to the United States in Congress as when agreed to by them and duly confirmed by the several States will effectually provide for the same. AND BE IT FURTHER ENACTED that in case of the death of any of the said Deputies or of their declining their appointments the Executive are hereby authorized to supply such

Vacancies. AND the Governor is requested to transmit forthwith a Copy of this Act to the United States in Congress and to the Executives of each of the States in the Union.

JOHN JONES Speaker of the Senate

Signed JOSEPH PRENTIS, Speaker of the House of Delegates.

A true Copy from the Inrollment

JOHN BECKLEY Clk House Dels.

In the House of Delegates
Monday the 4th of December 1786.

THE HOUSE according to the Order of the Day proceeded by joint Ballot with the Senate to the appointment of Seven Deputies from this Commonwealth to a Convention proposed to be held in the City of Philadelphia in May next for the purpose of revising the Fœderal Constitution, and the Members having prepared Tickets with the names of the Persons to be appointed, and deposited the same in the Ballot-boxes, Mr. Corbin, Mr. Matthews, Mr. David Stuart, Mr. George Nicholas, Mr. Richard Lee, Mr. Wills, Mr. Thomas Smith, Mr. Goodall and Mr. Turberville were nominated a Committee to meet a Committee from the Senate in the Conference-Chamber and jointly with them to examine the Ballot-boxes and report to the House on whom the Majority of Votes should fall. The Committee then withdrew and after some time returned into the House and reported that the Committee had, according to order, met a Committee from the Senate in the Conference-Chamber, and jointly with them examined the Ballot-boxes and found a majority of Votes in favor of George Washington, Patrick Henry, Edmund Randolph, John Blair, James Madison, George Mason and George Wythe Esquires.

Extract from the Journal,

JOHN BECKLEY Clk House Dels.

Attest JOHN BECKLEY
Clk. H. Dels.

In the House of Senators
Monday the 4th of December 1786.

THE SENATE according to the Order of the Day proceeded by joint ballot with the House of Delegates to the Appointment of Seven Deputies from this Commonwealth to a Convention proposed to be held in the City of Philadelphia in May next for the purpose of revising the Fœderal Constitution, and the Members having prepared Tickets with the names of the Persons to be appointed, and deposited the same in the Ballot-boxes, Mr. Anderson, Mr. Nelson and Mr Lee were nominated a Committee to meet a Committee from the House of Delegates in the Conference-Chamber and joinly with them to examine the Ballot-boxes and report to the House on whom the Majority of Votes should fall. The Committee then withdrew and after some time returned into the House and reported that the Committee had, according to order, met a Committee from the House of Delegates in the Conference-Chamber, and jointly with them examined the Ballot-boxes and found a Majority of Votes in favor of George Washington, Patrick Henry, Edmund Randolph, John Blair, James Madison George Mason and George Wythe Esquires.

Extract from the Journal
John Beckley Clk. H. Ds.

Attest,
    H. Brook Clk S.

VIRGINIA TO WIT

               I do Certify and make known, to all whom it (Seal)   may Concern, that John Beckley Esquire, is Clerk of the House of Delegates for this Commonwealth, and the proper Officer for attesting the proceedings of the General Assembly of the said Commonwealth, And that full Faith and Credit ought to be given to all things attested by the said John Beckley Esquire, by Virtue of his Office aforesaid.

    Given under my hand as Governor of the Commonwealth of Virginia and under the Seal thereof, at Richmond this fourth day of May, one thousand seven hundred and Eighty seven.

Edm: Randolph.

VIRGINIA TO WIT

    (Seal)   I do hereby Certify, that Patrick Henry, Esquire, one of the seven Commissioners appointed by joint ballot of both Houses of Assembly of the Commonwealth of Virginia, authorized as a Deputy therefrom, to meet such Deputies as might be appointed and authorized by other States to assemble in Philadelphia and to join with them in devising and discussing all such Alterations and further provisions, as might be necessary to render the Fœderal Constitution adequate to the exigencies of the Union; and in reporting such an Act for that purpose to the United States in Congress, as when agreed to by them and duly confirmed by the several States, might effectually provide for the same, did decline his appointment aforesaid; and thereupon in pursuance of an Act of the General Assembly of the said Commonwealth intituled "An Act for appointing Deputies from this Commonwealth to a Convention proposed to be held in the City of Philadelphia in May next, for the purpose of revising the Fœderal Constitution" I do hereby with the advice of the Council of State, supply the said Vacancy by nominating James McClurg, Esquire, a Deputy for the Purposes aforesaid.

Given under my Hand as Governor of the said Commonwealth and under the Seal thereof this second day of May in the Year of our Lord One thousand seven hundred and eighty seven.

—————— EDM: RANDOLPH

NEW JERSEY

The STATE OF NEW JERSEY.

(Seal) To the Honorable David Brearly, William Churchill Houston, William Patterson and John Neilson Esquires. Greeting.

The Council and Assembly reposing especial trust and confidence in your integrity, prudence and ability, have at a joint meeting appointed you the said David Brearley, William Churchill Houston, William Patterson and John Neilson Esquires, or any three of you, Commissioners to meet such Commissioners, as have been or may be appointed by the other States in the Union, at the City of Philadelphia in the Commonwealth of Pensylvania, on the second Monday in May next for the purpose of taking into Consideration the state of the Union, as to trade and other important objects, and of devising such other Provisions as shall appear to be necessary to render the Constitution of the Federal Government adequate to the exigencies thereof.

In testimony whereof the Great Seal of the State is hereunto affixed. Witness William Livingston Esquire, Governor, Captain General and Commander in Chief in and over the State of New Jersey and Territories thereunto belonging Chancellor and Ordinary in the same, at Trenton the Twenty third day of November in the Year of our Lord One thousand seven hundred and Eighty six and of our Sovereignty and Independence the Eleventh.

WIL: LIVINGSTON.

By His Excellency's Command
BOWES REED Secy.

The STATE OF NEW JERSEY.

(Seal) To His Excellency William Livingston and the Honorable Abraham Clark Esquires Greeting.

The Council and Assembly reposing especial trust and Confidence in your integrity, prudence and ability have at a joint Meeting appointed You the said William Livingston and Abraham Clark Esquires, in conjunction with the Honorable David Brearley, William Churchill Houston & William Patterson Esquires, or any three of you, Commissioners to meet such Commissioners as have been appointed by the other States in the Union at the City of Philadelphia in the Commonwealth of Pensylvania on the second Monday of this present month for the purpose of taking into consideration the state of the Union as to trade and other important Objects, and of devising such other Provisions as shall appear to be necessary to render the Constitution of the federal Government adequate to the exigencies thereof.

In Testimony whereof the Great Seal of the State is hereunto affixed. Witness William Livingston Esquire, Governor, Captain General and Commander in Chief in and over the State of New Jersey and Territories thereunto belonging Chancellor and Ordinary in the same at Burlington the Eighteenth day of May in the Year of our Lord One thousand seven hundred and Eighty seven and of our Sovereignty and Independence the Eleventh.

WIL: LIVINGSTON

By His Excellency's Command
    BOWES REED Secy.

THE STATE OF NEW JERSEY.

To the Honorable Jonathan Dayton Esquire

The Council and Assembly reposing especial trust and confidence in your integrity, prudence and ability have at a joint Meeting appointed You the said Jonathan Dayton Esquire, in conjunction with His Excellency William Livingston, the Honorable David Brearley, William Churchill Houston, William Patterson and Abraham Clark Esquires, or any three of you, Commissioners to meet such Commissioners as have been appointed by the other States in the Union at the City of Philadelphia in the Commonwealth of Pensylvania, for the purposes of taking into consideration the state of the Union as to trade and other important objects, and of devising such other Provision as shall appear to be necessary to render the Constitution of the federal Government adequate to the exigencies thereof.

In Testimony whereof the Great Seal of the State is hereunto affixed:—Witness Robert Lettis Hooper Esquire, Vice-President, Captain General and Commander in Chief in and over the State of New Jersey and Territories thereunto belonging, Chancellor and Ordinary in the same at Burlington the fifth day of June in the Year of our Lord One thousand seven hundred and Eighty seven and of our Sovereignty and Independence the Eleventh.

ROBT L. HOOPER.

By his Honor's Command
BOWES REED Secy.

PENNSYLVANIA

Pensylvania

An Act appointing Deputies to the Convention intended to be held in the City of Philadelphia for the purpose of revising the fœderal Constitution.

Section 1st Whereas the General Assembly of this Commonwealth taking into their serious Consideration the Representations heretofore made to the Legislatures of the several States in the Union by the United States in Congress Assembled, and also weighing the difficulties under which the Confederated States now labour, are fully convinced of the necessity of revising the federal Constitution for the purpose of making such Alterations and amendments as the exigencies of our Public Affairs require. And Whereas the Legislature of the State of Virginia have already passed an Act of that Commonwealth empowering certain Commissioners to meet at the City of Philadelphia in May next, a Convention of Commissioners or Deputies from the different States; And the Legislature of this State are fully sensible of the important advantages which may be derived to the United States, and every of them from co-operating with the Commonwealth of Virginia, and the other States of the Confederation in the said Design.

Section 2nd Be it enacted, and it is hereby enacted by the Representatives of the Freemen of the Commonwealth of Pensylvia in General Assembly met, and by the Authority of the same, That Thomas Mifflin, Robert Morris, George Clymer, Jared Ingersoll, Thomas Fitzsimmons, James Wilson and Governeur Morris Esquires, are hereby appointed Deputies from this State to meet in the Convention of the Deputies of the respective States of North America to be held at the City of Philadelphia on the second day of the Month of May next; And the said Thomas Mifflin, Robert Morris, George Clymer, Jared Ingersoll, Thomas Fitzsimmons, James Wilson and Governeur Morris Esquires, or any four of them, are hereby constituted and appointed Deputies from this State, with Powers to meet such Deputies as may be appointed and authorized by the other States, to assemble in the said Convention at the City aforesaid, and to join with them in devising, deliberating on, and discussing, all such alterations and further Provisions, as may be necessary to render the fœderal Constitution fully adequate to the exigencies of the Union, and in reporting such Act or Acts for that purpose to the United States in Congress Assembled, as when agreed to by them and duly confirmed by the several States, will effectually provide for the same.

Section 3d And be it further enacted by the Authority aforesaid, That in case any of the sd Deputies hereby nominated, shall happen to die, or to resign his or their said Appointment or Appointments, the Supreme Executive Council shall be and hereby are empowered and required, to nominate and appoint other Person or Persons in lieu of him or them so deceased, or who has or have so resigned, which Person or Persons, from and after such Nomination and Appointment, shall be and hereby are declared to be vested with the same Powers respectively, as any of the Deputies Nominated and Appointed by this Act, is vested with by the same: Provided Always, that the Council are not hereby authorised, nor shall they make any such Nomination or Appointment, except in Vacation and during the Recess of the General Assembly of this State.

Signed by Order of the House

{ Seal of the Laws }   THOMAS MIFFLIN Speaker
{ of Pensylvania }

Enacted into a Law at Philadelphia on Saturday December the thirtieth in the Year of our Lord one thousand seven hundred and Eighty six.

PETER ZACHARY LLOYD
Clerk of the General Assembly.

I Mathew Irwin Esquire Master of the Rolls for the State of Pensylvania Do Certify the Preceding Writing to be a true Copy (or Exemplification) of a certain Act of Assembly lodged in my Office.

(Seal)   In Witness whereof I have hereunto set my Hand and Seal of Office the 15 May A. D. 1787.

MATHW. IRWINE
M. R.

(Seal)   A Supplement to the Act entitled "An Act appointing Deputies to the Convention intended to be held in the City of Philadelphia for the purpose of revising the Federal Constitution.

Section 1st Whereas by the Act to which this Act is a Supplement, certain Persons were appointed as Deputies from this State to sit in the said Convention: And Whereas it is the desire of the General Assembly that His Excellency Benjamin Franklin Esquire, President of this State should also sit in the said Convention as a Deputy from this State — therefore

Section 2d Be it enacted and it is hereby enacted by the Representatives of the Freemen of the Commonwealth of Pensylvania, in General Assembly met, and by the Authority of the same, that His Excellency Benjamin Franklin Esquire, be, and he is hereby, appointed and authorised to sit in the said Convention as a Deputy from this State in addition to the Persons heretofore appointed; And that he be, and he hereby is invested with like Powers and authorities as are invested in the said Deputies or any of them.

Signed by Order of the House

THOMAS MIFFLIN Speaker.

Enacted into a Law at Philadelphia on Wednesday the twenty eighth day of March, in the Year of our Lord one thousand seven hundred & eighty seven.

PETER ZACHARY LLOYD
Clerk of the General Assembly.

I Mathew Irwine Esquire, Master of the Rolls for the State of Pensylvania Do Certify the above to be a true Copy (or Exemplification) of a Supplement to a certain Act of Assembly which Supplement is lodged in my Office

(Seal)   In Witness whereof I have hereunto set my Hand and Seal of Office the 15 May Ao D. 1787.

MATHW IRWINE

M. R.

NORTH CAROLINA

The State of NORTH CAROLINA

To the Honorable Alexander Martin Esquire, Greeting.

WHEREAS our General Assembly, in their late session holden at Fayette-ville, by adjournment, in the Month of January last, did by joint ballot of the Senate and House of Commons, elect Richard Caswell, Alexander Martin, William Richardson Davie, Richard Dobbs Spaight, and Willie Jones, Esquires, Deputies to attend a Convention of Delegates from the several United States of America, proposed to be held at the City of Philadelphia in May next for the purpose of revising the Fœderal Constitution.

We do therefore by these Presents, nominate, Commissionate and appoint you the said ALEXANDER MARTIN, one of the Deputies for and in our behalf to meet with our other Deputies at Philadelphia on the first day of May next and with them or any two of them to confer with such Deputies as may have been or shall be appointed by the other States, for the purpose aforesaid: *To hold*, exercise and enjoy the appointment aforesaid, with all Powers, Authorities and Emoluments to the same belonging or in any wise appertaining,[4] You conforming, in every instance, to the Act of our said Assembly under which you are appointed.

> WITNESS Richard Caswell Esquire, our Governor, Captain-General and Commander in Chief, under his Hand and our Great Seal at Kinston the 24th day of February in the XI Year of our Independence

> > RICD (Seal) CASWELL.

Ao Di 1787.
> By His Excellency's
Command.
> WINSTON CASWELL P. Secy

The State of NORTH-CAROLINA
> To the Honorable WILLIAM RICHARDSON DAVIE Esquire Greeting.

Whereas our General Assembly in their late session holden at Fayette-ville, by adjournment, in the Month of January last, did by joint-ballot of the Senate and House of Commons, elect Richard Caswell, Alexander Martin, William Richardson Davie, Richard Dobbs Spaight & Willie Jones Esquires, Deputies to attend a Convention of Delegates from the several United States of America proposed to be held in the City of Philadelphia in May next for the purpose of revising the Fœderal Constitution.

We do therefore, by these Presents, nominate Commissionate and appoint you the said WILLIAM RICHARDSON DAVIE one of the Deputies for and in our behalf to meet with our other Deputies at Philadelphia on the first day of May next and with them or any two of them to confer with such Deputies as may have been or shall be appointed by the other States for the Purposes aforesaid *To hold*, exercise and enjoy the said appointment with all Powers authorities and emoluments to the same belonging or in any wise appertaining, You conforming, in every instance, to the Act of our said Assembly under which you are appointed.

> WITNESS Richard Caswell Esquire, our Governor, Captain-General and Commander in Chief under his Hand and our

---

[4] "The Assembly have directed the same allowance to be made the Deputies as is granted to the Delegates to Congress to be paid by the Governor's Warrant on the Collectors of Imports out of the monies now due for Goods Imported." (Governor Caswell to each Delegate, January 7, 1787, *North Carolina State Records*, XX, 600.)

Great Seal at Kinston the 24th day of February in the XI.
Year of our Independence, Anno. Dom. 1787:

RD (Seal.) CASWELL

By His Excellency's Command
WINSTON CASWELL P. Secy.

The State of NORTH CAROLINA
   To the Honorable *Richard Dobbs Spaight* Esquire, Greeting.
   WHEREAS our General Assembly in their late session holden at
Fayette-ville, by adjournment, in the month of January last, did
elect you the said Richard Dobbs Spaight with Richard Caswell,
Alexander Martin, William Richardson Davie, and Willie Jones
Esquires, Deputies to attend a Convention of Delegates from the
several United States of America proposed to be held in the City of
Philadelphia in May next, for the purpose of revising the Fœderal
Constitution.
   We do therefore by these Presents nominate, Commissionate
and appoint you the said RICHARD DOBBS SPAIGHT one of the Deputies for and in behalf of us to meet with our other Deputies at
Philadelphia on the first day of May next and with them or any two
of them to confer with such Deputies as may have been or shall be
appointed by the other States for the purpose aforesaid. *To hold,*
exercise and enjoy the said Appointment with all Powers, Authorities
and Emoluments to the same incident and belonging or in any wise
appertaining. You conforming in every instance, to the Act of
our said Assembly under which you are appointed.
      WITNESS Richard Caswell Esquire, our Governor Captain-
      General and Commander in Chief under his Hand and our
      Great Seal at Kinston the 14th day of April in the XIth Year
      of our Independence Anno. Dom. 1787.

RD. (Seal) CASWELL.

By His Excellency's Command
WINSTON CASWELL P. Secy

State of NORTH-CAROLINA
   His Excellency Richard Caswell Esquire Governor, Captain
   General and Commander in Chief in and over the State afore-
   said.
   To all to whom these Presents shall come
                              Greeting.
   WHEREAS by an Act of the General Assembly of the said State
passed the sixth day of January last, entitled "An Act for appoint-
ing Deputies from this State, to a Convention proposed to be held

in the City of Philadelphia in May next, for the purpose of Revising the Fœderal Constitution" among other things it is Enacted "That five Commissioners be appointed by joint-ballot of both Houses of Assembly who, or any three of them, are hereby authorized as Deputies from this State to meet at Philadelphia on the first day of May next, then and there to meet and confer with such Deputies as may be appointed by the other States for similar purposes, and with them to discuss and decide upon the most effectual means to remove the defects of our Fœderal Union, and to procure the enlarged Purposes which it was intended to effect, and that they report such an Act to the General Assembly of this State as when agreed to by them, will effectually provide for the same." And it is by the said Act, further Enacted, "That in case of the death or resignation of any of the Deputies or of their declining their Appointments, His Excellency the Governor for the Time being, is hereby authorized to supply such Vacancies." And Whereas, in consequence of the said Act, Richard Caswell, Alexander Martin, William Richardson Davie, Richard Dobbs Spaight and Willie Jones Esquires, were by joint-ballot of the two Houses of Assembly, elected Deputies for the purposes aforesaid: And Whereas the said Richard Caswell hath resigned his said Appointment as one of the Deputies aforesaid.

Now know Ye that I have appointed and by these Presents do appoint the Honorable William Blount Esquire, one of the Deputies to represent this State in the Convention aforesaid, in the room and stead of the aforesaid Richard Caswell, hereby giving and granting to the said William Blount the same Powers, Privileges and Emoluments which the said Richard Caswell would have been vested with or entitled to, had he continued in the Appointment aforesaid.

> Given under my Hand and the Great Seal of the State, at Kinston, the 23d day of April Anno Dom 1787. And in the Eleventh Year of American Independence.
>
> > > > > Rid. (Seal) Caswell.

By His Excellency's Command
  Winston Caswell P. Secy

State of North-Carolina
> His Excellency Richard Caswell Esquire, Governor, Captain-General and Commander in Chief, in and over the State aforesaid.

To all to whom these Presents shall come
> > > Greeting.

Whereas by an Act of the General Assembly of the said State, passed the sixth day of January last, entitled "An Act for appointing Deputies from this State, to a Convention proposed to be held in the City of Philadelphia in May next for the purpose of revising the Fœderal Constitution" among other things it is enacted "That five Commissioners be appointed by joint-ballot of both Houses of Assembly, who, or any three of whom, are hereby authorized as Deputies from this State, to meet at Philadelphia on the first day of May next, then and there to meet and confer with such Deputies as may be appointed by the other States for similar purposes and with them to discuss and decide upon the most effectual means to remove the defects of our Fœderal Union, and to procure the enlarged purposes, which it was intended to effect, and that they report such an Act to the General Assembly of this State, as when agreed to by them, will effectually provide for the same." And it is by the said Act, further enacted "That in case of the death or resignation of any of the Deputies, or their declining their Appointments His Excellency the Governor for the Time being is hereby authorized to supply such Vacancies."

AND WHEREAS in consequence of the said Act Richard Caswell, Alexander Martin, William Richardson Davie, Richard Dobbs Spaight and Willie Jones Esquires, were by joint-ballot of ye two Houses of Assembly elected Deputies for the purposes aforesaid. And Whereas the said Willie Jones hath declined his Appointment as one of the Deputies aforesaid

Now KNOW YE that I have appointed and by these Presents do appoint the Honorable HUGH WILLIAMSON Esquire, one of the Deputies to represent this State in the Convention aforesaid in the room and stead of the aforesaid Willie Jones, hereby giving and granting to the said HUGH WILLIAMSON the same Powers, Privileges and emoluments which the said Willie Jones would have been vested with and entitled to had he acted under the Appointment aforesaid.

Given under my Hand and the Great Seal of the State at Kinston the third day of April Anno Dom. 1787. and in the Eleventh Year of American Independence

RID (Seal) CASWELL

By His Excellency's Command
DALLAM CASWELL Pro
Secretary

NEW HAMPSHIRE

State of New ⎱
Hampshire ⎰

In the House of Representatives
Jany 17th 1787—

Resolved, that any two of the Delegates of this State to the Congress of the United States, be & hereby are appointed and authorized as Deputies from this State, to meet such Deputies as may be appointed & authorized by other States in the Union, to assemble in Convention at Philadelphia on the second day of May next, and to join with them in devising & discussing all such alterations & further provisions as to render the federal Constitution adequate to the Exigencies of the Union & in reporting such an Act to the United States in Congress, as when agreed to by them, & duly confirmed by the several States, will effectually provide for the same, But in case of the Death of any of said Deputies, or their declining their Appointments, the Executive is hereby authorized to supply such vacancies, and the President is requested to transmit forthwith a copy of this Resolve to the United States in Congress and to the Executive of each of the States in the Union. —

Sent up for Concurrence

John Langdon Speaker

In Senate the same day read & concurred with this Amendment that the said Delegates shall proceed to join the Convention aforesaid, in case Congress shall signify to them, that they approve of the Convention, as advantageous to the Union and not an infringement of the Powers granted to Congress by the Confederation.

Jno Sullivan President

In the House of Representatives the same day read & concurred

John Langdon Speaker

A true Copy
Attest Joseph Pearson Secy

State of New Hampshire[5]

In the Year of our Lord One thousand seven hundred and Eighty seven.

An Act for appointing Deputies from this State to the Convention, proposed to be holden in the City of Philadelphia in May 1787 for the purpose of revising the federal Constitution

Whereas in the formation of the federal Compact, which frames the bond of Union of the American States, it was not possible in

---

[5] No action was taken under the previous resolution, and a further act became necessary.

"The representations of this State, even at that late day, were secured only by urgent efforts from abroad and extraordinary efforts at home. The finances of the State were in a deplorable condition and it is impossible to realize at the present time what the undertaking was to provide cash for any considerable public enterprise. It was currently reported in the newspapers of the day that the expenses of Mr. Gillman and himself were defrayed out of Mr. Langdon's private purse." *New Hampshire State Papers*, XX, 842, citing 2 New Hampshire Historical Society *Proceedings*, 28.

the infant state of our Republic to devise a system which in the course of time and experience, would not manifest imperfections that it would be necessary to reform.

And Whereas the limited powers, which by the Articles of Confederation, are vested in the Congress of the United States, have been found far inadequate, to the enlarged purposes which they were intended to produce. And Whereas Congress hath, by repeated and most urgent representations, endeavoured to awaken this, and other States of the Union, to a sense of the truly critical and alarming situation in which they may inevitably be involved, unless timely measures be taken to enlarge the powers of Congress, that they may be thereby enabled to avert the dangers which threaten our existence as a free and independent People. And Whereas this State hath been ever desirous to act upon the liberal system of the general good of the United States, without circumscribing its views, to the narrow and selfish objects of partial convenience; and has been at all times ready to make every concession to the safety and happiness of the whole, which justice and sound policy could vindicate.

BE IT THEREFORE ENACTED, by the Senate and House of Representatives in General Court convened that JOHN LANGDON, JOHN PICKERING, NICHOLAS GILMAN & BENJAMIN WEST ESQUIRES be and hereby are appointed Commissioners, they or any two of them, are hereby authorized, and empowered, as Deputies from this State to meet at Philadelphia said Convention or any other place, to which the Convention may be adjourned, for the purposes aforesaid, there to confer with such Deputies, as are, or may be appointed by the other States 'for similar purposes; and with them to discuss and decide upon the most effectual means to remedy the defects of our federal Union; and to procure, and secure, the enlarged purposes which it was intended to effect, and to report such an Act, to the United States in Congress, as when agreed to by them, and duly confirmed by the several States, will effectually provide for the same.

State of New ⎱ In the House of Representatives June 27th
Hampshire ⎰ 1787.

The foregoing Bill having been read a third time, Voted that it pass to be enacted.

Sent up for Concurrence
JOHN SPARHAWK Speaker

In Senate, the same day — This Bill having been read a third time, — Voted that the same be enacted.

JNO SULLIVAN President.

Copy Examined
Pr JOSEPH PEARSON Secy. (Seal appendt.)

DELAWARE

Delaware

His Excellency Thomas Collins, Esquire, President, Captain General, and Commander in Chief of the Delaware State; To all to whom these Presents shall come, Greeting. Know Ye, that among the Laws of the said State, passed by the General Assembly of the same, on the third day of February, (Seal) in the Year of our Lord One thousand seven hundred and Eighty seven, it is thus inrolled.

In the Eleventh Year of the Independence of the Delaware State

An Act appointing Deputies from this State to the Convention proposed to be held in the City of Philadelphia for the Purpose of revising the Federal Constitution.

Whereas the General Assembly of this State are fully convinced of the Necessity of revising the Federal Constitution, and adding thereto such further Provisions, as may render the same more adequate to the Exigencies of the Union; And Whereas the Legislature of Virginia have already passed an Act of that Commonwealth, appointing and authorizing certain Commissioners to meet, at the City of Philadelphia, in May next, a Convention of Commissioners or Deputies from the different States: And this State being willing and desirous of co-operating with the Commonwealth of Virginia, and the other States in the Confederation, in so useful a design.

Be it therefore enacted by the General Assembly of Delaware, that George Read, Gunning Bedford, John Dickinson, Richard Bassett and Jacob Broom, Esquires, are hereby appointed Deputies from this State to meet in the Convention of the Deputies of other States, to be held at the City of Philadelphia on the Second day of May next: And the said George Read, Gunning Bedford, John Dickinson, Richard Bassett and Jacob Broom, Esquires, or any three of them, are hereby constituted and appointed Deputies from this State, with Powers to meet such Deputies as may be appointed and authorized by the other States to assemble in the said Convention at the City aforesaid, and to join with them in devising, deliberating on, and discussing, such Alterations and further Provisions as may be necessary to render the Fœderal Constitution adequate to the Exigencies of the Union; and in reporting such Act or Acts for that purpose to the United States in Congress Assembled, as when agreed to by them, and duly confirmed by the several States, may effectually provide for the same: So always and Provided, that such Alterations or further Provisions, or any of them, do not extend to that part of the Fifth Article of the Confederation of the said States, finally

ratified on the first day of March, in the Year One thousand seven
hundred and eighty one, which declares that "In determining Ques-
"tions in the United States in Congress Assembled each State shall
"have one Vote." [6]

And be it enacted, that in Case any of the said Deputies hereby
nominated, shall happen to die, or to resign his or their Appointment, the President or Commander in Chief with the Advice of the
Privy Council, in the Recess of the General Assembly, is hereby
authorized to supply such Vacancies

Passed at Dover, } Signed by Order of the House of Assembly
February 3d. 1787. }   JOHN COOK, Speaker

Signed by Order of the Council

GEO CRAGHEAD, Speaker.

All and singular which Premises by the Tenor of these Presents,
I have caused to be Exemplified. In Testimony whereof I have
hereunto subscribed my Name, and caused the Great-Seal of the
said State to be affixed to these Presents, at New Castle the Second
day of April in the Year of our Lord One thousand seven hundred
and eighty seven, and in the Eleventh Year of the Independence of
the United States of America

                                        THOS COLLINS

Attest

    Ja Booth Secy.

---

[6] GEORGE READ TO JOHN DICKINSON.[a]

                      New Castle, January 17th, 1787.

Dear Sir, — Finding that Virginia hath again taken the lead in the proposed
convention at Philadelphia in May, as recommended in our report when at Annapolis,
as by an act of their Assembly, passed the 22d of November last, and inserted in Dunlap's paper of the 15th of last month, it occurred to me, as a prudent measure on the
part of our State, that its Legislature should, in the act of appointment, so far restrain
the powers of the commissioners, whom they shall name on this service, as that they
may not extend to any alteration in that part of the fifth article of the present Confederation, which gives each State *one vote* in determining questions in Congress, and
the latter part of the thirteenth article, as to future alterations, — that is, that such
clause shall be preserved or inserted, for the like purpose, in any revision that shall
be made and agreed to in the proposed convention. I conceive our existence as a
State will depend upon our preserving such rights, for I consider the acts of Congress
hitherto, as to the ungranted lands in most of the larger States, as sacrificing the just
claims of the smaller and bounded States to a proportional share therein, for the purpose of discharging the national debt incurred during the war; and such is my jealousy
of most of the larger States, that I would trust nothing to their candor, generosity,
or ideas of public justice in behalf of this State, from what has heretofore happened,
and which, I presume, hath not escaped your notice. But as I am generally distrust-
ful of my own judgment, and particularly in public matters of consequence, I wish your

---

[a] W. T. Read, *Life and Correspondence of George Read*, pp. 438–439.

GEORGIA

By the Honorable GEORGE MATHEWS Esquire, Captain General, Governor and Commander in Chief, in and over the said State aforesaid.

To all to whom these Presents shall come Greeting.

KNOW YE that JOHN MILTON Esquire, who hath Certified the annexed Copy of an Ordinance intitled "An Ordinance for "the appointment of Deputies from this State for the purpose "of revising the Fœderal Constitution" — is Secretary of the said State in whose Office the Archives of the same are deposited. Therefore all due faith, Credit and Authority are and ought to be had and given the same.

IN TESTOMONY whereof I have hereunto set my hand and caused the Great Seal of the said State to be put and affixed at *Augusta*, this Twenty fourth day of April in the Year of our Lord One thousand seven hundred and eighty seven and of our Sovereignty and Independence the Eleventh.

GEO: (Seal) MATHEWS

By his Honor's Command
J. MILTON Secy

AN ORDINANCE for the appointment of Deputies from this State for the purpose of revising the Fœderal Constitution.

BE IT ORDAINED by the Representatives of the Freemen of the State of Georgia in General Assembly met and by the Authority of the same, that WILLIAM FEW, ABRAHAM BALDWIN, WILLIAM PIERCE, GEORGE WALTON WILLIAM HOUSTOUN AND NATHANIEL PENDLETON ESQUIRES, Be, and they are hereby appointed Com-

---

consideration of the prudence or propriety of the Legislature's adopting such a measure, and more particularly for that I do suppose you will be one of its commissioners. Persuaded I am, from what I have seen occasionally in the public prints and heard in private conversations, that the voice of the States will be one of the subjects of revision, and in a meeting where there will be so great an interested majority, I suspect the argument or oratory of the smaller State commissioners will avail little.   In such circumstances I conceive it will relieve the commissioners of the State from disagreeable argumentation, as well as prevent the downfall of the State, which would at once become a cypher in the union, and have no chance of an accession of district, or even citizens; for, as we presently stand, our quota is increased upon us, in the requisition of this year, more than thirteen-eightieths since 1775, without any other reason that I can suggest than a promptness in the Legislature of this State to comply with all the Congress requisitions from time to time. This increase alone, without addition, would in the course of a few years banish many of its citizens and impoverish the remainder; therefore, clear I am that every guard that can be devised for this State's protection against future encroachment should be preserved or made. I wish your opinion on the subject as soon as convenient.

missioners, who, or any two or more of them are hereby authorized as Deputies from this State to meet such deputies as may be
appointed and authorized by other States to assemble in *Convention*
at *Philadelphia* and to join with them in devising and discussing
all such Alterations and farther Provisions as may be necessary to
render the *Federal Constitution* adequate to the exigencies of the
Union, and in reporting such an Act for that purpose to the United
States in Congress Assembled as when agreed to by them, and duly
confirmed by the several States, will effectually provide for the same.
In case of the death of any of the said Deputies, or of their declining
their appointments, the Executive are hereby authorized to supply
such Vacancies.

By Order of the House
(signed) WM GIBBONS Speaker.

Augusta the 10 February 1787.
    Georgia.
        Secretary's Office
    The above is a true Copy from the Original Ordinance deposited
in my Office.
    Augusta ⎱
24 April 1787 ⎰   J: MILTON Secy.

The State of Georgia by the grace of God, free, Sovereign and Independent.
    To the Honorable WILLIAM PIERCE Esquire.
    WHEREAS you the said William Pierce, are in and by an Ordi-
nance of the General Assembly of our said State Nominated and
Appointed a Deputy to represent the same in a Convention of the
United States to be assembled at Philadelphia, for the Purposes
of devising and discussing all such Alterations and farther Provisions as may be necessary to render the Fœderal Constitution adequate to the Exigencies of the Union.
    You are therefore hereby Commissioned to proceed on the duties
required of you in virtue of the said Ordinance

WITNESS our trusty and well beloved *George Mathews* Esquire, our Captain General, Governor and Commander in
Chief, under his hand and our Great Seal at Augusta this
Seventeenth day of April in the Year of our Lord one thousand seven hundred and eighty seven and of our Sovereignty
and Independence the Eleventh.

GEO: MATHEWS (Seal.)

By His Honor's Command.
J. MILTON. Secy.

The State of Georgia by the grace of God free, Sovereign and Independent.

To the Honorable WILLIAM FEW Esquire.

WHEREAS you the said William Few, are in and by an Ordinance of the General Assembly of our said State Nominated and appointed a Deputy to represent the same in a Convention of the United States to be assembled at Philadelphia, for the Purposes of devising and discussing all such Alterations and farther Provisions as may be necessary to render the Fœderal Constitution adequate to the Exigencies of the Union.

You are therefore hereby Commissioned to proceed on the duties required of you in virtue of the said Ordinance.

> WITNESS our trusty and well-beloved GEORGE MATHEWS Esquire our Captain-General, Governor and Commander in Chief, under his hand and our Great Seal at Augusta, this seventeenth day of April in the Year of our Lord One thousand seven hundred and eighty Seven, and of our Sovereignty and Independence the Eleventh.
>
> GEO: (Seal.) MATHEWS.

By His Honor's Command
    J. MILTON Secy

The State of Georgia by the grace of God, free, Sovereign and Independent.

To the Honorable WILLIAM HOUSTOUN Esquire

WHEREAS you the said *William Houstoun*, are in and by an Ordinance of the General Assembly of our said State nominated and appointed a Deputy to represent the same in a Convention of the United States to be assembled at Philadelphia, for the purposes of devising and discussing all such Alterations and farther Provisions as may be necessary to render the Fœderal Constitution adequate to the Exigencies of the Union.

You are therefore hereby Commissioned to proceed on the Duties required of you in virtue of the said Ordinance.

> WITNESS our trusty and well-beloved GEORGE MATHEWS Esquire, our Captain-General, Governor and Commander in Chief, under his hand and our Great Seal at Augusta, this seventeenth day of April in the Year of our Lord one thousand seven hundred and eighty seven, and of our Sovereignty and Independence the Eleventh.
>
> GEO: (*Seal.*) MATHEWS

By his Honor's Command
    J. MILTON   Secy

New-York.

NEW YORK [7]

By His Excellency George Clinton Esquire Governor of the State of New York General and Commander in Chief of all the Militia and Admiral of the Navy of the same.

(Seal)

To all to whom these Presents shall come

It is by these Presents certified that John McKesson who has subscribed the annexed Copies of Resolutions is Clerk of the Assembly of this State.

In Testimony whereof I have caused the Privy Seal of the said State to be hereunto affixed this Ninth day of May in the Eleventh Year of the Independence of the said State.

GEO: CLINTON.

State of New York

In Assembly February 28th 1787.

A Copy of a Resolution of the honorable the Senate, delivered by Mr Williams, was read, and is in the Words following, vizt.

Resolved, if the honorable the Assembly concur herein, that three Delegates be appointed on the part of this State, to meet such Delegates as may be appointed on the part of the other States respectively, on the second Monday in may next, at Philadelphia, for the sole and express purpose of revising the Articles of Confederation, and reporting to Congress, and to the several Legislatures, such

---

[7] Before New York took action, Congress formally authorized the convention in Philadelphia. As subsequent credentials were to some extent influenced by the Resolution of Congress, it seems best to insert it here, although it is given in Appendix A, I.

By

The United States in Congress Assembled

February 21st 1787.

Whereas there is provision in the Articles of Confederation and perpetual Union, for making alterations therein, by the assent of a Congress of the United States, and of the legislatures of the several States; and whereas experience hath evinced, that there are defects in the present confederation, as a mean to remedy which, several of the States, and particularly the State of New-York, by express instructions to their Delegates in Congress, have suggested a Convention for the purposes expressed in the following Resolution; and such Convention appearing to be the most probable means of establishing in these States a firm national Government.

Resolved, That in the opinion of Congress, it is expedient, that on the second Monday in May next, a Convention of Delegates, who shall have been appointed by the several States, be held at Philadelphia, for the sole and express purpose of revising the Articles of Confederation, and reporting to Congress and the several Legislatures, such alterations and provisions therein, as shall, when agreed to in Congress, and confirmed by the States, render the federal Constitution adequate to the exigencies of Government, and the preservation of the Union.

alterations and Provisions therein, as shall, when agreed to in Congress, and confirmed by the several States, render the federal Constitution adequate to the Exigencies of Government, and the preservation of the Union; and that in case of such concurrence, the two Houses of the Legislature, will, on Tuesday next, proceed to nominate and appoint the said Delegates, in like manner as is directed by the Constitution of this State, for nominating and appointing Delegates to Congress.

Resolved, that this House do concur with the honorable the Senate, in the said Resolution.

In Assembly March 6th 1787.

Resolved, that the Honorable Robert Yates Esquire, and Alexander Hamilton and John Lansing, Junior Esquires, be, and they are hereby nominated by this House, Delegates on the part of this State, to meet such Delegates as may be appointed on the part of the other States respectively, on the second Monday in May next, at Philadelphia, pursuant to concurrent Resolutions of both Houses of the Legislature, on the 28th Ultimo.

Resolved, that this House will meet the Honorable the Senate, immediately, at such place as they shall appoint, to compare the Lists of Persons nominated by the Senate and Assembly respectively, as Delegates on the part of this State, to meet such Delegates as may be appointed on the part of the other States respectively, on the second Monday in May next, at Philadelphia, pursuant to concurrent Resolutions, of both Houses of the Legislature, on the 28t Ultimo.

Ordered That Mr. N. Smith deliver a Copy of the last preceding Resolution, to the Honorable the Senate.

A Copy of a Resolution of the Honorable the Senate, was delivered by Mr. Vanderbilt, that the Senate will immediately meet this House in the Assembly Chamber, to compare the Lists of Persons nominated by the Senate and Assembly respectively, as Delegates, pursuant to the Resolutions before mentioned.

The Honorable the Senate accordingly attended in the Assembly Chamber, to compare the Lists of Persons nominated for Delegates, as above mentioned.

The list of Persons nominated by the Honorable the Senate, were the Honorable Robert Yates Esquire, and John Lansing Junior, and Alexander Hamilton Esquires; and on comparing the Lists of the Persons nominated by the Senate and Assembly respectively, it appeared that the same Persons were nominated in both Lists. Thereupon, Resolved that the Honorable Robert Yates, John Lansing Junior and Alexander Hamilton Esquires, be, and they are hereby declared duly nominated and appointed Delegates, on the part of this State, to meet such Delegates as may be appointed on the part of the other States respectively, on the second Monday in May next, at Philadelphia, for the sole and express purpose of revising the Articles of Confederation, and reporting to Congress, and to the several Legislatures, such alterations and provisions therein, as shall, when agreed to in Congress, and confirmed by the several States, render the federal Constitution adequate to the exigencies of Government, and the preservation of the Union.

> True Extracts from the Journals of the Assembly
> _____ JOHN McKESSON Clk.

SOUTH CAROLINA

State of SOUTH CAROLINA.

> By His Excellency Thomas Pinckney Esquire, Governor and Commander in Chief in and over the State aforesaid.

To the Honorable John Rutledge Esquire

> Greeting.

By Virtue of the Power and Authority in me vested by the Legislature of this State in their Act passed the eighth day of March last I do hereby Commission You the said John Rutledge as one of the Deputies appointed from this State to meet such Deputies or Commissioners as may be appointed and authorized by other of the United States to assemble in Convention at the City of Philadelphia in the Month of May next, or as soon thereafter as may be, and to join with such Deputies or Commissioners (they being duly authorized and empowered) in devising and discussing all such Alterations, Clauses, Articles and Provisions, as may be thought necessary to render the Fœderal Constitution entirely adequate to the actual Situation and future good Government of the confederated States, and that you together with the said Deputies or Commissioners or a Majority of them who shall be present (provided the State be not represented by less than two) do join in reporting such an Act, to the United States in Congress Assembled as when approved and agreed to by them, and duly ratified and confirmed by the several States will effectually provide for the Exigencies of the Union.

> Given under my hand and the Great Seal of the State in the City of Charleston, this tenth day of April in the Year of our Lord, One thousand seven hundred and eighty seven and of the Sovereignty and Independence of the United States of America the Eleventh.
> THOMAS (Seal.) PINCKNEY.

By his Excellency's Command
    PETER FRENEAU Secretary

State of SOUTH CAROLINA
>   By His Excellency Thomas Pinckney Esquire, Governor
>   and Commander in Chief in and over the State aforesaid.
To the Honorable Charles Pinckney Esquire.
>   Greeting.

By Virtue of the Power and Authority in me vested by the Legislature of this State in their Act passed the eighth day of March last, I do hereby Commission you the said Charles Pinckney, as one of the Deputies appointed from this State to meet such Deputies or Commissioners as may be appointed and authorized by other of the United States to assemble in Convention at the City of Philadelphia in the Month of May next, or as soon thereafter as may be, and to join with such Deputies or Commissioners (they being duly authorized and empowered) in devising and discussing all such Alterations, Clauses, Articles and Provisions, as may be thought necessary to render the Fœderal Constitution entirely adequate to the actual Situation and future good Government of the confederated States, and that you together with the said Deputies or Commissioners or a Majority of them who shall be present (provided the State be not represented by less than two) do join in reporting such an Act, to the United States in Congress Assembled as when approved and agreed to by them and duly ratified and confirmed by the several States will effectually provide for the Exigencies of the Union.

>   Given under my hand and the Great Seal of the State in the
>   City of Charleston this Tenth day of April in the Year of our
>   Lord One thousand seven hundred and Eighty Seven and of
>   the Sovereignty and Independence of the United States of
>   America the Eleventh.

>   THOMAS (Seal.) PINCKNEY

By His Excellency's Command
>   PETER FRENEAU Secretary.

State of South-Carolina.
>   By His Excellency Thomas Pinckney Esquire, Governor
>   and Commander in Chief in and over the State aforesaid.
To the Honorable Charles Cotesworth Pinckney Esquire,
>   Greeting.

By Virtue of the Power and Authority in me vested by the Legislature of this State in their Act passed the eighth day of March last, I do hereby Commission you the said Charles Cotesworth Pinckney as one of the Deputies appointed from this State to meet such Deputies or Commissioners as may be appointed and authorized by other of the United States to assemble in Convention at the City of Philadelphia in the Month of May next or as soon thereafter as may be, and to join with such Deputies or Commissioners (they being duly authorized and empowered) in devising and discussing all such Alterations, Clauses, Articles and Provisions as may be thought necessary to render the Fœderal Constitution entirely adequate to the actual Situation and future good Government of the Confederated States, and that you together with the said Deputies or Commissioners, or a Majority of them, who shall be present (provided the State be not represented by less than two) do join in reporting such an Act to the United States in Congress Assembled as when approved and agreed to by them and duly ratified and confirmed by the several States will effectually provide for the Exigencies of the Union.

Given under my hand and the Great Seal of the State in the City of Charleston this tenth day of April in the Year of our Lord one thousand seven hundred and eighty seven and of the Sovereignty and Independence of the United States of America the Eleventh.

THOMAS (Seal.) PINCKNEY.

By His Excellency's Command
PETER FRENEAU Secretary.

State of South Carolina
By His Excellency Thomas Pinckney Esquire, Governor and Commander in Chief in and over the State aforesaid.
To the Honorable Pierce Butler Esquire
Greeting.

By Virtue of the Power and authority in me vested by the Legislature of this State in their Act passed the eighth day of March last, I do hereby Commission you the said Pierce Butler, as one of the Deputies appointed from this State to meet such Deputies or Commissioners as may be appointed and authorized by other of the United States to assemble in Convention at the City of Philadelphia in the Month of May next, or as soon thereafter as may be and to join with with such Deputies or Commissioners (they being duly authorised and empowered) in devising and discussing, all such Alterations, Clauses, Articles and Provisions as may be thought necessary to render the Fœderal Constitution entirely adequate to the actual Situation and future good government of the confederated States, and that you together with the said Deputies or Commissioners or a Majority of them who shall be present (provided the State be not represented by less than two) do join in reporting such an Act, to the United States in Congress Assembled as when approved and agreed to by them and duly ratified and confirmed by the several States will effectually provide for the Exigencies of the Union.

Given under my hand and the Great Seal of the State in the City of Charleston this Tenth day of April in the Year of our Lord one thousand seven hundred and Eighty seven, and of the Sovereignty and Independence of the United States of America the Eleventh.

THOMAS (Seal.) PINCKNEY.

By His Excellency's Command
PETER FRENEAU Secretary.

MASSACHUSETTS

COMMONWEALTH OF MASSACHUSETTS.

(Seal Appendt.) By His Excellency James Bowdoin Esquire Governor of the Commonwealth of Massachusetts.

To the Honorable Francis Dana, Elbridge Gerry, Nathaniel Gorham, Rufus King and Caleb Strong Esquires. Greeting.

Whereas Congress did on the twenty first day of February Ao Di 1787, Resolve "that in the opinion of Congress it is expedient that on the second Monday in May next a Convention of Delegates who shall have been appointed by the several States to be held at Philadelphia for the sole and express purpose of revising the Articles of Confederation and reporting to Congress and the several Legislatures, such alterations and provisions therein as shall when agreed to in Congress, and confirmed by the States render the federal Constitution adequate to the exigencies of government and the preservation of the Union." And Whereas the General Court have constituted and appointed you their Delegates to attend and represent this Commonwealth in the said proposed Convention; and have by a Resolution of theirs of the tenth of March last, requested me to Commission you for that purpose.

Now therefore Know Ye, that in pursuance of the resolutions aforesaid, I do by these presents, commission you the said Francis Dana, Elbridge Gerry Nathaniel Gorham, Rufus King & Caleb Strong Esquires or any three of you to meet such Delegates as may be appointed by the other or any of the other States in the Union to meet in Convention at Philadelphia at the time and for the purposes aforesaid.

In Testimony whereof I have caused the Public Seal of the Commonwealth aforesaid to be hereunto affixed.

Given at the Council Chamber in Boston the Ninth day of

April Ao Dom. 1787 and in the Eleventh Year of the Independence of the United States of America.

By His Excellency's Command JAMES BOWDOIN.
JOHN AVERY Junr., Secretary

CONNECTICUT

STATE OF CONNECTICUT.

(Seal.) At a General Assembly of the State of Connecticut in America, holden at Hartford on the second Thursday of May, Anno Domini 1787.

An Act for appointing Delegates to meet in a Convention of the States to be held at the City of Philadelphia on the second Monday of May instant.

Whereas the Congress of the United States by their Act of the twenty first of February 1787 have recommended that on the second Monday of May instant, a Convention of Delegates, who shall have been appointed by the several States, be held at Philadelphia for the sole and express purpose of revising the Articles of Confederation.

Be it enacted by the Governor, Council and Representatives in General Court Assembled and by the Authority of the same.

That the Honorable William Samuel Johnson, Roger Sherman, and Oliver Ellsworth Esquires, be and they hereby are appointed Delegates to attend the said Convention, and are requested to proceed to the City of Philadelphia for that purpose without delay; And the said Delegates, and in case of sickness or accident, such one or more of them as shall actually attend the said Convention, is and are hereby authorized and empowered to Represent this State therein, and to confer with such Delegates appointed by the several States, for the purposes mentioned in the said Act of Congress that may be present and duly empowered to act in said Convention, and to discuss upon such Alterations and Provisions agreeable to the general principles of Republican Government as they shall think proper to render the federal Constitution adequate to the exigencies of Government and, the preservation of the Union; And they are further directed, pursuant to the said Act of Congress to report such alterations and provisions as may be agreed to by a majority of the United States represented in Convention to the Congress of the United States, and to the General Assembly of this State.

A true Copy of Record
Examd
By GEORGE WYLLYS Secy.

MARYLAND

Maryland.

An Act for the Appointment of, and conferring Powers in Deputies from this State to the fœderal Convention.

Be it enacted by the General Assembly of Maryland, That the Honorable James McHenry, Daniel of Saint Thomas Jenifer, Daniel Carroll, John Francis Mercer and Luther Martin Esquires, be appointed and authorised on behalf of this State, to meet such Deputies as may be appointed and authorised by any other of the United States to assemble in Convention at Philadelphia for the purpose of revising the Fœderal System, and to join with them in considering such Alterations and further Provisions as may be necessary to render the Fœderal Constitution adequate to the Exigencies of the Union and in reporting such an Act for that purpose to the United States in Congress Assembled as when agreed to by them, and duly confirmed by the several States will effectually provide for the same, and the said Deputies or such of them as shall attend the said Convention shall have full Power to represent this State for the Purposes aforesaid, and the said Deputies are hereby directed to report the Proceedings of the said Convention, and any Act agreed to therein, to the next session of the General Assembly of this State.

By the Senate May 26. 1787.[1]	By the House of Delegates
Read and Assented to	May 26d 1787.
By Order J. Dorsey Clk.	Read and Assented to
True Copy from the Original	By Order Wm Harwood Clk.
J. Dorsey Clk. Senate.	True Copy from the Original
	Wm Harwood Clk Ho Del.

W. Smallwood.

ATTENDANCE OF DELEGATES.

The following list of delegates to the Federal Convention, with the available data of their attendance, has been compiled from the *Records*.[2] The sources of information are so readily found that

---

[1] The delegates had been previously elected by the legislature, April 23–May 22. "The assembly had voted to pay the delegates as delegates in congress were paid." (Steiner, *Life and Correspondence of James McHenry*, 98 note 1.)

[2] Although the number of delegates who were at any time present in Philadelphia amounts to fifty-five, the average attendance at the sessions was decidedly smaller. The editor estimates the average attendance at forty or less. In his *History of the Virginia Federal Convention of 1788* (Vol. I, p. 34) H. B. Grigsby states that that body consisted of one hundred and seventy members. He adds: "It was more than four times greater than the Convention which formed the Federal Constitution when that body was full, and it exceeded it, as it ordinarily was, more than six times."

references have been omitted, but in a footnote attached to each name have been given references to those items in the *Records* which may throw some light upon the character of the delegate in question, or upon the part taken by him in the Convention.[1] The names of those who signed the Constitution are prefixed with numbers.

1. BALDWIN, ABRAHAM,[2] of Georgia. Attended on June 11, and probably regularly thereafter.
2. BASSETT, RICHARD,[3] of Delaware. Attended as early as May 21.
3. BEDFORD, GUNNING,[3] of Delaware. First attendance, May 28.
4. BLAIR, JOHN,[3] of Virginia. Attended as early as May 15.
5. BLOUNT, WILLIAM,[3] of North Carolina. Attended June 20—July 2; August 7 and thereafter. He was present in Congress in New York, July 4—August 3.
6. BREARLEY, DAVID,[4] of New Jersey. Attended as early as May 25.
7. BROOM, JACOB, of Delaware. Attended as early as May 21.
8. BUTLER, PIERCE,[3] of South Carolina. Attended as early as May 25.
9. CARROLL, DANIEL,[3] of Maryland. First attended on July 9.
10. CLYMER, GEORGE, of Pennsylvania. Attended May 28, but probably before, although absent on May 25.
    DAVIE, WILLIAM RICHARDSON, of North Carolina. Attended on May 22 or May 23; left on August 13. Approved the Constitution.
11. DAYTON, JONATHAN,[5] of New Jersey. Appointed, June 5; first attended on June 21.
12. DICKINSON, JOHN,[2] of Delaware. Attended on May 29. His remarks on July 25 imply previous absence. Absent on September 15. Read signed Dickinson's name to the Constitution.
    ELLSWORTH, OLIVER,[6] of Connecticut. First attended on May 28. Was present in Convention August 23. Was in New Haven August 27. Approved the Constitution.
13. FEW, WILLIAM,[2] of Georgia. Attended as early as May 19. Present in Congress in New York July 4—August 3. Probably returned to Convention after August 6.

---

[1] The following items deal with the delegates in general rather than with individuals: Appendix A, III, XXXII, XXXIV, XXXVII, XL, XLVIII, XLIX, LIX, LXXVI, XCVIII, CXIX, CCXXXIII, CCXLIII, CCCCI.

[2] Appendix A, CXIX, CLIX.   [3] Appendix A, CXIX.

[4] Appendix A, CXIX, CCCLXXVII.

[5] Appendix A, CXIX, CLIX, CCCLXXVI.

[6] Appendix A, CXIX, CLIX, CCCXCIX.

14. FITZSIMONS, THOMAS,[1] of Pennsylvania. Attended on May 25, and probably earlier.

15. FRANKLIN, BENJAMIN,[2] of Pennsylvania. Attended on May 28, and probably earlier, although absent on May 25.

GERRY, ELBRIDGE,[3] of Massachusetts. First attended on May 29. Absent on August 6. Refused to sign Constitution.

16. GILMAN, NICHOLAS,[4] of New Hampshire. Appointed June 27; first attended on July 23.

17. GORHAM, NATHANIEL,[1] of Massachusetts. Attended on May 28.

18. HAMILTON, ALEXANDER,[5] of New York. Attended on May 18; left Convention June 29; was in New York after July 2; appears to have been in Philadelphia on July 13; attended Convention August 13; was in New York August 20—September 2.

HOUSTON, WILLIAM CHURCHILL,[6] of New Jersey. Attended as early as May 25; was absent on June 6.

HOUSTOUN, WILLIAM,[1] of Georgia. Attended first on June 1, and probably thereafter until July 23. He probably left on July 26 or after Few's return.

19. INGERSOLL, JARED,[1] of Pennsylvania. Attended on May 28, and probably earlier, although absent on May 25.

20. JENIFER, DANIEL OF ST. THOMAS,[1] of Maryland. Commissioned on May 26; first attended on June 2.

21. JOHNSON, WILLIAM SAMUEL,[7] of Connecticut. Attended on June 2, and thereafter.

22. KING, RUFUS,[1] of Massachusetts. Attended as early as May 21.

23. LANGDON, JOHN,[4] of New Hampshire. Appointed June 27; first attended on July 23.

LANSING, JOHN,[8] of New York. First attended on June 2, though he may have been present before May 25; left on July 10. Opposed to the Constitution.

24. LIVINGSTON, WILLIAM,[9] of New Jersey. First attended on June 5; absent on June 28, and July 3–19.

---

[1] Appendix A, CXIX.

[2] *Records* of September 17 (McHenry's note), and Appendix A, XXXIV,CXIX, CLVIII (8), CLIX, CCCLXXX.

[3] Appendix A, CXIX, CXXVIII, CLVII, CLVIII (16), CLIX, CCCLXXXIX.

[4] Appendix A, CXIX, CLIX.

[5] Appendix A, CXIX, CLIX, CCCXIII, CCCXXV, CCCLXVII.

[6] Appendix A, CCCLXXVI.

[7] Appendix A, CCCCII.

[8] Appendix A, CXIX, CCCXXXIX, CCCXCII.

[9] Appendix A, CXIX, CLIX, CCCLXXVI.

McClurg, James,[1] of Virginia. Attended as early as May 15; was present July 20; and absent after August 5. Favored the Constitution.

25. McHenry, James,[2] of Maryland. Commissioned May 26; attended May 28–31; left on June 1; present August 6 and thereafter.

26. Madison, James, Jr.,[3] of Virginia. Attended on May 14 and thereafter.

Martin, Alexander,[2] of North Carolina. Attended as early as May 25; left in the latter part of August.

Martin, Luther,[4] of Maryland. Commissioned May 26; first attended June 9; absent August 7–12; left Convention September 4. Opposed to the Constitution.

Mason, George,[5] of Virginia. Attended on May 17 and thereafter. Refused to sign the Constitution.

Mercer, John Francis, of Maryland. First attended August 6; last recorded attendance August 17. Opposed to the Constitution.

27. Mifflin, Thomas,[6] of Pennsylvania. Attended on May 28, and probably before, although absent on May 25.

28. Morris, Gouverneur,[7] of Pennsylvania. Attended on May 25, and probably before; he left the Convention a few days after and was absent until July 2.

29. Morris, Robert,[6] of Pennsylvania. Attended May 25, and probably before.

30. Paterson, William,[8] of New Jersey. Attended as early as May 25, and thereafter until July 23. There is no evidence of his attendance after that date. August 21, Brearley wrote urging him to return. He probably returned to sign the Constitution.

Pierce, William,[2] of Georgia. Attended May 31; absent after July 1. He favored the Constitution.

31. Pinckney, Charles,[9] of South Carolina. Attended May 17 and thereafter.

---

[1] *Records* of July 17 (Madison's note) and Appendix A, CXIX.
[2] Appendix A, CXIX.
[3] Appendix A, CXIX, CLIX, CCCXXV.
[4] Appendix A, CXIX, CLIX, CLXXXIX, CCCLXXVII, CCCXCII.
[5] Appendix A, CXIX, CXXXVII, CLI, CLVII, CLVIII (16), CXCIV, CCCXVII.
[6] Appendix A, CXIX, CLIX.
[7] Appendix A, CXVII, CXIX, CLIX, CCCLXXVIII, CCCLXXIX, CCCXCV.
[8] Appendix A, CXIX, CCCLXXVI.
[9] Appendix A, CXIX, CXXXV, CCCLXXXIII.

32. PINCKNEY, CHARLES COTESWORTH,[2] of South Carolina. At-
    tended at least as early as May 25, and thereafter.

    RANDOLPH, EDMUND,[1] of Virginia. Attended May 15 and there-
    after. He refused to sign the Constitution.

33. READ, GEORGE,[2] of Delaware. Attended at least as early as
    May 19.

34. RUTLEDGE, JOHN,[1] of South Carolina. Attended on May 17,
    and thereafter.

35. SHERMAN, ROGER,[3] of Connecticut. Appointed May 17;
    attended May 30 and thereafter.

36. SPAIGHT, RICHARD DOBBS,[2] of North Carolina. Attended as
    early as May 19, and thereafter.

    STRONG, CALEB,[2] of Massachusetts. Attended on May 28;
    was present on August 15, but left before August 27. He
    favored the Constitution.

37. WASHINGTON, GEORGE,[4] of Virginia. Attended on May 14
    and thereafter.

38. WILLIAMSON, HUGH,[5] of North Carolina. Attended as early as
    May 25, and thereafter.

39. WILSON, JAMES,[1] of Pennsylvania. Attended as early as May
    25 (probably before) and thereafter.

    WYTHE, GEORGE,[2] of Virginia. Attended as early as May 15;
    left Convention June 4; resigned June 16. He approved
    the Constitution.

    YATES, ROBERT,[6] of New York. Attended May 18; left Con-
    vention July 10. Opposed to the Constitution.

---

[1] Appendix A, CXIX, CLIX.

[2] Appendix A, CXIX.

[3] Appendix A, XXXV, CXIX.

[4] Appendix A, XVII, CXIX, CLVIII (8), CCLXXXV, CCXCIII, CCCLIX.

[5] Appendix A, CLIX.

[5] Appendix A, CXIX, CCCXXXIX, CCCLVII, CCCLXV, CCCLXXVII,
CCCLXXXVIII, CCCXCII.

PLANS OF GOVERNMENT SUBMITTED TO THE CONVENTION

APPENDIX C
THE VIRGINIA PLAN OR RANDOLPH RESOLUTIONS

APPENDIX D
THE PINCKNEY PLAN

APPENDIX E
THE NEW JERSEY PLAN OR PATERSON RESOLUTIONS

APPENDIX F
THE HAMILTON PLAN

APPENDIX C

THE VIRGINIA PLAN OR RANDOLPH RESOLUTIONS.

As their state had taken the lead in calling the Federal Convention, the Virginia delegates felt a sense of responsibility. They accordingly prepared an outline of a new government, which was presented on May 29 in the form of a series of resolutions by Randolph, the governor of the state.[1] These resolutions, commonly known as the Randolph Resolutions, but more properly designated as the Virginia Plan, became the basis of the work of the Convention and, expanded and developed, eventually grew into the Constitution as adopted.

In the later stages of the proceedings of the Convention the delegates were provided with printed copies of the more important documents, but in the earlier stages the delegates were forced to make their own copies. As the importance of the Virginia Plan was early recognized and was the subject of discussion for two weeks in a committee of the whole house, not a few of the delegates made copies of this plan, of which several are still in existence, — e.g., Madison's, Washington's, Brearley's, McHenry's *et al.* The original document is missing,[2] and the various copies differ among themselves. There are inevitable slight variations in wording, spelling, and punctuation, but the most significant differences are found in the sixth and ninth resolutions.

The sixth resolution reads: "That the National Legislature ought to be empowered . . . to negative all laws passed by the several states, contravening in the opinion of the National Legislature the articles of Union", and at this point some of the texts add "or any treaty subsisting under the authority of the Union". The records show clearly that this additional clause was not in the original, as it was inserted on the motion of Franklin, May 31.[3] Madison's copy gives the correct reading.

In Madison's copy the ninth resolution reads:

"9. Resd. that a National Judiciary be established to consist of one or more supreme tribunals, and of inferior tribunals to be chosen by the National Legislature, . . . that the jurisdiction of the inferior tribunals shall be to hear & determine in the first instance,

---

[1] See *Records*, May 29, note 8.　　　[2] See *Records*, May 29, note 3
[3] See *Records*, May 31.

593

and of the supreme tribunal to hear and determine in the dernier resort, all piracies & felonies on the high seas, captures from an enemy;" etc. The other texts vary in the reading of the second, third, and fourth clauses, either by omitting them altogether, or by modifying or omitting one or more of them. Mr. Jameson argues that the specification of supreme and inferior tribunals could not have been in the original document because it was voted, on June 4, "to add these words to the first clause of the ninth resolution, namely: 'To consist of one supreme tribunal, and of one or more inferior tribunals.'" In support of this he cites the authority of both the Journal and Madison's notes.[1] By referring to the *Records* of that date, however, it will be seen that Madison's entry was copied from *Journal* and this evidence, therefore, rests upon the somewhat doubtful authority of the Journal alone. In the next place, it will be noticed that the wording of June 4 is slightly different from that of the original resolution (as reported by Madison), and so the phrase "to add" might well be used instead of "to accept" or "to agree to". And finally, the texts that in other respects prove to be the most accurate — Madison's, Washington's, McHenry's — all agree in the wording of this resolution.

The same reasoning applies to the latter part of the resolution respecting the jurisdiction of the inferior and superior tribunals, which Mr. Jameson argues is corrupted in the Madison copy.

In the editor's judgment, then, the Madison text of the Virginia Plan or Randolph Resolutions as given in the *Records* (May 29) is an accurate copy of the original.

---

[1] *Studies*, pp. 105–106.

APPENDIX D

THE PINCKNEY PLAN

On May 29, after Randolph had presented the Virginia Plan to the Convention, "Mr. Charles Pinckney . . . laid before the House for their consideration, the draught of a fœderal government to be agreed upon between the free and independent States of America." This plan was referred to the Committee of the Whole House, which was to take the Virginia Plan into consideration. Nothing more is recorded of it, except that on July 24 the Committee of the Whole was formally discharged from further consideration of it and it was referred to the Committee of Detail which was appointed to draft a constitution upon the basis of the proceedings of the Convention at that date.

When John Quincy Adams was preparing the Journal for publication, the Pinckney Plan was not to be found among the secretary's papers, and Pinckney himself was appealed to for a copy of the missing document.[1] In response Pinckney stated:

"I have already informed you I have several rough draughts of the Constitution I proposed & that they are all substantially the same differing only in words & the arrangement of the Articles — at the distance of nearly thirty two Years it is impossible for me now to say which of the 4 or 5 draughts I have was the one but enclosed I send you the one I believe was it — I repeat however that they are substantially the same differing only in form & unessentials — —".[2]

Adams accepted this statement and printed the following document: —

We the People of the States of New Hampshire Massachusetts Rhode Island & Providence Plantations —Connecticut New York New Jersey Pennyslvania Delaware Maryland Virginia North Caroline South Carolina & Georgia do ordain, declare & establish the following Constitution for the Government of Ourselves & Posterity.

Article 1:
The Stile of This Government shall be The United States of America & The Government shall consist of supreme legislative Executive and judicial Powers—

---

[1] Appendix A, CCCXXVIII.　　　　[2] Appendix A, CCCXXVI.

2

The Legislative Power shall be vested in a Congress to consist of
Two separate Houses—One to be called The House of Delegates &
the other the Senate who shall meet on the   Day of   in
every Year

3

The members of the House of Delegates shall be chosen every
Year by the people of the several States & the qualifications of the
electors shall be the same as those of the Electors in the several
States for their legislatures—each member shall have been a citizen
of the United States for   Years —shall be of   Yea of age
& a resident of the State he is chosen for—until a census of the people
shall be taken in the manner herein aftermentioned the House of
Delegates shall consist of   to be chosen from the different states
in the following proportions * — & the Legislature shall hereafter
regulate the number of delegates by the number of inhabitants
according to the Provisions herein after made at the rate of one for
every   thousand — all money bills of every kind shall originate
in the house of Delegates & shall not be altered by the Senate —
The House of Delegates shall exclusively possess the power of impeachment & shall choose it's own Officers & Vacancies therein shall
be supplied by the executive authority of the State in the representation from which they shall happen —

4

The Senate shall be elected & chosen by the House of Delegates
which house immediately after their meeting shall choose by ballot
     Senators from among the Citizens & residents of New Hamp-
shire.   from among those of Massachusetts. .   from among
those of Rhode Island   from among those of Connecticut.   from
among those of New York.   from among those of New Jersey
from among those of Pennsylvanie   from among those of Delaware —   from among those of Maryland.   from among those
of Virginia   from among those of North Caroline   from among
those of South Caroline   &   from among those of Georgia —
     The Senators chosen from New Hampshire Massachusetts Rhode
Island & Connecticut shall form one class — those from New York

* [In margin:]

for New Hampshire.	for Massachusetts	for New York
for Rhode Island —	for Connecticut.	for Delaware
for New Jersey.	for Pennsylvania.	for North Caroline
for Maryld:	for Virginie.	for Georgia
	for South Carolina—	

New Jersey Pennsylvanie & Delaware one class — & those from Maryland Virginia North Caroline South Caroline & Georgia one class —

The House of Delegates shall number these Classes one two & three & fix the times of their service by Lot — the first Class shall serve for   Years — the second for   Years & the third for   Years — as their Times of service expire the House of Delegates shall fill them up by Elections for   Years & they shall fill all Vacancies that arise from death or resignation for the Time of service remaining of the members so dying or resigning —

Each Senator shall be   Years of age at leest — shall have been a Citizen of the United States 4 Years before his Election & shall be a resident of the state he is chosen from — —

The Senate shall choose it's own Officers

5

Each State shall prescribe the time & manner of holding Elections by the People for the house of Delegates & the House of Delegates shall be the judges of the Elections returns & Qualifications of their members

In each House a Majority shall constitute a Quorum to do business — Freedom of Speech & Debate in the legislature shall not be impeached or Questioned in any place out of it & the Members of both Houses shall in all cases except for Treason Felony or breach of the Peace be free from arrest during their attendance at Congress & in going to & returning from it — both houses shall keep journals of their Proceedings & publish them except on secret occasions & the yeas & nays may be entered thereon at the desire of one   of the members present.

Neither house without the consent of the other shall adjourn for more than   days nor to any Place but where they are sitting

t The members of each house shall not be eligible to or capable of holding any office under the Union during the time for which they have been respectively elected nor the members of the Senate for one Year after —

The members of each house shall be paid for their services by the State's which they represent —

Every bill which shall have passed the Legislature shall be presented to the President of the United States for his revision — if he approves it he shall sign it — but if he does not approve it he shall return it with his objections to the house it originated in, which house if two thirds of the members present, notwithstanding the Presidents objections agree to pass it, shall send it to the other house with the Presidents Objections, where if two thirds of the members present also agree to pass it, the same shall become a law — & all bills sent to the President & not returned by him within days shall be laws unless the Legislature by their adjournment prevent their return in which case they shall not be laws

6

The Legislature of the United States shall have the power to lay & collect Taxes Duties Imposts & Excises

To regulate Commerce with all nations & among the several states. —

To borrow money & emit bills of Credit

To establish Post Offices

To raise armies

To build & equip Fleets

To pass laws for arming organizing & disciplining the Militia of the United States. —

To subdue a rebellion in any state on application of its legislature

To coin money & regulate the Value of all coins & fix the Standard of Weights & measures

To provide such Dock Yards & arsenals & erect such fortifications as may be necessary for the United States & to exercise exclusive Jurisdiction therein

To appoint a Treasurer by ballott

To constitute Tribunals inferior to the Supreme Court

To establish Post & military Roads

To establish and provide for a national University at the Seat of the Government of the United States —

To establish uniform rules of Naturalization

To provide for the establishment of a Seat of Government for the United States not exceeding   miles square in which they shall have exclusive jurisdiction

To make rules concerning Captures from an Enemy

To declare the law & Punishment of piracies & felonies at sea & of counterfieting Coin & of all offences against the Laws of Nations

To call forth the aid of the Militia to execute the laws of the Union enforce treaties suppress insurrections & repel invasions

And to make all laws for carrying the foregoing powers into execution. —

The Legislature of the United States shall have the Power to declare the Punishment of Treason which shall consist only in levying War against the United States or any of them or in adhering to their Enemies. — No person shall be convicted of Treason but by the Testimony of two Witnesses. —

The proportions of direct Taxation shall be regulated by the whole number of inhabitants of every description which number shall within   Years after the first meeting of the Legislature & within the term of every   Years after be taken in the manner to be prescribed by the legislature

No Tax shall be laid on articles exported from the States — nor capitation tax but in proportion to the Census before directed

All Laws regulating Commerce shall require the assent of two thirds of the members present in each house —

The United States shall not grant any title of Nobility — —

The Legislature of the United States shall pass no Law on the subject of Religion, nor touching or abridging the Liberty of the Press nor shall the Privilege of the Writ of Habeas Corpus ever be suspended except in case of Rebellion or Invasion

All acts made by the Legislature of the United States pursuant to this Constitution & all Treaties made under the authority of the United States shall be the Supreme Law of the Land & all Judges shall be bound to consider them as such in their decisions

7

The Senate shall have the sole & exclusive power to declare War & to make treaties & to appoint Ambassadors & other Ministers to Foreign nations & Judges of the Supreme Court

They shall have the exclusive power to regulate the manner of deciding all disputes & Controversies now subsisting or which may arise between the States respecting Jurisdiction or Territory

8

The Executive Power of the United States shall be vested in a President of the United States of America which shall be his stile & his title shall be His Excellency — — He shall be elected for   Years & shall be reeligible

He shall from time give information to the Legislature of the state of the Union & recommend to their consideration the measures he may think necessary — he shall take care that the laws of the United States be duly executed: he shall commission all the Officers of the United States & except as to Ambassadors other ministers & Judges of the Supreme Court he shall nominate & with the consent of the Senate appoint all other Officers of the United States — He shall recieve public Ministers from foreign nations & may correspond with the Executives of the different states — He shall have power to grant pardons & reprieves except in impeachments — He shall be Commander in chief of the army & navy of

the United States & of the Militia of the several states & shall
recieve a compensation which shall not be increased or diminished
during his continuance in office — At Entering on the Duties of his
office he shall take an Oath to faithfully execute the duties of a
President of the United States — He shall be removed from his
office on impeachment by the house of Delegates & Conviction in
the supreme Court of Treason bribery or Corruption — In case of
his removal death resignation or disability The President of the
Senate shall exercise the duties of his office until another President
be chosen — & in case of the death of the President of the Senate
the Speaker of the House of Delegates s shall do so — —

9

The Legislature of the United States shall have the Power & it shall
be their duty to establish such Courts of Law Equity & Admiralty as
shall be necessary — the Judges of these Courts shall hold their
Offices during good behaviour & recieve a compensation which shall
not be increased or diminished during their continuance in office —
One of these Courts shall be termed the Supreme Court whose Juris-
diction shall extend to all cases arising under the laws of the United
States or affecting ambassadors other public Ministers & Consuls —
To the trial of impeachments of Officers of the United States —
To all cases of Admiralty & maritime jurisdiction — In cases of
impeachment affecting Ambassadors & other public Ministers the
Jurisdiction shall be original & in all the other cases appellate —
All Criminal offenses, (except in cases of impeachment) shall
be tried in the State where they shall be committed — the trial shall
be open & public & be by Jury —

10

Immediately after the first census of the people of United States the
House of Delegates shall apportion the Senate by electing for each
State out of the Citizens resident therein One Senator for every
members such state shall have in the house of Delegates —
Each State however shall be entitled to have at least one member
in the Senate — —

11

No State shall grant letters of marque & reprisal or enter into treaty
or alliance or confederation nor grant any title of nobility nor without the Consent of the Legislature of the United States lay any
impost on imports — nor keep Troops or Ships of War in Time of
peace — nor enter into compacts with other states or foreign powers
or emit bills of Credit or make any thing but Gold Silver or Copper

a Tender in payment of debts nor engage in War except for self defence when actually invaded or the danger of invasion is so great as not to admit of a delay until the Government of the United States can be informed thereof — & to render these prohibitions effectual the Legislature of the United States shall have the power to revise the laws of the several states that may be supposed to infringe the Powers exclusively delegated by the Constitution to Congress & to negative & annul such as do

12

The Citizens of each state shall be entitled to all privileges & immunities of Citizens in the several states —

Any person charged with Crimes in any State fleeing from Justice to another shall on demand of the Executive of the State from which he fled be delivered up & removed to the State having jurisdiction of the Offense —

13

Full faith shall be given in each State to the acts of the Legislature & to the records & judicial Proceedings of the Courts & Magistrates of every State

14

The Legislature shall have power to admit new States into the Union on the same terms with the original States provided two thirds of the members present in both houses agree

15

On the application of the legislature of a State the United States shall protect it against domestic insurrections

16

If Two Thirds of the Legislatures of the States apply for the same The Legislature of the United States shall call a Convention for the purpose of amending the Constitution — Or should Congress with the Consent of Two thirds of each house propose to the States amendments to the same — the agreement of Two Thirds of the Legislatures of the States shall be sufficient to make the said amendments Parts of the Constitution

The Ratifications of the Conventions of   States shall be sufficient for organizing this Constitution — — [1]

Only a few of the members of the Convention were still living when the *Journal* was published in 1819, but two of those, King and Madison, expressed privately their conviction that the docu-

---

[1] [Endorsed:] in Mr. Pinckney's letter of Dec. 30, 1819.

ment printed in the *Journal* was not the same as that originally presented by Pinckney in 1787.[1]   Madison also prepared a somewhat elaborate criticism to be appended to the document, which he evidently intended to include in his Debates.[2]

It does not seem necessary in this connection to do anything more than point out the lines of evidence followed in disproving the document in question.   In the first place, the writing, the ink, and the paper of the document are the same as the letter accompanying it — the paper bearing the watermark of 1797 — so that it cannot be the original, but was probably copied or prepared in 1818.   In the second place, its provisions, in several important particulars, are directly at variance with Pinckney's opinions as expressed in the Convention.   In the next place, the document embodies several provisions that were only reached after weeks of bitter disputes — compromises and details, that it was impossible for any human being to have forecast accurately.   And finally, shortly after the Convention was over, Pinckney printed for private circulation a pamphlet entitled "*Observations on the Plan of Government submitted to the Federal Convention, by Mr. Charles Pinckney*", etc.,[3] which seems to have been a speech prepared in advance to be delivered in presenting his plan to the Convention,[4] but which never was delivered, owing probably to lack of time.   This speech outlines the principal features of the plan which differ radically from the provisions of the document sent to John Quincy Adams.

The problem then presents itself to determine as accurately as possible what Pinckney's original plan was.   In 1786, Pinckney was a delegate to the Continental Congress and obtained the appointment of a grand committee, of which he became a member, to recommend amendments to the Articles of Confederation.   He was the chairman of a sub-committee of three that drew up a report, which was accepted by the grand committee, and which proposed seven important changes or new articles to the original Articles of Confederation.   George Bancroft in his *History of the Constitution*, remarks that "these amended resolutions may well be taken as representing the intentions of Charles Pinckney at that time".[5]   Here, at least, is a starting-point, and as one proceeds in this investigation he becomes more and more convinced that Pinckney's working motive in his original proposals in the Federal Convention was a reform of

---

[1] Appendix A, CCCLXVII–CCCLXIX, CCCLXXXVII, CCCXCIII, CCCXCVI.
[2] Appendix A, CCCLXXXI–CCCLXXXV.
[3] Appendix A, CXXIX.
[4] A. C. McLaughlin, *American Historical Review*, July, 1904. IX, 735–741.
[5] Vol I, p. 258–263.

the Articles of Confederation.[1] These amendments, therefore, which he endorsed in 1786 and probably originated, are not merely a starting-point, they show somewhat of the character of the Pinckney Plan.

In the debates of the Federal Convention itself, during the discussion of the Randolph Resolutions in the Committee of the Whole — that is, during approximately the first two weeks of the Convention's work — Pinckney's attitude upon the various questions may be taken as fairly representing his original ideas, especially when his position was opposed to that of the leaders or to the general sentiment of the Convention. His later attitude was undoubtedly modified by the development of proceedings and can only be used with caution, although some suggestions may be obtained therefrom.[2]

While the delegates were gathering in Philadelphia and were waiting for a sufficient number to commence proceedings, George Read, of Delaware, wrote to his colleague Dickinson that he was "in possession of a copied draft of a federal system intended to be proposed," and he outlined a few of the conspicuous features. These do not at all correspond to the features of the Virginia Plan, but they do tally exactly with certain characteristics of the Pinckney Plan that have been obtained from the study of the debates. There can be no doubt that it is the latter plan that is here described, especially as we have on other authority that Pinckney prepared his plan in advance of his going to Philadelphia.[3] From this letter of Read's we get a few additional particulars, and the helpful suggestion that "some of its principal features are taken from the New York system of government." [4]

The pamphlet entitled *"Observations"* must be used with some caution, as it was not printed until after the Convention was over, and Pinckney may have modified some of his statements or added somewhat to his speech as originally prepared.

And there is also the draft sent to John Quincy Adams in 1818. In the light of the documents already noticed, it is established beyond all doubt that this draft does not represent "Pinckney's original plan with some additions and modifications." It does not even have

---

[1] See Mr. McLaughlin's confirmation of this position, *American Historical Review, loc. cit.*

[2] Mr. Jameson has made a careful analysis of this material; see his *Studies in the History of the Federal Convention of 1787*, pp. 117–120.

[3] "'W. S. E. of S. C.' (W. S. Elliot, grandson of Pinckney) in DeBow's *Review* XXXIV, 63, says: This draft was made in Charleston before the writer thereof had any opportunity of conference with his co-workers, and carried with him to the Convention.'" Jameson, *Studies*, p. 120, note.

[4] Appendix A, XVII.

Pinckney's original plan as its basis. Not only does it radically differ from the original plan in several essential matters, it is constructed on an entirely different framework. Indeed, when one notes its striking resemblance to the draft reported by the Committee of Detail on August 6, it is difficult not to agree with Mr. Jameson's conclusion that if Pinckney had copied "the printed report of the Committee of Detail, paraphrasing to a small extent here and there, and interweaving as he went along some of the best remembered features of his own plan," the results would have been precisely like the document that was sent to John Quincy Adams.[1] There is no proof, however, it is only a possible hypothesis, that in the points of difference from the draft of the Committee of Detail the document sent to Adams reproduces portions of the original plan. The most that can be said is, that when other evidence confirms the inclusion of such provisions, a possible reading of those clauses may here be found.

Following the same line of argument, although ignoring the amendments to the Articles of Confederation and treating the *Observations* with "considerable skepticism," Mr. Jameson was able to establish the main points of Pinckney's original plan. By a piece of brilliant criticism Mr. Jameson was thus enabled to identify a document among the Wilson drafts of the Committee of Detail as a series of extracts from the Pinckney Plan,[2] and Mr. McLaughlin was able to identify another document among the same papers as an outline of the entire plan.[3]

Combining all of these sources of information it is possible to obtain a fairly good idea of the Pinckney Plan in its original from. The following is the plan thus reconstructed. (Italics and quotation marks indicate respectively the outline and extracts used by Wilson in the Committee of Detail; statements based upon the "Observations" are placed in parentheses; numbers attached to the different articles have little significance).

THE DRAUGHT OF A FOEDERAL GOVERNMENT TO BE AGREED UPON BETWEEN THE FREE AND INDEPENDENT STATES OF AMERICA.[4]

A Confederation between the free and independent States of N. H. &c. is hereby solemnly made uniting them together under one general superintending Government for their common Benefit and for their

---

[1] *Studies,* p. 124.

[2] *Studies,* p. 117–132. See *Records,* July 27–August 4, Committee of Detail, VII.

[3] *American Historical Review, loc. cit.* See *Records,* July 27–August 4, Committee of Detail, III.   [4] *Records* of May 29.

Defense and Security against all Designs and Leagues that may be in-
jurious to their interests and against all Forc [Foes?] and Attacks offered
to or made upon them or any of them.

[I]

The Stile of this government shall be The United States of America,[1] and (the legislative, executive and judiciary powers shall be
separate and distinct).

[II]

"The *Legislature* shall consist of *two* distinct *Branches* — a
Senate and a *House of Delegates*, each of which shall have a Negative
on the other, and shall be stiled *the U. S. in Congress assembled.*"

The House of Delegates to be elected by the State Legislatures,[2]
and *to consist of one Member for every*   *thousand inhabi-*
tants ⅗ *of Blacks included.*[3]

For the forming of the Senate the United States to be divided
into *four* great *districts*,[4] (so apportioned as to give to each its due
weight). The *Senate to be elected by the House of Delegates either from*
among themselves or the people at large.[5] When so formed, the Senate to be divided into four classes, — *to serve by Rotation of four*
years.[3]

The Members of S. & H. D. shall each have one Vote,[6] *and shall*
be paid out of the common Treasury.

The Time of the Election of the Members of the H. D. and of the
meeting of the U. S. in C. assembled.

"Each House shall appoint its own Speaker and other Officers,
and settle its own Rules of Proceeding; but neither the Senate nor
H. D. shall have the power to adjourn for more than   Days
without the Consent of both."

[Freedom of speech and protection from arrest as in Article V of
the Articles of Confederation.]

(Attendance compulsory provided no punishment shall be further extended than to disqualifications) any longer to be members
of Congress or to hold any office of trust or profit under the United
States or any individual State.[7]

---

[1] Articles of Confederation.

[2] *Records* of June 6, Appendix A, CCXXXVII, CCXXXVIII, and letter of Read
to Dickinson.   [3] Confirmed by Read.

[4] Read, confirmed by *Observations* and *Records* of July 2. *Cf.* Constitution of
New York of 1777.

[5] Confirmed by Read and *Observations.*

[6] Confirmed by *Observations.*

[7] Amendment to Articles of Confederation proposed in 1786.

[III]

The Senate and H. D. shall by joint Ballot annually (septennially) *chuse the Presidt. U. S. from among themselves or the People at large. — In the Presidt. "the executive Authority of the U. S. shall be vested."*

"It shall be his Duty to inform the Legislature [at every session] [1] of the condition of the United States, so far as may respect his Department — to recommend Matters to their Consideration [such as shall appear to him to concern their good government, welfare and prosperity] [1] — to correspond with the Executives of the several States — to attend to the Execution of the Laws of the U S" (by the several States) — "to transact Affairs with the Officers of Government, civil and military — to expedite all such Measures as may be resolved on by the Legislature" — (to acquire from time to time, as perfect a knowledge of the situation of the Union, as he possibly can, and to be charged with all the business of the home department. He will be empowered, whenever he conceives it necessary) "to inspect the Departments of foreign Affairs — War — Treasury —" (and when instituted of the) "Admiralty — to reside where the Legislature shall sit — to commission all Officers, and keep the Great Seal of the United States."

"He shall, by Virtue of his Office, be Commander in chief of the Land Forces of U. S. and Admiral of their Navy." [2]

"He shall have Power to convene the Legislature on extraordinary occasions — to prorogue them," (when they cannot agree as to the time of their adjournment,) "provided such Prorogation shall not exceed   Days in the space of any   — He may suspend Officers, civil and military."

(He shall be removable by impeachment.[3]   The Legislature shall fix his salary on permanent principles.)

He shall have a Right to advise with the Heads of the different Departments as his Council.[4]

Council of Revision, consisting of the Presdt. S. for for. Affairs, S. of War, Heads of the Departments of Treasury and Admiralty or any two of them togr wt the Presidt.[4]

(IV)

(The 4th article . . . is formed exactly upon the principles of the 4th article of the present confederation, except with this difference, that the demand of the Executive of a State for any fugitive

---

[1] New York Constitution of 1777, Article XIX.

[2] Confirmed by *Observations. Cf.* New York Constitution, Article XVIII.

[3] Pinckney was opposed to impeachment on July 20. See *Records* of that date.

[4] Confirmed by *Observations. Cf. Records* of June 6.

criminal offender shall be complied with. It is now confined to treason, felony, or other high misdemeanor.)

· *Mutual Intercourse — Community of Privileges — Surrender of Criminals — Faith to Proceedings, &c.*

(V)

(The 5th article, declaring that individual States shall not exercise certain powers, is founded on the same principles as the 6th of the confederation.)

No State to make Treaties — lay interfering Duties — keep a naval or land Force Militia excepted to be disciplined &c according to the Regulations of the U. S.

Each State retains its Rights not expressly delegated — But no Bill of the Legislature of any State shall become a law till it shall have been laid before S. & H. D. in C. assembled and received their approbation.[1]

(VI)

The S. & H. D. in C. Assembled "shall have the exclusive Power — of raising a military Land Force" (and of appointing all the officers) — "of equiping a Navy — of rating and causing public Taxes to be levied" (agreeable to the rule now in use, an enumeration of the white inhabitants, and three-fifths of other descriptions.)

(VII)

The S. & H. D. in C. assembled shall have the exclusive power "*of regulating* the *Trade* of the several States as well with Foreign Nations as with each other — of *levying* Duties upon Imports and Exports" — *Each State may lay Embargoes in Time of Scarcity.*[2]

(VIII)

The S. & H. D. in C. assembled shall have exclusive power "*of establishing Post-Offices,* and raising a Revenue from them — of regulating Indian Affairs — of coining Money" — *regulating its Alloy and Value* — "*fixing the Standard of Weights and Measures*" *throughout U. S.* — "of determining in what species of Money the public Treasury shall be supplied."[3]

(IX)

S. & H. D. in C. ass. shall be the last Resort on Appeal in Disputes between two or more States; which Authority shall be exercised in the following Manner &c. (the same with that in the Confederation.)

---

[1] Confirmed by *Observations. Cf. Records* of June 8.

[2] Confirmed by *Observations*, and probably modelled upon amendment to Articles of Confederation proposed in 1786. [3] Confirmed by *Observations*.

(X)

S. & H. D. in C. ass. shall institute offices and appoint officers for the Departments of for. Affairs, War, Treasury and Admiralty—

They shall have the exclusive Power of declaring what shall be Treason and Misp. of Treason agt. U. S. — and of instituting a federal judicial Court, which "shall try Officers of the U. S. for all Crimes &c in their Offices — and to this Court *an Appeal shall be allowed from the*" judicial "*Courts of*" *the several States in all Causes wherein Questions shall arise on the Construction of Treaties made by U. S. — or on the Law of Nations — or on the Regulations of U. S. concerning Trade and Revenue or wherein U. S. shall be a Party — The Court shall consist of   Judges to be appointed during good Behaviour.*[1]

S. & H. D. in C. ass. "*shall have the exclusive Right of instituting in each State a Court of Admiralty,*" *and appointing the Judges &c of the same,* "for hearing and determining" all "*maritime Causes*" *which may arise therein respectively.*[2]

[XI]

Points in which the Assent of more than a bare Majority shall be necessary. (The Assent of Two-Thirds of both Houses, where the present Confederation has made the assent of Nine States necessary, and added the Regulation of Trade, and Acts for levying an Impost and raising a Revenue.)

[XII]

"The power of impeaching shall be vested in the H. D. — The Senators and Judges of the foederal Court, be a Court for trying Impeachments."[3]

[XIII]

S. & H. D. in C. ass. shall regulate "possess the exclusive Right of establishing the Government and Discipline of the *Militia*" *thro the U. S.* — "and of ordering the Militia of any State to any Place within U. S."[2]

[XIV]

Means of enforcing and compelling the Payment of the Quota of each State.[1]

[XV]

Manner and Conditions of admitting new States.

Power of dividing annexing and consolidating States, on the Consent and Petition of such States.

---

[1] Confirmed by *Observations*, and probably modelled upon amendment to Articles of Confederation proposed in 1786.   [2] Confirmed by *Observations*.

[3] Substance of this article was in the Wilson Outline. *Cf.* New York Constitution, Articles XXXII and XXXIII.

(Federal Government should also possess the exclusive right of declaring on what terms the privileges of citizenship and naturalization should be extended to foreigners.) [1]

(XVI)

The assent of the Legislature of   States shall be sufficient to invest future additional Powers in U. S. in C. ass. and shall bind the whole confederacy.[2]

[XVII]

The said States of N. H. &c guarrantee mutually each other and their Rights against all other Powers and against all Rebellion &c.

[XVIII]

(The next article provides for the privilege of the writ of habeas corpus — the trial by jury in all cases, criminal as well as civil — the freedom of the press and the prevention of religious tests as qualifications to offices of trust or emolument. . . .

There is also an authority to the national legislature, permanently to fix the seat of the general government, to secure to authors the exclusive right to their performances and discoveries, and to establish a Federal University.) [3]

[XIX]

The Articles of Confederation shall be inviolably observed unless altered as before directed, and the Union shall be perpetual.

---

[1] It is doubtful whether this paragraph should be included.

[2] Confirmed by *Observations*.

[3] These two paragraphs occur in a somewhat irrelevant way near the end of the pamphlet Observations. The provisions they embody were among those proposed by Pinckney on August 20. It is quite possible that they were not a part of the original plan

APPENDIX E

THE NEW JERSEY PLAN OR PATERSON RESOLUTIONS

When the Convention, in Committee of the Whole was evidently coming to a favorable conclusion in its consideration of the Virginia Plan, various representatives of the opposition — mainly from the smaller states — met together and drafted a series of resolutions, which was presented to the Convention on June 15. Paterson of New Jersey had apparently taken the lead in this movement and he was chosen to present the resolutions to the Convention. These resolutions have accordingly been known as the New Jersey Plan, or the Paterson Resolutions.[1]

Several copies of the New Jersey Plan are in existence, containing the usual minor differences in wording, spelling, and punctuation. But they also differ in more important particulars: — The Madison and Washington copies are practically identical, but the other copies contain two additional resolutions: a sixth, "that the legislative, executive, and judiciary powers within the several States ought to be bound by oath to support the Articles of Union;" and a ninth, "that provision ought to be made for hearing and deciding upon all disputes arising between the United States and an individual State respecting territory." Also in the fourth resolution, the Madison and Washington copies read, that the Executive shall be "removable by Congress on application by a majority of the executives of the several States," while the Brearley and Paterson copies read "removable on impeachment and conviction for malpractice or neglect of duty by Congress on application by a majority of the executives of the several States." [2]

As already stated, the presentation of the New Jersey Plan resulted from a conference of several delegates, in which Paterson seemed to have been a leading spirit. Among the Paterson Papers, each in Paterson's handwriting on a separate sheet of foolscap, are found the following documents: —

I

1. Resolved, That a union of the States merely federal ought to be the sole Object of the Exercise of the Powers vested in this Convention.[3]

---

[1] See *Records*, June 14–15, and Appendix A, CLVIII (5) and (10), CCXXXIII, CCCLXXVI.   [2] See Madison's note at the end of his copy (*Records*, June 15).
[3] This resolution is partly crossed out in the original.

2. Resolved, That the Articles of the Confederation ought to be so revised, corrected, and enlarged as to render the federal Constitution adequate to the Exigencies of Government, and the Preservation of the Union —

3. Resolved, That the federal Government of the United States ought to consist of a Supreme Legislative, Executive, and Judiciary —

4. Resolved, That the Powers of Legislation ought to be vested in Congress.

5. Resolved, That in Addition to the Powers vested in the United States in Congress by the present existing Articles of Confederation, they be authorized to pass Acts for levying a Duty or Duties on all Goods and Merchandize of foreign Growth or Manufacture imported into any Part of the United States not exceeding   per Cent. ad Valorem to be applied to such federal Purposes as they shall deem proper and expedient, and to make Rules and Regulations for the Collection thereof; and the same from Time to Time to alter and amend in such Manner as they shall think proper. Provided, That all Punishments, Fines, Forfeitures, and Penalties to be incurred for contravening such Rules and Regulations shall be adjudged and decided upon by the Judiciaries of the State in which any Offence contrary to the true Intent and Meaning of such Rules and Regulations shall be committed or perpetrated; subject nevertheless to an Appeal for the Correction of any Errors in rendering Judgment to the Judiciary of the United States.

That the United States in Congress be also authorized to pass Acts for the Regulation of Trade as well with foreign Nations as with each other, and for laying such Prohibitions, [In margin: " Imposts Excise — Stamps — Post-Office — Poll-Tax — "] and such Imposts and Duties upon Imports as may be necessary for the Purpose; Provided, That the Legislatures of the several States shall not be restrained from laying Embargoes in Times of Scarcity; and provided further that such Imposts and Duties so far forth as the same shall exceed . . . per Centum ad Valorem on the Imports shall accrue to the Use of the State in which the same may be collected

II

1. Resolved, That the Articles of the confederation ought[1] to[1] be so revised, corrected, and enlarged as to render the federal constitution adequate to the exigencies of government, and the preservation of the union —

2. Resolved, That the alterations, additions, and provisions made in and to the articles of the confederation shall be reported

---

[1] Added in different ink.

to the united states in congress and to the individual states composing the union, agreeably to the 13th [1] article of the confederation —

3. Resolved, That the federal government of the united states
ought to consist of a supreme [1] legislative, executive, and judiciary —

4. Resolved, That the powers of legislation be vested in Congress —

5. [In margin: " See Mr. Lansing— "]

6. [In margin: " See Governor Randolph's. 7th Prop."]

7. [In margin: " Same — 9th."]

Resolved, That every State in the Union as a State possesses an
equal Right to, and Share of, Sovereignty, Freedom, and Independance —

Resolved, therefore, that the Representation in the supreme
Legislature ought to be by States, otherwise some of the States in
the Union will possess a greater Share of Sovereignty, Freedom, and
Independance than others —

Whereas it is necessary in Order to form the People of the U. S.
of America into a Nation, that the States should be consolidated,
by which means all the Citizens thereof will become equally intitled
to and will equally participate in the same Privileges and Rights,
and in all waste, uncultivated, and back Territory and Lands; it is
therefore resolved, that all the Lands contained within the Limits
of each State individually, and of the U. S. generally be considered
as constituting one Body or Mass, and be divided into thirteen or
more integral Parts.

Resolved, That such Divisions or integral Parts shall be styled
Districts.

III

[A fair copy of the first four resolutions of II, but not numbered,
and in the second resolution "shall" is changed to "ought to".]

These documents evidently represent preliminary sketches of
the New Jersey Plan, and a careful study of the probable origin of
the various provisions shows clearly that the completed New Jersey Plan was doubtless a joint product.[2]

Paterson's copy of the plan is to be found in a little book into
which he also copied the Virginia Plan, the Report of the Committee
of the Whole, and Hamilton's Plan. The resolutions are written on
the right-hand pages; certain phrases omitted in copying or changes
in wording are written on the left-hand pages with marks to show
the places of their insertion. For example, in the doubtful reading
of the fourth article, the right-hand page has the words " and remove-

---

[1] Added in different ink.   [2] Jameson, *Studies*, 140–143.

able on Impeachment and Conviction for Mal-Practice, or Neglect of Duty," and opposite them on the left-hand page "by Congress on Application by a Majority of the executives of the several States." In this instance there are no asterisks, and the two phrases probably represent alternative proposals upon which no conclusion was reached. In copying, some of the members doubtless ran the two phrases together.[1] It is probable that most of the other variations could be accounted for in a similar way.

In his *Genuine Information*, Luther Martin states that a question was proposed and negatived "that a union of the States, merely federal, ought to be the sole object of the exercise of the powers vested in the convention." [2] Mr. Jameson identifies this with the action of the Convention on June 19 in rejecting the first of the resolutions presented by Paterson. He therefore concludes that we have in this the correct reading of the first article of the New Jersey Plan.

Martin also stated in his *Genuine Information* that he had a copy of the New Jersey Plan, which he asked leave to read.[3] Shortly afterward (February 15, 1788) there appeared in the Maryland *Gazette and Baltimore Advertiser* [4] a copy of the "Resolves proposed to the Convention by the Honorable Mr. Paterson, and mentioned in Mr. Martin's Information to the House of Assembly." It is altogether probable that the printer obtained the document from Martin. This copy consists of sixteen articles. The first is identical with the resolution Martin stated was negatived in the Convention and which Mr. Jameson thinks was the first article of the New Jersey Plan. It is the same as the first resolution partially crossed out in Paterson's first preliminary draft. The others correspond to those of the Paterson and Brearley copies, except that they differ in order and subdivisions and there is an extra article ("Resolved, that it is necessary to define what offences, committed in any State, shall be deemed high treason against the United States."), which was included but crossed out in Paterson's little book.

Assuming that this is Martin's copy, it would seem to have been compiled like those made by others of the group which formulated the New Jersey Plan, embodying various suggested articles and phrases which appealed to him personally.

Instead of regarding Martin's statement to be conclusive as to the identity of the first resolution of the New Jersey Plan, it would seem to be more likely that Martin had noted or remembered simply

---

[1] *Ibid*, 136–137.   [2] Appendix A, CLVIII (35).

[3] Appendix A, CLVIII (10).

[4] In which the *Genuine Information* had been printed, December 28, 1787–February 8, 1788. At the point where Martin referred to the New Jersey plan, the printer added a note: "these will be inserted in a future number."

that the first resolution had been rejected, and had then turned to his own copy for the exact wording of it.

The editor's final conclusion is that the Madison copy fairly reproduces the original, and is probably the most accurate copy in existence of the New Jersey Plan presented to the Convention. This conclusion is confirmed by Madison's line of argument when insisting upon the correctness of his text as compared with that in the *Journal*,[1] and by King's summary [2] which seems to have been taken down hastily as the plan was read in the Convention.

SHERMAN'S PROPOSALS

Among the Sherman papers was found a document containing a series of propositions,[3] which has been variously interpreted: The members of the Connecticut delegation to the Federal Convention had served upon several different committees of Congress that had proposed amendments to the Articles of Confederation, and this document embodies some of the amendments thus proposed.[4] L. H. Boutell, in his *Life of Roger Sherman*, treats it as having been prepared in the latter part of Sherman's service in Congress and "as embodying the amendments which he deemed necessary to be made to the existing government." [5]   Bancroft, on the other hand, regards it as a plan of government presented to the Federal Convention "which in importance stands next to that of Virginia." [6]

Neither of these interpretations is acceptable to the editor, who is inclined to consider this document as more probably presenting the ideas of the Connecticut delegation in forming the New Jersey Plan.[7]   It is accordingly reprinted here, and is as follows: —

"That, in addition to the legislative powers vested in congress by the articles of confederation, the legislature of the United States be authorised to make laws to regulate the commerce of the United States with foreign nations, and among the several states in the union; to impose duties on foreign goods and commodities imported into the United States, and on papers passing through the post office, for raising a revenue, and to regulate the collection thereof, and apply the same to the payment of the debts due from the United States, and for supporting the government, and other necessary charges of the Union.

---

[1] Note at end of his copy, *Records*, June 15.

[2] See above, *Records*, June 15.

[3] Printed in Sanderson, *Biography of the Signers of the Declaration of Independence* (1823), III, 269–274, and reprinted in Boutell, *Life of Roger Sherman* (1896), 132–134.

[4] Bancroft, *History of the Formation of the Constitution* II, 37–38, note.

[5] Boutell, *loc. cit.*, p. 132.

[6] Bancroft, *loc. cit.*, p. 37.   [7] See Jameson, *Studie*, p. 150.

To make laws binding on the people of the United States, and on the courts of law, and other magistrates and officers, civil and military, within the several states, in all cases which concern the common interests of the United States: but not to interfere with the government of the individual states, in matters of internal police which respect the government of such states only, and wherein the general welfare of the United States is not affected.

That the laws of the United States ought, as far as may be consistent with the common interests of the Union, to be carried into execution by the judiciary and executive officers of the respective states, wherein the execution thereof is required.

That the legislature of the United States be authorised to institute one supreme tribunal, and such other tribunals as they may judge necessary for the purpose aforesaid, and ascertain their respective powers and jurisdictions.

That the legislatures of the individual states ought not to possess a right to emit bills of credit for a currency, or to make any tender laws for the payment or discharge of debts or contracts, in any manner different from the agreement of the parties, unless for payment of the value of the thing contracted for, in current money, agreeable to the standard that shall be allowed by the legislature of the United States, or in any manner to obstruct or impede the recovery of debts, whereby the interests of foreigners, or the citizens of any other state, may be affected.

That the eighth article of the confederation ought to be amended agreeably to the recommendation of congress of the   day of   .[1]

That, if any state shall refuse or neglect to furnish its quota of supplies, upon requisition made by the legislature of the United States, agreeably to the articles of the Union, that the said legislature be authorised to order the same to be levied and collected of the inhabitants of such state, and to make such rules and orders as may be necessary for that purpose.

That the legislature of the United States have power to make laws calling forth such aid from the people, from time to time, as may be necessary to assist the civil officers in the execution of the laws of the United States; and annex suitable penalties to be inflicted in case of disobedience.

That no person shall be liable to be tried for any criminal offence, committed within any of the United States, in any other state than that wherein the offence shall be committed, nor be deprived of the privilege of trial by a jury, by virtue of any law of the United States."

---

[1] These blanks should evidently be filled with "18th of April, 1783."

APPENDIX F

THE HAMILTON PLAN [1]

In connection with his important speech of June 18, Hamilton read a sketch of a plan of government which "was meant only to give a more correct view of his ideas, and to suggest the amendments which he should probably propose to the plan of Mr. R. in the proper stages of its future discussion." [2]

Although this plan was not formally before the Convention in any way, several of the delegates made copies that show considerable differences in certain articles, — namely, the fourth, seventh and eighth.

In the fourth article, which relates to the executive, the variations are in that part which prescribes the (indirect) mode of his election. Hamilton's own copy (found among his papers, but may have been retouched by its author) provides for "his election to be made by electors chosen by electors chosen by the people in the election districts aforesaid," meaning the single-member districts arranged for the choice of senators. That is to say, it provides not that his election shall be secondary, but that it shall be, if the phrase is permissible, a tertiary election. An alternative is provided, which appears in no other of the texts, namely, "or by electors chosen for that purpose by the respective legislatures" — an election still tertiary. The Brearley and Paterson copies, though they do not give the second member of this alternative, agree exactly with the phraseology of the first. In Madison's copy the process becomes simply that of secondary election — "the election to be made by electors chosen by the people in the election districts aforesaid." Read's copy agrees with this. Arguments from one or another of these texts derived from expressions used in the subsequent debates seem to be lacking. The more intricate form in which the Hamilton copy provides for the election of the executive is sustained by the longer plan which Hamilton gave to Madison at the close of the Convention, for this provided for a tertiary rather than a secondary election,

---

[1] In preparing this criticism, the editor has used freely, with Mr. Jameson's permission, "The text of Hamilton's Plan," in J. F. Jameson, *Studies in the History of the Federal Convention of 1787*, pp. 143-150.

[2] See *Records* of June 18, and Appendix A, CCXXXIII, CCLXXI, CCXCII, CCXCIV — CCXCVI, CCCIX, CCCXI, CCCXII, CCCXXIV, CCCXXVIII, CCCXXIX, CCCLIV, CCCLXVII, CCCLXXX, CCCXCVII, CCCCI.

and it is easy in copying to omit one of two similar phrases when the repetition is not perfectly well known to be intentional. On the other hand, it is not easy to imagine that the alternative method which is suggested in Hamilton's copy was really the document read on June 18, yet escaped all notice on the part of all of those whose versions have come down to us.

In the seventh article, relating to the judiciary, the number of judges in the Supreme Court is left blank in the others, whereas in Hamilton's copy the blank is filled with the word twelve. Much the most probable conclusion is that the document originally read had a blank at this point, which Hamilton subsequently filled in with the number. In his longer plan he provides for a court of from six to twelve judges.

The eighth article in Hamilton's copy reads:

" The Legislature of the United States to have power to institute courts in each State for the determination of all causes of capture and of all matters relating to their revenue, or in which the citizens of foreign nations are concerned."

In the other copies we find a less specific definition of their jurisdiction: "for the determination of all matters of general concern." It would be natural, according to the usual rules respecting copying, to suppose that the more specific phrase was the original, the more general derivative; but this presumption is much weakened when we find several independent texts agreeing exactly in their phrasing of this provision.

Finally, in the ninth article, the various texts differ markedly in respect to the composition of the court for trying impeachments. Hamilton's copy provides that they shall be tried by a court consisting "of the judges of the Federal Supreme Court, chief or senior judge of the superior court of law of each State." The others make no mention of the judges of the Federal Supreme Court. Once they were introduced, it is easy to see why the blank in Article 7 should be filled with the word twelve, lest in impeachments of Federal officers they be quite outnumbered by the thirteen chief justices of the States, or so many of them as could attend. But the other copies, while they confine the tribunal to the State judges, have minor variations in their definition of them — Madison, "to consist of the chief   or judge of the superior court of law of each State"; Read, "chief   or judges"; Brearley and Paterson, "chief or senior judge". It is not difficult to imagine that, if the writer did not feel perfectly acquainted with the judicial systems of all the States, and therefore could not in advance of discussion decide what phrase should be used to cover the case of States which did not precisely have a chief judge, he might at first write "chief or   judge," and afterward fill in the blank with the word "senior". In Hamilton's longer plan, the court for the trial of impeachments in the case of the higher officials is composed of the Supreme Court of the United States, (which was to consist of from six to twelve judges), plus the chief or senior judge of each State, any twelve to constitute a court.

No other data being available, it is impossible to reach a positive conclusion upon the correct reading of any of these variations, but the editor is inclined to rely upon the accuracy of the Madison copy.

The document that has just been discussed is to be distinguished from the following, which was not submitted to the Convention and has no further value than attaches to the personal opinions of Hamilton.[1]

Copy of a paper Communicated to J. M. by Col. Hamilton, about the close of the Convention in Philada. 1787, which he said delineated the Constitution which he would have wished to be proposed by the Convention: He had stated the principles of it in the course of the deliberations. See

The people of the United States of America do ordain & establish this Constitution for the government of themselves and their posterity.

Article I

§. 1. The Legislative power shall be vested in two distinct bodies of men, one to be called the Assembly, the other the Senate, subject to the negative hereinafter mentioned.

§ 2. The Executive power, with the qualifications hereinafter specified, shall be vested in a President of the United States.

§. 3. The supreme Judicial authority, except in the cases otherwise provided for in this Constitution, shall be vested in a Court to be called the SUPREME COURT, to consist of not less than six or more than twelve Judges.

Article II

§ 1. The Assembly shall consist of persons to be called representatives, who shall be chosen, except in the first instance, by the free male citizens & inhabitants of the several States comprehended

---

[1] See references under note 2, above.

in the Union, all of whom of the age of twenty one years & upwards shall be entitled to an equal vote.

§ 2. But the first Assembly shall be chosen in the manner prescribed in the last article and shall consist of one hundred members of whom N. Hamshire shall have five, Massachussetts thirteen, Rhode Island two, Connecticut seven, N. York nine, N. Jersey six, Pennsylvania twelve, Delaware two, Maryland eight, Virginia sixteen, N. Carolina eight, S. Carolina eight, Georgia 4.

§ 3. The Legislature shall provide for the future elections of Representatives, apportioning them in each State, from time to time as nearly as may be to the number of persons described in the 4 § of the VII article, so as that the whole number of Representatives shall never be less than one hundred, nor more than   hundred. There shall be a Census taken for this purpose within three years after the first meeting of the Legislature, and within every successive period of ten years. The term for which Representatives shall be elected shall be determined by the Legislature but shall not exceed three years. There shall be a general election at least once in three years, and the time of service of all the members in each Assembly shall begin, (except in filling vacancies) on the same day, and shall always end on the same day.

§ 4. Forty members shall make a House sufficient to proceed to business; but their number may be increased by the Legislature, yet so as never to exceed a majority of the whole number of Representatives.

§ 5. The Assembly shall choose its President and other Officers, shall judge of the qualifications & elections of its own members, punish them for improper conduct in their capacity as Representatives not extending to life or limb; and shall exclusively possess the power of impeachment except in the case of the President of the United States; but no impeachment of a member of the Senate shall be by less than two thirds of the Representatives present.

§. 6. Representatives may vote by proxy; but no Representative present shall be proxy for more than one who is absent.[x]   [In margin: "Quera? (× to provide for distant States)"].

§ 7. Bills for raising revenue, and bills for appropriating monies for the support of fleets and armies, and for paying the salaries of the Officers of Government, shall originate in the Assembly; but may be altered and amended by the Senate —

§ 8. The acceptance of an office under the United States by a Representative shall vacate his seat in the Assembly.

Article III

§ 1. The Senate shall consist of persons to be chosen, except in the first instance, by Electors elected for that purpose by the Citizens and inhabitants of the several States comprehended in the Union who shall have in their own right, or in the right of their wifes, an estate in land for not less than life, or a term of years, whereof at the time of giving their votes there shall be at least fourteen years unexpired.

§ 2. But the first Senate shall be chosen in the manner prescribed in the last Article and shall consist of forty members to be called Senators, of whom N. Hampshire shall have   Massts.
R. Island   Connecticut   N. York   N. Jersey   Pena.
        Delaware   Maryld.   Virga.   N. Carola.   S.
Carol.   Geo.

§ 3. The Legislature shall provide for the future elections of Senators, for which purpose the States respectively, which have more than one Senator, shall be divided into convenient districts to which the Senators shall be apportioned. A State having but one Senator shall be itself a district. On the death, resignation or removal from office of a Senator his place shall be supplied by a new election in the district from which he came. Upon each election there shall be not less than six nor more than twelve electors chosen in a district

§ 4. The number of Senators shall never be less than forty, nor shall any State, if the same shall not hereafter be divided, ever have less than the number allotted to it in the second section of this article; but the Legislature may increase the whole number of Senators, in the same proportion to the whole number of Representatives as forty is to one hundred; and such increase beyond the present number, shall be apportioned to the respective States in a ratio to the respective numbers of their representatives.

§ 5. If States shall be divided, or if a new arrangement of the boundaries of two or more States shall take place, the Legislature shall apportion the number of Senators (in elections succeeding such division or new arrangement) to which the constituent parts were entitled according to the change of situation, having regard to the number of persons described in the 4. § of the VII article.

§ 6. The Senators shall hold their places during good behaviour, removeable only by conviction on impeachment for some crime or misdemeanor. They shall continue to exercise their offices when impeached untill a conviction shall take place. Sixteen Senators attending in person shall be sufficient to make a House to transact business, but the Legislature may increase this number, yet so as never to exceed a majority of the whole number of Senators. The Senators may vote by proxy, but no Senator who is present shall be proxy for more than two who are absent.

§. 7. The Senate shall choose its President and other Officers; shall judge of the qualifications and electons of its members, and shall punish them for improper conduct in their capacity of Senators; but such punishment shall not extend to life or limb; nor to expulsion. In the absence of their President they may choose a temporary President. The President shall only have a casting vote when the House is equally divided.

§. 8. The Senate shall exclusively possess the power of declaring war. No Treaty shall be made without their advice and consent; which shall also be necessary to the appointment of all officers, except such for which a different provision is made in this Constitution

Article IV

§ 1. The President of the United States of America, (except in the first instance) shall be elected in manner following — The Judges of the Supreme Court shall within sixty days after a vacancy shall happen, cause public notice to be given in each State, of such vacancy, appointing therein three several days for the several purposes following, to wit, a day for commencing the election of electors for the purposes hereinafter specified, to be called the first electors, which day shall not be less than forty, nor more than sixty days, after the day of the publication of the notice in each State — — another day for the meeting of the electors not less than forty nor more than ninety days from the day for commencing their election — — another day for the meeting of electors to be chosen by the first electors, for the purpose hereinafter specified, and to be called the second Electors, which day shall be not less than forty nor more than sixty days after the meeting of the first electors.

§. 2. After notice of a vacancy shall have been given there shall be chosen in each State a number of persons, as the first electors in the preceding section mentioned, equal to the whole number of the Representatives and Senators of such State in the Legislature of the United States; which electors shall be chosen by the Citizens of such State having an estate of inheritance or for three lives in land, or a clear personal estate of the value of one thousand Spanish milled dollars of the present Standard.

§ 3. These first electors shall meet in their respective States at the time appointed, at one place; and shall proceed to vote by ballot for a President, who shall not be one of their own number, unless the Legislature upon experiment should hereafter direct otherwise. They shall cause two lists to be made of the name or names of the person or persons voted for, which they or the major part of them shall sign & certify. They shall then proceed each to nominate openly in the presence of the others, two persons as for second electors, and out of the persons who shull have the four highest numbers of Nominations, they shall afterwards by ballot by plurality of votes choose two who shall be the second electors, to each of whom shall be delivered one of the lists before mentioned. These second electors shall not be any of the persons voted for as President. A copy of the same list signed and certified in like manner shall be transmitted by the first electors to the Seat of the Government of the United States, under a sealed cover directed to the President of the Assembly, which after the meeting of the second electors shall be opened for the inspection of the two House of the Legislature

§ 4. The second electors shall meet precisely on the day appointed and not on another day, at one place. The Chief Justice of the Supreme Court, or if there be no Chief Justice, the Judge senior in office in such Court, or if there be no one Judge senior in office, some other Judge of that Court, by the choice of the rest of the Judges or of a majority of them, shall attend at the same place and shall preside at the meeting, but shall have no vote. Two thirds of the whole number of the Electors shall constitute a sufficient meeting for the execution of their trust. At this meeting the lists delivered to the respective electors shall be produced and inspected, and if there be any person who has a majority of the whole number of votes given by the first electors, he shall be the President of the United States; but if there be no such person, the second electors so met shall proceed to vote, by ballot for one of the persons named in the lists who shall, have the three highest numbers of the votes of the first electors; and if upon the first or any succeeding ballot on the day of their meeting, either of those persons shall have a number of votes equal to a majority of the whole number of second electors chosen, he shall be the President. But if no such choice be made on the day appointed for the meeting either by reason of the nonattendance of the second electors, or their not agreeing, or any other matter, the person having the greatest number of votes of the first electors shall be the President.

§ 5. If it should happen that the Chief-Justice or some other Judge of the Supreme Court should not attend in due time, the second electors shall proceed to the execution of their trust without him.

§ 6. If the Judges should neglect to cause the notice required by the first section of this article to be given within the time therein limited, they may nevertheless cause it to be afterwards given; but their neglect if wilful, is hereby declared to be an offence for which they may be impeached, and if convicted they shall be punished as in other cases of conviction on impeachment.

§ 7. The Legislature shall by permanent laws provide such further regulations as may be necessary for the more orderly election of the President, not contravening the provisions herein contained.

§ 8. The President before he shall enter upon the execution of his office shall take an oath or affirmation, faithfully to execute the same, and to the utmost of his Judgment & power to protect the rights of the people, and preserve the Constitution inviolate. This oath or affirmation shall be administered by the President of the Senate for the time being in the presence of both Houses of the Legislature.

§. 9. The Senate and the Assembly shall always convene in Session on the day appointed for the meeting of the second electors and shall continue sitting till the President take the oath or affirmation of office. He shall hold his place during good behavior, removeable only by conviction upon an impeachment for some crime or misdemeanor.

§ 10. The President at the beginning of every meeting of the Legislature as soon as they shall be ready to proceed to business, shall convene them together at the place where the Senate shall sit, and shall communicate to them all such matters as may be necessary for their information, or as may require their consideration. He may by message during the Session communicate all other matters which may appear to him proper. He may, whenever in his opinion the public business shall require it, convene the Senate and Assembly, or either of them, and may prorogue them for a time not exceeding forty days at one prorogation; and if they should disagree about their adjournment, he may adjourn them to such time as he shall think proper. He shall have a right to negative all bills, Resolutions or acts of the two Houses of the Legislature about to be passed into laws. He shall take care that the laws be faithfully executed. He shall be the commander in chief of the army and Navy of the United States and of the Militia within the several States, and shall have the direction of war when commenced, but he shall not take the actual command in the field of an army without the consent of the Senate and Assembly. All treaties, conventions and agreements with foreign nations shall be made by him, by and with the advice and consent of the Senate. He shall have the appointment of the principal or Chief officer of each of the departments of War, naval Affairs, Finance, and Foreign Affairs; and shall have the nomination; and by and with the Consent of the Senate, the appointment of all other officers to be appointed under the authority of the United States, except such for whom different provision is made by this Constitution; and provided that this shall not be construed to prevent the Legislature, from appointing by name in their laws, persons to special & particular trusts created in such laws, nor shall be construed to prevent principals in offices merely ministerial, from constituting deputies. — In the recess of the Senate he may fill vacancies in offices by appointments to continue in force until the end of the next Session of the Senate. And he shall commission all Officers. He shall have power to pardon all offences except treason, for which he may grant reprieves, untill the opening of the Senate & Assembly can be had; and with their concurrence may pardon the same.

§ 11. He shall receive a fixed compensation for his Services to be paid to him at stated times, and not to be increased nor diminished during his continuance in office –

§ 12. If he depart out of the United States without the Consent of the Senate and Assembly, he shall thereby abdicate his office –

§. 13. He may be impeached for any crime or misdemeanor by the two Houses of the Legislature, two thirds of each House concurring, and if convicted shall be removed from office. He may be afterwards tried & punished in the ordinary course of law – His impeachment shall operate as a suspension from office until the determination thereof.

§ 14. The President of the Senate shall be vice President of the United States. On the death, resignation, impeachment, removal from office, or absence from the United States, of the President thereof, the Vice President shall exercise all the powers by this Constitution vested in the President, until another shall be appointed, or untill he shall return within the United States, if his absence was with the Consent of the Senate and Assembly.

Article V

§ 1. There shall be a chief Justice of the Supreme Court, who together with the other Judges thereof, shall hold their offices during good behaviour, removeable only by conviction on impeachment for some crime or misdemeanor – Each Judge shall have a competent Salary to be paid to him at stated times, and not to be diminished during his continuance in office.

The Supreme Court shall have original jurisdiction in all causes in which the United States shall be a party, in all controversies between the United States, and a particular State, or between two or more States, except such as relate to a claim of territory between the United States, and one or more States, which shall be determined in the mode prescribed in the VI article; in all cases affecting foreign Ministers, Consuls and Agents; and an appellate jurisdiction both as to law and fact in all cases which shall concern the Citizens of foreign nations, in all questions between the Citizens of different States, and in all others in which the fundamental rights of this Constitution are involved, subject to such exceptions as are herein contained and to such regulations as the Legislature shall provide.

The Judges of all Courts which may be constituted by the Legislature shall also hold their places during good behaviour, removeable only by conviction on impeachment for some crime or misdemeanor, and shall have competent salaries to be paid at stated times and not to be diminished during their continuance in office; but nothing herein contained shall be construed to prevent the Legislature from abolishing such Courts themselves.

All crimes, except upon impeachment, shall be tried by a Jury of twelve men; and if they shall have been committed within any State, shall be tried within such State; and all civil causes arising under this Constitution of the like kind with those which have been heretofore triable by Jury in the respective States, shall in like manner be tried by jury; unless in special cases the Legislature shall think proper to make different provision, to which provision the concurrence of two thirds of both Houses shall be necessary.

§   Impeachments of the President and and Vice President of the U– States, members of the Senate, the Governours and Presidents of the several States, the principal or chief Officers of the Departments enumerated in the 10 §. of the 4th. Article, Ambassadors and other like public Ministers, the Judges of the Supreme Court, Generals and Admirals of the Navy shall be tried by a Court to consist of the Judges of the Supreme Court, and the Chief Justice or first senior Judge of the superior Court of law in each State, of whom twelve shall constitute a Court. A majority of the Judges present may convict. All other persons shall be tried on impeachment by a court to consist of the Judges of the supreme Court and six Senators drawn by lot, a majority of whom may convict.

Impeachments shall clearly specify the particular offence for which the party accused is to be tried, and judgment on conviction upon the trial thereof shall be either removal from office singly, or removal from office and disqualification for holding any future

Office or place of trust; but no Judgment on impeachment shall prevent prosecution and punishment in the ordinary course of law; provided that no Judge concerned in such conviction shall sit as Judge on the second trial. The Legislature may remove the disabilities incurred by conviction on impeachment.

Article VI

Controversies about the rights of territory between the United States and particular States shall be determined by a Court to be constituted in manner following. The State or States claiming in opposition to the United States as parties shall nominate a number of persons, equal to double the number of Judges of the Supreme Court for the time being, of whom none shall be citizens by birth of the States which are parties, nor inhabitants thereof when nominated, and of whom not more than two shall have their actual residence in one State. Out of the persons so nominated the Senate shall elect one half, who together with the Judges of the supreme Court, shall form the Court. Two thirds of the whole number may hear and determine the controversy, by plurality of voices. The States concerned may at their option claim a decision by the Supreme Court only. All the members of the Court hereby instituted, shall, prior to the hearing of the Cause take an Oath impartially, and according to the best of their judgments and consciences, to hear and determine the controversy.

Article VII.

§ 1. The Legislature of the United States shall have power to pass all laws which they shall judge necessary to the common defence and general welfare of the Union: But no Bill, Resolution, or act of the Senate and Assembly shall have the force of a law until it shall have received the Assent of the President, or of the vice-President when exercising the powers of the President; and if such assent shall not have been given within ten days, after such bill, resolution or other act shall have been presented to him for that purpose, the same shall not be a law— No bill, resolution or other act not assented to shall be revived in the same Session of the Legislature. The mode of signifying such assent, shall be by signing the bill act of resolution, and returning it so signed to either House of the Legislature.

§ 2. The enacting stile of a laws shall be " Be it enacted by the people of the United States of America ".

§ 3. No bill of attainder shall be passed, nor any ex post facto law; nor shall any title of nobility be granted by the United States, or by either of them; nor shall any person holding an office or place of trust under the United States without the permission of the Legislature accept any present, emolument Office or title from a foreign prince or State.   Nor shall any Religious Sect, or denomination, or religious test for any office or place, be ever established by law.

§ 4.   Taxes on lands, houses and other real estate, and capitation taxes shall be proportioned in each State by the whole number of free persons, except Indians not taxed. and by three fifths of all other persons.

§. 5.   The two Houses of the Legislature may by joint ballot appoint a Treasurer of the United States- Neither House in the Session of both Houses, without the consent of the other shall adjourn for more than three days at a time.   The Senators and Representatives, in attending, going to and coming from the Session of their respective houses shall be privileged from arrest except for crimes and breaches of the peace.   The place of meeting shall always be at the seat of Government which shall be fixed by law.

§ 6.   The laws of the United States, and the treaties which have been made under the articles of the confederation, and which shall be made under this Constitution shall be the supreme law of the Land, and shall be so construed by the Courts of the several States.

§ 7.   The Legislature shall convene at least once in each year, which unless otherwise provided for by law, shall be the first Monday in December.

§ 8.   The members of the two Houses of the Legislature shall receive a reasonable compensation for their services, to be paid out of the Treasury of the United States and ascertained by law.   The law for making such provision shall be passed with the concurrence of the first Assembly and shall extend to succeeding Assemblies; and no succeeding Assembly shall concur in an alteration of such provision, so as to increase its own compensation; but there shall be always a law in existence for making such provision.

Article VIII

§ 1.   The Governour or President of each State shall be appointed under the authority of the United States, and shall have a right to negative all laws about to be passed in the State of which he shall be Governour or President, subject to such qualifications and regutaions, as the Legislature of the United States shall prescribe—   He shall in other respects have the same powers only which the Constitution of the State does or shall allow to its Governour or President, except as to appointment of Officers of the Militia.

§ 2. Each Governour or President of a State shall hold his office until a successor be actually appointed, unless he die, or resign or be removed from office by conviction on impeachment. There shall be no appointment of such Governor or President in the Recess of the Senate.

The Governours and Presidents of the several States at the time of the ratification of this Constitution shall continue in office in the same manner and with the same powers as if they had been appointed pursuant to the first section of this article.

The officers of the Militia in the several States may be appointed under the authority of the U– States; the Legislature whereof may authorize the Governors or Presidents of States to make such appointments with such restrictions as they shall think proper.

Article IX

§. 1. No person shall be eligible to the office of President of the United States unless he be now a Citizen of one of the States, or hereafter be born a Citizen of the United States.

§. 2. No person shall be eligible as a Senator or Representative unless at the time of his election he be a Citizen and inhabitant of the State in which he is chosen; provided that he shall not be deemed to be disqualified by a temporary absence from the State.

§ 3. No person entitled by this Constitution to elect or to be elected President of the United States, or a Senator or Representative in the Legislature thereof, shall be disqualified but by the conviction of some offence for which the law shall have previously ordained the punishment of disqualification. But the Legislature may by law provide that persons holding offices under the United States or either of them shall not be eligible to a place in the Assembly or Senate, and shall be during their continuance in office suspended from sitting in the Senate.

§ 4. No person having an office or place of trust under the United States shall without permission of the Legislature accept any present emolument Office or title from any foreign Prince or State.

§ 5. The citizens of each State shall be entitled to the rights privileges and immunities of citizens in every other State; and full faith and credit shall be given in each State to the public acts, records and judicial proceedings of another.

§ 6. Fugitives from justice from one State who shall be found in another shall be delivered up on the application of the State from which they fled.

§ 7. No new State shall be erected within the limits of another, or by the junction of two or more States, without the concurrent consent of the Legislatures of the United States and of the States concerned. The Legislature of the United States may admit new States into the Union–

§ 8. The United States are hereby declared to be bound to guarantee to each State a Republican form of Government, and to protect each State as well against domestic violence as foreign invasion.

§ 9. All Treaties, Contracts and engagements of the United States of America under the articles of Confederation and perpetual Union, shall have equal validity under this Constitution.

§ 10. No State shall enter into a Treaty, alliance, or contract with another, or with a foreign power without the consent of the United States

§ 11. The members of the Legislature of the United States and of each State, and all officers Executive & Judicial of the one and of the other shall take an oath or affirmation to support the Constitution of the United States –

§ 12. This Constitution may receive such alterations and amendments as may be proposed by the Legislature of the United States, with the concurrence of two thirds of the members of both Houses, and ratified by the Legislatures of, or by Conventions of deputies chosen by the people in, two thirds of the States composing the Union.

Article X

This Constitution shall be submitted to the consideration of Conventions in the several States, the members whereof shall be chosen by the people of such States respectively under the direction of their respective Legislatures– Each Convention which shall ratify the same, shall appoint the first representatives and Senators from such State according to the rule prescribed in the   § of the   Article. The representatives so appointed shall continue in office for one year only. Each Convention so ratifying shall give notice thereof to the Congress of the United States, transmitting at the same time a list of the Representatives and Senators chosen. When the Constitution shall have been duly ratified, Congress shall give notice of a day and place for the meeting of the Senators and Representatives from the several States; and when these or a majority of them shall have assembled according to such notice, they shall by joint ballot, by plurality of votes, elect a President of the United States; and the Constitution thus organized shall be carried into effect.